The Liturgy Compared With The Bible

THE

LITURGY

COMPARED WITH THE BIBLE;

OR,

AN ILLUSTRATION AND CONFIRMATION,

BY SCRIPTURE QUOTATIONS AND REFERENCES,

OF SUCH PARTS OF THE

BOOK OF COMMON PRAYER,

ADMINISTRATION OF THE SACRAMENTS,

AND OTHER RITES AND CEREMONIES OF THE

UNITED CHURCH OF ENGLAND AND IRELAND,

AS ARE NOT DIRECT EXTRACTS FROM THE HOLY SCRIPTURES.

BY THE REV. HENRY IVES BAILEY,

PERPETUAL CURATE OF DRIGHLINGTON, NEAR LEEDS.

IN TWO VOLUMES.

VOL. II.

In the day of your gladness, and in your solemn days, and in the beginnings of your months, ye shall blow with the trumpets over your burnt offerings, and over the sacrifices of your peace offerings; that they may be to you for a memorial before your God: I am the Lord your God. NUM. x. 10.

Hold fast the form of sound words. 2 TIM. i. 13.

LONDON:

PUBLISHED AND SOLD BY RIVINGTONS, SEELEY AND SONS,

HATCHARD AND CO., AND HAMILTON AND CO.

MDCCCXXXV.

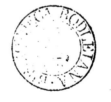

PREFACE.

THE favourable manner in which the *First* Volume of the *Liturgy compared with the Bible* has been received, and the request of several respected Individuals that the Compiler would complete the Work, have induced him to offer the *Second* to the Public.

The *Identification* of the Liturgy of the Church of England with the Holy Scriptures might, probably, have been rendered more apparent, had the Work been undertaken by an abler hand. Yet as several persons have expressed the satisfaction they have received from the First Volume, and as the same kind clerical friend who revised that portion of the Compilation has given his valuable aid in examining and arranging the present Volume, the Writer trusts that candid minds will not rise unedified from its perusal. He also hopes that the devout worshipper will thereby be assisted to use, yet more spiritually than he has been accustomed, those Occasional Services of our Scriptural Church, in which it may be his duty and his privilege to join.

It is too apparent that by great numbers of persons these Services are not regarded as acts of Divine Worship, and that they do not attend the celebration of them with even a remote view of reaping spiritual advantage from their use. *The loss,* to such persons, *is incalculable.* For as our " Church is a witness and keeper of Holy Writ," and as so large a portion of God's Word is embodied in each of her Offices, we are authorized* to believe that much personal benefit would accrue to those, who, with due preparation of mind, should seek and expect in them a blessing from the Lord, the God of Israel. There can be no doubt, however, that the reverent, devout,

---

* Is. lv, 10, 11.—Luke viii. 15.—2 Tim. iii. 15, 16.—Rom. xiv. 4.—Rev. i. 3.

and impressive ministration of these Offices affords a most excellent means of *testifying* to thousands, who, perhaps, never attend the more stated Ordinances of the Sanctuary, *the Gospel of the Grace of God.*

The Compiler would, in conclusion, earnestly urge his fellow Christians—*to wait for the lovingkindness of the Lord* IN THE MIDST OF HIS TEMPLE;—*to walk about Zion, and go round about her;—to tell the towers thereof;—to mark well her bulwarks;—to consider her palaces, that they may tell it to the generation following. For this God is our God for ever and ever: He will be our guide even unto death.*

THE MINISTRATION OF

PUBLIC

BAPTISM OF INFANTS.

CLIV. Exhortation to the Congregation in behalf of the Candidate for Baptism.

1. Dearly beloved, forasmuch as all men are conceived and born in sin;

1. Behold, I was shapen in iniquity; and in sin did my mother conceive me. *Ps. li.* 5. How can he be clean that is born of a woman? *Job xxv.* 4. Among whom also we all had our conversation in times past in the lusts of our flesh, fulfilling the desires of the flesh and of the mind; and were by nature the children of wrath, even as others. *Ep. ii.* 3. As by one man sin entered into the world, and death by sin; and so death passed upon all men, for that all have sinned. By the offence of one judgment came upon all men to condemnation. *Rom. v.* 12. 18. That which is born of the flesh is flesh.

2. and that our Saviour Christ saith, None can enter into the kingdom of God, except he be regenerate and born anew of Water and of the Holy Ghost;

John iii. 6.

2. Jesus answered and said unto him, Verily, verily, I say unto thee, Except a man be born again, he cannot see the kingdom of God. Verily, verily, I say unto thee, Except a man be born of water and of the Spirit, he cannot enter into the kingdom of God. *John iii.* 3. 5.

3. I beseech you to call upon God the Father, through our Lord Jesus Christ, that of his bounteous mercy he will grant to *this* Child that thing which by nature *he* cannot have;

3. In every thing by prayer and supplication with thanksgiving, let your requests be made known unto God. *Ph. iv.* 6. If ye call on the Father, who without respect of persons judgeth according to every man's work, pass the time of your sojourning here in fear. 1 *Pe. i.* 17. No man cometh unto the Father, but by me. *John xiv.* 6. Again I say unto you, that if two of you shall agree on earth, as touching any thing that they shall ask, it shall be done for them of my Father which is in heaven. For where two or three are gathered together in my name, there am I in the midst of them. *Mat. xviii.* 19, 20. That in the ages to come he might shew the exceeding riches of his grace, in his kindness to-

B

wards us through Christ Jesus. *Ep. ii.* 7. According to his mercy he saved us. *Tit. iii.* 5. Of his fulness have all we received. As many as received him, to them gave he power to become the sons of God, which were born not of blood, nor of the will of the flesh, nor of the will of man, but of God. *John i.* 16. 12, 13. Who can bring a clean thing out of an unclean? *Job xiv.* 4. They which are the children of the flesh, these are not the children of God. *Ro. ix.* 8. For we are his workmanship, created in Christ Jesus unto good works. *Ep. ii.* 10. The new man, which after God is created in righteousness and true holiness. *Ep. iv.* 24.

4. that *he* may be baptized with Water and the Holy Ghost, and received into Christ's holy Church, and be made *a lively member* of the same.

4. Can any man forbid water, that these should not be baptized? *Ac. x.* 47. John truly baptized with water, but ye shall be baptized with the Holy Ghost. *Ac. i.* 5. Then they that gladly received his word were baptized : and the same day there were added unto them about three thousand souls. And the Lord added to the Church daily such as should be saved. *Ac. ii.* 41. 47. By one Spirit are we all baptized into one body. 1 *Co. xii.* 13. The Church which is his body. *Ep. i.* 22, 23. Now ye are the body of Christ, and members in particular. 1 *Co. xii.* 27. Know ye not, that so many of us as were baptized into Jesus Christ were baptized into his death? Now if we be dead with Christ, we believe that we shall also live with him : knowing that Christ being raised from the dead dieth no more; death hath no more dominion over him. Likewise reckon ye also yourselves to be dead indeed unto sin, but alive unto God through Jesus Christ our Lord. *Ro. vi.* 3. 8, 9. 11. And when they were come up out of the water, the Eunuch went on his way rejoicing. *Ac. viii.* 39.

CLV. *Prayer that Spiritual Benefits may be conferred upon the Candidate in the Sacrament of Baptism. No.* 1.

1. Almighty and everlasting God, who of thy great mercy didst save Noah and his family in the ark from

1. If God spared not the old world, but saved Noah the eighth person, a preacher of righteousness, bringing in the flood upon the world of the ungodly; the Lord knoweth how to deliver the godly out of temptations. 2 *Pe. ii.* 4, 5. 9. And God looked upon the earth, and, behold, it was corrupt;

perishing by water; and also didst safely lead the Children of Israel thy people through the Red Sea, figuring thereby thy holy Baptism;

for all flesh had corrupted his way upon the earth. And God said unto Noah, The end of all flesh is come before me; for the earth is filled with violence through them; and, behold, I, even I, do bring a flood of waters upon the earth, to destroy all flesh; but with thee will I establish my covenant; and thou shalt come into the ark, thou, and thy sons, and thy wife, and thy sons' wives with thee. *Ge. vi.* 12, 13. 17, 18. Fifteen cubits upward did the waters prevail; and the mountains were covered: and all flesh died; all, in whose nostrils was the breath of life, of all that was in the dry land, died. And every living substance was destroyed which was upon the face of the ground; and Noah only remained alive, and they that were with him in the ark. *Ge. vii.* 20 *to* 23. The spirits in prison, which sometime were disobedient, when once the long suffering of God waited in the days of Noah, while the ark was a preparing, wherein few, that is, eight souls were saved by water. The like figure whereunto even baptism doth also now save us, (not the putting away of the filth of the flesh, but the answer of a good conscience toward God,) by the resurrection of Jesus Christ. 1 *Pe. iii.* 19, 20, 21. He rebuked the Red Sea, and it was dried up; so he led them through the depths. *Ps. cvi.* 9. The children of Israel walked upon dry land in the midst of the sea; and the waters were a wall unto them on their right hand and on their left. *Ex. xiv.* 29. Brethren, I would not that ye should be ignorant, how that all our fathers were under the cloud, and all passed through the sea; and were all baptized unto Moses in the cloud and in the sea. 1 *Co. x.* 1, 2.

2. and by the Baptism of thy well-beloved Son, Jesus Christ, in the river Jordan, didst sanctify Water to the mystical washing away of sin;

2. Then cometh Jesus from Galilee to Jordan unto John, to be baptized of him. But John forbade him, saying, I have need to be baptized of thee, and comest thou to me? And Jesus answering said unto him, Suffer it to be so now; for thus it becometh us to fulfil all righteousness. Then he suffered him. *Mat. iii.* 13, 14, 15. In whom also ye are circumcised with the circumcision made without hands, in putting off the body of the sins of the flesh by the circumcision of Christ; buried with him in baptism, wherein also ye are risen with him through the faith of the operation of God, who hath raised him from the dead. *Col. ii.* 11, 12.

This is he that came by water and blood, even Jesus Christ. 1 *John v.* 6. Why tarriest thou? arise, and be baptized, and wash away thy sins, calling on the name of the Lord. *Ac. xxii.* 16.

3. We beseech thee, for thine infinite mercies, that thou wilt mercifully look upon this child; wash him and sanctify him with the Holy Ghost; that he, being delivered from thy wrath, may be received into the ark of Christ's Church;

3. His tender mercies are over all his works. *Ps. cxlv.* 9. It is not the will of your Father which is in heaven, that one of these little ones should perish. *Mat. xviii.* 14. He shall gather the lambs with his arm, and carry them in his bosom. *Is. xl.* 11. They brought young children to him that he should touch them: and Jesus said, Suffer the little children to come unto me, and forbid them not: for of such is the kingdom of God. *Mar. x.* 13, 14. Ye are washed, ye are sanctified, ye are justified in the name of the Lord Jesus, and by the Spirit of our God. 1 *Co. vi.* 11. He that believeth and is baptized shall be saved. *Mar. xvi.* 16. For God so loved the world, that he gave his only begotten Son, that whosoever believeth in him should not perish, but have everlasting life. *John iii.* 16. Being now justified by his blood, we shall be saved from wrath through him. *Ro. v.* 9. And the Lord said unto Noah, Come thou and all thy house into the ark. *Ge. vii.* 1. The Lord added to the Church daily such as should be saved. *Ac. ii.* 47.

4. and being stedfast in faith, joyful through hope, and rooted in charity, may so pass the waves of this troublesome world, that finally he may come to the land of everlasting life, there to reign with thee world without end; through Jesus Christ our Lord. Amen.

4. Now abideth faith, hope, charity. 1 *Co. xiii.* 13. We are made partakers of Christ, if we hold the beginning of our confidence stedfast unto the end. Christ, whose house are we, if we hold fast the confidence and the rejoicing of the hope firm unto the end. *He. iii.* 14. 6.—Which hope we have as an anchor of the soul, both sure and stedfast, and which entereth into that within the veil. *He. vi.* 19. Stedfast in the faith. 1 *Pe. v.* 9. Now the God of hope fill you with all joy and peace in believing, that ye may abound in hope, through the power of the Holy Ghost. *Ro. xv.* 13. And above all these things put on charity, which is the bond of perfectness. *Col. iii.* 14. Being rooted and grounded in love. [charity.] *Ep. iii.* 17. All thy waves and thy billows are gone over me. *Ps. xlii.* 7. The floods lift up their waves. The Lord on high is mightier than the noise of many waters, yea, than the mighty waves of the sea. *Ps. xciii.* 3, 4. Which stilleth the noise of the seas, the noise of their waves, and the tumult of the people. *Ps. lxv.* 7. The waters prevailed,

and were increased greatly upon the earth; and the ark went upon the face of the waters. *Ge. vii.* 18. The Lord your God dried up the waters of Jordan from before you, until ye were passed over, as the Lord your God did to the Red Sea, which he dried up before us, until we were gone over. *Jos. iv.* 23. We are troubled on every side. 2 *Co. iv.* 8. In the world ye shall have tribulation: but be of good cheer; I have overcome the world. *John xvi.* 33. If we suffer, we shall also reign with him. 2 *Ti. ii.* 12. When even was now come, his disciples went down unto the sea, and entered into a ship, and went over the sea toward Capernaum. And it was now dark, and Jesus was not come to them. And the sea arose by reason of a great wind that blew. So when they had rowed about five and twenty or thirty furlongs, they see Jesus walking on the sea, and drawing nigh unto the ship: and they were afraid. But he saith unto them, It is I; be not afraid. Then they willingly received him into the ship; and immediately the ship was at the land whither they went. *John vi.* 16 *to* 21. They returned, confirming the souls of the disciples, and exhorting them to continue in the faith, and that we must through much tribulation enter into the kingdom of God. *Ac. xiv.* 21, 22. These are they which came out of great tribulation, and have washed their robes, and made them white in the blood of the Lamb. Therefore are they before the throne of God, and serve him day and night in his temple; and he that sitteth on the throne shall dwell among them. *Re. vii.* 14, 15. They shall reign for ever and ever. *Re. xxii.* 5.

CLVI. Prayer that Spiritual Benefits may be conferred upon the Candidate in the Sacrament of Baptism. No. 2.

1. Almighty and immortal God, the aid of all that need, the helper of all that flee to thee for succour,

1. The blessed and only Potentate, the King of kings, and Lord of lords; who only hath immortality, dwelling in the light which no man can approach unto; whom no man hath seen, nor can see. 1 *Ti. vi.* 15, 16. The Lord looseth the prisoners; the Lord openeth the eyes of the blind; the Lord raiseth them that are bowed down; the Lord loveth the righteous; the Lord preserveth the strangers; he relieveth the fatherless and widow. *Ps. cxlvi.* 7, 8, 9. Deliver me, O

Lord, from mine enemies; I flee unto thee to hide me. *Ps. cxliii.* 9. I have heard thee in a time accepted, in the day of salvation have I succoured thee. *2 Co. vi.* 2. Thou hast been a strength to the poor, a strength to the needy in his distress, a refuge from the storm, a shadow from the heat. *Is. xxv.* 4. Our help is in the name of the Lord, who made heaven and earth. *Ps. cxxiv.* 8. He shall deliver the needy when he crieth; the poor also, and him that hath no helper. *Ps. lxxii.* 12. They that know thy name will put their trust in thee; for thou, Lord, hast not forsaken them that seek thee. *Ps. ix.* 10.

2. the life of them that believe, and the resurrection of the dead;

2. With thee is the fountain of life. *Ps. xxxvi.* 9. This is the record, that God hath given to us eternal life, and this life is in his Son. He that hath the Son hath life: and he that hath not the Son of God hath not life. *1 John v.* 11, 12. He that believeth on the Son hath everlasting life: and he that believeth not the Son shall not see life; but the wrath of God abideth on him. *John iii.* 36. Your life is hid with Christ in God. *Col. iii.* 3. Jesus said unto her, I am the Resurrection, and the Life; he that believeth in me, though he were dead, yet shall he live; and whosoever liveth and believeth in me shall never die. *John xi.* 25, 26.

3. We call upon thee for *this Infant*, that *he*, coming to thy holy Baptism, may receive remission of *his* sins by spiritual regeneration.

3. Pray one for another: the effectual fervent prayer of a righteous man availeth much. *Ja. v.* 16. The Lord is nigh unto all them that call upon him, to all that call upon him in truth. He will fulfil the desire of them that fear him; he also will hear their cry, and will save them. *Ps. cxlv.* 18, 19. Then were there brought unto him little children, that he should put his hands on them, and pray. *Mat. xix.* 13. There came to him a certain man, kneeling down to him, and saying, Lord, have mercy on my son. *Mat. xvii.* 14, 15. A woman of Canaan cried unto him, saying, Have mercy on me, O Lord, thou son of David; my daughter is grievously vexed with a devil. *Mat. xv.* 22. Peter said unto them, Repent, and be baptized every one of you in the name of Jesus Christ for the remission of sins. *Ac. ii.* 38. Not by works of righteousness which we have done, but according to his mercy he saved us, by the washing of regeneration, and renewing of the Holy Ghost. *Tit. iii.* 5. Buried with him in baptism, wherein also

ye are risen with him through the faith of the operation of God, who hath raised him from the dead. And you, being dead in your sins and the uncircumcision of your flesh, hath he quickened together with him, having forgiven you all trespasses. *Col. ii.* 12, 13.

4. Receive him, O Lord, as thou hast promised by thy well-beloved Son, saying, Ask, and ye shall have; seek, and ye shall find; knock, and it shall be opened unto you: So give now unto us that ask; let us that seek find; open the gate unto us that knock; that *this Infant* may enjoy the everlasting benediction of thy heavenly washing, and may come to the eternal kingdom which thou hast promised by Christ our Lord. *Amen.*

4. I beseech thee, look upon my son. *Lu. ix.* 38. And when she had weaned him, she took him up with her, with three bullocks, and one ephah of flour, and a bottle of wine, and brought him unto the house of the Lord in Shiloh; and the child was young. And she said [to Eli,] For this child I prayed; and the Lord hath given me my petition which I asked of him; therefore also I have lent him to the Lord; as long as he liveth he shall be lent unto the Lord. And he worshipped the Lord there. 1 *Sa. i.* 24. 26, 27, 28. Ask, and it shall be given you; seek, and ye shall find; knock, and it shall be opened unto you: for every one that asketh receiveth; and he that seeketh findeth; and to him that knocketh it shall be opened. *Mat. vii.* 7, 8. If ye being evil, know how to give good gifts unto your children; how much more shall your heavenly Father give the Holy Spirit to them that ask him? *Lu. xi.* 13. Ye are washed, ye are sanctified, ye are justified in the name of the Lord Jesus, and by the Spirit of our God. 1 *Co. vi.* 11. As many of you as have been baptized into Christ have put on Christ. There is neither Jew nor Greek, there is neither bond nor free, there is neither male nor female: for ye are all one in Christ Jesus. And if ye be Christ's, then are ye Abraham's seed, and heirs according to the promise. *Ga. iii.* 27, 28, 29. Unto him that loved us, and washed us from our sins in his own blood, and hath made us kings and priests unto God and his Father; to him be glory and dominion for ever and ever. Amen. *Re. i.* 5, 6.

Hear the words of the Gospel, written by Saint *Mark*, in the tenth Chapter, at the thirteenth Verse.

They brought young children to Christ, that he should touch them; and his disciples rebuked those that brought them. But when Jesus saw it, he was much displeased, and said unto them, Suffer the little children to come unto me, and forbid them not; for of such is the kingdom of God. Verily I say unto you, Whosoever shall not receive the kingdom of God as a little child, he shall not enter therein.   And he took them up in his arms, put his hands upon them, and blessed them. Mar. x. 13 to 16.

CLVII. The Exhortation founded on the Gospel.

Beloved, ye hear in this Gospel the words of our Saviour Christ, that he commanded the children to be brought unto him; how he blamed those that would have kept them from him; how he exhorteth all men to follow their innocency.   Ye perceive how by his outward gesture and deed he declared his good will toward them; for he embraced them in his arms, he laid his hands upon them, and blessed them.   Doubt ye not therefore, but earnestly believe, that he will likewise favourably receive *this* present *Infant;* that he will embrace *him* in the arms of his mercy; that he will give unto *him* the blessing of eternal life and make *him partaker* of his everlasting kingdom.   Wherefore we being thus persuaded of the good will of our heavenly Father towards *this Infant,* declared by his Son Jesus Christ; and nothing doubting but that he favourably alloweth this charitable work of ours in bringing *this Infant* to his holy Baptism; let us faithfully and devoutly give thanks unto him.

Let him ask in faith, nothing wavering. *Ja. i.* 6.   I will that men pray every where, lifting up holy hands, without wrath and doubting. 1 *Ti. ii.* 8.   Jesus saith unto them, Have faith in God.   For verily I say unto you, That whosoever shall say unto this mountain, Be thou removed, and be thou cast into the sea; and shall not doubt in his heart, but shall believe that those things which he saith shall come to pass; he shall have whatsoever he saith.   Therefore I say unto you, What things soever ye desire, when ye pray, believe that ye receive them, and ye shall have them. *Mar. xi.* 22, 23, 24.   Jesus answered and said unto them, Verily I say unto you, If ye have faith, and doubt not, ye shall not only do this which is done to the fig-tree, but also if ye shall say unto this mountain, Be thou removed, and be thou cast into the sea, it shall be done.   And all things, whatsoever ye shall ask in prayer believing, ye shall receive. *Mat. xxi.* 21, 22.   Take heed that ye despise not one of these little ones.   It is not the will of your Father which is in heaven, that one of these little ones should perish.— *Mat. xviii.* 10. 14.

CLVIII. Thanksgiving and Prayer for Spiritual blessings.

1. Almighty and everlasting God, heavenly   1. I am the Almighty God. *Ge. xvii.* 1. Blessed be the Lord God of Israel from everlasting, and to everlasting.—

Father, we give thee humble thanks, for that thou hast vouchsafed to call us to the knowledge of thy grace, and faith in thee:

Ps. xli. 13. Blessed be the God and Father of our Lord Jesus Christ, which according to his abundant mercy hath begotten us again unto a lively hope by the resurrection of Jesus Christ from the dead. 1 *Pe. i.* 3. Who hath saved us, and called us with an holy calling, not according to our works, but according to his own purpose and grace, which was given us in Christ Jesus before the world began. 2 *Ti. i.* 9. According as his divine power hath given unto us all things that pertain unto life and godliness, through the knowledge of Him that hath called us to glory and virtue. 2 *Pe. i.* 3. The new man which is renewed in knowledge after the image of Him that created him. *Col. iii.* 10. Ye know the grace of our Lord Jesus Christ. 2 *Co. viii.* 9. In whom are hid all the treasures of wisdom and knowledge. *Col. ii.* 3. Faith cometh by hearing, and hearing by the word of God. *Ro. x.* 17. The preaching of Jesus Christ, according to the revelation of the mystery, which was kept secret since the world began, but now is made manifest, and by the Scriptures of the prophets, according to the commandment of the everlasting God, made known to all nations for the obedience of faith. *Ro. xvi.* 25, 26. This is his commandment, That we should believe on the name of his Son Jesus Christ. 1 *John iii.* 23. The word of the truth of the Gospel, which is come unto you, as it is in all the world. *Col. i.* 5, 6. Ye are a chosen generation, a royal priesthood, an holy nation, a peculiar people; that ye should shew forth the praises of him who hath called you out of darkness into his marvellous light. 1 *Pe. ii.* 9.

2. Increase this knowledge, and confirm this faith in us evermore.

2. Wherefore I also, after I heard of your faith in the Lord Jesus, and love unto all the saints, cease not to give thanks for you, making mention of you in my prayers; that the God of our Lord Jesus Christ, the Father of Glory, may give unto you the spirit of wisdom and revelation in the knowledge of him: the eyes of your understanding being enlightened; that ye may know what is the hope of his calling, and what the riches of the glory of his inheritance in the saints, and what is the exceeding greatness of his power to us-ward who believe, according to the working of his mighty power. *Ep. i.* 15 *to* 19. Being fruitful in every good work, and increasing in the knowledge of God. *Col. i.* 10. Rooted

and built up in Him, and stablished in the faith, as ye have been taught. *Col. ii.* 7. I bow my knees unto the Father of our Lord Jesus Christ, of whom the whole family in heaven and earth is named, that he would grant you, according to the riches of his glory, to be strengthened with might by his Spirit in the inner man; that Christ may dwell in your hearts by faith; that ye, being rooted and grounded in love, may be able to comprehend with all saints what is the breadth, and length, and depth, and height; and to know the love of Christ, which passeth knowledge, that ye might be filled with all the fulness of God. *Ep. iii.* 14 *to* 19. Grow in grace, and in the knowledge of our Lord and Saviour Jesus Christ. 2 *Pe. iii.* 18. I count not myself to have apprehended; but this one thing I do, forgetting those things which are behind, and reaching forth unto those things which are before, I press toward the mark for the prize of the high calling of God in Christ Jesus. *Ph. iii.* 13, 14. The righteous shall flourish like the palm tree; he shall grow like a cedar in Lebanon. Those that be planted in the house of the Lord shall flourish in the courts of our God. *Ps. xcii.* 12, 13. Our Lord Jesus Christ shall also confirm you unto the end, that ye may be blameless in the day of our Lord Jesus Christ. 1 *Co. i.* 7, 8.

3. Give thy Holy Spirit to *this Infant,* that *he* may be born again and be made an *heir* of everlasting salvation; through our Lord Jesus Christ, who liveth and reigneth with thee and the Holy Spirit, now and for ever. *Amen.*

3. If ye then, being evil, know how to give good gifts unto your children; how much more shall your heavenly Father give the Holy Spirit to them that ask him. *Lu. xi.* 13. Except a man be born again, he cannot see the kingdom of God. Jesus answered, Verily, verily, I say unto thee, Except a man be born of water and of the Spirit, he cannot enter into the kingdom of God. That which is born of the flesh is flesh; and that which is born of the Spirit is spirit. Marvel not that I said unto thee, Ye must be born again. *John iii.* 3. 5, 6, 7. God hath from the beginning chosen you to salvation through sanctification of the Spirit and belief of the truth, whereunto he called you by our Gospel, to the obtaining of the glory of our Lord Jesus Christ. 2 *Thes. ii.* 13, 14. For God so loved the world, that he gave his only begotten Son, that whosoever believeth in him should not perish, but have everlasting life. *John iii.* 16. And being made perfect, he became the author of eternal salvation unto all them that obey him. *He. v.* 9.

Are they [the angels] not all ministering spirits, sent forth to minister for them who shall be heirs of salvation ? *He. i.* 14. Heirs according to the hope of eternal life. *Tit. iii.* 7. Heirs according to the promise. *Ga. iii.* 29. An heir of God through Christ. *Ga. iv.* 7. For as many of you as have been baptized into Christ have put on Christ. *Ga. iii.* 27. Now, therefore, O our God, hear the prayer of thy servant, and his supplications, for the Lord's sake. *Da. ix.* 17.—*See also, Is. xl.* 3.—*Ga. vi.* 15.—*John vii.* 37. 39.—*Ac. xxvi.* 18.

CLIX. *Particular Address to the Sponsors.*

1. Dearly beloved, ye have brought *this Child* here to be baptized, ye have prayed that our Lord Jesus Christ would vouchsafe to receive *him*, to release *him* of *his* sins, to sanctify *him* with the Holy Ghost, to give *him* the kingdom of heaven, and everlasting life. Ye have heard also that our Lord Jesus Christ hath promised in his Gospel to grant all these things that ye have prayed for: which promise he, for his part will most surely keep and perform.

1. Men verily swear by the greater, and an oath for confirmation is to them an end of all strife. Wherein God, willing more abundantly to shew unto the heirs of promise the immutability of his counsel, confirmed it by an oath : that by two immutable things, in which it was impossible for God to lie, we might have a strong consolation, who have fled for refuge to lay hold upon the hope set before us : which hope we have as an anchor of the soul, both sure and stedfast, and which entereth into that within the vail ; whither the forerunner is for us entered, even Jesus. *He. vi.* 16 *to* 20.—*See also, Ac. vii.* 8.—*Ro. iv.* 11, 12.—*Ep. i.* 7.—1 *Pe. i.* 2.—*Tit. i.* 1, 2. 4.—*De. vii.* 9.—2 *Cor. iv.* 16.

2. Wherefore, after this promise made by Christ, *this Infant* must also faithfully, for *his* part, promise by you that are *his* sureties, (until *he* come of age to take it upon *himself,*) that *he* will renounce the

2. Keep the words of this covenant, and do them, that ye may prosper in all that ye do. *De. xxix.* 9. Let every one that nameth the name of Christ depart from iniquity. 2 *Ti. ii.* 19. He that committeth sin is of the devil; for the devil sinneth from the beginning. For this purpose the Son of God was manifested, that he might destroy the works of the devil. In this the children of God are manifest, and the children of the devil ; whosoever doeth not righteousness is not of God, neither he that loveth not his brother. 1 *John iii.* 8. 10. Ye are of your father the devil, and the lusts of your father ye

devil and all his works, and constantly believe God's Holy Word, and obediently keep his commandments. — He was a murderer from the beginning, and abode not in the truth, because there is no truth in him. When he speaketh a lie, he speaketh of his own; for he is a liar, and the father of it. *John viii.* 44.   Now the works of the flesh are manifest, which are these ; Adultery, fornication, uncleanness, lasciviousness, idolatry, witchcraft, hatred, variance, emulations, wrath, strife, seditions, heresies, envyings, murders, drunkenness, revellings, and such like. They that are Christ's have crucified the flesh with the affections and lusts. *Ga. v.* 19, 20, 21. 24.   As they went on their way, they came unto a certain water; and the eunuch said, See, here is water; what doth hinder me to be baptized? And Philip said, If thou believest with all thine heart, thou mayest. *Ac. viii.* 36, 37. And you, that were sometime alienated and enemies in your mind by wicked works, yet now hath he reconciled in the body of his flesh through death, to present you holy and unblameable and unreproveable in his sight : if ye continue in the faith grounded and settled, and be not moved away from the hope of the Gospel. *Col. i.* 21, 22, 23.   The holy Scriptures which are able to make thee wise unto salvation through faith which is in Christ Jesus. *2 Ti. iii.* 15.   Not every one that saith unto me, Lord, Lord, shall enter into the kingdom of heaven; but he that doeth the will of my Father which is in heaven. *Mat. vii.* 21.   If ye love me, keep my commandments. *John xiv.* 15.

CLX. *Particular questions addressed to each Sponsor : and the Sponsor's Answer.*

I demand therefore, Dost thou, in the name of this Child, renounce the devil and all his works, the vain pomp and glory of the world, with all covetous desires of the same, and the carnal desires of the flesh, so — He that committeth sin is of the devil; for the devil sinneth from the beginning. For this purpose the Son of God was manifested, that he might destroy the works of the devil. Whosoever is born of God doth not commit sin; for his seed remaineth in him : and he cannot sin, because he is born of God. In this the children of God are manifest, and the children of the devil; whosoever doeth not righteousness is not of God. *1 John iii.* 8, 9, 10.   Resist the devil, and he will flee from you. *Ja. iv.* 7.   My people are gone into captivity, because they have no knowledge; and their honourable men

that thou wilt not follow, nor be led by them?

I renounce them all.

are famished, and their multitude dried up with thirst. Therefore hell hath enlarged herself, and opened her mouth without measure: and their glory, and their multitude, and their pomp, and he that rejoiceth, shall descend into it. *Is. v.* 13, 14. The fashion of this world passeth away. 1 *Co. vii.* 31. Love not the world, neither the things that are in the world. If any man love the world, the love of the Father is not in him. For all that is in the world, the lust of the flesh, and the lust of the eyes, and the pride of life, is not of the Father, but is of the world. 1 *John ii.* 15, 16. We know that we are of God, and the whole world lieth in wickedness. 1 *John v.* 19. To be carnally minded is death ; but to be spiritually minded is life and peace. We are debtors not to the flesh to live after the flesh. For if ye live after the flesh, ye shall die; but if ye through the Spirit do mortify the deeds of the body, ye shall live. For as many as are led by the Spirit of God, they are the sons of God. *Ro. viii.* 6. 12, 13, 14. For the grace of God that bringeth salvation, hath appeared to all men, teaching us that, denying ungodliness and worldly lusts, we should live soberly, righteously, and godly, in this present world; looking for that blessed hope, and the glorious appearing of the great God and our Saviour Jesus Christ; who gave himself for us, that he might redeem us from all iniquity, and purify unto himself a peculiar people zealous of good works. *Tit. ii.* 11 *to* 14.

CLXI. Questions to each Sponsor respecting his Faith: and the Sponsor's Answer.

Dost thou believe in God

1. Lord, I believe, help thou mine unbelief. *Mark ix.* 24. Believe in the Lord your God, so shall ye be established. 2 *Ch. xx.* 20. Without faith it is impossible to please him ; for he that cometh to God must believe that he is. *He. xi.* 6. There is none other God but one. 1 *Co. viii.* 4. Ye turned to God from idols, to serve the living and true God. 1 *Th. i.* 9. Unto thee it was shewed, that thou mightest know that the Lord he is God; there is none else beside him. *De. iv.* 35. See also, *John iv.* 24.

2. the Father Almighty,

2. Have we not all one Father? hath not one God created us? *Mal. ii.* 10. To us there is but one God, the Father, of whom are all things, and we in him; and one Lord Jesus Christ, by whom are all things, and we by him. 1 *Co. viii.* 6. With God all things are possible. *Mat. xix.* 26. There is nothing too hard for thee; the Great, the Mighty God, the Lord of hosts, is his name: I am the Lord, the God of all flesh; Is there any thing too hard for me? *Je. xxxii.* 17, 18. 27. My Father is greater than all; and no man is able to pluck my sheep out of my Father's hand. *John x.* 29. The Lord God omnipotent reigneth. *Re. xix.* 6.

3. Maker of heaven and earth?

3. In the beginning God created the heaven and the earth. *Ge. i.* 1. In six days the Lord made heaven and earth. *Ex. xx.* 11. Of old hast thou laid the foundation of the earth; and the heavens are the work of thy hands. *Ps. cii.* 25. Thus saith the Lord that created the heavens; God himself that formed the earth and made it; he hath established it, he created it not in vain, he formed it to be inhabited. *Is. xlv.* 18.— *See also, Mal. ii.* 10. *as in* § 2.—*Is. xlviii.* 12, 13.

4. And in Jesus Christ his only-begotten Son, our Lord?

4. Thou shalt call his name JESUS, for he shall save his people from their sins. *Mat. i.* 21. Unto you is born this day, in the city of David, a Saviour, which is Christ the Lord. *Lu. ii.* 11. God sent his only begotten Son into the world. 1 *John iv.* 9. Then said Jesus unto the twelve, Will ye also go away? Then Simon Peter answered him, Lord, to whom shall we go? thou hast the words of eternal life: and we believe and are sure that thou art that Christ, the Son of the living God. *John vi.* 67, 68, 69. Ye believe in God, believe also in me. *John xiv.* 1. I believe that Jesus Christ is the Son of God. *Ac. viii.* 37. These are written, that ye might believe that Jesus is the Christ, the Son of God; and that believing, ye might have life through his name. *John xx.* 31. —*See also, John iii.* 18.—*John xiii.* 13.

5. And that he was conceived by the Holy Ghost; born of the Virgin Mary;

5. The Holy Ghost shall come upon thee, and the power of the Highest shall overshadow thee; therefore also that holy thing which shall be born of thee, shall be called the Son of God. *Lu. i.* 35. Behold, a virgin shall conceive, and bear a Son, and shall call his name Immanuel. *Is. vii.* 14. Fear not to take unto thee Mary thy wife; for that which is con-

ceived in her is of the Holy Ghost. Now all this was done, that it might be fulfilled which was spoken of the Lord by the prophet, saying, Behold, a virgin shall be with child, and shall bring forth a Son. Joseph knew her not till she had brought forth her firstborn Son; and he called his name JESUS. *Mat. i.* 20. 22 *to* 25.

6. that he suffered under Pontius Pilate, was crucified, dead, and buried ;

6. It is written of the Son of Man, that he must suffer many things, and be set at nought. *Mar. ix.* 12. Christ hath suffered for us in the flesh. 1 *Ps. iv.* 1. The chief priests and elders of the people took counsel against Jesus to put him to death: and when they had bound him, they led him away, and delivered him to Pontius Pilate the governor; and when he had scourged Jesus, he delivered him to be crucified ; and they stripped him and put on him a scarlet robe; and when they had platted a crown of thorns, they put it upon his head, and a reed in his right hand ; and they spit upon him, and took the reed, and smote him on the head ; and after that they had mocked him, they led him away to crucify him. Jesus, when he had cried again with a loud voice, yielded up the ghost. And when Joseph had taken the body, he wrapped it in a clean linen cloth, and laid it in his own new tomb. *Mat. xxvii.* 1, 2. 26 *to* 31. 50. 59, 60.—*See also, Mat. xxvi.* 38.—*Lu. xxii.* 44.—*Mat. xii.* 40.

7. that he went down into hell, and also did rise again the third day ;

7. Thou wilt not leave my soul in hell, neither wilt thou suffer thine Holy One to see corruption. *Ps. xvi.* 10. What is it but that he also descended into the lower parts of the earth? *Ep. iv.* 9. Having loosed the pains of death, because it was not possible that he should be holden of it. *Ac. ii.* 24. He rose again the third day according to the Scriptures. 1 *Co. xv.* 4. Jesus our Lord was delivered for our offences, and was raised again for our justification. *Ro. iv.* 24, 25.—*See also, Ac. ii.* 27 *to* 32.—*Is. v.* 14.

8. that he ascended into heaven, and sitteth at the right hand of God the Father Almighty ;

8. While they beheld, he was taken up ; and a cloud received him out of their sight. *Ac. i.* 9: And it came to pass, while he blessed them, he was parted from them, and carried up into heaven. *Lu. xxiv.* 51. He that descended is the same also that ascended up far above all heavens, that he might fill all things. *Ep. iv.* 10. After the Lord had spoken unto them, he was received up into heaven, and sat on the right

hand of God. *Mar. xvi.* 19. Jesus Christ is gone into heaven and is on the right hand of God, angels and authorities and powers being made subject unto him. 1 *Pe. iii.* 21, 22.—*See also, Ac. vii.* 56.—*He. vi.* 20.—*x.* 12.

9. and from thence shall come again at the end of the world, to judge the quick and the dead ?

9. The Father judgeth no man, but hath committed all judgement unto the Son. *John v.* 22. It is he which was ordained of God to be the Judge of quick and dead. *Ac. x.* 42. The Lord Jesus Christ shall judge the quick and the dead at his appearing and his kingdom. 2 *Ti. iv.* 1.—*See also,* 1 *Th. iv.* 16, 17.—*Mat. xxv.* 31 *to* 46.

10. And dost thou believe in the Holy Ghost ;

10. Go ye therefore and teach all nations, baptizing them in the name of the Father, and of the Son, and of the Holy Ghost. *Mat. xxviii.* 19. Peter said, Ananias, why hath Satan filled thine heart to lie to the Holy Ghost? thou hast not lied unto men, but unto God. *Ac. v.* 3, 4. He that shall blaspheme against the Holy Ghost hath never forgiveness, but is in danger of eternal damnation. *Mar. iii.* 29.—*See also, Ac. xix.* 1 *to* 6.—2 *Co. xiii.* 14.

11. the holy Catholic Church;

11. Upon this rock I will build my Church. *Mat. xvi.* 18. Ye are come to the general assembly and Church of the firstborn, which are written in heaven. *He. xii.* 22, 23. The body is one, and hath many members, and all the members of that one body, being many, are one body, so also is Christ. 1 *Co. xii.* 12. And he is the head of the body, the Church. *Col. i.* 18. Who hath saved us, and called us with an holy calling. 2 *Ti. i.* 9. Thou wast slain, and hast redeemed us to God by thy blood out of every kindred, and tongue, and people, and nation. *Re. v.* 9. That he might present it to himself a glorious Church, not having spot, or wrinkle, or any such thing ; but that it should be holy and without blemish. *Ep. v.* 27.—*See also, Mat. xiii.* 24 *to* 30. 47, 48.—*xxii.* 9, 10.—*John x.* 16.—*xvii.* 20, 21.—*Ep. ii.* 19 *to* 22.—1 *Cor. x.* 17.—*He. xi.* 40.

12. the communion of Saints;

12. There is one body, and one Spirit, even as ye are called in one hope of your calling. *Ep. iv.* 4. Beloved of God, called to be saints. *Ro. i.* 7. They are many members, yet but one body. 1 *Cor. xii.* 20. Our conversation is in heaven. *Ph. iii.* 20. That which we have seen and heard declare we unto you, that ye also may have fellowship with us ; and truly our fellowship is with the Father, and with his Son Jesus Christ ; if we walk in the light, as he is in the light, we have fellow-

ship one with another. 1 *John i.* 3. 7. That they all may be one; as thou, Father, art in me, and I in thee, that they also may be one in us. *John xvii.* 21. I John, who also am your brother and companion in tribulation, and in the kingdom and patience of Jesus Christ. *Re. i.* 9. And they continued stedfastly in the apostles' doctrine and fellowship, and in breaking of bread, and in prayers. *Ac. ii.* 42.—*See also*, 1 *Pe. i.* 15, 16. —1 *Cor. xii.* 12 *to* 27.

13. the Remission of sins;

13. There is forgiveness with thee, that thou mayest be feared. *Ps. cxxx.* 4. That repentance and remission of sins should be preached in his name among all nations. *Lu. xxiv.* 47. In whom we have redemption through his blood, the forgiveness of sins. *Ep. i.* 7. Blessed are they whose iniquities are forgiven, whose sins are covered; blessed is the man to whom the Lord will not impute sin. *Ro. iv.* 7, 8.—*See also*, 1 *John ii.* 1, 2.—*He. ix.* 22.—*Ac. xiii.* 38.

14. the Resurrection of the flesh;

14. Ourselves also, which have the firstfruits of the Spirit, even we ourselves groan within ourselves, waiting for the adoption, to wit, the redemption of our body. *Ro. viii.* 23. Thy dead men shall live, together with my dead body shall they arise. *Is. xxvi.* 19. The trumpet shall sound, and the dead shall be raised incorruptible. 1 *Cor. xv.* 52. The hour is coming, in the which all that are in the graves shall hear his voice, and shall come forth, they that have done good unto the resurrection of life. *John v.* 28, 29. I saw the dead, small and great, stand before God; and the sea gave up the dead which were in it; and death and hell delivered up the dead which were in them. *Re. xx.* 12, 13.

15. and everlasting life after death?

15. He gave his only begotten Son, that whosoever believeth in him should not perish, but have everlasting life. *John iii.* 16. Then shall the righteous shine forth as the sun in the kingdom of their Father. *Mat. xiii.* 43. And the smoke of their (of those that worship the beast) torment ascendeth up for ever and ever, and they have no rest day nor night. *Re. xiv.* 11. Where their worm dieth not, and the fire is not quenched. *Mar. ix.* 44. The servants of God shall serve him, and they shall reign for ever and ever. *Re. xxii.* 3. 5. These shall go away into everlasting punishment; but the righteous into life eternal. *Mat. xxv.* 46.

16. All this I stedfastly believe.

16. As they went on their way, they came unto a certain water; and the Eunuch said, See, here is water; what doth hinder me to be baptized? And Philip said, If thou believest with all thine heart, thou mayest. And he answered and said, I believe that Jesus Christ is the Son of God. *Ac. viii.* 36, 37. Ye believe in God, believe also in me. *John xiv.* 1. We believe and are sure that thou art that Christ, the Son of the living God. *John vi.* 69. They believed the Scripture, and the word which Jesus had said. *John ii.* 22.

17. Wilt thou be baptized in this faith?

18. That is my desire.

17, 18. And they said, Believe on the Lord Jesus Christ, and thou shalt be saved, and thy house. And they spake unto him the word of the Lord, and to all that were in his house. And he took them the same hour of the night, and washed their stripes; and was baptized, he and all his, straightway. *Ac. xvi.* 31, 32, 33. Then they that gladly received his word were baptized. *Ac. ii.* 41.

19. Wilt thou then obediently keep God's holy will and commandments, and walk in the same all the days of thy life?

20. I will.

19, 20. Fear God, and keep his commandments: for this is the whole duty of man. *Ec. xii.* 13. Thou hast commanded us to keep thy precepts diligently. O that my ways were directed to keep thy statutes! Teach me, O Lord, the way of thy statutes; and I shall keep it unto the end; I hate every false way. I will keep the commandments of my God; I do not forget thy law. I will run the way of thy commandments, when thou shalt enlarge my heart. *Ps. cxix.* 4, 5. 33. 104. 115. 153. 32. How shall we, that are dead to sin, live any longer therein? *Ro. vi.* 2. Hereby we do know that we know him, if we keep his commandments. He that saith, I know him, and keepeth not his commandments, is a liar, and the truth is not in him. He that saith he abideth in him, ought himself also so to walk even as he walked. 1 *John ii.* 3, 4. 6. So shall I keep thy law continually for ever and ever. *Ps. cxix.* 44.

CLXII. Short Prayers.

1. O merciful God, grant that the old Adam in *this* Child may be so buried, that the new man

1. The first man Adam was made a living soul; the last Adam was made a quickening Spirit. For as in Adam all die, even so in Christ shall all be made alive. 1 *Co. xv.* 45. 22. We are buried with him by baptism into death; that like as Christ was raised up from the dead by the glory of the Father,

may be raised
up in *him.*
Amen.

even so we also should walk in newness of life. *Ro. vi.* 4. God, who is rich in mercy, for his great love wherewith he loved us, even when we were dead in sins, hath quickened us together with Christ, (by grace are ye saved;) and hath raised us up together, and made us sit together in heavenly places. *Ep. ii.* 4, 5, 6. Ye have not so learned Christ ; if so be that ye have heard him, and been taught by him, as the truth is in Jesus : that ye put off concerning the former conversation the old man, which is corrupt according to the deceitful lusts ; and be renewed in the spirit of your mind : and that ye put on the new man, which after God is created in righteousness and true holiness. *Ep. iv.* 20 *to* 24.

2. Grant
that all carnal
affections may
die in *him,* and
that all things
belonging to
the Spirit may
live and grow
in *him. Amen.*

2. To be carnally minded is death ; but to be spiritually minded is life and peace. *Ro. viii.* 6. Likewise reckon ye also yourselves to be dead indeed unto sin, but alive unto God through Jesus Christ our Lord. *Ro. vi.* 11. If ye through the Spirit do mortify the deeds of the body, ye shall live. *Ro. viii.* 13. They that are Christ's have crucified the flesh with the affections and lusts. *Ga. v.* 24. Mortify therefore your members which are upon the earth. *Col. iii.* 5. Knowing this, that our old man is crucified with him, that the body of sin might be destroyed, that henceforth we should not serve sin. *Ro. vi.* 6. The fruit of the Spirit is love, joy, peace, longsuffering, gentleness, goodness, faith, meekness, temperance ; against such there is no law. *Ga. v.* 22, 23. Put on therefore, as the elect of God, holy and beloved, bowels of mercies, kindness, humbleness of mind, meekness, longsuffering ; forbearing one another, and forgiving one another, if any man have a quarrel against any : even as Christ forgave you, so also do ye. And above all these things put on charity. *Col. iii.* 12, 13, 14. Having therefore these promises, dearly beloved, let us cleanse ourselves from all filthiness of the flesh and spirit, perfecting holiness in the fear of God. 2 *Co. vii.* 1. Grow in grace and in the knowledge of our Lord and Saviour Jesus Christ. 2 *Pe. iii.* 18.

3. Grant
that *he* may
have power and
strength to
have victory,
and to triumph,

3. He giveth power to the faint ; and to them that have no might he increaseth strength. They that wait upon the Lord shall renew their strength. *Is. xl.* 29. 31. He said unto me, My grace is sufficient for thee ; for my strength is made per-

against the de-
vil, the world,
and the flesh.
Amen.

fect in weakness. 2 *Cor. xii.* 9.   Strengthened with might by his Spirit in the inner man. *Ep. iii.* 16.   Resist the devil, and he will flee from you. *Ja. iv.* 7.   The God of peace shall bruise satan under your feet shortly. *Ro. xvi.* 20.   Whatsoever is born of God overcometh the world: and this is the victory that overcometh the world, even our faith. 1 *John v.* 4. Hating even the garment spotted by the flesh. *Jude* 23. Finally, my brethren, be strong in the Lord, and in the power of his might.   Put on the whole armour of God, that ye may be able to stand against the wiles of the devil.   Take unto you the whole armour of God, that ye may be able to withstand in the evil day, and having done all, to stand. *Ep. vi.* 10, 11. 13.   Thanks be to God, which giveth us the victory through our Lord Jesus Christ. 1 *Co. xv.* 57.   Thanks be unto God, which always causeth us to triumph in Christ. 2 *Co. ii.* 14.   In all these things we are more than conquerors through him that loved us. *Ro. viii.* 37.

4. Grant that
whosoever is
here dedicated
to thee by our
office and min-
istry may also
be endued with
heavenly vir-
tues, and ever-
lastingly
rewarded,
through thy
mercy, O bless-
ed Lord God,
who dost live,
and govern all
things, world
without end.
Amen.

4. Ye are all the children of God by faith in Christ Jesus.   For as many of you as have been baptized into Christ have put on Christ. *Ga. iii.* 26, 27.   Let a man so account of us, as of the ministers of Christ, and stewards of the mysteries of God. 1 *Co. iv.* 1.   Who then is Paul, and who is Apollos, but ministers by whom ye believed, even as the Lord gave to every man?   I have planted, Apollos watered; but God gave the increase.   So neither is he that planteth any thing, neither he that watereth; but God that giveth the increase. 1 *Co. iii.* 5, 6, 7.   Grace and peace be multiplied unto you through the knowledge of God, and of Jesus our Lord, according as his divine power hath given unto us all things that pertain unto life and godliness, through the knowledge of him that hath called us to glory and virtue. 2 *Pe. i.* 2, 3.   And this I pray, that your love may abound yet more and more in knowledge and in all judgment; that ye may approve things that are excellent; that ye may be sincere and without offence till the day of Christ; being filled with the fruits of righteousness, which are by Jesus Christ, unto the glory and praise of God. *Ph. i.* 9, 10, 11.   For this cause we also, since the day we heard it, do not cease to pray for you, and to desire that ye might be filled with the knowledge

of his will in all wisdom and spiritual understanding ; that ye might walk worthy of the Lord unto all pleasing, being fruitful in every good work, and increasing in the knowledge of God. Warning every man, and teaching every man in all wisdom ; that we may present every man perfect in Christ Jesus. *Col. i.* 9, 10. 28. Knowing that of the Lord ye shall receive the reward of the inheritance, for ye serve the Lord Christ. *Col. iii.* 24. Behold, I come quickly ; and my reward is with me, to give to every man according as his work shall be. *Re. xxii.* 12. The gift of God is eternal life through Jesus Christ our Lord. *Ro. vi.* 23. According to his mercy he saved us. *Tit. iii.* 5. Keep yourselves in the love of God, looking for the mercy of our Lord Jesus Christ unto eternal life. *Jude* 21. Then shall the king say unto them on his right hand, Come, ye blessed of my Father, inherit the kingdom prepared for you from the foundation of the world. *Mat. xxv.* 34. The Lord hath prepared his throne in the heavens ; and his kingdom ruleth over all. *Ps. ciii.* 19. Who is the blessed and only Potentate, the King of kings, and Lord of lords. 1 *Ti. vi.* 15. He ruleth by his power for ever. *Ps. lxvi.* 7.

CLXIII. *Prayer of Consecration.*

1. Almighty, everliving God, whose most dearly beloved Son Jesus Christ, for the forgiveness of our sins, did shed out of his most precious side both water and blood ;

1. And Jesus, when he was baptized, went up straightway out of the water : and, lo, the heavens were opened unto him, and he saw the Spirit of God descending like a dove, and lighting upon him : and, lo, a voice from heaven, saying, This is my beloved Son, in whom I am well pleased. *Mat. iii.* 16, 17. In that day there shall be a fountain opened to the house of David and to the inhabitants of Jerusalem for sin and for uncleanness. *Zech. xiii.* 1. One of the soldiers with a spear pierced his side, and forthwith came thereout blood and water. *John xix.* 34. This is he that came by water and blood, even Jesus Christ ; not by water only, but by water and blood. 1 *John v.* 6. In whom we have redemption through his blood, the forgiveness of sins, according to the riches of his grace. *Ep. i.* 7. The blood of Jesus Christ his Son cleanseth us from all sin. 1 *John i.* 7. Unto him that loved us, and washed us from our sins in his own blood, to him be glory

and dominion for ever and ever. *Re. i.* 5, 6.—*See also, Zec. xii.* 10.—*He. ix.* 12, 13, 14.

2. and gave commandment to his disciples, that they should go teach all nations, and baptize them In the Name of the Father, theSon, and the Holy Ghost;

2. Jesus came and spake unto them, saying, All power is given unto me in heaven and in earth. Go ye therefore, and teach all nations, baptizing them in the name of the Father, and of the Son, and of the Holy Ghost. *Mat. xxviii.* 18, 19.— *See also, Mar. xvi.* 20.—*Ac. v.* 42.—*xi.* 26.

3. Regard, we beseech thee, the supplications of thy congregation; sanctify this water to the mystical washing away of sin;

3. Hearken thou to the supplication of thy servant, and of thy people Israel, when they shall pray toward this place. 1 *Ki. viii.* 30. Verily, verily, I say unto you, whatsoever ye shall ask the Father in my name, he will give it you. Ask, and ye shall receive, that your joy may be full. *John xvi.* 23, 24. Again I say unto you, That if two of you shall agree on earth as touching any thing that they shall ask, it shall be done for them of my Father which is in heaven. *Mat. xviii.* 19. This is the confidence that we have in him, that, if we ask any thing according to his will, he heareth us. 1 *John v.* 14. Elisha sent a messenger unto Naaman, saying, Go and wash in Jordan seven times, and thy flesh shall come again to thee, and thou shalt be clean. But Naaman said, Are not Abana and Pharpar, rivers of Damascus, better than all the waters of Israel? May I not wash in them, and be clean? So he turned and went away in a rage. And his servants came near, and spake unto him, and said, My father, if the prophet had bid thee do some great thing, wouldest thou not have done it? how much rather then, when he saith to thee, Wash, and be clean? Then went he down, and dipped himself seven times in Jordan, according to the saying of the man of God: and his flesh came again like unto the flesh of a little child, and he was clean. 2 *Ki. v.* 10 *to* 14. It is sanctified by the word of God and prayer. 1 *Ti. iv.* 5. Great is the mystery of godliness. 1 *Ti. iii.* 16. Now why tarriest thou? arise, and be baptized, and wash away thy sins, calling on the name of the Lord. *Ac. xxii.* 16.

4. And grant that this Child now to be bap- tized therein, may receive the fulness of thy grace, and

4. Repent, and be baptized every one of you in the name of Jesus Christ, for the remission of sins, and ye shall receive the gift of the Holy Ghost. *Ac. ii.* 38. But ye are washed, but ye are sanctified, but ye are justified in the name of the Lord Jesus, and by the Spirit of our God. 1 *Co. vi.* 11. He

ever remain in the number of thy faithful and elect children; through Jesus Christ our Lord. *Amen.*

saved us by the washing of regeneration, and renewing of the Holy Ghost; which he shed on us abundantly through Jesus Christ our Saviour. *Tit. iii.* 5, 6. And of his fulness have all we received, and grace for grace. *John i.* 16. My God shall supply all your need according to his riches in glory by Christ Jesus. *Ph. iv.* 19. Then they that gladly received his word were baptized: and they continued stedfastly in the apostles' doctrine and fellowship, and in breaking of bread, and in prayers. *Ac. ii.* 41, 42. Ye have received the Spirit of adoption, whereby we cry, Abba, Father. The Spirit itself beareth witness with our spirit, that we are the children of God. *Ro. viii.* 15, 16. Elect according to the foreknowledge of God the Father, through sanctification of the Spirit, unto obedience and sprinkling of the blood of Jesus Christ. 1 *Pe. i.* 2. Now unto him that is able to keep you from falling, and to present you faultless before the presence of his glory with exceeding joy, to the only wise God our Saviour, be glory and majesty, dominion and power, both now and ever. Amen. *Jude* 24, 25. I pray God your whole spirit and soul and body be preserved blameless unto the coming of our Lord Jesus Christ. 1 *Th. v.* 23. Be thou faithful unto death, and I will give thee a crown of life. *Re. ii.* 10. He is Lord of lords, and King of kings; and they that are with him are called, and chosen, and faithful. *Re. xvii.* 14.—*See also, Ac. iv.* 32, 33.

CLXIV. Naming and Baptizing the Infant.

1. Name this Child.

N. I baptize thee In the Name of the Father, and of the Son, and of the Holy Ghost. *Amen.*

1. And it came to pass, that on the eighth day they came to circumcise the child; and they called him Zacharias, after the name of his father. And his mother answered and said, Not so, but he shall be called John. And they said unto her, There is none of thy kindred that is called by this name. And they made signs to his father, how he would have him called. And he asked for a writing-table, and wrote, saying, His name is John. *Lu. i.* 59 *to* 63. And when eight days

were accomplished for the circumcising of the child, his name was called JESUS, which was so named of the angel before he was conceived in the womb. *Lu. ii.* 21. Teach all nations, baptizing them in the name of the Father, and of the Son, and of the Holy Ghost. *Mat. xxviii.* 19.

CLXV. The Receiving of the baptized Infant into the Congregation.

1. We receive this Child into the Congregation of Christ's flock,

1. I am the good shepherd: the good shepherd giveth his life for the sheep. And other sheep I have, which are not of this fold : them also I must bring, and they shall hear my voice; and there shall be one fold, and one shepherd. *John x.* 11. 16. By one Spirit are we all baptized into one body. 1 *Co. xii.* 13. And the Lord added to the Church daily such as should be saved. *Ac. ii.* 47. Fear not, little flock; for it is your Father's good pleasure to give you the kingdom. *Lu. xii.* 32. See also, *Jere. xxiii.* 3.—*Ac. v.* 14.—*John xvii.* 21, 22, 23.

2. and do sign *him* with the sign of the Cross, in token that hereafter *he* shall not be ashamed to confess the faith of Christ crucified,

2. And they shall see his face ; and his name shall be in their foreheads. *Re. xxii.* 4. Abraham received the sign of circumcision. *Ro. iv.* 11. God forbid that I should glory, save in the cross of our Lord Jesus Christ, by whom the world is crucified unto me, and I unto the world. *Ga. vi.* 14. I am not ashamed of the Gospel of Christ : for it is the power of God unto salvation to every one that believeth ; to the Jew first, and also to the Greek. *Ro. i.* 16. We preach Christ crucified. 1 *Co. i.* 23. Whosoever therefore shall be ashamed of me and of my words, of him also shall the Son of Man be ashamed, when he cometh in the glory of his Father. *Mar. viii.* 38. Whosoever shall confess me before men, him will I confess also before my Father which is in heaven. *Mat. x.* 32.

3. and manfully to fight under his banner, against sin, the world, and the devil ; and to continue Christ's faithful soldier and servant unto *his* life's end. *Amen.*

3. Jesus said unto his disciples, If any man will come after me, let him deny himself, and take up his cross, and follow me. *Mat. xvi.* 24. His banner over me was love. *Sol. Song ii.* 4. Be strong in the Lord, and in the power of his might. Put on the whole armour of God, that ye may be able to stand against the wiles of the devil. Take unto you the whole armour of God, that ye may be able to withstand in the evil

day, and having done all, to stand. *Ep. vi.* 10, 11. 13. Fight the good fight of faith, lay hold on eternal life, whereunto thou art also called, and hast professed a good profession before many witnesses. 1 *Ti. vi.* 12. Thou therefore endure hardness, as a good soldier of Jesus Christ. No man that warreth entangleth himself with the affairs of this life; that he may please him who hath chosen him to be a soldier. 2 *Ti. ii.* 3, 4. When the enemy shall come in like a flood, the Spirit of the Lord shall lift up a standard against him. *Is. lix.* 19. Let not sin therefore reign in your mortal body, that ye should obey it in the lusts thereof. Knowing this, that our old man is crucified with him, that the body of sin might be destroyed, that henceforth we should not serve sin. *Ro. vi.* 12. 6. Ye have not yet resisted unto blood, striving against sin. *He. xii.* 4. Whatsoever is born of God overcometh the world: and this is the victory that overcometh the world, even our faith. Who is he that overcometh the world, but he that believeth that Jesus is the Son of God? 1 *John v.* 4, 5. Be sober, be vigilant; because your adversary the devil, as a roaring lion, walketh about, seeking whom he may devour; whom resist stedfast in the faith. 1 *Pe. v.* 8, 9. Let us hold fast our profession. *He. iv.* 14. I have fought a good fight, I have finished my course, I have kept the faith; henceforth there is laid up for me a crown of righteousness, which the Lord, the righteous Judge, shall give me at that day. 2 *Ti. iv.* 7, 8. Be thou faithful unto death, and I will give thee a crown of life. *Re. ii.* 10.

CLXVI. *Address to the people after the receiving of the Baptized into the Congregation.*

1. Seeing now, dearly beloved brethren, that *this Child* is regenerate, and grafted into the body of Christ's Church,

1. If any man be in Christ, he is a new creature: old things are passed away; behold, all things are become new. 2 *Co. v.* 17. For as many of you as have been baptized into Christ have put on Christ. *Ga. iii.* 27. Being born again, not of corruptible seed, but of incorruptible. 1 *Pe. i.* 23. 'I am the vine, ye are the branches. *John xv.* 5. Thou wilt say then, The branches were broken off, that I might be graffed in. Well; because of unbelief they were broken off;

E

and thou standest by faith. Be not high minded, but fear. *Ro. xi.* 19, 20. By one Spirit are we all baptized into one body. 1 *Co. xii.* 13. The Church which is his [Christ's] body, the fulness of him that filleth all in all. *Ep. i.* 22, 23.

2. let us give thanks unto Almighty God for these benefits;

2. Oh that men would praise the Lord for his goodness, and for his wonderful works to the children of men! let them sacrifice the sacrifices of thanksgiving, and declare his works with rejoicing. *Ps. cvii.* 21, 22. What shall I render unto the Lord for all his benefits toward me ? *Ps. cxvi.* 12. Bless the Lord, O my soul, and forget not all his benefits. *Ps. ciii.* 2. Blessed be the Lord, who daily loadeth us with benefits, even the God of our salvation. *Ps. lxviii.* 19.

3. and with one accord make our prayers unto him, that *this Child* may lead the rest of *his* life according to this beginning.

3. And when they heard that, they lifted up their voice to God with one accord. *Ac. iv.* 24. Pray one for another. The effectual fervent prayer of a righteous man availeth much. *Ja. v.* 16. I thank my God upon every remembrance of you, being confident of this very thing, that he which hath begun a good work in you will perform it until the day of Jesus Christ: and this I pray, that your love may abound yet more and more in knowledge and in all judgment; that ye may be sincere and without offence till the day of Christ ; being filled with the fruits of righteousness. *Ph. i.* 3. 6. 9, 10, 11. Then shall we know, if we follow on to know the Lord. *Ho. vi.* 3. Grow in grace, and in the knowledge of our Lord and Saviour Jesus Christ. 2 *Pe. iii.* 18. As newborn babes, desire the sincere milk of the word, that ye may grow thereby. 1 *Pe. ii.* 2. As ye have therefore received Christ Jesus the Lord, so walk ye in him : rooted and built up in him, and stablished in the faith, as ye have been taught. *Col. ii.* 6, 7. For we are made partakers of Christ, if we hold the beginning of our confidence stedfast unto the end. *He. iii.* 14.

CLXVII. *Concluding Thanksgiving and Prayer.*

1. We yield thee hearty thanks, most merciful Father,

1. I thank my God always on your behalf, for the grace of God which is given you by Jesus Christ. 1 *Co. i.* 4. Always in every prayer of mine for you all making request with joy, for your fellowship in the gospel ; being confident of this very thing, that he which hath begun a good work in you will

perform it until the day of Jesus Christ. *Ph. i.* 4, 5, 6. Giving thanks unto the Father, which hath made us meet to be partakers of the inheritance of the saints in light. *Col. i.* 12. I will praise the Lord with my whole heart, in the assembly of the upright, and in the congregation. *Ps. cxi.* 1. Blessed be God, even the Father of our Lord Jesus Christ, the Father of mercies, and the God of all comfort. 2 *Co. i.* 3.—*See also,* 1 *Th. v.* 18.—1 *Pe. ii.* 5.—*Ep. v.* 20.—*Ps. xxxv.* 18.

2. that it hath pleased thee to regenerate *this Infant* with thy Holy Spirit,

2. Verily, verily, I say unto thee, Except a man be born again he cannot see the kingdom of God ; except a man be born of water and of the Spirit, he cannot enter into the kingdom of God. That which is born of the flesh is flesh ; and that which is born of the Spirit is spirit : marvel not. *John iii.* 3. 5, 6, 7. Peter said unto them, Repent, and be baptized every one of you in the name of Jesus Christ for the remission of sins, and ye shall receive the gift of the Holy Ghost. For the promise is unto you, and to your children, and to all that are afar off, even as many as the Lord our God shall call. *Ac. ii.* 38, 39. I will pour my Spirit upon thy seed, and my blessing upon thine offspring. *Is. xliv.* 3. Ye also are builded together for an habitation of God through the Spirit. *Ep. ii.* 22. Not by works of righteousness which we have done, but according to his mercy he saved us, by the washing of regeneration and renewing of the Holy Ghost. *Tit. iii.* 5. *See also, Je. i.* 5.—*Lu. i.* 15.

3. to receive *him* for thine own *Child* by adoption, and to incorporate *him* into thy holy Church.

3. The Spirit itself beareth witness with our spirit, that we are the children of God. *Ro. viii.* 16. It shall come to pass, that in the place where it was said unto them, Ye are not my people ; there shall they be called the children of the living God. They which are the children of the flesh, these are not the children of God : but the children of the promise are counted for the seed. *Ro. ix.* 26. 8. When the fulness of the time was come, God sent forth his Son, made of a woman, made under the law, to redeem them that were under the law, that we might receive the adoption of sons. *Ga. iv.* 4, 5. As many as received him, to them gave he power to become the sons of God, even to them that believe on his name. *John i.* 12. As the body is one, and hath many members, and all the members of that one body, being many, are one body ;

so also is Christ. For by one Spirit are we all baptized into one body whether we be Jews or Gentiles, whether we be bond or free. For the body is not one member, but many. 1 *Co. xii.* 12, 13, 14. The Church which is his body. *Ep. i.* 22, 23.

4. And humbly we beseech thee to grant, that *he*, being dead unto sin, and living unto righteousness, and being buried with Christ in his death, may crucify the old man, and utterly abolish the whole body of sin; and that, as *he is* made *partaker* of the death of thy Son, *he* may also be *partaker* of his resurrection;

4. Reckon ye also yourselves to be dead indeed unto sin, but alive unto God through Jesus Christ our Lord. Neither yield ye your members as instruments of unrighteousness unto sin: but yield yourselves unto God, as those that are alive from the dead, and your members as instruments of righteousness unto God. I speak after the manner of men because of the infirmity of your flesh; for as ye have yielded your members servants to uncleanness and to iniquity unto iniquity; even so now yield your members servants to righteousness unto holiness. *Ro. vi.* 11. 13. 19. I am crucified with Christ: nevertheless I live; yet not I, but Christ liveth in me: and the life which I now live in the flesh, I live by the faith of the Son of God, who loved me, and gave himself for me. *Ga. ii.* 20. Who his own self bare our sins in his own body on the tree, that we, being dead to sins, should live unto righteousness. 1 *Pe. ii.* 24. Buried with him in baptism, wherein also ye are risen with him through the faith of the operation of God, who hath raised him from the dead. And you, being dead in your sins and the uncircumcision of your flesh, hath he quickened together with him, having forgiven you all trespasses. *Col. ii.*12, 13. Therefore we are buried with him by baptism into death: that like as Christ was raised up from the dead by the glory of the Father, even so we also should walk in newness of life. For if we have been planted together in the likeness of his death, we shall be also in the likeness of his resurrection: knowing this, that our old man is crucified with him, that the body of sin might be destroyed, that henceforth we should not serve sin. *Ro. vi.* 4, 5, 6. If ye then be risen with Christ, seek those things which are above, where Christ sitteth on the right hand of God. Set your affection on things above, not on things on the earth: for ye are dead, and your life is hid with Christ in God. When Christ, who is our life, shall appear, then shall ye also appear with him in glory. Mortify therefore your members which are upon the earth;

fornication, uncleanness, inordinate affection, evil concupiscence, and covetousness, which is idolatry. Now ye also put off all these; anger, wrath, malice, blasphemy, filthy communication out of your mouth. Lie not one to another, seeing ye have put off the old man with his deeds; and have put on the new man, which is renewed in knowledge after the image of him that created him. Put on therefore, as the elect of God, holy and beloved, bowels of mercies, kindness, humbleness of mind, meekness, longsuffering, forbearing one another, and forgiving one another, if any man have a quarrel against any : even as Christ forgave you, so also do ye. And above all these things put on charity, which is the bond of perfectness. And let the peace of God rule in your hearts, to the which also ye are called in one body; and be ye thankful. *Col. iii.* 1 *to* 5. 8 *to* 15.

5. so that finally, with the residue of thy holy Church, he may be an inheritor of thine everlasting kingdom, through Jesus Christ our Lord. Amen.

5. We are made partakers of Christ, if we hold the beginning of our confidence stedfast unto the end. *He. iii.* 14. These all, having obtained a good report through faith, received not the promise : God having provided some better thing for us, that they without us should not be made perfect. *He. xi.* 39, 40. After this I will return, and will build again the tabernacle of David, which is fallen down; and I will build again the ruins thereof, and I will set it up : that the residue of men might seek after the Lord, and all the Gentiles, upon whom my name is called, saith the Lord, who doeth all these things. *Ac. xv.* 16, 17. If we believe that Jesus died and rose again, even so them also which sleep in Jesus will God bring with him. The dead in Christ shall rise first : then we which are alive and remain shall be caught up together with them in the clouds, to meet the Lord in the air : and so shall we ever be with the Lord. 1 *Th. iv.* 14. 16, 17. And now, brethren, I commend you to God, and to the word of his grace, which is able to build you up, and to give you an inheritance among all them which are sanctified. *Ac. xx.* 32. That they may receive forgiveness of sins, and inheritance among them which are sanctified by faith that is in me. *Ac. xxvi.* 18. He is the Head of the body, the Church : who is the firstborn from the dead. *Col. i.* 18. Fear not, little flock ; for it is your Father's good pleasure to give you the kingdom. *Lu. xii.* 32. If children, then heirs ; heirs of God, and joint-heirs with Christ ;

if so be that we suffer with him, that we may be also glorified together. *Ro. viii.* 17. Ye are come unto mount Sion, and unto the city of the living God, the heavenly Jerusalem, and to an innumerable company of angels, to the general assembly and Church of the firstborn, which are written in heaven, and to God the Judge of all, and to the spirits of just men made perfect, and to Jesus the mediator of the new covenant. *He. xii.* 22, 23. 26. Blessed be the God and Father of our Lord Jesus Christ, which according to his abundant mercy hath begotten us again unto a lively hope by the resurrection of Jesus Christ from the dead, to an inheritance incorruptible, and undefiled, and that fadeth not away, reserved in heaven for you, who are kept by the power of God through faith unto salvation ready to be revealed in the last time. 1 *Pe. i.* 3, 4, 5.

CLXVIII & CLXIX. The Exhortation to the Godfathers and Godmothers.

1. Forasmuch as *this Child hath* promised by you *his* sureties, to renounce the devil and all his works, to believe in God, and to serve him; ye must remember, that it is your parts and duties to see that *this Infant* be taught, so soon as *he* shall be able to learn, what a solemn vow, promise, and profession, *he hath* here made by you.

1. Offer unto God thanksgiving; and pay thy vows unto the Most High. *Ps. l.* 14. Now 1 say, that the heir, as long as he is a child, differeth nothing from a servant, though he be lord of all; but is under tutors and governors until the time appointed of the father. *Ga. iv.* 1, 2. Set your hearts unto all the words which I testify among you this day, which ye shall command your children to observe to do, all the words of this law. For it is not a vain thing for you; because it is your life: and through this thing ye shall prolong your days in the land. *De. xxxii.* 46, 47. Thou shalt teach them diligently unto thy children, and shalt talk of them when thou sittest in thine house, and when thou walkest by the way, and when thou liest down, and when thou risest up. *De. vi.* 7. Only take heed to thyself, and keep thy soul diligently, lest thou forget the things which thine eyes have seen, and lest they depart from thy heart all the days of thy life: but teach them thy sons and thy son's sons; specially the day that thou stoodest before the Lord thy God in Horeb, when the Lord said unto me, Gather me the people together, and I will make them hear my words, that they may learn to fear me all the days

that they shall live upon the earth, and that they may teach
their children. *De. iv.* 9, 10. The father to the children
shall make known thy truth. *Is. xxxviii.* 19. I know him,
that he will command his children and his household after
him, and they shall keep the way of the Lord. *Ge. xviii.* 19.
Train up a child in the way he should go. *Pr. xxii.* 6. When
thou vowest a vow unto God, defer not to pay it; for he hath
no pleasure in fools: pay that which thou hast vowed. *Ec. v.* 4.
Come, ye children, hearken unto me: I will teach you the
fear of the Lord. *Ps. xxxiv.* 11.

2. And that *he* may know these things the better, ye shall call upon *him* to hear sermons;

2. Faith cometh by hearing, and hearing by the word of
God. *Ro. x.* 17. And all the people gathered themselves
together as one man. And Ezra the Priest brought the law
before the congregation both of men and women, and all that
could hear with understanding; and he read therein. And
Ezra the scribe stood upon a pulpit of wood; and he opened
the book in the sight of all the people; (for he was above all
the people;) and when he opened it, all the people stood up.
And the Levites caused the people to understand the law.
So they read in the book in the law of God distinctly, and
gave the sense, and caused them to understand the reading.
Ne. viii. 1 *to* 5. 7, 8. Gather the people together, men, and
women, and children, and thy stranger that is within thy
gates, that they may hear, and that they may learn, and fear
the Lord your God, and observe to do all the words of this
law: and that their children, which have not known any
thing, may hear, and learn to fear the Lord your God. *De.
xxxi.* 12, 13. Now his parents went to Jerusalem every year
at the feast of the passover. And when he was twelve years
old, they went up to Jerusalem after the custom of the feast.
Lu. ii. 41, 42. The next Sabbath day came almost the whole
city together to hear the word of God. *Ac. xiii.* 44.

3. and chiefly ye shall provide, that *he* may learn the Creed, the Lord's Prayer, and the Ten Commandments the in vulgar tongue,

3. He established a testimony in Jacob, and appointed a
law in Israel, which he commanded our fathers, that they
should make them known to their children: that the generation to come might know them, even the children which
should be born; who should arise and declare them to their
children: that they might set their hope in God, and not
forget the works of God, but keep his commandments. *Ps.*

and all other things which a Christian ought to know and believe to his soul's health; and that *this Child* may be virtuously brought up to lead a godly and a Christian life; remembering always, that Baptism doth represent unto us our profession; which is, to follow the example of our Saviour Christ, and to be made like unto him; that, as he died, and rose again for us, so should we, who are baptized, die from sin, and rise again unto righteousness; continually mortifying all our evil and corrupt affections, and daily proceeding in all virtue and godliness of living.

lxxviii. 5, 6, 7. These words, which I command thee this day, shall be in thine heart: and thou shalt teach them diligently unto thy children. *De. vi.* 6, 7. Go ye therefore, and teach all nations, baptizing them in the name of the Father, and of the Son, and of the Holy Ghost: teaching them to observe all things whatsoever I have commanded you. *Mat. xxviii.* 19, 20. Without faith it is impossible to please God. *He. xi.* 6. Believe on the Lord Jesus Christ. *Ac. xvi.* 31. Lord, teach us to pray, as John also taught his disciples. And he said unto them, When ye pray, say, Our Father which art in heaven, hallowed be thy name. Thy kingdom come. Thy will be done, as in heaven so in earth. *Lu. xi.* 1, 2. And, behold, one came to him and said unto him, Good Master, what good thing shall I do, that I may have eternal life? He said unto him, If thou wilt enter into life, keep the commandments. *Mat. xix.* 16, 17. Except ye utter by the tongue words easy to be understood, how shall it be known what is spoken? If I know not the meaning of the voice, I shall be unto him that speaketh a barbarian, and he that speaketh shall be a barbarian unto me. *1 Co. xiv.* 9. 11. Incline your ear, and come unto me: hear, and your soul shall live. *Is. lv.* 3. Their souls shall be as a watered garden. *Je. xxxi.* 12. Heal my soul, for I have sinned against thee. *Ps. xli.* 4. Ye fathers, provoke not your children to wrath: but bring them up in the nurture and admonition of the Lord. *Ep. vi.* 4. Train up a child in the way he should go: and when he is old, he will not depart from it. *Pr. xxii.* 6. Continue thou in the things which thou hast learned and hast been assured of; that from a child thou hast known the holy Scriptures which are able to make thee wise unto salvation through faith which is in Christ Jesus. *2 Ti. iii.* 14, 15. Remember ye the words which were spoken before of the apostles of our Lord Jesus Christ. *Jude* 17. I think it meet to stir you up by putting you in remembrance. *2 Pe. i.* 13. As many of you as have been baptized into Christ have put on Christ. *Ga. iii.* 27. Let us hold fast the profession of our faith without wavering. *He. x.* 23. For even hereunto were ye called: because Christ also suffered for us, leaving an example, that ye should follow his steps. *1 Pe. ii.* 21. Know ye not, that so many of us as were baptized into Jesus Christ were baptized into his death? therefore we are buried with him by baptism into death : that like as Christ was raised up from the dead by the glory of the Father, even so we also should walk in newness of life. For if we have been planted together in the likeness of his death, we shall be also in the likeness of his resurrection: knowing this, that our old man is crucified with him, that the body of sin might be destroyed, that henceforth we should not serve sin. Likewise reckon ye also yourselves to be dead indeed unto sin, but alive unto God through Jesus Christ our Lord. *Ro. vi.* 3 *to* 6. 11. Mortify therefore your members which are upon the earth. For ye are dead, and your life is hid with Christ in God. *Col. iii.* 5. 3. According as his divine power hath given unto us all things that pertain unto life and godliness, through the knowledge of him that hath called us to glory and virtue : whereby are given unto us exceeding great and precious promises : that by these ye might be partakers of the divine nature, having escaped the corruption that is in the world through lust. And beside this, giving all diligence, add to your faith virtue ; and to virtue knowledge ; and to knowledge temperance ; and to temperance patience ; and to patience godliness ; and to godliness brotherly kindness ; and to brotherly kindness charity. 2 *Pe. i.* 3 *to* 7.

4. Ye are to take care that *this Child* be brought to the Bishop to be confirmed by him, so soon as *he* can say the Creed, the Lord's Prayer, and the Ten Commandments in the vulgar tongue, and be further instructed in the Church. Catechism set forth for that purpose.

4. Now when the Apostles which were at Jerusalem heard that Samaria had received the word of God, they sent unto them Peter and John: who, when they were come down, prayed for them, that they might receive the Holy Ghost: (for as yet he was fallen upon none of them: only they were baptized in the name of the Lord Jesus.) Then laid they their hands on them, and they received the Holy Ghost. *Ac. viii.* 14 *to* 17. And when they had preached the gospel to that city, and had taught many, they returned again to Lystra, and to Iconium, and Antioch, confirming the souls of the disciples, and exhorting them to continue in the faith, and that we must through much tribulation enter into the kingdom of God. *Ac. xiv.* 21, 22.

F

THE MINISTRATION OF PRIVATE BAPTISM OF CHILDREN IN HOUSES.
AND OF BAPTISM TO SUCH AS ARE OF RIPER YEARS.

Note.—The two offices for Baptism which follow, contain much of what is found in the preceding office for the Public Baptism of Infants. *The difference that exists between them arises from the varying circumstances of the Baptized; as such, it is thought unnecessary to adduce quotations from Scripture, but merely to insert those portions of these services which are verbally different. The following are those portions.*

PRIVATE BAPTISM OF INFANTS.

CLXX. *The Receiving of the Baptized Infant into the Congregation.*

We yield thee hearty thanks, most merciful Father, that it hath pleased thee to re-generate *this Infant* with thy holy Spirit, to receive *him* for thine own Child by adoption, and to incorporate *him* into thy holy Church. And we humbly beseech thee to grant, that as *he* is now made *partaker* of the death of thy Son, so *he* may be also of his resurrection; and that finally, with the residue of thy Saints, *he* may inherit thine everlasting kingdom; through the same thy Son Jesus Christ our Lord. *Amen.*

CLXXI. CLXXII. *Certificates and Enquiries concerning the due Baptizing of the Infant.*

1. I certify you, that according to the due and prescribed Order of the Church, *at such a time*, and *at such a place*, before divers witnesses I baptized this Child.

2. By whom was this Child baptized?
3. Who was present when this Child was baptized?
4. Because some things essential to this Sacrament may happen to be omitted through fear or haste, in such times of extremity; therefore I demand further of you,
5. With what matter was this Child baptized?
6. With what words was this Child baptized?

7. I certify you, that in this case all is well done, and according unto due order, concern-ing the baptizing of this Child; who being born in original sin, and in the wrath of God, is now, by the laver of Regeneration in Baptism, received into the number of the children of God, and heirs of everlasting life, for our Lord Jesus Christ doth not deny his grace and mercy unto such Infants, but most lovingly doth call them unto him, as the holy Gospel doth witness to our comfort on this wise.

Then follows the Gospel from St. Mark x. 13.

CLXXIII. *The Exhortation upon the words of the Gospel.*

Beloved, ye hear in this Gospel the words of our Saviour Christ, that he commanded the children to be brought unto him; how he blamed those that would have kept them from him; how he exhorted all men to follow their innocency. Ye perceive how by his outward gesture and deed he declared his good will toward them; for he embraced them in his arms, he laid his hands upon them, and blessed them. Doubt ye not therefore, but earnestly believe, that he hath likewise favourably received *this* present *Infant;* that he hath embraced *him* with the arms of his mercy; and (as he hath promised in his holy Word) will give unto *him* the blessing of eternal life, and make *him partaker* of his everlasting kingdom. Wherefore, we being thus persuaded of the good will of our heavenly Father, declared by his Son Jesus Christ, towards *this Infant,* let us faithfully and devoutly give-thanks unto him, and say the Prayer which the Lord himself taught us.

CLXXIV. Thanksgiving and Prayer.

Almighty and everlasting God, heavenly Father, we give thee humble thanks, that thou hast vouchsafed to call us to the knowledge of thy grace, and faith in thee: Increase this knowledge, and confirm this faith in us evermore. Give thy Holy Spirit to *this Infant*, that *he*, being born again, and being made *an heir* of everlasting salvation, through our Lord Jesus Christ, may continue thy *servant*, and attain thy promise ; through the same our Lord Jesus Christ thy Son, who liveth and reigneth with thee and the Holy Spirit, now and for ever. *Amen.*

PUBLIC BAPTISM OF SUCH AS ARE OF RIPER YEARS.

CLXXV. Exhortation to the Congregation in behalf of the Candidates for Baptism.

Dearly beloved, forasmuch as all men are conceived and born in sin, (and that which is born of the flesh is flesh,) and they that are in the flesh cannot please God, but live in sin, committing many actual transgressions ; and that our Saviour Christ saith, None can enter into the kingdom of God, except he be regenerate and born anew of Water and of the Holy Ghost ; I beseech you to call upon God the Father, through our Lord Jesus Christ, that of his bounteous goodness he will grant to *these persons* that which by nature *they* cannot have ; that *they* may be baptized with Water and the Holy Ghost, and received into Christ's holy Church, and be made lively *members* of the same.

CLXXVI. The Gospel from St. John iii. 1. and the Exhortation founded on the Gospel.

There was a man of the Pharisees, named Nicodemus, a ruler of the Jews. The same came to Jesus by night, and said unto him, Rabbi, we know that thou art a teacher come from God ; for no man can do these miracles that thou doest, except God be with him. Jesus answered and said unto him, Verily, verily I say unto thee, Except a man be born again, he cannot see the kingdom of God. Nicodemus saith unto him, How can a man be born when he is old? Can he enter the second time into his mother's womb, and be born? Jesus answered, Verily, verily I say unto thee, Except a man be born of water and of the Spirit, he cannot enter into the kingdom of God. That which is born of the flesh is flesh ; and that which is born of the Spirit is spirit. Marvel not that I said unto thee, Ye must be born again. The wind bloweth where it listeth, and thou hearest the sound thereof ; but canst not tell whence it cometh, and whither it goeth : so is every one that is born of the Spirit.

Beloved, ye hear in this Gospel the express words of our Saviour Christ, that except a man be born of water and of the Spirit, he cannot enter into the kingdom of God. Whereby ye may perceive the great necessity of this Sacrament, where it may be had. Likewise, immediately before his ascension into heaven, (as we read in the last Chapter of Saint Mark's Gospel,) he gave command to his disciples, saying, Go ye into all the world, and preach the Gospel to every creature. He that believeth, and is baptized, shall be saved ; but he that believeth not, shall be damned. Which also sheweth unto us the great benefit we reap thereby. For which cause Saint Peter the Apostle, when upon his first preaching of the Gospel many were pricked at the heart, and said to him and the rest of the Apostles, Men and brethren, what shall we do ? he replied and said unto them, Repent, and be baptized every one of you for the remission of sins, and ye shall receive the gift of the Holy Ghost. For the promise is to you and your children, and to all that are afar off, even as many as the Lord our God shall call. And with many other words exhorted he them, saying, Save yourselves from this untoward generation. For (as the same Apostle testifieth in another place) even Baptism doth also now save us, (not the putting away of the filth of the flesh, but the answer of a good conscience towards God,) by the resurrection of Jesus Christ. Doubt ye not therefore, but earnestly believe, that he will favourably receive *these present persons*, truly repenting, and coming unto him by faith ;

that he will grant *them* remission of *their* sins, and bestow upon *them* the Holy Ghost; that he will give *them* the blessing of eternal life, and make *them* *partakers* of his everlasting kingdom.

Wherefore we being thus persuaded of the good will of our heavenly Father towards *these persons*, declared by his Son Jesus Christ; let us faithfully and devoutly give thanks to him.

CLXXVII. The Minister's particular Address to the Persons to be Baptized.

Well-beloved, who are come hither desiring to receive holy Baptism, *ye* have heard how the congregation hath prayed, that our Lord Jesus Christ would vouchsafe to receive you and bless you, to release you of your sins, to give you the kingdom of heaven, and everlasting life. *Ye* have heard also, that our Lord Jesus Christ hath promised in his holy Word to grant all those things that we have prayed for; which promise he, for his part, will most surely keep and perform.

Wherefore, after this promise made by Christ, *ye* must also faithfully, for your part, promise in the presence of these your witnesses, and this whole congregation, that *ye* will renounce the devil and all his works, and constantly believe God's holy Word, and obediently keep his commandments.

CLXXVIII. Concluding Thanksgiving and Prayer.

We yield thee humble thanks, O heavenly Father, that thou hast vouchsafed to call us to the knowledge of thy grace, and faith in thee: Increase this knowledge, and confirm this faith in us evermore. Give thy Holy Spirit to *these Persons*; that, being now born again, and made *heirs* of everlasting salvation, through our Lord Jesus Christ, *they* may continue thy *servants*, and attain thy promises; through the same Lord Jesus Christ thy Son, who liveth and reigneth with thee, in the unity of the same Holy Spirit, everlastingly. *Amen.*

CLXXIX. CLXXX. Concluding Address to the Godfathers and Godmothers, and to the Newly-baptized.

Forasmuch as *these persons have* promised in your presence to renounce the devil and all his works, to believe in God, and to serve him; ye must remember, that it is your part and duty to put *them* in mind, what a solemn vow, promise, and profession *they have* now made before this congregation, and especially before you *their* chosen witnesses. And ye are also to call upon *them* to use all diligence to be rightly instructed in God's holy Word; that so *they* may grow in grace, and in the knowledge of our Lord Jesus Christ, and live godly, righteously, and soberly in this present world.

And as for you, who have now by Baptism put on Christ, it is your part and duty also, being made the *children* of God and of the light, by faith in Jesus Christ, to walk answerably to your Christian calling, and as becometh the children of light; remembering always that Baptism representeth unto us our profession; which is, to follow the example of our Saviour Christ, and to be made like unto him; that as he died, and rose again for us; so should we, who are baptized, die from sin, and rise again unto righteousness; continually mortifying all our evil and corrupt affections, and daily proceeding in all virtue and godliness of living.

CATECHISM.

A CATECHISM, that is to say, an Instruction to be learned of every person, before he be brought to be confirmed by the Bishop.

That thou mightest know the certainty of those things, wherein thou hast been instructed. [*Greek*, catechized.] *Lu. i.* 4. This man was instructed [*Gr.* catechized] in the way of the Lord. *Ac. xviii.* 25. Being instructed [*Gr.* catechized] out of the law. *Ro. ii.* 18. I had rather speak five words with my understanding, that by my voice I might teach [*Gr.* catechize] others, than ten thousand words in an unknown tongue. 1 *Co. xiv.* 19. Let him that is taught [*Gr.* catechized] in the word communicate unto him that teacheth in all good things. *Ga. vi.* 6.

CLXXXI. The Baptismal Vow, or Engagement.

1 What is your Name?

2. Who gave you this Name?

1. 2. Neither shall thy name any more be called Abram, but thy name shall be Abraham; for a father of many nations have I made thee. And God said unto Abraham, As for Sarai thy wife, thou shalt not call her name Sarai, but Sarah shall her name be. *Ge. xvii.* 5. 15. And it came to pass, that on the eighth day they came to circumcise the child; and they called him Zacharias, after the name of his father. And his mother answered and said, Not so; but he shall be called John. *Lu. i.* 59, 60. And when Jesus beheld him, he said, Thou art Simon the son of Jona; thou shalt be called Cephas, which is by interpretation, A stone. *John i.* 42.

3. My Godfathers and Godmothers, in my Baptism; wherein I was made a member of Christ, the child of God, and an inheritor of the kingdom of heaven.

3. Jesus came and spake unto them, saying, Go and teach all nations, baptizing them. *Mat. xxviii.* 18, 19. Jesus said, Suffer little children and forbid them not, to come unto me: for of such is the kingdom of heaven. *Mat. xix.* 14. As the body is one, and hath many members, and all the members of that one body, being many, are one body: so also is Christ. For by one Spirit are we all baptized into one body, whether we be Jews or Gentiles, whether we be bond or free; and have

been all made to drink into one Spirit. For the body is not one member, but many. Now ye are the body of Christ and members in particular. 1 *Co. xii.* 12, 13, 14. 27. Ye are all the children of God by faith in Christ Jesus. For as many of you as have been baptized into Christ have put on Christ. *Ga. iii.* 26, 27. As many as received him, to them gave he power to become the sons of God, even to them that believe on his name : which were born, not of blood, nor of the will of the flesh, nor of the will of man, but of God. *John i.* 12, 13. And if children, then heirs ; heirs of God, and joint-heirs with Christ ; if so be that we suffer with him, that we may be also glorified together. *Ro. viii.* 17. He that believeth, and is baptized, shall be saved. *Mar. xvi.* 16. Not by works of righteousness which we have done, but according to his mercy he saved us, by the washing of regeneration, and renewing of the Holy Ghost ; which he shed on us abundantly through Jesus Christ our Saviour ; that being justified by his grace, we should be made heirs according to the hope of eternal life. *Tit. iii.* 5, 6, 7. Blessed be the God and Father of our Lord Jesus Christ, which according to his abundant mercy hath begotten us again unto a lively hope by the resurrection of Jesus Christ from the dead, to an inheritance incorruptible and undefiled, and that fadeth not away, reserved in heaven. 1 *Pet. i.* 3, 4. Our conversation* is in heaven. *Ph. iii.* 20.

4. What did your Godfathers and Godmothers then for you ?

5. They did promise and vow three things in my name. First, that I should renounce the devil and all his works, the pomps and vanity of this wicked world, and all the sinful lusts of the flesh. Secondly, that I should

4. 5. Promise unto the Lord your God, and keep it, all ye that are round about him. *Ps. lxxvi.* 11. They shall vow a vow unto the Lord, and perform it. *Is. xix.* 21. If ye will obey my voice indeed, and keep my covenant, then ye shall be a peculiar treasure unto me. And Moses came and called for the elders of the people, and laid before their faces all these words which the Lord commanded him. And all the people answered together and said, All that the Lord hath spoken we will do. *Ex. xix.* 5. 7, 8. He that committeth sin is of the devil ; for the devil sinneth from the beginning. For this purpose the Son of God was manifested, that he might destroy the works of the devil. 1 *John iii.* 8. The great dragon was cast out, that old serpent, called the Devil, and Satan, which deceiveth the whole world : and they overcame him by the

* Citizenship.

believe all the Articles of the Christian Faith. And thirdly, that I should keep God's holy will and commandments, and walk in the same all the days of my life.

blood of the Lamb, and by the word of their testimony. *Re. xii.* 9. 11. The spirit that now worketh in the children of disobedience. *Ep. ii.* 2. Be sober, be vigilant; because your adversary the devil, as a roaring lion, walketh about, seeking whom he may devour: whom resist stedfast in the faith. 1 *Pe. v.* 8, 9. Put on the whole armour of God, that ye may be able to stand against the wiles of the devil. *Ep. vi.* 11. Resist the devil and he will flee from you. *Ja. iv.* 7. Ye are of your father the devil, and the lusts of your father ye will do. He was a murderer from the beginning, and abode not in the truth, because there is no truth in him. When he speaketh a lie, he speaketh of his own; for he is a liar, and the father of it. *John viii.* 44. If ye have bitter envying and strife in your hearts, glory not, and lie not against the truth. This wisdom descendeth not from above, but is earthly, sensual, devilish. *Ja. iii.* 14, 15. Have no fellowship with the unfruitful works of darkness, but rather reprove them. *Ep. v.* 11. Be not conformed to this world. *Ro. xii.* 2. Know ye not that the friendship of the world is enmity with God? whosoever therefore will be a friend of the world is the enemy of God. *Ja. iv.* 4. The world hateth me because I testify of it, that the works thereof are evil. *John vii.* 7. Love not the world, neither the things that are in the world. If any man love the world, the love of the Father is not in him. For all that is in the world, the lust of the flesh, and the lust of the eyes, and the pride of life, is not of the Father, but is of the world. 1 *John ii.* 15, 16. The whole world lieth in wickedness. 1 *John v.* 19. Therefore hell hath enlarged herself, and opened her mouth without measure: and their glory, and their multitude, and their pomp, and he that rejoiceth, shall descend into it. *Is. v.* 14. Vanity of vanities, saith the Preacher, vanity of vanities, all is vanity. *Ec. i.* 2. Christ gave himself for our sins, that he might deliver us from this present evil world. *Ga. i.* 4. They that are Christ's have crucified the flesh with the affections and lusts. *Gal. v.* 24. Now the works of the flesh are manifest, which are these; Adultery, fornication, uncleanness, lasciviousness, idolatry, witchcraft, hatred, variance, emulations, wrath, strife, seditions, heresies, envyings, murders, drunkenness, revellings, and such like; of the which I tell you before, as I have also told you in time past, that they which do such things shall not inherit the kingdom of God. *Ga. v.* 19, 20, 21. Mortify therefore your members which are upon the earth. *Col. iii.* 5. Denying ungodliness and worldly lusts, we should live soberly, righteously, and godly, in this present world. *Tit. ii.* 12. Ye believe in God, believe also in me. *John xiv.* 1. Without faith it is impossible to please him : for he that cometh to God must believe that he is, and that he is a rewarder of them that diligently seek him. *He. xi.* 6. These are written, that ye might believe that Jesus is the Christ, the Son of God; and that believing ye might have life through his name. *John xx.* 31. As many as received him, to them gave he power to become the sons of God, even to them that believe on his name. *John i.* 12. Repent ye, and believe the gospel. *Mar. i.* 15. For therein is the righteousness of God revealed from faith to faith : as it is written, The just shall live by faith. *Ro. i.* 17. Teaching them [*the baptized*] to observe all things whatsoever I have commanded you. *Mat. xxviii.* 20. Jesus said unto him, Thou shalt love the Lord thy God with all thy heart, and with all thy soul, and with all thy mind. This is the first and great commandment. And the second is like unto it, Thou shalt love thy neighbour as thyself. *Mat. xxii.* 37, 38, 39. Owe no man any thing, but to love one another : for he that loveth another hath fulfilled the law. For this, Thou shalt not commit adultery, Thou shalt not kill, Thou shalt not steal, Thou shalt not bear false witness, Thou shalt not covet; and if there be any other commandment, it is briefly comprehended in this saying, namely, Thou shalt love thy neighbour as thyself. *Ro. xiii.* 8, 9. Whosoever shall keep the whole law, and yet offend in one point, he is guilty of all. For he that said, Do not commit adultery, said also, Do not kill. Now if thou commit no adultery, yet if thou kill, thou art become a transgressor of the law. *Ja. ii.* 10, 11. Hereby we do know that we know him, if we keep his commandments. He that saith, I know him, and keepeth not his commandments, is a liar, and the truth is not in him. But whoso keepeth his word, in him verily is the love of God perfected: hereby know we that we are in him. He that saith he abideth in him ought himself also so to walk, even as he walked. 1 *John ii.* 3 *to* 6. Doing the will of God from the heart. *Ep. vi.* 6. Epaphras, who is one of you, a servant of Christ, saluteth you, always labouring fervently for you in prayers, that ye may stand perfect and complete in all the will of God. *Col. iv.* 12. When a righteous man turneth away from his righteousness, and committeth iniquity, and dieth in them ; for his iniquity that he hath done shall he die. *Ez. xviii.* 26. We are made partakers of Christ, if we hold the beginning of our confidence stedfast unto the end. *He. iii.* 14. That he would grant unto us, that we being delivered out of the hand of our enemies might serve him without fear, in holiness and righteousness before him all the days of our life. *Lu. i.* 74, 75.

6. Dost thou not think that thou art bound to believe, and to do, as they have promised for thee ?

7. Yes verily ; and by God's help so I will. And I heartily thank our heavenly Father, that he hath called me to this state of salvation, through Jesus Christ our Saviour. And I pray unto God to give me his grace, that I may continue in the same unto my life's end.

6. 7. He that believeth, and is baptized, shall be saved ; but he that believeth not, shall be damned. *Mar. xvi.* 16. Thou hast avouched the Lord this day to be thy God, and to walk in his ways, and to keep his statutes, and his commandments, and his judgments, and to hearken unto his voice : and the Lord hath avouched thee this day to be his peculiar people, as he hath promised thee, and that thou shouldest keep all his commandments ; that thou mayest be a holy people unto the Lord thy God. *De. xxvi.* 17, 18, 19. And he took the book of the covenant, and read in the audience of the people : and they said, All that the Lord hath said will we do, and be obedient. *Ex. xxiv.* 7. Ye ought to say, If the Lord will, we shall live, and do this, or that. *Ja. iv.* 15. It is God which worketh in you both to will and to do of his good pleasure. *Ph. ii.* 13. Happy is he that hath the God of Jacob for his help, whose hope is in the Lord his God. *Ps. cxlvi.* 5. Giving thanks always for all things unto God and the Father in the name of our Lord Jesus Christ. *Ep. v.* 20. Who hath saved us, and called us with an holy calling. 2 *Ti. i.* 9. Look unto me, and be ye saved, all the ends of the earth : for I am God. *Is. xlv.* 22. I am not ashamed of the Gospel of Christ ; for it is the power of God unto salvation to every one that believeth. *Ro. i.* 16. The grace of God that bringeth salvation hath appeared to all men. *Tit. ii.* 11. By the name of Jesus Christ of Nazareth, doth this man stand

here before you whole. Neither is there salvation in any other : for there is none other name under heaven given among men, whereby we must be saved. *Ac. iv.* 10. 12. God hath not appointed us to wrath, but to obtain salvation by our Lord Jesus Christ. 1 *Th. v.* 9. Praying always with all prayer and supplication in the Spirit. *Ep. vi.* 18. In every thing by prayer and supplication with thanksgiving let your requests be made known unto God. *Ph. iv.* 6. Continue in prayer, and watch in the same with thanksgiving. *Col. iv.* 2. Whatsoever ye shall ask the Father in my name, he will give it you. *John xvi.* 23. If ye being evil, know how to give good gifts unto your children; how much more shall your heavenly Father give the Holy Spirit to them that ask him? *Lu. xi.* 13. The Lord is faithful, who shall stablish you, and keep you from evil. 2 *Th. iii.* 3. Then said Jesus to those Jews which believed on him, If ye continue in my word, then are ye my disciples indeed. *John viii.* 31. Grieve not the Holy Spirit of God, whereby ye are sealed unto the day of redemption. *Ep. iv.* 30. Being confident of this very thing, that he which hath begun a good work in you will perform it until the day of Jesus Christ. *Ph. i.* 6.—Grace be with thee. Amen. 1 *Ti. vi.* 21. *See also, Is. lv.* 1.—*Mat. xi.* 28.—*Lu. xxiv.* 47.—*John vii.* 37.

CLXXXII. The Christian's Belief or Creed.

1. Rehearse the Articles of thy Belief.

I Believe in God the Father Almighty, Maker of Heaven and Earth : And in Jesus Christ his only Son our Lord, Who was conceived by the Holy Ghost, Born of the Virgin Mary, Suffered under Pontius Pilate, Was crucified, dead, and buried, He descended into Hell; The third day he rose again from the dead, He ascended into Heaven, And sitteth on the right hand of God the Father Almighty ; From thence he shall come to judge the quick and the dead.

I believe in the Holy Ghost ; The holy Catholick Church : The Communion of Saints ; The Forgiveness of sins ; The Resurrection of the body ; And the Life everlasting. Amen.

For Quotations illustrating the Creed, see No. CLXI.

2. What dost thou chiefly learn in these Articles of thy Belief?

2. 3. Gather the people together, men, and women, and children, and thy stranger that is within thy gates, that they may hear, and that they may learn, and fear the Lord your God. *De. xxxi.* 12. At that time Jesus answered and said,

3. First, I learn to believe I thank thee, O Father, Lord of heaven and earth, because

in God the Father, who hath made me, and all the world.

thou hast hid these things from the wise and prudent, and hast revealed them unto babes. *Mat. xi.* 25. He that cometh to God must believe that he is. *He. xi.* 6. O Lord, thou art our Father; we are the clay, and thou our potter; and we all are the work of thy hand. *Is. lxiv.* 8. Lord, thou art God, which hast made heaven, and earth, and the sea, and all that in them is. *Ac. iv.* 24. To us there is but one God, the Father, of whom are all things. 1 *Co. viii.* 6.

4. Secondly, in God the Son, who hath redeemed me, and all mankind.

4. We have seen and do testify that the Father sent the Son to be the Saviour of the world. 1 *John iv.* 14. And we know that the Son of God is come, and hath given us an understanding, that we may know him that is true, and we are in him that is true, even in his Son Jesus Christ. This is the true God, and eternal life. 1 *John v.* 20. I and my Father are one. *John x.* 30. Without controversy great is the mystery of godliness; God was manifest in the flesh. 1 *Ti. iii.* 16. John seeth Jesus coming unto him, and saith, Behold the Lamb of God, which taketh away the sin of the world. *John i.* 29. Christ hath redeemed us from the curse of the law, being made a curse for us. *Ga. iii.* 13. Thou wast slain, and hast redeemed us to God by thy blood out of every kindred, and tongue, and people, and nation. *Re. v.* 9. If any man sin, we have an Advocate with the Father, Jesus Christ the righteous: and he is the Propitiation for our sins: and not for ours only, but also for the sins of the whole world. 1 *John ii.* 1, 2.

5. Thirdly, in God the Holy Ghost, who sanctifieth me, and all the elect people of God.

5. John saw the Spirit of God descending like a dove, and lighting upon him. *Mat. iii.* 16. Peter said, Ananias, Why hath satan filled thine heart to lie to the Holy Ghost? Why hast thou conceived this thing in thine heart? thou hast not lied unto men, but unto God. *Ac. v.* 3, 4. Elect according to the foreknowledge of God the Father, through sanctification of the Spirit, unto obedience. 1 *Pe. i.* 2. We are bound to give thanks always to God for you, brethren beloved of the Lord, because God hath from the beginning chosen you to salvation, through sanctification of the Spirit and belief of the truth. 2 *Th. ii.* 13. That the offering up of the Gentiles might be acceptable, being sanctified by the Holy Ghost. *Ro. xv.* 16.

CLXXXIII. A Summary of Christian Duties.

1. You said, that your Godfathers and Godmothers did promise for you, that you should keep God's Commandments. Tell me how many there be? Ten.

1. And God spake all these words, saying, I am the Lord thy God, which have brought thee out of the land of Egypt, out of the house of bondage. *Ex. xx.* 1, 2. And the Lord spake unto you out of the midst of the fire, and he declared unto you his covenant, which he commanded you to perform, even ten commandments; and he wrote them upon two tables of stone. *De. iv.* 12, 13.

Which be they? The same which God spake in the twentieth chapter of Exodus.

2. 3. And he gave unto Moses, when he had made an end of communing with him upon mount Sinai, two tables of testimony, tables of stone, written with the finger of God. *Ex. xxxi.* 18. He wrote upon the tables the words of the covenant, the ten commandments. *Ex. xxxiv.* 28. The weightier matters of the law, judgment, mercy, and faith. *Mat. xxiii.* 23.

2. What dost thou chiefly learn by these Commandments?

Jesus said unto him, Thou shalt love the Lord thy God with all thy heart, and with all thy soul, and with all thy mind. This is the first and great commandment. And the second is

3. I learn two things: my duty towards God, and my duty towards my neighbour.

like unto it, Thou shalt love thy neighbour as thyself. On these two commandments hang all the Law and the Prophets. *Mat. xxii.* 37 *to* 40. Continue thou in the things which thou hast learned and hast been assured of, knowing of whom thou hast learned them. 2 *Ti. iii.* 14.

The Christian's Duty towards God.

4. What is thy duty towards God?

4. 5. As they went forth, Jehoshaphat stood and said, Hear me, O Judah, and ye inhabitants of Jerusalem: Believe in the Lord your God, so shall ye be established; believe his

5. My duty towards God, is to believe in him, to fear him, and to love him with all my heart, with all my mind, with all my soul, and with all my strength; to worship him, to give him thanks, to put my whole trust

prophets, so shall ye prosper. 2 *Ch. xx.* 20. Without faith it is impossible to please him; for he that cometh to God must believe that he is. *He. xi.* 6. Ye believe in God, believe also in me. *John xiv.* 1. Holding faith, and a good conscience: which some having put away concerning faith have made shipwreck. 1 *Ti. i.* 19. If ye believe not that I am he, ye shall die in your sins. *John viii.* 24. If we believe not, yet God abideth faithful: he cannot deny himself. 2 *Ti. ii.* 13. Now, Israel, what doth the Lord thy God require of thee, but to fear the Lord thy God, to walk in all his ways, and to love

in him, to call
upon him, to
honour his
holy Name and
his Word; and
to serve him
truly all the
days of my
life.
him, and to serve the Lord thy God, with all thy heart, and
with all thy soul. *De. x.* 12. I will forewarn you whom ye
shall fear: Fear him, which after he hath killed hath power
to cast into hell: yea, I say unto you, Fear him. *Lu. xii.* 5.,
So did not I, because of the fear of God. *Ne. v.* 15. Wherefore we receiving a kingdom which cannot be moved, let us
have grace, whereby we may serve God acceptably, with
reverence and godly fear. *He. xii.* 28. Take diligent heed to
love the Lord your God, and to keep his commandments, and
to serve him with all your heart and with all your soul. *Jos.
xxii.* 5. And he answering said, Thou shalt love the Lord
thy God with all thy heart, and with all thy soul, and with all
thy strength, and with all thy mind. *Lu. x.* 27. This is the
love of God, that we keep his commandments. 1 *John v.* 3.
If any man love not the Lord Jesus Christ, let him be Anathema Maran-atha. 1 *Co. xvi.* 22. My son, give me thine heart,
and let thine eyes observe my ways. *Pr. xxiii.* 26.

The Lord, him shall ye fear, and him shall ye worship.
2 *Ki. xvii.* 36. Then saith Jesus unto him, Get thee hence,
Satan: for it is written, Thou shalt worship the Lord thy
God, and him only shalt thou serve. *Mat. iv.* 10. The hour
cometh, and now is, when the true worshippers shall worship
the Father in spirit and in truth: for the Father seeketh such
to worship him. *John iv.* 23. Worship the Lord in the
beauty of holiness. *Ps. xxix.* 2. If any man be a worshipper
of God, and doeth his will, him he heareth. *John ix.* 31. And
I fell at his feet to worship him. [the angel.] And he said
unto me, See thou do it not: I am thy fellow-servant, and of
thy brethren that have the testimony of Jesus: Worship God.
Re. xix. 10.

Offer unto God thanksgiving. *Ps. l.* 14. In every thing
give thanks: for this is the will of God in Christ Jesus concerning you. 1 *Th. v.* 18. Giving thanks always for all things
unto God and the Father in the name of our Lord Jesus
Christ. *Ep. v.* 20. Father, I thank thee that thou hast heard
me. *John xi.* 41.

Trust ye in the Lord for ever. *Is. xxvi.* 4. Trust in him at
all times. *Ps. lxii.* 8. Trust in the Lord with all thine heart;
and lean not unto thine own understanding. *Pr. iii.* 5. Who is

among you that feareth the Lord, that obeyeth the voice of his servant, that walketh in darkness, and hath no light? let him trust in the name of the Lord, and stay upon his God. *Is. l.* 10. O Israel, trust thou in the Lord ; he is their help and their shield. O house of Aaron, trust in the Lord ; he is their help and their shield. Ye that fear the Lord, trust in the Lord; he is their help and their shield. *Ps. cxv.* 9, 10, 11. Cursed be the man that trusteth in man, and maketh flesh his arm, and whose heart departeth from the Lord. Blessed is the man that trusteth in the Lord, and whose hope the Lord is. *Je. xvii.* 5. 7. He that trusteth in the Lord, mercy shall compass him about. *Ps. xxxii.* 10. We both labour and suffer reproach, because we trust in the living God, who is the Saviour of all men, specially of those that believe. 1 *Ti. iv.* 10.

O give thanks unto the Lord ; call upon his name. *Ps. cv.* 1. In every thing by prayer and supplication with thanksgiving let your requests be made known unto God. *Ph. iv.* 6. Pour out your heart before him : God is a refuge for us. *Ps. lxii.* 8. Call upon me in the day of trouble; I will deliver thee, and thou shalt glorify me. *Ps. l.* 15. Seek ye the Lord while he may be found, call ye upon him while he is near. *Is. lv.* 6. Whosoever shall call upon the name of the Lord shall be saved. *Ro. x.* 13.

How excellent is thy Name in all the earth! *Ps. viii.* 1. Blessed be thy glorious name, which is exalted above all blessing and praise. *Ne. ix.* 5. Let thy name be magnified for ever. 2 *Sam. vii.* 26. Sing forth the honour of his name. *Ps. lxvi.* 2. Ye shall not swear by my name falsely, neither shalt thou profane the name of thy God : I am the Lord. *Le. xix.* 12. Who shall not fear thee, O Lord, and glorify thy name ? for thou only art holy. *Re. xv.* 4. Give unto the Lord the glory due unto his name. *Ps. xxix.* 2. Let them praise thy great and terrible name, for it is holy. *Ps. xcix.* 3. He will magnify the Law, and make it honourable. *Is. xlii.* 21. Thou hast magnified thy Word above all thy name. *Ps. cxxxviii.* 2. Whoso despiseth the word shall be destroyed. *Pr. xiii.* 13. Hear the word of the Lord, ye that tremble at his word ; he shall appear to your joy. *Is. lxvi.* 5. My heart standeth in awe of thy word. I rejoice at thy word, as one that findeth great spoil. *Ps. cxix.* 161, 162. Wherefore lay apart all filthiness and superfluity of naughtiness, and receive with meekness the engrafted word, which is able to save your souls. But be ye doers of the word, and not hearers only, deceiving your own selves. *Ja. i.* 21, 22. Whoso keepeth his word, in him verily is the love of God perfected. 1 *John ii.* 5.

Thou shalt fear the Lord thy God, and serve him, and shalt swear by his name. *De. vi.* 13. Now therefore fear the Lord, and serve him in sincerity and in truth. *Jos. xxiv.* 14. Only fear the Lord, and serve him in truth with all your heart : for consider how great things he hath done for you. 1 *Sa. xii.* 24. And thou, Solomon my son, know thou the God of thy father, and serve him with a perfect heart and with a willing mind : for the Lord searcheth all hearts, and understandeth all the imaginations of the thoughts : if thou seek him, he will be found of thee : but 'if thou forsake him, he will cast thee off for ever. 1 *Ch. xxviii.* 9. Then said Jesus unto him, Get thee hence, Satan : for it is written, Thou shalt worship the Lord thy God, and him only shalt thou serve. *Mat. iv.* 10. Let us have grace, whereby we may serve God acceptably with reverence and godly fear. *He. xii.* 28. Therefore are they before the throne of God, and serve him day and night in his temple. *Re. vii.* 15. Let us hear the conclusion of the whole matter : Fear God, and keep his commandments : for this is the whole duty of man. *Ec. xii.* 13.

CLXXXIV. *The Christian's duty towards his Neighbour.*

1. What is thy duty towards thy Neighbour ?

My duty towards my Neighbour, is to love him as myself, and to do to all men, as I would they should do unto me :

1. Thou shalt love thy neighbour as thyself : I am the Lord. *Le. xix.* 18. The second [commandment] is like unto it, [*the first,*] Thou shalt love thy neighbour as thyself. *Mat. xxii.* 39. Owe no man any thing but to love one another ; for he that loveth another hath fulfilled the law. For this, Thou shalt not commit adultery, Thou shalt not kill, Thou shalt not steal, Thou shalt not bear false witness, Thou shalt not covet ; and if there be any other commandment, it is briefly comprehended in this saying, namely, Thou shalt love thy neighbour as thyself. Love worketh no ill to his neighbour : therefore love is the fulfilling of the law. *Ro. xiii.* 8, 9, 10.

By love serve one another: for all the law is fulfilled in one word, even in this; Thou shalt love thy neighbour as thyself. *Ga. v.* 13, 14. Therefore all things whatsoever ye would that men should do to you, do ye even so to them: for this is the Law and the Prophets. *Mat. vii.* 12.

2. To love, honour, and succour my father and mother.

2. God commanded, saying, Honour thy father and mother: and, He that curseth father or mother, let him die the death. *Mat. xv.* 4. Honour thy father and mother; which is the first · commandment with promise; that it may be well with thee, and thou mayest live long on the earth. *Ep. vi.* 2, 3. Speak unto all the congregation of the children of Israel and say unto them, Ye shall be holy: for I the Lord your God am holy. Ye shall fear every man his mother and his father: I am the Lord your God. *Le. xix.* 2, 3. Cursed be he that setteth light by his father or his mother. *De. xxvii.* 16. If a man have a stubborn and rebellious son, which will not obey the voice of his father, or the voice of his mother, and that, when they have chastened him, will not hearken unto them: then shall his father and his mother lay hold on him, and bring him out unto the elders of his city, and unto the gate of his place; and they shall say unto the elders of his city, This our son is stubborn and rebellious, he will not obey our voice; he is a glutton, and a drunkard. And all the men of his city shall stone him with stones, that he die: so shalt thou put evil away from among you; and all Israel shall hear, and fear. *De. xxi.* 18 *to* 21. Moses said, Honour thy father and thy mother; and, whoso curseth father or mother, let him die the death: but ye say, If a man shall say to his father or mother, It is Corban, that is to say, a gift, by whatsoever thou mightest be profited by me; he shall be free. And ye suffer him no more to do ought for his father or his mother; making the word of God of none effect through your tradition, which ye have delivered. *Mar. vii.* 10 *to* 13. Hearken unto thy father that begat thee, and despise not thy mother when she is old. *Pr. xxiii.* 22. A wise son heareth his father's instruction. *Pr. xiii.* 1. A foolish man despiseth his mother. *Pr. xv.* 20. If any widow have children or nephews, let them first learn to shew piety at home, and to requite their parents: for that is good and acceptable before God. 1 *Ti. v.* 4. Joseph nourished his

father, and his brethren, and all his father's household. *Ge. xlvii.* 12. Children, obey your parents in all things: for this is well pleasing unto the Lord. *Col. iii.* 20. And he [Jesus] went down with them, [his parents,] and was subject unto them. *Lu. ii.* 51. *See also, Ge. xlvi.* 29.—*Ex. xxi.* 15. 17.—*Pr. i.* 8, 9.

'3. To honour and obey the King, and all that are put in authority under him:

3. Submit yourselves to every ordinance of man for the Lord's sake: whether it be to the king, as supreme; or unto governors, as unto them that are sent by him for the punishment of evil doers, and for the praise of them that do well. Honour all men. Love the brotherhood. Fear God. Honour the King. 1 *Pe. ii.* 13, 14. 17. Thou shalt not revile the gods, [*marginal reading*, judges,] nor curse the ruler of thy people. *Ex. xxii.* 28. Let every soul be subject unto the higher powers. For there is no power but of God: the powers that be are ordained of God. Whosoever therefore resisteth the power, resisteth the ordinance of God: and they that resist shall receive to themselves damnation. For rulers are not a terror to good works, but to the evil. Wilt thou then not be afraid of the power? do that which is good, and thou shalt have praise of the same: for he is the minister of God to thee for good. But if thou do that which is evil, be afraid; for he beareth not the sword in vain: for he is the minister of God, a revenger to execute wrath upon him that doeth evil. Wherefore ye must needs be subject, not only for wrath, but also for conscience sake. For for this cause, pay ye tribute also; for they are God's ministers, attending continually upon this very thing. Render therefore to all their dues: tribute to whom tribute is due; custom to whom custom; fear to whom fear; honour to whom honour. *Ro. xiii.* 1 *to* 7. Then saith he unto them, Render therefore unto Cæsar the things which are Cæsar's; and unto God the things that are God's. *Mat. xxii.* 21. By me kings reign, and princes decree justice. By me princes rule, and nobles, even all the judges of the earth. *Pr. viii.* 15, 16. And thou shalt come unto the priests the Levites, and unto the judge that shall be in those days, and enquire; and they shall shew thee the sentence of judgment: and thou shalt do according to the sentence; and thou shalt observe to do according to all that they inform thee: accord-

H

ing to the sentence of the law which they shall teach thee, and according to the judgment which they shall tell thee, thou shalt do : thou shalt not decline from the sentence which they shall shew thee, to the right hand, nor to the left. *De. xvii.* 9, 10, 11. And David said unto his men, The Lord forbid that I should do this thing unto my master, the Lord's anointed, to stretch forth mine hand against him, seeing he is the anointed of the Lord. So David stayed his servants with these words, and suffered them not to rise against Saul. 1 *Sa. xxiv.* 6, 7. Put them in mind to be subject to principalities and powers, to obey magistrates. *Tit. iii.* 1. I exhort therefore, that, first of all, supplications, prayers, intercessions, and giving of thanks, be made for all men ; for kings, and for all that are in authority ; that we may lead a quiet and peaceable life in all godliness and honesty. For this is good and acceptable in the sight of God our Saviour. 1 *Ti. ii.* 1, 2, 3. *See also, Nu. xvi.* 12, 13, 14. 28 *to* 32.—*Jude* 8.

4. To submit myself to all my governors, teachers, spiritual pastors and masters :

4. They cast lots, ward against ward, as well the small as the great, the teacher as the scholar. 1 *Ch. xxv.* 8. Now I say, That the heir, as long as he is a child, differeth nothing from a servant, though he be lord of all; but is under tutors and governors until the time appointed of the father. *Ga. iv.* 1, 2. Lest thou mourn at the last, and say, How have I hated instruction, and my heart despised reproof; and have not obeyed the voice of my teachers, nor inclined mine ear to them that instructed me. *Pr. v.* 10 *to* 13. And he gave some, apostles; and some, prophets ; and some, evangelists; and some, pastors and teachers. *Ep. iv.* 11. Let a man so account of us, as of the ministers of Christ, and stewards of the mysteries of God. 1 *Co. iv.* 1. The priest's lip should keep knowledge, and they should seek the law at his mouth : for he is the messenger of the Lord of hosts. *Mal. ii.* 7. Remember them which have the rule over you, who have spoken unto you the word of God : whose faith follow. Obey them that have the rule over you, and submit yourselves : for they watch for your souls, as they that must give account. *He. xiii.* 7. 17. We beseech you, brethren, to know them which labour among you, and are over you in the Lord, and admonish you ; and to esteem them very highly in love for their work's sake. 1 *Th. v.* 12, 13. Let

him that is taught in the word communicate unto him that teacheth in all good things. *Ga. vi.* 6. Who goeth a warfare any time at his own charges? Who planteth a vineyard, and eateth not of the fruit thereof? or who feedeth a flock, and eateth not of the milk of the flock? Do ye not know that they which minister about holy things live of the things of the temple? and they which wait at the altar are partakers with the altar? even so hath the Lord ordained that they which preach the Gospel should live of the Gospel. 1 *Co. ix.* 7. 13, 14. Let the elders that rule well be counted worthy of double honour, especially they who labour in the word and doctrine. 1 *Ti. v.* 17. Receive him [Epaphroditus] therefore in the Lord with all gladness; and hold such in reputation. *Ph. ii.* 29. He that heareth you heareth me; and he that despiseth you despiseth me; and he that despiseth me despiseth him that sent me. *Lu. x.* 16. But they [*the Jews*] mocked the messengers of God, and despised his words, and misused his prophets, until the wrath of the Lord arose against his people, till there was no remedy. 2 *Ch. xxxvi.* 16. He therefore that despiseth, despiseth not man, but God. 1 *Th. iv.* 8. Servants, be subject to your masters with all fear; not only to the good and gentle but also to the froward. 1 *Pe. ii.* 18. Servants, obey in all things your masters according to the flesh; not with eyeservice, as menpleasers; but in singleness of heart, fearing God: and whatsoever ye do, do it heartily, as to the Lord, and not unto men; knowing that of the Lord ye shall receive the reward of the inheritance: for ye serve the Lord Christ. But he that doeth wrong shall receive for the wrong which he hath done: and there is no respect of persons. *Col. iii.* 22 *to* 25. Exhort servants to be obedient unto their own masters, and to please them well in all things; not answering again; not purloining, but shewing all good fidelity; that they may adorn the doctrine of God our Saviour in all things. *Tit. ii.* 9, 10. Let as many servants as are under the yoke count their own masters worthy of all honour, that the name of God and his doctrine be not blasphemed. And they that have believing masters, let them not despise them, because they are brethren; but rather do them service, because they are faithful and beloved, partakers of the benefit. These things teach and exhort. 1 *Ti. vi.* 1, 2. See also, *Ep. vi.* 5, 6.

5. To order myself lowly and reverently to all my betters:

5. Likewise, ye younger, submit yourselves unto the elder. Yea, all of you be subject one to another. 1 *Pe. v.* 5. Thou shalt rise up before the hoary head, and honour the face of the old man, and fear thy God: I am the Lord. *Le. xix.* 32. Bathsheba therefore went unto king Solomon, to speak unto him for Adonijah. And the king rose up to meet her, and bowed himself unto her. 1 *Ki. ii.* 19. Honour all men. 1 *Pe. ii.* 17. Render therefore to all their dues: fear to whom fear; honour to whom honour. *Ro. xiii.* 7. Rebuke not an elder, but intreat him as a father. 1 *Ti. v.* 1. Now Elihu had waited till Job had spoken, because they were elder than he. And Elihu the son of Barachel the Buzite answered and said, I am young, and ye are very old; wherefore I was afraid, and durst not shew you mine opinion. *Job xxxii.* 4. 6. The people shall be oppressed, every one by another, and every one by his neighbour: the child shall behave himself proudly against the ancient, and the base against the honourable. *Is. iii.* 5.

6. To hurt nobody by word nor deed:

6. Ye have heard that it was said by them of old time, Thou shalt not kill; and whosoever shall kill shall be in danger of the judgment: but I say unto you, That whosoever is angry with his brother without a cause shall be in danger of the judgment: and whosoever shall say to his brother, Raca, shall be in danger of the council: but whosoever shall say, Thou fool, shall be in danger of hell fire. *Mat. v.* 21, 22. Whosoever hateth his brother is a murderer. 1 *John iii.* 15. And the soldiers demanded of him, saying, And what shall we do? And he said unto them, Do violence to no man, neither accuse any falsely. *Lu. iii.* 14. I say unto you, Love your enemies, bless them that curse you, do good to them that hate you. *Mat. v.* 44. Be ye angry, and sin not: let all bitterness, and wrath, and anger, and clamour, and evil-speaking, be put away from you, with all malice: and be ye kind one to another, tender-hearted. *Ep. iv.* 26. 31, 32. Recompense to no man evil for evil. If it be possible, as much as lieth in you, live peaceably with all men. Dearly beloved, avenge not yourselves, but rather give place unto wrath: for

it is written, Vengeance is mine; I will repay, saith the Lord. If thine enemy hunger, feed him; if he thirst, give him drink. Be not overcome of evil, but overcome evil with good. *Ro. xii.* 17 *to* 21. Put on, as the elect of God, holy and beloved, bowels of mercies, kindness; forbearing one another, and forgiving one another, if any man have a quarrel against any. *Col. iii.* 12, 13. Love worketh no ill to his neighbour: therefore love is the fulfilling of the law. *Ro. xiii.* 10. Blessed are the peacemakers: for they shall be called the children of God. *Mat. v.* 9.—*See also, Mar. vii.* 21.

7. To be true and just in all my dealing:

7. Thou knowest the commandments, Do not steal, Defraud not. *Mar, x.* 19. Thou shalt not defraud thy neighbour, neither rob him: the wages of him that is hired shall not abide with thee all night until the morning. Ye shall do no unrighteousness in judgment, in meteyard, in weight, or in measure. Just balances, just weights, a just ephah, and a just hin, shall ye have: I am the Lord your God. *Le. xix.* 13. 35, 36. Divers weights, and divers measures, both of them are alike abomination to the Lord. It is nought, it is nought, saith the buyer: but when he is gone his way, then he boasteth. Bread of deceit is sweet to a man; but afterwards his mouth shall be filled with gravel. *Pr. xx.* 10. 14. 17. The wicked borroweth, and payeth not again: but the righteous sheweth mercy, and giveth. *Ps. xxxvii.* 21. If thou sell ought unto thy neighbour, or buyest ought of thy neighbour's hand, ye shall not oppress one another. *Le. xxv.* 14. Thou shalt not have in thy bag divers weights, a great and a small. Thou shalt not have in thine house divers measures, a great and a small. But thou shalt have a perfect and just weight, a perfect and just measure shalt thou have: for all that do such things, are an abomination unto the Lord thy God. *De. xxv.* 13 *to* 16. Exhort servants to be obedient, not purloining, but shewing all good fidelity; that they may adorn the doctrine of God our Saviour in all things. *Tit. ii.* 9, 10. Masters, give unto your servants that which is just and equal; knowing that ye also have a Master in heaven. *Col. iv.* 1. Finally, brethren, whatsoever things are true, whatsoever things are honest, whatsoever things are just, whatsoever things are pure, whatsoever things are lovely, whatsoever things are of

good report; if there be any virtue, and if there be any praise, think on these things. *Ph. iv.* 8.

8. To bear no malice nor hatred in my heart:

8. But now ye also put off all these; anger, wrath, malice, blasphemy. *Col. iii.* 8. Thou shalt not hate thy brother in thine heart. *Le. xix.* 17. Brethren, be not children in understanding : howbeit in malice be ye children. 1 *Co. xiv.* 20. From within, out of the heart of men, proceed evil thoughts, adulteries, fornications, murders, thefts, covetousness, wickedness, deceit, lasciviousness, an evil eye, blasphemy, pride, foolishness : all these evil things come from within, and defile the man. *Mar. vii.* 21,22, 23. But if ye have bitter envying and strife in your hearts, glory not, and lie not against the truth: for where envying and strife is, there is confusion and every evil work. *Ja. iii.* 14. 16.

9. To keep my hands from picking and stealing,

9. Ye shall not steal, neither deal falsely. Thou shalt not defraud thy neighbour, neither rob him. *Le. xix.* 11. 13. This is the curse that goeth forth over the face of the whole earth : for every one that stealeth shall be cut off as on this side according to it. I will bring it forth, saith the Lord of hosts, and it shall enter into the house of the thief. *Zec. v.* 3, 4. Know ye not that the unrighteous shall not inherit the kingdom of God ? Be not deceived : neither fornicators, nor thieves, nor covetous, nor drunkards, nor revilers, nor extortioners, shall inherit the kingdom of God. 1 *Co. vi.* 9, 10. As the partridge sitteth on eggs, and hatcheth them not; so he that getteth riches, and not by right, shall leave them in the midst of his days, and at his end shall be a fool. *Je. xvii.* 11.| Let him that stole steal no more, but rather let him labour, working with his hands the thing which is good, that he may have to give to him that needeth. *Ep. iv.* 28. We have renounced the hidden things of dishonesty. 2 *Co. iv.* 2.—*See more quotations on this subject in* § 7.

10. and my tongue from evil-speaking, lying, and slandering:

10. Thou shalt not bear false witness against thy neighbour. *Ex. xx.* 16. Put them in mind to be ready to every good work, to speak evil of no man, to be no brawlers. *Tit. iii.* 1, 2. Putting away lying, speak every man truth with his neighbour : let all evil-speaking be put away from you. *Ep. iv.* 25. 31. Lie not one to another, seeing that ye have put off the old man with his deeds. *Col. iii.* 9. Speak ye every

man the truth to his neighbour. *Zec. viii.* 16. These things doth the Lord hate; a lying tongue, an heart that deviseth wicked imaginations, a false witness that speaketh lies, and he that soweth discord among brethren. *Pr. vi.* 16 *to* 19. If any man among you seem to be religious, and bridleth not his tongue, but deceiveth his own heart, this man's religion is vain. *Ja. i.* 26. Ye are of your father the devil; he was a murderer from the beginning, and abode not in the truth, because there is no truth in him. When he speaketh a lie, he speaketh of his own: for he is a liar, and the father of it. *John viii.* 44. All liars shall have their part in the lake which burneth with fire and brimstone. There shall in no wise enter into it [the holy Jerusalem] any thing that defileth, neither whatsoever worketh abomination, or maketh a lie. *Re. xxi.* 8. 27. Remove from me the way of lying; and grant me thy law graciously. I hate and abhor lying; but thy law do I love. *Ps. cxix.* 29. 163. Deliver my soul, O Lord, from lying lips, and from a deceitful tongue. *Ps. cxx.* 2. Thou shalt not go up and down as a talebearer among thy people: neither lie one to another. *Le. xix.* 16. 11. He that uttereth a slander, is a fool. *Pr. x.* 18. Whoso privily slandereth his neighbour, him will I cut off. *Ps. ci.* 5. Wherefore laying aside all malice, and all guile, and hypocrisies, and envies, and all evil speakings, as newborn babes, desire the sincere milk of the word, that ye may grow thereby. 1 *Pe. ii.* 1, 2. Not rendering evil for evil, or railing for railing: but contrariwise blessing. For he that will love life, and see good days, let him refrain his tongue from evil, and his lips that they speak no guile. 1 *Pe. iii.* 9, 10. For with what judgment ye judge, ye shall be judged: and with what measure ye mete, it shall be measured to you again. *Mat. vii.* 2. See also, *Pr. xii.* 19. 22.—*Ja. iv.* 11.—*Ac. v.* 1 *to* 10.—*Ps. lviii.* 3.—*Re. xxii.* 15.

11. To keep my body in temperance, soberness, and chastity:

11. Take heed to yourselves, lest at any time your hearts be overcharged with surfeiting, and drunkenness, and cares of this life. *Lu. xxi.* 34. The time past of our life may suffice us to have wrought the will of the Gentiles, when we walked in lasciviousness, lusts, excess of wine, revellings, banquetings, and abominable idolatries. 1 *Pe. iv.* 3. Beside this, giving all diligence, add to your knowledge, temperance. 2 *Pe. i.* 5, 6.

Every man that striveth for the mastery is temperate in all things. I keep under my body, and bring it into subjection. 1 *Co. ix.* 25. 27. The end of all things is at hand; be ye therefore sober, and watch unto prayer. 1 *Pe. iv.* 7. Let us walk honestly, as in the day; not in rioting and drunkenness, not in chambering and wantonness, not in strife and envying. But put ye on the Lord Jesus Christ, and make not provision for the flesh, to fulfil the lusts thereof. *Ro. xiii.* 13, 14. Meats for the belly, and the belly for meats: but God shall destroy both it and them. Now the body is not for fornication, but for the Lord: and the Lord for the body. 1 *Co. vi.* 13. Ye have heard that it was said by them of old time, Thou shalt not commit adultery: but I say unto you, That whosoever looketh on a woman to lust after her hath committed adultery with her already in his heart. *Mat. v.* 27, 28. Ye know what commandments we gave you by the Lord Jesus. For this is the will of God, even your sanctification, that ye should abstain from fornication: that every one of you should know how to possess his vessel in sanctification and honour. 1 *Th. iv.* 2, 3, 4. Fornication, and all uncleanness, or covetousness, let it not be once named among you, as becometh saints; neither filthiness, nor foolish talking, nor jesting, which are not convenient. For this ye know, that no whoremonger, nor unclean person, nor covetous man, who is an idolater, hath any inheritance in the kingdom of Christ and of God. *Ep. v.* 3, 4, 5. Dearly beloved, I beseech you as strangers and pilgrims, abstain from fleshly lusts, which war against the soul. 1 *Pe. ii.* 11. How can I do this great wickedness, and sin against God ? *Ge. xxxix.* 9. Every man is tempted, when he is drawn away of his own lust, and enticed. Then when lust hath conceived, it bringeth forth sin: and sin, when it is finished, bringeth forth death. *Ja. i.* 14, 15. Dearly beloved, let us cleanse ourselves from all filthiness of the flesh and spirit, perfecting holiness in the fear of God. 2 *Co. vii.* 1.

12. Not to covet nor desire other men's goods;

12. Thou shalt not covet thy neighbour's house, thou shalt not covet thy neighbour's wife, nor his man-servant, nor his maid-servant, nor his ox, nor his ass, nor any thing that is thy neighbour's. *Ex. xx.* 17. Let your conversation be without covetousness; and be content with such things as ye have.

He. xiii. 5. And he said unto them, Take heed and beware of covetousness : for a man's life consisteth not in the abundance of the things which he possesseth. *Lu. xii.* 15. They covet fields, and take them by violence ; and houses, and take them away. *Mi. ii.* 2. The wicked blesseth the covetous, whom the Lord abhorreth. *Ps. x.* 3. For the iniquity of his covetousness was I wroth, and smote him. *Is. lvii.* 17. Woe to him that coveteth an evil covetousness to his house, that he may set his nest on high. Woe to him that increaseth that which is not his! *Hab. ii.* 9. 6. Be not deceived ; neither thieves, nor covetous, shall inherit the kingdom of God. 1 *Co. vi.* 9, 10. This ye know, that no covetous man, who is an idolater, hath any inheritance in the kingdom of Christ and of God. *Ep. v.* 5. All that is in the world, the lust of the flesh, and the lust of the eyes, and the pride of life, is not of the Father, but is of the world. 1 *John ii.* 16. Mortify therefore your members which are upon the earth: evil concupiscence, and covetousness which is idolatry.—*Col. iii.* 5. *See also, the account of Gehazi,* 2 *Ki. v.* 20 *to* 27. *and Mat. vi.* 19 *to* 24.—*Ro. vii.* 8.—2 *Pe. ii.* 15.—*Mar. vii.* 21, 22.

13. but to learn and labour truly to get mine own living, and to do my duty in that state of life, unto which it shall please God to call me.

13. That ye study to be quiet, and to do your own business, and to work with your own hands, as we commanded you ; that ye may walk honestly toward them that are without, and that ye may have lack of nothing. 1 *Th. iv.* 11, 12. Provide things honest in the sight of all men. *Ro. xii.* 17. If any provide not for his own, and specially for those of his own house, he hath denied the faith, and is worse than an infidel. 1 *Ti. v.* 8. After these things Paul departed from Athens, and came to Corinth ; and found a certain Jew named Aquila, born in Pontus. And because he was of the same craft, he abode with them, and wrought: for by their occupation they were tent-makers. *Ac. xviii.* 1, 2, 3. Neither did we eat any man's bread for nought; but wrought with labour and travail night and day, that we might not be chargeable to any of you : not because we have not power, but to make ourselves an ensample unto you to follow us. For even when we were with you, this we commanded you, that if any would not work, neither should he eat. Now them that are such we command and exhort by our Lord Jesus Christ, that with

I

quietness they work, and eat their own bread. *2 Th. iii.* 8, 9, 10. 12. The soul of the sluggard desireth, and hath nothing : but the soul of the diligent shall be made fat. *Pr. xiii.* 4. I went by the field of the slothful, and by the vineyard of the man void of understanding ; and, lo, it was all grown over with thorns, and nettles had covered the face thereof, and the stone wall thereof was broken down. Then I saw, and considered it well ; I looked upon it, and received instruction. Yet a little sleep, a little slumber, a little folding of the hands to sleep: so shall thy poverty come as one that travelleth ; and thy want as an armed man. *Pr. xxiv.* 30 *to* 34. Whatsoever thy hand findeth to do, do it with thy might ; for there is no work, nor device, nor knowledge, nor wisdom, in the grave, whither thou goest. *Ec. ix.* 10. Seekest thou great things for thyself? seek them not. *Je. xlv.* 5. Godliness with contentment is great gain. For we brought nothing into this world, and it is certain we can carry nothing out. And having food and raiment let us be therewith content. But they that will be rich fall into temptation and a snare, and into many foolish and hurtful lusts, which drown men in destruction and perdition. For the love of money is the root of all evil : which while some coveted after, they have erred from the faith, and pierced themselves through with many sorrows. 1 *Ti. vi.* 6 *to* 10. Peter saith to Jesus, Lord, and what shall this man do? Jesus saith unto him, If I will that he tarry till I come, what is that to thee? follow thou me. *John xxi.* 21, 22. Let every man abide in the same calling wherein he was called. Art thou called being a servant? care not for it : but if thou mayest be made free, use it rather. For he that is called in the Lord, being a servant, is the Lord's free man : likewise also he that is called, being free, is Christ's servant. 1 *Co. vii.* 20, 21, 22. Whatsoever things are honest, whatsoever things are just, whatsoever things are of good report, think on these things. *Ph. iv.* 8. Let us hear the conclusion of the whole matter : Fear God, and keep his commandments ; for this is the whole duty of man. *Ec. xii.* 13. *See also, Job xxviii.* 28.—*Ep. iv.* 28.—*Mat. vi.* 19, 20.

CLXXXV. Address concerning the Necessity and Duty of Prayer.

1. My good child, know this, that thou art not able to do these things of thyself, nor to walk in the Commandments of God, and to serve him, without his special grace;

1. Not that we are sufficient of ourselves to think any thing as of ourselves; but our sufficiency is of God. *2 Co. iii.* 5. How to perform that which is good I find not. *Ro. vii.* 18. No man can come to me, except the Father which hath sent me draw him. *John vi.* 44. Without me ye can do nothing. *John xv.* 5. O Lord, I know that the way of man is not in himself: it is not in man that walketh to direct his steps. *Jer. x.* 23. It is God which worketh in you both to will and to do of his good pleasure. *Ph. ii.* 13. God is able to make all grace abound toward you. *2 Co. ix.* 8. He said unto me, My grace is sufficient for thee: for my strength is made perfect in weakness. *2 Co. xii.* 9. By the grace of God I am what I am: and his grace which was bestowed on me was not in vain; but I laboured more abundantly than they all: yet not I, but the grace of God which was with me. *1 Co. xv.* 10. I can do all things through Christ which strengtheneth me. *Ph. iv.* 13. My soul cleaveth unto the dust: quicken thou me according to thy word. I will run the way of thy commandments, when thou shalt enlarge my heart. Teach me, O Lord, the way of thy statutes; and I shall keep it unto the end. Give me understanding, and I shall keep thy law; yea, I shall observe it with my whole heart. Make me to go in the path of thy commandments; for therein do I delight. Incline mine heart unto thy testimonies. *Ps. cxix.* 25. 32 *to* 36. Every good gift and every perfect gift is from above, and cometh down from the Father of lights. *Ja. i.* 17. Let us therefore come boldly unto the throne of grace, that we may obtain mercy, and find grace to help in time of need. *He. iv.* 16.

2. which thou must learn at all times to call for by diligent prayer. Let me hear therefore, if thou canst say the Lord's Prayer.

2. I will that men pray every where. *1 Ti. ii.* 8. Ask, and it shall be given you; seek, and ye shall find; knock, and it shall be opened unto you: for every one that asketh receiveth; and he that seeketh findeth; and to him that knocketh it shall be opened. *Mat. vii.* 7, 8. If any of you lack wisdom, let him ask of God, that giveth to all men liberally, and upbraideth not; and it shall be given him. *Ja. i.* 5. Whatsoever ye shall ask in my name, that will I do. *John xiv.* 13. This

is the confidence that we have in him, that, if we ask any thing according to his will, he heareth us. 1 *John v.* 14. And whatsoever we ask, we receive of him, because we keep his commandments, and do those things that are pleasing in his sight. 1 *John iii.* 22. Pray without ceasing. 1 *Th. v.* 17. Continue in prayer, and watch in the same with thanksgiving. *Col. iv.* 2. Praying always with all prayer and supplication in the Spirit, and watching thereunto with all perseverance. *Ep. vi.* 18. And all things, whatsoever ye shall ask in prayer believing, ye shall receive. *Mat. xxi.* 22. Evening, and morning, and at noon, will I pray, and cry aloud : and he shall hear my voice. *Ps. lv.* 17. Jacob said, I will not let thee go, except thou bless me. *Ge. xxxii.* 26. When ye pray, use not vain repetitions, as the heathen do : for they think that they shall be heard for their much speaking. *Mat. vi.* 7. One of his disciples said unto him, Lord, teach us to pray. And he said unto them, When ye pray, say, Our Father which art in heaven, Hallowed be thy name. Thy kingdom come. Thy will be done, as in heaven, so in earth. Give us day by day our daily bread. And forgive us our sins ; for we also forgive every one that is indebted to us. And lead us not into temptation ; but deliver us from evil. *Lu. xi.* 1 *to* 4.

CLXXXVI. *A Paraphrase on the Lord's Prayer.*

1. What desirest thou of God in this Prayer?

I desire my Lord God our heavenly Father, who is the giver of all goodness, to send his grace unto me, and to all people ;

1. Jesus said unto them, What would ye that I should do for you ? *Mar. x.* 36. The desire of our soul is to thy name. With my soul have I desired thee. *Is. xxvi.* 8, 9. What things soever ye desire, when ye pray, believe that ye receive them, and ye shall have them. *Mar. xi.* 24. And the Lord descended in the cloud, and proclaimed the name of the Lord. The Lord, The Lord God, merciful and gracious, long-suffering, and abundant in goodness and truth. *Ex. xxxiv.* 5, 6. Behold what manner of love the Father hath bestowed upon us, that we should be called the sons of God. 1 *John iii.* 1. And because ye are sons, God hath sent forth the Spirit of his Son into your hearts, crying, Abba, Father. Wherefore thou art no more a servant but a son. *Ga. iv.* 6, 7. Every good gift and every perfect gift is from above, and cometh

down from the Father of lights, with whom is no variableness, neither shadow of turning. *Ja. i.* 17. The Lord is good to all; and his tender mercies are over all his works. *Ps. cxlv.* 9. Let us lift up our heart with our hands unto God in the heavens. *La. iii.* 41. Unto thee lift I up mine eyes, O thou that dwellest in the heavens. *Ps. cxxiii.* 1. I will pour upon the house of David, and upon the inhabitants of Jerusalem, the spirit of grace and of supplications. *Zec. xii.* 10. This shall be the covenant that I will make with the house of Israel; After those days, saith the Lord, I will put my law in their inward parts, and write it in their hearts; and will be their God, and they shall be my people. They shall all know me, from the least of them unto the greatest of them, saith the Lord: for I will forgive their iniquity, and I will remember their sin no more. *Je. xxxi.* 33, 34. What prayer and supplication soever be made by any man, or by all thy people Israel, which shall know every man the plague of his own heart, and spread forth his hands toward this house: then hear thou in heaven thy dwelling place, and forgive, and do, and give to every man according to his ways: that they may fear thee all the days that they live. 1 *Ki. viii.* 38, 39, 40. Praying always with all prayer and supplication for all saints. *Ep. vi.* 18. God be merciful unto us, and bless us; and cause his face to shine upon us. That thy way may be known upon earth, thy saving health among all nations. *Ps. lxvii.* 1, 2.

2. that we may worship him, serve him, and obey him, as we ought to do.

2. O come, let us worship and bow down: let us kneel before the Lord our Maker. *Ps. xcv.* 6. O worship the Lord in the beauty of holiness. *Ps. xcvi.* 9. Exalt the Lord our God, and worship at his holy hill; for the Lord our God is holy. *Ps. xcix.* 9. Holy and reverend is his name. *Ps. cxi.* 9. Give unto the Lord the glory due unto his name; worship the Lord in the beauty of holiness. In his temple doth every one speak of his glory. *Ps. xxix.* 2. 9. Sanctify the Lord God in your hearts. 1 *Pe. iii.* 15. God is greatly to be feared in the assembly of the saints, and to be had in reverence of all them that are about him. *Ps. lxxxix.* 7. Glorify God in your body, and in your spirit, which are God's. 1 *Co. vi.* 20. Serve the Lord with fear, and rejoice with trembling. *Ps. ii.* 11. Serve the Lord with gladness: come before his presence with

singing. *Ps. c.* 2. Thy will be done in earth, as it is in heaven. *Mat. vi.* 10. Hath the Lord as great delight in burnt offerings and sacrifices, as in obeying the voice of the Lord? Behold, to obey is better than sacrifice, and to hearken than the fat of rams. 1 *Sa. xv.* 22. Amend your ways and your doings, and obey the voice of the Lord your God. *Je. xxvi.* 13. Now, therefore, if ye will obey my voice indeed, and keep my covenant, then ye shall be a peculiar treasure unto me above all people: for all the earth is mine. *Ex. xix.* 5. Whosoever shall keep the whole law, and yet offend in one point, he is guilty of all. *Ja. ii.* 10. Blessed are the undefiled in the way, who walk in the law of the Lord. Blessed are they that keep his testimonies, and that seek him with the whole heart. Then shall I not be ashamed, when I have respect unto all thy commandments. *Ps. cxix.* 1, 2. 6.

3. and I pray unto God, that he will send us all things that be needful both for our souls and bodies;

3. Give us this day our daily bread. *Mat. vi.* 11. In the sweat of thy face shalt thou eat bread. *Ge. iii.* 19. He humbled thee, and suffered thee to hunger, and fed thee with manna, which thou knewest not, neither did thy fathers know; that he might make thee know that man doth not live by bread only, but by every word that proceedeth out of the mouth of the Lord doth man live. *De. viii.* 3. Labour not for the meat which perisheth, but for that meat which endureth unto everlasting life, which the Son of man shall give unto you. *John vi.* 27. As newborn babes, desire the sincere milk of the word, that ye may grow thereby. 1 *Pe. ii.* 2. My God shall supply all your need according to his riches in glory by Christ Jesus. *Ph. iv.* 19. We labour, working with our own hands. 1 *Co. iv.* 12. When we were with you, this we commanded you, that if any would not work, neither should he eat. Now them that are such we command and exhort by our Lord Jesus Christ, that with quietness they work, and eat their own bread. 2 *Th. iii.* 10. 12. Not slothful in business; fervent in spirit; serving the Lord. *Ro. xii.* 11. The young lions do lack, and suffer hunger: but they that seek the Lord shall not want any good thing. *Ps. xxxiv.* 10. Let your conversation be without covetousness; and be content with such things as ye have: for he hath said, I will never leave thee, nor forsake thee. *He. xiii.* 5. Casting all your

care upon him ; for he careth for you. 1 *Pe. v.* 7. Therefore I say unto you, Take no thought for your life, what ye shall eat, or what ye shall drink; nor yet for your body, what ye shall put on. Is not the life more than meat, and the body than raiment? Behold the fowls of the air: for they sow not, neither do they reap, nor gather into barns; yet your heavenly Father feedeth them. Are ye not much better than they? And why take ye thought for raiment? Consider the lilies of the field, how they grow; they toil not, neither do they spin: and yet I say unto you, That even Solomon in all his glory was not arrayed like one of these. Wherefore, if God so clothe the grass of the field, which to day is, and to morrow is cast into the oven, shall he not much more clothe you, O ye of little faith? Therefore take no thought, saying, What shall we eat? or, What shall we drink? or, Wherewithal shall we be clothed? (For after all these things do the Gentiles seek:) for your heavenly Father knoweth that ye have need of all these things. But seek ye first the kingdom of God, and his righteousness; and all these things shall be added unto you. *Mat. vi.* 25, 26. 28 *to* 33. Remove far from me vanity and lies : give me neither poverty nor riches; feed me with food convenient for me. *Pr. xxx.* 8. Godliness with contentment is great gain. Having food and raiment let us be therewith content. 1 *Ti. vi.* 6. 8.

4. and that he will be merciful unto us, and forgive us our sins; 4. And forgive us our debts as we forgive our debtors. And lead us not into temptation, but deliver us from evil. For if ye forgive men their trespasses, your heavenly Father will also forgive you. *Mat. vi.* 12, 13, 14. If thou, Lord, shouldest mark iniquities, O Lord, who shall stand? but there is forgiveness with thee, that thou mayest be feared. *Ps. cxxx.* 3, 4. The mercy of the Lord is from everlasting to everlasting upon them that fear him. *Ps. ciii.* 17. If we confess our sins, he is faithful and just to forgive us our sins. 1 *John i.* 9. In whom we have redemption through his blood, the forgiveness of sins. *Ep. i.* 7. Have mercy upon me, O God, according unto thy lovingkindness: according unto the multitude of thy tender mercies blot out my transgressions. Hide thy face from my sins, and blot out all mine iniquities. *Ps. li.* 1. 9. For thy name's sake, O Lord,

pardon mine iniquity ; for it is great. Look upon mine
affliction and my pain ; and forgive all my sin. *Ps. xxv.* 11.
18. Blessed are they whose iniquities are forgiven, and whose
sins are covered. Blessed is the man unto whom the Lord
will not impute sin. *Ro. iv.* 7, 8.

5. and that
it will please
him to save
and defend us
in all dangers
ghostly and
bodily ;

5. Lead us not into temptation. *Mat. vi.* 13. Watch and
pray, that ye enter not into temptation. *Mat. xxvi.* 41. Keep
back thy servant also from presumptuous sins ; let them not
have dominion over me. *Ps. xix.* 13. There hath no temptation taken you but such as is common to man : but God is
faithful, who will not suffer you to be tempted above that ye
are able ; but will with the temptation also make a way to
escape, that ye may be able to bear it. 1 *Co. x.* 13. For in
that he himself hath suffered being tempted, he is able to
succour them that are tempted. *He. ii.* 18. The Lord knoweth
how to deliver the godly out of temptations. 2 *Pe. ii.* 9. For
this purpose the Son of God was manifested, that he might
destroy the works of the devil. 1 *John iii.* 8. Innumerable
evils have compassed me about : mine iniquities have taken
hold upon me, so that I am not able to look up ; they are
more than the hairs of mine head : therefore my heart faileth
me. *Ps. xl.* 12. The Lord shall preserve thee from all evil :
he shall preserve thy soul. The Lord shall preserve thy
going out and thy coming in from this time forth, and even
for evermore. *Ps. cxxi.* 7, 8. Yea, though I walk through
the valley of the shadow of death, I will fear no evil : for
thou art with me ; thy rod and thy staff they comfort me.
Ps. xxiii. 4. He that dwelleth in the secret place of the Most
High shall abide under the shadow of the Almighty. Because
thou hast made the Lord which is my refuge, even the Most
High, thy habitation ; there shall no evil befall thee, neither
shall any plague come nigh thy dwelling. *Ps. xci.* 1. 9, 10.

6. and that
he will keep us
from all sin
and wicked-
ness, and from
our ghostly
enemy, and
from everlast-
ing death.
⁀᾽ᴛ᾽ᴊ ᴍ ᴦ

6. Deliver us from evil. *Mat. vi.* 13. Who can understand
his errors ? cleanse thou me from secret faults. Keep back
thy servant also from presumptuous sins ; let them not have
dominion over me. *Ps. xix.* 12, 13. I pray not that thou
shouldest take them out of the world, but that thou shouldest
keep them from the evil. *John xvii.* 15. The whole world
lieth in wickedness. 1 *John v.* 19. And Jabez called on the

God of Israel, saying, Oh that thou wouldest bless me indeed, and enlarge my coast, and that thine hand might be with me, and that thou wouldest keep me from evil, that it may not grieve me! 1 *Ch. iv.* 10. Be sober, be vigilant; because your adversary the devil, as a roaring lion, walketh about, seeking whom he may devour. 1 *Pe. v.* 8. And the serpent said unto the woman, Yea, hath God said, Ye shall not eat of every tree in the garden? Ye shall not surely die: for God doth know that in the day ye eat thereof, then your eyes shall be opened, and ye shall be as gods, knowing good and evil. *Ge. iii.* 1. 4, 5. The Lord said unto Satan, Hast thou considered my servant Job, that there is none like him in the earth, a perfect and an upright man, one that feareth God, and escheweth evil. Then Satan answered the Lord, and said, Doth Job fear God for nought? Hast not thou made an hedge about him, and about his house, and about all that he hath on every side? thou hast blessed the work of his hands, and his substance is increased in the land. But put forth thine hand now, and touch all that he hath, his bone and his flesh—and he will curse thee to thy face. *Job i.* 8 *to* 11. *ii.* 5. And he shewed me Joshua the high priest standing before the angel of the Lord, and Satan standing at his right hand to resist him. *Zec. iii.* 1. And Jesus was there in the wilderness forty days tempted of Satan. *Mar. i.* 13. Put on the whole armour of God, that ye may be able to stand against the wiles of the devil. *Ep. vi.* 11. He that is begotten of God keepeth himself, and that wicked one toucheth him not. 1 *John v.* 18. Kept by the power of God through faith unto salvation. 1 *Pe. i.* 5. The wages of sin is death; but the gift of God is eternal life through Jesus Christ our Lord. *Ro. vi.* 23. He that overcometh shall not be hurt of the second death. *Re. ii.* 11. The lake which burneth with fire and brimstone; which is the second death. *Re. xxi.* 8. The Lord shall deliver me from every evil work, and will preserve me unto his heavenly kingdom. 2 *Ti. iv.* 18. *See also*, 1 *Sa. ii.* 9.—*Ge. xxxix.* 9.

7. And this I trust he will do of his mercy and goodness, through our Lord Jesus

7. O Israel, thou hast destroyed thyself; but in me is thine help. *Ho. xiii.* 9. The mercy of the Lord is from everlasting to everlasting upon them that fear him. *Ps. ciii.* 17. The goodness of God endureth continually. *Ps. lii.* 1. O how great

K

Christ. And therefore I say, Amen. So be it.

is thy goodness, which thou hast laid up for them that fear thee; which thou hast wrought for them that trust in thee before the sons of men! *Ps. xxxi.* 19. I trust in the mercy of God for ever and ever. *Ps. lii.* 8. The Lord redeemeth the soul of his servants: and none of them that trust in him shall be desolate. *Ps. xxxiv.* 22. Surely goodness and mercy shall follow me all the days of my life. *Ps. xxiii.* 6. Now unto him that is able to keep you from falling, and to present you faultless before the presence of his glory with exceeding joy, To the only wise God our Saviour, be glory and majesty, dominion and power, both now and ever. Amen. *Jude* 24, 25. No man cometh unto the Father, but by me. *John xiv.* 6. Through him we both have access by one Spirit unto the Father. *Ep. ii.* 18. Behold the Lamb of God, which taketh away the sin of the world. *John i.* 29. Our Lord Jesus Christ who gave himself for our sins, that he might deliver us from this present evil world, according to the will of God and our Father. *Ga. i.* 3, 4. For in that he himself hath suffered being tempted, he is able to succour them that are tempted. *He. ii.* 18. There is one God, and one mediator between God and men, the man Christ Jesus; who gave himself a ransom for all, to be testified in due time. 1 *Ti. ii.* 5, 6. Jesus our Lord, who was delivered for our offences, and was raised again for our justification. *Ro. iv.* 24, 25. Through sanctification of the Spirit unto obedience, and sprinkling of the blood of Jesus Christ. 1 *Pe. i.* 2. Justified freely by his grace through the redemption that is in Christ Jesus. *Ro. iii.* 24. Christ is all, and in all. *Col. iii.* 11. All the promises of God in him are yea, and in him amen, unto the glory of God. 2 *Co. i.* 20. Then answered I, and said, So be it, O Lord. *Je. xi.* 5.

CLXXXVII. *Concerning the Sacraments.*

1. How many Sacraments hath Christ ordained in his Church?

2. Two only, as generally

1 *to* 6. And ye shall circumcise the flesh of your foreskin; and it shall be a token of the covenant betwixt me and you. *Ge. xvii.* 11. And the Lord said unto Moses and Aaron, This is the ordinance of the passover: There shall no stranger eat thereof: and ye shall observe this thing for an ordinance to

necessary to salvation, that is to say, Baptism; and the Supper of the Lord.

3. What meanest thou by this word Sacrament?

4. I mean an outward and visible sign of an inward and spiritual grace given unto us, ordained by Christ himself, as a means whereby we receive the same, and a pledge to assure us thereof.

5. How many parts are there in a Sacrament?

6. Two: the outward visible sign, and the inward spiritual grace.

thee and to thy sons for ever. *Ex. xii.* 43. 24. Now I say that Jesus Christ was a minister of the circumcision for the truth of God, to confirm the promises made unto the fathers: and that the Gentiles might glorify God for his mercy. *Ro. xv.* 8, 9. Elect according to the foreknowledge of God the Father, through sanctification of the Spirit unto obedience, and sprinkling of the blood of Jesus Christ. 1 *Pe. i.* 2. And Jesus came, and spake unto them, saying, All power is given unto me in heaven and in earth. Go ye therefore, and teach all nations, baptizing them. *Mat. xxviii.* 18, 19. Jesus came and his disciples into the land of Judea ; and there he tarried with them and baptized. *John iii.* 22. He that believeth and is baptized shall be saved. *Mar. xvi.* 16. Except a man be born of water and of the Spirit, he cannot enter into the kingdom of God. *John iii.* 5. And he took bread, and gave thanks, and brake it, and gave unto them saying, This is my body which was given for you : this do in remembrance of me. Likewise also the cup after supper, saying, This cup is the new testament in my blood, which is shed for you. *Lu. xxii.* 19, 20. Then Jesus said unto them, Verily, verily, I say unto you, Except ye eat the flesh of the Son of man, and drink his blood, ye have no life in you. Whoso eateth my flesh, and drinketh my blood, hath eternal life ; and I will raise him up at the last day. *John vi.* 53, 54. Can any man forbid water, that these should not be baptized, which have received the Holy Ghost as well as we ? *Ac. x.* 47. Not by works of righteousness which we have done, but according to his mercy he saved us, by the washing of regeneration, and renewing of the Holy Ghost. *Tit. iii.* 5. Know ye not, that so many of us as were baptized into Jesus Christ were baptized into his death ? *Ro. vi.* 3. The cup of blessing which we bless, is it not the communion of the blood of Christ ? The bread which we break, is it not the communion of the body of Christ ? 1 *Co. x.* 16. This do in remembrance of me. *Lu. xxii.* 19. Buried with him in baptism, wherein also ye are risen with him through the faith of the operation of God, who hath raised him from the dead, *Col. ii.* 12. He that eateth my flesh, and drinketh my blood, dwelleth in me, and I in him. *John vi.* 56.

7. What is the outward visible sign or form in Baptism?

8. Water, wherein the person is baptized in the Name of the Father, and of the Son, and of the Holy Ghost.

7; 8. Go ye therefore, and teach all nations, baptizing them in the name of the Father, and of the Son, and of the Holy Ghost. *Mat. xxviii.* 19. And Jesus, when he was baptized, went up straightway out of the water : and, lo, the heavens were opened unto him, and he saw the Spirit of God descending like a dove, and lighting upon him. *Mat. iii.* 16. Can any man forbid water, that these should not be baptized, which have received the Holy Ghost as well as we ? *Ac. x.* 47. And as they went on their way, they came unto a certain water : and the eunuch said, See here is water; what doth hinder me to be baptized ? And he commanded the chariot to stand still; and they went down both into the water, both Philip and the eunuch; and he baptized him. *Ac. viii.* 36. 38.

9. What is the inward and spiritual grace?

10. A death unto sin, and a new birth unto righteousness: for being by nature born in sin, and the children of wrath, we are hereby made the children of grace.

9, 10. Know ye not, that so many of us as were baptized into Jesus Christ were baptized into his death? Therefore we are buried with him by baptism into death: that like as Christ was raised up from the dead by the glory of the Father, even so we also should walk in newness of life. For he that is dead is freed from sin. Likewise reckon ye also yourselves to be dead indeed unto sin, but alive unto God through Jesus Christ our Lord. *Ro. vi.* 3, 4. 7. 11. Except a man be born again, he cannot see the kingdom of God : except a man be born of water and of the Spirit, he cannot enter into the kingdom of God. *John iii.* 3. 5. Which were born, not of blood, nor of the will of the flesh, nor of the will of man, but of God. *John i.* 13. Who his own self bore our sins in his own body on the tree, that we, being dead to sins, should live unto righteousness. 1 *Pe. ii.* 24. Not by works of righteousness which we have done, but according to his mercy he saved us, by the washing of regeneration, and renewing of the Holy Ghost. *Tit. iii.* 5. Being then made free from sin, ye became the servants of righteousness. For as ye have yielded your members servants to uncleanness and to iniquity unto iniquity ; even so now yield yourselves servants to righteousness unto holiness. *Ro. vi.* 18, 19. And you hath he quickened, who were dead in trespasses and sins; wherein in time past ye walked according to the course of this world, according to the prince of the power of the air, the spirit that now worketh in the children of disobedience : among whom also we all had our conversation in times past in the lusts of our flesh, fulfilling the desires of the flesh and of the mind; and were by nature the children of wrath, even as others. *Ep. ii.* 1, 2, 3. Behold, I was shapen in iniquity; and in sin did my mother conceive me. *Ps. li.* 5. As it is written, There is none righteous, no, not one. *Ro. iii.* 10. Wherefore, as by one man sin entered into the world, and death by sin; and so death passed upon all men. *Ro. v.* 12. He that believeth and is baptized shall be saved. *Mar. xvi.* 16. By one Spirit are we all baptized into one body. 1 *Co. xii.* 13. Ye are all the children of God by faith in Christ Jesus. For as many of you as have been baptized into Christ have put on Christ. *Ga. iii.* 26, 27. They which are the children of the flesh, these are not the children of God: but the children of the promise are counted for the seed. *Ro. ix.* 8. And of his fulness have all we received, and grace for grace. *John i.* 16. For sin shall not have dominion over you: for ye are not under the law, but under grace. *Ro. vi.* 14.

11. What is required of persons to be baptised?

12. Repentance, whereby they forsake sin; and Faith, whereby they stedfastly believe the promises of God made to them in that Sacrament.

11, 12. Then Peter said unto them, Repent, and be baptized every one of you in the name of Jesus Christ for the remission of sins, and ye shall receive the gift of the Holy Ghost. *Ac. ii.* 38. Repent ye therefore, and be converted, that your sins may be blotted out. *Ac. iii.* 19. But shewed first unto them of Damascus, and at Jerusalem, and throughout all the coasts of Judea, and then to the Gentiles, that they should repent and turn to God, and do works meet for repentance. *Ac. xxvi.* 20. Godly sorrow worketh repentance to salvation not to be repented of: for behold this selfsame thing, that ye sorrowed after a godly sort, what carefulness it wrought in you, yea, what clearing of yourselves, yea, what indignation, yea, what fear, yea, what vehement desire, yea, what zeal, yea, what revenge! 2 *Co. vii.* 10, 11. He that believeth and is baptized shall be saved. *Mar. xvi.* 16. But when they believed Philip preaching the things concerning the kingdom of God, and the name of Jesus Christ, they were baptized, both men and women. And the eunuch said, What doth hinder me to be baptized? And Philip said, If thou believest with all thine heart, thou mayest. And he answered and said, I believe that Jesus Christ is the Son of God. *Ac.*

viii. 12. 36, 37. Let us draw near with a true heart in full assurance of faith, having our hearts sprinkled from an evil conscience, and our bodies washed with pure water. Let us hold fast the profession of our faith without wavering; for he is faithful that promised. *He. x.* 22, 23. The promise is unto you, and to your children, and to all that are afar off, even as many as the Lord our God shall call. *Ac. ii.* 39.

13. Why then are Infants baptized, when by reason of their tender age they cannot perform them?

14. Because they promise them both by their Sureties; which promise, when they come to age, themselves are bound to perform.

13, 14. Jesus said, Suffer little children, and forbid them not, to come unto me: for of such is the kingdom of heaven. *Mat. xix.* 14. Ye stand this day all of you before the Lord your God; your captains of your tribes, your elders, and your officers, with all the men of Israel, your little ones, your wives, and thy stranger that is in thy camp, from the hewer of thy wood unto the drawer of thy water: that thou shouldest enter into covenant with the Lord thy God, and into his oath, which the Lord thy God maketh with thee this day: that he may establish thee to-day for a people unto himself, and that he may be unto thee a God, as he hath said unto thee, and as he hath sworn unto thy fathers, to Abraham, to Isaac, and to Jacob. Neither with you only do I make this covenant and this oath; but with him that standeth here with us before the Lord our God, and also with him that is not here with us this day. *De. xxix.* 10 *to* 15. And he that is eight days old shall be circumcised among you, every man child in your generations, he that is born in the house, or bought with money of any stranger, which is not of thy seed. He that is born in thy house, and he that is bought with thy money, must needs be circumcised: and my covenant shall be in your flesh for an everlasting covenant. *Ge. xvii.* 12, 13. In whom also ye are circumcised with the circumcision made without hands, in putting off the body of the sins of the flesh by the circumcision of Christ: buried with him in baptism, wherein also ye are risen with him through the faith of the operation of God. *Col. ii.* 11, 12. I will establish my covenant between me and thee and thy seed after thee in their generations for an everlasting covenant, to be a God unto thee, and to thy seed after thee. *Ge. xvii.* 7. Wherefore hath the Lord done thus unto this land? what meaneth the heat of this great anger? Then men shall say, Because they have forsaken the covenant of the Lord God of their fathers, which he made with them. *De. xxix. 24, 25. See also, the case of St. Paul engaging himself as Surety to Philemon for Onesimus:—and, 2 Ki. xxiii. 2, 3.*

15. Why was the Sacrament of the Lord's Supper ordained?

16. For the continual remembrance of the sacrifice of the death of Christ, and of the benefits which we receive thereby.

17. What is the outward part or sign of the Lord's Supper?

18. Bread and Wine, which the Lord hath commanded to be received.

15 to 18. And he took bread, and gave thanks, and brake it, and gave unto them, saying, This is my body which is given for you: this do in remembrance of me. Likewise also the cup after supper, saying, This cup is the new testament in my blood, which is shed for you. *Lu. xxii. 19, 20.* I have received of the Lord that which also I delivered unto you, That the Lord Jesus the same night in which he was betrayed took bread: and when he had given thanks, he brake it, and said, Take, eat: this is my body, which is broken for you: this do in remembrance of me. After the same manner also he took the cup, when he had supped, saying, This cup is the new testament in my blood: this do ye, as oft as ye drink it, in remembrance of me. For as often as ye eat this bread, and drink this cup, ye do shew the Lord's death till he come. *1 Co. xi. 23 to 26.* Christ our Passover is sacrificed for us. *1 Co. v. 7.* Now once in the end of the world hath he appeared to put away sin by the sacrifice of himself. *He. ix. 26.* This is my blood of the new testament, which is shed for many for the remission of sins. *Mat. xxvi. 28.* Behold the Lamb of God, which taketh away the sin of the world. *John i. 29.* Now in Christ Jesus ye who sometimes were far off are made nigh by the blood of Christ. *Ep. ii. 13.* Having made peace through the blood of his cross. *Col. i. 20.* We also joy in God through our Lord Jesus Christ, by whom we have now received the atonement. *Ro. v. 11.* When Christ, who is our life, shall appear, then shall ye also appear with him in glory. *Col. iii. 4.—See also, He. ix. 26.—John xv. 13.—Ep. v. 2.*

19. What is the inward part or thing signified?

20. The Body and Blood of Christ, which are verily and indeed taken and received by the faithful in the Lord's Supper.

19, 20. And as they were eating, Jesus took bread, and blessed it, and brake it, and gave it to the disciples, and said, Take, eat: this is my body. And he took the cup, and gave thanks, and gave it to them, saying, Drink ye all of it; for this is my blood of the new testament, which is shed for many for the remission of sins. *Mat. xxvi. 26, 27, 28.* The cup of blessing which we bless, is it not the communion of the blood of Christ? The bread which we break, is it not the communion of the body of Christ? 1 *Co. x.* 16. Then Jesus said unto them, Verily, verily, I say unto you, Except ye eat the flesh of the Son of man, and drink his blood, ye have no life in you. He that believeth on me hath everlasting life. *John vi.* 53. 47.

21. What are the benefits whereof we are partakers thereby?
22. The strengthening and refreshing of our souls by the Body and Blood of Christ, as our bodies are by the Bread and Wine.

21, 22. Wine that maketh glad the heart of man, and oil to make his face to shine, and bread which strengtheneth man's heart. *Ps. civ.* 15. Jesus said unto them, I am the bread of life: he that cometh to me shall never hunger; and he that believeth on me shall never thirst. I am the living bread which came down from heaven: if any man eat of this bread, he shall live for ever: and the bread that I will give is my flesh, which I will give for the life of the world. For my flesh is meat indeed, and my blood is drink indeed. He that eateth my flesh, and drinketh my blood, dwelleth in me, and I in him. *John vi.* 35. 51. 55, 56.

23. What is required of them who come to the Lord's Supper?
24. To examine themselves, whether they repent them truly of their former sins, stedfastly purposing to lead a new life; have a lively faith in God's mercy through Christ, with a thankful remembrance of his death; and be in charity with all men.

23, 24. But let a man examine himself, and so let him eat of that bread, and drink of that cup. 1 *Co. xi.* 28. Examine yourselves whether ye be in the faith; prove your own selves. Know ye not your own selves, how that Jesus Christ is in you, except ye be reprobates? 2 *Co. xiii.* 5. Examine me, O Lord, and prove me; try my reins and my heart. *Ps. xxvi.* 2. Search me, O God, and know my heart: try me, and know my thoughts: and see if there be any wicked way in me, and lead me in the way everlasting. *Ps. cxxxix.* 23, 24. For behold this selfsame thing, that ye sorrowed after a godly sort, what carefulness it wrought in you, yea, what clearing of yourselves, yea, what indignation, yea, what fear, yea, what vehement desire, yea, what zeal, yea, what revenge! 2 *Co. vii.* 11. Let us search and try our ways, and turn again to the Lord. *La. iii.* 40. For the grace of God that bringeth salvation hath appeared to all men, teaching us that, denying ungodliness and worldly lusts, we should live soberly, righteously, and godly, in this present world. *Tit. ii.* 11, 12. He hath shewed thee, O man, what is good; and what doth the Lord require of thee, but to do justly, and to love mercy, and to walk humbly with thy God? *Mi. vi.* 8. And having an High Priest over the house of God; let us draw near with a true heart in full assurance of faith, having our hearts sprinkled

from an evil conscience, and our bodies washed with pure
water. *He. x.* 21, 22. Surely he hath borne our griefs, and
carried our sorrows: yet we did esteem him stricken, smitten
of God, and afflicted. But he was wounded for our transgressions, he was bruised for our iniquities: the chastisement
of our peace was upon him; and with his stripes we are
healed. Yet it pleased the Lord to bruise him; he hath put
him to grief: when thou shalt make his soul an offering for
sin, he shall see his seed, he shall prolong his days. *Is. liii.*
4, 5. 10. He that spared not his own Son, but delivered him
up for us all, how shall he not with him also freely give us all
things? *Ro. viii.* 32. For as often as ye eat this bread, and
drink this cup, ye do shew the Lord's death till he come. 1 *Co.*
xi. 26. Giving thanks unto the Father, which hath made us
meet to be partakers of the inheritance of the saints in light:
who hath delivered us from the power of darkness, and hath
translated us into the kingdom of his dear Son: in whom we
have redemption through his blood, even the forgiveness of
sins. *Col. i.* 12, 13, 14. If thou bring thy gift to the altar,
and there rememberest that thy brother hath ought against
thee; leave there thy gift before the altar, and go thy way;
first be reconciled to thy brother, and then come and offer thy
gift. *Mat. v.* 23, 24. Beloved, if God so loved us, we ought
also to love one another. 1 *John iv.* 11. Let all bitterness, and
wrath, and anger, and clamour, and evil speaking, be put
away from you, with all malice: and be ye kind one to another,
tender hearted, forgiving one another, even as God for Christ's
sake hath forgiven you. *Ep. iv.* 31, 32. Purge out therefore
the old leaven, that ye may be a new lump, as ye are unleavened. For even Christ our passover is sacrificed for us:
therefore let us keep the feast, not with old leaven, neither
with the leaven of malice and wickedness; but with the
unleavened bread of sincerity and truth. 1 *Co. v.* 7, 8. Charity
suffereth long, and is kind; charity envieth not; charity
vaunteth not itself, is not puffed up, doth not behave itself
unseemly, seeketh not her own, is not easily provoked, thinketh
no evil; rejoiceth not in iniquity, but rejoiceth in the truth;
beareth all things, believeth all things, hopeth all things,
endureth all things. Charity never faileth: but whether there

be prophecies, they shall fail; whether there be tongues, they shall cease; whether there be knowledge, it shall vanish away. And now abideth faith, hope, charity; these three; but the greatest of these is charity. 1 *Co. xiii.* 4 *to* 8. 13. Finally, be perfect, be of good comfort, be of one mind, live in peace; and the God of love and peace shall be with you. The grace of the Lord Jesus Christ, and the love of God, and the communion of the Holy Ghost, be with you all. Amen. 2 *Co. xiii.* 11. 14.

ORDER OF CONFIRMATION,

OR LAYING ON OF HANDS UPON THOSE THAT ARE BAPTIZED, AND ARE COME TO YEARS OF DISCRETION.

CLXXXVIII. *A serious Address to the Congregation.*

To the end that Confirmation may be ministered to the more edifying of such as shall receive it, the Church hath thought good to order, That none hereafter shall be Confirmed, but such as can say the Creed, the Lord's Prayer, and the Ten Commandments; and can also answer to such other Questions, as in the short Catechism are contained: which order is very convenient to be observed; to the end that children, being now come to the years of discretion, and having learned what their Godfathers and Godmothers promised for them in Baptism, they may themselves, with their own mouth and consent, openly before the Church, ratify and confirm the same; and also promise, that by the grace of God they will evermore endeavour themselves, faithfully to observe such things as they, by their own confession, have assented unto.

Now when the apostles which were at Jerusalem heard that Samaria had received the word of God, they sent unto them Peter and John: who, when they were come down, prayed for them, that they might receive the Holy Ghost: (for as yet he was fallen upon none of them: only they were baptized in the name of the Lord Jesus.) Then laid they their hands on them, and they received the Holy Ghost. *Ac.* *viii.* 14 *to* 17.

CLXXXIX. *The Solemn Stipulation.*

Q. Do you here in the presence of God, and of this Congregation, renew the solemn promise and vow, that was made in your name at your Baptism; ratifying and confirming the same in your own persons, and acknowledging yourselves bound to believe, and to do all those things which your Godfathers and Godmothers then undertook for you?—*A.* I do.

And the king went up into the house of the Lord, and all the men of Judah, and the inhabitants of Jerusalem, and the priests, and the Levites, and all the people, great and small: and he read in their ears all the words of the book of the covenant that was found in the house of the Lord. And the king stood in his place, and made a covenant before the Lord, to walk after the Lord, and to keep his commandments, and his testimonies, and his statutes, with all his heart, and with all his soul, to perform the words of the covenant which are written in this book, and he caused all that were present in

Jerusalem and Benjamin to stand to it. And the inhabitants of Jerusalem did according to the covenant of God, the God of their fathers. *2 Ch. xxxiv.* 30, 31, 32. *See also, 2 Ki. xvii.* 13, 14, 15.

CXC. *Acts of Praise.*

1. Our help is in the Name of the Lord ;

2. Who hath made heaven and earth.

1, 2. Our help is in the Name of the Lord, who made heaven and earth. *Ps. cxxiv.* 8. I will lift up mine eyes unto the hills, from whence cometh my help. My help cometh from the Lord, which made heaven and earth. *Ps. cxxi.* 1, 2. Happy is he that hath the God of Jacob for his help, whose hope is in the Lord his God : which made heaven, and earth, the sea, and all that therein is : which keepeth truth for ever. *Ps. cxlvi.* 5, 6.

3. Blessed be the Name of the Lord ;

4. Henceforth, world without end.

3, 4. Blessed be the Name of the Lord from this time forth and for evermore. *Ps. cxiii.* 2. Daniel said, Blessed be the name of God for ever and ever. *Da. ii.* 20. Blessed be the Lord God of Israel from everlasting to everlasting : and let all the people say, Amen. Praise ye the Lord. *Ps. cvi.* 48. *See also, Eze. iii.* 12.

5. Lord, hear our prayers ;

6. And let our cry come unto thee.

5, 6. Hear my prayer, O Lord, and let my cry come unto thee. *Ps. cii.* 1. Out of the depths have I cried unto thee, O Lord. Lord, hear my voice : let thine ears be attentive to the voice of my supplications. *Ps. cxxx.* 1, 2. *See also, 2 Ch. xxx.* 27.

CXCI. *Supplication for the Gifts and Grace of the Holy Spirit.*

1. Let us pray, Almighty and everliving God, who hast vouchsafed to regenerate these thy servants by Water and the Holy Ghost, and hast given unto them forgiveness of all their sins ;

1. Except a man be born of water and of the Spirit, he cannot enter into the kingdom of God. *John iii.* 5. But ye are washed, ye are sanctified, ye are justified in the name of the Lord Jesus, and by the Spirit of our God. *1 Co. vi.* 11. Not by works of righteousness which we have done, but according to his mercy he saved us, by the washing of regeneration and renewing of the Holy Ghost. *Tit. iii.* 5. Now we have received, not the spirit of the world, but the Spirit which is of God. *1 Co. ii.* 12. Peter said unto them, Repent, and be baptized every one of you in the name of Jesus Christ

for the remission of sins, and ye shall receive the gift of the Holy Ghost. *Ac.* ii. 38. God for Christ's sake hath forgiven you. *Ep.* iv. 32. I write unto you, little children, because your sins are forgiven you for his name's sake. 1 *John* ii. 12. You, being dead in your sins and the uncircumcision of your flesh, hath he quickened together with him, having forgiven you all trespasses. *Col.* ii. 13. *See also, other quotations in the office for Public Baptism of Infants.*

2. Strengthen them, we beseech thee, O Lord, with the Holy Ghost the Comforter, 2. Thy God hath sent forth strength for thee, stablish the thing, O God, that thou hast wrought in us. *Ps.* lxviii. 28. For this cause I bow my knees unto the Father of our Lord Jesus Christ, of whom the whole family in heaven and earth is named, that he would grant you, according to the riches of his glory, to be strengthened with might by his Spirit in the inner man. *Ep.* iii. 14, 15, 16. Strengthened with all might, according to his glorious power. *Col.* i. 11. The God of all grace, who hath called us unto his eternal glory by Christ Jesus, after that ye have suffered awhile, make you perfect, stablish, strengthen, settle you. 1 *Pe.* v. 10. I will pray the Father, and he shall give you another Comforter, that he may abide with you for ever; even the Spirit of truth; the Comforter, which is the Holy Ghost, whom the Father will send in my name. *John* xiv. 16, 17. 26. Surely, shall one say, in the Lord have I righteousness and strength. *Is.* xlv. 24.

3. and daily increase in them thy manifold gifts of grace; 3. The head from which all the body by joints and bands having nourishment ministered, and knit together, increaseth with the increase of God. *Col.* ii. 19. Every good gift and every perfect gift is from above. *Ja.* i. 17. There are diversities of gifts, but the same Spirit. Covet earnestly the best gifts. 1 *Co.* xii. 4. 31. Grow in grace, and in the knowledge of our Lord and Saviour Jesus Christ. 2 *Pe.* iii. 18. And this I pray, that your love may abound yet more and more in knowledge and in all judgment; that ye may approve things that are excellent; that ye may be sincere and without offence, till the day of Christ; being filled with the fruits of righteousness, which are by Jesus Christ, unto the glory and praise of God. *Ph.* i. 9, 10, 11. Brethren, I count not myself to have apprehended: but this one thing I do, forgetting those things which are behind, and reaching forth unto those things which are before, I press toward the mark for the prize of the high calling of God in Christ Jesus. *Ph. iii.* 13, 14.   As every man hath received the gift, even so minister the same one to another, as good stewards of the manifold grace of God. 1 *Pe. iv.* 10.

4. the Spirit of wisdom and understanding; the Spirit of counsel and ghostly strength; the Spirit of know-ledge and true godliness;   4. The Spirit of the Lord shall rest upon him, the Spirit of wisdom and understanding, the Spirit of counsel and might, the Spirit of knowledge and of the fear of the Lord. *Is. xi.* 2. Making mention of you in my prayers ; That the God of our Lord Jesus Christ, the Father of glory, may give unto you the Spirit of wisdom and revelation in the knowledge of him : the eyes of your understanding being enlightened ; that ye may know what is the hope of his calling, and what the riches of the glory of his inheritance in the saints. *Ep. i.* 16, 17, 18. That ye might walk worthy of the Lord unto all pleasing, being fruitful in every good work, and increasing in the know-ledge of God. *Col. i.* 10.   Grace and peace be multiplied unto you through the knowledge of God, and of Jesus our Lord, according as his divine power hath given unto us all things that pertain unto life and godliness, through the knowledge of him that hath called us to glory and virtue. 2 *Pe. i.* 2, 3.   If any of you lack wisdom, let him ask of God, that giveth to all men liberally, and upbraideth not ; and it shall be given him. *Ja. i.* 5.   I would have you wise unto that which is good, and simple concerning evil. *Ro. xvi.* 19.   Happy is the man that findeth wisdom, and the man that getteth understanding. *Pr. iii.* 13.   Through thy precepts I get understanding. *Ps. cxix.* 104.   Counsel is mine, and sound wisdom ; I am un-derstanding ; I have strength. *Pr. viii.* 14.   I will bless the Lord, who hath given me counsel. *Ps. xvi.* 7.   And the child grew, and waxed strong in spirit. *Lu. i.* 80.   Be strong in the Lord, and in the power of his might. *Ep. vi.* 10.   I bow my knees unto the Father of our Lord Jesus Christ, that he would grant you, according to the riches of his glory, to be strength-ened with might by his Spirit in the inner man. *Ep. iii.* 14. 16.   Teach me good judgment and knowledge ; for I have believed thy commandments. *Ps. cxix.* 66.   I will give you pastors according to mine heart, which shall feed you with knowledge and understanding. *Je. iii.* 15.   And Joshua, the son of Nun was full of the spirit of wisdom ; for Moses had laid his hands upon him. *De. xxxiv.* 9. Add to your faith virtue; and to virtue knowledge; and to knowledge temperance; and to temperance patience; and to patience godliness; and to godliness brotherly kindness; and to brotherly kindness charity. *2 Pe. i.* 5, 6, 7.

5. and fill them, O Lord, with the Spirit of thy holy fear, now and for ever. Amen.

5. I will make an everlasting covenant with them, that I will not turn away from them, to do them good; I will put my fear in their hearts, that they shall not depart from me. *Je. xxxii.* 40. The Spirit of the Lord shall rest upon him; and shall make him of quick understanding in the fear of the Lord. *Is. xi.* 2, 3. The fear of the Lord is the beginning of wisdom: a good understanding have all they that do his commandments. *Ps. cxi.* 10. The fear of the Lord is clean, enduring for ever. *Ps. xix.* 9. The fear of the Lord tendeth to life: and he that hath it shall abide satisfied; he shall not be visited with evil. *Pr. xix.* 23. Wherefore we receiving a kingdom which cannot be moved, let us have grace, whereby we may serve God acceptably with reverence and godly fear. *He. xii.* 28. *See also, Pr. i.* 7.—*xiv.* 27.—*Job xxviii.* 28.

CXCII. *Prayer, with the Laying on of the Hands of the Bishop.*

1, Defend, O Lord, this thy child, [or this thy servant] with thy heavenly grace, that he may continue thine for ever;

1. The Lord God is a sun and shield: the Lord will give grace and glory: no good thing will he withhold from them that walk uprightly. *Ps. lxxxiv.* 11. The name of the God of Jacob defend thee. *Ps. xx.* 1. The Lord bless thee, and keep thee. *Nu. vi.* 24. I am thine, save me; for I have sought thy precepts. *Ps. cxix.* 94. Hold up my goings in thy paths, that my footsteps slip not. Keep me as the apple of the eye, hide me under the shadow of thy wings. *Ps. xvii.* 5. 8. Fear thou not; for I am with thee: be not dismayed; for I am thy God: I will strengthen thee; yea, I will help thee; yea, I will uphold thee with the right hand of my righteousness. *Is. xli.* 10. I am continually with thee: thou hast holden me by my right hand. Thou shalt guide me with thy counsel, and afterward receive me to glory. *Ps. lxxiii.* 23, 24. *See also, Is. xlix.* 2.—*John x.* 28, 29.—*He. iii.* 14.—*Ps. xlviii.* 14.

2. and daily increase in thy

2. By one Spirit are we all baptized into one body. *1 Co. xii.* 13. The God of all grace, make you perfect, stablish,

Holy Spirit more and more, until he come unto thy everlasting kingdom. Amen.

strengthen, settle you. 1 *Pe. v.* 10. The Lord make you to increase and abound in love one toward another, and toward all men, even as we do toward you : to the end he may stablish your hearts unblameable in holiness before God, even our Father, at the coming of our Lord Jesus Christ with all his saints. 1 *Th. iii.* 12, 13. Grow in grace. 2 *Pe. iv.* 18. The very God of peace sanctify you wholly ; and I pray God your whole spirit and soul and body be preserved blameless unto the coming of our Lord Jesus Christ. 1 *Th. v.* 23. The Lord shall deliver me from every evil work, and will preserve me unto his heavenly kingdom. 2 *Ti. iv.* 18. Now unto him that is able to keep you from falling, and to present you faultless before the presence of his glory with exceeding joy, to the only wise God our Saviour, be glory and majesty, dominion and power, both now and ever. Amen. *Jude* 24, 25. *See also, John xiv.* 26.

3. The Lord be with you : And with thy spirit.

3. The Lord be with you. 2 *Th. iii.* 16. The Lord Jesus Christ be with thy spirit. 2 *Ti. iv.* 22.

Our Father, &c.

CXCIII. *A Prayer for the Exercise of God's Providence and Grace towards the Confirmed.*

1. Almighty and everliving God, who makest us both to will and to do those things that be good and acceptable unto thy divine Majesty ;

2. We make our humble supplications unto thee, for these thy servants,

3. upon whom (after the example of the holy apostles) we have now laid our hands, to certify them (by this sign) of

1. O Lord, I know that the way of man is not in himself; it is not in man that walketh to direct his steps. *Je. x.* 23. It is God which worketh in you both to will and to do of his good pleasure. *Ph. ii.* 13. Good and acceptable before God. 1 *Ti. v.* 4. *See also,* 1 *Ch. xxix.* 14.—*Pr. xvi.* 1.

2. Pray one for another. *Ja. v.* 16. God giveth grace unto the humble. *Ja. iv.* 6. The effectual fervent prayer of a righteous man availeth much. *Ja. v.* 16.

3. The holy apostles. *Ep. iii.* 5. Now when the apostles which were at Jerusalem heard that Samaria had received the word of God, they sent unto them Peter and John; who, when they were come down, prayed for them, that they might receive the Holy Ghost : for as yet he was fallen upon none of them : only they were baptized in the name of the Lord Jesus. Then laid they their hands on them, and they received the Holy Ghost. *Ac. viii.* 14 *to* 17. When they heard this, they

thy favour and gracious goodness towards them.

were baptized in the name of the Lord Jesus. And when Paul had laid his hands upon them, the Holy Ghost came on them. *Ac. xix.* 5, 6. God hath not given us the spirit of fear; but of power, and of love, and of a sound mind. 2 *Ti. i.* 7. *See also, Ps. cvi.* 4.—1 *Ti. iv.* 14.—2 *Ti. i.* 6.—*Ph. iv.* 19.—*Ac. vi.* 6.

4. Let thy fatherly hand, we beseech thee, ever be over them ; let thy Holy Spirit ever be with them ;

4. I am a Father to Israel. *Je. xxxi.* 9. Like as a father pitieth his children, so the Lord pitieth them that fear him. *Ps. ciii.* 13. The Lord careth for the righteous. *Ps. cxlvi.* 8. The hand of our God is upon all them for good that seek him. *Ezr. viii.* 22. Let thine hand help me; for I have chosen thy precepts. *Ps. cxix.* 173. Come out from among them, and be ye separate, saith the Lord, and touch not the unclean thing; and I will receive you, and will be a Father unto you, and ye shall be my sons and daughters, saith the Lord Almighty. 2 *Co. vi.* 17, 18. And I give unto thee eternal life; and they shall never perish, neither shall any man pluck them out of my hand. My Father which gave them me, is greater than all; and no man is able to pluck them out of my Father's hand. *John x.* 28, 29. I will pray the Father, and he shall give you another Comforter, that he may abide with you for ever; even the Spirit of truth. *John xiv.* 16, 17. Every one that asketh receiveth; and he that seeketh findeth; and to him that knocketh, it shall be opened. If ye being evil, know how to give good gifts unto your children, how much more shall your heavenly Father give the Holy Spirit to them that ask him. *Lu. xi.* 10. 13.

5. And so lead them in the knowledge and obedience of thy Word, that in the end they may obtain everlasting life; through our Lord Jesus Christ, who with thee and the Holy Ghost liveth and reigneth, ever one God, world without end. Amen.

5. Wherefore I also, after I heard of your faith in the Lord Jesus, and love unto all the saints, cease not to give thanks for you, making mention of you in my prayers; that the God of our Lord Jesus Christ, the Father of glory, may give unto you the Spirit of wisdom and revelation in the knowledge of him: the eyes of your understanding being enlightened; that ye may know what is the hope of his calling, and what the riches of the glory of his inheritance in the saints, and what is the exceeding greatness of his power to us-ward who believe, according to the working of his mighty power. *Ep. i.* 15 *to* 19. For this cause I bow my knees unto the Father of our Lord Jesus Christ, of whom the whole family in heaven and earth is named, that he would grant you, according to the riches

M

of his glory, to be strengthened with might by his Spirit in the inner man; that Christ may dwell in your hearts by faith; that ye, being rooted and grounded in love, may be able to comprehend with all saints what is the breadth, and length, and depth, and height; and to know the love of Christ, which passeth knowledge, that ye might be filled with all the fulness of God. *Ep. iii.* 14 *to* 19. From a child thou hast known the Holy Scriptures, which are able to make thee wise unto salvation through faith which are in Christ Jesus. 2 *Ti. iii.* 15. Lead me in thy truth, and teach me: for thou art the God of my salvation. *Ps. xxv.* 5. Teach me to do thy will. *Ps. cxliii.* 10. Thy word have I hid in mine heart, that I might not sin against thee. *Ps. cxix.* 11. For this cause also thank we God without ceasing, because, when ye received the word of God which ye heard of us, ye received it not as the word of men, but as it is in truth, the word of God, which effectually worketh also in you that believe. 1 *Th. ii.* 13. Not every one that saith unto me, Lord, Lord, shall enter into the kingdom of heaven; but he that doeth the will of my Father which is in heaven. *Mat. vii.* 21. I give thee charge in the sight of God, who quickeneth all things, and before Christ Jesus, who before Pontius Pilate witnessed a good confession; that thou keep this commandment without spot, unrebukable, until the appearing of our Lord Jesus Christ. 1 *Ti. vi.* 13, 14. I have fought a good fight, I have finished my course, I have kept the faith: henceforth there is laid up for me a crown of righteousness, which the Lord, the righteous Judge, shall give me at that day: and not to me only, but unto all them also that love his appearing. 2 *Ti. iv.* 7, 8. Now unto him that is able to keep you from falling, and to present you faultless before the presence of his glory with exceeding joy, to the only wise God our Saviour, be glory and majesty, dominion and power, both now and ever. Amen. *Jude* 24, 25. See also, *John vii.* 17.

SOLEMNIZATION OF MATRIMONY.

CXCIV.

*I publish the Banns of Marriage between M. of—— and N. of——.
If any of you know cause, or just impediment, why these two Persons should
not be joined together in holy Matrimony, ye are to declare it. This is the
first,* [second, *or* third,] *time of asking.*

CXCV. The Address to the Congregation.

I. Dearly beloved, we are gathered together here in the sight of God, and in the face of this congregation, to join together this Man and this Woman in holy Matrimony;

1. Now are we all here present before God. *Ac. x.* 33. The eyes of the Lord are in every place, beholding the evil and the good. *Pr. xv.* 3. All things are naked and opened unto the eyes of him with whom we have to do. *He. iv.* 13. And Boaz said unto the elders, and unto all the people, ye are witnesses this day. *Ru. iv.* 9. There was a marriage in Cana of Galilee; and the mother of Jesus was there : and both Jesus was called, and his disciples, to the marriage. *John ii.* 1, 2. To avoid fornication, let every man have his own wife, and let every woman have her own husband. 1 *Co. vii.* 2.

2. which is an honourable estate, instituted of God in the time of man's innocency, signifying unto us the mystical union that is betwixt Christ and his Church;

2. Marriage is honourable in all. *He. xiii.* 4. Whoso findeth a wife findeth a good thing, and obtaineth favour of the Lord. *Pr. xviii.* 22. The Lord God said, It is not good that the man should be alone; I will make him an help meet for him. And the Lord God caused a deep sleep to fall upon Adam, and he slept : and he took one of his ribs, and closed up the flesh instead thereof; and the rib, which the Lord God had taken from man, made he a woman, and brought her unto the man. And Adam said, This is now bone of my bones, and flesh of my flesh : she shall be called Woman, because she was taken out of Man. Therefore shall a man leave his father and his mother, and shall cleave unto his wife : and they shall be one flesh. *Ge. ii.* 18. 21 *to* 24. Have ye not read, that he which made them at the beginning made them male and female? and said, For this cause shall a man leave father and mother, and shall cleave to his wife : and they twain shall be one flesh? *Mat. xix.* 4, 5. Wives, submit yourselves unto your own husbands, as unto the Lord. For the husband is the

head of the wife, even as Christ is the Head of the Church : and he is the Saviour of the body. Therefore as the Church is subject unto Christ, so let the wives be to their own husbands in every thing. Husbands, love your wives, even as Christ also loved the Church, and gave himself for it ; that he might sanctify and cleanse it with the washing of water by the word, that he might present it to himself a glorious Church, not having spot, or wrinkle, or any such thing ; but that it should be holy and without blemish. So ought men to love their wives as their own bodies. He that loveth his wife loveth himself. For no man ever yet hated his own flesh ; but nourisheth and cherisheth it, even as the Lord the Church : for we are members of his body, of his flesh, and of his bones. For this cause shall a man leave his father and mother, and shall be joined unto his wife, and they two shall be one flesh. This is a great mystery : but I speak concerning Christ and the Church. Nevertheless let every one of you in particular so love his wife even as himself ; and the wife see that she reverence her husband. *Ep. v.* 22 *to* 33.

3. which holy estate Christ adorned and beautified with his presence, and first miracle that he wrought, in Cana of Galilee ; and is commended of St. Paul to be honourable among all men:

3. And the third day there was a marriage in Cana of Galilee ; and the mother of Jesus was there : and both Jesus was called, and his disciples, to the marriage. And when they wanted wine, the mother of Jesus saith unto him, They have no wine. Jesus saith unto them, [the servants,] Fill the waterpots with water. And they filled them up to the brim. And he saith unto them, Draw out now, and bear unto the governor of the feast. And they bare it. When the ruler of the feast had tasted the water that was made wine, and knew not whence it was ; (but the servants which drew the water knew ;) the governor of the feast called the bridegroom, and saith unto him, Every man at the beginning doth set forth good wine ; and when men have well drunk, then that which is worse : but thou hast kept the good wine until now. This beginning of miracles did Jesus in Cana of Galilee. *John ii.* 1, 2, 3. 7 *to* 11. Marriage is honourable in all, and the bed undefiled ; but whoremongers and adulterers God will judge. *He. xiii.* 4.

4. and therefore is not by

4. And it came to pass, when men began to multiply on the face of the earth, and daughters were born unto them, that

uny to be enterprised, not taken in hand, unadvisedly, lightly, or wantonly, to satisfy men's carnal lusts and appetites, like brute beasts that have no understanding; but reverently, discreetly, advisedly, soberly, and in the fear of God; duly considering the causes for which Matrimony was ordained.

the sons of God saw the daughters of men that they were fair; and they took them wives of all which they chose. And the Lord said, My Spirit shall not always strive with man. And also after that, when the sons of God came in unto the daughters of men, and they bare children to them, the same became mighty men which were of old, men of renown. And God saw that the wickedness of man was great in the earth. *Ge. vi.* 1 *to* 5. Esau was forty years old when he took to wife Judith the daughter of Beeri the Hittite, and Bashemath the daughter of Elon the Hittite, which were a grief of mind unto Isaac and to Rebekah. *Ge. xxvi.* 34, 35. And Rebekah said to Isaac, I am weary of my life because of the daughters of Heth: if Jacob take a wife of the daughters of Heth, such as these which are the daughters of the land, what good shall my life do me? And Isaac called Jacob, and blessed him, and charged him, and said unto him, Thou shalt not take a wife of the daughters of Canaan. *Ge. xxvii.* 46. *xxviii.* 1. When the Lord thy God shall bring thee into the land whither thou goest to possess it, and hath cast out many nations before thee, thou shalt make no covenant with them; neither shalt thou make marriages with them; for they will turn away thy son from following me. *De. vii.* 1 *to* 4. But king Solomon loved many strange women. And it came to pass, when Solomon was old, that his wives turned away his heart after other gods. 1 *Ki. xi.* 1. 4. These filthy dreamers defile the flesh. What they know naturally as brute beasts, in those things they corrupt themselves. *Jude* 8. 10. Be not as the horse, or as the mule, which hath no understanding, *Ps. xxxii.* 9. Who can find a virtuous woman? for her price is far above rubies. *Pr. xxxi.* 10. A prudent wife is from the Lord. *Pr. xix.* 14. In all thy ways acknowledge him, and he shall direct thy paths. *Pr. iii.* 6. See that ye walk circumspectly, not as fools, but as wise. *Ep. v.* 15. The wife is bound by the law as long as her husband liveth; but if her husband be dead, she is at liberty to be married to whom she will; only in the Lord. 1 *Co. vii.* 39. Be ye not unequally yoked together with unbelievers: for what fellowship hath righteousness with unrighteousness? and what communion hath light with darkness? and what concord hath Christ with

Belial? or what part hath he that believeth with an infidel? 2 *Co. vi.* 14, 15. And Abraham said unto his eldest servant of his house, that ruled over all that he had, Put, I pray thee, thy hand under my thigh: and I will make thee swear by the Lord, the God of heaven, and the God of the earth, that thou shalt not take a wife unto my son of the daughters of the Canaanites, among whom I dwell: but thou shalt go unto my country, and to my kindred, and take a wife unto my son Isaac. And the servant went to Mesopotamia, unto the city of Nahor. And it came to pass, that, behold, Rebekah came out, who was born to Bethuel, son of Milcah, the wife of Nahor, Abraham's brother. And the man wondering at her held his peace, to wit whether the Lord had made his journey prosperous or not. And said, Whose daughter art thou? And she said unto him, I am the daughter of Bethuel the son of Milcah, which she bare unto Nahor. And Rebekah had a brother, and his name was Laban: and Laban ran out unto the man, and said, Come in, thou blessed of the Lord. And he said, I will not eat until I have told mine errand.—And now if ye will deal kindly and truly with my master, tell me; and if not, tell me. Then Laban and Bethuel answered and said, The thing proceedeth from the Lord; we cannot speak unto thee bad or good. Behold, Rebekah is before thee, take her, and go, and let her be thy master's son's wife, as the Lord hath spoken. And they called Rebekah, and said unto her, Wilt thou go with this man? And she said, I will go. And they sent away Rebekah their sister. And Isaac brought her into his mother Sarah's tent, and she became his wife. *Ge. xxiv.* 2, 3, 4, 10. 15, 21, 23, 24. 29. 31, 33, 49, 50, 51. 58, 59. 67.

5. First, It was ordained for the procreation of children, to be brought up in the fear and nurture of the Lord, and to the praise of his holy Name.

5. God created man in his own image, in the image of God created he him; male and female created he them. And God blessed them, and God said unto them, be fruitful, and multiply and replenish the earth. *Ge. i.* 27, 28. Ye fathers, provoke not your children to wrath; but bring them up in the nurture and admonition of the Lord. *Ep. vi.* 4. Then Manoah entreated the Lord, and said, O my Lord, let the man of God which thou didst send come again unto us, and teach us what we shall do unto the child that shall be born. And Manoah said, Now let thy words come to pass. How shall we order

the child, and how shall we do unto him ? *Jud. xiii.* 8. 12. Both young men, and maidens; old men, and children; let them praise the name of the Lord. *Ps. cxlviii.* 12, 13.

6. Secondly,
It was or-
dained for a
remedy against
sin, and to
avoid fornica-
tion ; that such
persons as have
not the gift of
continency
might marry,
and keep them-
selves undefiled
members of
Christ's body.
Thirdly, It
was ordained
for the mutual
society, help,
and comfort,
that the one
ought to have
of the other,
both in pros-
perity and ad-
versity. Into
which holy e-
state these two
persons present
come now to be
joined. There-
fore if any man
can shew any
just cause, why
they may not
lawfully be
joined toge-
ther, let him
now speak, or
else hereafter
for ever hold
his peace.

6. To avoid fornication, let every man have his own wife, and let every woman have her own husband. 1 *Co. vii.* 2. This is the will of God, even your sanctification, that ye should abstain from fornication. 1 *Th. iv.* 3. Know ye not that your bodies are the members of Christ ? Shall I then take the members of Christ, and make them the members of an harlot? God forbid. 1 *Co. vi.* 15. We know that, when he shall appear, we shall be like him. And every man that hath this hope in him, purifieth himself, even as he is pure. 1 *John iii.* 2, 3. And the Lord God said, It is not good that the man should be alone; I will make him an help meet for him. *Ge. ii.* 18. Two are better than one; because they have a good reward for their labour. For if they fall, the one will lift up his fellow : but woe to him that is alone when he falleth ; for he hath not another to help him up. *Ec. iv.* 9, 10. Let every one of you in particular so love his wife even as himself; and the wife see that she reverence her husband. He that loveth his wife loveth himself. For no man ever yet hated his own flesh ; but nourisheth and cherisheth it. *Ep. v.* 33. 28, 29. The unbelieving husband is sanctified by the wife, and the unbelieving wife is sanctified by the husband. 1 *Co. vii.* 14. And Isaac took Rebekah, and she became his wife ; and he loved her: and Isaac was comforted after his mother's death. *Ge. xxiv.* 67. And David comforted Bathsheba his wife. 2 *Sa. xii.* 24. The Pharisees came unto him, tempting him, and saying unto him, Is it lawful for a man to put away his wife for every cause? And he answered and said unto them, Have ye not read, that he which made them at the beginning made them male and female, and said, For this cause shall a man leave father and mother, and shall cleave to his wife: and they twain shall be one flesh? Wherefore they are no more twain but one flesh. What therefore God hath joined together, let not man put asunder. And I say unto you, Whosoever shall put away his wife, except it be for fornication, and shall marry another, committeth adultery : and whoso marrieth her which is put away doth commit adultery. *Mat. xix.* 3 to 6. 9.

CXCVI. The Charge to the two persons now to be joined together in holy Matrimony.

1. I require and charge you both, as ye will answer at the dreadful day of judgment when the secrets of all hearts shall be disclosed, that if either of you know any impediment, why ye may not be lawfully joined together in Matrimony, ye do now confess it.

1. The priest shall charge her by an oath. *Nu. v.* 19. The high priest answered and said unto him, I adjure thee by the living God. *Mat. xxvi* 63. I say unto you, that every idle word that men shall speak, they shall give account thereof in the day of judgment. *Mat. xii.* 36. God shall bring every work into judgment, with every secret thing, whether it be good, or whether it be evil. *Ec. xii.* 14. In the day when God shall judge the secrets of men by Jesus Christ. *Ro. ii.* 16. There is nothing covered, that shall not be revealed; neither hid, that shall not be known. *Lu. xii.* 2. He that covereth his sins shall not prosper: but whoso confesseth and forsaketh them shall have mercy. *Pr. xxviii.* 13.

2. For be ye well assured, that so many as are coupled together otherwise than God's Word doth allow, are not joined together by God; neither is their Matrimony lawful.

2. Be sure your sin will find you out. *Nu. xxxii.* 23. Though hand join in hand, the wicked shall not be unpunished. *Pr. xi.* 21. Herod himself had sent forth and laid hold upon John, and bound him in prison for Herodias's sake, his brother Philip's wife: for he had married her. For John had said unto Herod, It is not lawful for thee to have thy brother's wife. *Mar. vi.* 17, 18. Should we again break thy commandments, and join in affinity with the people of these abominations? wouldest not thou be angry with us till thou hadst consumed us? *Ezr. ix.* 14. And Shechaniah the son of Jehiel, one of the sons of Elam, answered and said unto Ezra, We have trespassed against our God, and have taken strange wives of the people of the land: yet now there is hope in Israel concerning this thing. Now therefore let us make a covenant with our God to put away all the wives, and such as are born of them, according to the counsel of my lord, and of those that tremble at the commandment of our God; and let it be done according to the law. Arise; for this matter belongeth unto thee; be of good courage, and do it. Then arose Ezra, and made the chief priests, the Levites, and all Israel, to swear that they should do according to this word. And they sware. And Ezra the priest stood up, and said unto them, Ye have transgressed, and taken strange wives, to increase the trespass of Israel. Now therefore make confession unto the Lord God of your

fathers, and do his pleasure: and separate yourselves from the people of the land, and from the strange wives. Then all the congregation answered and said with a loud voice, As thou hast said, so must we do. *Ezr. x.* 2 *to* 5. 10, 11, 12.

CXCVII.—*Enquiries respecting the mutual consent of the parties in contracting Matrimony. No.* 1.

M. Wilt thou have this Woman to thy wedded wife, to live together after God's ordinance, in the holy estate of Matrimony? Wilt thou love her, comfort her, honour, and keep her in sickness and in health; and, forsaking all other, keep thee only unto her, so long as ye both shall live?

I will.

And he answered and said unto them, Have ye not read, that he which made them at the beginning made them male and female, and said, For this cause shall a man leave father and mother, and shall cleave to his wife: and they twain shall be one flesh? Wherefore they are no more twain but one flesh. *Mat. xix.* 4, 5, 6. So ought men to love their wives as their own bodies. He that loveth his wife loveth himself. For no man ever yet hated his own flesh; but nourisheth and cherisheth it, even as the Lord the Church. *Ep. v.* 28, 29. Likewise, ye husbands, dwell with them according to knowledge, giving honour unto the wife, as unto the weaker vessel, and as being heirs together of the grace of life; that your prayers be not hindered. 1 *Pe. iii.* 7. To avoid fornication, let every man have his own wife, and let every woman have her own husband. Let the husband render unto the wife due benevolence: and likewise also the wife unto the husband. 1 *Co. vii.* 2, 3. Live joyfully with the wife whom thou lovest all the days of the life of thy vanity. *Ec. ix.* 9. Drink waters out of thine own cistern, and running waters out of thine own well. Let thy fountains be dispersed abroad, and rivers of waters in the streets. Let them be only thine own, and not strangers with thee. Let thy fountain be blessed: and rejoice with the wife of thy youth, and be thou ravished always with her love. And why wilt thou, my son, be ravished with a strange woman, and embrace the bosom of a stranger? *Pr. v.* 15 *to* 20. Take heed to your spirit, and let none deal treacherously against the wife of his youth. The Lord, the God of Israel, saith that he hateth putting away. *Mal. ii.* 15, 16. Let not the husband put away his wife. 1 *Co. vii.* 11. And now, my daughter, fear not; I will do to thee all that thou requirest. So Boaz took Ruth, and she was his wife. *Ru. iii.* 11. *iv,* 13.

N

CXCVIII. *Enquiries, &c. No. 2.*

1. *N.* Wilt thou have this Man to thy wedded husband, to live together after God's ordinance, in the holy estate of Matrimony? Wilt thou obey him, and serve him, love, honour, and keep him in sickness and in health; and, forsaking all other, keep thee only unto him, so long as ye both shall live?

1 will.

1. And they called Rebekah, and said unto her, Wilt thou go with this man? And she said, I will go. *Ge. xxiv.* 58. And the Lord God said, It is not, good that the man should be alone; I will make him an help meet for him. *Ge. ii.* 18. Sara obeyed Abraham, calling him lord. 1 *Pe. iii.* 6. Wives, submit yourselves unto your own husbands, as it is fit in the Lord. *Col. iii.* 18. Wives, submit yourselves unto your own husbands, as unto the Lord. Therefore as the Church is subject unto Christ, so let the wives be to their own husbands in every thing. Let the wife see that she reverence her husband. *Ep. v.* 22. 24. 33. That they [the aged women] may teach the young women to be sober, to love their husbands, to love their children, to be discreet, chaste, keepers at home, good, obedient to their own husbands, that the word of God be not blasphemed. *Tit. ii.* 4, 5. The heart of her husband doth safely trust in her, so that he shall have no need of spoil. She will do him good and not evil all the days of her life. *Pr. xxxi.* 11, 12. The strange woman, which forsaketh the guide of her youth, and forgetteth the covenant of her God. *Pr. ii.* 16, 17. The wife is bound by the law as long as her husband liveth. 1 *Co. vii.* 39. See also, 1 *Sa. xxv.* 39, 40.

2. Who giveth this Woman to be married to this Man?

2. And the rib, which the Lord God had taken from man, made he a woman, and brought her unto the man. *Ge. ii.* 22. He that giveth her in marriage doeth well. 1 *Co. vii.* 38.

CXCIX and CC. *The Mutual Stipulation.*

1 *M.* take thee *N.* to my wedded wife, to have and to hold from this day forward, for better for worse for richer for poorer, in sickness and in health, to love and to cherish, till death us do part, according to God's holy ordinance; and thereto 1 plight thee my troth.

1 *N.* take thee *M.* to my wedded husband, to have and to hold from this day forward, for better for worse, for richer for poorer, in sickness and in health, to love, cherish, and to obey, till death us do part, according to God's holy ordinance; and thereto I give thee my troth.

The Pharisees came to him, and asked him, Is it lawful for a man to put away his wife? tempting him. Jesus answered and said unto them, From the beginning of the creation God made them male and female. For this cause shall a man leave father and mother, and cleave to his wife; and they twain shall be one flesh: so then they are no more twain, but one flesh. And he saith unto them, Whosoever shall put away his wife, and marry another, committeth adultery against her· And if a woman shall put away her husband, and be married to another, she committeth adultery. *Mar. x.* 2. *5 to* 8. 11, 12. He saith unto them, Moses, because of the hardness of your hearts suffered you to put away your wives: but from the beginning it was not so. *Mat. xix.* 8. *See also,* 1 *Co. vii.* 5.

CCI. The *Giving and the Receiving of the Ring as the solemn Pledge of the mutual Engagement.*

With this Ring I thee wed, with my body I thee worship, and with all my worldly goods I thee endow: In the name of the Father, and of the Son, and of the Holy Ghost. Amen.

Now this was the manner in former time in Israel concerning redeeming and concerning changing, for to confirm all things; a man plucked off his shoe, and gave it to his neighbour: and this was a testimony in Israel.—Boaz drew off his shoe, and said unto the elders, and unto all the people, Ye are witnesses this day. And all the people that were in the gate, and the elders, said, We are witnesses. The Lord make the woman that is come into thine house like Rachel and like Leah, which two did build the house of Israel. So Boaz took Ruth, and she was his wife. *Ru. iv.* 7, 8, 9. 11. 13. Then Laban and Bethuel answered and said, Behold, Rebekah is before thee, let her be thy master's son's wife, as the Lord hath spoken. And the servant brought forth jewels of silver, and jewels of gold, and raiment, and gave them to Rebekah. And Isaac brought her into his mother Sarah's tent, and took Rebekah, and she became his wife; and he loved her: and Isaac was comforted after his mother's death. *Ge. xxiv.* 50, 51. 53. 67. Whatsoever ye do in word or deed, do all in the name of the Lord Jesus. *Col. iii.* 17. Do all to the glory of God. 1 *Co. x.* 31. A faithful witness will not lie. *Pr. xiv.* 5. If thou shalt afflict my daughters, or if thou take other wives beside my daughters, no man is with us; see, God is witness betwixt me and thee. *Ge. xxxi.* 50.

CCII. *A Prayer for a Blessing on the Parties making the mutual Engagement.*

Let us pray.
1. O Eternal God, Creator and Pre-

1. Before the mountains were brought forth, or ever thou hadst formed the earth and the world, even from everlasting to everlasting, thou art God. *Ps, xc.* 2. Thou art worthy, O

server of all mankind,

Lord, to receive glory and honour and power : for thou hast created all things, and for thy pleasure they are and were created. *Re. iv.* 11. What shall I do unto thee, O thou Preserver of men? *Job vii.* 20. *See also, Ne. ix.* 6.—*Je. xxvii.* 5. —*Is. xlv.* 12.—*Ps. xxxvi.* 6.

2. Giver of all spiritual grace, the Author of everlasting life ;

2. The God of all grace, who hath called us unto his eternal glory by Christ Jesus, make you perfect, stablish, strengthen, settle you. 1 *Pe. v.* 10. I will pour upon the house of David, and upon the inhabitants of Jerusalem, the spirit of grace. *Zec. xii.* 10. The Lord God is a Sun and Shield : the Lord will give grace and glory. *Ps. lxxxiv.* 11. We know that the Son of God is come, and hath given us an understanding, that we may know him that is true, and we are in him that is true. This is the true God and eternal life. 1 *John v.* 20. And being made perfect, he became the Author of eternal salvation unto all them that obey him. *He. v.* 9. *See also, John i.* 14. 17.

3. Send thy blessing upon these thy servants, this man and this woman whom we bless in thy Name ;

3. God blessed them. *Ge. i.* 28. God Almighty bless thee, and give thee the blessing of Abraham, to thee, and to thy seed with thee. *Ge. xxviii.* 3, 4. Even by the God of thy father, who shall help thee ; and by the Almighty, who shall bless thee with blessings of heaven above, blessings of the deep that lieth under, blessings of the breasts, and of the womb. *Ge. xlix.* 25. He will bless them that fear the Lord, both small and great. The Lord shall increase you more and more, you and your children. *Ps. cxv.* 13, 14. Behold, that thus shall the man be blessed that feareth the Lord. *Ps. cxxviii.* 4. And the Lord spake unto Moses, saying, Speak unto Aaron and unto his sons, saying, On this wise ye shall bless the children of Israel, saying unto them, The Lord bless thee, and keep thee : The Lord make his face shine upon thee, and be gracious unto thee : The Lord lift up his countenance upon thee, and give thee peace. And they shall put my name upon the children of Israel ; and I will bless them. *Nu. vi.* 22 *to* 27. Let it please thee to bless the house of thy servant, that it may continue for ever before thee ; and with thy blessing let the house of thy servant be blessed for ever. 2 *Sa. vii.* 29.

4. that, as Isaac and Rebekah lived faithfully toge-

4. And Isaac brought her into his mother Sarah's tent, and took Rebekah and she became his wife, and he loved her, and Isaac was comforted after his mother's death. *Ge. xxiv.* 67.

ther, so these persons may surely perform and keep the vow and covenant betwixt them made, (whereof this Ring given and received is a token and pledge,)

When thou vowest a vow unto God, defer not to pay it; for he hath no pleasure in fools: pay that which thou hast vowed. *Ec. v.* 4. When thou shalt vow a vow unto the Lord thy God, thou shalt not slack to pay it: for the Lord thy God will surely require it of thee; and it would be sin in thee. That which is gone out of thy lips thou shalt keep and perform. *De. xxiii.* 21. 23. If a man vow a vow unto the Lord, or swear an oath to bind his soul with a bond; he shall not break his word, he shall do according to all that proceedeth out of his mouth. *Nu. xxx.* 2. Keep therefore the words of this covenant, and do them, that ye may prosper in all that ye do. *De. xxix.* 9.

5. and may ever remain in perfect love and peace together, and live according to thy laws; through Jesus Christ our Lord. Amen.

5. Wives, submit yourselves unto your own husbands, as it is fit in the Lord. Husbands, love your wives, and be not bitter against them. *Col. iii.* 18, 19. The aged women likewise, that they may teach the young women to be sober, to love their husbands, to love their children, to be discreet, chaste, keepers at home, good, obedient to their own husbands, that the word of God be not blasphemed. *Tit. ii.* 3, 4, 5. Live joyfully with the wife whom thou lovest all the days of the life of thy vanity, which he hath given thee under the sun, all the days of thy vanity. *Ec. ix.* 9. Be ye kind one to another, tender hearted, forgiving one another, even as God for Christ's sake hath forgiven you. *Ep. iv.* 32. Be perfect, be of good comfort, be of one mind, live in peace; and the God of love and peace shall be with you. *2 Co. xiii.* 11. Zacharias and his wife Elisabeth were both righteous before God, walking in all the commandments and ordinances of the Lord blameless. *Lu. i.* 5, 6. Great peace have they which love thy law. Make me to go in the path of thy commandments; for therein do I delight. *Ps. cxix.* 165, 35. If two of you shall agree on earth as touching any thing that they shall ask, it shall be done for them of my Father which is in heaven. *Mat. xviii.* 19. Whatsoever ye shall ask in my name, that will I do. *John xiv.* 13,

CCIII. *The Church's Ratification of the Matrimonial engagement.*

Those whom God hath joined together let For this cause shall a man leave father and mother, and shall cleave to his wife; and they twain shall be one flesh.

no man put asunder.

Forasmuch as *M.* and *N.* have consented together in holy wedlock, and have witnessed the same before God and this company, and thereto have given and pledged their troth either to other, and have declared the same by giving and receiving of a Ring, and by joining of hands; I pronounce that they be Man and Wife together, In the Name of the Father, and of the Son, and of the HolyGhost. Amen.

Wherefore they are no more twain but one flesh. What therefore God hath joined together, let not man put asunder. *Mat. xix.* 5, 6. Because the Lord hath been witness between thee and the wife of thy youth, against whom thou hast dealt treacherously: yet is she thy companion, and the wife of thy covenant. And did not he make one? Yet had he the residue of the Spirit. And wherefore one? That he might seek a godly seed. Therefore take heed to your spirit, and let none deal treacherously against the wife of his youth. For the Lord, the God of Israel, saith that he hateth putting away. *Mal. ii.* 14, 15, 16. Unto the married I command, yet not I, but the Lord, Let not the wife depart from her husband. 1 *Co. vii.* 10. And they called Rebekah, and said unto her, Wilt thou go with this man? And she said, I will go. And Isaac took Rebekah and she became his wife. *Ge. xxiv.* 58. 67. And Boaz said unto the elders, and unto all the people, Ye are witnesses this day, that Ruth the Moabitess, have I purchased to be my wife. *Ru. iv.* 9, 10. Whatsoever ye do in word or deed, do all in the name of the Lord Jesus. *Col. iii.* 17. Verily I say unto you, Whatsoever ye shall bind on earth shall be bound in heaven: and whatsoever ye shall loose on earth shall be loosed in heaven. *Mat. xviii.* 18.

CCIV. The Blessing.

1. God the Father, God the Son, God the Holy Ghost, bless, preserve, and keep you; the Lord mercifully with his favour look upon you;

1. And Eli blessed Elkanah and his wife. 1 *Sa. ii.* 20. The grace of the Lord Jesus Christ, and the love of God, and the communion of the Holy Ghost, be with you all. 2 *Co. xiii.* 14. The Lord bless thee, and keep thee: The Lord make his face shine upon thee, and be gracious unto thee: The Lord lift up his countenance upon thee, and give thee peace. *Nu. vi.* 24, 25, 26. The Lord that made heaven and earth bless thee out of Zion. *Ps. cxxxiv.* 3. He preserveth the souls of his saints. *Ps. xcvii.* 10. The Lord is thy keeper; the Lord shall preserve thee from all evil: he shall preserve thy soul. *Ps. cxxi.* 5. 7. I intreated thy favour with my whole heart. Look thou upon me, and be merciful unto me, as thou usest to do unto those that love thy name. *Ps. cxix.* 58. 132.—In his favour is life. *Ps. xxx.* 5.

2. and so fill
you with all
spiritual bene-
diction and
grace,

2. Blessed be the God and Father of our Lord Jesus Christ, who hath blessed us with all spiritual blessings in heavenly places in Christ. *Ep. i.* 3.　Grace be unto you, and peace, from God our Father, and from the Lord Jesus Christ. 1 *Co. i.* 3.　Grace unto you, and peace, be multiplied. 1 *Pe. i.* 2.　I bow my knees unto the Father of our Lord Jesus Christ, that he would grant you, according to the riches of his glory, to be strengthened with might by his Spirit in the inner man; that Christ may dwell in your hearts by faith; that ye, being rooted and grounded in love, may be able to comprehend with all saints what is the breadth, and length, and depth, and height; and to know the love of Christ, which passeth knowledge, that ye might be filled with all the fulness of God. *Ep. iii.* 14. 16 *to* 19.　This I pray, that your love my abound yet more and more in knowledge and in all judgment; that ye may approve things that are excellent; that ye may be sincere and without offence till the day of Christ. *Ph. i.* 9, 10.

3. that ye
may so live to-
gether in this
life, that in the
world to come
ye may have
life everlasting.
Amen.

3. Likewise, ye husbands, dwell with them according to knowledge, giving honour unto the wife, as unto the weaker vessel, and as being heirs together of the grace of life; that your prayers be not hindered. 1 *Pe. iii.* 7.　He that soweth to his flesh shall of the flesh reap corruption; but he that soweth to the Spirit shall of the Spirit reap life everlasting. *Ga. vi.* 8. Being made free from sin, and become servants to God, ye have your fruit unto holiness, and the end everlasting life. *Ro. vi.* 22.　See also, *Lu. xviii.* 29, 30.

Psalm CXXVIII. Blessed are all they that fear the Lord: and walk in his ways. —For thou shalt eat the labour of thine hands: O well is thee, and happy shalt thou be.— Thy wife shall be as the fruitful vine: upon the walls of thine house.—Thy children like the olive branches: round about thy table.—Lo, thus shall the man be blessed: that feareth the Lord.—The Lord from out of Sion shall so bless thee: that thou shalt see Jerusalem in prosperity all thy life long;—Yea, that thou shalt see thy children's children: and peace upon Israel.—Glory be to the Father, &c.　As it was in the, &c.

Psalm LXVII. God be merciful unto us, and bless us: and shew us the light of his countenance, and be merciful unto us.—That thy way may be known upon earth: thy saving health among all nations.—Let the people praise thee, O God: yea, let all the people praise thee.—O let the nations rejoice and be glad: for thou shalt judge the folk righteously, and govern the nations upon earth.—Let the people praise thee, O God: yea, let all the people praise thee.—Then shall the earth bring forth her increase; and God, even our own God, shall give us his blessing.—God shall bless us: and all the ends of the world shall fear him.

Glory be to the Father, &c.　As it was in the beginning, &c.

    Lord, have mercy upon us.
    Christ, have mercy upon us.
    Lord, have mercy upon us.

    Our Father, &c.

CCV. *Supplications and Prayers.* *No.* 1.

1, 2.   O Lord, save thy servant, and thy handmaid; who put their trust in thee.

> 1, 2. O thou my God, save thy servant that trusteth in thee. *Ps. lxxxvi.* 2.

3, 4.   O Lord, send them help from thy holy place; and evermore defend them.

> 3, 4. The Lord hear thee in the day of trouble; the name of the God of Jacob defend thee. Send thee help from the sanctuary, and strengthen thee out of Zion. *Ps. xx.* 1, 2.

5, 6.   Be unto them a tower of strength, from the face of their enemy.

> 5, 6. Thou hast been a shelter for me, and a strong tower from the enemy. *Ps. lxi.* 3.

7, 8.   O Lord, hear our prayer; and let our cry come unto thee.

> 7, 8. Hear my prayer, O Lord, and let my cry come unto thee. *Ps. cii.* 1.

CCVI. *Supplications and Prayers.* *No.* 2.

1. O God of Abraham, God of Isaac, God of Jacob, bless these thy servants,

1. Have ye not read that which was spoken unto you by God, saying, I am the God of Abraham, and the God of Isaac, and the God of Jacob? *Mat. xxii.* 31, 32. I am the God of thy father, the God of Abraham, the God of Isaac, and the God of Jacob. *Ex. iii.* 6. And God Almighty bless thee, and make thee fruitful, and multiply thee, that thou mayest be a multitude of people; and give thee the blessing of Abraham, to thee, and to thy seed with thee. *Ge. xxviii.* 3, 4. Thou, Lord, wilt bless the righteous. *Ps. v.* 12.

2. and sow the seed of eternal life in their hearts;

2. The seed is the word of God. That on the good ground are they, which in an honest and good heart, having heard the word, keep it, and bring forth fruit with patience. *Lu. viii.* 11. 15. The word of the truth of the Gospel; which is come unto you, as it is in all the world; and bringeth forth fruit, as it doth also in you, since the day ye heard of it, and knew the grace of God in truth. *Col. i.* 5, 6. Being made free from sin, and become servants to God, ye have your fruit unto holiness, and the end everlasting life. *Ro. vi.* 22.

Whosoever drinketh of the water that I shall give him shall never thirst; but the water that I shall give him shall be in him a well of water springing up into everlasting life. *John iv.* 14.

3. that what-
soever in thy
holy Word they
shall profitably
learn, they may
in deed fulfil
the same.

3. All Scripture is given by inspiration of God, and is profitable for doctrine, for reproof, for correction, for instruction in righteousness: that the man of God may be perfect, throughly furnished unto all good works. 2 *Ti. iii.* 16, 17. It is written in the prophets, And they shall be all taught of God. Every man therefore that hath heard, and hath learned of the Father, cometh unto me. *John vi.* 45. Be ye doers of the word, and not hearers only, deceiving your own selves. *Ja. i.* 22. If ye fulfil the royal law according to the Scripture, ye do well. *Ja. ii.* 8. Those things, which ye have both learned, and received, and heard, and seen in me, do: and the God of peace shall be with you. *Ph. iv.* 9. If ye know these things, happy are ye if ye do them. *John xiii.* 17. *See also, Mat. xxviii.* 20.

4. Look, O
Lord, merci-
fully upon them
from heaven,
and bless them.
And as thou
didst send thy
blessing upon
Abraham and
Sarah, to their
great comfort;
so vouchsafe to
send thy bless-
ing upon these
thy servants;
that they obey-
ing thy will,
and alway being
in safety under
thy protection,
may abide in
thy love unto
their lives' end;
through Jesus
Christ our Lord.
Amen.

4. Look down from thy holy habitation, from heaven, and bless thy people Israel. *De. xxvi.* 15. Look thou upon me, and be merciful unto me, as thou usest to do unto those that love thy name. *Ps. cxix.* 132. And the Lord had blessed Abraham in all things. *Ge. xxiv.* 1. I will bless her, and give thee a son also of her: yea, I will bless her, and she shall be a mother of nations. *Ge. xvii.* 16. God Almighty bless thee, and give thee the blessing of Abraham. *Ge. xxviii.* 3, 4. Blessed is the man that feareth the Lord, that delighteth greatly in his commandments. His seed shall be mighty upon earth: the generation of the upright shall be blessed. Wealth and riches shall be in his house; and his righteousness endureth for ever. *Ps. cxii.* 1, 2, 3. Who shall ascend into the hill of the Lord? or who shall stand in his holy place? He that hath clean hands and a pure heart; who hath not lifted up his soul unto vanity, nor sworn deceitfully. He shall receive the blessing from the Lord, and righteousness from the God of his salvation. *Ps. xxiv.* 3, 4, 5. Whoso hearkeneth unto me shall dwell safely, and shall be quiet from fear of evil. *Pr. i.* 33. He that doeth the will of God abideth for ever. 1 *John ii.* 17. O love the Lord, all ye his saints: for the Lord preserveth the

o

faithful. *Ps. xxxi.* 23. Abide in me, and I in you. As the branch cannot bear fruit of itself, except it abide in the vine; no more can ye, except ye abide in me. *John xv.* 4.

CCVII. Supplications and Prayers. No. 3.

1. O merciful Lord, and heavenly Father, by whose gracious gift mankind is increased; We beseech thee, assist with thy blessing these two persons, that they may both be fruitful in procreation of children,

1. And God blessed them, and God said unto them, Be fruitful, and multiply, and replenish the earth. *Ge. i.* 28. And God said unto Abraham, As for Sarai thy wife, thou shalt not call her name Sarai, but Sarah shall her name be. And I will bless her, and give thee a son also of her: yea, I will bless her, and she shall be a mother of nations; kings of people shall be of her. *Ge. xvii.* 15, 16. Is any thing too hard for the Lord? *Ge. xviii.* 14. And they blessed Rebekah, and said unto her, Thou art our sister, be thou the mother of thousands of millions. *Ge. xxiv.* 60. Who are those with thee? And he said, The children which God hath graciously given thy servant. *Ge. xxxiii.* 5. And all the people that were in the gate, and the elders, said, We are witnesses. The Lord make the woman that is come into thine house like Rachel and like Leah, which two did build the house of Israel: and do thou worthily in Ephratah, and be famous in Bethlehem: and let thy house be like the house of Pharez, whom Tamar bare unto Judah, of the seed which the Lord shall give thee of this young woman. *Ru. iv.* 11, 12. Thy wife shall be as a fruitful vine by the sides of thine house, thy children like olive plants round about thy table. *Ps. cxxviii.* 3. Lo children are an heritage of the Lord; and the fruit of the womb is his reward. *Ps. cxxvii.* 3. For this child I [Hannah] prayed; and the Lord hath given me my petition which I asked of him. *1 Sa. i.* 27. And Eli blessed Elkanah and his wife, and said, The Lord give thee seed of this woman, for the loan which is lent to the Lord. And the Lord visited Hannah, so that she conceived, and bare three sons and two daughters. *1 Sa. ii.* 20, 21. He maketh the barren woman to keep house, and to be a joyful mother of children. *Ps. cxiii.* 9.

2. and also live together so long in godly love, and be-

2. I pray to God that ye do no evil; not that we should appear approved, but that ye should do that which is honest. *2 Co. xiii.* 7. Blessed is every one that feareth the Lord; that

nesty,that they may see their children christianly and virtuously brought up, to thy praise and honour; through Jesus Christ our Lord. Amen.

walketh in his ways. For thou shalt eat the labour of thine hands: happy shalt thou be, and it shall be well with thee. Thy wife shall be as a fruitful vine by the sides of thine house: thy children like olive plants round about thy table. Behold that thus shall the man be blessed that feareth the Lord. The Lord shall bless thee out of Zion; and thou shalt see the good of Jerusalem all the days of thy life. Yea, thou shalt see thy children's children, and peace upon Israel. *Ps. cxxviii.* Defraud ye not one the other, except it be with consent for a time. 1 *Co. vii.* 5. Who can find a virtuous woman? The heart of her husband doth safely trust in her, so that he shall have no need of spoil. Her children arise up, and call her blessed; her husband also, and he praiseth her. *Pr. xxxi.* 10, 11. 28. There was in the days of Herod, a certain Priest named Zacharias, and his wife was of the daughters of Aaron, and her name was Elisabeth. And they were both righteous before God, walking in all the commandments and ordinances of the Lord blameless. *Lu. i.* 5, 6. Train up a child in the way he should go; and when he is old, he will not depart from it. *Pr. xxii.* 6. Jesus said unto them, Suffer the little children to come unto me, and forbid them not: for of such is the kingdom of God. *Mar. x.* 14. Ye fathers, provoke not your children to wrath: but bring them up in the nurture and admonition of the Lord. *Ep. vi.* 4. I know him, that he will command his children and his houshold after him, and they shall keep the way of the Lord. *Ge. xviii.* 19. That our sons may grow up as the young plants; and that our daughters may be as the polished corners of the temple. Happy is that people, whose God is the Lord. *Ps. cxliv.* 12. 15. Do all to the glory of God. 1 *Co. x.* 31. Herein is my Father glorified, that ye bear much fruit. *John xv.* 8. See also, *De. vi.* 7. 1 *Co. xiii.* 4 to 7.

CCVIII. *Supplications and Prayers. No.* 4.

1. O God, who by thy mighty power hast made all things of nothing; who also (after

1. In the beginning God created the heaven and the earth. *Ge. i.* 1. Thou hast created all things, and for thy pleasure they are and were created. *Re. iv.* 11. Through faith we understand that the worlds were framed by the word of God,

other things set in order) didst appoint, that out of man (created after thine own image and similitude) woman should take her beginning;

so that things which are seen were not made of things which do appear. *He. xi.3.* These are the generations of the heavens and of the earth when they were created, in the day that the Lord God made the earth and the heavens, and every plant of the field before it was in the earth, and every herb of the field before it grew. *Ge. ii. 4, 5.* God created man in his own image, in the image of God created he him; male and female created he them. *Ge. i. 27.* And the Lord God caused a deep sleep to fall upon Adam, and he slept: and he took one of his ribs, and closed up the flesh instead thereof; and the rib, which the Lord God had taken from man, made he a woman, and brought her unto the man, and Adam said, This is now bone of my bones, and flesh of my flesh: she shall be called Woman, because she was taken out of Man. *Ge. ii. 21, 22, 23.* The man is not of the woman; but the woman of the man. *1 Co. xi. 8.* Adam was first formed, then Eve. *1 Ti. ii. 13.*

2. and, knitting them together, didst teach that it should never be lawful to put asunder, those whom thou by Matrimony hadst made one:

2. He answered and said unto them, Have ye not read, that he which made them at the beginning made them male and female, and said, For this cause shall a man leave father and mother, and shall cleave to his wife: and they twain shall be one flesh? Wherefore they are no more twain but one flesh. What therefore God hath joined together, let not man put asunder. *Mat. xix. 4, 5, 6.* Unto the married I command, yet not I, but the Lord, Let not the wife depart from her husband. *1 Co. vii. 10.*

3. O God, who hast consecrated the state of Matrimony to such an excellent mystery, that in it is signified and represented the spiritual marriage and unity betwixt Christ and his Church; Look mercifully upon these thy servants, that both this man may love his wife, according to thy Word, (as

3. As a young man marrieth a virgin, so shall thy sons marry thee: and as the bridegroom rejoiceth over the bride, so shall thy God rejoice over thee. *Is. lxii. 5.* And I John saw the holy city, new Jerusalem, coming down from God out of heaven, prepared as a bride adorned for her husband. *Re. xxi. 2.* Let us be glad and rejoice, and give honour to him; for the marriage of the Lamb is come, and his wife hath made herself ready. And to her was granted that she should be arrayed in fine linen, clean and white: for the fine linen is the righteousness of saints. *Re. xix. 7, 8.* The King shall greatly desire thy beauty, for he is thy Lord; and worship thou him. *Ps. xlv. 11.* The husband is the head of the wife, even as Christ is the Head of the Church: and he is the Saviour of the body. Therefore as the Church is subject unto

Christ did love his spouse the Church, who gave himself for it, loving and cherishing it even as his own flesh,)

Christ, so let the wives be to their own husbands in every thing. Husbands, love your wives, even as Christ also loved the Church, and gave himself for it; that he might sanctify and cleanse it with the washing of water by the word, that he might present it to himself a glorious Church, not having spot, or wrinkle, or any such thing; but that it should be holy and without blemish. So ought men to love their wives as their own bodies. He that loveth his wife loveth himself. For no man ever yet hated his own flesh; but nourisheth and cherisheth it, even as the Lord the Church: for we are members of his body, of his flesh, and of his bones. For this cause shall a man leave his father and mother, and shall be joined unto his wife, and they two shall be one flesh. This is a great mystery: but I speak concerning Christ and the Church. *Ep. v. 23 to 32.* Likewise, ye husbands, dwell with them according to knowledge, giving honour unto the wife, as unto the weaker vessel, and as being heirs together of the grace of life. 1 *Pe. iii.* 7.

4. and also that this woman may be loving and amiable, faithful and obedient to her husband; and in all quietness, sobriety, and peace, be a follower of holy and godly matrons. O Lord, bless them both, and grant them to inherit thy everlasting kingdom; through Jesus Christ our Lord. Amen.

4. Teach the young women to be sober, to love their husbands, to love their children, to be discreet, chaste, keepers at home, good, obedient to their own husbands. *Tit. ii.* 4, 5. A prudent wife is from the Lord. *Pr. xix.* 14. Let the woman learn in silence with all subjection. 1 *Ti. ii.* 11. Likewise, ye wives, be in subjection to your own husbands. 1 *Pe. iii.* 1. Be of one mind, live in peace; and the God of love and peace shall be with you. 2 *Co. xiii.* 11. Being heirs together of the grace of life. 1 *Pe. iii.* 7. Behold, how good and how pleasant it is for brethren to dwell together in unity! It is like the precious ointment upon the head, that ran down upon the beard, even Aaron's beard: that went down to the skirts of his garments; as the dew of Hermon, and as the dew that descended upon the mountains of Zion: for there the Lord commanded the blessing, even life for evermore. *Ps. cxxxiii.*

CCIX. *Supplications and Prayers. No.* 5.

1. Almighty God, who at the beginning did create our first

1. And the Lord God formed man of the dust of the ground, and breathed into his nostrils the breath of life; and man became a living soul. And the Lord God said, It is not good

parents, Adam and Eve, and did sanctify and join them together in marriage ;

that the man should be alone ; I will make him an help meet for him. And the Lord God caused a deep sleep to fall upon Adam, and he slept : and he took one of his ribs, and closed up the flesh instead thereof ; and the rib, which the Lord God had taken from man, made he a woman, and brought her unto the man. And Adam said, This is now bone of my bones, and flesh of my flesh; she shall be called Woman, because she was taken out of Man. *Ge. ii.* 7. 18. 21, 22, 23. And Adam called his wife's name Eve ; because she was the mother of all living. *Ge. iii.* 20.

2. Pour upon you the riches of his grace, sanctify and bless you ; that ye may please him both in body and soul, and live together in holy love unto your lives' end. *Amen.*

2. The exceeding riches of his grace in his kindness toward us through Christ Jesus. *Ep. ii.* 7. The very God of peace sanctify you wholly ; and I pray God your whole spirit and soul and body be preserved blameless unto the coming of our Lord Jesus Christ. Faithful is he that calleth you, who also will do it. 1 *Th. v.* 23, 24. Ye are bought with a price, therefore glorify God in your body, and in your spirit, which are God's. 1 *Co. vi.* 20. As the Father hath loved me, so have I loved you : continue ye in my love. If ye keep my commandments, ye shall abide in my love. This is my commandment, That ye love one another, as I have loved you. *John xv.* 9, 10. 12. He will bless them that fear the Lord, both small and great. The Lord shall increase you more and more, you and your children. *Ps. cxv.* 13, 14.

CCX. The Exhortation to the newly married, taken out of the holy Scriptures.

1. All ye that are married, or that intend to take the holy estate of Matrimony upon you, hear what the holy Scripture doth say as touching the duty of husbands towards their wives, and wives towards their husbands.

2. Saint Paul in his Epistle to the Ephesians, the fifth Chapter, doth give this commandment to all married men, *Husbands, love your wives, even as Christ also loved the Church, and gave himself for it, that he might sanctify and cleanse it with the washing of water, by the Word ; that he might present it to himself a glorious Church, not having spot, or wrinkle, or any such thing ; but that it should be holy, and without blemish. So ought men to love their wives as their own bodies : he that loveth his wife, loveth himself. For no man ever yet hated his own flesh, but nourisheth and cherisheth it, even as the Lord the Church : for we are members of his body, of his flesh, and of his bones. For this cause shall a man leave his father and mother, and shall be joined unto his wife ; and they two shall be one flesh. This is a great mystery ; but I speak concerning Christ and the Church. Nevertheless, let every one of you in particular so love his wife, even as himself.* Ep. v. 25 to 33.

3. Likewise, the same Saint Paul, writing to the Colossians, speaketh thus to all men that are married : *Husbands, love your wives, and be not bitter against them.* Col. iii. 19.

4. Hear also what Saint Peter, the Apostle of Christ, who was himself a married man, saith unto them that are married ; *Ye husbands, dwell with your wives according to know-*

ledge, giving honour unto the wife, as unto the weaker vessel, and as being heirs together of the grace of life, that your prayers be not hindered. 1 Pet. iii. 7.

5. Hitherto ye have heard the duty of the husband toward the wife. Now likewise, ye wives, hear and learn your duties toward your husbands, even as it is plainly set forth in holy Scripture.

6. Saint Paul, in the aforenamed Epistle to the Ephesians, teacheth you thus; *Wives, submit yourselves unto your own husbands, as unto the Lord. For the husband is the head of the wife, even as Christ is the head of the Church : and he is the Saviour of the body. Therefore as the Church is subject unto Christ, so let the wives be to their own husbands in every thing. And again he saith, let the wife see that she reverence her husband.* Ep. v. 22, 23, 24. And in his Epistle to the Colossians, Saint Paul giveth you this short lesson ; *Wives, submit yourselves unto your own husbands, as it is fit in the Lord.* Col. iii. 18 .

7. Saint Peter also doth instruct you very well, thus saying, *Ye wives, be in subjection to your own husbands ; that if any obey not the word, they also may without the word be won by the conversation of the wives ; while they behold your chaste conversation coupled with fear. Whose adorning let it not be that outward adorning of plaiting the hair, and of wearing of gold, or of putting on of apparel ; but let it be the hidden man of the heart, in that which is not corruptible, even the ornament of a meek and quiet spirit, which is in the sight of God of great price. For after this manner in the old time the holy women also, who trusted in God, adorned themselves, being in subjection unto their own husbands ; even as Sarah obeyed Abraham, calling him lord ; whose daughters ye are as long as ye do well, and are not afraid with any amazement.* 1 Pe. iii. 1. 3 to 6.

THE VISITATION OF THE SICK.

CCXI. The Salutation and Responsals.

1. Peace be
to this house,
and to all that
dwell in it.
2. Remem-
ber not, Lord,
our iniquities,
nor the iniqui-
ties of our
forefathers:
spare us, good
Lord, spare thy
people, whom
thou hast re-
deemed with
thy most pre-
cious blood,
and be not
angry with us
for ever.
3. Spare us,
good Lord.

1. And into whatsoever house ye enter, first say, **Peace be to this house.** *Lu. x.* 5.

2, 3. I the Lord thy God am a jealous God, visiting the iniquity of the fathers upon the children unto the third and fourth generation of them that hate me. *Ex. xx.* 5. We have sinned with our fathers, we have committed iniquity, we have done wickedly. *Ps. cvi.* 6. We acknowledge, O Lord, our wickedness, and the iniquity of our fathers: for we have sinned against thee: do not abhor us, for thy name's sake. *Je. xiv.* 20, 21. O remember not against us former iniquities: [*marginal reading,* remember not the iniquities of them that were before us.] *Ps. lxxix.* 8. Be not wroth very sore, O Lord, neither remember iniquity for ever. *Is. lxiv.* 9. Remember not the sins of my youth, nor my transgressions. *Ps. xxv.* 7. Hide thy face from my sins, and blot out all mine iniquities. *Ps. li.* 9. I will be merciful to their unrighteousness, and their sins and their iniquities will I remember no more. *He. viii.* 12. Ye know that ye were not redeemed with corruptible things, as silver and gold, from your vain conversation received by tradition from your fathers; but with the precious blood of Christ, as of a lamb without blemish and without spot. 1 *Pe. i.* 18, 19. Who gave himself for us, that he might redeem us from all iniquity, and purify unto himself a peculiar people, zealous of good works. *Tit. ii.* 14. Without shedding of blood is no remission. *He. ix.* 22. O my God, spare me according to the greatness of thy mercy. *Ne. xiii.* 22. O spare me, that I may recover my strength, before I go hence, and be no more. *Ps. xxxix.* 13. *See also, Joel ii.* 17.—*Ex. xxxii.* 11, 12.—*Ps. lxxviii.* 38.

Let us pray.
Lord, have mercy upon us.
Christ, have mercy upon us.
Lord, have mercy upon us.
Our Father, &c.

P

4, 5. O Lord, save thy servant; which putteth his trust in thee.

4, 5. Preserve my soul; for I am holy: O thou my God, save thy servant that trusteth in thee. *Ps. lxxxvi.* 2.

6, 7. Send him help from thy holy place; and evermore mightily defend him.

6, 7. The Lord hear thee in the day of trouble, the name of the God of Jacob defend thee. Send thee help from the sanctuary, and strengthen thee out of Zion. *Ps. xx.* 1, 2. Help us, O God of our salvation, and deliver us. *Ps. lxxix.* 9.

8, 9. Let the enemy have no advantage of him; nor the wicked approach to hurt him.

8, 9. My hand shall hold him fast: and my arm shall strengthen him. The enemy shall not exact upon him: the son of wickedness shall not hurt him. *Ps. lxxxix.* 22, 23.

10, 11. Be unto him, O Lord, a strong tower; from the face of his enemy.

10, 11. Thou hast been a shelter for me, and a strong tower from the enemy. *Ps. lxi.* 3. The name of the Lord is a strong tower: the righteous runneth into it, and is safe. *Pr. xviii.* 10.

12, 13. O Lord, hear our prayers; and let our cry come unto thee.

12, 13. Hear my prayer, O Lord, and let my cry come unto thee. *Ps. cii.* 1.

CCXII. *A Prayer for Support under Affliction.*

1. O Lord, look down from heaven, behold, visit, and relieve this thy servant.

1. Return, we beseech thee, O God of hosts: look down from heaven, and behold, and visit this vine. *Ps. lxxx.* 14. Look down from heaven, and behold from the habitation of thy holiness and of thy glory. *Is. lxiii.* 15. Remember me, O Lord, with the favour that thou bearest unto thy people: O visit me with thy salvation. *Ps. cvi.* 4. Mine eyes fail for thy word, saying, When wilt thou comfort me? *Ps. cxix.* 82. Make thy face to shine upon thy servant: save me for thy mercies' sake. *Ps. xxxi.* 16. Let thy mercies come also unto me, O Lord, even thy salvation, according to thy word. *Ps. cxix.* 41.

2. Look upon him with

2. The eyes of the Lord are over the righteous, and his ears are open unto their prayers. 1 *Pe. iii.* 12. The Lord is

the eyes of thy mercy, give him comfort and sure confidence in thee, defend him from the danger of the enemy,

merciful and gracious, slow to anger, and plenteous in mercy. He will not always chide: neither will he keep his anger for ever. *Ps. ciii.* 8, 9. Let, I pray thee, thy merciful kindness be for my comfort, according to thy word unto thy servant. Mine eyes fail for thy word, saying, When wilt thou comfort me? *Ps. cxix.* 76. 82. Make us glad according to the days wherein thou hast afflicted us, and the years wherein we have seen evil. *Ps. xc.* 15. I have seen his ways, and will heal him: I will lead him also, and restore comforts unto him and to his mourners. *Is. lvii.* 18. I, even I, am he that comforteth you. *Is. li.* 12. Blessed are they that mourn: for they shall be comforted. *Mat. v.* 4. In the fear of the Lord is strong confidence. *Pr. xiv.* 26. O God of our Salvation, who art the confidence of all the ends of the earth. *Ps. lxv.* 5. If our heart condemn us not, then have we confidence toward God. 1 *John iii.* 21. And this is the confidence, that we have in him, that, if we ask any thing according to his will, he heareth us. 1 *John v.* 14. Your adversary the devil, as a roaring lion, walketh about, seeking whom he may devour. 1 *Pe.* 5. 8. Hear my voice, O God, in my prayer: preserve my life from fear of the enemy. *Ps. lxiv.* 1. Defend me from them that rise up against me. *Ps. lix.* 1.

3. and keep him in perpetual peace and safety, through Jesus Christ our Lord. *Amen.*

3. Thou wilt keep him in perfect peace, whose mind is stayed on thee; because he trusteth in thee. *Is. xxvi.* 3. The peace of God, which passeth all understanding, shall keep your hearts and minds through Christ Jesus. *Ph. iv.* 7. Hold thou me up, and I shall be safe. *Ps. cxix.* 117. Whoso putteth his trust in the Lord shall be safe. *Pr. xxix.* 25. For in the time of trouble he shall hide me in his pavilion: in the secret of his tabernacle shall he hide me; he shall set me upon a rock. *Ps. xxvii.* 5. Withhold not thou thy tender mercies from me, O Lord; let thy lovingkindness and thy truth continually preserve me. *Ps. xl.* 11. Cast thy burden upon the Lord, and he shall sustain thee; he shall never suffer the righteous to be moved. *Ps. lv.* 22. Whatsoever ye shall ask the Father in my name, he will give it you. *John xvi.* 23. He is able also to save them to the uttermost that come unto God by him. *He. vii.* 25.

CCXIII.—*A Prayer for the sanctifying of Affliction.*

Almighty and most merciful God and Saviour;

1. If thou wouldest seek unto God betimes, and make thy supplication to the Almighty; surely now he would awake for thee. *Job viii.* 5, 6. Behold happy is the man whom God correcteth: therefore despise not thou the chastening of the Almighty. *Job v.* 17. Mighty to save. *Is. lxiii.* 1. The Lord is good; his mercy is everlasting; and his truth endureth to all generations. *Ps. c.* 5. Let them now that fear the Lord say, that his mercy endureth for ever. *Ps. cxviii.* 4. The Lord passed by before him, and proclaimed, The Lord, The Lord God, merciful and gracious, longsuffering, and abundant in goodness and truth, keeping mercy for thousands, forgiving iniquity and transgression and sin, and that will by no means clear the guilty; visiting the iniquity of the fathers upon the children, and upon the children's children, unto the third and to the fourth generation. *Ex. xxxiv.* 6, 7. As for me, my prayer is unto thee, O Lord, in an acceptable time: O God, in the multitude of thy mercy hear me, in the truth of thy salvation. *Ps. lxix.* 13. Verily thou art a God that hidest thyself, O God of Israel, the Saviour. *Is. xlv.* 15. He said, Surely they are my people, children that will not lie: so he was their Saviour. *Is. lxiii.* 8. Thou shalt know that I the Lord am thy Saviour and thy Redeemer, the Mighty One of Jacob. *Is. lx.* 16.

thy accustomed goodness. Remember this thy servant who is grieved with sickness.

2. Look thou upon me, and be merciful unto me, as thou usest to do unto those that love thy name. *Ps. cxix.* 132. Remember me, O Lord, with the favour that thou bearest unto thy people: O visit me with thy salvation. *Ps. cvi.* 4. Bring my soul out of prison, that I may praise thy name: the righteous shall compass me about; for thou shalt deal bountifully with me. *Ps. cxlii.* 7. The sorrows of death compassed me, and the pains of hell gat hold upon me: I found trouble and sorrow. Then called I upon the name of the Lord; O Lord, I beseech thee, deliver my soul. *Ps. cxvi.* 3, 4. O Lord, I am oppressed; undertake for me. *Is. xxxviii.* 14. Look upon mine affliction and my pain; and forgive all my sins. *Ps. xxv.* 18. Deal with thy servant according unto thy mercy. *Ps. cxix.* 124. Hezekiah was sick unto death. And

the prophet Isaiah said unto him, Thus saith the Lord, Set thine house in order; for thou shalt die, and not live. Then he prayed unto the Lord; and Hezekiah wept sore. *2 Ki. xx.* 1, 2, 3.

3. Sanctify the Lord God in your hearts. *1 Pe. iii.* 15. Blessed is the man that endureth temptation: for when he is tried, he shall receive the crown of life, which the Lord hath promised to them that love him. *Ja. i.* 12. Whom the Lord loveth he chasteneth, and scourgeth every son whom he receiveth. If ye endure chastening, God dealeth with you as with sons; for what son is he whom the father chasteneth not? But if ye be without chastisement, whereof all are partakers, then are ye bastards, and not sons. Furthermore we have had fathers of our flesh which corrected us, and we gave them reverence: shall we not much rather be in subjection unto the Father of spirits, and live? For they verily for a few days chastened us after their own pleasure; but he for our profit, that we might be partakers of his holiness. Now no chastening for the present seemeth joyous, but grievous: nevertheless afterward it yieldeth the peaceable fruit of righteousness unto them which are exercised thereby. *He. xii.* 6 *to* 11. Like as a father pitieth his children, so the Lord pitieth them that fear him. *Ps. ciii.* 13.

4. I said in the cutting off of my days, I shall go to the gates of the grave: I am deprived of the residue of my years. *Is. xxxviii.* 10. Thou holdest mine eyes waking: I am so troubled that I cannot speak. Hath God forgotten to be gracious? hath he in anger shut up his tender mercies? And I said, This is my infirmity: but I will remember the years of the right hand of the Most High. *Ps. lxxvii.* 4: 9, 10. Have mercy upon me, O Lord, for I am in trouble: my strength faileth because of mine iniquity. *Ps. xxxi.* 9, 10. Mine eyes fail with looking upward: O Lord, I am oppressed; undertake for me. *Is. xxxviii.* 14. Why art thou cast down, O my soul? and why art thou disquieted within me? hope thou in God: for I shall yet praise him, who is the health of my countenance, and my God. *Ps. xlii.* 11. He said unto me, My grace is sufficient for thee: for my strength is made perfect in weakness. *2 Co. xii.* 9. Lord, I believe; help thou

Marginal notes:

3. Sanctify, we beseech thee, this thy Father-ly correction to him;

4. that the sense of his weakness may add strength to his faith, and seriousness to his repentance:

mine unbelief. *Mar. ix.* 24. This is my comfort in my affliction: for thy word hath quickened me. *Ps. cxix.* 50. I had
fainted, unless I had believed to see the goodness of the Lord
in the land of the living. *Ps. xxvii.* 13. Blind Bartimeus, the
son of Timeus, sat by the high-way side begging. And when
he heard that it was Jesus of Nazareth, he began to cry out,
and say, Jesus, thou son of David, have mercy on me, and
many charged him that he should hold his peace : but he
cried the more a great deal, Thou son of David, have mercy
on me. *Mar. x.* 46, 47, 48. Except ye repent, ye shall
all likewise perish. *Lu. xiii.* 3. I have sinned ; what shall I
do unto thee, O thou preserver of men? *Job vii.* 20. I have
heard of thee by the hearing of the ear : but now mine eye
seeth thee. Wherefore I abhor myself, and repent in dust
and ashes. *Job xlii.* 5, 6. If I have done iniquity, I will do
no more. *Job xxxiv.* 32. I know, O Lord, that thy judgments are right, and that thou in faithfulness hast afflicted me.
Before I was afflicted I went astray : but now have I kept thy
word. I thought on my ways, and turned my feet unto thy
testimonies. I made haste, and delayed not to keep thy commandments. *Ps. cxix.* 75. 67. 59, 60.

5. That, if it
shall be thy
good pleasure
to restore him
to his former
health, he may
lead the residue
of his life in thy
fear, and to thy
glory :

5. O Lord, let it be thy pleasure to deliver me : make
haste, O Lord, to help me. *Ps. xl.* 16. O spare me, that I
may recover strength, before I go hence, and be no more.
Ps. xxxix. 13. Not my will, but thine, be done. *Lu. xxii.* 42.
The word of the Lord came to Isaiah saying, Tell Hezekiah
the captain of my people, Thus saith the Lord, the God of
David thy father, I have heard thy prayer, I have seen thy
tears : behold I will heal thee ; and I will add unto thy days
fifteen years. *2 Ki. xx.* 4, 5, 6. Behold, thou art made whole :
sin no more, lest a worse thing come unto thee. *John v.* 14.
Let not thine heart envy sinners : but be thou in the fear of
the Lord all the day long. *Pr. xxiii.* 17. What shall I render
unto the Lord for all his benefits toward me? I will walk
before the Lord in the land of the living. I will take the cup
of salvation, and call upon the name of the Lord. *Ps. cxvi.*
12. 9. 13. The living, the living, he shall praise thee, as I do
this day : the father to the children shall make known thy
truth. The Lord was ready to save me : therefore we will
sing my songs to the stringed instruments all the days of our
life in the house of the Lord. *Is. xxxviii.* 19, 20.

6. or else, give him grace so to take thy [visitation, that] after this pain-ful life ended, he may dwell with thee in life everlasting; through Jesus Christ our Lord. Amen.

6. What will ye do in the day of visitation? *Is. x.* 3. God is able to make all grace abound toward you. *2 Co. ix.* 8. My grace is sufficient for thee. *2 Co. iii.* 9. I was dumb, I opened not my mouth; because thou didst it. *Ps. xxxix.* 9. Wherefore doth a living man complain, a man for the punish-ment of his sins? Let us search and try our ways, and turn again to the Lord. *La. iii.* 39, 40. Naked came I out of my mother's womb, and naked shall I return thither: the Lord gave, and the Lord hath taken away; blessed be the name of the Lord. *Job i.* 21. All the days of my appointed time will I wait, till my change come. *Job xiv.* 14. Though I walk through the valley of the shadow of death, I will fear no evil: for thou art with me. *Ps. xxiii.* 4. Man is born unto trouble, as the sparks fly upward. *Job v.* 7. His flesh upon him shall have pain, and his soul within him shall mourn. *Job xiv.* 22. I would not live alway. *Job vii.* 16. I know that my Redeemer liveth, and that he shall stand at the latter day upon the earth: and though after my skin worms destroy this body, yet in my flesh shall I see God: whom I shall see for myself, and mine eyes shall behold, and not another; though my reins be consumed within me. *Job xix.* 25, 26, 27. In my Father's house are many mansions: if it were not so, I would have told you. I go to prepare a place for you, and if I go and prepare a place for you, I will come again, and receive you unto myself; that where I am there ye may be also. *John xiv.* 2, 3. Blessed is the man whom thou chastenest, O Lord, and teachest him out of thy law; that thou mayest give him rest from the days of adversity. *Ps. xciv.* 12, 13. Blessed is the man that endureth temptation: for when he is tried, he shall receive the crown of life, which the Lord hath promised to them that love him. *Ja. i.* 12. For if we believe that Jesus died and rose again, even so them also which sleep in Jesus will God bring with him; and so shall we ever be with the Lord. *1 Th. iv.* 14. 17.

CCXIV. *The First Part of the Exhortation to the Sick Person.*

1. Dearly beloved, know this, that Al-

1. Know therefore this day, and consider it in thine heart, that the Lord he is God in heaven above, and upon the earth

the Lord of life and death, and of all things to them pertaining, as youth, strength, health, age, weakness, and sickness.

mighty God is beneath: there is none else. *De. iv.* 39. See now that I, even I, am he, and there is no God with me: I kill, and I make alive; I wound, and I heal: neither is there any that can deliver out of my hand. For I lift up my hand to heaven, and say, I live for ever. *De. xxxii.* 39, 40. Who knoweth not in all these, that the hand of the Lord hath wrought this? in whose hand is the soul of every living thing, and the breath of all mankind. *Job xii.* 9, 10. Unto God the Lord belong the issues from death. *Ps. lxviii.* 20. The Lord killeth, and the Lord maketh alive, he bringeth down to the grave, and bringeth up. *1 Sa. ii.* 6. He giveth to all life, and breath, and all things. *Ac. xvii.* 25. The days of his youth hast thou shortened. *Ps. lxxxix.* 45. The Lord satisfieth thy mouth with good things; so that thy youth is renewed like the eagle's. *Ps. ciii.* 5. Both riches and honour come of thee, and thou reignest over all; and in thine hand is power and might; and in thine hand it is to make great, and to give strength unto all. *1 Ch. xxix.* 12. Hope thou in God; for I shall yet praise him, who is the health of my countenance, and my God. *Ps. xlii.* 11. Thus saith the Lord, I will add unto thy days fifteen years. *Is. xxxviii.* 5. Thou shalt be buried in a good old age. *Ge. xv.* 15. He weakened my strength in the way; he shortened my days. *Ps. cii.* 23. The Lord struck the child that Uriah's wife bare unto David, and it was very sick. *2 Sa. xii.* 15.

2. Wherefore, whatsoever your sickness is, know you certainly, that it is God's visitation.

2. Shall there be evil in a city, and the Lord hath not done it? *Am. iii.* 6. And Eli said, It is the Lord; let him do what seemeth him good. *1 Sa. iii.* 18. The Lord smote the king, so that he was a leper unto the day of his death. *2 Ki. xv.* 5. I will visit their transgression with the rod. *Ps. lxxxix.* 32. Are not two sparrows sold for a farthing? and one of them shall not fall on the ground without your Father. But the very hairs of your head are all numbered. *Mat. x.* 29, 30.

3. And for what cause, soever this sickness is sent unto you; whether it be to try your patience for the example of others,

3. Thou, O God, hast proved us: thou hast tried us, as silver is tried. *Ps. lxvi.* 10. My brethren, count it all joy when ye fall into divers temptations; knowing this, that the trying of your faith worketh patience. But let patience have her perfect work, that ye may be perfect and entire, wanting nothing. *Ja. i.* 2, 3, 4. Rejoicing in hope, patient in tribula-

L

tion. *Ro. xii.* 12. Take, my brethren, the prophets, who have spoken in the name of the Lord, for an example of suffering affliction, and of patience. *Ja. v.* 10. Be not slothful, but followers of them who through faith and patience inherit the promises. *He. vi.* 12. I waited patiently for the Lord; and he inclined unto me, and heard my cry. He brought me up also out of an horrible pit, out of the miry clay, and set my feet upon a rock. Many shall see it, and fear, and shall trust in the Lord. *Ps. xl.* 1, 2, 3. See also, *John xi.* 4.

4. and that your faith may be found in the day of the Lord, laudable, glorious, and honourable to the increase of glory and endless felicity;

4. Wherein ye greatly rejoice, though now for a season, if need be, ye are in heaviness through manifold temptations: that the trial of your faith, being much more precious than of gold that perisheth, though it be tried with fire, might be found unto praise and honour and glory at the appearing of Jesus Christ. 1 *Pe. i.* 6, 7. Our light affliction, which is but for a moment, worketh for us a far more exceeding and eternal weight of glory; while we look not at the things which are seen, but at the things which are not seen: for the things which are seen are temporal; but the things which are not seen are eternal. 2 *Co. iv.* 17, 18. Receiving the end of your faith, even the salvation of your souls. 1 *Pe. i.* 9. See also, 2 *Th. i.* 10, 11, 12.—*Jude* 24, 25.—*Re. ii.* 10.

5. or else it be sent unto you to correct and amend in you whatsoever doth offend the eyes of your heavenly Father;

5. When thou with rebukes dost correct man for iniquity, thou makest his beauty to consume away, like a moth. *Ps. xxxix.* 11. If his children forsake my law, and walk not in my judgments; then will I visit their transgression with the rod, and their iniquity with stripes. Nevertheless my loving kindness will I not utterly take from him. *Ps. lxxxix.* 30, 32, 33. Whom the Lord loveth he chasteneth,—for our profit, that we might be partakers of his holiness. *He. xii.* 6, 10. I will go and return to my place, till they acknowledge their offence, and seek my face: in their affliction they will seek me early. *Ho. v.* 15. As many as I love, I rebuke and chasten. *Re. iii.* 19. The Lord trieth the righteous. *Ps. xi.* 5. Thou art of purer eyes than to behold evil, and canst not look on iniquity. *Hab. i.* 13. Before I was afflicted I went astray: but now have I kept thy word. It is good for me that I have been afflicted; that I might learn thy statutes. *Ps. cxix.* 67, 71.

6. know you certainly, that if you truly repent you of your sins, and bear your sickness patiently, trusting in God's mercy, for his dear Son Jesus Christ's sake,

6. In the day of adversity consider. *Ec. vii.* 14. Come and let us return unto the Lord: for he hath torn, and he will heal us; he hath smitten, and he will bind us up. *Ho. vi.* 1. I will declare mine iniquity; I will be sorry for my sin. *Ps. xxxviii.* 18. I will arise and go to my father, and will say unto him, Father, I have sinned against heaven, and before thee, and am no more worthy to be called thy son. *Lu. xv.* 18, 19. Surely it is meet to be said unto God, I have borne chastisement; I will not offend any more: that which I see not, teach thou me: if I have done iniquity, I will do no more. *Job xxxiv.* 31, 32. Godly sorrow worketh repentance to salvation not to be repented of. *2 Co. vii.* 10. Wherefore doth a living man complain, a man for the punishment of his sins? *La. iii.* 39. I was dumb, I opened not my mouth; because thou didst it. *Ps. xxxix.* 9. I will bear the indignation of the Lord, because I have sinned against him. *Mi. vii.* 9. Casting all your care upon him, for he careth for you. *1 Pe. v.* 7. I have trusted in thy mercy. *Ps. xiii.* 5. Unto you first, God, having raised up his Son Jesus, sent him to bless you, in turning away every one of you from his iniquities. *Ac. iii.* 26. If any man sin, we have an Advocate with the Father, Jesus Christ the righteous: and he is the Propitiation for our sins: and not for ours only, but also for the sins of the whole world. *1 John ii.* 1, 2.

7. and render unto him humble thanks for his fatherly visitation, submitting yourself wholly unto his will,

7. I will thank the Lord for giving me warning: my reins also chasten me in the night season. *Ps. xvi.* 8. I know, O Lord, that thy judgments are right, and that thou in faithfulness hast afflicted me. *Ps. cxix.* 75. Job arose, and worshipped, and said, Naked came I out of my mother's womb, and naked shall I return thither: the Lord gave, and the Lord hath taken away; blessed be the name of the Lord. *Job i.* 20, 21. It is the Lord; let him do what seemeth him good. *1 Sa. iii.* 18.

8. it shall turn to your profit, and help you forward in the right way that leadeth unto everlasting life.

8. They cried unto the Lord in their trouble, and he delivered them out of their distresses, and he led them forth by the right way. *Ps. cvii.* 6, 7. It is good for me that I have been afflicted; that I might learn thy statutes. *Ps. cxix.* 71. Knowing that tribulation worketh patience; and patience, experience; and experience, hope; and hope maketh not

ashamed ; because the love of God is shed abroad in our hearts by the Holy Ghost which is given unto us. *Ro. v.* 3, 4, 5. They [our fathers] verily for a few days chastened us after their own pleasure : but he for our profit, that we might be partakers of his holiness. Now no chastening for the present seemeth to be joyous, but grievous : nevertheless afterward it yieldeth the peaceable fruit of righteousness unto them which are exercised thereby. *He. xii.* 10, 11. Our light affliction, which is but for a moment, worketh for us a far more exceeding and eternal weight of glory. 2 *Co. iv.* 17. Blessed is the man that endureth temptation : for when he is tried, he shall receive the crown of life, which the Lord hath promised to them that love him. *Ja. i.* 12.

CCXV. The second part of the Exhortation to the sick person.

1. Take therefore in good part the chastisement of the Lord : For, (as St. Paul saith in the twelfth Chapter to the Hebrews,) *whom the Lord loveth he chasteneth, and scourgeth every son whom he receiveth. If ye endure chastening, God dealeth with you as with sons ; for what son is he whom the father chasteneth not ? But if ye be without chastisement, whereof all are partakers, then are ye bastards, and not sons. Furthermore, we have had fathers of our flesh, which corrected us, and we gave them reverence : shall we not much rather be in subjection unto the Father of spirits, and live ? For they verily for a few days chastened us after their own pleasure ; but he for our profit, that we might be partakers of his holiness.*

1. My son, despise not the chastening of the Lord; neither be weary of his correction. *Pr. iii.* 11. For whom the Lord loveth he chasteneth, and scourgeth every son whom he receiveth. If ye endure chastening, God dealeth with you as with sons ; for what son is he whom the father chasteneth not? But if ye be without chastisement, whereof all are partakers, then are ye bastards, and not sons. Furthermore, we have had fathers of our flesh which corrected us, and we gave them reverence : shall we not much rather be in subjection unto the Father of spirits, and live ? For they verily for a few days chastened us after their own pleasure ; but he for our profit, that we might be partakers of his holiness. *He. xii.* 6 *to* 10.

2. These words, good brother, are written in holy Scripture for our comfort

2. Whatsoever things were written aforetime were written for our learning, that we through patience and comfort of the Scriptures might have hope. *Ro. xv.* 4. All Scripture is given by inspiration of God, and is profitable for doctrine, for re-

and instruction; that we should patiently, and with thanksgiving, bear our heavenly Father's correction, whensoever by any manner of adversity, it shall please his gracious goodness to visit us.

3 And there should be no greater comfort to Christian persons, than to be made like unto Christ, by suffering patiently adversities, troubles, and sicknesses. For he himself went not up to joy, but first he suffered pain; he entered not into his glory before he was crucified.

proof, for correction, for instruction in righteousness. 2 *Ti. iii.* 16. Remember the word unto thy servant, upon which thou hast caused me to hope. This is my comfort in my affliction: for thy word hath quickened me. Thy testimonies have I taken as an heritage for ever: for they are the rejoicing of my heart. *Ps. cxix.* 49, 50. 111. And Samuel told Eli every whit, and hid nothing from him. And he said, It is the Lord: let him do what seemeth him good. 1 *Sa. iii.* 18. Then said Hezekiah unto Isaiah, Good is the word of the Lord which thou hast spoken. 2 *Ki. xx.* 19. Patient in tribulation. *Ro. xii.* 12. My brethren, count it all joy when ye fall into divers temptations. *Ja. i.* 2. Not only so, but we glory in tribulations also. *Ro. v.* 3. Giving thanks always for all things unto God and the Father in the name of our Lord Jesus Christ. *Ep. v.* 20. And the king said, Let him curse, because the Lord hath said unto him, Curse David. Who shall then say, Wherefore hast thou done so? It may be that the Lord will look on mine affliction, and that the Lord will requite me good for his cursing this day. 2 *Sa. xvi.* 10. 12. For unto you it is given in the behalf of Christ, not only to believe on him, but also to suffer for his sake. *Ph. i.* 29. Even hereunto were ye called: because Christ also suffered for us, leaving us an example, that ye should follow his steps: who did no sin, neither was guile found in his mouth: who, when he was reviled, reviled not again; when he suffered, he threatened not; but committed himself to him that judgeth righteously: who his own self bare our sins in his own body on the tree, that we, being dead to sins, should live unto righteousness: by whose stripes ye were healed. 1 *Pe. ii.* 21 to 24. He was afflicted, yet he opened not his mouth: he is brought as a lamb to the slaughter, and as a sheep before her shearers is dumb, so he openeth not his mouth. *Is. liii.* 7. Most gladly will I glory in mine infirmities, that the power of Christ may rest upon me. Therefore I take pleasure in infirmities, in reproaches, in necessities, in persecutions, in distresses for Christ's sake. 2 *Co. xii.* 9, 10. I am filled with comfort, I am exceeding joyful in all our tribulation. 2 *Co. vii.* 4. Our Lord Jesus Christ himself, and God, even our Father, hath loved us, and hath given us everlasting consolation. 2 *Th. ii.* 16. Let them that suffer according to the will of God commit the keeping of their souls to him in well doing, as unto a faithful Creator. 1 *Pe. iv.* 19. That I may know him, and the fellowship of his sufferings, being made conformable unto his death. *Ph. iii.* 10. Looking unto Jesus the Author and Finisher of our faith, who for the joy that was set before him endured the cross, despising the shame, and is set down at the right hand of the throne of God. *He. xii.* 2. Ought not Christ to have suffered these things, and to enter into his glory? *Lu. xxiv.* 26. For it became him, for whom are all things, and by whom are all things, in bringing many sons unto glory, to make the Captain of their salvation perfect through sufferings. *He. ii.* 10. Though he were a Son, yet learned he obedience by the things which he suffered; and being made perfect, he became the Author of eternal salvation unto all them that obey him. *He. v.* 8, 9. For though he was crucified through weakness, yet he liveth by the power of God. 2 *Co. xiii.* 4.

4. So truly our way to eternal joy is to suffer here with Christ; and our door to enter into eternal life is gladly to die with Christ, that we may rise again from death, and dwell with him in everlasting life.

4. Jesus saith unto him, I am the Way, and the Truth, and the Life. *John xiv.* 6. I am the Door: by me if any man enter in, he shall be saved. *John x.* 9. It is a faithful saying: For if we be dead with him, we shall also live with him: if we suffer we shall also reign with him: if we deny him, he also will deny us. 2 *Ti. ii.* 11, 12. If we be dead with Christ, we believe that we shall also live with him. Know ye not, that so many of us as were baptized into Jesus Christ were baptized into his death? If we have been planted together in the likeness of his death, we shall be also in the likeness of his resurrection: knowing that Christ being raised from the dead dieth no more; death hath no more dominion over him. *Ro. vi.* 3. 5. 9. Ye are dead, and your life is hid with Christ in God. When Christ, who is our life, shall appear, then shall ye also appear with him in glory. *Col. iii.* 3, 4. I reckon that the sufferings of this present time are not worthy to be compared with the glory which shall be revealed in us. *Ro. viii.* 18. For as in Adam all die, even so in Christ shall all be made alive. 1 *Co. xv.* 22. If the Spirit of him that raised up Jesus from the dead dwell in you, he that raised up Christ from the dead shall also quicken your mortal bodies by

his Spirit that dwelleth in you. *Ro. viii.* 11. These are they which came out of great tribulation, and have washed their robes, and made them white in the blood of the Lamb. Therefore are they before the throne of God, and serve him day and night in his temple. *Re. vii.* 14, 15.

5. Now, therefore, taking your sickness, which is thus profitable for you, patiently,

5. Rest in the Lord, and wait patiently for him. *Ps. xxxvii.* 7. I waited patiently for the Lord; and he inclined unto me, and heard my cry. *Ps. xl.* 1. It is good for me that I have been afflicted; that I might learn thy statutes. *Ps. cxix.* 71. The Lord is good unto them that wait for him, to the soul that seeketh him. It is good that a man should both hope and quietly wait for the salvation of the Lord. *La. iii.* 25, 26. By this shall the iniquity of Jacob be purged; and this is all the fruit to take away his sin. *Is. xxvii.* 9.

6. I exhort you, in the Name of God, to remember the profession which you made unto God in your Baptism.

6. Fight the good fight of faith, lay hold on eternal life, whereunto thou art also called, and hast professed a good profession before many witnesses. 1 *Ti. vi.* 12. Let us hold fast the profession of our faith without wavering. *He. x.* 23. For we are made partakers of Christ if we hold the beginning of our confidence stedfast unto the end. *He. iii.* 14.—*See also, Nos. CLX. CLXI.*

7. And forasmuch as after this life there is an account to be given unto the righteous Judge, by whom all must be judged, without respect of persons,

7. It is appointed unto men once to die, but after this the judgment. *He. ix.* 27. We shall all stand before the judgment seat of Christ. Every one of us shall give account of himself to God. *Ro. xiv.* 10. 12. He hath appointed a day, in the which he will judge the world in righteousness by that man whom he hath ordained. *Ac. xvii.* 31. Then Peter opened his mouth, and said, Of a truth I perceive that God is no respecter of persons. *Ac. x.* 34. Who shall give account to him that is ready to judge the quick and the dead. 1 *Pe. iv.* 5. If ye call on the Father, who without respect of persons judgeth according to every man's work, pass the time of your sojourning here in fear. 1 *Pe. i.* 17.

8. I require you to examine yourself and your estate, both toward God and man; so that, accusing and condemning your-

8. Knowing therefore the terror of the Lord, we persuade men. 2 *Co. v.* 11. Set thine house in order. 2 *Ki. xx.* 1. Let a man examine himself. 1 *Co. xi.* 28. Thus saith the Lord of hosts; Consider your ways. *Hag. i.* 5. Confess your faults one to another. *Ja. v.* 16. He that covereth his sins shall not prosper; but whoso confesseth and forsaketh them shall have

self for your own faults, you may find mercy at our heavenly Father's hand for Christ's sake,

mercy. *Pr. xxviii.* 13. Let us search and try our ways, and turn again to the Lord. *La. iii.* 40. Examine me, O Lord, and prove me; try my reins and my heart. *Ps. xxvi.* 2. I acknowledge my transgressions: and my sin is ever before me. *Ps. li.* 3. I abhor myself, and repent in dust and ashes. *Job xlii.* 6. When I kept silence, my bones waxed old through my roaring all the day long. I acknowledged my sin unto thee, and mine iniquity have I not hid. I said, I will confess my transgressions unto the Lord; and thou forgavest the iniquity of my sin. *Ps. xxxii.* 3. 5. If we would judge ourselves, we should not be judged. 1 *Co. xi.* 31. For God so loved the world, that he gave his only begotten Son, that whosoever believeth in him should not perish, but have everlasting life. *John iii.* 16. Be it known unto you, men and brethren, that through this Man is preached unto you the forgiveness of sins. *Ac. xiii.* 38. If we confess our sins, he is faithful and just to forgive us our sins, and to cleanse us from all unrighteousness. 1 *John i.* 9.

9. and not be accused and condemned in that fearful judgment

9. If our heart condemn us not, then have we confidence toward God. 1 *John iii.* 21. When we are judged, we are chastened of the Lord, that we should not be condemned with the world. 1 *Co. xi.* 32. But the day of the Lord will come as a thief in the night; in the which the heavens shall pass away with a great noise, and the elements shall melt with fervent heat, the earth also and the works that are therein shall be burned up. 2 *Pe. iii.* 10. The fearful, and unbelieving, and the abominable, and murderers, and whoremongers, and sorcerers, and idolaters, and all liars, shall have their part in the lake which burneth with fire and brimstone: which is the second death. *Re. xxi.* 8. A certain fearful looking for of judgment and fiery indignation. *He. x.* 27. And the kings of the earth, and the great men, and the rich men, and the chief captains, and the mighty men, and every bond man, and every free man, hid themselves in the dens and in the rocks of the mountains; and said to the mountains and rocks, Fall on us, and hide us from the face of him that sitteth on the throne, and from the wrath of the Lamb: for the great day of his wrath is come; and who shall be able to stand? *Re. vi.* 15, 16, 17. The Lord grant unto him that he may find mercy of the Lord in that day. 2 *Ti. i.* 18.

10. There-
fore I shall re-
hearse to you
the Articles of
our Faith, that
ye may know
whether you do
believe as a
Christian man
should, or no.

10. Remember how thou hast received and heard. *Re. iii.* 3.
Examine yourselves, whether ye be in the faith; prove your
own selves. Know ye not your own selves? 2 *Co. xiii.* 5.
To the law and to the testimony: if they speak not according
to this word, it is because there is no light in them. *Is. xiii.* 20.
Search me, O God, and know my heart: try me and know
my thoughts: and see if there be any wicked way in me, and
lead me in the way everlasting. *Ps. cxxix.* 23, 24.

The Creed.—Dost thou believe in God the Father Almighty, Maker of heaven and earth?
And in Jesus Christ his only begotten Son our Lord? And that he was conceived by
the Holy Ghost, born of the Virgin Mary; that he suffered under Pontius Pilate, was
crucified, dead, and buried; that he went down into hell, and also did rise again the third
day; that he ascended into heaven, and sitteth at the right hand of God the Father Almighty; and from thence shall come again at the end of the world, to judge the quick
and the dead?
And dost thou believe in the Holy Ghost; the Holy Catholic Church; the Communion
of Saints; the Remission of sins; the Resurrection of the flesh; and everlasting Life
after death?
All this I stedfastly believe.

CCXVI. *The ministerial Absolution.*

Our Lord
Jesus Christ,
who hath left
power to his
Church to ab-
solve sinners
who truly re-
pent and believe
in him, of his
great mercy
forgive thee
thine offences:
And by his au-
thority com-
mitted to me,
I absolve thee
from all thy
sins, In the
Name of the
Father, and of
the Son, and of
the Holy Ghost.
Amen.

All things are of God, who hath reconciled us to himself by
Jesus Christ, and hath given to us the ministry of reconciliation: Now then we are ambassadors for Christ. 2 *Co. v.* 18. 20.
Is any sick among you? let him call for the elders of the
Church; and let them pray over him: and the prayer of faith
shall save the sick, and the Lord shall raise him up; and if he
have committed sins, they shall be forgiven him. *Ja. v.* 14, 15.
Whosoever sins ye remit, they are remitted unto them; and
whosoever sins ye retain, they are retained. *John xx.* 23.
Whatsoever ye shall bind on earth shall be bound in heaven:
and whatsoever ye shall loose on earth shall be loosed in heaven. Again I say unto you, That if two of you shall agree
on earth as touching any thing that they shall ask, it shall be
done for them of my Father which is in heaven. *Mat. xviii.*
18, 19. Lo, I am with you alway, even unto the end of the
world. *Mat. xxviii.* 20. Paul, a servant of Jesus Christ, called
to be an Apostle, separated unto the Gospel of God; by whom
we have received grace and apostleship, for obedience to the
faith among all nations, for his name. *Ro. i.* 1, 5. Testifying
both to the Jews, and also to the Greeks, repentance toward
God, and faith toward our Lord Jesus Christ. *Ac. xx.* 21.

To whom ye forgive any thing, I forgive also : for if I forgive any thing, to whom I forgave it, for your sakes forgave I it in the person of Christ. 2 Co. ii. 10. *compared with.* In the name of our Lord Jesus Christ, when ye are gathered together, and my spirit, with the power of our Lord Jesus Christ, to deliver such an one unto Satan for the destruction of the flesh. 1 Co. v. 4, 5. When the wicked man turneth away from his wickedness that he hath committed, and doeth that which is lawful and right, he shall save his soul alive. *Eze. xviii.* 27. Him that cometh to me I will in no wise cast out. *John vi.* 37. Ye shall know them by their fruits. *Mat. vii.* 16. If we confess our sins, he is faithful and just to forgive us our sins, and to cleanse us from all unrighteousness. 1 *John i.* 9. To the Lord our God belong mercies and forgivenesses, though we have rebelled against him. *Da. ix.* 9. Thou, Lord, art good, and ready to forgive ; and plenteous in mercy unto all them that call upon thee. *Ps. lxxxvi.* 5. Christ died for our sins. 1 *Co. xv.* 3. Through this man is preached unto you the forgiveness of sins. *Ac. xiii.* 38. Through his name whosoever believeth in him shall receive remission of sins. *Ac. x.* 43. Having therefore, brethren, boldness to enter into the holiest by the blood of Jesus, and having an High Priest over the house of God ; let us draw near with a true heart in full assurance of faith, having our hearts sprinkled from an evil conscience, and our bodies washed with pure water. *Heb. x.* 19, 21, 22. The Lord bless thee, and keep thee : The Lord make his face shine upon thee, and be gracious unto thee : The Lord lift up his countenance upon thee, and give thee peace. *Nu.* 24, 25, 26. See also, quotations in No. III. and the following Le. xiii. 3. 8. 11. 15. 20. 22. 25. 27. 30. *The priest shall look on him, and pronounce him unclean.—*44, 45. *The priest shall pronounce him utterly unclean, and the leper shall cry, Unclean, unclean.—*13. *The priest shall consider ; he shall pronounce him clean, he is clean.—*17. *The priest shall see him ; and the priest shall pronounce him clean, he is clean.—*23. 28. 34. 37. *The priest shall pronounce him clean.—*Nu. vi. 23. 27. Aaron and his sons shall put my name upon the children of Israel ; and I will bless them.—Isa. vi. 9, 10. Go, make the heart of this people fat, and make their ears heavy, and shut their eyes.

R

—Je. i. 10. *See, I have this day set thee over the nations and over the kingdoms, to root out, and to pull down, and to destroy, and to throw down, to build, and to plant.*—Eze. xxxii. 18. *Son of man, cast them down, [the multitude of Egypt,] even her, and the daughters of the famous nations, unto the nether parts of the earth.*—Je. xv. 1. to 4. *Then said the Lord unto me, Cast them out of my sight, and let them go forth; such as are for death, to death; and such as are for the sword, to the sword; and such as are for the famine, to the famine; and such as are for the captivity, to the captivity. And I will appoint over them four kinds, saith the Lord: the sword to slay, and the dogs to tear, and the fowls of the heaven, and the beasts of the earth, to devour and destroy. And I will cause them to be removed into all kingdoms of the earth.*—Lev. xiv. 2. 11. *The leper shall be brought unto the priest; and the priest that maketh him clean, shall present the man that is to be made clean.*—Ex. xiv. 16. *But lift thou up thy rod, [the ensign of Moses' office,] and stretch out thine hand over the sea, and divide it.*

CCXVII. *A Prayer for the Exercise of the Divine Mercy, and of renewing Grace.*

1. Let us lift up our heart with our hands unto God in the heavens. La. iii. 41. Draw nigh to God, and he will draw nigh to you. Ja. iv. 8. Have mercy upon me, O God, according to thy lovingkindness: according unto the multitude of thy tender mercies blot out my transgressions. Ps. li. 1. The Lord will not cast off for ever: but though he cause grief, yet will he have compassion according to the multitude of his mercies. For he doth not afflict willingly nor grieve the children of men. La. iii. 31, 32, 33. Repent ye, and be converted, that your sins may be blotted out, when the times of refreshing shall come from the presence of the Lord. Ac. iii. 19. Godly sorrow worketh repentance to salvation not to be repented of: but the sorrow of the world worketh death. For behold this selfsame thing, that ye sorrowed after a godly sort, what carefulness it wrought in you, yea, what vehement desire, yea, what zeal, yea, what revenge, yea, what clearing

of yourselves, yea, what indignation, yea, what fear! 2 *Co. vii.* 10, 11. And David said unto Nathan, I have sinned against the Lord. And Nathan said unto David, The Lord also hath put away thy sin; thou shalt not die. 2 *Sa. xii.* 13. He will turn again, he will have compassion upon us; he will subdue our iniquities; and thou wilt cast all their sins into the depths of the sea. *Mi. vii.* 19. I, even I, am he that blotteth out thy transgressions for mine own sake, and will not remember thy sins. *Is. xliii.* 25. For I will be merciful to their unrighteousness, and their sins and their iniquities will I remember no more. *He. viii.* 12. Thou hast cast all my sins behind thy back. *Is. xxxviii.* 17. Their sins and iniquities will I remember no more. *He. x.* 17. *See also, Je. l.* 20.

2. Open thine eye of mercy upon this thy servant, who most earnestly desireth pardon and forgiveness.

2. Lord, bow down thine ear, and hear; open, Lord, thine eyes, and see. 2 *Ki. xix.* 16. That thine eyes may be open unto the supplication of thy servant, and unto the supplication of thy people, to hearken unto them in all that they call for unto thee. 1 *Ki. viii.* 52. For thy name's sake, O Lord, pardon mine iniquity; for it is great. *Ps. xxv.* 11. O Lord, hear; O Lord, forgive; O Lord, hearken and do; defer not, for thine own sake, O my God. *Da. ix.* 19. Look thou upon me, and be merciful unto me, as thou usest to do unto those that love thy name. *Ps. cxix.* 132. *See also, Nu. xiv.* 19.

3. Renew in him, most loving Father, whatsoever hath been decayed by the fraud and malice of the devil, by his own carnal will and frailness;

3. After the kindness and love of God our Saviour toward man appeared, not by works of righteousness which we have done, but according to his mercy he saved us, by the washing of regeneration, and renewing of the Holy Ghost; which he shed on us abundantly through Jesus Christ our Saviour. *Tit. iii.* 4, 5, 6. That ye put off concerning the former conversation the old man, which is corrupt according to the deceitful lusts; and be renewed in the spirit of your mind. *Ep. iv.* 22, 23. The Lord is loving unto every man. *Ps. cxlv.* 9. Like as a father pitieth his children, so the Lord pitieth them that fear him. *Ps. ciii.* 13. Create in me a clean heart, O God, and renew a right spirit within me. *Ps. li.* 10. Behold, satan hath desired to have you, that he may sift you as wheat. *Lu. xxii.* 31. That old serpent, called the devil, and satan, which deceiveth the whole world. *Re. xii.* 9. I fear, lest by any means, as the serpent beguiled Eve through his subtilty, so

your minds should be corrupted from the simplicity that is in Christ. 2 *Co. xi.* 3. Be sober, be vigilant, because your adversary the devil, as a roaring lion, walketh about, seeking whom he may devour. 1 *Pe. v.* 8. Lest satan should get an advantage of us: for we are not ignorant of his devices. 2 *Co. ii.* 11. I am carnal, sold under sin. For that which I do, I allow not: for what I would, that do I not; but what I hate, that do I. When I would do good, evil is present with me. *Ro. vii.* 14, 15, 21. How weak is thine heart, saith the Lord God. *Eze. xvi.* 30. Watch and pray, that ye enter not into temptation. *Mat. xxvi.* 41.

4. preserve and continue this sick member in the unity of the Church;

4. Holy Father, keep through thine own name those whom thou hast given me, that they may be one, as we are. Neither pray I for these alone, but for them also, which shall believe on me through their word; that they all may be one. *John xvii.* 11. 20, 21. Endeavouring to keep the unity of the Spirit in the bond of peace. *Ep. iv.* 3. Who are kept by the power of God through faith unto salvation ready to be revealed in the last time. Wherein ye greatly rejoice, though now for a season, if need be, ye are in heaviness through manifold temptations. 1 *Pe. i.* 5, 6. The afflictions of Christ in my flesh for his body's sake, which is the Church. *Col. i.* 24.

5. consider his contrition, accept his tears, assuage his pain, as shall seem to thee most expedient for him.

5. Consider mine affliction. *Ps. cxix.* 153. Wash me throughly from mine iniquity, and cleanse me from my sin. For I acknowledge my transgressions: and my sin is ever before me. A broken and a contrite heart, O God, thou wilt not despise. *Ps. li.* 2, 3. 17. To this man will I look, even to him that is poor and of a contrite spirit. *Is. lxvi.* 2. My tears have been my meat day and night. *Ps. xlii.* 3. Put my tears into thy bottle: are they not in thy book? *Ps. lvi.* 8. Thou hast known my soul in adversities. *Ps. xxxi.* 7. Look upon mine affliction and my pain; and forgive all my sins. *Ps. xxv.* 18. Mine eyes fail with looking upward; O Lord, I am oppressed, undertake for me. [*marginal reading, ease me.*] Then Hezekiah prayed unto the Lord, and said, Remember now, O Lord, I beseech thee, how I have walked before thee in truth and with a perfect heart, and have done that which is good in thy sight. And Hezekiah wept sore. Then came the word of the Lord to Isaiah, saying, Go, and say to Hezekiah,

Thus saith the Lord, the God of David thy father, I have heard thy prayer; I have seen thy tears. *Is. xxxviii.* 14. 2 *to* 5. Mine eyes are unto thee, O God, the Lord: in thee is my trust; leave not my soul destitute. *Ps. cxli.* 8. Deliver me. Deal with thy servant according unto thy mercy. *Ps. cxix.* 153. 124. The Lord comfort him, when he lieth sick upon his bed: make thou all his bed in his sickness. *Ps. xli.* 3. Wherein ye greatly rejoice, though now for a season, if need be, ye are in heaviness through manifold temptations. 1 *Pe. i.* 6. There was given to me a thorn in the flesh, the messenger of satan to buffet me. For this thing I besought the Lord thrice, that it might depart from me. And he said unto me, My grace is sufficient for thee: for my strength is made perfect in weakness. Therefore I take pleasure in infirmities. 2 *Co. xii.* 7 *to* 10. And he kneeled down, and prayed, saying, Father, if thou be willing, remove this cup from me: nevertheless not my will, but thine, be done. *Lu. xxii.* 41, 42.

6. And forasmuch as *he putteth his* full *trust only in* thy mercy, im*pute not unto him his* former sins,

6. I trust in the mercy of God for ever and ever. *Ps. lii.* 8. In thee, O Lord, do I put my trust: let me never be put to confusion. Deliver me in thy righteousness, and cause me to escape; incline thine ear unto me, and save me. *Ps. lxxi.* 1, 2. If thou, Lord, shouldest mark iniquities, O Lord, who shall stand? But there is forgiveness with thee, that thou mayest be feared. I wait for the Lord, my soul doth wait, and in his word do I hope. Let Israel hope in the Lord: for with the Lord there is mercy, and with him is plenteous redemption. And he shall redeem Israel from all his iniquities. *Ps. cxxx.* 3, 4, 5. 7; 8. O remember not against us former iniquities. *Ps. lxxix.* 8. Remember not the sins of my youth, nor my transgressions: according to thy mercy remember thou me for thy goodness' sake, O Lord. *Ps. xxv.* 7. Blessed are they whose iniquities are forgiven, and whose sins are covered. Blessed is the man to whom the Lord will not impute sin. *Ro. iv.* 7, 8.

7. *but* strengthen *him* with thy blessed Spirit;

7. The Lord will strengthen him upon the bed of languishing. *Ps. xli.* 3. Strengthened with might by his Spirit in the inner man. *Ep. iii.* 16. Strengthened with all might, according to his glorious power, unto all patience and longsuffering with joyfulness. *Col. i.* 11. Will he plead against me with his great power? No; but he would put strength

in me. *Job xxiii.* 6. In the day when I cried thou answeredst me, and strengthenedst me with strength in my soul. *Ps. cxxxviii.* 3. Be strong in the Lord, and in the power of his might. *Ep. vi.* 10.

8. and, when thou art pleased to take him hence, take him unto thy favour, through the merits of thy most dearly beloved Son Jesus Christ our Lord. *Amen.*

8. Knowest thou that the Lord will take away thy master from thy head to day? *2 Ki. ii.* 3. All the days of my appointed time will I wait, till my change come. *Job xiv.* 14. I am in a strait betwixt two, having a desire to depart, and to be with Christ. *Ph. i.* 23. In his favour is life : weeping may endure for a night, but joy cometh in the morning. *Ps. xxx.* 5. As for me, I will behold thy face in righteousness : I shall be satisfied, when I awake, with thy likeness. *Ps. xvii.* 15. Thou wilt shew me the path of life : in thy presence is fulness of joy; at thy right hand there are pleasures for evermore. *Ps. xvi.* 11. Remember me, O Lord, with the favour that thou bearest unto thy people : O visit me with thy salvation. *Ps. cvi.* 4. Into thine hand I commit my spirit : thou hast redeemed me, O Lord God of truth. *Ps. xxxi.* 5. The beggar died, and was carried by the angels into Abraham's bosom. *Lu. xvi.* 22. I heard a voice from heaven saying unto me, Write, Blessed are the dead, which die in the Lord from henceforth : Yea, saith the Spirit, that they may rest from their labours ; and their works do follow them. *Re. xiv.* 13. In my Father's house are many mansions : if it were not so, I would have told you. I go to prepare a place for you, and if I go and prepare a place for you, I will come again, and receive you unto myself; that where I am, there ye may be also. *John xiv.* 2, 3. This is my beloved Son, in whom I am well pleased. *Mat. xvii.* 5. The Author of eternal salvation unto all them that obey him. *He. v.* 9.

Psalm lxxi. In thee, O Lord, have I put my trust; let me never be put to confusion: but rid me, and deliver me in thy righteousness ; incline thine ear unto me, and save me.—Be thou my strong hold, whereunto I may alway resort : thou hast promised to help me, for thou art my house of defence, and my castle.—Deliver me, O my God, out of the hand of the ungodly : out of the hand of the unrighteous and cruel man.—For thou, O Lord God, art the thing that I long for : thou art my hope, even from my youth.—Through thee have I been holden up ever since I was born: thou art he that took me out of my mother's womb ; my praise shall alway be of thee.—I am become as it were a monster unto many : but my sure trust is in thee.—O let my mouth be filled with thy praise: that I may sing of thy glory and honour all the day long.—Cast me not away in the time of age : forsake me not when my strength faileth me.—For mine enemies speak against me, and they that lay wait for my soul, take their counsel together, saying : God hath forsaken him, persecute him, and take him ; for there is none to deliver him.—Go not far from me, O God : my God, haste thee to help me.—Let them be confounded and perish that are against my soul : let them be *covered with shame and dishonour that seek to do me evil.—As for me, I will patiently abide alway: and will praise thee more and more.—My mouth shall daily speak of thy righteous-ness and salvation: for I know no end thereof. I will go forth in the strength of the Lord God: and will make mention of thy righteousness only.—Thou, O God, hast taught me from my youth up until now: therefore will I tell of thy wondrous works.—Forsake me not, O God, in mine old age, when I am gray-headed: until I have shewed thy strength unto this generation, and thy power to all them that are yet for to come.—Thy righteousness, O God, is very high, and great things are they that thou hast done: O God, who is like unto thee?*—Glory be to the Father, &c. As it was in, &c.

CCXVIII.—*A Prayer to the Redeemer.*

1. O Saviour of the world, who by thy Cross and precious Blood hast redeemed us, save us, and help us, we humbly beseech thee, O Lord.

1. O the Hope of Israel, The Saviour thereof in time of trouble. *Je. xiv. 8.* The Father sent the Son to be the Saviour of the world. *1 John iv. 14.* If any man sin, we have an Advocate with the Father, Jesus Christ the righteous: and he is the Propitiation for our sins: and not for ours only, but also for the sins of the whole world. *1 John ii. 1, 2.* Now we believe, and know that this is indeed the Christ, the Saviour of the world. *John iv. 42.* Having made peace through the blood of his cross. *Col. i. 20.* Ye were not redeemed with corruptible things, as silver and gold; but with the precious blood of Christ, as of a lamb without blemish and without spot. *1 Pe. i. 18, 19.* Save now, I beseech thee, O Lord. *Ps. cxviii. 25.* Help us, O God of our salvation, for the glory of thy name. *Ps. lxxix. 9.* Help me, O Lord my God: O save me according to thy mercy. *Ps. cix. 26.* The sorrows of death compassed me, and the pains of hell gat hold upon me: I found trouble and sorrow. Then called I upon the name of the Lord; O Lord, I beseech thee, deliver my soul. *Ps. cxvi. 3, 4.*

CCXIX. *The Form of Benediction.*

1. The Almighty Lord, who is a most strong tower to them that put their trust in him,

1. Lord God Almighty, which was, and is, and is to come. *Re. iv. 8.* The Almighty shall be thy defence. *Job xxii. 25.* The Name of the Lord is a strong tower: the righteous runneth into it, and is safe. *Pr. xviii. 10.* Trust ye in the Lord for ever: for in the Lord JEHOVAH is everlasting strength. *Is. xxvi. 4.* They that trust in the Lord shall be as mount Zion, which cannot be removed, but abideth for ever. *Ps. cxxv. 1. See also, Ps. v. 11, 12.—1 Sa. ii. 6.—Na. i. 7.* 2. Thine is the kingdom, and the power, and the glory, for ever. Amen. *Mat. vi. 13.* And Jesus came and spake unto

heaven, in earth, and under the earth, do bow and obey,

3. be now and evermore thy defence;

4. and make thee know and feel, that there is none other Name under heaven given to man, in whom, and through whom, thou mayest receive health and salvation, but only the Name of our Lord Jesus Christ. Amen.

them, saying, All power is given unto me in heaven, and in earth. *Mat. xxviii.* 18. God also hath highly exalted him, and given him a name which is above every name: that at the name of Jesus every knee should bow, of things in heaven, and things in earth, and things under the earth. *Ph. ii.* 9, 10. Even the winds and the sea obey him! *Mat. viii.* 27. Who is gone into heaven, and is on the right hand of God; angels and authorities and powers being made subject unto him. *1 Pe. iii.* 22.

3. The Lord hear thee in the day of trouble; the name of the God of Jacob defend thee. Send thee help from the sanctuary, and strengthen thee out of Zion. *Ps. xx.* 1, 2. Bow down thine ear to me; deliver me speedily: be thou my strong rock, for an house of defence to save me. *Ps. xxxi.* 2. Cast me not off in the time of old age; forsake me not when my strength faileth. *Ps. lxxi.* 9. See also, *Ps. xxxvii.* 40.—cxxi. 8.—*2 Ti. iv.* 18.

4. Be it known unto you all, and to all the people of Israel, that by the name of Jesus Christ of Nazareth, whom ye crucified, whom God raised from the dead, even by him doth this man stand here before you whole. Neither is there salvation in any other: for there is none other name under heaven given among men, whereby we must be saved. *Ac. iv.* 10. 12. And his name through faith in his name hath made this man strong; yea, the faith which is by him hath given him this perfect soundness in the presence of you all. *Ac. iii.* 16. Be it known unto you therefore, men and brethren, that through this man is preached unto you the forgiveness of sins: and by him all that believe are justified from all things, from which ye could not be justified by the law of Moses. *Ac. xiii.* 38, 39. Other foundation can no man lay than that is laid, which is Jesus Christ. *1 Co. iii.* 11. There is no God else beside me; a just God and a Saviour; there is none beside me. Look unto me, and be ye saved, all the ends of the earth: for I am God, and there is none else. Israel shall be saved in the Lord with an everlasting salvation: ye shall not be ashamed nor confounded world without end. *Is. xlv.* 21, 22. 17. Heal me, O Lord, and I shall be healed; save me, and I shall be saved. *Je. xvii.* 14.

CCXX. *The second Form of Benediction.*

Unto God's gracious mercy and protection we commit thee. The Lord bless thee, and keep thee. The Lord make his face to shine upon thee, and be gracious unto thee. The Lord lift up his countenance upon thee, and give thee peace, both now and evermore. *Amen.*

And now, brethren, I commend you to God, and to the word of his grace, which is able to build you up, and to give you an inheritance among all them which are sanctified. *Ac. xx.* 32. Thou, O Lord, art a God full of compassion, and gracious, longsuffering, and plenteous in mercy and truth. *Ps. lxxxvi.* 15. O Lord, be gracious unto us; we have waited for thee: be thou their arm every morning, our salvation also in the time of trouble. *Is. xxxiii.* 2. Let them that suffer according to the will of God commit the keeping of their souls to him in well doing, as unto a faithful Creator. *1 Pe. iv.* 19. There be many that say, Who will shew us any good? Lord, lift thou up the light of thy countenance upon us. *Ps. iv.* 6. Thou wilt keep him in perfect peace, whose mind is stayed on thee: because he trusteth in thee. *Is. xxvi.* 3. Peace I leave with you, my peace I give unto you. Let not your heart be troubled, neither let it be afraid. *John xiv.* 27. The work of righteousness shall be peace; and the effect of righteousness quietness and assurance for ever. *Is. xxxii.* 17. The Lord bless thee, and keep thee: The Lord make his face shine upon thee, and be gracious unto thee: The Lord lift up his countenance upon thee, and give thee peace. *Nu. vi.* 24, 25, 26. *See also, De. xxxiii.* 27.

CCXXI. *A Prayer for a sick Child.*

1. O Almighty God, and merciful Father, to whom alone belong the issues of life and death;

1. He that is our God is the God of salvation; and unto God the Lord belong the issues from death. *Ps. lxviii.* 20. Thou hidest thy face, they are troubled: thou takest away their breath, they die, and return to their dust. Thou sendest forth thy Spirit, they are created. *Ps. civ.* 29, 30. He maketh sore, and bindeth up: he woundeth, and his hands make whole. *Job v.* 18. The Lord killeth, and maketh alive: he bringeth down to the grave, and bringeth up. *1 Sa. ii.* 6. He was sick nigh unto death: but God had mercy on him. *Ph. ii.* 27. And he said, While the child was yet alive, I fasted and wept: for I said, Who can tell whether God will be gracious to me, that the child may live? *2 Sa. xii.* 22. *See also, the account of the Shunammite's son. 2 Ki. iv.*

S

2. Look down from heaven, we humbly beseech thee, with the eyes of mercy upon this Child, now lying upon the bed of sickness:

2. David besought God for the child; and David fasted, and went in, and lay all night upon the earth. *2 Sa. xii.* 16. Look down from heaven and behold. *Ps. lxxx.* 14. The eyes of the Lord are upon the righteous, and his ears are open unto their cry. *Ps. xxxiv.* 15. Let thy tender mercies speedily prevent us. *Ps. lxxix.* 8. Let my prayer come before thee; incline thine ear unto my cry; for my soul is full of troubles: and my life draweth nigh unto the grave. I am afflicted and ready to die. *Ps. lxxxviii.* 2, 3. 15. And, behold, there cometh one of the rulers of the synagogue, Jairus by name; and when he saw him, he fell at his feet, and besought him greatly, saying, My little daughter lieth at the point of death : I pray thee, come and lay thy hands on her, that she may be healed; and she shall live. And Jesus went with him; and much people followed him, and thronged him. While he yet spake, there came from the ruler of the synagogue's house certain which said, Thy daughter is dead : why troublest thou the Master any further? As soon as Jesus heard the word that was spoken, he saith unto the ruler of the synagogue, Be not afraid, only believe. And he cometh to the house of the ruler of the synagogue, and seeth the tumult, and them that wept and wailed greatly. And when he was come in, he saith unto them, Why make ye this ado, and weep? the damsel is not dead, but sleepeth. And he took the damsel by the hand, and said unto her, Damsel, I say unto thee, arise. And straightway the damsel arose, and walked. *Mar. v.* 22, 23, 24. 35, 36. 38, 39. 41, 42.

3. Visit *him*, O Lord, with thy salvation; deliver *him* in thy good appointed time from *his* bodily pain, and save *his* soul for thy mercies' sake:

3. Remember me, O Lord, with the favour that thou bearest unto thy people : O visit me with thy salvation. *Ps. cvi.* 4. Consider mine affliction, and deliver me. *Ps. cxix.* 153. Is there not an appointed time to man upon earth? *Job vii.* 1. It is good that a man should both hope and quietly wait for the salvation of the Lord. *La. iii.* 26. I waited patiently for the Lord; and he inclined unto me, and heard my cry. *Ps. xl.* 1. Have mercy upon me, O Lord; for I am weak; O Lord, heal me; for my bones are vexed. Return, O Lord, deliver my soul : O save me for thy mercies' sake. *Ps. vi.* 2. 4. They brought to him a man sick of the palsy, lying on a bed : and Jesus said unto the sick of the palsy, Son, be of good cheer;

thy sins be forgiven thee. That ye may know that the Son of man hath power on earth to forgive sins, (then saith he to the sick of the palsy,) Arise, take up thy bed, and go unto thine house. And he arose, and departed to his house. *Mat. ix.* 2. 6, 7. *See also, Ps. xlix.* 15.—*cxvi.* 3, 4.

4. That, if it shall be thy pleasure to prolong *his* days here on earth, *he* may live to thee, and be an instrument of thy glory, by serving thee faithfully, and doing good in *his* generation:

4. Who can tell whether God will be gracious to me, that the child may live? 2 *Sa. xii.* 22. In him we live, and move, and have our being. *Ac. xvii.* 28. He is thy life, and the length of thy days. *De. xxx.* 20. There is no man that hath power over the spirit to retain the spirit. *Ec. viii.* 8. He was sick nigh unto death; but God had mercy on him. *Ph. ii.* 27. I shall not die, but live, and declare the works of the Lord. *Ps. cxviii.* 17. Forasmuch as Christ hath suffered for us in the flesh, arm yourselves likewise with the same mind: for he that hath suffered in the flesh hath ceased from sin; that he no longer should live the rest of his time in the flesh to the lusts of men, but to the will of God. 1 *Pe. iv.* 1, 2. They which live should not henceforth live unto themselves, but unto him which died for them, and rose again. 2 *Co. v.* 15. Come and hear, all ye that fear God, and I will declare what he hath done for my soul. *Ps. lxvi.* 16. O God, forsake me not; until I have shewed thy strength unto this generation, and thy power to every one that is to come. *Ps. lxxi.* 18. To do good and to communicate forget not: for with such sacrifices God is well pleased. *He. xiii.* 16. As we have therefore opportunity, let us do good unto all men, especially unto them who are of the household of faith. *Ga. vi.* 10. *See also,* 2 *Ch. xxiv.* 16.—*Ph. i.* 20 to 24.

5. or else receive *him* into those heavenly habitations, where the souls of them that sleep in the Lord Jesus enjoy perpetual rest and felicity. Grant this, O Lord, for thy mercies' sake, in the same thy Son our Lord Jesus Christ, who

5. In my Father's house are many mansions: I go to prepare a place for you. I will receive you unto myself. *John xiv.* 2, 3. Lord Jesus, receive my spirit. *Ac. vii.* 59. We know that if our earthly house of this tabernacle were dissolved, we have a building of God, an house not made with hands, eternal in the heavens. 2 *Co. v.* 1. If we believe that Jesus died and rose again, even so them also which sleep in Jesus will God bring with him. 1 *Th. iv.* 14. I heard a voice from heaven saying unto me, Write, Blessed are the dead which die in the Lord from henceforth: Yea, saith the Spirit, that they may rest from their labours; and their works do follow them. *Re.*

liveth and
reigneth with
thee and the
Holy Ghost,
ever one God,
world without
end. Amen.

xiv. 13. He shall enter into peace. *Is. lvii.* 2. There the
wicked cease from troubling; and there the weary be at rest.
Job iii. 17. Thou wilt shew me the path of life: in thy
presence is fulness of joy; at thy right hand there are pleasures for evermore. *Ps. xvi.* 11. Do thou for me, O God the
Lord, for thy name's sake: because thy mercy is good. *Ps.
cix.* 21. Arise for our help, and redeem us for thy mercies'
sake. *Ps. xliv.* 26. Alleluia: for the Lord God omnipotent
reigneth. *Re. xix.* 6. *See also,* 1 *Th. iv.* 17.—*Re. vii.* 14 *to* 17.—
Lu. xvi. 9.

CCXXII. *A Prayer for a sick person, when there appeareth small hope of recovery.*

1. O Father
of mercies, and
God of all com-
fort, our only
help in time
of need;

1. My prayer is unto thee, O Lord, in an acceptable time:
O God, in the multitude of thy mercy hear me. *Ps. lxix.* 13.
Great are thy tender mercies, O Lord, quicken me according
to thy judgments. *Ps. cxix.* 156. Blessed be God, even the
Father of our Lord Jesus Christ, the Father of mercies, and
the God of all comfort; who comforteth us in all our tribulation, that we may be able to comfort them which are in any
trouble, by the comfort wherewith we ourselves are comforted,
of God. 2 *Cor.* 3, 4. My soul, wait thou only upon God;
for my expectation is from him. *Ps. lxii.* 5. God is our refuge
and strength, a very present help in trouble. *Ps. xlvi.* 1. Give
us help from trouble: for vain is the help of man. *Ps. cviii.* 12.
Happy is he that hath the God of Jacob for his help, whose
hope is in the Lord his God. *Ps. cxlvi.* 5. Let us therefore
come boldly unto the throne of grace, that we may obtain
mercy, and find grace to help in time of need. *He. iv.* 16.

2. We fly unto
thee for suc-
cour in behalf
of this thy serv-
ant, here lying
under thy hand
in great weak-
ness of body.

2. O thou that hearest prayer, unto thee shall all flesh come.
Ps. lxv. 2. Come unto me, all ye that labour and are heavy
laden. *Mat. xi.* 28. In that he himself hath suffered being
tempted, he is able to succour them that are tempted. *He.
ii.* 18. Is any among you afflicted? let him pray. Is any
sick among you? let him call for the elders of the Church;
and let them pray over him: and the prayer of faith shall
save the sick. The effectual fervent prayer of a righteous

man availeth much. *Ja. v.* 13 *to* 16. And when Jesus was entered into Capernaum, there came unto him a centurion, beseeching him, and saying, Lord, my servant lieth at home sick of the palsy, grievously tormented. And Jesus saith unto him, I will come and heal him. *Mat. viii.* 5, 6, 7.

3. Look graciously upon him, O Lord; and the more the outward man decayeth, strengthen him, we beseech thee, so much the more continually with thy grace and Holy Spirit in the inner man.

3. The Lord make his face shine upon thee, and be gracious unto thee. *Nu. vi.* 25. Look thou upon me, and be merciful unto me. *Ps. cxix.* 132. My strength is dried up like a potsherd. *Ps. xxii.* 15. I am gone like the shadow when it declineth. *Ps. cix.* 23. When we cried unto the Lord God of our fathers, the Lord heard our voice, and looked on our affliction. *De. xxvi.* 7. The Lord will strengthen him upon the bed of languishing: thou wilt make all his bed in his sickness. *Ps. xli.* 3. For which cause we faint not: but though our outward man perish, yet the inward man is renewed day by day. *2 Co. iv.* 16. I bow my knees unto the Father of our Lord Jesus Christ, that he would grant you, according to the riches of his glory, to be strengthened with might by his Spirit in the inner man. *Ep. iii.* 14, 16.

4. Give him unfeigned repentance for all the errors of his life past, and stedfast faith in thy Son Jesus;

4. Repentance toward God, and faith toward our Lord Jesus Christ. *Ac. xx.* 21. Him hath God exalted, to give repentance to Israel, and forgiveness of sins. *Ac. v.* 31. Repentance to salvation not to be repented of. *2 Co. vii.* 10. Repentance unto life. *Ac. xi.* 18. Remember not the sins of my youth, nor my transgressions. For thy name's sake, O Lord, pardon mine iniquity; for it is great. *Ps. xxv.* 7, 11. God, having raised up his Son Jesus, sent him to bless you, in turning away every one of you from his iniquities. *Ac. iii.* 26. We are made partakers of Christ, if we hold the beginning of our confidence stedfast unto the end. *He. iii.* 14. Stedfast in the faith. *1 Pe. v.* 9.

5. that his sins may be done away by thy mercy, and his pardon sealed in heaven, before he go hence, and be no more seen.

5. According to the multitude of thy mercies do away mine offences. *Ps. li.* 1. Repent, and be converted, that your sins may be blotted out. *Ac. iii.* 19. By grace are ye saved through faith; and that not of yourselves: it is the gift of God. *Ep. ii.* 8. To him give all the prophets witness, that through his name whosoever believeth in him shall receive remission of sins. *Ac. x.* 43. Whatsoever ye shall bind on earth shall be bound in heaven: and whatsoever ye shall loose

on earth, shall be loosed in heaven. *Mat. xviii.* 18. Sealed with that Holy Spirit of promise, which is the earnest of our inheritance. *Ep. i.* 13, 14. Having this seal, The Lord knoweth them that are his. *2 Ti. ii.* 19. I heard the number of them which were sealed. *Re. vii.* 4. Man dieth, and wasteth away : yea, man giveth up the ghost, and where is he? As the waters fail from the sea, and the flood decayeth and drieth up : so man lieth down, and riseth not : till the heavens be no more, they shall not awake, nor be raised out of their sleep. *Job xiv.* 10, 11, 12. Whatsoever thy hand findeth to do, do it with thy might ; for there is no work, nor device, nor knowledge, nor wisdom, in the grave, whither thou goest. *Ec. ix.* 10. O spare me a little, that I may recover my strength : before I go hence, and be no more seen. *Ps. xxxix.* 15.

6. We know, O Lord, that there is no word impossible with thee ; and that, if thou wilt, thou canst even yet raise him up, and grant him a longer continuance amongst us :

6. Lord God, behold, thou hast made the heaven and the earth, by thy great power and stretched out arm, and there is nothing too hard for thee. *Je. xxxii.* 17. Speak the word only, and my servant shall be healed. *Mat. viii.* 8. With God nothing shall be impossible. *Lu. i.* 37. Lord, if thou hadst been here, my brother had not died. *John xi.* 32. By faith Abraham, when he was tried, offered up Isaac ; accounting that God was able to raise him up, even from the dead. *He. xi.* 17. 19. The prayer of faith shall save the sick, and the Lord shall raise him up. *Ja. v.* 15. Tell Hezekiah, Thus saith the Lord, the God of David thy father, I have heard thy prayer, I have seen thy tears : behold, I will heal thee : on the third day thou shalt go up unto the house of the Lord. And I will add unto thy days fifteen years. *2 Ki. xx.* 5, 6.

7. Yet forasmuch as in all appearance the time of *his* dissolution draweth near, so fit and prepare *him,* we beseech thee, against the hour of death, that after *his* departure hence in peace, and in thy favour, *his* soul may be received into

7. The time of my departure is at hand. I have fought a good fight, I have finished my course, I have kept the faith : henceforth there is laid up for me a crown of righteousness, which the Lord, the righteous Judge, shall give me at that day. *2 Ti. iv.* 6, 7, 8. Thus saith the Lord, Set thine house in order : for thou shalt die, and not live. *Is. xxxviii.* 1. Beloved, now are we the sons of God, and it doth not yet appear what we shall be : but we know that, when he shall appear, we shall be like him ; for we shall see him as he is. And every man that hath this hope in him, purifieth himself, even as he is pure. 1 *John iii.* 2, 3. Let your loins be girded

thine everlasting kingdom, through the merits and mediation of Jesus Christ, thine only Son, our Lord and Saviour. *Amen.*

about, and your lights burning; and ye yourselves like unto men that wait for their lord, when he will return from the wedding; that when he cometh and knocketh, they may open unto him immediately. Blessed are those servants, whom the lord when he cometh shall find watching: Be ye therefore ready also: for the Son of man cometh at an hour when ye think not. *Lu. xii.* 35, 36, 37. 40. They that were foolish took their lamps, and took no oil with them: but the wise took oil in their vessels with their lamps. *Mat. xxv.* 3, 4. Brethren, give diligence to make your calling and election sure: for if ye do these things, ye shall never fall: for so an entrance shall be ministered unto you abundantly into the everlasting kingdom of our Lord and Saviour Jesus Christ. *2 Pe. i.* 10, 11. He shall enter into peace: they shall rest in their beds. *Is. lvii.* 2. Mark the perfect man, and behold the upright: for the end of that man is peace. *Ps. xxxvii.* 37. Where sin abounded, grace did much more abound: that as sin hath reigned unto death, even so might grace reign through righteousness unto eternal life by Jesus Christ our Lord. *Ro. v.* 20, 21. I heard a voice from heaven, saying unto me, Write, Blessed are the dead which die in the Lord from henceforth: Yea, saith the Spirit, that they may rest from their labours; and their works do follow them. *Re. xiv.* 12. Father, I will that they also, whom thou hast given me, be with me where I am; that they may behold my glory. *John xvii.* 24. Come, ye blessed of my Father, inherit the kingdom prepared for you from the foundation of the world. *Mat. xxv.* 34. *See also, Lu. vii.* 2.—*Ge. v.* 24.—*Ro. viii.* 29, 30.—*2 Ti. i.* 10.

CCXXIII. A Commendatory Prayer for a sick person at the point of departure.

1. O Almighty God, with whom do live the spirits of just men made perfect, after they are delivered from their earthly prisons;

1. God spake, saying, I am the God of Abraham, and the God of Isaac, and the God of Jacob. He is not the God of the dead, but the God of the living. *Mar. xii.* 26, 27. Then shall the dust return to the earth as it was: and the spirit shall return unto God who gave it. *Ec. xii.* 7. Ye are come to the general assembly and Church of the firstborn, which are written in heaven, and to God the Judge of all, and to the spirits of

just men made perfect. *He. xii.* 22, 23: We that are in this tabernacle do groan, being burdened: not for that we would be unclothed, but clothed upon, that mortality might be swallowed up of life. We are always confident, knowing that, whilst we are at home in the body, we are absent from the Lord: we are confident, I say, and willing rather to be absent from the body, and to be present with the Lord. *2 Co. v.* 4. 6. 8.

2. We humbly commend the soul of this thy servant, our dear *brother,* into thy hands, as into the hands of a faithful Creator, and most merciful Saviour;.

2. And now, I commend you to God. *Ac. xx.* 32. The Lord Jesus Christ be with thy spirit. *2. Ti. iv.* 22. I know whom I have believed, and am persuaded that he is able to keep that which I have committed unto him against that day. *2 Ti. i.* 12. Lord Jesus, receive my spirit. *Ac. vii.* 59. Into thine hand I commit my spirit: thou hast redeemed me, O Lord God of truth. *Ps. xxxi.* 5. Let them that suffer according to the will of God commit the keeping of their souls to him in well doing, as unto a faithful Creator. *1 Pe. iv.* 19. The Father sent the Son to be the Saviour of the world. *1 John iv.* 14. In all things it behoved him to be made like unto his brethren, that he might be a merciful and faithful High Priest in things pertaining to God, to make reconciliation for the sins of the people. *He. ii.* 17. Greater love hath no man than this, that a man lay down his life for his friends. *John xv.* 13. *See also, Ep. ii.* 4, 5.

3. most humbly beseeching thee, that it may be precious in thy sight.

3. Hide not thy face from thy servant; hear me speedily. Draw nigh unto my soul, and redeem it. *Ps. lxix.* 17, 18. Say unto my soul, I am thy salvation. *Ps. xxxv.* 3. All souls are mine. *Eze. xviii.* 4. Gather not my soul with sinners, nor my life with bloody men. Redeem me, and be merciful unto me. *Ps. xxvi.* 9. 11. Let my life now be precious in thy sight. *2 Ki. i.* 14. My soul was precious in thine eyes this day. *1 Sa. xxvi.* 21.

4. Wash it, we pray thee, in the blood of that immaculate Lamb, that was slain to take away the sins of the world:

4. Wash me throughly from mine iniquity, and cleanse me from my sin. Wash me, and I shall be whiter than snow. *Ps. li.* 2. 7. Ye are washed, ye are sanctified, ye are justified in the Name of the Lord Jesus, and by the Spirit of our God. *1 Co. vi.* 11. Behold the Lamb of God, which taketh away the sin of the world. *John i.* 29. Ye know that ye were not redeemed with corruptible things, as silver and gold, but with the precious blood of Christ, as of a lamb without blemish and without

spot. 1 Pe. i. 18, 19. And they sung a new song, saying, Thou art worthy to take the book, and to open the seals thereof: for thou wast slain, and hast redeemed us to God by thy blood out of every kindred, and tongue, and people, and nation. Re. v. 9. These are they which came out of great tribulation, and have washed their robes, and made them white in the blood of the Lamb. Re. vii. 14. Unto him that loved us, and washed us from our sins in his own blood, and hath made us kings and priests unto God and his Father; to him be glory and dominion for ever and ever. Amen. Re. i. 5, 6.

5. That whatsoever defilements it may have contracted in the midst of this miserable and naughty world, through the lusts of the flesh, or the wiles of satan, being purged and done away,

5. The whole world lieth in wickedness. 1 John v. 19. Who can bring a clean thing out of an unclean? Job xiv. 4. There is not a just man upon earth, that doeth good, and sinneth not. Ec. vii. 20. Christ gave himself for our sins, that he might deliver us from this present evil world. Ga. 1. 4. The flesh lusteth against the Spirit and the Spirit against the flesh: and these are contrary the one to the other : so that ye cannot do the things that ye would. Ga. v. 17. Be sober, be vigilant; because your adversary the devil, as a roaring lion, walketh about, seeking whom he may devour. 1 Pe. v. 8. Lest satan should get an advantage of us: for we are not ignorant of his devices. 2 Co. ii. 11. The wiles of the devil. Ep. vi. 11. If any man sin, we have an Advocate with the Father, Jesus Christ the righteous. 1 John ii. 1. The blood of Jesus Christ his Son cleanseth us from all sin. 1 John i. 7. Have mercy upon me, O God, after thy great goodness : according to the multitude of thy mercies do away mine offences. Ps. li. 1.

6. it may be presented pure and without spot before thee.

6. Christ also loved the Church, and gave himself for it; that he might sanctify and cleanse it with the washing of water by the word, that he might present it to himself a glorious Church, not having spot, or wrinkle, or any such thing; but that it should be holy and without blemish. Ep. v. 25, 26, 27. And you, that were sometime alienated and enemies in your mind by wicked works, yet now hath he reconciled in the body of his flesh through death; to present you holy and unblameable and unreproveable in his sight. Col. i. 21, 22. Now unto him that is able to keep you from falling, and to present you faultless before the presence of his glory with exceeding joy, to the only wise God our Saviour, be glory and majesty. Jude 24, 25.

T

7. And teach us who survive, in this and other like daily spectacles of mortality, to see how frail and uncertain our own condition is;

7. It is better to go to the house of mourning, than to go to the house of feasting : for that is the end of all men ; and the living will lay it to his heart. *Ec. vii.* 2. As for man, his days are as grass : as a flower of the field, so he flourisheth. For the wind passeth over it, and it is gone ; and the place thereof shall know it no more. *Ps. ciii.* 15, 16. Lord, what is man, that thou takest knowledge of him ! or the son of man, that thou makest account of him ! Man is like to vanity : his days are as a shadow that passeth away. *Ps. cxliv.* 3, 4. Man dieth, and wasteth away : yea, man giveth up the ghost, and where is he ? As the waters fail from the sea, and the flood decayeth and drieth up; so man lieth down, and riseth not. *Job xiv.* 10, 11, 12. One dieth in his full strength, being wholly at ease and quiet. Another dieth in the bitterness of his soul, and never eateth with pleasure. *Job xxi.* 23. 25. They are destroyed from morning to evening : they perish for ever without any regarding it. *Job iv.* 20. Oh that they were wise, that they understood this, that they would consider their latter end ! *De. xxxii.* 29. Lord, make me to know mine end, and the measure of my days, what it is ; that I may know how frail 1 am. Behold, thou hast made my days as an handbreadth ; and mine age is as nothing before thee : verily every man at his best state is altogether vanity. *Ps. xxxix.* 4, 5.

8. and so to number our days, that we may seriously apply our hearts to that holy and heavenly wisdom, whilst we live here, which may in the end bring us to life everlasting, through the merits of Jesus Christ thine only Son our Lord. *Amen.*

8. Their days did he consume in vanity, and their years in trouble. When he slew them, then they sought him : and they returned and enquired early after God. And they remembered that God was their rock, and the high God their Redeemer. *Ps. lxxviii.* 33, 34, 35. So teach us to number our days, that we may apply our hearts unto wisdom. *Ps. xc.* 12. Redeeming the time, because the days are evil. See then that ye walk circumspectly, not as fools, but as wise. *Ep. vi.* 16. 15. Behold, the fear of the Lord, that is wisdom ; and to depart from evil is understanding. *Job xxviii.* 28. The law of the wise is a fountain of life, to depart from the snares of death. *Pr. xiii.* 14. Set your hearts unto all the words which I testify among you this day : for it is not a vain thing for you ; because it is your life. *De. xxxii.* 46, 47. God will render to every man according to his deeds : to them who by patient continuance in well doing seek for glory and honour

and immortality, eternal life. *Ro. ii.* 6, 7. As sin hath reigned unto death, even so might grace reign through righteousness unto eternal life by Jesus Christ our Lord. *Ro. v.* 21. The gift of God is eternal life through Jesus Christ our Lord. *Ro. vi.* 23.

CCXXIV. A Prayer for persons troubled in mind or in conscience.

1. O Blessed Lord, the Father of mercies, and the God of all comforts; We beseech thee, look down in pity and compassion upon this thy afflicted servant.

1. Blessed be God, even the Father of our Lord Jesus Christ, the Father of mercies, and the God of all comfort. 2 *Co. i.* 3. Great are thy tender mercies, O Lord. *Ps. cxix.* 156. Many are the afflictions of the righteous: but the Lord delivereth him out of them all. *Ps. xxxiv.* 19. Like as a father pitieth his children, so the Lord pitieth them that fear him. *Ps. ciii.* 13. Ye have heard of the patience of Job, and have seen the end of the Lord; that the Lord is very pitiful, and of tender mercy. *Ja. v.* 11. Look down from heaven, and behold from the habitation of thy holiness and of thy glory: where is thy zeal and thy strength, the sounding of thy bowels and of thy mercies toward me? are they restrained? Doubless thou art our Father;—thou, O Lord, art our Father, our Redeemer; thy name is from everlasting. *Is. lxiii.* 15, 16. Though he cause grief, yet will he have compassion according to the multitude of his mercies. For he doth not afflict willingly nor grieve the children of men. It is of the Lord's mercies that we are not consumed, because his compassions fail not. *La. iii.* 32, 33. 22. *See also, Is. xlix.* 15, 16.

2. Thou writest bitter things against him, and makest him to possess his former iniquities; thy wrath lieth hard upon him, and his soul is full of trouble.

2. Thou writest bitter things against me, and makest me to possess the iniquities of my youth. *Job xiii.* 26. And she said unto Elijah, What have I to do with thee, O thou man of God? art thou come unto me to call my sin to remembrance, and to slay my son? 1 *Ki. xvii.* 18. My soul is full of troubles: and my life draweth nigh unto the grave. I am counted with them that go down into the pit: I am as a man that hath no strength: free among the dead, like the slain that lie in the grave, whom thou rememberest no more: and they are cut off from thy hand. Thou hast laid me in the lowest pit, in darkness, in the deeps. Thy wrath lieth hard upon me, and thou hast afflicted me with all thy waves. *Ps. lxxxviii.* 3 *to* 7. *See also, Ps.* xxxviii.—*Is. xxxviii.* 10 *to* 15.

3. But, O merciful God, who hast written, thy holy Word for our learning, that we, through patience and comfort of thy holy Scriptures, might have hope; give him a right understanding of himself, and of thy threats and promises; that he may neither cast away his confidence in thee, nor place it any where but in thee.

3. Whatsoever things were written aforetime were written for our learning, that we through patience and comfort of the Scriptures might have hope. *Ro. xv.* 4. I also cease not to give thanks for you, making mention of you in my prayers; that the God of our Lord Jesus Christ, the Father of glory, may give unto you the spirit of wisdom and revelation in the knowledge of him: the eyes of your understanding being enlightened. *Ep. i.* 15 to 18. Examine yourselves; prove your ownselves. Know ye not your ownselves? 2 *Co. xiii.* 5. If our heart condemn us, God is greater than our heart, and knoweth all things. Beloved, if our heart condemn us not, then have we confidence toward God. 1 *John iii.* 20, 21. Who will render to every man according to his deeds: to them who by patient continuance in well doing seek for glory and honour and immortality, eternal life: but unto them that are contentious, and do not obey the truth, but obey unrighteousness, indignation and wrath, tribulation and anguish, upon every soul of man that doeth evil; but glory, honour, and peace, to every man that worketh good. *Ro. ii.* 6 to 10. If we would judge ourselves, we should not be judged. 1 *Co. xi.* 31. Open thou mine eyes, that I may behold wondrous things out of thy law. Make me to understand the way of thy precepts. Give me understanding, and I shall keep thy law; yea, I shall observe it with my whole heart. Teach me good judgment and knowledge. *Ps. cxix.* 18. 27. 34. 66. The Son of God, Jesus Christ, was not yea and nay, but in him was yea. For all the promises of God in him are yea, and in him Amen, unto the glory of God by us. 2 *Co. i.* 19, 20. Cast not away therefore your confidence, which hath great recompense of reward. For ye have need of patience, that, after ye have done the will of God, ye might receive the promise. *He. x.* 35, 36. O Lord of hosts, blessed is the man that trusteth in thee. *Ps. lxxxiv.* 12. Trust ye in the Lord for ever: for in the Lord JEHOVAH is everlasting strength. *Is. xxvi.* 4. Put not your trust in princes, nor in the son of man, in whom there is no help. His breath goeth forth, he returneth to his earth; in that very day his thoughts perish. Happy is he that hath the God of Jacob for his help, whose hope is in the Lord his God: which made heaven, and earth, the sea, and all that therein is: which keepeth truth for ever.

Ps. cxlvi. 3 *to* 6. O Lord our God, other lords beside thee have had dominion over us: but by thee only will we make mention of thy name. *Is. xxvi.* 13. Thou art my hope, O Lord God: thou art my trust from my youth. *Ps. lxxi.* 5. Blessed is the man that trusteth in the Lord, and whose hope the Lord is. *Je. xvii.* 7.

4. Give *him* strength against all *his* temptations, and heal all his distempers.

4. He said unto me, My grace is sufficient for thee: for my strength is made perfect in weakness. *2 Co. xii.* 9. For in that he himself hath suffered being tempted, he is able to succour them that are tempted. *He. ii.* 18. Though now for a season, if need be, ye are in heaviness through manifold temptations. 1 *Pe. i.* 6. My brethren, count it all joy when ye fall into divers temptations. Blessed is the man that endureth temptation. *Ja. i.* 2. 12. The God of all grace, who hath called us unto his eternal glory by Christ Jesus, after that ye have suffered awhile, make you perfect, stablish, strengthen, settle you. 1 *Pe. v.* 10. I said, Lord, be merciful unto me: heal my soul. *Ps. xli.* 4. I have seen his ways, and will heal him. *Is. lvii.* 18. I will heal their backsliding, I will love them freely: for mine anger is turned away from him. *Ho. xiv.* 4. Heal me, O Lord, and I shall be healed; for thou art my praise. *Je. xvii.* 14. I will restore health unto thee, and I will heal thee of thy wounds, saith the Lord. *Je. xxx.* 17. Bless the Lord, O my soul, and forget not all his benefits: who forgiveth all thine iniquities; who healeth all thy diseases; who redeemeth thy life from destruction. *Ps. ciii.* 2, 3, 4.

5. Break not the bruised reed, nor quench the smoking flax. Shut not up thy tender mercies in displeasure; but make *him* to hear of joy and gladness, that the bones which thou hast broken may rejoice.

5. A bruised reed shall he not break, and smoking flax shall he not quench, till he send forth judgment unto victory. *Mat. xii.* 20. Hath God forgotten to be gracious: and will he shut up his lovingkindness in displeasure? *Ps. lxxvii.* 9. Make me to hear joy and gladness; that the bones which thou hast broken may rejoice. The sacrifices of God are a broken spirit: a broken and a contrite heart, O God, thou wilt not despise. *Ps. li.* 8. 17. Come unto me, all ye that labour and are heavy laden, and I will give you rest. *Mat. xi.* 28. The Lord will not cast off for ever: but though he cause grief, yet will he have compassion according to the multitude of his mercies. For he doth not afflict willingly nor grieve the

children of men. *La. iii.* 31, 32, 33. Wherefore lift up the hands which hang down, and the feeble knees. *He. xii.* 12. Thou hast turned for me my mourning into dancing: thou hast put off my sackcloth, and girded me with gladness. *Ps. xxx.* 11. They that sow in tears shall reap in joy. He that goeth forth and weepeth, bearing precious seed, shall doubtless come again with rejoicing, bringing his sheaves with him. *Ps. cxxvi.* 5, 6.

6. Deliver *him* from fear of the enemy, and lift up the light of thy countenance upon *him*, and give *him* peace, through the merits and mediation of Jesus Christ our Lord. *Amen.*

6. Hear my voice, O God, in my prayer: preserve my life from fear of the enemy. *Ps. lxiv.* 1. From the end of the earth will I cry unto thee, when my heart is overwhelmed: lead me to the rock that is higher than I. For thou hast been a shelter for me, and a strong tower from the enemy. *Ps. lxi.* 2, 3. I will set him in safety from him that puffeth at him. *Ps. xii.* 5. Because he hath set his love upon me, therefore will I deliver him: I will set him on high, because he hath known my name. He shall call upon me, and I will answer him: I will be with him in trouble. I will deliver him, and honour him. With long life will I satisfy him, and shew him my salvation. *Ps. xci.* 14, 15, 16. There be many that say, Who will shew us any good? Lord, lift thou up the light of thy countenance upon us. *Ps. iv.* 6. The Lord lift up his countenance upon thee, and give thee peace. *Nu. vi.* 26. Being justified by faith, we have peace with God through our Lord Jesus Christ. *Ro. v.* 1. The peace of God, which passeth all understanding, shall keep your hearts and minds through Christ Jesus. *Ph. iv.* 7.

THE COMMUNION OF THE SICK.

CCXXV. *A Prayer for patience under affliction.*

1. Almighty, everliving God, Maker of mankind, who dost correct those whom thou dost love, and chastise every one whom thou dost receive;

1. I, even I, am he, and there is no god with me: I kill, and I make alive; I wound, and I heal: neither is there any that can deliver out of my hand. For I lift up my hand to heaven, and say, I live for ever. *De. xxxii.* 39, 40. Now, O Lord, thou art our Father; we are the clay, and thou our potter, and we all are the work of thy hand. Be not wroth very sore, O Lord, neither remember iniquity for ever: behold, see, we beseech thee, we are all thy people. *Is. lxiv.* 8, 9. My son, despise

THE COMMUNION OF THE SICK.—*A Prayer for patience, &c.* 143

not thou the chastening of the Lord, nor faint when thou art rebuked of him: for whom the Lord loveth he chasteneth, and scourgeth every son whom he receiveth. If ye endure chastening, God dealeth with you as with sons. *He. xii.* 5, 6, 7. Behold, happy is the man whom God correcteth: therefore despise not thou the chastening of the Almighty: for he maketh sore, and bindeth up: he woundeth, and his hands make whole. *Job v.* 17, 18.

2. We beseech thee to have mercy upon this thy servant visited with thine hand,

2. Thou, O Lord, art a God full of compassion, and gracious, longsuffering, and plenteous in mercy and truth. O turn unto me, and have mercy upon me; give thy strength unto thy servant, and save the son of thine handmaid. *Ps. lxxxvi.* 15, 16. Let thy mercies come also unto me, O Lord, even thy salvation, according to thy word. Let thy tender mercies come unto me, that I may live: for thy law is my delight. *Ps. cxix.* 41. 77. Day and night thy hand was heavy upon me. My moisture is turned into the drought of summer. *Ps. xxxii.* 4. Remove thy stroke away from me: I am consumed by the blow of thine hand. *Ps. xxxix.* 10. *See also,* 1 *Sa. v.* 9.—*Job xix.* 27.

3. and to grant that *he* may take *his* sickness patiently, and recover *his* bodily health, (if it be thy gracious will;) and whensoever *his* soul shall depart from the body, it may be without spot presented unto thee; through Jesus Christ our Lord. *Amen.*

3. My brethren, count it all joy when ye fall into divers temptations; knowing this, that the trying of your faith worketh patience. But let patience have her perfect work, that ye may be perfect and entire, wanting nothing. *Ja. i.* 2, 3, 4. Humble yourselves therefore under the mighty hand of God, that he may exalt you in due time. 1 *Pe. v.* 6. Then Hezekiah turned his face toward the wall, and prayed unto the Lord, and said, Remember now, O Lord, I beseech thee, how I have walked before thee in truth and with a perfect heart, and have done that which is good in thy sight. And Hezekiah wept sore. Then came the word of the Lord to Isaiah, saying, Go and say to Hezekiah, Thus saith the Lord, the God of David thy father, I have heard thy prayer, I have seen thy tears: behold, I will add unto thy days fifteen years. *Is. xxxviii.* 2 *to* 5. O spare me, that I may recover strength, before I go hence, and be no more. *Ps. xxxix.* 13. Father, if thou be willing, remove this cup from me: nevertheless not my will, but thine, be done. *Lu. xxii.* 42. We that are in this tabernacle do groan, being burdened: not for that we would be unclothed, but clothed upon, that mortality

might be swallowed up of life. 2 *Co. v.* 4. Then shall the dust return to the earth as it was: and the spirit shall return unto God who gave it. *Ec. xii.* 7. I am in a strait betwixt two, having a desire to depart, and to be with Christ; which is far better. *Ph. i.* 23. To day shalt thou be with me in paradise. *Lu. xxiii.* 43. Christ loved the Church, and gave himself for it; that he might sanctify and cleanse it with the washing of water by the word, that he might present it to himself a glorious Church, not having spot, or wrinkle, or any such thing; but that it should be holy and without blemish. *Ep. v.* 25, 26, 27. Ye are the body of Christ, and members in particular. 1 *Co. xii.* 27. Now unto him that is able to keep you from falling, and to present you faultless before the presence of his glory with exceeding joy, to the only wise God our Saviour, be glory and majesty, dominion and power, both now and ever. Amen. *Jude* 24, 25.

The Epistle. Hebrews xii. 5, 6.—*My son, despise not thou the chastening of the Lord, nor faint when thou art rebuked of him. For whom the Lord loveth he chasteneth; and scourgeth every son whom he receiveth.*

The Gospel. John v. 24.—*Verily, verily I say unto you, He that heareth my word, and believeth on him that sent me, hath everlasting life, and shall not come into condemnation; but is passed from death unto life.*

THE ORDER FOR

THE BURIAL OF THE DEAD.

The introductory Sentences, Psalms, and Lesson.

I am the resurrection and the life, saith the Lord: he that believeth in me, though he were dead, yet shall he live. And whosoever liveth and believeth in me, shall never die. John xi. 25, 26. *I know that my Redeemer liveth, and that he shall stand at the latter day upon the earth. And though after my skin worms destroy this body; yet in my flesh shall I see God: whom I shall see for myself, and mine eyes shall behold, and not another.* Job xix. 25, 26, 27. *We brought nothing into this world, and it is certain we can carry nothing out. The Lord gave, and the Lord hath taken away; blessed be the Name of the Lord.* 1 Tim. vi. 7. Job i. 21.

Psalm xxxix.—I said, I will take heed to my ways: that I offend not in my tongue.—I will keep my mouth as it were with a bridle: while the ungodly is in my sight.—I held my tongue, and spake nothing: I kept silence, yea, even from good words; but it was pain and grief to me.—My heart was hot within me, and while I was thus musing, the fire kindled: and at the last I spake with my tongue.—Lord, let me know my end, and the number of my days: that I may be certified how long I have to live.—Behold, thou hast made my days as it were a span long: and mine age is even as nothing in respect of thee, and verily every man living is altogether vanity.—For man walketh in a vain shadow, and disquieteth himself in vain: he heapeth up riches, and cannot tell who shall gather them.—And now, Lord, what is my hope: truly my hope is even in thee.—Deliver me from all mine offences: and make me not a rebuke unto the foolish.—I became dumb, and opened not my mouth: for it was thy doing.—Take thy plague away from me: I am even consumed by means of thy heavy hand.—When thou with rebukes dost chasten man for sin, thou makest his beauty to consume away, like as it were a moth fretting a garment: every man therefore is but vanity. —Hear my prayer, O Lord, and with thine ears consider my calling: hold not thy peace at my tears.—For I am a stranger with thee: and a sojourner, as all my fathers were.—O spare me a little, that I may recover my strength: before I go hence, and be no more seen.— Glory be to the Father, &c. As it was in the, &c.

Psalm xc.—Lord, thou hast been our refuge: from one generation to another.—Before the mountains were brought forth, or ever the earth and the world were made: thou art God from everlasting, and world without end.—Thou turnest man to destruction: again thou sayest, Come again, ye children of men.—For a thousand years in thy sight are but as yesterday: seeing that is past as a watch in the night.—As soon as thou scatterest them, they are even as a sleep: and fade away suddenly like the grass.—In the morning it is green, and groweth up: but in the evening it is cut down, dried up, and withered.—For we consume away in thy displeasure: and are afraid at thy wrathful indignation.—Thou hast set our misdeeds before thee: and our secret sins in the light of thy countenance.—For when thou art angry, all our days are gone: we bring our years to an end, as it were a tale that is told.— The days of our age are threescore years and ten, and though men be so strong that they come to fourscore years: yet is their strength then but labour and sorrow; so soon passeth it away, and we are gone.—But who regardeth the power of thy wrath: for even thereafter as a man feareth, so is thy displeasure.—So teach us to number our days: that we may apply our hearts unto wisdom.—Turn thee again, O Lord, at the last: and be gracious unto thy servants.—O satisfy us with thy mercy, and that soon: so shall we rejoice and be glad all the days of our life.—Comfort us again, now after the time that thou hast plagued us: and for the years wherein we have suffered adversity.—Shew thy servants thy work: and their children thy glory.—And the glorious Majesty of the Lord our God be upon us: prosper thou the work of our hands upon us, O prosper thou our handy-work.—Glory be to the Father, &c. As it was in the, &c.

1 Cor. xv. 20.—Now is Christ risen from the dead, and become the first-fruits of them that slept. For since by man came death, by man came also the resurrection of the dead.

U

For as in Adam all die, even so in Christ shall all be made alive. But every man in his own order : Christ the first-fruits ; afterward they that are Christ's, at his coming. Then cometh the end, when he shall have delivered up the kingdom to God, even the Father ; when he shall have put down all rule, and all authority, and power. For he must reign till he hath put all enemies under his feet. The last enemy that shall be destroyed is death : For he hath put all things under his feet. But when he saith, All things are put under him, it is manifest that he is excepted which did put all things under him. And when all things shall be subdued unto him, then shall the Son also himself be subject unto him that put all things under him, that God may be all in all. Else what shall they do which are baptized for the dead, if the dead rise not at all? Why are they then baptized for the dead? And why stand we in jeopardy every hour? I protest by your rejoicing which I have in Christ Jesus our Lord, I die daily. If after the manner of men I have fought with beasts at Ephesus, what advantageth it me if the dead rise not? Let us eat and drink, for to morrow we die. Be not deceived ; evil communications corrupt good manners. Awake to righteousness, and sin not ; for some have not the knowledge of God: I speak this to your shame. But some man will say, How are the dead raised up? and with what body do they come? Thou fool, that which thou sowest is not quickened except it die. And that which thou sowest, thou sowest not that body that shall be, but bare grain, it may chance of wheat, or of some other grain. But God giveth it a body, as it hath pleased him, and to every seed his own body. All flesh is not the same flesh, but there is one kind of flesh of men, another flesh of beasts, another of fishes, and another of birds. There are also celestial bodies, and bodies terrestrial ; but the glory of the celestial is one, and the glory of the terrestrial is another. There is one glory of the sun, and another glory of the moon, and another glory of the stars ; for one star differeth from another star in glory. So also is the resurrection of the dead : It is sown in corruption ; it is raised in incorruption : It is sown in dishonour ; it is raised in glory : It is sown in weakness ; it is raised in power : It is sown a natural body ; it is raised a spiritual body. There is a natural body, and there is a spiritual body. And so it is written, The first man Adam was made a living soul, the last Adam was made a quickening spirit. Howbeit, that was not first which is spiritual ; but that which is natural, and afterward that which is spiritual. The first man is of the earth, earthy : the second man is the Lord from heaven. As is the earthy, such are they that are earthy : and as is the heavenly, such are they also that are heavenly. And as we have borne the image of the earthy, we shall also bear the image of the heavenly. Now this I say, brethren, that flesh and blood cannot inherit the kingdom of God : neither doth corruption inherit incorruption. Behold, I shew you a mystery : We shall not all sleep, but we shall all be changed, in a moment, in the twinkling of an eye, at the last trump ; (for the trumpet shall sound, and the dead shall be raised incorruptible, and we shall be changed.) For this corruptible must put on incorruption, and this mortal must put on immortality. So when this corruptible shall have put on incorruption, and this mortal shall have put on immortality, then shall be brought to pass the saying that is written, Death is swallowed up in victory. O death, where is thy sting? O grave, where is thy victory? The sting of death is sin, and the strength of sin is the law. But thanks be to God which giveth us the victory, through our Lord Jesus Christ. Therefore, my beloved brethren, be ye stedfast, unmoveable, always abounding in the work of the Lord, forasmuch as ye know that your labour is not in vain in the Lord.

CCXXVI. Meditations preparatory to the placing the corpse in the earth.

1. Man that is born of a woman is of few days, and full of trouble. He cometh forth like a flower, and is cut down: he fleeth also as a shadow, and continueth not. *Job xiv.* 1, 2. For all flesh is as grass, and all the glory of man as the flower of grass. 1 *Pe. i.* 24. As for man, his days are as grass : as a flower of the field, so he flourisheth. For the wind passeth over it, and it is gone ; and the place thereof shall know it no more. *Ps. ciii.* 15, 16. Man is born unto

1. Man that is born of a woman hath but a short time to live, and is full of misery. He cometh up, and is cut down, like a flower ; he fleeth as it were a shadow, and never continueth in one stay.

trouble, as the sparks fly upward. *Job v.* 7. For all his days are sorrows, and his travail grief; yea, his heart taketh not rest in the night. *Ec. ii.* 23. And Jacob said unto Pharaoh, The days of the years of my pilgrimage are an hundred and thirty years : few and evil have the days of the years of my life been. *Ge. xlvii.* 9. Behold, thou hast made my days as an handbreadth ; and mine age is as nothing before thee. *Ps. xxxix.* 5. My days are swifter than a post : they flee away, they see no good. They are passed away as the swift ships : as the eagle that hasteth to the prey. *Job ix.* 25, 26. The days of our years are threescore years and ten; and if by reason of strength they be fourscore years, yet is their strength labour and sorrow ; for it is soon cut off, and we fly away. Thou carriest them away as with a flood ; they are as a sleep : in the morning they are like grass which groweth up. In the morning it flourisheth, and groweth up ; in the evening it is cut down, and withereth. For we are consumed by thine anger, and by thy wrath are we troubled. *Ps. xc.* 10. 5, 6, 7. We are sojourners as were all our fathers : our days on the earth are as a shadow, and there is none abiding. *1 Ch. xxix.* 15. One generation passeth away, and another cometh. *Ec. i.* 4. See also, *Is. xl.* 5 to 8.—*Ja. i.* 10, 11.

2. In the midst of life we are in death : of whom may we seek for succour, but of thee, O Lord, who for our sins art justly displeased ?

2. Boast not thyself of to-morrow ; for thou knowest not what a day may bring forth. *Pr. xxvii.* 1. Ye know not what shall be on the morrow. For what is your life ? It is even a vapour, that appeareth for a little time, and then vanisheth away. *Ja. iv.* 14. There is but a step between me and death. *1 Sa. xx.* 3. We had the sentence of death in ourselves. *2 Co. i.* 9. As the partridge sitteth on eggs, and hatcheth them not ; so he that getteth riches, and not by right, shall leave them in the midst of his days, and at his end shall be a fool. *Je. xvii.* 11. In those days was Hezekiah sick unto death. And the prophet Isaiah the son of Amoz came to him, and said unto him, Thus saith the Lord, Set thine house in order ; for thou shalt die, and not live. *2 Ki. xx.* 1. Lord, to whom shall we go ? thou hast the words of eternal life. *John vi.* 68. O God, thou hast cast us off, thou hast scattered us, thou hast been displeased ; O turn thyself to us again. *Ps. lx.* 1. Thou hast set our iniquities before

then, our secret sins in the light of thy countenance. Who knoweth the power of thine anger? even according to thy fear, so is thy wrath. *Ps. xc. 8. 11.* I said, Lord, be merciful unto me: heal my soul; for I have sinned against thee. *Ps. xli. 4.* O Lord, my strength, and my fortress, and my refuge in the day of affliction. *Je. xvi. 19.* God is our refuge and strength, a very present help in trouble. *Ps. xlvi. 1.* Who is a rock save our God? *Ps. xviii. 31.* All have sinned, and come short of the glory of God. *Ro. iii. 23.* God is angry with the wicked every day. *Ps. vii. 11.* Look unto me, and be ye saved, all the ends of the earth: for I am God, and there is none else. *Is. xlv. 22.* I, even I, am he that blotteth out thy transgressions. *Is. xliii. 25.*

3. Who is like unto thee, O Lord, among the gods? who is like thee, glorious in holiness. *Ex. xv. 11.* There is none holy as the Lord: for there is none beside thee: neither is there any rock like our God. *1 Sa. ii. 2.* Who in the heaven can be compared unto the Lord? who among the sons of the mighty can be likened unto the Lord? O Lord God of hosts, who is a strong Lord like unto thee? *Ps. lxxxix. 6. 8.* The Lord thy God in the midst of thee is mighty; he will save, he will rejoice over thee with joy; he will rest in his love. *Zep. iii. 17.* O the hope of Israel, the Saviour thereof in time of trouble, why shouldest thou be as a stranger in the land, and as a wayfaring man that turneth aside to tarry for a night? why shouldest thou be as a man astonied, as a mighty man that cannot save? *Je. xiv. 8, 9.* Thou art a God ready to pardon, gracious and merciful, slow to anger, and of great kindness. Thou art a gracious and merciful God. *Ne. ix. 17. 31.* Thou shalt know that I the Lord am thy Saviour and thy Redeemer, the mighty one of Jacob. *Is. lx. 16.* Forasmuch as the children are partakers of flesh and blood, he also himself likewise took part of the same; that through death he might destroy him that had the power of death, that is, the devil; and deliver them who through fear of death were all their lifetime subject to bondage. *He. ii. 14, 15.* The Lord knoweth how to deliver the godly out of temptations. *2 Ps. ii. 9.* Deliver us from evil. *Mat. vi. 13.* Gather not my soul with sinners, nor my life with bloody men. *Ps. xxvi. 9.*

Marginal note: 3. Yet, O Lord God most holy, O Lord most mighty, O holy and most merciful Saviour, deliver us not into the bitter pains of eternal death.

These shall go away into everlasting punishment. *Mat. xxv.*
46. Who among us shall dwell with the devouring fire? who
among us shall dwell with everlasting burnings? *Is. xxxiii.*
14. He that overcometh shall not be hurt of the second
death. *Re. ii. 11.*

4. Lord, all my desire is before thee; and my groaning
is not hid from thee. *Ps. xxxviii. 9.* Neither is there any
creature that is not manifest in his sight: but all things are
naked and opened unto the eyes of him with whom we have
to do: *He. iv. 13.* Lord, bow down thine ear, and hear.
2 Ki. xix. 16. Hear, O Lord, and have mercy upon me,
Lord, be thou my helper. *Ps. xxx. 10.* Lord, hear my voice:
let thine ears be attentive to the voice of my supplications.
Ps. cxxx. 2. The eyes of the Lord are over the righteous,
and his ears are open unto their prayers. *1 Pe. iii. 12.* Let
the priests, the ministers of the Lord, weep between the
porch and the altar, and let them say, Spare thy people, O
Lord, and give not thine heritage to reproach. *Joel ii. 17.*
They shall be mine, saith the Lord of hosts, in that day when
I make up my jewels; and I will spare them, as a man spareth his own son that serveth him. *Mal. iii. 17.* Thou art holy,
O thou that inhabitest the praises of Israel. *Ps. xxii. 3.* The
mighty God, even the Lord, hath spoken, and called the earth
from the rising of the sun unto the going down thereof. *Ps. l. 1.*
The waves of the sea are mighty, and rage horribly: but
yet the Lord, who dwelleth on high, is mightier. *Ps. xciii. 5.*
Ye denied the Holy One and the Just. *Ac. iii. 14.* The
Saviour of all men. *1 Ti. iv. 10.* It behoved him to be made
like unto his brethren, that he might be a merciful and faithful
High Priest, in things pertaining to God, to make reconcili-
nation for the sins of the people. *He. ii. 17.* It is he which
was ordained of God to be the Judge of quick and dead. *Ac.*
x. 42. Thou art worthy, O Lord, to receive glory and honour
and power. *Re. iv. 11.* The sorrows of death compassed me,
and the pains of hell gat hold upon me: I found trouble and
sorrow. Then called I upon the name of the Lord; O Lord,
I beseech thee, deliver my soul. *Ps. cxvi. 3, 4.* But now thus
saith the Lord that created thee, O Jacob, and he that formed
thee, O Israel, Fear not. When thou passest through the

waters I will be with thee; and through the rivers, they shall not overflow thee. For I am the Lord thy God, the Holy One of Israel, thy Saviour. *Is. xliii.* 1, 2, 3. Yea, though I walk through the valley of the shadow of death, I will fear no evil: for thou art with me. *Ps. xxiii.* 4. They stoned Stephen, calling upon God, and saying, Lord Jesus, receive my spirit. And he kneeled down, and cried with a loud voice, Lord, lay not this sin to their charge. And when he had said this, he fell asleep. *Ac. vii.* 59, 60.

CCXXVII. *The Solemn Interment.*

1. Forasmuch as it hath pleased Almighty God of his great mercy to take unto himself the soul of our dear *brother* here departed,

1. The Lord killeth, and maketh alive: he bringeth down to the grave, and bringeth up. 1 *Sa. ii.* 6. Thou takest away their breath, they die, and are turned to their dust. *Ps. civ.* 29. Why died I not from the womb? For now should I have lain still and been quiet, I should have slept: then had I been at rest. There the wicked cease from troubling; and there the weary be at rest. *Job iii.* 11. 13. 17. In very deed for this cause have I raised thee up, for to shew in thee my power. *Ex. ix.* 16. Though a sinner do evil an hundred times, and his days be prolonged, yet surely I know that it shall be well with them that fear God: but it shall not be well with the wicked. *Ec. viii.* 12, 13. Because thine heart was tender, and thou hast humbled thyself before the Lord, I will gather thee unto thy fathers, and thou shalt be gathered into thy grave in peace; and thine eyes shall not see all the evil which I will bring upon this place. 2 *Ki. xxii.* 19, 20. Him that dieth of Jeroboam in the city shall the dogs eat; and him that dieth in the field shall the fowls of the air eat: for the Lord hath spoken it. Arise thou therefore, get thee to thine own house: and when thy feet enter into the city, the child shall die. And all Israel shall mourn for him, and bury him: for he only of Jeroboam shall come to the grave. 1 *Ki. xiv.* 11, 12, 13. Merciful men are taken away, from the evil to come. *Is. lvii.* 1. I am in a strait betwixt two, having a desire to depart, and to be with Christ; which is far better. *Ph. i.* 23. Then shall the spirit return unto God who gave it. *Ec. xii.* 7. In the sweat of thy face shalt thou eat bread, till

thou return unto the ground; for out of it wast thou taken : for dust thou art, and unto dust shalt thou return. *Ge. iii.* 19.

2. We therefore commit *his* body to the ground; earth to earth, ashes to ashes, dust to dust;

2. And Sarah died: and Abraham stood up before his dead, and spake unto the sons of Heth, saying, Give me a possession of a burying place with you, that I may bury my dead out of my sight. And the children of Heth answered, In the choice of our sepulchres bury thy dead: none of us shall withhold from thee his sepulchre, but that thou mayest bury thy dead. And Abraham spake unto Ephron in the audience of the people of the land, saying, I will give thee money for the field; take it of me, and I will bury my dead there. And after this, Abraham buried Sarah his wife in the cave of the field of Machpelah before Mamre; the same is Hebron in the land of Canaan. *Ge. xxiii.* 2 to 6. 12, 13. 19. This man [Joseph of Arimathea] went unto Pilate, and begged the body of Jesus. And he took it down, and wrapped it in linen, and laid it in a sepulchre that was hewn in stone, wherein never man before was laid. *Lu. xxiii.* 52, 53. The first man is of the earth, earthy. 1 *Co. xv.* 47. Then shall the dust return to the earth as it was. *Ec. xii.* 7. And Abraham answered and said, Behold, now, I have taken upon me to speak unto the Lord, which am but dust and ashes. *Ge. xviii.* 27. All are of the dust, and all turn to dust again. *Ec. iii.* 20.

3. In sure and certain hope of the Resurrection to eternal life, through our Lord Jesus Christ; who shall change our vile body, that it may be like unto his glorious body, according to the mighty working, whereby he is able to subdue all things to himself.

3. And have hope toward God, which they themselves also allow, that there shall be a resurrection of the dead, both of the just and unjust. *Ac. xxiv.* 15. Now, that the dead are raised, even Moses showed at the bush, when he called the Lord the God of Abraham, and the God of Isaac, and the God of Jacob. For he is not a God of the dead, but of the living : for all live unto him. *Lu. xx.* 37, 38. And many of them that sleep in the dust of the earth shall awake, some to everlasting life, and some to shame and everlasting contempt. *Da. xii.* 2. Since by man came death, by man came also the resurrection of the dead. For as in Adam all die, even so in Christ shall all be made alive. The trumpet shall sound, and the dead shall be raised. 1 *Co. xv.* 21, 22. 52. Jesus said, I am the resurrection, and the life. *John xi.* 25. The Lord Jesus Christ, who shall change our vile body, that it may be fashioned like unto his glorious body, according to the work-

ing whereby he is able even to subdue all things unto himself: *Ph. iii. 20, 21.* This is the Father's will which hath sent me, that of all which he hath given me I should lose nothing; but should raise it up again at the last day. And this is the will of him that sent me, that every one which seeth the Son, and believeth on him, may have everlasting life; and I will raise him up at the last day. *John vi. 39, 40.* Beloved, now are we the sons of God, and it doth not yet appear what we shall be: but we know that, when he shall appear, we shall be like him; for we shall see him as he is. *1 John iii. 2.*

I heard a voice from heaven, saying unto me, Write, From henceforth blessed are the dead which die in the Lord: even so saith the Spirit; for they rest from their labours. Re. xiv. 13.

Lord, have mercy upon us.
Christ, have mercy upon us.
Lord, have mercy upon us.

Our Father, &c.

CCXXVIII. *A Prayer for the complete happiness of God's Church.*

L. Almighty God, with whom do live the spirits of them that depart hence in the Lord, and with whom the souls of the faithful, after they are delivered from the burden of the flesh, are in joy and felicity;

1. I am the God of thy father, the God of Abraham, the God of Isaac, and the God of Jacob. *Ex. iii. 6.* He is not a God of the dead, but of the living: for all live unto him. *Lu. xx. 38.* Then shall the dust return to the earth as it was: and the spirit shall return unto God who gave it. *Ec. xii. 7.* Jesus said unto him, Verily, I say unto thee, To day shalt thou be with me in paradise. *Lu. xxiii. 46.* It came to pass, that the beggar died, and was carried by the angels into Abraham's bosom. *Lu. xvi. 22.* I am in a strait betwixt two, having a desire to depart, and to be with Christ; which is far better. *Ph. i. 23.* We that are in this tabernacle do groan, being burdened: not for that we would be unclothed, but clothed upon, that mortality might be swallowed up of life. *2 Co. v. 4.* Thou shalt guide me with thy counsel, and afterward receive me to glory. *Ps. lxxiii. 24.* I will behold thy face in righteousness: I shall be satisfied, when I awake, with thy likeness. *Ps. xvii. 15.* Thou wilt shew me the path of life: in thy presence is fulness of joy; at thy right hand there are pleasures for evermore. *Ps. xvi. 11.* I heard a voice from heaven, saying unto me, Write, Blessed are the dead which die in the Lord from henceforth. *Re. xiv. 13.*

2. We give thee hearty thanks, for that it hath pleased thee to deliver this our brother out of the miseries of this sinful world;

2. The Lord gave, and the Lord hath taken away; blessed be the name of the Lord. *Job i.* 21. Thou takest away their breath, they die, and return to their dust. *Ps. civ.* 29. It is the Lord: let him do what seemeth him good. 1 *Sa. iii.* 18. The righteous perisheth, and no man layeth it to heart: and merciful men are taken away from the evil to come. He shall enter into peace: they shall rest in their beds. *Is. lvii.* 1, 2. David said unto his servants, Is the child dead? And they said, He is dead. Then David arose from the earth, and washed, and anointed himself, and changed his apparel, and came into the house of the Lord, and worshipped: then he came to his own house; and when he required, they set bread before him, and he did eat. 2 *Sa. xii.* 19, 20. I will gather thee unto thy fathers, and thou shalt be gathered into thy grave in peace; and thine eyes shall not see all the evil which I will bring upon this place. 2 *Ki. xxii.* 20. Man is born unto trouble. *Job v.* 7. In the world ye shall have tribulation. *John xvi.* 33.

3. beseeching thee, that it may please thee of thy gracious goodness, shortly to accomplish the number of thine elect, and to hasten thy kingdom;

3. I saw under the altar the souls of them that were slain for the word of God, and for the testimony which they held: and they cried with a loud voice, saying, How long, O Lord, holy and true, dost thou not judge and avenge our blood on them that dwell on the earth? And white robes were given unto every one of them, and it was said unto them, that they should rest yet for a little season, until their fellow-servants also and their brethren, that should be killed as they were, should be fulfilled. *Re. vi.* 9, 10, 11. He will finish the work, and cut it short in righteousness: because a short work will the Lord make upon the earth. *Ro. ix.* 28. He shall send his angels with a great sound of a trumpet, and they shall gather together his elect from the four winds, from one end of heaven to the other. *Mat. xxiv.* 31. He shall see of the travail of his soul, and shall be satisfied. *Is. liii.* 11. Thy kingdom come. *Mat. vi.* 10. I the Lord will hasten it in his time. *Is. lx.* 22. He which testifieth these things saith, Surely I come quickly; Amen. Even so, come, Lord Jesus. *Re. xxii.* 20. See also, *Is. ii.* 2, 3, 4—*Da. ii.* 44.—*Mat. xiii.* 41, 42. 49, 50.

4. that we, with all those that are depart-

4. These all died in faith, not having received the promises, but having seen them afar off, and were persuaded of them,

x

ed in the true faith of thy holy Name, may have our perfect consummation and bliss, both in body and soul, in thy eternal and everlasting glory, through Jesus Christ our Lord. *Amen.*

and embraced them, and confessed that they were strangers and pilgrims on the earth. These all, having obtained a good report through faith received not the promise; God having provided some better thing for us, that they without us should not be made perfect. *He. xi.* 13. 39, 40. Henceforth there is laid up for me a crown of righteousness, which the Lord, the righteous Judge shall give me at that day: and not to me only, but unto all them also that love his appearing. *2 Ti. iv.* 8. Beloved, now are we the sons of God, and it doth not yet appear what we shall be: but we know that, when he shall appear, we shall be like him. *1 John iii.* 2. The Lord Jesus Christ, who shall change our vile body that it may be fashioned like unto his glorious body, according to the working whereby he is able even to subdue all things unto himself. *Ph. iii.* 20, 21. These are they which came out of great tribulation, and have washed their robes, and made them white in the blood of the Lamb. Therefore are they before the throne of God, and serve him day and night in his temple: and he that sitteth on the throne shall dwell among them. They shall hunger no more, neither thirst any more; neither shall the sun light on them, nor any heat. For the Lamb which is in the midst of the throne shall feed them, and shall lead them unto living fountains of waters: and God shall wipe away all tears from their eyes. *Re. vii.* 14 *to* 17. Then we which are alive and remain, shall be caught up together with them in the clouds, to meet the Lord in the air: and so shall we ever be with the Lord. *1 Th. iv.* 17. Father, I will that they also, whom thou hast given me, be with me where I am; that they may behold my glory, which thou hast given me: for thou lovedst me before the foundation of the world. *John xvii.* 24. I saw in the night visions, and, behold, one like the Son of Man came with the clouds of heaven, and came to the Ancient of days, and they brought him near before him. And there was given him dominion, and glory, and a kingdom, that all people, nations, and languages, should serve him: his dominion is an everlasting dominion, which shall not pass away, and his kingdom that which shall not be destroyed. *Da. vii.* 13, 14. There were great voices in heaven, saying, The kingdoms of this world are become the kingdoms of our

Lord, and of his Christ; and he shall reign for ever and ever. *Re. xi.* 15.

CCXXIX. *A Prayer for spiritual life here, and eternal life in the world to come.*

1. O merciful God, the Father of our Lord Jesus Christ, who is the Resurrection and the Life; in whom whosoever believeth shall live, though he die; and whosoever liveth, and believeth in him, shall not die eternally;

1. Blessed be God, even the Father of our Lord Jesus Christ, the Father of mercies, and the God of all comfort. *2 Co. i.* 3. Blessed be the God and Father of our Lord Jesus Christ, which according to his abundant mercy hath begotten us again unto a lively hope by the resurrection of Jesus Christ from the dead, to an inheritance incorruptible, and undefiled. *1 Pe. i.* 3, 4. Jesus said unto her, I am the resurrection, and the life: he that believeth in me, though he were dead, yet shall he live: and whosoever liveth and believeth in me shall never die. *John xi.* 25, 26. God so loved the world, that he gave his only begotten Son, that whosoever believeth in him should not perish, but have everlasting life. *John iii.* 16. This is the Father's will which hath sent me, that of all which he hath given me I should lose nothing, but should raise it up again at the last day. *John vi.* 39. For as the Father raiseth up the dead, and quickeneth them; even so the Son quickeneth whom he will. As the Father hath life in himself; so hath he given to the Son to have life in himself. He that heareth my word, and believeth on him that sent me, hath everlasting life, and shall not come into condemnation; but is passed from death unto life. *John v.* 21. 26. 24. Verily, verily, I say unto you, If a man keep my saying, he shall never see death. *John viii.* 51. See also, *Ro. viii.* 11.—*He. xi.* 13 *to* 16.

2. Who also hath taught us, by his holy Apostle Saint Paul, not to be sorry as men without hope, for them that sleep in him;

2. I would not have you to be ignorant, brethren, concerning them which are asleep, that ye sorrow not, even as others which have no hope. For if we believe that Jesus died and rose again, even so them also which sleep in Jesus will God bring with him. *1 Th. iv.* 13, 14. And all his sons and all his daughters rose up to comfort him; but he refused to be comforted; and he said, For I will go down into the grave unto my son mourning. Thus his father wept for him. *Ge. xxxvii.* 35. The king was much moved, and went up to the chamber over the gate, and wept: and as he went, thus he said, O my son Absalom, my son, my son

Absalom! would God I had died for thee, O Absalom, my son, my son! 2 *Sa. xviii.* 33. As for me, I will behold thy face in righteousness: I shall be satisfied, when I awake, with thy likeness. *Ps. xvii.* 15. I know that my Redeemer liveth, and that he shall stand at the latter day upon the earth; and though after my skin worms destroy this body, yet in my flesh shall I see God: whom I shall see for myself, and mine eyes shall behold, and not another. *Job xix.* 25, 26, 27.

3. *we meekly beseech thee, O Father, to raise us from the death of sin unto the life of righteousness;*

3. Then cried I unto thee, O Lord: and get me to my Lord right humbly. *Ps. xxx.* 8. And you hath he quickened who were dead in trespasses and sins; wherein in time past ye walked according to the course of this world, according to the prince of the power of the air, the spirit that now worketh in the children of disobedience. But God, who is rich in mercy, for his great love wherewith he loved us, even when we were dead in sins, hath quickened us together with Christ. *Ep. ii.* 1, 2. 4, 5. Reckon yourselves to be dead indeed unto sin, but alive unto God through Jesus Christ our Lord. *Ro. vi.* 11. Who his ownself bare our sins in his own body on the tree, that we, being dead to sins, should live unto righteousness. 1 *Pe. ii.* 24.

4. *that, when we shall depart this life, we may rest in him, as our hope is this our brother doth;*

4. Yea doubtless, and I count all things but loss for the excellency of the knowledge of Christ Jesus my Lord: for whom I have suffered the loss of all things, and do count them but dung, that I may win Christ, and be found in him, not having mine own righteousness, which is of the law, but that which is through the faith of Christ, the righteousness which is of God by faith: that I may know him, and the power of his resurrection, and the fellowship of his sufferings, being made conformable unto his death; if by any means I might attain unto the resurrection of the dead. *Ph. iii.* 8 *to* 11. It is appointed unto men once to die. *He. ix.* 27. What man is he that liveth, and shall not see death? Shall he deliver his soul from the hand of the grave? *Ps. lxxxix.* 48. Come unto me, all ye that labour and are heavy laden, and I will give you rest. *Mat. xi.* 28. There remaineth therefore a rest to the people of God. For we which have believed do enter into rest. *He. iv.* 9. 3. The righteous is taken away from the evil to come. He shall enter into peace; they shall rest in

their beds. *Ia. lvii.* 1, 2. Charity thinketh no evil : believeth all things, hopeth all things. 1 *Co. iii.* 5, 7. The Lord taketh pleasure in them that fear him, in those that hope in his mercy. *Ps. cxlvii.* 11. Judge not, and ye shall not be judged : condemn not, and ye shall not be condemned. *Lu. vi.* 37. Who art thou that judgest another man's servant ? to his own master he standeth or falleth. *Ro. xiv.* 4. We must all appear before the judgment seat of Christ. 2 *Co. v.* 10. *See also,* *Ge. iii.* 19.—*Ec. iii.* 20.

5. and that, at the general Resurrection in the last day, we may be found acceptable in thy sight;

5. There shall be a resurrection of the dead, both of the just and unjust. *Ac. xxiv.* 15. I will raise him up at the last day. *John vi.* 40. I know that he shall rise again in the resurrection at the last day. *John xi.* 24. The Lord grant unto him that he may find mercy of the Lord in that day. 2 *Ti. i.* 18. The word that I have spoken, the same shall judge him in the last day. *John xii.* 48. God accepteth no man's person. *Ga. ii.* 6. Wherefore we labour, that, whether present or absent, we may be accepted of him. 2 *Co. v.* 9. He hath made us accepted in the beloved. *Ep. i.* 6. *See also,* *Ro. xvi.* 10.—2 *Co. x.* 18.

6. and receive that blessing, which thy well-beloved Son shall then pronounce to all that love and fear thee, saying, Come, ye blessed children of my Father, receive the kingdom prepared for you from the beginning of the world: Grant this, we beseech thee, O merciful Father, through Jesus Christ, our Mediator and Redeemer. *Amen.*

6. Blessed are the dead which die in the Lord. *Re. xiv.* 13. I go to prepare a place for you. And if I go and prepare a place for you, I will come again, and receive you unto myself; that where I am, there ye may be also. *John xiv.* 2, 3. It is written, Eye hath not seen, nor ear heard, neither have entered into the heart of man, the things which God hath prepared for them that love him. 1 *Co. ii.* 9. Continue ye in my love. *John xv.* 9. Fear not them which kill the body, but are not able to kill the soul: but rather fear him which is able to destroy both soul and body in hell. *Mat. x.* 28. The Father judgeth no man, but hath committed all judgment unto the Son. *John v.* 22. He received from God the Father honour and glory, when there came such a voice to him from the excellent glory, This is my beloved Son, in whom I am well pleased. 2 *Pe. i.* 17. Verily, verily, I say unto you, The hour is coming, and now is, when the dead shall hear the voice of the Son of God: and they that hear shall live. *John v.* 25. Then shall the King say unto them on his right hand, Come, ye blessed of my Father, inherit the kingdom prepared

for you from the foundation of the world. *Mat. xxv.* 34. Blessed be the God and Father of our Lord Jesus Christ, which according to his abundant mercy hath begotten us again unto a lively hope by the resurrection of Jesus Christ from the dead, to an inheritance incorruptible, and undefiled, and that fadeth not away, reserved in heaven for you, who are kept by the power of God through faith unto salvation ready to be revealed in the last time. 1 *Pe. i.* 3, 4, 5. Where sin abounded, grace did much more abound : that as sin hath reigned unto death, even so might grace reign through righteousness unto eternal life by Jesus Christ our Lord. *Ro. v.* 20, 21. *See also,* *Jo. i.* 12.—*Ps. cxxxiii.* 3.—*Lu. xii.* 32.—*2 Ti. ii.* 12.

The grace of our Lord Jesus Christ, and the love of God, and the fellowship of the Holy Ghost, be with us all evermore. Amen. 2 Co. xiii. 14.

THE
THANKSGIVING OF WOMEN AFTER CHILD-BIRTH,

COMMONLY CALLED

THE CHURCHING OF WOMEN.

CCXXX. Address to the Woman.

Forasmuch as it hath pleased Almighty God of his goodness to give you safe deliverance, and hath preserved you in the great danger of childbirth; you shall therefore give hearty thanks unto God, and say,

Unto the woman he said, I will greatly multiply thy sorrow and thy conception ; in sorrow thou shalt bring forth children; and thy desire shall be to thy husband, and he shall rule over thee. *Ge. iii.* 16. When the days of her purifying are fulfilled, for a son, or for a daughter, she shall bring a lamb of the first year for a burnt offering, and a young pigeon, or a turtle dove, for a sin offering, unto the door of the tabernacle of the congregation, unto the priest: who shall offer it before the Lord, and make an atonement for her. *Le. xii.* 6, 7. And when eight days were accomplished for the circumcising of the child, his name was called JESUS, which was so named of the angel before he was conceived in the womb. And when the days of her purification according to the law of Moses were accomplished, they brought him to Jerusalem, to present him to the Lord ; and to offer a sacrifice according to that which is said in the law of the Lord. *Lu. ii.* 21, 22. 24. The woman being deceived was in the transgression. Notwithstanding she shall be saved in childbearing, if they continue in faith and charity and holiness with sobriety. 1 *Ti. ii.* 14, 15. Call upon me in the day of trouble : I will deliver thee, and thou shalt glorify me. *Ps. l.* 15. The sorrows of death compassed me, and the pains of hell gat hold upon me : I found trouble and sorrow. Then called I upon the name of the Lord : O Lord, I beseech thee, deliver my soul. Gracious is the Lord, and righteous ; yea, our God is merciful. The Lord preserveth the simple : I was brought low, and he helped me. Return unto thy rest, O my soul; for the Lord hath dealt bountifully with thee. *Ps. cxvi. 3 to 7.*

Psalm cxvi.—*I am well pleased : that the Lord hath heard the voice of my prayer ;—That he hath inclined his ear unto me : therefore will I call upon him as long as I live.—The snares of death compassed me round about : and the pains of hell gat hold upon me.—I found trouble and heaviness, and I called upon the name of the Lord : O Lord, I beseech thee, deliver my soul.—Gracious is the Lord, and righteous: yea, our God is merciful.—The Lord preserveth the simple: I was in misery, and he helped me.—Turn again then unto thy rest, O my soul: for the Lord hath rewarded thee.—And why? thou hast delivered my soul from death: mine eyes from tears, and my feet from falling.—I will walk before the Lord: in the land of the living.—I believed, and therefore will I speak; but I was sore troubled: I said in my haste, All men are liars.—What reward shall I give unto the Lord: for all the benefits that he hath done unto me?—I will receive the cup of salvation: and call upon the Name of the Lord.—I will pay my vows now in the presence of all his people: in the courts of the Lord's house, even in the midst of thee, O Jerusalem. Praise the Lord.*

Glory be to the Father, &c. As it was in the beginning, &c.

Psalm cxxvii.—*Except the Lord build the house: their labour is but lost that build it.—Except the Lord keep the city: the watchman waketh but in vain.—It is but lost labour that ye haste to rise up early, and so late take rest, and eat the bread of carefulness; for so he giveth his beloved sleep.—Lo, children and the fruit of the womb: are an heritage and gift that cometh of the Lord.—Like as the arrows in the hand of the giant: even so are the young children.—Happy is the man that hath his quiver full of them: they shall not be ashamed when they speak with their enemies in the gate.*

Glory be to the Father, &c. As it was in the beginning, &c.

> Lord, have mercy upon us.
> Christ, have mercy upon us.
> Lord, have mercy upon us.
> *Our Father, &c.*

CCXXXI. *The Intercession or Suffrages.*

1, 2. O Lord, save this woman thy servant; who putteth her trust in thee.

> 1, 2. Preserve my soul; for I am holy: O thou my God, save thy servant that trusteth in thee. *Ps. lxxxvi. 2.*

3, 4. Be thou to her a strong tower; from the face of her enemy.

> 3, 4. Thou hast been a shelter for me, and a strong tower from the enemy. *Ps. lxi. 3.*

5, 6. Lord, hear our prayer; and let our cry come unto thee.

> 5, 6. Hear my cry, O God; attend unto my prayer. *Ps. lxi. 1.*

CCXXXII. *A Prayer that the woman may live a holy life.*

1. O Almighty God, we give thee humble thanks for that thou hast vouchsafed to deliver this woman thy servant from the great pain and peril of Childbirth;

1. I will offer to thee the sacrifice of thanksgiving, and will call upon the name of the Lord. I will pay my vows unto the Lord now in the presence of all his people, in the courts of the Lord's house, in the midst of thee, O Jerusalem. Praise ye the Lord. *Ps. cxvi. 17, 18, 19.* A woman when she is in travail hath sorrow, because her hour is come: but as soon as she is delivered of the child, she remembereth no more the anguish, for joy that a man is born into the world. *John*

xvi. 21. Thou hast delivered my soul from death, mine eyes from tears, and my feet from falling. I was greatly afflicted. What shall I render unto the Lord for all his benefits toward me? *Ps. cxvi.* 8. 10. 12.

2. The Lord hear thee in the day of trouble; the name of the God of Jacob defend thee. Send thee help from the sanctuary, and strengthen thee out of Zion. *Ps. xx.* 1, 2. I can do all things through Christ which strengtheneth me. *Ph. iv.* 13. Our help is in the name of the Lord. *Ps. cxxiv.* 8. Let us come boldly unto the throne of grace, that we may obtain mercy, and find grace to help in time of need. *He. iv.* 16. Deal bountifully with thy servant, that I may live, and keep thy word. Order my steps in thy word: and let not any iniquity have dominion over me. *Ps. cxix.* 17. 133. That which is gone out of thy lips thou shalt keep and perform; even a freewill offering, according as thou hast vowed unto the Lord thy God, which thou hast promised with thy mouth. *De. xxiii.* 23. Thus shall ye do in the fear of the Lord, faithfully, and with a perfect heart. 2 *Chi. xix.* 9. I live by the faith of the Son of God. *Ga. ii.* 20. For we walk by faith, not by sight. 2 *Co. v.* 7. Teach me to do thy will; for thou art my God. *Ps. cxliii.* 10. As ye have therefore received Christ Jesus the Lord, so walk ye in him: rooted and built up in him, and stablished in the faith, as ye have been taught, abounding therein with thanksgiving. *Col. ii.* 6, 7. If ye do these things, ye shall never fall: for so an entrance shall be ministered unto you abundantly into the everlasting kingdom of our Lord and Saviour Jesus Christ. 2 *Pe. i.* 10, 11.

2. Grant, we beseech thee, most merciful Father, that she, through thy help, may both faithfully live, and walk according to thy will, in this life present; and also may be partaker of everlasting glory in the life to come; through Jesus Christ our Lord. Amen.

Y

A COMMINATION,

OR DENOUNCING OF GOD'S ANGER AND JUDGMENTS AGAINST

SINNERS, WITH CERTAIN PRAYERS.

To be used on the first Day of Lent, and at other times, as the Ordinary shall appoint.

CCXXXIII. The minister's address to the congregation.

1. Brethren, in the Primitive Church there was a godly discipline, that, at the beginning of Lent, such persons as stood convicted of notorious sin were put to open penance, and punished in this world, that their souls might be saved in the day of the Lord; and that others, admonished by their example, might be the more afraid to offend.

1. In the name of our Lord Jesus Christ, when ye are gathered together, and my spirit, with the power of our Lord Jesus Christ, to deliver such an one unto satan for the destruction of the flesh, that the spirit may be saved in the day of the Lord Jesus. Know ye not that a little leaven leaveneth the whole lump? Purge out therefore the old leaven, that ye may be a new lump, as ye are unleavened. Now I have written unto you not to keep company, if any man that is called a brother be a fornicator, or covetous, or an idolater, or a railer, or a drunkard, or an extortioner; with such an one no not to eat. Therefore put away from among yourselves that wicked person. 1 *Co. v.* 4 *to* 7. 11. 13. Them that sin rebuke before all, that others also may fear. 1 *Ti. v.* 20. If there arise a matter too hard for thee in judgment, being matters of controversy within thy gates: then shalt thou arise, and get thee up into the place which the Lord thy God shall choose, and thou shalt come unto the priests the Levites, and unto the judge that shall be in those days, and enquire, and they shall shew thee the sentence of judgment: and thou shalt do according to the sentence. And the man that will do presumptuously, and will not hearken unto the priest that standeth to minister there before the Lord thy God, or unto the judge, even that man shall die: and thou shalt put away the evil from Israel. And all the people shall hear, and fear, and do no more presumptuously. *De. xvii.* 8, 9, 10. 12, 13. See also, *Mat. xviii.* 15 *to* 18.—*John* IX.

2. Instead whereof, (until the said disci-

2. Moses charged the people the same day, saying, These shall stand upon Mount Gerizim to bless the people; and these

pline may be restored again, which is much to be wished,) it is thought good, that at this time (in the presence of you all) should be read the general sentences of God's curse against impenitent sinners, gathered out of the seven and twentieth Chapter of Deuteronomy, and other places of Scripture; and that ye should answer to every Sentence, Amen: To the intent that, being admonished of the great indignation of God against sinners, ye may the rather be moved to earnest and true repentance; and may walk more warily in these dangerous days; fleeing from such vices, for which ye affirm with your own mouths the curse of God to be due.....

shall stand upon Mount Ebal to curse. And the Levites shall speak unto all the men of Israel with a loud voice. And all the people shall answer and say, Amen. *De. xxvii.* 11 *to* 15. And all the people gathered themselves together as one man into the street that was before the watergate ; and they spake unto Ezra the scribe to bring the book of the law of Moses which the Lord had commanded to Israel. And Ezra the priest brought the law before the congregation both of men and women, and all that could hear with understanding, upon the first day of the seventh month. And he read therein before the street that was before the watergate from the morning until midday, before the men and the women, and those that could understand; and the ears of all the people were attentive unto the book of the law. *Ne. viii.* 1, 2, 3. Now in the twenty and fourth day of this month the children of Israel were assembled with fasting, and with sackclothes, and earth upon them. And the seed of Israel separated themselves from all strangers, and stood and confessed their sins, and the iniquities of their fathers. And they stood up in their place, and read in the book of the law of the Lord their God one fourth part of the day; and another fourth part they confessed, and worshipped the Lord their God. *Ne. ix.* 1, 2, 3. Unto them that are contentious, and do not obey the truth, but obey unrighteousness, indignation and wrath, tribulation and anguish, upon every soul of man that doeth evil. *Ro. ii.* 8, 9. God is angry with the wicked every day. If he turn not, he will whet his sword; he hath bent his bow, and made it ready. *Ps. vii.* 11, 12. There remaineth a certain fearful looking for of judgment and fiery indignation, which shall devour the adversaries. *He. x.* 26, 27. Gather the people, sanctify the congregation, assemble the elders, gather the children, and those that suck the breasts: let the bridegroom go forth of his chamber, and the bride out of her closet. Let the priests, the ministers of the Lord, weep between the porch and the altar, and let them say, Spare thy people, O Lord, and give not thine heritage to reproach. *Joel ii.* 16, 17. And Jonah began to enter into the city a day's journey, and he cried, and said, Yet forty days, and Nineveh shall be overthrown. So the people of Nineveh

believed God, and proclaimed a fast, and put on sackcloth,
from the greatest of them even to the least of them. For
word came unto the king of Nineveh, and he arose from his
throne, and he laid his robe from him, and covered him with
sackcloth, and sat in ashes. And he caused it to be proclaimed
and published through Nineveh by the decree of the king and
his nobles, saying, Let neither man nor beast, herd nor flock,
taste any thing : let them not feed, nor drink water : but let
man and beast be covered with sackcloth, and cry mightily
unto God : yea, let them turn every one from his evil way,
and from the violence that is in their hands. Who can tell if
God will turn and repent, and turn away from his fierce anger,
that we perish not? And God saw their works, that they
turned from their evil way ; and God repented of the evil,
that he had said that he would do unto them ; and he did it
not. *Jon. iii.* 4 *to* 10. Thus saith the Lord, Stand ye in the
ways, and see, and ask for the old paths, where is the good
way, and walk therein, and ye shall find rest for your souls.
Je. vi. 16. Depart from evil, and do good ; seek peace, and
pursue it. *Ps. xxxiv.* 14. Neither let us commit fornication,
as some of them committed, and fell in one day three and
twenty thousand. Neither let us tempt Christ, as some of
them also tempted, and were destroyed of serpents. Neither
murmur ye, as some of them also murmured, and were destroyed of the destroyer. 1 *Co. x.* 8, 9, 10. Seek good, and
not evil, that ye may live : and so the Lord, the God of hosts,
shall be with you, as ye have spoken. Hate the evil, and
love the good, and establish judgment in the gate. The
prudent shall keep silence in that time, for it is an evil time.
Am. v. 14, 15. 13. This know also, that in the last days
perilous times shall come. For men shall be lovers of their
ownselves, covetous, boasters, proud, blasphemers, disobedient
to parents, unthankful, unholy, without natural affection, trucebreakers, false accusers, incontinent, fierce, despisers of those
that are good, traitors, heady, highminded, lovers of pleasures more than lovers of God ; having a form of godliness,
but denying the power thereof : from such turn away. 2 *Ti.
iii.* 1 *to* 5. O that I had in the wilderness a lodging place of
wayfaring men ; that I might leave my people, and go from

them! for they be all adulterers, an assembly of treacherous men. And they bend their tongues like their bow for lies; but they are not valiant for the truth upon the earth; for they proceed from evil to evil, and they know not me, saith the Lord. Take ye heed every one of his neighbour, and trust ye not any brother: for every brother will utterly supplant, and every neighbour will walk with slanders. And they will deceive every one his neighbour, and will not speak the truth: they have taught their tongue to speak lies, and weary themselves to commit iniquity. Through deceit they refuse to know me, saith the Lord. *Je. ix.* 2 *to* 6. And in those times there was no peace to him that went out, nor to him that came in, but great vexations were upon all the inhabitants of the countries. And nation was destroyed of nation, and city of city: for God did vex them with all adversity. 2 *Ch. xv.* 5, 6. See then that ye walk circumspectly, not as fools, but as wise. *Ep. v.* 15. Let every one that nameth the name of Christ depart from iniquity. *Ti. ii.* 19. Abstain from all appearance of evil. 1 *Th. v.* 22.

CCXXXIV. *The Sentences of cursing.*

1. Cursed is the man that maketh any carved or molten image, to worship it. Amen. *De. xxvii.* 15.

2. Cursed is he that curseth his father or mother. Amen. *De. xxvii.* 16.

3. Cursed is he that removeth his neighbour's landmark. Amen. *De. xxvii.* 17.

4. Cursed is he that maketh the blind to go out of his way. Amen. *xxvii.* 18.

5. Cursed is he that perverteth the judgment of the stranger, the fatherless, and widow. Amen. *De. xxvii.* 19.

6. Cursed is he that smiteth his neighbour secretly. Amen. *De. xxvii.* 24.

7. Cursed is he that lieth with his neighbour's wife. Amen. *Lev. xx.* 10.

8. Cursed is he that taketh reward to slay the innocent. Amen. *De. xxvii.* 25.

9. Cursed is he that putteth his trust in man, and taketh man for his defence, and in his heart goeth from the Lord. Amen. *Je. xvii.* 5.

10. Cursed are the unmerciful, fornicators, and adulterers, covetous persons, idolaters, slanderers, drunkards, and extortioners. Amen. *St. Matt. xxv.* 41.—1 *Cor. vi.* 9, 10.

CCXXXV. *The Application and Exhortation.*

1. Now seeing that all they are accursed (as the prophet David beareth witness) who do err and go astray from the

1. Thou hast rebuked the proud: and cursed are they that do err from thy commandments. My flesh trembleth for fear of thee; and I am afraid of thy judgments. *Ps. cxix.* 21. 120. Lord, when thy hand is lifted up, they will not see: but they shall see, and be ashamed for their envy at the people; yea, the fire of thine enemies shall devour them. *Is. xxvi.* 11. Re-

commandments of God; let us (remembering the dreadful judgment hanging over our heads, and always ready to fall upon us) return unto our Lord God, with all contrition and meekness of heart;

member Lot's wife. *Lu. xvii.* 32. God is angry with the wicked every day. If he turn not, he will whet his sword; he hath bent his bow, and made it ready. He hath also prepared for him the instruments of death. *Ps. vii.* 11, 12, 13. Our God is a consuming fire. *He. xii.* 29. Repent, and turn yourselves from all your transgressions; so iniquity shall not be your ruin. *Eze. xviii.* 30. Let us search and try our ways, and turn again to the Lord. Let us lift up our heart with our hands unto God in the heavens. *La. iii.* 40, 41. Turn us, O God of our salvation, and cause thine anger toward us to cease. *Ps. lxxxv.* 4. Turn thou me, and I shall be turned; for thou art the Lord my God. *Je. xxxi.* 18. The sacrifices of God are a broken spirit: a broken and a contrite heart, O God, thou wilt not despise. *Ps. li.* 17.

2. bewailing and lamenting our sinful life, acknowledging and confessing our offences, and seeking to bring forth worthy fruits of penance [*repentance.*]

2. I will bewail with the weeping of Jazer. *Is. xvi.* 9. I prayed unto the Lord my God, and made my confession, and said, O Lord, the great and dreadful God, keeping the covenant and mercy to them that love him, and to them that keep his commandments: we have sinned, and have committed iniquity, and have done wickedly, and have rebelled, even by departing from thy precepts and from thy judgments: neither have we hearkened unto thy servants the prophets, which spake in thy name. *Da. ix.* 4, 5, 6. Surely after that I was turned, I repented; and after that I was instructed, I smote upon my thigh: I was ashamed, yea, even confounded, because I did bear the reproach of my youth. *Je. xxxi.* 19. O my God, I am ashamed and blush to lift up my face to thee, my God: for our iniquities are increased over our head, and our trespass is grown up into the heavens. *Ezr. ix.* 6. I acknowledge my transgressions: and my sin is ever before me. *Ps. li.* 3. I have borne chastisement, I will not offend any more: that which I see not teach thou me: if I have done iniquity, I will do no more. *Job xxxiv.* 31, 32. Create in me a clean heart, O God; and renew a right spirit within me. *Ps. li.* 10. Bring forth therefore fruits meet for repentance: [*marginal reading, answerable to amendment of life.*] *Mat. iii.* 8.

3. For now is the axe put unto the root of the trees, so

3. And now also the axe is laid unto the root of the trees: therefore every tree which bringeth not forth good fruit is hewn down, and cast into the fire. *Mat. iii.* 10. Behold, the

that every tree day cometh, that shall burn as an oven; and all the proud,
that bringeth
not forth good yea, and all that do wickedly, shall be stubble: and the day
fruit is hewn
down, and cast that cometh shall burn them up, saith the Lord of hosts, that
into the fire. it shall leave them neither root nor branch. *Mal. iv.* 1.   He
It is a fearful
thing to fall that despised Moses' law died without mercy under two or
into the hands three witnesses: of how much sorer punishment, suppose ye,
of the living
God: He shall shall he be thought worthy, who hath trodden under foot the
pour down rain Son of God, and hath counted the blood of the covenant,
upon the sin-
ners, snares, wherewith he was sanctified, an unholy thing, and hath done
fire and brim-
stone, storm despite unto the spirit of grace?   For we know him that hath
and tempest; said, Vengeance belongeth unto me, I will recompense, saith
this shall be
their portion the Lord.   It is a fearful thing to fall into the hands of the
to drink. living God. *He. x.* 28 *to* 31.   For our God is a consuming
fire. *He. xii.* 29.   The Lord thy God is a consuming fire, even
a jealous God. *De. iv.* 24.   Upon the ungodly he shall rain
snares, fire and brimstone, storm and tempest, this shall be
their portion to drink. *Ps. xi.* 7.   The Lord rained upon
Sodom and upon Gomorrah brimstone and fire from the Lord
out of heaven. *Ge. xix.* 24.   *See also, Is. xxiv.* 17, 18.—*Ze.
xiii.* 13.—*Job xx.* 11. 25. 27. 29.

4. For lo,   4. For, behold, the Lord cometh out of his place to punish
the Lord is
come out of the inhabitants of the earth for their iniquity. *Is. xxvi.* 21.
his place to
visit the wick- But who may abide the day of his coming? and who shall
edness of such stand when he appeareth? for he is like a refiner's fire, and
as dwell upon
the earth. But like fuller's sope. *Mal. iii.* 2.   The mighty God, even the
who may abide
the day of his Lord, hath spoken, and called the earth from the rising of the
coming? who
shall be able to sun unto the going down thereof.   Out of Zion, the perfection
endure when he of beauty, God hath shined.   Our God shall come, and shall
appeareth?
not keep silence: a fire shall devour before him, and it shall
be very tempestuous round about him,   He shall call to the
heavens from above, and to the earth, that he may judge his
people.   Call upon me in the day of trouble: I will deliver
thee, and thou shalt glorify me.   But unto the wicked God
saith, What hast thou to do to declare my statutes, or that
thou shouldest take my covenant in thy mouth? seeing thou
hatest instruction, and castest my words behind thee.   When
thou sawest a thief, then thou consentedst with him, and hast
been partaker with adulterers.   Thou givest thy mouth to evil,
and thy tongue frameth deceit.   Thou sittest and speakest

against thy brother; thou slanderest thine own mother's son. Now consider this, ye that forget God, lest I tear you in pieces, and there be none to deliver. *Ps. l.* 1 *to* 4. 15 *to* 20. 22. The great day of his wrath is come; and who shall be able to stand. *Re. vi.* 17. And he shall sit as a refiner and purifier of silver: and he shall purify the sons of Levi, and purge them as gold and silver. *Mal. iii.* 3.

5. His fan is in his hand, and he will purge his floor, and gather his wheat into the barn; but he will burn the chaff with unquenchable fire.

5. Whose fan is in his hand, and he will throughly purge his floor, and gather his wheat into the garner; but he will burn up the chaff with unquenchable fire. *Mat. iii.* 12. I will fan them with a fan in the gates of the land; I will bereave them of children, I will destroy my people, since they return not from their ways. *Je. xv.* 7. Every branch in me that beareth not fruit he taketh away: and every branch that beareth fruit, he purgeth it, that it may bring forth more fruit. *John xv.* 2. In the time of harvest I will say to the reapers, Gather ye together first the tares, and bind them in bundles to burn them: but gather the wheat into my barn. *Mat. xiii.* 30. The wicked are as stubble before the wind, and as chaff that the storm carrieth away. *Job xxi.* 18. The ungodly are like the chaff which the wind driveth away. Therefore the ungodly shall not stand in the judgment, nor sinners in the congregation of the righteous. For the Lord knoweth the way of the righteous: but the way of the ungodly shall perish. *Ps. i.* 4, 5, 6. The wicked shall be turned into hell. *Ps. ix.* 17. As the fire devoureth the stubble, and the flame consumeth the chaff, so their root shall be as rottenness, and their blossom shall go up as dust. *Is. v.* 44. Their worm shall not die, neither shall their fire be quenched. *Is. lxvi.* 24.

6. The day of the Lord cometh as a thief in the night: and when men shall say, Peace, and all things are safe, then shall sudden destruction come upon them, as sorrow cometh upon a woman

6. Yourselves know perfectly that the day of the Lord so cometh as a thief in the night. For when they shall say, Peace and safety; then sudden destruction cometh upon them, as travail upon a woman with child; and they shall not escape. *1 Th. v.* 2, 3. As the days of Noe were, so shall also the coming of the Son of man be. For as in the days that were before the flood they were eating and drinking, marrying and giving in marriage, until the day that Noe entered into the ark, and knew not until the flood came, and took them all

z

travailing with child, and they shall not escape.

away; so shall also the coming of the Son of man be. *Mat. xiv.* 37, 38, 39. Likewise also as it was in the days of Lot; they did eat, they drank, they bought, they sold, they planted, they builded; but the same day that Lot went out of Sodom, it rained fire and brimstone from heaven, and destroyed them all. Even thus shall it be in the day when the Son of man is revealed. *Lu. xvii.* 28, 29, 30. They shall be afraid: pangs and sorrows shall take hold of them; they shall be in pain as a woman that travaileth: they shall be amazed one at another; their faces shall be as flames. *Is. xiii.* 8. How are they brought into desolation, as in a moment! they are utterly consumed with terrors: yea, even like as a dream when one awaketh, so shalt thou make their image to vanish out of the city. *Ps. lxxiii.* 19. See that ye refuse not him that speaketh. For if they escaped not who refused him that spake on earth, much more shall not we escape, if we turn away from him that speaketh from heaven. *He. xii.* 25. How shall we escape, if we neglect so great salvation? *He. ii.* 3. See also, *Mat. xiii.* 41, 42, 43.—*xxiii.* 33.

7. Then shall appear the wrath of God in the day of vengeance, which obstinate sinners, through the stubbornness of their heart, have heaped unto themselves; which despised the goodness, patience, and long-suffering of God, when he calleth them continually to repentance.

7. Then shall appear the sign of the Son of man in heaven: and then shall all the tribes of the earth mourn, and they shall see the Son of man coming in the clouds of heaven with power and great glory. *Mat. xxiv.* 30. He will not spare in the day of vengeance. *Pr. vi.* 34. [They] said to the mountains and rocks, Fall on us, and hide us from the face of him that sitteth on the throne, and from the wrath of the Lamb: for the great day of his wrath is come; and who shall be able to stand? *Re. vi.* 16, 17. The hypocrites in heart heap up wrath. *Job xxxvi.* 13. He that being often reproved hardeneth his neck, shall suddenly be destroyed, and that without remedy. *Pr. xxix.* 1. They refused to hearken, and pulled away the shoulder, and stopped their ears, that they should not hear. Yea, they made their hearts as an adamant stone: therefore came a great wrath from the Lord of hosts. *Zec. vii.* 11, 12. After thy hardness and impenitent heart treasurest up unto thyself wrath against the day of wrath and revelation of the righteous judgment of God. Or despisest thou the riches of his goodness and forbearance and longsuffering; not knowing that the goodness of God leadeth thee to repentance? *Ro. ii.*

5. 4. Harden not your heart. *Ps. xcv.* 8. Account that the longsuffering of our Lord is salvation. The Lord is not slack concerning his promise, as some men count slackness; but is longsuffering to usward, not willing that any should perish, but that all should come to repentance. *2 Pe. iii.* 15. 9.

8. Then shall they call upon me, (saith the Lord,) but I will not hear; they shall seek me early, but they shall not find me; and that, because they hated knowledge, and received not the fear of the Lord, but abhorred my counsel, and despised my correction. Then shall it be too late to knock when the door shall be shut; and too late to cry for mercy when it is the time of justice. O terrible voice of most just judgment, which shall be pronounced upon them, when it shall be said unto them, Go, ye cursed, into the fire everlasting, which is prepared for the devil and his angels.

8. Then shall they call upon me, but I will not answer; they shall seek me early, but they shall not find me: for that they hated knowledge, and did not choose the fear of the Lord: they would none of my counsel: they despised all my reproof. *Pr. i.* 28, 29, 30. While they went to buy, the bridegroom came; and they that were ready went in with him to the marriage: and the door was shut. Afterward came also the other virgins, saying, Lord, Lord, open to us. But he answered and said, Verily, I say unto you, I know you not. *Mat. xxv.* 10, 11, 12. And Noah went in, and his sons, and his wife, and his sons' wives with him, into the ark, because of the waters of the flood. And the Lord shut him in. And the flood was forty days upon the earth; and the waters increased, and bare up the ark, and it was lift up above the earth. And the waters prevailed exceedingly upon the earth. And all flesh died that moved upon the earth, every man, all in whose nostrils was the breath of life, of all that was in the dry land, died. *Ge. vii.* 7. 16, 17. 19. 21, 22. Behold, now is the accepted time; behold, now is the day of salvation. *2 Co. vi.* 2. It is appointed unto men once to die, but after this the judgment. *He. ix.* 27. Whatsoever thy hand findeth to do, do it with thy might; for there is no work, nor device, nor knowledge, nor wisdom, in the grave, whither thou goest. *Ec. ix.* 10. The Lord thy God is among you, a mighty God and terrible. *De. vii.* 21. The voice of the Lord is full of majesty, the voice of the Lord shaketh the wilderness. *Ps. xxix.* 4. 8. Righteousness and judgment are the habitation of his throne. *Ps. xcvii.* 2. Not every one that saith unto me, Lord, Lord, shall enter into the kingdom of heaven, but he that doeth the will of my Father which is in heaven. Many will say to me in that day, Lord, Lord, have we not prophesied in thy name? and in thy name have cast out devils? and in thy name done many wonderful works? and then will I profess unto

them, I never knew you: depart from me; ye that work iniquity. *Mat. vii.* 21, 22, 23. Then shall he say also unto them on the left hand, Depart from me, ye cursed, into everlasting fire, prepared for the devil and his angels. And these shall go away into everlasting punishment. *Mat. xxv.* 41. 46.

9. Therefore we ought to give the more earnest heed to the things which we have heard, lest at any time we should let them slip. For if the word spoken by angels was stedfast, and every transgression and disobedience received a just recompense of reward; how shall we escape, if we neglect so great salvation. *He. ii.* 1, 2, 3. See that ye refuse not him that speaketh. For if they escaped not who refused him that spake on earth, much more shall not we escape, if we turn away from him that speaketh from heaven. *He. xii.* 25. For he saith, I have heard thee in a time accepted, and in the day of salvation have I succoured thee: behold, now is the accepted time; behold, now is the day of salvation. *2 Co. vi.* 2. Take heed, brethren, lest there be in any of you an evil heart of unbelief, in departing from the living God. *He. iii.* 12. Watch ye therefore, and pray always, that ye may be accounted worthy to escape all these things that shall come to pass, and to stand before the Son of man. *Lu. xxi.* 36. I must work the works of him that sent me, while it is day; the night cometh, when no man can work. As long as I am in the world, I am the light of the world. *John ix.* 4, 5. Walk while ye have the light, lest darkness come upon you: for he that walketh in darkness knoweth not whither he goeth. While ye have light, believe in the light, that ye may be the children of light. *John xii.* 35, 36. Redeeming the time, because the days are evil. *Ep. x.* 16. Take the talent from him, and give it unto him which hath ten talents. And cast ye the unprofitable servant into outer darkness: there shall be weeping and gnashing of teeth. *Mat. xxv.* 28. 30. Woe unto them! to whom is reserved the blackness of darkness for ever. *Jude* 11. 13.

10. Despisest thou the riches of his goodness and forbearance and longsuffering; not knowing that the goodness of God leadeth thee to repentance? *Ro. ii.* 4. Seeing that thou

Margin:

9. Therefore, brethren, take we heed betime, while the day of salvation lasteth; for the night cometh, when none can work. But let us, while we have the light, believe in the light, and walk as children of the light, that we be not cast into utter darkness, where is weeping and gnashing of teeth.

10. Let us not abuse the goodness of God, who call-

eth us merci-
fully to amend-
ment, and of
his endless pity
promiseth us
forgiveness of
that which is
past, if with a
perfect and
true heart we
return unto
him.

our God hast punished us less than our iniquities deserve, and hast given us such deliverance as this; should we again break thy commandments, wouldest not thou be angry with us till thou hadst consumed us? *Ezr. ix.* 13, 14. The mercy of the Lord is from everlasting to everlasting upon them that fear him. *Ps. ciii.* 17. In his love and in his pity he redeemed them. *Is. lxiii.* 9. I will forgive their iniquity, and I will remember their sin no more. *Je. xxxi.* 34. Return unto me; for I have redeemed thee. *Is. xliv.* 22. Return, ye backsliding children, and I will heal your backslidings. *Je. iii.* 22. Therefore now amend your ways and your doings, and obey the voice of the Lord your God; and the Lord will repent him of the evil that he hath pronounced against you. *Je. xxvi.* 13. Let the wicked forsake his way, and the unrighteous man his thoughts: and let him return unto the Lord, and he will have mercy upon him. *Is. lv.* 7. The eyes of the Lord run to and fro throughout the whole earth, to shew himself strong in the behalf of them whose heart is perfect toward him. 2 *Ch. xvi.* 9.

11. For though our sins be as red as scarlet, they shall be made white as snow; and though they be like purple, yet they shall be made white as wool. Turn ye (saith the Lord) from all your wickedness, and your sin shall not be your destruction. Cast away from you all your ungodliness that ye have done: Make you new hearts, and a new spirit: Wherefore will ye die, O ye house of Israel, seeing that I have no pleasure in the death of him that dieth, saith the Lord God? Turn ye then, and ye shall live.

11. Come now, and let us reason together, saith the Lord: though your sins be as scarlet, they shall be as white as snow; though they be red like crimson, they shall be as wool. *Is. i.* 18. Repent, and turn yourselves from all your transgressions; so iniquity shall not be your ruin. Cast away from you all your transgressions, whereby ye have transgressed; and make you a new heart and a new spirit; for why will ye die, O house of Israel? For I have no pleasure in the death of him that dieth, saith the Lord God; wherefore turn yourselves, and live ye. *Eze. xviii.* 30 *to* 32. Purge me with hyssop and I shall be clean: wash me, and I shall be whiter than snow. *Ps. li.* 7. Turn thou me, and I shall be turned; for thou art the Lord my God. *Je. xxxi.* 18.

12. Although we have sinned, yet have we an Advocate with the Father, Jesus Christ the righteous; and he is the Propitiation for our sins. For he was wounded for our offences, and smitten for our wickedness.

12. My little children, these things write I unto you, that ye sin not. And if any man sin, we have an Advocate with the Father, Jesus Christ the righteous : and he is the Propitiation for our sins : and not for ours only, but also for the sins of the whole world. 1 *John ii.* 1, 2. Surely he hath borne our griefs, and carried our sorrows : he was wounded for our transgressions, he was bruised for our iniquities : the chastisement of our peace was upon him ; and with his stripes we are healed. The Lord hath laid on him the iniquity of us all. *Is. liii.* 4, 5, 6. We have sinned, we have done wickedly. *Da. ix.* 15. All have sinned, and come short of the glory of God ; being justified freely by his grace through the redemption that is in Christ Jesus : whom God hath set forth to be a Propitiation through faith in his blood. *Ro. iii.* 23, 24, 25. Ye know that he was manifested to take away our sins. 1 *John iii.* 5. It is Christ that died, who is even at the right hand of God, who also maketh intercession for us. *Ro. viii.* 34. Herein is love, not that we loved God, but that he loved us, and sent his Son to be the Propitiation for our sins. 1 *John iv.* 10. Christ hath once suffered for sins, the just for the unjust, that he might bring us to God. 1 *Pe. iii.* 18.

13. Let us therefore return unto him, who is the merciful receiver of all true penitent sinners;

13. Come, and let us return unto the Lord : for he hath torn, and he will heal us ; he hath smitten, and he will bind us up. *Ho. vi.* 1. Go and proclaim these words toward the north, and say, Return, thou backsliding Israel, saith the Lord ; and I will not cause mine anger to fall upon you : for I am merciful, saith the Lord, and I will not keep anger for ever. Only acknowledge thine iniquity, that thou hast transgressed against the Lord thy God. *Je. iii.* 12, 13. O Israel, return unto the Lord thy God ; for thou hast fallen by thine iniquity. Take with you words, and turn to the Lord : say unto him, Take away all iniquity, and receive us graciously. *Ho. xiv.* 1, 2. I will arise and go unto my father, and will say unto him. Father, I have sinned against heaven, and before thee, and am no more worthy to be called thy son. And he arose, and came to his father. But when he was a great way off, his father saw him, and had compassion, and ran, and fell on his neck, and kissed him. *Lu. xv.* 18, 19, 20. Return unto me, and I will return unto you, saith the Lord of hosts. *Mal. iii.* 7.

They shall return even to the Lord, and he shall be intreated of them, and shall heal them. *Is. xix.* 22.

14. Thou, Lord, art good, and ready to forgive, and plenteous in mercy unto all them that call upon thee. *Ps. lxxxvi.* 5. The Lord was ready to save me. *Is. xxxviii.* 20. Him that cometh unto me I will in no wise cast out. *John vi.* 37. Repent, and turn yourselves from all your transgressions. *Eze. xviii.* 30. Let the wicked forsake his way, and the unrighteous man his thoughts : and let him return unto the Lord, for he will abundantly pardon. *Is. lv.* 7. I say unto you, that likewise joy shall be in heaven over one sinner that repenteth. *Lu. xv.* 7. If the wicked will turn from all his sins that he hath committed, and do that which is lawful and right, he shall surely live, he shall not die. All his transgressions that he hath committed, they shall not be mentioned unto him : in his righteousness that he hath done he shall live. *Eze. xviii.* 21, 22. The Lord will speak peace unto his people, and to his saints : but let them not turn again to folly. *Ps. lxxxv.* 8. Now be not stiffnecked, but yield yourselves unto the Lord. *2 Ch. xxx.* 8. Yield yourselves unto God, as those that are alive from the dead, and your members as instruments of righteousness unto God. *Ro. vi.* 13. And many people shall go and say, Come ye, and let us go up to the mountain of the Lord, to the House of the God of Jacob : and he will teach us of his ways, and we will walk in his paths. *Is. ii.* 3. Now, Israel, what doth the Lord thy God require of thee, but to fear the Lord thy God, to walk in all his ways, and to love him, and to serve the Lord thy God with all thy heart, and with all thy soul. *De. x.* 12. Blessed are they that keep his testimonies, and that seek him with the whole heart. They also do no iniquity : they walk in his ways. *Ps. cxix.* 2, 3. Wherefore come out from among them, and be ye separate, saith the Lord, and touch not the unclean thing ; and I will receive you, and will be a Father unto you, and ye shall be my sons and daughters, saith the Lord Almighty. *2 Co. vi.* 17, 18. Come unto me, all ye that labour and are heavy laden, and I will give you rest. Take my yoke upon you, and learn of me ; for I am meek and lowly in heart : and ye shall find rest unto your souls. For my yoke is easy, and my burden

14. Assuring ourselves that he is ready to receive us, and most willing to pardon us, if we come unto him with faithful repentance; if we submit ourselves unto him, and from henceforth walk in his ways; if we will take his easy yoke, and light burden upon us, to follow him in lowliness, patience, and charity, and be ordered by the governance of his Holy Spirit; seeking always his glory, and serving him duly in our vocation with thanksgiving:

is light. *Mat. xi.* 28, 29, 30. With all lowliness and meekness. *Ep. iv.* 2. In lowliness of mind let each esteem other better than themselves. *Phi. ii.* 3. Let us run with patience the race that is set before us, looking unto Jesus. *He. xii.* 1, 2. Above all things put on charity, which is the bond of perfectness. *Col. iii.* 14. If we live in the Spirit, let us also walk in the Spirit. *Ga. v.* 25. As many as are led by the Spirit of God, they are the sons of God. *Ro. viii.* 14. Glorify God in your body, and in your spirit, which are God's. *1 Co. vi.* 20. Whether therefore ye eat, or drink, or whatsoever ye do, do all to the glory of God. *1 Co. x.* 31. I therefore, the prisoner of the Lord, beseech you that ye walk worthy of the vocation wherewith ye are called. *Ep. iv.* 1. Serving the Lord with all humility of mind. *Ac. xx.* 19. Abounding therein with thanksgiving. *Col. ii.* 7. Continue in prayer, and watch in the same with thanksgiving. *Col. iv.* 2.

15. This if we do, Christ will deliver us from the curse of the law, and from the extreme malediction which shall light upon them that shall be set on the left hand; and he will set us on his right hand, and give us the gracious benediction of his Father, commanding us to take possession of his glorious kingdom: Unto which he vouchsafe to bring us all, for his infinite mercy. Amen.

15. There is therefore now no condemnation to them which are in Christ Jesus, who walk not after the flesh, but after the spirit. *Ro. viii.* 1. It is written, Cursed is every one that continueth not in all things which are written in the book of the law to do them. Christ hath redeemed us from the curse of the law, being made a curse for us. *Ga. iii.* 10. 13. The Lord Jesus shall be revealed from heaven with his mighty angels, in flaming fire taking vengeance on them that know not God, and that obey not the gospel of our Lord Jesus Christ: who shall be punished with everlasting destruction from the presence of the Lord, and from the glory of his power. *2 Th. i.* 7, 8, 9. He shall set the sheep on his right hand, but the goats on the left. Then shall he say unto them on the left hand, Depart from me, ye cursed, into everlasting fire, prepared for the devil and his angels. Then shall the King say unto them on his right hand, Come, ye blessed of my Father, inherit the kingdom prepared for you from the foundation of the world. *Mat. xxv.* 33. 41. 34. If these things be in you, and abound, they make you that ye shall neither be barren nor unfruitful in the knowledge of our Lord Jesus Christ. Wherefore the rather, brethren, give diligence to make your calling and election sure: for if ye do these things, ye shall never fall: for so an entrance shall be ministered unto

you abundantly into the everlasting kingdom of our Lord and
Saviour Jesus Christ. 2 *Pet. i.* 8. 10, 11. Then shall the righteous shine forth as the sun in the kingdom of their Father.
Mat. xiii. 43. O send out thy light and thy truth: let them
lead me; let them bring me unto thy holy hill, and to thy
tabernacles. *Ps. xliii.* 3. Thy mercy, O Lord, endureth for
ever. *Ps. cxxxviii.* 8.

CCXXXVI.—*The Intercession or Suffrages.*

Psalm li.—*Have mercy upon me, O God, after thy great goodness: according to the multitude of thy mercies do away mine offences.—Wash me throughly from my wickedness: and
cleanse me from my sin.—For I acknowledge my faults: and my sin is ever before me.—
Against thee only have I sinned, and done this evil in thy sight: that thou mightest be justified in thy saying, and clear when thou art judged.—Behold, I was shapen in wickedness:
and in sin hath my mother conceived me.—But lo, thou requirest truth in the inward parts:
and shalt make me to understand wisdom secretly.—Thou shalt purge me with hyssop, and I
shall be clean: thou shalt wash me, and I shall be whiter than snow.—Thou shalt make me
hear of joy and gladness: that the bones which thou hast broken may rejoice.—Turn thy
face away from my sins: and put out all my misdeeds.—Make me a clean heart, O God:
and renew a right spirit within me.—Cast me not away from thy presence: and take not
thy holy Spirit from me.—O give me the comfort of thy help again: and stablish me with
thy free Spirit.—Then shall I teach thy ways unto the wicked: and sinners shall be converted
unto thee.—Deliver me from blood-guiltiness, O God, thou that art the God of my health: and
my tongue shall sing of thy righteousness.—Thou shalt open my lips, O Lord: and my mouth
shall shew thy praise.—For thou desirest no sacrifice, else would I give it thee: but thou
delightest not in burnt-offerings.—The sacrifice of God is a troubled spirit: a broken and
contrite heart, O God, shalt thou not despise.—O be favourable and gracious unto Sion: build
thou the walls of Jerusalem.—Then shalt thou be pleased with the sacrifice of righteousness,
with the burnt-offerings and oblations: then shall they offer young bullocks upon thine altar.*
Glory be to the Father, &c. As it was in the beginning, &c.

Lord, have mercy upon us.
Christ, have mercy upon us.
Lord, have mercy upon us.
Our Father, &c.

1, 2. O Lord, save thy servants; that put their trust in thee.

1, 2. Preserve my soul; for I am holy: O thou my God,
save thy servant that trusteth in thee. *Ps. lxxxvi.* 2.

3, 4. Send unto them help from above: and evermore mightily defend them.

3, 4. The Lord hear thee in the day of trouble; the name
of the God of Jacob defend thee. Send thee help from the
sanctuary, and strengthen thee out of Sion. *Ps. xx.* 1, 2.

5, 6. Help us, O God our Saviour, and for the glory of thy Name deliver us; be merciful to us sinners, for thy name's sake.

5, 6. Help us, O God of our salvation, for the glory of thy

name : and deliver us, and purge away our sins, for thy name's sake. *Ps. lxxix.* 9.

7, 8. O Lord, hear our prayer : and let our cry come unto thee.

7, 8. Hear my prayer, O Lord, and let my cry come unto thee. *Ps. cii.* 1.

CCXXXVII. *A Prayer for Absolution.*

O Lord, we beseech thee, mercifully hear our prayers, and spare all those who confess their sins unto thee; that they, whose consciences by sin are accused, by thy merciful pardon may be absolved; through Christ our Lord. *Amen.*

Hear me when I call, O God of my righteousness : have mercy upon me, and hear my prayer. *Ps. iv.* 1. Give ear to my prayer, O God ; and hide not thyself from my supplication. Attend unto me, and hear me. *Ps. lv.* 1, 2. Spare thy people, O Lord. *Joel ii.* 17. God be merciful to me a sinner. *Lu. xviii.* 13. I acknowledge my transgressions : and my sin is ever before me. Against thee, thee only, have I sinned, and done this evil in thy sight. Hide thy face from my sins, and blot out all mine iniquities. *Ps. li.* 3, 4. 9. He that covereth his sins shall not prosper : but whoso confesseth and forsaketh them shall have mercy. *Pr. xxviii.* 13. And when he [the Holy Spirit] is come, he will reprove the world of sin, *John xvi.* 8. If our heart condemn us, God is greater than our heart, and knoweth all things. 1 *John iii.* 20. Now when they heard this, they were pricked in their heart, and said unto Peter and to the rest of the apostles, Men and brethren, what shall we do ? *Ac. ii.* 37. For thy name's sake, O Lord, pardon mine iniquity ; for it is great. *Ps. xxv.* 11. And David said unto Nathan, I have sinned against the Lord. And Nathan said unto David, The Lord also hath put away thy sin ; thou shalt not die. 2 *Sa. xii.* 13. The Lord is nigh unto them that are of a broken heart ; and saveth such as be of a contrite spirit. *Ps. xxxiv.* 18. He healeth the broken in heart, and bindeth up their wounds. *Ps. cxlvii.* 3. I, even I, am he that blotteth out thy transgressions for mine own sake, and will not remember thy sins. *Is. xliii.* 25. Being justified by faith, we have peace with God through our Lord Jesus Christ. *Ro. v.* 1. Who his ownself bare our sins in his own body on the tree ; by whose stripes ye were healed. 1 *Pe. ii.* 24. Who is a God like unto thee, that pardoneth iniquity, and passeth by the transgression of the remnant of his heritage? he retaineth not his anger for ever, because he delighteth in mercy. *Mi. vii.* 18.

CCXXXVIII. *A Confession of Sin ; and Prayer for Pardon.*

1. O most mighty God, and merciful Father, who hast compassion upon all men, and hatest nothing that thou hast made; who wouldest not the death of a sinner, but that he should rather turn from his sin, and be saved;

1. The Lord, even the most mighty God, hath spoken. *Ps. l.* 1. Who is this that cometh from Edom, with dyed garments from Bozrah? this that is glorious in his apparel, travelling in the greatness of his strength? I that speak in righteousness, mighty to save. *Is. lxiii.* 1. The Lord is gracious, and full of compassion; slow to anger, and of great mercy. The Lord is good to all : and his tender mercies are over all his works. *Ps. cxlv.* 8, 9. The Father of mercies, and the God of all comfort. 2 *Co. i.* 3. He maketh his sun to rise on the evil and on the good, and sendeth rain on the just and on the unjust. *Mat. v.* 45. God our Saviour, who will have all men to be saved, and to come unto the knowledge of the truth. 1 *Ti. ii.* 3, 4. Say unto them, As I live, saith the Lord God, I have no pleasure in the death of the wicked; but that the wicked turn from his way and live : turn ye, turn ye from your evil ways ; for why will ye die, O house of Israel? *Eze. xxxiii.* 11. Look unto me, and be ye saved, all the ends of the earth. *Is. xlv.* 22. The Lord is not slack concerning his promise, as some men count slackness; but is longsuffering to us-ward, not willing that any should perish, but that all should come to repentance. 2 *Pe. iii.* 9.

2. Mercifully forgive us our trespasses ; receive and comfort us, who are grieved and wearied with the burden of our sins.

2. Have mercy upon me, O God, according to thy lovingkindness : according unto the multitude of thy tender mercies blot out my transgressions. *Ps. li.* 1. O Lord, hear; O Lord, forgive. *Da. ix.* 19. I will be merciful to their unrighteousness, and their sins and their iniquities will I remember no more. *He. viii.* 12. God was in Christ, reconciling the world unto himself, not imputing their trespasses unto them. 2 *Co. v.* 19. When ye stand praying, forgive, if ye have ought against any : that your Father also which is in heaven may forgive you your trespasses. *Mar. xi.* 25. Mine iniquities are gone over mine head : as an heavy burden they are too heavy for me. *Ps. xxxviii.* 4. The spirit of a man will sustain his in-

firmity; but a wounded spirit who can bear? *Pr. xviii.* 14. The sacrifices of God are a broken spirit: a broken and a contrite heart, O God, thou wilt not despise. *Ps. li.* 17. Come unto me, all ye that labour and are heavy laden, and I will give you rest. *Mat. xi.* 28. Take with you words, and turn to the Lord: say unto him, Receive us graciously. *Ho. xiv.* 2. Let, I pray thee, thy merciful kindness be for my comfort. *Ps. cxix.* 76. Now our Lord Jesus Christ himself, and God, even our Father, which hath loved us, and hath given us ever-lasting consolation and good hope through grace, comfort your hearts, and stablish you in every good word and work. *2 Th. ii.* 16, 17.

3. Thy pro-perty is always to have mercy; to thee only it appertaineth to forgive sins. Spare us there-fore, good Lord, spare thy peo-ple, whom thou hast redeemed;

3. The Lord, The Lord God, merciful and gracious, long-suffering, keeping mercy for thousands, forgiving iniquity and transgression and sin. *Ex. xxxiv.* 6, 7. His mercy endureth for ever. *Ps. cxxxvi.* 1. Who can forgive sins but God only? *Mat. ii.* 7. I, even I, am the Lord; and beside me there is no Saviour. I, even I, am he that blotteth out thy transgres-sions for mine own sake. *Is. xliii.* 11. 25. Let the priests, the ministers of the Lord, weep between the porch and the altar, and let them say, Spare thy people, O Lord, and give not thine heritage to reproach. *Joel ii.* 17. Hezekiah prayed for them, saying, The good Lord pardon every one that prepareth his heart to seek God, the Lord God of his fathers. *2 Ch. xxx.* 18, 19. Be merciful, O Lord, unto thy people Israel, whom thou hast redeemed. *De. xxi.* 8. Ye know that ye were not redeemed with corruptible things, as silver and gold; but with the precious blood of Christ, as of a Lamb without blemish and without spot. *1 Pe. i.* 18, 19.

4. enter not into judgment with thy ser-vants, who are vile earth, and miserable sin-ners;

4. Enter not into judgment with thy servant: for in thy sight shall no man living be justified. *Ps. cxliii.* 2. He knoweth our frame; he remembereth that we are dust. *Ps. ciii.* 14. When the breath of man goeth forth he shall turn again to his earth. *Ps. cxlvi.* 3. Man is like a thing of nought. *Ps. cxliv.* 4. Thine own wickedness shall correct thee, and thy backslidings shall reprove thee: know therefore and see that it is an evil thing and bitter, that thou hast forsaken the Lord thy God. *Je. ii.* 19. Woe unto us, that we have sinned! *La. v.* 16.

,5, but so turn thine anger from us, who meekly acknowledge our vileness, and truly repent us of our faults, and so make haste to help us in this world, that we may ever live with thee in the world to come; through Jesus Christ our Lord. Amen.

5. Turn us, O God of our salvation, and cause thine anger toward us to cease. Shew us thy mercy, O Lord, and grant us thy salvation. *Ps. lxxxv. 4. 7.* We acknowledge, O Lord, our wickedness. *Je. xiv. 20.* O Lord, to us belongeth confusion of face, because we have sinned against thee. *Da. ix. 8.* We lie down in our shame, and our confusion covereth us: for we have sinned against the Lord our God. *Je. iii. 25.* Behold I am vile. *Job xl. 4.* I have heard of thee by the hearing of the ear: but now mine eye seeth thee. Wherefore I abhor myself, and repent in dust and ashes. *Job xlii. 5, 6.* Wilt thou not revive us again: that thy people may rejoice in thee? *Ps. lxxxv. 6.* Be not thou far from me, O Lord: O my strength, haste thee to help me. *Ps. xxii. 19.* O spare me, that I may recover strength, before I go hence, and be no more. *Ps. xxxix. 13.* Work out your own salvation with fear and trembling. For it is God which worketh in you. *Ph. ii. 12, 13.* Him that overcometh will I make a pillar in the temple of my God, and he shall go no more out: and I will write upon him the name of my God, and the name of the city of my God, and I will write upon him my new name. *Re. iii. 12.* Where sin abounded, grace did much more abound: that as sin hath reigned unto death, even so might grace reign through righteousness unto eternal life by Jesus Christ our Lord. *Ro. v. 20, 21.* Let us therefore come boldly unto the throne of grace, that we may obtain mercy, and find grace to help in time of need. *He. iv. 16.*

CCXXXIX. *An earnest Prayer for Restoration to God's favour.*

1. Turn thou us, O good Lord, and so shall we be turned. Be favourable, O Lord, Be favourable to thy people, Who turn to thee in weeping, fasting, and praying. For thou art a merciful God, Full of compassion,

1. Turn thou us unto thee, O Lord, and we shall be turned. *La. v. 21.* Thou, Lord, art good, and ready to forgive. *Ps. lxxxvi. 5.* I have surely heard Ephraim bemoaning himself thus: Thou hast chastised me, and I was chastised, as a bullock unaccustomed to the yoke: turn thou me, and I shall be turned; for thou art the Lord my God. *Je. xxxi. 18.* He shall pray unto God, and he will be favourable unto him: and he shall see his face with joy. *Job xxxiii. 26.* In that time, saith the Lord, the children of Israel shall come, going and weeping: they shall go, and seek the Lord their God. *Je. l. 4.* There-

Longsuffering, and of great pity.

fore also now, saith the Lord, Turn ye even to me with all your heart, and with fasting, and with weeping, and with mourning: and rend your heart, and not your garments, and turn unto the Lord your God: for he is gracious and merciful, slow to anger, and of great kindness, and repenteth him of the evil. *Joel ii.* 12, 13. The children of Israel were assembled with fasting, and with sackclothes, and earth upon them: and stood and confessed their sins, and the iniquities of their fathers. And they stood up in their place, and read in the book of the law of the Lord their God one fourth part of the day; and another fourth part they confessed, and worshipped the Lord their God. *Ne. ix.* 1, 2, 3. I will pour upon the house of David, and upon the inhabitants of Jerusalem, the spirit of grace and of supplications: and they shall look upon me whom they have pierced, and they shall mourn for him, and shall be in bitterness for him, as one that is in bitterness for his firstborn. *Zec. xii.* 10. For with the Lord there is mercy. *Ps. cxxx.* 7. Thou, O Lord, art a God full of compassion, and gracious, longsuffering, and plenteous in mercy and truth. *Ps. lxxxvi.* 15.

2. Thou sparest when we deserve punishment, And in thy wrath thinkest upon mercy. Spare thy people, good Lord, spare them, And let not thine heritage be brought to confusion.

2. Thou our God hast punished us less than our iniquities deserve. *Ezr. ix.* 13. I will spare them, as a man spareth his own son that serveth him. *Mal. iii.* 17. O Lord, in wrath remember mercy. *Hab. iii.* 2. He, being full of compassion, forgave their iniquity, and destroyed them not: yea, many a time turned he his anger away, and did not stir up all his wrath. For he remembered that they were but flesh; a wind that passeth away, and cometh not again. *Ps. lxxviii.* 38, 39. I know the thoughts that I think toward you, saith the Lord, thoughts of peace, and not of evil. *Je. xxix.* 11. Let the priests, the ministers of the Lord, weep between the porch and the altar, and let them say, Spare thy people, O Lord, and give not thine heritage to reproach. *Joel ii.* 17. In thee, O Lord, do I put my trust: let me never be put to confusion. *Ps. lxxi.* 1. See also, *Ps. lxxix.* 19.

3. Hear us, O Lord, for thy mercy is great; And after the multitude of thy

3. Consider and hear me, O Lord my God. *Ps. xiii.* 3. Great are thy tender mercies, O Lord. *Ps. cxix.* 156. Have mercy upon me, O God, according to thy lovingkindness: according unto the multitude of thy tender mercies blot out

mercies look upon us; Through the merits and mediation of thy blessed Son, Jesus Christ our Lord. Amen.

my transgressions. *Ps. li.* 1. But as for me, my prayer is unto thee, O Lord, in an acceptable time: O God, in the multitude of thy mercy hear me, in the truth of thy salvation. *Ps. lxix.* 13. God, who is rich in mercy, for his great love wherewith he loved us, even when we were dead in sins, hath quickened us together with Christ. *Ep. ii.* 4, 5. Who gave himself for our sins, that he might deliver us from this present evil world, according to the will of God and our Father. *Ga. i.* 4. He is the Mediator of the new testament. *He. ix.* 15. I am the Way, no man cometh unto the Father, but by me. *John xiv.* 6. God is faithful, by whom ye were called unto the fellowship of his Son Jesus Christ our Lord. 1 *Co. i.* 9. Blessed be God, even the Father of our Lord Jesus Christ, the Father of mercies. 2 *Co. i.* 3.

The concluding Prayer for a Blessing.

The Lord bless us, and keep us; the Lord lift up the light of his countenance upon us, and give us peace now and for evermore. Amen. Nu. vi. 24, 25, 26.

FORMS OF

PRAYER TO BE USED AT SEA.

CCXL. A Daily Prayer.

1. O Eternal Lord God, who alone spreadest out the heavens, and rulest the raging of the sea; who hast compassed the waters with bounds until day and night come to an end: Be pleased to receive into thy Almighty and most gracious protection, the Persons of us thy servants, and the Fleet in which we serve.

1. Know this day, and consider it in thine heart, that the Lord he is God in heaven above, and upon the earth beneath: there is none else. *De. iv.* 39. From everlasting to everlasting, thou art God. *Ps. xc.* 2. Which alone spreadeth out the heavens, and treadeth upon the waves of the sea. *Job ix.* 8. Thou rulest the raging of the sea: when the waves thereof arise, thou stillest them. *Ps. lxxxix.* 9. Who shut up the sea with doors, when it brake forth, and said, Hitherto shalt thou come, but no further: and here shall thy proud waves be stayed? *Job xxxviii.* 8. 11. He hath compassed the waters with bounds, until the day and night come to an end. *Job xxvi.* 10. Happy is he that hath the God of Jacob for his help, whose hope is in the Lord his God. *Ps. cxlvi.* 5. Thus saith the Lord; Cursed be the man that trusteth in man, and maketh flesh his arm, and whose heart departeth from the Lord. Blessed is the man that trusteth in the Lord, and whose hope the Lord is. *Je. xvii.* 5. 7. I will therefore that men pray every where, lifting up holy hands, without wrath and doubting. 1 *Ti. ii.* 8. Wilt not thou, O God, go forth with our hosts? Give us help from trouble: for vain is the help of man. Through God we shall do valiantly: for he it is that shall tread down our enemies. *Ps. cviii.* 11, 12, 13 See also, *Ex. xvii.* 10, 11, 12.—*Ps. lvi.* 9.—*xliii.* 2, 3.—*Is. xl.* 12. 22.—*xlii.* 5.

2. Preserve us from the dangers of the sea, and from the violence of the enemy; that we may be a safeguard unto our most gracious Sovereign Lord, King *William*, and his Dominions,

2. Preserve me, O God; for in thee do I put my trust. *Ps. xvi.* 1. Which stilleth the noise of the seas, the noise of their waves, and the tumult of the people. *Ps. lxv.* 7. They that go down to the sea in ships, that do business in great waters; these see the works of the Lord, and his wonders in the deep. They cry unto the Lord in their trouble, and he bringeth them out of their distresses. *Ps. cvii.* 23, 24. 28. Deliver me, O Lord, from the evil man: preserve me from the violent man. *Ps. cxl.* 1. Now the Lord my God hath given me rest on

and a security for such as pass on the sea upon their lawful occasions;

every side, so that there is neither adversary nor evil occurrent. 1 *Ki. v.* 4. The horse is prepared against the day of battle: but safety is of the Lord. *Pr. xxi.* 31. *See also,* 1 *Ki. iv.* 24, 25.—2 *Ch. xxvi.* 8 *to* 12.

3. that the inhabitants of our Island may in peace and quietness serve thee our God; and that we may return in safety to enjoy the blessings of the land, with the fruits of our labours;

3. I exhort therefore, that, first of all, supplications, prayers, intercessions, and giving of thanks, be made for all men; for kings; and for all that are in authority; that we may lead a quiet and peaceable life in all godliness and honesty. 1 *Ti. ii.* 1, 2. The Lord will give strength unto his people; the Lord will bless his people with peace. *Ps. xxix.* 11. They shall sit every man under his vine and under his figtree; and none shall make them afraid: for the mouth of the Lord of hosts hath spoken it. *Mi. iv.* 4. Then Joshua called the Reubenites, and the Gadites, and the half tribe of Manasseh, and said unto them, Ye have kept all that Moses the servant of the Lord commanded you; ye have not left your brethren these many days unto this day. And now the Lord your God hath given rest unto your brethren, as he promised them: therefore now return ye, and get you unto your tents, and unto the land of your possession. Return with much riches unto your tents, and with very much cattle, with silver, and with gold, and with brass, and with iron, and with very much raiment: divide the spoil of your enemies with your brethren. *Jos. xxii.* 1 *to* 4. 8. Thou shalt eat the labour of thine hands: happy shalt thou be, and it shall be well with thee. *Ps. cxxviii.* 2. *See also, Is. iii.* 10.—*De. xxxiii.* 13 *to* 16.

4. and with a thankful remembrance of thy mercies to praise and glorify thy holy Name; through Jesus Christ our Lord. *Amen.*

4. Oh that men would praise the Lord for his goodness, and for his wonderful works to the children of men! *Ps. cvii.* 8. I will praise thee, O Lord, among the people: and I will sing praises unto thee among the nations. For thy mercy is great above the heavens. *Ps. cviii.* 3, 4. Rejoice in the Lord, ye righteous; and give thanks at the remembrance of his holiness. *Ps. xcvii.* 12. I will praise thee, O Lord my God, with all my heart: and I will glorify thy name for evermore. *Ps. lxxxvi.* 12. I will not trust in my bow, neither shall my sword save me. Thou hast saved us from our enemies, and hast put them to shame that hated us. In God we boast all the day long, and praise thy name for ever. *Ps. xliv.* 6, 7, 8. It is God that avengeth me, and that

bringeth down the people under me, and that bringeth me forth from mine enemies: thou also hast lifted me up on high above them that rose up against me: thou hast delivered me from the violent man. Therefore I will give thanks unto thee, O Lord, among the heathen, and I will sing praises unto thy name. *2 Sa. xxii.* 48, 49, 50. Giving thanks always unto God and the Father in the name of our Lord Jesus Christ. *Ep. v.* 20. I thank my God through Jesus Christ for you all. *Ro. i.* 8.

Prevent us, O Lord, &c. *as* CLI.

CCXLI. *A Prayer to be used during a Storm at Sea.* No. 1.

1. O Most powerful and glorious Lord God, at whose command the winds blow, and lift up the waves of the sea, and who stillest the rage thereof;

1. I am God Almighty. *Ge. xxxv.* 11. The Great, the Mighty God, the Lord of hosts, is his name. *Je. xxxii.* 18. Who is like unto thee, O Lord, among the gods? who is like thee, glorious in holiness? *Ex. xv.* 11. Give unto the Lord, O ye mighty, give unto the Lord glory and strength. Give unto the Lord the glory due unto his name; worship the Lord in the beauty of holiness. The voice of the Lord is upon the waters: the God of glory thundereth: the Lord is upon many waters. The voice of the Lord is powerful; the voice of the Lord is full of majesty. The Lord sitteth upon the flood; yea, the Lord sitteth King for ever. *Ps. xxix.* 1 *to* 4. 10. The Lord hath his way in the whirlwind and in the storm, and the clouds are the dust of his feet. He rebuketh the sea, and maketh it dry, and drieth up all the rivers. *Na. i.* 3, 4. The Lord on high is mightier than the noise of many waters, yea, than the mighty waves of the sea. *Ps. xciii.* 4. He commandeth, and raiseth the stormy wind, which lifteth up the waves thereof. *Ps. cvii.* 25. The floods have lifted up, O Lord, the floods have lifted up their voice: the floods lift up their waves. *Ps. xciii.* 3. Thou rulest the raging of the sea: when the waves thereof arise, thou stillest them. *Ps. lxxxix.* 9. He arose, and rebuked the winds and the sea; and there was a great calm. *Mat. viii.* 26. Is any thing too hard for the Lord? *Ge. xviii.* 14.

2. We thy creatures, but miserable sinners, do in this our great dis-

2. O Lord, thou art our Father; we are the clay, and thou our Potter; and we all are the work of thy hand. *Is. lxiv.* 8. We have sinned with our fathers, we have committed iniquity,

trees cry unto
thee for help:
Save, Lord, or
else we perish.

we have done wickedly. *Ps. cvi. 6.* Be not wroth very sore,
O Lord, neither remember iniquity for ever: behold, see, we
beseech thee, we are all thy people. *Is. lxiv. 9.* Now, our God,
thou art just in all that is brought upon us, for thou hast done
right, but we have done wickedly. *Ne. ix. 32, 33.* Behold,
O Lord; for I am in distress. *La. i. 20.* Lord, I cry unto
thee: make haste unto me; give ear unto my voice, when I
cry unto thee. *Ps. cxli. 1.* They mount up to the heaven,
they go down again to the depths: their soul is melted because
of trouble. They reel to and fro, and stagger like a drunken
man, and are at their wits' end. Then they cry unto the Lord
in their trouble, and he bringeth them out of their distresses.
Ps. cvii. 26, 27, 28. Help me, O Lord my God: O save me
according to thy mercy. *Ps. cix. 26.* In my distress I called
upon the Lord, and cried unto my God: he heard my voice
out of his temple, and my cry came before him, even into his
ears. *Ps. xviii. 6.* From the end of the earth will I cry unto
thee; when my heart is overwhelmed: lead me to the rock
that is higher than I. *Ps. lxi. 2.* When Peter saw the wind
boisterous, he was afraid; and beginning to sink, he cried,
saying, Lord, save me. *Mat. xiv. 30.* And his disciples came
to him, and awoke him, saying, Lord, save us: we perish.
Mat. viii. 25.

If, when we
fear, when we
have been safe,
and seeing all
things quiet
about us, we
have forgot
thee our God,
and refused to
hearken to the
still voice of
thy word, and
to obey thy
command-
ments.

In my prosperity I said, I shall never be moved. *Ps.
xxx. 6.* They soon forgat his works; they waited not for his
counsel. They forgat God their Saviour, which had done
great things in Egypt. *Ps. cvi. 13. 21.* He made him ride
on the high places of the earth, that he might eat the increase
of the fields; and he made him to suck honey out of the rock,
and oil out of the flinty rock; butter of kine, and milk of
sheep, with fat of lambs, and rams of the breed of Bashan,
and goats, with the fat of kidneys of wheat; and thou didst
drink the pure blood of the grape. But Jeshurun waxed fat,
and kicked: thou art waxen fat, thou art grown thick, thou
art covered with fatness; then he forsook God which made him,
and lightly esteemed the Rock of his salvation. Of the Rock
that begat thee thou art unmindful, and hast forgotten God
that formed thee. *De. xxxii. 13, 14, 15. 18.* [They] refused
to obey, neither were mindful of thy wonders that thou

didst among them; but hardened their necks. They were disobedient, and rebelled against thee, and cast thy law behind their backs, and they wrought great provocations. *Ne. ii.* 17. 26. Neither have we obeyed the voice of the Lord our God. *Da. ix.* 10. We have forsaken thy commandments. *Ezr. ix.* 10. When the Lord thy God shall have brought thee into the land which he sware unto thy fathers, to Abraham, to Isaac, and to Jacob, to give thee great and goodly cities, which thou buildedst not, and houses full of good things, which thou filledst not, and wells digged, which thou diggedst not, vineyards and olive trees, which thou plantedst not: when thou shalt have eaten, and be full; then beware lest thou forget the Lord. *De. vi.* 10, 11, 12. *See also, De. viii.* 10 *to* 14.— *Am. i.* 3 *to* 6.

4. But now we see, how terrible thou art in all thy works of wonder; the great God to be feared above all;

4. When they shall say, Peace and safety; then sudden destruction cometh upon them. 1 *Th. v.* 3. Say unto God, How terrible art thou in thy works! through the greatness of thy power shall thine enemies submit themselves unto thee. Come and see the works of God: he is terrible in his doing toward the children of men. *Ps. lxvi.* 3. 5. They that go down to the sea in ships, that do business in great waters; these see the works of the Lord, and his wonders in the deep. *Ps. cvii.* 23, 24. Our God, the great, the mighty, and the terrible God. *Ne. ix.* 32. Thou, even thou, art to be feared: and who may stand in thy sight when once thou art angry? *Ps. lxxvi.* 7. The Lord is great; he is to be feared above all gods. *Ps. xcvi.* 4.

5. And therefore we adore thy Divine Majesty, acknowledging thy power, and imploring thy goodness. Help, Lord, and save us for thy mercies' sake in Jesus Christ thy Son, our Lord. Amen.

5. The Lord is a great God, and a great King above all gods. The sea is his, and he made it. O come, let us worship and bow down: let us kneel before the Lord our Maker. *Ps. xcv.* 3. 5, 6. Thine, O Lord, is the greatness, and the power, and the glory, and the majesty: for all that is in the heaven and in the earth is thine; thine is the kingdom, O Lord, and thou art exalted as head above all. 1 *Ch. xxix.* 11. Oh how great is thy goodness, which thou hast laid up for them that fear thee; which thou hast wrought for them that trust in thee! *Ps. xxxi.* 19. According to thy mercy remember thou me for thy goodness' sake, O Lord. *Ps. xxv.* 7. Help me, O Lord my God; O save me according to thy mercy.

Ps. cix. 26. Hear, O Lord, and have mercy upon me : Lord, be thou my helper. *Ps. xxxi. 10.* Be not far from me ; for trouble is near. *Ps. xxii. 11.* God is our refuge and strength, a very present help in trouble. *Ps. xlvi. 1.* The wages of sin is death ; but the gift of God is eternal life through Jesus Christ our Lord. *Ro. vi. 23.* God so loved the world, that he gave his only begotten Son, that whosoever believeth in him should not perish, but have everlasting life. *John iii. 16.* Verily, verily, I say unto you, Whatsoever ye shall ask the Father in my name, he will give it you. *John xvi. 23.*

CCXLII. *A Prayer to be used during a Storm at Sea.* No. 2.

1. O most glorious and gracious Lord God, who dwellest in heaven, but beholdest all things below ; Look down, we beseech thee, and hear us, calling out of the depth of misery, and out of the jaws of this death, which is ready now to swallow us up : Save, Lord, or else we perish.

1. Thy right hand, O Lord, is become glorious in power. Who is like unto thee, O Lord, among the gods ? who is like thee, glorious in holiness ; fearful in praises, doing wonders ? *Ex. xv. 6. 11.* Thou, O Lord, art a God full of compassion, and gracious, longsuffering, and plenteous in mercy and truth. *Ps. lxxxvi. 15.* He will be very gracious unto thee at the voice of thy cry : when he shall hear it, he will answer thee. *Is. xxx. 19.* Unto thee lift I up mine eyes, O thou that dwellest in the heavens. *Ps. cxxiii. 1.* The Lord is in his holy. temple, the Lord's throne is in heaven: his eyes behold, his eyelids try, the children of men. *Ps. xi. 4.* The Lord looketh from heaven ; he beholdeth all the sons of men. From the place of his habitation he looketh upon all the inhabitants of the earth. *Ps. xxxiii. 13, 14.* Thus saith the High and Lofty One that inhabiteth eternity ; I dwell in the high and holy place, with him also that is of a contrite and humble spirit. *Is. lvii. 15.* Look down from heaven, and behold from the habitation of thy holiness and of thy glory. *Is. lxiii. 15.* Out of the depths have I cried unto thee, O Lord. Lord, hear my voice. *Ps. cxxx. 1, 2.* Deep calleth unto deep at the noise of thy waterspouts : all thy waves and thy billows are gone over me. *Ps. xlii. 7.* Out of the belly of hell cried I, and thou heardest my voice. For thou hadst cast me into the deep, in the midst of the seas ; and the floods compassed me about : all thy billows and thy waves passed over me. *Jon. ii. 2, 3.* The sorrows of death compassed me, and the pains of hell

gat hold upon me : I found trouble and sorrow. Then called I upon the name of the Lord ; O Lord, I beseech thee, deliver my soul. *Ps. cxvi.* 3, 4. Save me, O God ; for the waters are come in unto my soul. I sink in deep mire, where there is no standing : I am come into deep waters, where the floods overflow me. I am weary of my crying : mine eyes fail while I wait for my God. O God, in the multitude of thy mercy hear me. Deliver me out of the mire, and let me not sink : let me be delivered out of the deep waters. Let not the waterflood overflow me, neither let the deep swallow me up. *Ps. lxix.* 1, 2, 3. 13, 14, 15. Make haste, O God, to deliver me ; make haste to help me, O Lord. *Ps. lxx.* 1. The Lord sent out a great wind into the sea, and there was a mighty tempest in the sea, so that the ship was like to be broken. Then the mariners were afraid, and cried every man unto his god, and cast forth the wares that were in the ship into the sea to lighten it of them. But Jonah was fast asleep. So the shipmaster came to him, and said unto him, What meanest thou, O sleeper? arise, call upon thy God, if so be that God will think upon us, that we perish not. *Jon. i.* 4, 5, 6. And his disciples came to him, and awoke him, saying, Lord, save us : we perish. *Mat. viii.* 25.

2. The living, the living, shall praise thee. O send thy word of command to rebuke the raging winds and the roaring sea ; that we, being delivered from this distress, may live to serve thee, and to glorify thy Name all the days of our life.

2. The living, the living, he shall praise thee, as I do this day: the father to the children shall make known thy truth. *Is. xxxviii.* 19. And he saith unto them, Why are ye fearful, O ye of little faith? Then he arose, and rebuked the winds and the sea ; and there was a great calm. *Mat. viii.* 26. He rebuked the Red Sea also, and it was dried up. *Ps. cvi.* 9. By terrible things in righteousness wilt thou answer us, O God of our salvation ; who art the confidence of all the ends of the earth, and of them that are afar off upon the sea. Which stilleth the noise of the seas, the noise of their waves. *Ps. lxv.* 5. 7. They mount up to the heaven, they go down again to the depths : their soul is melted because of trouble. They reel to and fro, and stagger like a drunken man, and are at their wits' end. Then they cry unto the Lord in their trouble, and he bringeth them out of their distresses. He maketh the storm a calm, so that the waves thereof are still. Then are they glad because they be quiet ; so he bringeth them unto their desired haven. Oh that men would praise the Lord for his goodness, and for his wonderful works to the children of men! Let them exalt him also in the congregation of the people, and praise him in the assembly of the elders. *Ps. cvii.* 26 to 32. All people will walk every one in the name of his god, and we will walk in the name of the Lord our God for ever and ever. *Mi. iv.* 5. Bless the Lord, O my soul: and all that is within me, bless his holy name. Bless the Lord, O my soul, and forget not all his benefits: who forgiveth all thine iniquities; who healeth all thy diseases; who redeemeth thy life from destruction; who crowneth thee with loving-kindness and tender mercies. *Ps. ciii.* 1 to 4. While I live will I praise the Lord: I will sing praises unto my God while I have any being. *Ps. cxlvi.* 2. The Lord was ready to save me: therefore we will sing my songs to the stringed instruments all the days of our life in the house of the Lord. *Is. xxxviii.* 20. I will praise thee, O Lord my God, with all my heart: and I will glorify thy name for evermore. *Ps. lxxxvi.* 12. See also, *Ps. xcviii.* 7, 8, 9.—*Ac.* XXVII.

3. Hear, Lord, and save us, for the infinite merits of our blessed Saviour, thy Son, our Lord Jesus Christ. *Amen.*

3. Hear, O Lord, and have mercy upon me: Lord, be thou my helper. *Ps. xxx.* 10. Save us, O God of our salvation. *1 Ch. xvi.* 35. Arise, and help us: and deliver us for thy mercies' sake. *Ps. xliv.* 26. Whatsoever ye shall ask the Father in my name, he will give it you. Hitherto ye have asked nothing in my name: ask, and ye shall receive, that your joy may be full. *John xvi.* 23, 24. This is my beloved Son, in whom I am well pleased. *Mat. iii.* 17.

CCXLIII. A Prayer to be used before a Fight at Sea, against an Enemy.

1. O most powerful and glorious Lord God, the Lord of hosts, that rulest and commandest all things;

1. Lord God Almighty, which was, and is, and is to come. *Re. iv.* 8. Thine, O Lord, is the greatness, and the power, and the glory, and the victory, and the majesty: for all that is in the heaven and in the earth is thine; thine is the kingdom, O Lord, and thou art exalted as head above all. *1 Ch. xxix.* 11. Who is like unto thee, O Lord, among the gods? who is like thee, glorious in holiness, fearful in praises, doing wonders? *Ex. xv.* 11. The Great, the Mighty God, the Lord of hosts, is his name, great in counsel, and mighty in work. *Je. xxxii.*

18, 19. The Lord of hosts is with us; the God of Jacob is our refuge. *Ps. xlvi.* 11. The Lord which giveth the sun for a light by day, and the ordinances of the moon and of the stars for a light by night, which divideth the sea when the waves thereof roar; the Lord of hosts is his name. *Je. xxxi.* 35. He ruleth by his power for ever. *Ps. lxvi.* 7. His kingdom ruleth over all. *Ps. ciii.* 19. The Most High ruleth in the kingdom of men, and giveth it to whomsoever he will. He doeth according to his will in the army of heaven, and among the inhabitants of the earth. *Da. iv.* 17. 35. I, even my hands, have stretched out the heavens, and all their host have I commanded. *Is. xlv.* 12. He sendeth forth his commandment upon earth: his word runneth very swiftly. *Ps. cxlvii.* 15.

2, God is a righteous Judge, strong, and patient. *Ps. vii.* 12. Thou hast maintained my right and my cause; thou satest in the throne judging right. *Ps. ix.* 4. He is a God of truth and without iniquity, just and right is he. *De. xxxii.* 4. In my distress I called upon the Lord. *2 Sa. xxii.* 7. Hear the right, O Lord; let my sentence come forth from thy presence; let thine eyes behold the things that are equal. *Ps. xvii.* 1, 2. Stir up thyself, and awake to my judgment, even unto my cause, my God and my Lord. *Ps. xxxv.* 23. I know that the Lord will maintain the cause of the afflicted, and the right of the poor. *Ps. cxl.* 12. The Lord judge between me and thee, and the Lord avenge me of thee; but mine hand shall not be upon thee. The Lord therefore be Judge, and judge between me and thee, and see, and plead my cause, and deliver me out of thine hand. *1 Sa. xxiv.* 12. 15. Now, behold, the children of Ammon and Moab and Mount Seir, behold, I say, how they reward us, to come to cast us out of thy possession, which thou hast given us to inherit. O our God, wilt thou not judge them? for we have no might against this great company that cometh against us; neither know we what to do: but our eyes are upon thee. And all Judah stood before the Lord, with their little ones, their wives, and their children. *2 Ch. xx.* 10 to 13. Thus saith Jephthah, I have not sinned against thee, but thou doest me wrong to war against me: The Lord the Judge be Judge this day between the children of Israel and the children of Ammon. *Jud. xi.*

2. Thou sittest in the throne judging right, and therefore we make our address to thy Divine Majesty in this our necessity, that thou wouldest take the cause into thine own hand, and judge between us and our enemies.

c 2

15. 27. Dearly beloved, avenge not yourselves, but rather give place unto wrath: for it is written, Vengeance is mine: I will repay, saith the Lord. *Ro. xii.* 19. Christ, when he was reviled, reviled not again; when he suffered, he threatened not; but committed himself to him that judgeth righteously. 1 *Pe. ii.* 21. 23.

3. Stir up thy strength, O Lord, and come and help us; for thou givest not alway the battle to the strong, but canst save by many or by few.

3. Before Ephraim, Benjamin, and Manasses, stir up thy strength, and come, and help us. *Ps. lxxx.* 2. Stir up thyself, and awake to my judgment, even unto my cause, my God and my Lord. *Ps. xxxv.* 23. I returned, and saw under the sun, that the race is not to the swift, nor the battle to the strong. *Ec. ix.* 11. He sent all the rest of Israel every man unto his tent, and retained those three hundred men. And he divided the three hundred men into three companies. And [they] blew the trumpets, and brake the pitchers, and held the lamps in their left hands, and the trumpets in their right hands: and they cried, The sword of the Lord, and of Gideon. And they stood every man in his place round about the camp: and all the host ran, and cried, and fled. And the Lord set every man's sword against his fellow, even throughout all the host: and the host fled. *Jud. vii.* 8. 16. 20, 21, 22. And Asa cried unto the Lord his God, and said, Lord, it is nothing with thee to help, whether with many, or with them that have no power: help us, O Lord our God; for we rest on thee, and in thy name we go against this multitude. O Lord, thou art our God; let not man prevail against thee. 2 *Ch. xiv.* 11. And all this assembly shall know that the Lord saveth not with sword and spear: for the battle is the Lord's, and he will give you into our hands. So David prevailed over the Philistine with a sling and with a stone, and smote the Philistine, and slew him; and the men of Israel and of Judah pursued the Philistines, until thou come to the valley, and to the gates of Ekron. 1 *Sa. xvii.* 47. 50. 52. And Jonathan said to the young man that bare his armour, Come, and let us go over unto the garrison of these uncircumcised: it may be that the Lord will work for us: for there is no restraint to the Lord to save by many or by few. 1 *Sa. xiv.* 6. *See also,* 1 *Ch. xiv.* 14, 15, 16.—*De. xx.* 3, 4.

4. O let not our sins now

4. And he said, What hast thou done? the voice of thy brother's blood crieth unto me from the ground. *Ge. iv.* 10.

cry against us for vengeance; but hear us thy poor servants begging mercy, and imploring thy help, and that thou wouldest be a defence unto us against the face of the enemy.

And the Lord said, Because the cry of Sodom and Gomorrah is great, and because their sin is very grievous; I will go down now, and see whether they have done altogether according to the cry of it, which is come unto me; and if not, I will know. *Ge. xviii.* 20, 21. Behold, the hire of the labourers who have reaped down your fields, which is of you kept back by fraud, crieth : and the cries of them which have reaped are entered into the ears of the Lord of Sabaoth. *Ja. v.* 4. Jerusalem hath grievously sinned ; therefore she is removed. The Lord is righteous; for I have rebelled against his commandments. *La. i.* 8. 18. They mocked the messengers of God, and despised his words, and misused his prophets, until the wrath of the Lord arose against his people, till there was no remedy. 2 *Ch. xxxvi.* 16. O Lord, I beseech thee, let now thine ear be attentive to the prayer of thy servants, who desire to fear thy name. *Ne. i.* 11. I am poor and needy ; yet the Lord thinketh upon me : thou art my help and my deliverer ; make no tarrying, O my God. *Ps. xl.* 17. Bow down thine ear to me ; deliver me speedily : be thou my strong rock, for an house of defence to save me. *Ps. xxxi.* 2. Deliver me from mine enemies, O my God : defend me from them that rise up against me. *Ps. lix.* 1. Thou hast been a shelter for me, and a strong tower from the enemy. *Ps. lxi.* 3.

5. Make it appear that thou art our Saviour and mighty Deliverer, through Jesus Christ our Lord. Amen.

5. Let them be confounded and troubled for ever ; yea, let them be put to shame, and perish : that men may know that thou, whose name alone is JEHOVAH, art the Most High over all the earth. *Ps. lxxxiii.* 17, 18. All flesh shall know that I the Lord am thy Saviour and thy Redeemer, the Mighty One of Jacob. *Is. xlix.* 26. So that a man shall say, Verily there is a reward for the righteous : verily he is a God that judgeth in the earth. *Ps. lviii.* 11. Fear not, thou worm Jacob, and ye men of Israel ; I will help thee, saith the Lord, and thy Redeemer, the Holy One of Israel. That they may see, and know, and consider, and understand together, that the hand of the Lord hath done this, and the Holy One of Israel hath created it. *Is. xli.* 14. 20. The Lord is my rock, and my fortress, and my deliverer ; my God, my strength, in whom I will trust;

my buckler, and the horn of my salvation, and my high
tower. I will call upon the Lord, who is worthy to be
praised : so shall I be saved from mine enemies. *Ps. xviii.*
2, 3. See also, *Is. lx.* 16.—*Ps. xci.* 16.

CCXLIV. *General and Special prayers in a Storm; and, with respect to the Enemy.*

1. Lord, be merciful to us sinners, and save us for thy mercy's sake.

1. Lord, be merciful unto me ; heal my soul: for I have
sinned against thee. *Ps. xli.* 4. God be merciful to me a
sinner. *Lu. xviii.* 13. O Lord, deliver my soul: Oh save me
for thy mercies' sake. *Ps. vi.* 4.

2. Thou art the great God, thou hast made and rulest all things: O deliver us for thy Name's sake.

2. Thou, even thou, art Lord alone; thou hast made heaven, the heaven of heavens, with all their host, the earth, and
all things that are therein, and thou preservest them all. Our
God, the Great, the mighty God. *Ne. ix.* 6. 32. O Lord God
of our fathers, art not thou God in heaven ? and rulest not
thou over all the kingdoms of the heathen ? and in thine hand
is there not power and might, so that none is able to withstand
thee ? *2 Ch. xx.* 6. Help us, O God of our salvation, for the
glory of thy name : and deliver us, for thy name's sake. *Ps.
lxxix.* 9.

3. Thou art the great God to be feared above all : O save us, that we may praise thee.

3. O Lord my God, thou art very great. *Ps. civ.* 1. The
Lord is a great God, and a great King above all gods. *Ps.
xcv.* 3. Thou, even thou, art to be feared: and who may
stand in thy sight when once thou art angry ? *Ps. lxxvi.* 7.
I prayed before the God of heaven, and said, I beseech thee,
O God of heaven, the Great and terrible God, that keepeth
covenant and mercy for them that love him and observe his
commandments. *Ne. i.* 4, 5. Have mercy upon me, O Lord ;
consider my trouble, thou that liftest me up from the gates of
death : that I may shew forth all thy praise in the gates of
the daughter of Zion. *Ps. ix.* 13, 14. Let my soul live, and
it shall praise thee. *Ps. cxix.* 175. The Lord hath chastened
me sore : but he hath not given me over unto death. Open
to me the gates of righteousness: I will go into them, and I
will praise the Lord. *Ps. cxviii.* 18, 19.

4. Thou, O Lord, art just and powerful : O defend our

4. A God of truth and without iniquity, just and right is
he. *De. xxxii.* 4. Great is our Lord, and of great power. *Ps.
cxlvii.* 5. Defend my cause against the ungodly people: O

cause against the face of the enemy. deliver me from the deceitful and wicked man. *Ps. xliii.* 1. Plead my cause, O Lord, with them that strive with me : fight against them that fight against me. *Ps. xxxv.* 1.

5. O God, thou art a strong tower of defence to all that flee unto thee : O save us from the violence of the enemy. 5. Blessed be the Lord my strength ; my goodness, and my fortress ; my high tower, and my deliverer. *Ps. cxliv.* 1, 2. He only is my rock and my salvation : he is my defence, I shall not be moved. In God is my salvation and my glory : the rock of my strength, and my refuge, is in God. *Ps. lxii.* 6, 7. Deliver me, O Lord, from mine enemies : I flee unto thee to hide me. *Ps. cxliii.* 9. Thou hast been a shelter for me, and a strong tower from the enemy. *Ps. lxi.* 3. Deliver me, O Lord, from the evil man : preserve me from the violent man. *Ps. cxl.* 1.

6. O Lord of hosts, fight for us, that we may glorify thee. 6. O Lord of hosts. *Ps. lxxxiv.* 12. Plead my cause, O Lord, with them that strive with me : fight against them that fight against me. Take hold of shield and buckler, and stand up for mine help. Draw out also the spear, and stop the way against them that persecute me : say unto my soul, I am thy salvation. *Ps. xxxv.* 1, 2, 3. Ye shall not need to fight in this battle : set yourselves, stand ye still, and see the salvation of the Lord with you, O Judah and Jerusalem : fear not, nor be dismayed. *2 Ch. xx.* 17. One man of you shall chase a thousand : for the Lord your God, he it is that fighteth for you, as he hath promised you. *Jos. xxiii.* 10. Call upon me in the day of trouble : I will deliver thee, and thou shalt glorify me. *Ps. l.* 15. Be thou exalted, Lord, in thine own strength : so will we sing and praise thy power. *Ps. xxi.* 13.

7. O suffer us not to sink under the weight of our sins, or the violence of the enemy. 7. Mine iniquities are gone over mine head : as an heavy burden they are too heavy for me. *Ps. xxxviii.* 4. Deliver me out of the mire, and let me not sink : let me be delivered from them that hate me, and out of the deep waters. Let not the waterflood overflow me, neither let the deep swallow me up, and let not the pit shut her mouth upon me. *Ps. lxix.* 14, 15. The righteous cry, and the Lord heareth, and delivereth them out of all their troubles. The Lord is nigh unto them that are of a broken heart ; and saveth such as be of a contrite spirit. *Ps. xxxiv.* 17, 18. He shall redeem their soul from deceit and violence : and precious shall their blood be in his sight. *Ps. lxxii.* 14.

8. O Lord, arise, help us, and deliver us for thy Name's sake.

8. Arise, O Lord, in thine anger, lift up thyself because of the rage of mine enemies. *Ps. vii.* 6. Arise for our help, and redeem us for thy mercies' sake. *Ps. xliv.* 26. O Lord, though our iniquities testify against us, do thou it for thy name's sake. *Je. xiv.* 7. Do thou for me, O God the Lord, for thy name's sake : because thy mercy is good, deliver thou me. *Ps. cix.* 21. He saved them for his name's sake, that he might make his mighty power to be known. *Ps. cvi.* 8.

9. Thou, O Lord, that stillest the raging of the sea, hear, hear us, and save us, that we perish not.

9. By terrible things in righteousness wilt thou answer us, O God of our salvation ; who art the confidence of all the ends of the earth, and of them that are afar off upon the sea. Which stilleth the noise of the seas, the noise of their waves, and the tumult of the people. *Ps. lxv.* 5. 7. O Lord, hear ; O Lord, hearken and do ; defer not, for thine own sake, O my God. *Da. ix.* 19. Hear me, O Lord, hear me. 1 *Ki. xviii.* 37. Who can tell if God will turn and repent, and turn away from his fierce anger, that we perish not ? *Jon. iii.* 9.

10. O blessed Saviour, that didst save thy disciples ready to perish in a storm, hear us, and save us, we beseech thee.

10. He went into a ship with his disciples : but as they sailed he fell asleep : and there came down a storm of wind on the lake ; and they were filled with water, and were in jeopardy. And they came to him, and awoke him, saying, Master, master, we perish. Then he arose, and rebuked the wind and the raging of the water : and they ceased, and there was a calm. *Lu. viii.* 22, 23, 24. They cried unto the Lord and said, We beseech thee, O Lord, we beseech thee, let us not perish. *Jon. i.* 14. Hear, O Lord, and have mercy upon me : Lord, be thou my helper. *Ps. xxx.* 10. Save us, O God of our salvation. 1 *Ch. xvi.* 35. They lifted up their voices, and said, Jesus, Master, have mercy on us. *Lu. xvii.* 13. Help me, O Lord my God : O save me according to thy mercy. *Ps. cix.* 26.

Lord, have mercy upon us.
Christ, have mercy upon us.
Lord, have mercy upon us.

O Lord, hear us.
O Christ, hear us.

God the Father, God the Son, God the Holy Ghost, have mercy upon us, save us now and evermore. Amen.

Our Father, &c.

Almighty God, Father, &c. as *CXXXI.*

Almighty God, our, &c. as *CXXXII.*

Psalm lxvi.—*O be joyful in God, all ye lands : sing praises unto the honour of his Name, make his praise to be glorious.—Say unto God, O how wonderful art thou in thy works : through the greatness of thy power shall thine enemies be found liars unto thee.—For all the world shall worship thee : sing of thee, and praise thy Name.—O come hither, and behold the works of God : how wonderful he is in his doing toward the children of men.—He turned the sea into dry land : so that they went through the water on foot ; there did we rejoice thereof.—He ruleth with his power for ever ; his eyes behold the people : and such as will not believe shall not be able to exalt themselves.—O praise our God, ye people : and make the voice of his praise to be heard ;—Who holdeth our soul in life : and suffereth not our feet to slip.—For thou, O God, hast proved us : thou also hast tried us, like as silver is tried. —Thou broughtest us into the snare : and laidest trouble upon our loins.—Thou sufferedst men to ride over our heads : we went through fire and water, and thou broughtest us out into a wealthy place.—I will go into thine house with burnt-offerings : and will pay thee my vows, which I promised with my lips, and spake with my mouth, when I was in trouble.—I will offer unto thee fat burnt-sacrifices, with the incense of rams : I will offer bullocks and goats. —O come hither, and hearken, all ye that fear God : and I will tell you what he hath done for my soul.—I called unto him with my mouth : and gave him praises with my tongue.— If I incline unto wickedness with mine heart : the Lord will not hear me.—But God hath heard me : and considered the voice of my prayer.—Praised be God who hath not cast out my prayer : nor turned his mercy from me.*

Glory be to the Father, &c. As it was in the beginning, &c.

Psalm cvii.——*O give thanks unto the Lord, for he is gracious : and his mercy endureth for ever.—Let them give thanks whom the Lord hath redeemed : and delivered from the hand of the enemy.—And gathered them out of the lands, from the east, and from the west : from the north, and from the south.—They went astray in the wilderness out of the way : and found no city to dwell in ;—Hungry and thirsty : their soul fainted in them.—So they cried unto the Lord in their trouble : and he delivered them from their distress.—He led them forth by the right way : that they might go to the city where they dwelt.—O that men would therefore praise the Lord for his goodness : and declare the wonders that he doeth for the children of men !—For he satisfieth the empty soul : and filleth the hungry soul with goodness.—Such as sit in darkness, and in the shadow of death : being fast bound in misery and iron ; Because they rebelled against the words of the Lord : and lightly regarded the counsel of the Most Highest.—He also brought down their heart through heaviness : they fell down, and there was none to help them.—So when they cried unto the Lord in their trouble : he delivered them out of their distress.—For he brought them out of darkness, and out of the shadow of death : and brake their bonds in sunder.—O that men would therefore praise the Lord for his goodness : and declare the wonders that he doeth for the children of men !—For he hath broken the gates of brass : and smitten the bars of iron in sunder.—Foolish men are plagued for their offence : and because of their wickedness. —Their soul abhorred all manner of meat : and they were even hard at death's door.—So when they cried unto the Lord in their trouble : he delivered them out of their distress.— He sent his word, and healed them : and they were saved from their destruction.—O that men would therefore praise the Lord for his goodness : and declare the wonders that he doeth for the children of men !—That they would offer unto him the sacrifice of thanksgiving : and tell out his works with gladness !—They that go down to the sea in ships : and occupy their business in great waters ;—These men see the works of the Lord : and his wonders in the deep.—For at his word the stormy wind ariseth : which lifteth up the waves thereof.—They are carried up to the heaven, and down again to the deep : their soul melteth away because of the trouble.—They reel to and fro, and stagger like a drunken man : and are at their wit's end.—So when they cry unto the Lord in their trouble : he delivereth them out of their distress.—For he maketh the storm to cease : so that the waves thereof are still.—Then are they glad, because they are at rest : and so he bringeth them unto the haven where they would be.—O that men would therefore praise the Lord for his goodness : and declare the wonders that he doeth for the children of men !—That they would exalt him also in the congregation of the people : and praise him in the seat of the elders !—Who turneth the floods into a wilderness : and drieth up the water-springs.—A fruitful land maketh he barren ; for the wickedness of them that dwell therein.—Again, he maketh the wilderness a standing water : and water-springs of a dry ground.—And there he setteth the hungry : that they may build them a city to dwell in ;—That they may sow their land, and plant vineyards : to yield them fruits of increase.—He blesseth them, so that they multiply exceedingly : and suffereth not their cattle to decrease.—And again, when they are minished, and brought low ; through oppression, through any plague, or trouble ;—Though he suffer them to be evil intreated through tyrants : and let them wander out of the way in the wilderness;—Yet helpeth he the poor out of misery : and maketh him housholds like a flock of sheep.— The righteous will consider this and rejoice : and the mouth of all wickedness shall be stopped.— Whoso is wise will ponder these things ; and they shall understand the loving-kindness of the Lord.*

Glory be to the Father, &c. As it was in the beginning, &c.

CCXLV. *A Thanksgiving after a Storm. No.* 1.

1. O most blessed and glorious Lord God, who art of infinite goodness and mercy ;

1. And David said, Blessed be thou, Lord God of Israel our Father, for ever and ever. Thine, O Lord, is the power, and the glory, and the majesty; and thou reignest over all. And David said to all the congregation, Now bless the Lord your God. And all the congregation blessed the Lord God of their fathers, and bowed down their heads, and worshipped the Lord. 1 *Ch. xxix.* 10, 11, 12. 20. Who is like unto thee, O Lord, glorious in holiness, fearful in praises, doing wonders? *Ex. xv.* 11. Why boastest thou thyself in mischief, O mighty man? the goodness of God endureth continually. *Ps. lii.* 1. The mercy of the Lord is from everlasting to everlasting upon them that fear him, and his righteousness unto children's children. *Ps. ciii.* 17. Surely goodness and mercy shall follow me all the days of my life. *Ps. xxiii.* 6. See also, Ge. *xiv.* 20.—*Ex. xxxiv.* 6.

2. We thy poor creatures, whom thou hast made and preserved, holding our souls in life, and now rescuing us out of the jaws of death,

2. I am poor and needy. *Ps. lxx.* 5. This poor man cried, and the Lord heard him, and saved him out of all his troubles. *Ps. xxxiv.* 6. I am as a wonder unto many; but thou art my strong refuge. By thee have I been holden up from the womb : thou art he that took me out of my mother's bowels. *Ps. lxxi.* 7. 6. Which holdeth our soul in life, and suffereth not our feet to be moved. *Ps. lxvi.* 9. He delivereth and rescueth, and he worketh signs and wonders in heaven and in earth. *Da. vi.* 27. Unless the Lord had been my help, my soul had almost dwelt in silence. *Ps. xciv.* 17. He brought me up also out of an horrible pit, out of the miry clay, and set my feet upon a rock, and established my goings. *Ps. xl.* 2. See also, Job *xxxiv.* 19.—*Ps. xxxv.* 17.

3. humbly present ourselves again before thy, Divine Majesty, to offer a sacrifice of praise

3. O come, let us worship and bow down: let us kneel before the Lord our Maker. *Ps. xcv.* 6. I will go into thy house with burnt offerings : I will pay thee my vows, which my lips have uttered, and my mouth hath spoken, when I was in trouble. *Ps. lxvi.* 13, 14. I will offer to thee the sacrifice of

and thanksgiv- thanksgiving, and will call upon the name of the Lord. *Ps.*
ing,
cxvi. 17. Let them sacrifice the sacrifices of thanksgiving, and
declare his works with rejoicing. *Ps. cvii.* 22. David spake unto
the Lord the words of this song in the day that the Lord had
delivered him out of the hand of all his enemies. 2 *Sa. xxii.* 1.

4. for that thou
heardest us
when we called
in our trouble,
and didst not
cast out our
prayer, which
we made before
thee in our
great distress :

4. Call upon me in the day of trouble; I will deliver thee
and thou shalt glorify me. *Ps. l.* 15. Ye shall seek me and
find me, when ye shall search for me with all your heart.
And I will be found of you, saith the Lord. *Je. xxix.* 13, 14.
They cried unto the Lord in their trouble, and he delivered
them out of their distresses. *Ps. cvii.* 6. I waited patiently
for the Lord; and he inclined unto me, and heard my cry.
Ps. xl. 1. Praised be God, who hath not cast out my prayer :
nor turned his mercy from me. *Ps. lxvi.* 18. I will sing of thy
power ; yea, I will sing aloud of thy mercy in the morning:
for thou hast been my defence and refuge in the day of my
trouble. *Ps. lix.* 16.

5. Even
when we gave
all for lost, our
ship, our
goods, our
lives, then
didst thou mer-
cifully look
upon us, and
wonderfully
command a
deliverance ;
for which we,
now being in
safety, do give
all praise and
glory to thy
Holy Name ;
through Jesus
Christ our
Lord. *Amen.*

5. We had the sentence of death in ourselves, that we
should not trust in ourselves, but in God which raiseth the
dead: who delivered us from so great a death, and doth deliver : in whom we trust that he will yet deliver us. 2 *Co. i.*
9, 10. And falling into a place where two seas met, they
ran the ship aground; and the forepart stuck fast, and remained unmoveable, but the hinder part was broken with the
violence of the waves. And the centurion commanded that
they which could swim should cast themselves first into the sea
and get to land : and so it came to pass, that they escaped all
safe to land. *Ac. xxvii.* 41. 43, 44. Then they cry unto the
Lord in their trouble, and he bringeth them out of their distresses. He maketh the storm a calm, so that the waves
thereof are still. Then are they glad because they be quiet;
so he bringeth them unto their desired haven. *Ps. cvii.* 28,
29, 30. He sent from above, he took me; he drew me out
of many waters; he delivered me from my strong enemy,
and from them that hated me : for they were too strong for
me. 2 *Sa. xxii.* 17, 18. Thou art my King, O God: command deliverances for Jacob. *Ps. xliv.* 4. The Lord saved
them by a great deliverance. 1 *Ch. xi.* 14. Who remembered us in our low estate; and hath redeemed us from our

enemies: for his mercy endureth for ever. *Ps. cxxxvi.* 23, 24. Thou art my hiding-place; thou shalt preserve me from trouble; thou shalt compass me about with songs of deliverance. Be glad in the Lord, and rejoice, ye righteous: and shout for joy, all ye that are upright in heart. *Ps. xxxii.* 7. 11. Blessed be thou, Lord God of Israel our Father, for ever and ever. Now therefore, our God, we thank thee, and praise thy glorious name. 1 *Ch. xxix.* 10. 13.—*See also,* 1 *Sa. xxiii.* 26, 27, 28.—2 *Ki.* VI. VII. XVIII, XIX.

CCXLVI. *A Thanksgiving after a Storm. No. 2.*

1. O most mighty and gracious good God, thy mercy is over all thy works, but in special manner hath been extended toward us, whom thou hast so powerfully and wonderfully defended.

1. O Lord God of hosts, who is a strong Lord like unto thee? or to thy faithfulness round about thee? thou hast a mighty arm: strong is thy hand, and high is thy right hand. Thou rulest the raging of the sea: when the waves thereof arise, thou stillest them. *Ps. lxxxix.* 8. 13. 9. Thou, O Lord, art a God full of compassion, and gracious, longsuffering, and plenteous in mercy and truth. *Ps. lxxxvi.* 15. The Lord is good to all: and his tender mercies are over all his works. *Ps. cxlv.* 9. He rode upon a cherub, and did fly: and he was seen upon the wings of the wind. The Lord thundered from heaven, and the Most High uttered his voice. And the channels of the sea appeared, the foundations of the world were discovered, at the rebuking of the Lord, at the blast of the breath of his nostrils. He drew me out of many waters; he brought me forth also into a large place: he delivered me. 2 *Sa. xxii.* 11. 14. 16, 17. 20. The Lord is our defence. *Ps. lxxxix.* 18.

2. Thou hast shewed us terrible things, and wonders in the deep, that we might see how powerful and gracious a God thou art; how able and ready to help them that trust in thee.

2. By terrible things in righteousness wilt thou answer us, O God of our salvation; who art the confidence of all the ends of the earth, and of them that are afar off upon the sea. *Ps. lxv.* 5. Say unto God, How terrible art thou in thy works! *Ps. lxvi.* 3. They that go down to the sea in ships, that do business in great waters; these see the works of the Lord, and his wonders in the deep. *Ps. cvii.* 23, 24. The Lord God is thy praise, and he is thy God, that hath done for thee these great and terrible things, which thine eyes have seen. *De. x.* 20, 21. He saved them for his name's sake, that he might make his mighty power to be known. *Ps. cvi.* 8.

All men that see it, shall say, This hath God done; for they shall perceive that it is his work. *Ps. lxiv.* 9. And Peter beginning to sink, cried, saying, Lord, save me. And immediately Jesus stretched forth his hand, and caught him, and said unto him, O thou of little faith, wherefore didst thou doubt? *Mat. xiv.* 20. 31. Blessed is that man that maketh the Lord his trust. *Ps. xl.* 4. Our fathers trusted in thee; they trusted, and thou didst deliver them. *Ps. xxii.* 4. Oh how great is thy goodness, which thou hast laid up for them that fear thee; which thou hast wrought for them that trust in thee before the sons of men! *Ps. xxxi.* 19. The Lord shall help them, and deliver them: he shall save them, because they trust in him. *Ps. xxxvii.* 40.

3. *Thou hast shewed us how both winds and seas obey thy command;*

3. The men marvelled, saying, What manner of man is this, that even the winds and the sea obey him! *Mat. viii.* 27. He arose, and rebuked the wind, and said unto the sea, Peace, be still. And the wind ceased, and there was a great calm. And they said one to another, What manner of man is this, that even the wind and the sea obey him? *Mar. iv.* 39. 41. He commandeth, and raiseth the stormy wind, which lifteth up the waves thereof. He maketh the storm a calm, so that the waves thereof are still. *Ps. cvii.* 25, 29. And Moses stretched out his hand over the sea; and the Lord caused the sea to go back by a strong east wind all that night, and made the sea dry land. And the children of Israel went into the midst of the sea upon the dry ground: and the waters were a wall unto them on their right hand, and on their left. And the Egyptians pursued, and went in after them to the midst of the sea. And Moses stretched forth his hand over the sea, and the sea returned to his strength when the morning appeared. *Ex. xiv.* 21, 22, 23. 27.

4. *that we may learn, even from them, hereafter to obey thy voice, and to do thy will.*

4. Even the winds and the sea obey him. *Mar. iv.* 41. Thy will be done in earth, as it is in heaven. *Mat. vii.* 10. Whoso is wise, and will observe these things, even they shall understand the loving kindness of the Lord. *Ps. cvii.* 43. Therefore now amend your ways and your doings, and obey the voice of the Lord your God; and the Lord will repent him of the evil that he hath pronounced against you. *Je. xxvi.* 13. Teach me to do thy will; for thou art my God: thy Spirit is good; lead me into the land of uprightness. *Ps. cxliii.* 10.

5, We therefore bless and glorify thy Name, for this thy mercy in saving us, when we were ready to perish.

5. The Lord was ready to save me : therefore we will sing my songs to the stringed instruments all the days of our life in the house of the Lord. *Is. xxxviii.* 20. Not unto us, O Lord, not unto us, but unto thy name give glory, for thy mercy, and for thy truth's sake. *Ps. cxv.* 1. The Lord is my strength and song, and he is become my salvation : he is my God, and I will prepare him an habitation; my father's God, and I will exalt him. *Ex. xv.* 2. In God we boast all the day long, and praise thy name for ever. *Ps. xliv.* 8. For thy mercy is great above the heavens : and thy truth reacheth unto the clouds· Be thou exalted, O God, above the heavens : and thy glory above all the earth. *Ps. cviii.* 4, 5.

6. And, we beseech thee, make us as truly sensible now of thy mercy, as we were then of the danger ; and give us hearts always ready to express our thankfulness, not only by words, but also by our lives, in being more obedient to thy holy commandments.

6. Thy mercy is great unto the heavens. *Ps. lvii.* 10. They draw near unto the gates of death. Then they cry unto the Lord in their trouble, and he saveth them out of their distresses. Oh that men would praise the Lord for his goodness, and for his wonderful works to the children of men ! *Ps. cvii.* 18, 19. 21. The Egyptians marched after them; and they were sore afraid : and the children of Israel cried out unto the Lord. The Lord saved Israel that day out of the hand of the Egyptians ; and Israel saw the Egyptians dead upon the sea shore. And Israel saw that great work which the Lord did upon the Egyptians : and the people feared the Lord, and believed the Lord, and his servant Moses. *Ex. xiv.* 10. 30, 31. I will sacrifice unto thee with the voice of thanksgiving; I will pay that that I have vowed. Salvation is of the Lord. *Jon. ii.* 9. Then sang Moses and the children of Israel this song unto the Lord, and spake, saying, I will sing unto the Lord, for he hath triumphed gloriously : the horse and his rider hath he thrown into the sea. The Lord is my strength and song, and he is become my salvation. *Ex. xv.* 1, 2. Oh that there were such an heart in them, that they would fear me, and keep all my commandments always, that it might be well with them, and with their children for ever ! *De. v.* 29. He established a testimony in Jacob, and appointed a law in Israel, which he commanded our fathers, that they should make them known to their children : that they might set their hope in God, and not forget the works of God. They kept not the covenant of God, and refused to walk in his law : therefore their days did he consume in vanity, and their years

in trouble. When he slew them, then they sought him : and they returned and enquired early after God. Nevertheless they did flatter him with their mouth, and they lied unto him with their tongues. For their heart was not right with him, neither were they stedfast in his covenant. *Ps. lxxviii.* 5. 7. 10. 33, 34. 36, 37. In those days Hezekiah was sick to the death, and prayed unto the Lord : and he spake unto him, and he gave him a sign. But Hezekiah rendered not again according to the benefit done unto him. *2 Ch. xxxii.* 24, 25. I will run the way of thy commandments, when thou shalt enlarge my heart. *Ps. cxix.* 32.

7. Continue, we beseech thee, this thy goodness to us ; that we, whom thou hast saved, may serve thee in holiness and righteousness all the days of our life ; through Jesus Christ our Lord and Saviour. *Amen.*

7. O continue thy loving kindness unto them that know thee ; and thy righteousness to the upright in heart. *Ps. xxxvi.* 10. That we being delivered out of the hand of our enemies might serve him without fear, in holiness and righteousness before him, all the days of our life. *Lu.* 1. 74, 75. The mercy of the Lord is from everlasting to everlasting upon them that fear him, and his righteousness unto children's children ; to such as keep his covenant, and to those that remember his commandments to do them. *Ps. ciii.* 17, 18. Surely, shall one say, In the Lord have I righteousness and strength. *Is. xlv.* 24. Christ liveth in me : and the life which I now live in the flesh I live by the faith of the Son of God. *Ga. ii.* 20.

CCXLVII. *An Hymn of Praise and Thanksgiving after a dangerous Tempest.*

1. O come, let us give thanks unto the Lord, for he is gracious ; and his mercy endureth for ever.

1. O come, let us sing unto the Lord : let us make a joyful noise to the rock of our salvation. *Ps. xcv.* 1. O give thanks unto the Lord, for he is gracious : and his mercy endureth for ever. *Ps. cvii.* 1.

2. Great is the Lord, and greatly to be praised ; let the redeemed of the Lord say so ; whom he hath delivered from the merciless rage of the sea.

2. Great is the Lord, and greatly to be praised. *Ps. xlviii.* 1. Let the redeemed of the Lord say so, whom he hath redeemed from the hand of the enemy. *Ps. cvii.* 2.

3. The Lord is gracious and full of compassion ; slow to anger, and of great mercy.

3. The Lord is gracious, and full of compassion ; slow to anger, and of great mercy. *Ps. cxlv.* 8.

4, 5. He hath not dealt with us according to our sins, neither rewarded us according to our iniquities. But as the heaven is high above the earth : so great hath been his mercy towards us.

4, 5. He hath not dealt with us after our sins ; nor rewarded us according to our iniquities. As the heaven is high above the earth, so great is his mercy toward them that fear him. *Ps. ciii.* 10, 11.

6. We found trouble and heaviness : we were even at death's door.

6. The sorrows of death compassed me, and the pains of hell gat hold upon me : I found trouble and sorrow. *Ps. cxvi.* 3. Their soul abhorred all manner of meat : and they were even hard at death's door. *Ps. cvii.* 18.

7. The waters of the sea had well nigh covered us : the proud waters had well nigh gone over our soul.

7. The waters had overwhelmed us, the stream had gone over our soul : then the proud waters had gone over our soul. *Ps. cxxiv.* 4, 5. *See also, Ps. xlii.* 7.—*lxix.* 15.—*xciii.* 3, 4.— *Job xxxviii.* 8.

8. The sea roared, and the stormy wind lifted up the waves thereof.

8. Let the sea roar, and the fulness thereof ; the world, and they that dwell therein. *Ps. xcviii.* 7. He commandeth, and raiseth the stormy wind, which lifteth up the waves thereof. *Ps. cvii.* 25.

9, 10. We were carried up as it were to heaven, and then down again into the deep : our soul melted within us, because of trouble ; then cried we unto thee, O Lord, and thou didst deliver us out of our distress.

9, 10. They mount up to the heaven, they go down again to the depths : their soul is melted because of trouble. Then they cry unto the Lord in their trouble, and he bringeth them out of their distresses. *Ps. cvii.* 26. 28.

11. Blessed be thy name, who didst not despise the prayer of thy servants : but didst hear our cry, and hast saved us.

11. The righteous cry, and the Lord heareth, and delivereth them out of all their troubles. *Ps. xxxiv.* 17. He will fulfil the desire of them that fear him : he also will hear their cry, and will save them. *Ps. cxlv.* 19. Verily God hath heard me ; he hath attended to the voice of my prayer. Blessed be God, which hath not turned away my prayer, nor his mercy from me. *Ps. lxvi.* 19, 20.

12. Thou didst send forth thy commandment: and the windy storm ceased, and was turned into a calm.

> 12. He sendeth forth his commandment upon earth: his word runneth very swiftly. *Ps. cxlvii.* 15. He maketh the storm a calm, so that the waves thereof are still. *Ps. cvii.* 29. *See also, Ps. lxv. 7.—Lu. viii.* 24.

13. O let us therefore praise the Lord for his goodness: and declare the wonders that he hath done, and still doeth for the children of men!

> 13. O that men would praise the Lord for his goodness, and declare the wonders that he doeth for the children of men! *Ps. cvii.* 31. *See also, Ex. xv. 1.—Jud. v.* 1, 2.

14, 15. Praised be the Lord daily: even the Lord that helpeth us, and poureth his benefits upon us. He is our God, even the God of whom cometh salvation: God is the Lord, by whom we have escaped death.

> 14, 15. Praised be the Lord daily: even the God who helpeth us, and poureth his benefits upon us. He is our God, even the God of whom cometh salvation: God is the Lord, by whom we escape death. *Ps. lxviii.* 19, 20.

16. Thou, Lord, hast made us glad through the operation of thy hands: and we will triumph in thy praise.

> 16. I will rejoice in giving praise for the operations of thy hands. Thou, Lord, hast made me glad through thy works. *Ps. xcii.* 4.

17, 18. Blessed be the Lord God: even the Lord God, who only doeth wondrous things; and blessed be the Name of his Majesty for ever: and let every one of us say, Amen, Amen.

> 17, 18. Blessed be the Lord God, even the God of Israel: which only doeth wondrous things; and blessed be the name of his Majesty for ever: and all the earth shall be filled with his Majesty. Amen, Amen. *Ps. lxxii.* 18, 19. Blessed be the Lord God of Israel from everlasting to everlasting; and let all the people say, Amen. Praise ye the Lord. *Ps. cvi.* 4. 8.

The grace of our Lord Jesus Christ, and the love of God, and the fellowship of the Holy Ghost, be with us all evermore. Amen. 2 Co. xiii. 14.

CCXLVIII.—*A Psalm or Hymn of Praise and Thanksgiving after Victory.*

1, 2, 3, 4. If the Lord had not been on our side, now may we say: if the Lord himself had not been on our side, when men rose up against us; they had swallowed us up quick, when they were so wrathfully displeased at us : yea, the waters had drowned us, and the stream had gone over our soul : the deep waters of the proud had gone over our soul. But praised be the Lord, who hath not given us over as a prey unto them. *Ps. cxxiv.* 1 to 5.

5. The Lord hath wrought a mighty salvation for us.   5. The Lord wrought a great salvation for all Israel. 1 *Sa. xix.* 5. To day the Lord hath wrought salvation in Israel. 1 *Sa. xi.* 13.

6. We gat not this by our own sword, neither was it our own arm that saved us : but thy right hand, and thine arm, and the light of thy countenance, because thou hadst a favour unto us.

6. They got not the land in possession by their own sword, neither did their own arm save them : but thy right hand, and thine arm, and the light of thy countenance, because thou hadst a favour unto them. *Ps. xliv.* 3.

7, 8. The Lord hath appeared for us; the Lord hath covered our heads, and made us to stand in the day of battle. The Lord hath appeared for us, the Lord hath overthrown our enemies, and dashed in pieces those that rose up against us.   7, 8. O God the Lord, the strength of my salvation, thou hast covered my head in the day of battle. *Ps. cxl.* 7. Hear the word of the Lord, ye that tremble at his word; Your brethren that hated you, that cast you out for my Name's sake, said, Let the Lord be glorified : but he shall appear to your joy, and they shall be ashamed. *Is. lxvi.* 5. In the greatness of thine excellency thou hast overthrown them that rose up against thee. Thy right hand, O Lord, hath dashed in pieces the enemy. *Ex. xv.* 7. 6. Them that rose up against me hast thou subdued under me. 2 *Sa. xxii.* 40. They are brought down and fallen : but we are risen, and stand upright. *Ps. xx.* 8.

9. Therefore not unto us, O Lord, not unto us, but unto thy Name be given the glory.

9. Not unto us, O Lord, not unto us, but unto thy name, give glory, for thy mercy, and for thy truth's sake. *Ps. cxv.* 1.

10. The Lord hath done great things for us ; the Lord hath done great things for us, for which we rejoice.

10. The Lord hath done great things for them. Yea, the Lord hath done great things for us already : whereof we rejoice. *Ps. cxxvi.* 3, 4.

11. Our help standeth in the Name of the Lord : who hath made heaven and earth.

11. My help cometh from the Lord, which made heaven and earth. *Ps. cxxi.* 2. Our help is in the name of the Lord, who made heaven and earth. *Ps. cxxiv.* 8.

12. Blessed be the name of the Lord from this time forth and for evermore. *Ps. cxiii.* 2. Blessed be the Lord God of Israel from everlasting, and to everlasting. Amen, and Amen. *Ps. xli.* 13.

CCXLIX. *A Prayer for Grace to glorify God.*

1. O Almighty God, the Sovereign Commander of all the world, in whose hand is power and might which none is able to withstand ;

1. Great and marvellous are thy works, Lord God Almighty; just and true are thy ways, thou King of saints. *Re. xv.* 3. The Lord most high is terrible; he is a great King over all the earth. Sing praises to God, sing praises: sing praises unto our King, sing praises. For God is the King of all the earth: sing ye praises with understanding. God reigneth over the heathen: God sitteth upon the throne of his holiness. The princes of the people are gathered together, even the people of the God of Abraham: for the shields of the earth belong unto God. *Ps. xlvii.* 2. 6 *to* 9. Thine is the kingdom, and the power, and the glory. *Mat. vi.* 13. For he spake, and it was done; he commanded, and it stood fast. *Ps. xxxiii.* 9. The Lord reigneth; let the people tremble: he sitteth between the cherubims ; let the earth be moved. *Ps. xcix.* 1. O Lord God of our fathers, art not thou God in heaven? and rulest thou not over all the kingdoms of the heathen; and in thine hand is there not power and might, so that none is able to withstand thee? 2 *Ch. xx.* 6.

2. We bless and magnify thy great and glorious Name for this happy Victory, the whole glory whereof we do ascribe to thee, who art the only giver of Victory.

2. Stand up and bless the Lord your God for ever and ever : and blessed be thy glorious name, which is exalted above all blessing and praise. *Ne. ix.* 5. I will praise the name of God with a song, and will magnify him with thanksgiving. *Ps. lxix.* 30. Now, O Lord God, let thy name be magnified for ever. 2 *Sa. vii.* 25, 26. O sing unto the Lord a new song ; for he hath done marvellous things : his right hand, and his holy arm, hath gotten him the victory. *Ps. xcvii.* 1. Thou hast saved us from our enemies, and hast put them to shame that hated us. In God we boast all the day long, and praise thy name for ever. *Ps. xliv.* 7, 8. Not unto us, O Lord, not unto us, but unto thy name give glory, for thy mercy, and for thy truth's sake. *Ps. cxv.* 1. Truly my soul

E 2

waiteth upon God: from him cometh my salvation. He only is my rock and my salvation; he is my defence; I shall not be greatly moved. *Ps. lxii.* 1, 2. Thine, O Lord, is the greatness, and the power, and the glory, and the victory, and the majesty. 1 *Ch. xxix.* 11. Naaman, captain of the host of the king of Syria, was a great man with his master, and honourable, because by him the Lord had given deliverance [*marginal reading,* victory] unto Syria. 2 *Ki. v.* 1.—*See also, De. xxxii.* 39 *to* 42.

3. **And, we beseech thee, give us grace to improve this great mercy to thy glory, the advancement of thy Gospel, the honour of our Sovereign, and, as much as in us lieth, to the good of all mankind.**

3. I am the Lord thy God which teacheth thee to profit. *Is. xlvii.* 17. Behold, God exalteth by his power: who teacheth like him? Remember that thou magnify his work, which men behold. *Job xxxvi.* 22, 23. Whatsoever ye do, do all to the glory of God. 1 *Co. x.* 31. It came to pass, when the king sat in his house, and the Lord had given him rest round about from all his enemies; that the king said unto Nathan the prophet, See now, I dwell in an house of cedar, but the ark of God dwelleth within curtains.—And Solomon sent to Hiram, saying, Thou knowest how that David my father could not build an house unto the name of the Lord his God for the wars which were about him on every side, until the Lord put them under the soles of his feet. But now the Lord my God hath given me rest on every side. And, behold, I purpose to build an house unto the name of the Lord my God. 2 *Sa. vii.* 1, 2.—1 *Ki. v.* 2 *to* 5. And the Syrians became servants to David, and brought gifts. And David took the shields of gold that were on the servants of Hadadezer, and brought them to Jerusalem. And from [the] cities of Hadadezer, king David took exceeding much brass. And Joram brought with him vessels of silver, and vessels of gold, and vessels of brass; which also king David did dedicate unto the Lord, with the silver and gold that he had dedicated of all nations which he subdued. 2 *Sa. viii.* 6, 7, 8. 10, 11. And they offered unto the Lord the same time, of the spoil which they had brought, seven hundred oxen and seven thousand sheep. And they entered into a covenant to seek the Lord God of their fathers with all their heart and with all their soul; that whosoever would not seek the Lord God of Israel should be put to death, whether small or great, whe-

ther man or woman. And all Judah rejoiced at the oath : for they had sworn with all their heart, and sought him with their whole desire; and he was found of them. And Asa put away the abominable idols out of all the land of Judah and Benjamin, and out of the cities which he had taken from mount Ephraim, and renewed the altar of the Lord. 2 *Ch. xv.* 11, 12, 13. 15. 8. Let the people praise thee, O God; let all the people praise thee. That thy way may be known upon earth; thy saving health among all nations. *Ps. lxvii.* 3. 2. They shall hear of thy great name, and of thy strong hand, and of thy stretched out arm. 1 *Ki. viii.* 42. Then sang Deborah and Barak on that day, saying, Praise ye the Lord for the avenging of Israel. Hear, O ye kings; give ear, O ye princes; I, even I, will sing unto the Lord; I will sing praise to the Lord God of Israel. *Jud. v.* 1, 2, 3. And it came to pass as they came, when David was returned from the slaughter of the Philistine, that the women came out of all cities of Israel, singing and dancing, to meet king Saul, with tabrets, with joy, and with instruments of music. And the women answered one another as they played, and said, Saul hath slain his thousands, and David his ten thousands. 1 *Sa. xviii.* 6, 7. As we have therefore opportunity, let us do good unto all men, especially unto them who are of the houshold of faith. *Ga. vi.* 10. See that none render evil for evil unto any man ; but ever follow that which is good, both among yourselves, and to all men. 1 *Th. v.* 15.

4. *And, we beseech thee, give us such a sense of this great mercy, as may engage us to a true thankfulness,* 4. Return unto thy rest, O my soul ; for the Lord hath dealt bountifully with thee. For thou hast delivered my soul from death, mine eyes from tears, and my feet from falling. I will walk before the Lord in the land of the living. *Ps. cxvi.* 7, 8, 9. Our fathers understood not thy wonders in Egypt; they remembered not the multitude of thy mercies; but provoked him at the sea, even at the Red sea. Nevertheless he saved them for his name's sake, that he might make his mighty power to be known. *Ps. cvi.* 7, 8. I will praise thee, O Lord, with my whole heart ; I will shew forth all thy marvellous works. *Ps. ix.* 1. Only fear the Lord, and serve him in truth with all your heart : for consider how great things he hath done for you. 1 *Sa. xii.* 24. And when Jeho-

shaphat and his people came to take away the spoil, they found among them in abundance both riches with the dead bodies; and precious jewels, which they stripped off for themselves, more than they could carry away: and they were three days in gathering of the spoil, it was so much. And on the fourth day they assembled themselves in the valley of Berachah ; for there they blessed the Lord. Then they returned, every man of Judah and Jerusalem, and Jehoshaphat in the forefront of them, to go again to Jerusalem with joy ; for the Lord had made them to rejoice over their enemies. And they came to Jerusalem with psalteries and harps and trumpets unto the house of the Lord. *2 Ch. xx. 25 to 28.*

5. such as may appear in our lives by an humble, holy, and obedient walking before thee all our days, through Jesus Christ our Lord; to whom with thee and the Holy Spirit, as for all thy mercies, so in particular for this Victory, and Deliverance, be all glory and honour, world without end. *Amen.*

5. I beseech you therefore, brethren, by the mercies of God, that ye present your bodies a living sacrifice, holy, acceptable unto God, which is your reasonable service. *Ro. xii.* 1. That we, being delivered out of the hand of our enemies might serve him without fear, in holiness and righteousness before him, all the days of our life. *Lu. i. 74, 75.* He hath shewed thee, O man, what is good ; and what doth the Lord require of thee, but to do justly, and to love mercy, and to walk humbly with thy God? *Mi. vi. 8.* And now, Israel, what doth the Lord thy God require of thee, but to fear the Lord thy God, to walk in all his ways, and to love him, and to serve the Lord thy God, with all thy heart, and with all thy soul, to keep the commandments of the Lord, and his statutes, which I command thee this day for thy good? *De. x. 12, 13.* And David said, Blessed be thou, Lord God of Israel our father, for ever and ever. Thine, O Lord, is the greatness, and the power, and the glory, and the victory, and the majesty : for all that is in the heaven and in the earth is thine : thine is the kingdom, O Lord, and thou art exalted as head above all. *1 Ch. xxix. 10, 11.* O give thanks to the Lord of lords ; to him who alone doeth great wonders ; to him which smote great kings ; and slew famous kings ; and gave their land for an heritage ; who remembered us in our low estate : and hath redeemed us from our enemies. O give thanks unto the God of heaven : for his mercy endureth for ever. *Ps. cxxxvi. 3, 4. 17, 18. 21. 23, 24. 25.* Now unto the King eternal, immortal, invisible, the only wise God, be

honour and glory for ever and ever. Amen. 1 *Ti. i.* 17.

The Grace of our Lord Jesus Christ, &c. 2 Co. xiii. 14.

CCL. *A Prayer to be used at the burial of their dead at Sea.*

1. We therefore commit his body to the deep, to be turned into corruption, looking for the resurrection of the body, (when the sea shall give up her dead,)

1. Thou hast laid me in the lowest pit, in darkness, in the deeps. *Ps. lxxxviii.* 6. I went down to the bottoms of the mountains; the earth with her bars was about me for ever: yet hast thou brought up my life from corruption, O Lord my God. *Jon. ii.* 6. So also is the resurrection of the dead. It is sown in corruption; it is raised in incorruption. 1 *Co. xv.* 42. Jesus saith unto her, Thy brother shall rise again. Martha saith unto him, I know that he shall rise again in the resurrection at the last day. Jesus said unto her, I am the resurrection, and the life. *John xi.* 23, 24, 25. And the sea gave up the dead which were in it; and death and hell delivered up the dead which were in them: and they were judged every man according to their works. *Re. xx.* 13.

2. and the life of the world to come, through our Lord Jesus Christ; who at his coming shall change our vile body, that it may be like his glorious body, according to the mighty working, whereby he is able to subdue all things to himself.

2. Keep yourselves in the love of God, looking for the mercy of our Lord Jesus Christ unto eternal life. *Jude* 21. The trumpet shall sound, and the dead shall be raised incorruptible. 1 *Co. xv.* 52. Our conversation is in heaven; from whence also we look for the Saviour, the Lord Jesus Christ; who shall change our vile body, that it may be fashioned like unto his glorious body, according to the working whereby he is able even to subdue all things unto himself. *Ph. iii.* 20, 21.

THE FORM AND MANNER OF

MAKING, ORDAINING, AND CONSECRATING

OF

BISHOPS, PRIESTS, AND DEACONS,

According to the Order of the United Church of England and Ireland. *

CCLI. The Presentation of the Candidates for the Office of Deacon to the Bishop: his answer, and address to the Congregation.

1. Reverend Father in God, I present unto you these persons present, to be admitted Deacons.

1. Though ye have ten thousand instructors in Christ, yet have ye not many fathers; for in Christ Jesus I have begotten you through the gospel. 1 *Cor. iv.* 15. And Elisha saw it, and he cried, My father, my father. 2 *Ki. ii.* 12. Then saith he unto his disciples, The harvest truly is plenteous, but the labourers are few; pray ye therefore the Lord of the harvest, that he will send forth labourers into his harvest. *Mat. ix.* 37, 38. After these things the Lord appointed other seventy also. *Lu. x.* 1. In those days, when the number of the disciples was multiplied, the twelve called the multitude of the disciples unto them, and said, Look ye out among you seven men of honest report, full of the Holy Ghost and wisdom, whom we may appoint. And the saying pleased the whole multitude: and they chose Stephen, a man full of faith and of

---

* THE PREFACE.

It is evident unto all men, diligently reading holy Scripture and ancient Authors, that from the Apostles' time there have been these Orders of Ministers in Christ's Church; Bishops, Priests, and Deacons. Which Offices were evermore had in such reverend estimation, that no man might presume to execute any of them, except he were first called, tried, examined, and known to have such Qualities as are requisite for the same; and also by Public Prayer, with imposition of Hands, were approved and admitted thereunto by lawful Authority. And therefore, to the intent that these Orders may be continued, and reverently used and esteemed in the Church of England; no Man shall be accounted or taken to be a lawful Bishop, Priest, or Deacon in the Church of England; or suffered to execute any of the said Functions, except he be called, tried, examined, and admitted thereunto, according to the Form hereafter following, or hath had formerly Episcopal Consecration or Ordination.

And none shall be admitted a Deacon, except he be Twenty-three Years of age, unless he have a Faculty. And every man which is to be admitted a Priest, shall be full Four-and Twenty Years old. And every man which is to be ordained or consecrated Bishop, shall be full Thirty Years of age.

And the Bishop knowing, either by himself, or by sufficient Testimony, any Person to be a Man of virtuous Conversation, and without Crime; and, after Examination and Trial, finding him learned in the Latin Tongue, and sufficiently instructed in holy Scripture, may at the Times appointed in the Canon, or else, on urgent Occasion, upon some other Sunday or Holy-day, in the face of the Church, admit him a Deacon, in such Manner and Form as hereafter followeth.

the Holy Ghost, and Philip, and Prochorus, and Nicanor, and Timon, and Parmenas, and Nicolas a proselyte of Antioch: whom they set before the apostles: and when they had prayed, they laid their hands on them. *Ac. vi.* 1, 2, 3. 5, 6. No man taketh this honour unto himself, but he that is called of God, as was Aaron. So also Christ glorified not himself to be made an High Priest; but he that said unto him, Thou art my Son, to day have I begotten thee. *He. v.* 4, 5. And the Lord spake unto Moses, saying, Bring the tribe of Levi near, and present them before Aaron the priest, that they may minister unto him. *Nu. iii.* 5, 6. And the Lord spake unto Moses, saying, Take the Levites from among the children of Israel, and cleanse them. And Aaron shall offer the Levites before the Lord for an offering of the children of Israel, that they may execute the service of the Lord. And thou shalt set the Levites before Aaron, and before his sons, and offer them for an offering unto the Lord. Thus shalt thou separate the Levites from among the children of Israel: and the Levites shall be mine. *Nu. viii.* 5, 6. 11. 13, 14. Paul and Timotheus, the servants of Jesus Christ, to all the saints in Christ Jesus which are at Philippi, with the bishops and deacons. *Ph. i.* 1.

2. Take heed that the persons whom ye present unto us, be apt and meet, for their learning and godly conversation, to exercise their Ministry duly, to the honour of God, and the edifying of his Church.

3. I have enquired of them, and also examined them, and think them so to be.

4. Brethren, if there be any of you, who knoweth any Impediment, or notable Crime in any of these persons presented to be ordered Deacons, for the which he ought not to be admitted to that Office, let him come forth in the Name of God, and shew what the Crime or Impediment is.

2, 3, 4. Lay hands suddenly on no man, neither be partaker of other men's sins. 1 *Ti. v.* 22. Likewise must the Deacons be grave, not doubletongued, not given to much wine, not greedy of filthy lucre: holding the mystery of the faith in a pure conscience. And let these also first be proved; then let them use the office of a Deacon, being found blameless. Not a novice, lest being lifted up with pride he fall into the condemnation of the devil. 1 *Ti. iii.* 8, 9, 10. 6. The servant of the Lord must not strive; but be gentle unto all men, apt to teach, patient, in meekness instructing those that oppose themselves. 2 *Ti. ii.* 24, 25. Beloved, believe not every

spirit, but try the spirits whether they are of God. 1 *John iv.* 1.
He must have a good report of them which are without;
lest he fall into reproach and the snare of the devil. 1 *Ti. iii.* 7.
Look ye out among you seven men of honest report. *Ac. vi.* 3.
Herein do I exercise myself, to have always a conscience void
of offence toward God, and toward men. *Ac. xxiv.* 16. And
Jehoshaphat said to the judges, Take heed what ye do. Let
the fear of the Lord be upon you; for there is no iniquity
with the Lord our God, nor respect of persons. 2 *Ch. xix.* 6, 7.

O God the Father of heaven, &c.

CCLII. *Particular Petition in the Litany in behalf of the Candidates for the office of Deacon.*

That it may
please thee to
bless these thy
servants, now
to be admitted
to the Order of
Deacons
[*or Priests*]
and to pour thy
grace upon
them ; that
they may duly
execute their
Office, to the
edifying of thy
Church, and
the glory of thy
holy Name.

Bless thine inheritance. *Ps. xxviii.* 9. They shall put my
name upon the children of Israel; and I will bless them.
Nu. vi. 27. Thus shalt thou separate the Levites from among
the children of Israel: and the Levites shall be mine. And after
that shall the Levites go in to do the service of the tabernacle
of the congregation: for they are wholly given unto me from
among the children of Israel. *Nu. viii.* 14, 15, 16. I will
pour upon the house of David, and upon the inhabitants of
Jerusalem, the spirit of grace. *Zec. xii.* 10. It is a good
thing that the heart be established with grace. *He. xiii.* 9.
As every man hath received the gift, even so minister the
same one to another, as good stewards of the manifold grace
of God. 1 *Pe. iv.* 10. He gave some, apostles; and some,
prophets; and some, evangelists; and some, pastors and
teachers; for the perfecting of the saints, for the work of the
ministry, for the edifying of the body of Christ. *Ep. iv.* 11, 12.
The Church which is his body. *Ep. i.* 22, 23. Being filled
with the fruits of righteousness, which are by Jesus Christ,
unto the glory and praise of God. *Ph. i.* 11.

Our Father which art in heaven, &c.

O God, merciful Father, &c. *as* XVIII.

We humbly beseech thee, &c. *as* XIX.

CCLIII. *A Prayer for the Candidates for the office of Deacon.*

1. Almighty
God, who by

1. Jesus came and spake unto them, saying, All power is
given unto me in heaven and in earth. *Mat. xxviii.* 18. When

F 2

thy Divine Providence, hast appointed divers Orders of Ministers in thy Church, and didst inspire thine Apostles to choose into the order of Deacons the first Martyr Saint Stephen, with others;

he ascended up on high, he led captivity captive, and gave gifts unto men. He gave some, apostles; and some, prophets; and some, evangelists; and some pastors and teachers. *Ep. iv.* 8. 11. God hath set some in the church, first apostles, secondarily prophets, thirdly teachers. 1 *Co. xii.* 28. And no man taketh this honour unto himself, but he that is called of God, as was Aaron. *He. v.* 4. As my Father hath sent me, even so send I you. *John xx.* 21. And, lo, I am with you alway, even unto the end of the world. *Mat. xxviii.* 20. Wherefore, brethren, look ye out among you seven men of honest report, full of wisdom, whom we may appoint. And they chose Stephen, a man full of faith and of the Holy Ghost, and Philip, and Prochorus, and Nicanor, and Timon, and Parmenas, and Nicolas a proselyte of Antioch: whom they set before the apostles: and when they had prayed, they laid their hands on them. *Ac. vi.* 3. 5, 6.

2. Mercifully behold these thy servants now called to the like Office and Administration;

2. Look down from heaven, and behold from the habitation of thy holiness and of thy glory. *Is. lxiii.* 15. Grace, mercy, and peace, from God our Father and Jesus Christ our Lord. 1 *Ti. i.* 2. The Holy Ghost said, Separate me Barnabas and Saul for the work whereunto I have called them. *Ac. xiii.* 2.

3. replenish them so with the truth of thy Doctrine, and adorn them with innocency of life, that both by word and good example, they may faithfully serve thee in this Office, to the glory of thy Name, and the edification of thy Church, through the merits of our Saviour Jesus Christ, who liveth and reigneth with thee and the Holy Ghost, now and for ever. *Amen.*

3. For this cause we also, do not cease to pray for you, and to desire that ye might be filled with the knowledge of his will in all wisdom and spiritual understanding; that ye might walk worthy of the Lord unto all pleasing, being fruitful in every good work, and increasing in the knowledge of God: strengthened with all might, according to his glorious power. *Col. i.* 9, 10, 11. Sanctify them through thy truth: thy word is truth. *John xvii.* 17. He shall give you another Comforter, that he may abide with you for ever; even the Spirit of truth. The Comforter, which is the Holy Ghost, whom the Father will send in my name, he shall teach you all things. When He, the Spirit of truth, is come, He will guide you into all truth. *John xiv.* 16, 17, 26. *xvi.* 13. Be thou an example of the believers, in word, in conversation, in charity, in spirit, in faith, in purity. 1 *Ti. iv.* 12. Speak thou the things which become sound doctrine; in all things shewing thyself a pattern of good works: in doctrine shewing uncorruptness, gravity,

sincerity, sound speech, that cannot be condemned. *Tit. ii.* 1.
7, 8. Likewise must the Deacons be grave, not doubletongued, not given to much wine, not greedy of filthy lucre;
holding the mystery of the faith in a pure conscience. Let
them use the office of a Deacon, being found blameless.
Even so must their wives be grave, not slanderers, sober, faithful in all things. Let the Deacons be the husbands of one
wife, ruling their children and their own houses well. For
they that have used the office of a Deacon well, purchase to
themselves a good degree, and great boldness in the faith
which is in Christ Jesus. 1 *Ti. iii.* 8 *to* 13. Continue thou in
the things which thou hast learned and hast been assured of,
knowing of whom thou hast learned them. 2 *Ti. iii.* 14. Say
to Archippus, Take heed to the ministry which thou hast received in the Lord, that thou fulfil it. *Col. iv.* 17. Moreover
it is required in stewards, that a man be found faithful. 1 *Co.
iv.* 2. Be thou faithful unto death. *Re. ii.* 10. Let your light
so shine before men, that they may see your good works, and
glorify your Father which is in heaven. *Mat. v.* 16. Herein
is my Father glorified, that ye bear much fruit. *John xv.* 8.
We have this treasure in earthen vessels, that the excellency
of the power may be of God, and not of us. 2 *Co. iv.* 7. Seek
that ye may excel to the edifying of the Church. 1 *Co. xiv.* 12.
If any man speak, let him speak as the oracles of God; if
any man minister, let him do it as of the ability which God
giveth: that God in all things may be glorified through Jesus
Christ, to whom be praise and dominion for ever and ever.
Amen. 1 *Pe. iv.* 11.

The Epistle. 1 Tim. iii. 8 *to*13.—*Likewise must the Deacons be grave, not double-tongued, not
given to much wine, not greedy of filthy lucre; holding the mystery of the faith in a pure
conscience. And let these also first be proved; then let them use the Office of a Deacon,
being found blameless. Even so must their wives be grave, not slanderers, sober, faithful in
all things. Let the Deacons be the husbands of one wife, ruling their children and their
own houses well. For they, that have used the Office of a Deacon well, purchase to themselves a good degree, and great boldness in the faith which is in Christ Jesus.*

Or else this, out of the Sixth Chapter of the Acts of the Apostles. *Acts. vi.* 2 *to* 7.—
*Then the twelve called the multitude of the disciples unto them, and said, It is not reason that
we should leave the Word of God, and serve tables. Wherefore, brethren, look ye out among
you seven men of honest report, full of the Holy Ghost and wisdom, whom we may appoint
over this business. But we will give ourselves continually to prayer, and to the ministry of
the Word. And the saying pleased the whole multitude: And they chose Stephen, a man
full of faith and of the Holy Ghost, and Philip, and Prochorus, and Nicanor, and Timon,
and Parmenas, and Nicolas a proselyte of Antioch; whom they set before the Apostles: and
when they had prayed, they laid their hands on them. And the Word of God increased;
and the number of the disciples multiplied in Jerusalem greatly; and a great company of
the Priests were obedient to the faith.*

CCLIV. *The Oath of the King's Sovereignty.*

I A. B. do swear, That I do from my heart, abhor, detest, and abjure, as impious and heretical, that damnable doctrine, and position, That Princes excommunicated or deprived by the Pope, or any Authority of the See of Rome, may be deposed or murthered by their subjects, or any other whatsoever. And I do declare, That no foreign Prince, Person, Prelate, State, or Potentate hath, or ought to have, any jurisdiction, power, superiority, pre-eminence, or authority, Ecclesiastical or Spiritual, within this Realm.

Thou shalt do no murder. *Mat. xix.* 18. Honour all men. Honour the King. 1 *Pe. ii.* 17. And David said, Destroy him not: for who can stretch forth his hand against the Lord's anointed, and be guiltless? 1 *Sa. xxvi.* 9. And David said to Solomon his son, Be strong and of good courage, fear not, nor be dismayed: for the Lord God, even my God, will be with thee; he will not fail thee nor forsake thee, until thou hast finished all the work for the service of the house of the Lord. And, behold, the courses of the priests and the Levites, even they shall be with thee for all the service of the house of God. 1 *Ch. xxviii.* 20, 21. Solomon thrust out Abiathar from being priest unto the Lord. 1 *Ki. ii.* 27. *See also,* 2 *Ch. viii.* 14, 15.—*xx.* 21.

CCLV. *The solemn Questions to the Candidates for the Office of Deacon.*

The Bishop. 1. Do you trust, that you are inwardly moved by the Holy Ghost, to take upon you this Office and Ministration, to serve God for the promoting of his glory, and the edifying of his people?

Ans. I trust so.

The Bishop. 2. Do you think, that you are truly called according to the Will of our Lord Jesus Christ, and the

1, 2. I have not sent these prophets, yet they ran; I have not spoken to them, yet they prophesied: *Je. xxiii.* 21. Examine yourselves, whether ye be in the faith; prove your ownselves. 2 *Co. xiii.* 5. If a man think himself to be something, when he is nothing, he deceiveth himself. But let every man prove his own work, and then shall he have rejoicing in himself alone, and not in another. For every man shall bear his own burden. *Ga. vi.* 3, 4, 5. The fruit of the Spirit is in all goodness and righteousness and truth. *Ep. v.* 9. The Spirit itself beareth witness with our spirit, that we are the children of God. *Ro. viii.* 16. I seek not mine own glory. *John viii.* 50. We preach not ourselves. 2 *Co. iv.* 5. We do all things, dearly beloved, for your edifying. 2 *Co. xii.* 19. For the love of Christ constraineth us. 2 *Co. v.* 14. Yea, and if I be offered upon the sacrifice and service of your faith, I joy, and rejoice with you all. *Ph. ii.* 17. And Jesus, walking by

due Order of this Realm to the Ministry of the Church?

Ans. I think so.

the sea of Galilee, saw two brethren, Simon called Peter, and Andrew his brother, casting a net into the sea: for they were fishers. And he saith unto them, Follow me, and they straightway left their nets, and followed him. And going on from thence, he saw two other brethren, mending their nets; and he called them. And they immediately left the ship and their father, and followed him. *Mat. iv.* 18 *to* 22. Many will say to me in that day, Lord, Lord, have we not prophesied in thy name? and in thy name have cast out devils? and in thy name done many wonderful works? And then will I profess unto them, I never knew you: depart from me, ye that work iniquity. *Mat. vii.* 22, 23. No man taketh this honour unto himself, but he that is called of God, as was Aaron. So also Christ glorified not himself to be made an High Priest; but he that said unto him, Thou art my Son, to day have I begotten thee. *He. v.* 4, 5. Let every man be fully persuaded in his own mind. *Ro. xiv.* 5. *See also, Eze. xiii.* 3.— *Ex,* xix.—*Ac. xiii.* 2.

The Bishop.
3. Do you unfeignedly believe all the Canonical Scriptures of the Old and New Testament?

Ans. I do believe them.

3. Be mindful of the words which were spoken before of the holy prophets, and of the commandment of us the apostles of the Lord and Saviour. *2 Pe. iii.* 2. But continue thou in the things which thou hast learned and hast been assured of, knowing of whom thou hast learned them, and that from a child thou hast known the holy Scriptures, which are able to make thee wise unto salvation through faith which is in Christ Jesus. All Scripture is given by inspiration of God, and is profitable for doctrine, for reproof, for correction, for instruction in righteousness. *2 Ti. iii,* 14, 15, 16. For this cause thank we God without ceasing, because, when ye received the word of God which ye heard of us, ye received it not as the word of men, but as it is in truth the word of God. *1 Th. ii.* 13.

The Bishop.
4. Will you diligently read the same unto the People assembled in the Church, where you shall be appointed to serve?

Ans. I will.

4. And he came to Nazareth; and, as his custom was, he went into the synagogue on the Sabbath day, and stood up for to read. *Lu. iv.* 16. And Moses took the book of the covenant, and read in the audience of the people. *Ex. xxiv.* 7. And Ezra the priest brought the law before the congregation both of men and women, and all that could hear with understanding. And he read therein from morning until midday,

before the men and the women, and those that could understand; and the ears of all the people were attentive unto the
book of the law. And Ezra the scribe stood upon a pulpit
of wood, which they had made for the purpose ; and Ezra
opened the book in the sight of all the people ; and when he
opened it, all the people stood up : and Ezra blessed the Lord,
the great God : and all the people answered, Amen, Amen,
with lifting up their hands; and they bowed their heads, and
worshipped the Lord. And the Levites caused the people to
understand the law : and the people stood in their place. So
they read in the book in the law of God distinctly, and gave
the sense, and caused them to understand the reading. *Ne.
viii. 2 to 8.* They stood up in their place, and read in the
book of the law of the Lord their God one fourth part of the
day. *Ne. ix. 3.* When all Israel is come to appear before the
Lord thy God in the place which he shall choose, thou shalt
read this law before all Israel in their hearing. *De. xxxi. 11.*
When this epistle is read among you, cause that it be read
also in the Church of the Laodiceans; and that ye likewise
read the epistle from Laodicea. *Col. iv. 16. See also,* 1 *Co.*
xiv.—*Acts xiii.* 14, 15. 27.

*CCLVI. The Duties of Deacons ; and further Questions to the
Candidates.*

The Bishop.—1. It appertaineth to the Office of Deacon in the Church, where he shall be
appointed to serve, to assist the Priest in Divine Service, and especially when he ministereth
the holy Communion ; and to help him in the distribution thereof, and to read Holy Scriptures and Homilies in the Church ; and to instruct the Youth in the Catechism ; in the absence
of the Priest to baptize Infants ; and to preach, if he be admitted thereto by the Bishop.
And furthermore, it is his Office, where provision is so made, to search for the sick, poor,
and impotent people of the Parish, to intimate their estates, names, and places where
they dwell, unto the Curate, that by his exhortation they may be relieved with the alms
of the Parishioners, or others. Will you do this gladly and willingly ?—*Ans.* I will do
so, by the help of God.

1. And the Lord spake unto Moses, saying, Bring the
tribe of Levi near, and present them before Aaron the priest
that they may minister unto him. And they shall keep his
charge, and the charge of the whole congregation before the
tabernacle of the congregation, to do the service of the tabernacle. *Nu. iii.* 5, 6, 7. In those days, when the number of
the disciples was multiplied, there arose a murmuring of
the Grecians against the Hebrews, because their widows were

neglected in the daily ministration. Then the twelve called the multitude of the disciples unto them, and said, It is not reason that we should leave the word of God, and serve tables. Wherefore, brethren, look ye out among you seven men of honest report, full of the Holy Ghost and wisdom, whom we may appoint over this business. But we will give ourselves continually unto prayer, and to the ministry of the word. And they chose Stephen, a man full of faith and of the Holy Ghost, and Philip. *Ac. vi.* 1 *to* 5. Then Philip went down to the city of Samaria, and preached Christ unto them. When they believed Philip preaching the things concerning the kingdom of God, and the name of Jesus Christ, they were baptized, both men and women. *Ac. viii.* 5. 12.

The Bishop.
2. Will you apply all your diligence to frame and fashion your own lives, and the lives of your families, according to the Doctrine of Christ; and to make both yourselves and them, as much as in you lieth, wholesome examples of the flock of Christ?

Ans. I will do so, the Lord being my helper.

2. Likewise must the Deacons be grave, not doubletongued, not given to much wine, not greedy of filthy lucre; holding the mystery of the faith in a pure conscience. And let these also first be proved : then let them use the office of a Deacon, being found blameless. Even so must their wives be grave, not slanderers, sober, faithful in all things. Let the Deacons be the husbands of one wife, ruling their children and their own houses well. For they that have used the office of a Deacon well purchase to themselves a good degree, and great boldness in the faith which is in Christ Jesus. 1 *Ti. iii.* 8 *to* 13. Giving no offence in any thing, that the ministry be not blamed : but in all things approving ourselves as the ministers of God, in much patience, in afflictions, in necessities, in distresses, in stripes, in imprisonments, in tumults, in labours, in watchings, in fastings; by pureness, by knowledge, by longsuffering, by kindness, by the Holy Ghost, by love unfeigned, by the word of truth, by the power of God, by the armour of righteousness on the right hand and on the left, by honour and dishonour, by evil report and good report: as deceivers and yet true; as unknown, and yet well known; as dying, and, behold, we live ; as chastened, and not killed ; as sorrowful, yet alway rejoicing ; as poor, yet making many rich ; as having nothing, and yet possessing all things. 2 *Co. vi.* 3 *to* 10. Flee youthful lusts: but follow righteousness, faith, charity, peace, with them that call on the Lord out of a pure heart. 2 *Ti. ii.* 22. Let no man despise thy youth ; but be thou an

example of the believers, in word, in conversation, in charity,
in spirit, in faith, in purity.   Take heed unto thyself, and unto
the doctrine ; continue in them : for in doing this thou shalt
both save thyself, and them that hear thee. 1 *Ti. iv.* 12. 16.
Feed the flock of God which is among you : neither as being
lords over God's heritage, but being ensamples to the flock.
1 *Pe. v.* 2, 3.   Wherewithal shall a young man cleanse his
way ? by taking heed thereto according to thy word. *Ps.*
cxix. 9.   I beseech you therefore, brethren, by the mercies of
God, that you present your bodies a living sacrifice, holy, acceptable unto God, which is your reasonable service.   And be
not conformed to this world : but be ye transformed by the
renewing of your mind. *Ro. xii.* 1, 2.   Know ye not that
they which run in a race run all, but one receiveth the prize ?
so run, that ye may obtain.   I therefore so run, not as uncertainly : so fight I, not as one that beateth the air : but I keep
under my body, and bring it into subjection : lest that by any
means, when I have preached to others, I myself should be a
cast-away. 1 *Co. ix.* 24. 26, 27.

The Bishop.—3. Will you reverently obey your Ordinary, and other chief Ministers of
the Church, and them to whom the charge and government over you is committed; following with a glad Mind and Will their godly admonitions?—*Ans.* I will endeavour
myself, the Lord being my helper.

3. Ye younger, submit yourselves unto the elder. 1 *Pe. v.* 5.
Obey them that have the rule over you, and submit yourselves.
He. xiii. 17.   Submit yourselves to every ordinance of man
for the Lord's sake. 1 *Pe. ii.* 13.   Ye must needs be subject,
not only for wrath, but also for conscience sake. *Ro. xiii.* 5.
For God is not the Author of confusion, but of peace, as in all
Churches of the saints. 1 *Co. xiv.* 33.

CCLVII. *The Giving of authority to execute the Office of a Deacon.*

*Then the Bishop, laying his hands severally upon the head of every one of them humbly
kneeling before him, shall say*—Take thou, &c.

*The Lord said unto Moses, Take thee Joshua the son of
Nun, a man in whom is the Spirit, and lay thine hand upon
him ; and thou shalt put some of thine honour upon him.*

And he laid his hands upon him, and gave him a charge, as the Lord commanded by the hand of Moses. Nu. xxvii. 18. 20. 23. *And they brought young children to Jesus, that he should touch them: and he took them up in his arms, put his hands upon them, and blessed them.* Mar. x. 13. 16. See also, Ac. xiii. 3.—1 Ti. iv. 14.—v. 22.

1. Take thou authority to execute the office of a Deacon in the Church of God committed unto thee; In the name of the Father, and of the Son, and of the Holy Ghost. Amen.

1. Let these first be proved, then let them use the office of a Deacon, being found blameless. 1 Ti. iii. 10. The things that thou hast heard of me among many witnesses, the same commit thou to faithful men, who shall be able to teach others also. 2 Ti. ii. 2. I put thee in remembrance that thou stir up the gift of God, which is in thee by the putting on of my hands. 2 Ti. i. 6. Whatsoever ye do in word or deed, do all in the name of the Lord Jesus, giving thanks to God and the Father by him. Col. iii. 17. See also, Mat. xxviii. 19.

2. Take thou authority to read the Gospel in the Church of God, and to preach the same, if thou be thereto licensed by the Bishop himself.

2. Study to shew thyself approved unto God, a workman that needeth not to be ashamed, rightly dividing the word of truth. 2 Ti. ii. 15. Having then gifts differing according to the grace that is given to us, whether prophecy, let us prophesy according to the proportion of faith; or ministry, let us wait on our ministering: or he that teacheth, on teaching; or he that exhorteth, on exhortation. Ro. xii. 6, 7, 8. And they chose Stephen, and Philip, whom they set before the apostles: and when they had prayed, they laid their hands on them. Ac. vi. 5, 6. Philip went down to the city of Samaria, and preached Christ unto them. Ac. viii. 5. See also, Mar. xvi. 15.—Lu. ix. 6.—1 Co. ix. 17.—Is. xxxiv. 16.

The Gospel. Lu. xii. 35 to 38.—*Let your loins be girded about, and your lights burning; and ye yourselves like unto men that wait for their Lord, when he will return from the wedding; that when he cometh and knocketh, they may open unto him immediately. Blessed are those servants, whom the Lord, when he cometh, shall find watching. Verily I say unto you, that he shall gird himself, and make them to sit down to meat, and will come forth and serve them. And if he shall come in the second watch, or come in the third watch, and find them so, blessed are those servants.*

CCLVIII. A Prayer for God's special grace upon the Newly-ordained.

1. Almighty God, giver of all good things, who of thy great goodness

1. I am the Almighty God; walk before me, and be thou perfect. Ge. xvii. 1. Every good gift and every perfect gift is from above, and cometh down from the Father of lights. Ja. i. 17. Thou openest thine hand and satisfiest the

hast vouch-
safed to accept
and take these
thy servants
unto the Office
of Deacons in
thy Church;
Make them,
we beseech
thee, O Lord,
to be modest,
humble, and
constant in
their Ministra-
tion, to have a
ready will to
observe all spi-
ritual Disci-
pline;

desire of every living thing. *Ps. cxlv.* 16. He hath filled the hungry with good things. *Lu. i.* 53. Good and upright is the Lord: therefore will he teach sinners in the way. *Ps. xxv.* 8. If ye being evil, know how to give good gifts unto your children, how much more shall your Father which is in heaven give good things to them that ask him? *Mat. vii.* 11. All of you be subject one to another, and be clothed with humility. 1 *Pe. v.* 5. I say, through the grace given unto me, to every man that is among you, not to think of himself more highly than he ought to think; but to think soberly, according as God hath dealt to every man the measure of faith. *Ro. xii.* 3. He that humbleth himself shall be exalted. *Lu. xviii.* 14. Neglect not the gift that is in thee, which was given thee by prophecy, with the laying on of the hands of the presbytery. Meditate upon these things; give thyself wholly to them: that thy pro-fiting may appear to all. Take heed unto thyself, and unto the doctrine; continue in them; for in doing this thou shalt both save thyself, and them that hear thee. 1 *Ti. iv.* 14, 15, 16. Preach the word; be instant in season, out of season; re-prove, rebuke, exhort, with all longsuffering and doctrine. 2 *Ti. iv.* 2. Unto the Jews I became as a Jew, that I might gain the Jews; to them that are under the law, as under the law, that I might gain them that are under the law; to the weak became I as weak, that I might gain the weak: I am made all things to all men, that I might by all means save some. And this I do for the Gospel's sake. 1 *Co. ix.* 20. 22, 23· Let all things be done decently and in order. The spirits of the prophets are subject to the prophets. 1 *Co. xiv.* 40. 32. Uphold me with thy free Spirit. Then will I teach transgres-sors thy ways; and sinners shall be converted unto thee. *Ps. li.* 12, 13.

2. that they
having always
the testimony
of a good con-
science, and
continuing ever
stable and
strong in thy
Son Christ,
may so well
behave them-
selves in this

2. Herein do I exercise myself, to have always a conscience void of offence toward God and toward men. *Ac. xxiv.* 16· Our rejoicing is this, the testimony of our conscience, that in simplicity and godly sincerity, not with fleshly wisdom, but by the grace of God, we have had our conversation in the world, and more abundantly to you-ward. 2 *Co. i.* 12. Holding the mystery of the faith in a pure conscience. 1 *Ti. iii.* 9. If our heart condemn us, God is greater than our heart, and knoweth

inferior Office, that they may be found worthy to be called unto the higher Ministries in thy Church, through the same thy Son our Saviour Jesus Christ; to whom be glory and honour, world without end. Amen.

all things. Beloved, if our heart condemn us not, then have we confidence toward God. 1 *John iii.* 20, 21. Now the end of the commandment is charity out of a pure heart, and of a good conscience, and of faith unfeigned. Holding faith, and a good conscience; which some having put away concerning faith, have made shipwreck. 1 *Ti. i.* 5. 19. Pray for us: for we trust we have a good conscience, in all things willing to live honestly. *He. xiii.* 18. Say to them that are of a fearful heart, Be strong. *Is. xxxv.* 4. Be strong in the Lord, and in the power of his might. *Ep. vi.* 10. It is a good thing that the heart be established with grace. *He. xiii.* 9. I can do all things through Christ which strengtheneth me. *Ph. iv.* 13. Thou therefore, my son, be strong in the grace that is in Christ Jesus. Endure hardness, as a good soldier of Jesus Christ. 2 *Ti. ii.* 1. 3. Rooted and built up in him, and stablished in the faith, as ye have been taught. *Col. ii.* 7. The God of all grace, who hath called us unto his eternal glory by Christ Jesus, after that ye have suffered awhile, make you perfect, stablish, strengthen, settle you. 1 *Pe. v.* 10. Brethren, whatsoever things are true, whatsoever things are honest, whatsoever things are just, whatsoever things are pure, whatsoever things are lovely, whatsoever things are of good report; if there be any virtue, and if there be any praise, think on these things. *Ph. iv.* 8. He that is faithful in that which is least is faithful also in much: and he that is unjust in the least is unjust also in much. *Lu. xvi.* 10. These things write I unto thee, that thou mayest know how thou oughtest to behave thyself in the house of God: for they that have used the office of a Deacon well purchase to themselves a good degree, and great boldness in the faith which is in Christ Jesus. 1 *Ti. iii.* 14, 15. 13. Now our Lord Jesus Christ himself, and God, even our Father, which hath loved us, stablish you in every good word and work. 2 *Th. ii.* 16, 17. And the Lord make you to increase and abound in love one toward another, and toward all men, even as we do toward you: to the end he may stablish your hearts unblameable in holiness before God, even our Father, at the coming of our Lord Jesus Christ with all his saints. 1 *Th. iii.* 12, 13.

Prevent us, O Lord, &c. *as* CLI.
The peace of God which, &c. *as* CXLVII.

THE ORDERING OF PRIESTS.

CCLIX. The Presentation of the Candidates for the Office of Priest to the Bishop, his answer, and address to the congregation. Nearly the same as CCLI.

1. Reverend Father in God, I present unto you these persons present, to be admitted to the Order of Priesthood.

2. Take heed that the persons, whom ye present unto us, be apt and meet, for their learning and godly conversation, to exercise their Ministry duly, to the honour of God, and the edifying of his Church.

3. I have enquired of them, and also examined them, and think them so to be.

4. Good people, these are they, whom we purpose, God willing, to receive this Day into the holy Office of Priesthood : for after due examination, we find not to the contrary, but that they be lawfully called to their Function and Ministry, and that they be persons meet for the same. But yet if there be any of you, who knoweth any Impediment, or notable Crime in any of them, for the which he ought not to be received into this holy Ministry, let him come forth in the Name of God, and shew what the Crime or Impediment is.

1, 2, 3, 4. Ye shall be named the Priests of the Lord. *Is. lxi.* 6. Let thy Priests be clothed with righteousness. I will clothe her Priests with salvation. *Ps. cxxxii.* 8. 16. The Priest's lips should keep knowledge. *Mal. ii.* 7. *See also the quotations under CCLI. and* 1 *Ki. xii.* 31.—*xiii.* 33, 34.

CCLX. nearly the same as CCLIII.

Almighty God, giver of all good things, who, by thy Holy Spirit, hast appointed divers Orders of Ministers in the Church ; Mercifully behold these thy servants, now called to the Office of Priesthood ; and replenish them so with the truth of thy Doctrine, and adorn them with innocency of life, that both by word and good example they may faithfully serve thee in this Office, to the glory of thy Name, and the edification of thy Church, through the merits of our Saviour Jesus Christ, who liveth and reigneth with thee and the Holy Ghost, world without end. *Amen.*

The Epistle. Ephes. iv. 7 to 15.—*Unto every one of us is given grace according to the measure of the gift of Christ. Wherefore he saith, When he ascended up on high, he led captivity captive, and gave gifts unto men. (Now that he ascended, what is it, but that he also descended first into the lower parts of the earth? He that descended is the same also that ascended up far above all heavens, that he might fill all things.) And he gave some, Apostles ; and some, Prophets ; and some, Evangelists ; and some, Pastors and Teachers ; for the perfecting of the Saints, for the work of the Ministry, for the edifying of the body of Christ : till we all come in the unity of the faith, and of the knowledge of the Son of God, unto a perfect man, unto the measure of the stature of the fulness of Christ.*

After this shall be read, for the Gospel, part of the ninth Chapter of Saint Matthew, as followeth.—Matth. ix. 36, 37, 38.—*When Jesus saw the multitudes, he was moved with compassion on them, because they fainted, and were scattered abroad, as sheep having no shepherd. Then saith he unto his disciples, The harvest truly is plenteous, but the labourers are few : Pray ye therefore the Lord of the harvest, that he will send forth labourers into his harvest.*

Or else this that followeth out of the tenth Chapter of Saint John.—John x. 1 to 16. *Verily, verily, I say unto you, He that entereth not by the door into the sheepfold, but climbeth up some other way, the same is a thief and a robber. But he that entereth in by the door is the shepherd of the sheep. To him the porter openeth ; and the sheep hear his voice : and he calleth his own sheep by name, and leadeth them out. And when he putteth forth his own sheep, he goeth before them, and the sheep follow him : for they know his voice. And a stranger will they not follow, but will flee from him : for they know not the voice of strangers. This parable spake Jesus unto them : but they understood not, what things they were, which he spake unto them. Then said Jesus unto them again, Verily, verily, I say unto you, I am the door of the sheep. All, that ever came before me, are thieves and robbers : but the sheep did not hear them. I am the door : by me if any man enter in, he shall be saved, and shall go in and out, and find pasture. The thief cometh not, but for to steal, and to kill, and to destroy : I am come, that they might have life, and that they might have it more abundantly. I am the good Shepherd : the good Shepherd giveth his life for the sheep. But he that is an hireling, and not the shepherd, whose own the sheep are not, seeth the wolf coming, and leaveth the sheep, and fleeth : and the wolf catcheth them, and scattereth the sheep : The hireling fleeth, because he is an hireling, and careth not for the sheep. I am the good Shepherd, and know my sheep, and am known of mine. As the Father knoweth me, even so know I the Father ; and I lay down my life for the sheep. And other sheep I have which are not of this fold : them also I must bring ; and they shall hear my voice : and there shall be one fold, and one Shepherd.*

CCLXI. The Bishop's comprehensive Exhortation to Candidates for the Office of Priest.

1. You have heard, brethren, as well in your private examination, as in the exhortation which was now made to you, and in the holy Lessons taken out of the Gospel, and the writings of the Apostles, of what Dignity, and of how great Importance this Office is, whereunto ye are called. And now again we exhort you in the name of our Lord Jesus Christ, that you have in remembrance, into how high a Dignity, and to how weighty an Office and Charge ye are called ;

1. If ye know these things, happy are ye if ye do them. *John xiii.* 17. Let a man so account of us, as of the ministers of Christ, and stewards of the mysteries of God. 1 *Co. iv.* 1. All things are of God, who hath reconciled us to himself by Jesus Christ, and hath given to us the ministry of reconciliation ; to wit, that God was in Christ reconciling the world unto himself, not imputing their trespasses unto them; and hath committed unto us the word of reconciliation. Now then we are ambassadors for Christ, as though God did beseech you by us : we pray you in Christ's stead, be ye reconciled to God. 2 *Co. v.* 18, 19, 20. We then, as workers together with him, beseech you also that ye receive not the grace of God in vain. 2 *Co. vi.* 1. We are unto God a sweet savour of Christ, in them that are saved, and in them that perish : to the one we are the savour of death unto death ; and to the other the savour of life unto life. And who is sufficient for these things? 2 *Co. ii.* 15, 16. Not that we are sufficient of ourselves to think any thing as of ourselves; but our sufficiency is of God. 2 *Co. iii.* 5. We have this treasure in earthen vessels, that the excellency of the power may be of God, and not of us. 2 *Co. iv.* 7.

2. that is to say, To be Messengers, Watchmen, and Stewards of the Lord;

2. Whether any do enquire of Titus, he is my partner and fellowhelper concerning you : or our brethren be enquired of, they are the messengers of the churches, and the glory of Christ. 2 *Co. viii.* 23. Then spake Haggai the Lord's messenger in the Lord's message unto the people. *Hag. i.* 13. The priest's lips should keep knowledge : he is the messenger of the Lord of hosts. *Mal. ii.* 7. Thus saith the Lord, thy Redeemer, that confirmeth the word of his servant, and performeth the counsel of his messengers. *Is. xliv.* 24. 26. Son of man, I have made thee a watchman unto the house of Israel : therefore hear the word at my mouth, and give them warning from me. *Eze. iii.* 17. Watch thou in all things, endure afflictions, do the work of an evangelist, make full proof of thy ministry. 2 *Ti. iv.* 5. Let a man so account of us, as of the ministers of Christ and stewards of the mysteries of God. Moreover it is required in stewards, that a man be found faithful. 1 *Co. iv* 1, 2. And the Lord said, Who then is that faithful and wise steward, whom his Lord shall make ruler over his houshold, to give them their portion of meat in due season ? *Lu. xii.* 42. As every man hath received the gift, even so minister the same one to another, as good stewards of the manifold grace of God. If any man speak, let him speak as the oracles of God ; if any man minister, let him do it as of the ability which God giveth. 1 *Pe. iv.* 10, 11. *See also,* He. *xiii.* 17.—*Eze. xxxiv.* 2.

3. to teach, and to premonish, to feed and provide for the Lord's Family;

3. And daily in the temple, and in every house, they ceased not to teach and preach Jesus Christ. *Ac. v.* 42. These things teach and exhort. 1 *Ti. vi.* 2. The things that thou hast heard of me among many witnesses, the same commit thou to faithful men, who shall be able to teach others also. 2 *Ti. ii.* 2. And the Lord spake unto Aaron, saying, Do not drink wine nor strong drink, thou, nor thy sons with thee, when ye go into the tabernacle of the congregation, lest ye die : that ye may teach the children of Israel all the statutes which the Lord hath spoken unto them by the hand of Moses. *Le. x.* 8, 9. 11. Remember, that by the space of three years I ceased not to warn every one night and day with tears. *Ac. xx.* 31. Now we exhort you, brethren, warn them that are unruly. 1 *Th. v.* 14. Hear the word at my mouth, and give them warning from me. When

I say unto the wicked, Thou shalt surely die ; and thou givest
him not warning, nor speakest to warn the wicked from his
wicked way, to save his life; the same wicked man shall die
in his iniquity ; but his blood will I require at thine hand.
Yet if thou warn the wicked, and he turn not from his wickedness, nor from his wicked way, he shall die in his iniquity ;
but thou hast delivered thy soul.   Again, When a righteous
man doth turn from his righteousness, and commit iniquity,
and I lay a stumbling block before him, he shall die : because
thou hast not given him warning, he shall die in his sin ; his
blood will I require at thine hand. *Eze. iii.* 17 *to* 20.   We beseech you, brethren, to know them which labour among you,
and are over you in the Lord, and admonish you. 1 *Th. v.* 12.
These things speak, and exhort. *Tit. ii.* 15.   Take heed to all
the flock, over the which the Holy Ghost hath made you overseers, to feed the Church of God. *Ac. xx.* 28.   I will give you
pastors according to mine heart, which shall feed you with
knowledge and understanding. *Je. iii.* 15.   And the Lord
said, Who then is that faithful and wise steward, whom his
lord shall make ruler over his houshold, to give them their
portion of meat in due season ?   Blessed is that servant, whom
his lord when he cometh shall find so doing. *Lu. xii.* 42, 43.
Now ye are no more strangers and foreigners, but fellow-
citizens with the saints, and of the houshold of God. *Ep. ii.* 19.
The Father of our Lord Jesus Christ, of whom the whole family
in heaven and earth is named. *Ep. iii.* 14, 15.   *See also, John
x.* 11 *to* 16.—xvii.—*Gal. vi.* 10.

4. to seek for
Christ's sheep,
that are dis-
persed abroad,
and for his chil-
dren who are in
the midst of this
naughty world,
that they may
be saved
through Christ
for ever.

4. Thus saith the Lord God unto the shepherds ; Woe be
to the shepherds of Israel that do feed themselves ! should not
the shepherds feed the flocks?   The diseased have ye not
strengthened, neither have ye healed that which was sick, neither have ye bound up that which was broken, neither have ye
brought again that which was driven away, neither have ye
sought that which was lost; but with force and with cruelty
have ye ruled them.   My sheep wandered through all the
mountains, and upon every high hill: yea, my flock was scattered upon all the face of the earth, and none did search or
seek after them. Therefore, ye shepherds, hear the word of the
Lord; as I live, saith the Lord God, surely because my flock be-

came a prey, and my flock became meat to every beast of the field, because there was no shepherd, neither did my shepherds search for my flock, but the shepherds fed themselves, and fed not my flock; therefore, O ye shepherds, hear the word of the Lord; Thus saith the Lord God; Behold, I am against the shepherds; and I will require my flock at their hand, and cause them to cease from feeding the flock; neither shall the shepherds feed themselves any more; for I will deliver my flock from their mouth, that they may not be meat for them. For thus saith the Lord God; Behold, I, even I, will both search my sheep, and seek them out. I will feed my flock, and I will cause them to lie down, saith the Lord God. I will seek that which was lost, and bring again that which was driven away, and will bind up that which was broken, and will strengthen that which was sick: I will feed them with judgment. *Eze. xxxiv.* 2. 4. 6 *to* 11. 15, 16. Go rather to the lost sheep of the house of Israel. *Mat. x.* 6. I am not sent but unto the lost sheep of the house of Israel. *Mat. xv.* 24. The Son of man is come to seek and to save that which was lost. *Lu. xix.* 10. Then said Jesus to them again, As my Father hath sent me, even so send I you. *John xx.* 21. Ye were as sheep going astray; but are now returned unto the Shepherd and Bishop of your souls. 1 *Pe. ii.* 25. He prophesied that Jesus should die for that nation; and not for that nation only, but that also he should gather together in one the children of God that were scattered abroad. *John xi.* 51, 55. Ye were all the children of God by faith in Christ Jesus. *Ga. iii.* 26. The whole world lieth in wickedness. 1 *John v.* 19. I pray not that thou shouldest take them out of the world, but that thou shouldest keep them from the evil. *John xvii.* 15. Brethren, my heart's desire and prayer to God for Israel is, that they might be saved. *Ro. x.* 1. This is a faithful saying, and worthy of all acceptation, that Christ Jesus came into the world to save sinners; of whom I am chief. 1 *Ti. i.* 15. Being made perfect, he became the Author of eternal salvation unto all them that obey him. *He. v.* 9. Perhaps he therefore departed for a season, that thou shouldest receive him for ever. *Phile.* 15. Take heed unto thyself, and unto the doctrine; continue in them: for in doing this thou shalt both save thyself, and them that hear thee. 1 *Ti. iv.* 16. For God hath not appointed us to wrath, but to obtain salvation by our Lord Jesus Christ. 1 *Th. v.* 9. *See also, Lu. xv.* 3 *to* 7. *Ps.* xxiii.

5. Have always therefore printed in your remembrance, how great a treasure is committed to your charge. For they are the sheep of Christ, which he bought with his death, and for whom he shed his blood.

5. I put thee in remembrance that thou stir up the gift of God, which is in thee by the putting on of my hands. 2 *Ti. i.* 6. Remember how thou hast received and heard. *Re. iii.* 3. Thus shalt thou say to the house of Jacob, and tell the children of Israel; if ye will obey my voice indeed, then ye shall be a peculiar treasure unto me above all people. *Ex. xix.* 3. 5. And they shall be mine, saith the Lord of hosts, in that day when I make up my jewels. *Mal. iii.* 17. Feed the Church of God, which he hath purchased with his own blood. *Ac. xx.* 28. Ye know that ye were not redeemed with corruptible things, as silver and gold, from your vain conversation; but with the precious blood of Christ. 1 *Pe. i.* 18, 19. We are sanctified through the offering of the body of Jesus Christ once for all. *He. x.* 10. In whom we have redemption through his blood, the forgiveness of sins. *Ep. i.* 7. I am the good Shepherd: the good Shepherd giveth his life for the sheep. I am come that they might have life, and that they might have it more abundantly. I am the good Shepherd, and know my sheep, and am known of mine. As the Father knoweth me, even so know I the Father: and I lay down my life for the sheep. *John x.* 11. 10. 14, 15. *See also, Ep. v.* 2. —*Is. liii.* 10, 11.—2 *Pe. i.* 12.—*Ac. xxvi.* 16, 17, 18.

6. The Church and Congregation whom you must serve, is his Spouse, and his Body.

6. Ye shall be named the Priests of the Lord; men shall call you the Ministers of our God. *Is. lxi.* 6. We preach not ourselves, but Christ Jesus the Lord; and ourselves your servants for Jesus' sake. 2 *Co. iv.* 5. Even as the Son of Man came not to be ministered unto, but to minister. *Mat. xx.* 28. I have espoused you to one husband, that I may present you as a chaste virgin to Christ. 2 *Co. xi.* 2. The husband is the head of the wife, even as Christ is the head of the Church: and he is the Saviour of the body. Christ also loved the Church, and gave himself for it; that he might present it to himself a glorious Church, not having spot, or wrinkle, or any such thing; but that it should be holy and without blemish. For we are members of his body, of his flesh, and of his

H 2

bones. For this cause shall a man leave his father and mother, and shall be joined unto his wife, and they two shall be one flesh. This is a great mystery : but I speak concerning Christ and the Church. *Ep. v.* 23. 25. 27. 30, 31, 32. He is the head of the body, the Church. *Col. i.* 18. We being many are one body. 1 *Co. x.* 17.

7. And if it shall happen, the same Church, or any member thereof, do take any hurt or hindrance, by reason of your negligence, ye know the greatness of the fault, and also the horrible punishment that will ensue.

7. But and if that servant say in his heart, My lord delayeth his coming; and shall begin to beat the men-servants and maidens, and to eat and drink, and to be drunken ; the lord of that servant will come in a day when he looketh not for him, and at an hour when he is not aware, and will cut him in sunder, and will appoint him his portion with the unbelievers. And that servant, which knew his lord's will, and prepared not himself, neither did according to his will, shall be beaten with many stripes. But he that knew not, and did commit things worthy of stripes, shall be beaten with few stripes. For unto whomsoever much is given, of him shall be much required: and to whom men have committed much, of him they will ask the more. *Lu. xii.* 45 *to* 48. And now, O ye priests, this commandment is for you. If ye will not hear, and if ye will not lay it to heart, to give glory unto my name, saith the Lord of hosts, I will even send a curse upon you, and I will curse your blessings: yea, I have cursed them already, because ye do not lay it to heart. Behold, I will corrupt your seed, and spread dung upon your faces, even the dung of your solemn feasts; and one shall take you away with it. And ye shall know that I have sent this commandment unto you, that my covenant might be with Levi, saith the Lord of hosts. My covenant was with him of life and peace; and I gave them to him for the fear wherewith he feared me, and was afraid before my name. The law of truth was in his mouth, and iniquity was not found in his lips: he walked with me in peace and equity, and did turn many away from iniquity. For the priest's lips should keep knowledge, and they should seek the law at his mouth : for he is the messenger of the Lord of hosts. But ye are departed out of the way; ye have caused many to stumble at the law; ye have corrupted the covenant of Levi, saith the Lord of hosts. Therefore have I also made you contemptible and base before all

the people, according as ye have not kept my ways, but have been partial in the law. *Mal. ii.* 1 *to* 9. My tabernacle is spoiled, and all my cords are broken: my children are gone forth of me, and they are not: there is none to stretch forth my tent any more, and to set up my curtains. For the pastors are become brutish, and have not sought the Lord: therefore they shall not prosper, and all their flocks shall be scattered. *Je. x.* 20, 21. O Son of Man, I have set thee a watchman unto the house of Israel; therefore thou shalt hear the word at my mouth, and warn them from me. When I say unto the wicked, O wicked man, thou shalt surely die; if thou dost not speak to warn the wicked from his way, that wicked man shall die in his iniquity; but his blood will I require at thine hand. *Eze. xxxiii.* 7, 8. Thus saith the Lord God unto the shepherds, Woe be to the shepherds of Israel that do feed themselves! should not the shepherds feed the flocks? Thus saith the Lord God; Behold, I am against the shepherds; and I will require my flock at their hand, and cause them to cease from feeding the flock; neither shall the shepherds feed themselves any more; for I will deliver my flock from their mouth, that they may not be meat for them. *Eze. xxxiv.* 2. 10. Woe to the idol-shepherd that leaveth the flock! the sword shall be upon his arm, and upon his right eye: his arm shall be clean dried up, and his right eye shall be utterly darkened. *Zec. xi.* 17. Woe be unto the pastors that destroy and scatter the sheep of my pasture! saith the Lord. Therefore thus saith the Lord God of Israel against the pastors that feed my people; Ye have scattered my flock, and driven them away, and have not visited them: behold, I will visit upon you the evil of your doings, saith the Lord. Both prophet and priest are profane; yea, in my house have I found their wickedness, saith the Lord. Wherefore their ways shall be unto them as slippery ways in the darkness: they shall be driven on, and fall therein: for I will bring evil upon them, even the year of their visitation, saith the Lord. *Je. xxiii.* 1, 2. 11, 12.

8. Where-fore consider with yourselves the end of the ministry towards the chil-

8. Oh that they were wise, that they understood this, that they would consider their latter end! *De. xxxii.* 29. We are ambassadors for Christ, as though God did beseech you by us: we pray you in Christ's stead, be ye reconciled to God; who

dren of God, towards the spouse and Body of Christ; and see that you never cease your labour, your care and diligence, until you have done all that lieth in you, according to your bounden duty, to bring all such as are or shall be committed to your charge, unto that agreement in the faith and knowledge of God, and to that ripeness and perfectness of age in Christ, that there be no place left among you, either for error in Religion, or for viciousness in Life.

hath given to us the ministry of reconciliation. 2 Co. v. 20. 18. We are labourers together with God. 1 Co. iii. 9. He gave some, apostles; and some, prophets ; and some, evangelists ; and some, pastors and teachers ; for the perfecting of the saints, for the work of the ministry, for the edifying of the body of Christ : till we all come in the unity of the faith, and of the knowledge of the Son of God, unto a perfect man, unto the measure of the stature of the fulness of Christ. *Ep. iv.* 11, 12, 13. They watch for your souls, as they that must give account, that they may do it with joy, and not with grief : for that is unprofitable for you. *He. xiii.* 17. The children of God by faith in Christ Jesus. *Ga. iii.* 26. I have espoused you to one husband, that I may present you as a chaste virgin to Christ. *2 Co. xi.* 2. The Church which is his body. *Ep. i.* 22, 23. This charge I commit unto thee, son Timothy, that thou mightest war a good warfare; holding faith, and a good conscience. 1 *Ti. i.* 18, 19. Till I come, give attendance to reading, to exhortation, to doctrine. Neglect not the gift that is in thee. Meditate upon these things; give thyself wholly to them ; that thy profiting may appear to all. Take heed unto thyself and unto the doctrine; continue in them : for in doing this thou shalt both save thyself, and them that hear thee. 1 *Ti. iv.* 13 *to* 16. Study to shew thyself approved unto God, a workman that needeth not to be ashamed, rightly dividing the word of truth. In meekness instructing those that oppose themselves. 2 *Ti. ii.* 15. 25. Be instant in season, out of season; reprove, rebuke, exhort with all longsuffering and doctrine. 2 *Ti. iv.* 2. Whereunto I also labour, striving according to his working, which worketh in me mightily. *Col. i.* 29. Epaphras, who is one of you, a servant of Christ, saluteth you, always labouring fervently for you in prayers, that ye may stand perfect and complete in all the will of God. *Col. iv.* 12. We labour, that, whether present or absent, we may be accepted of him. For whether we be beside ourselves, it is to God : or whether we be sober, it is for your cause. 2 *Co. v.* 9. 13. None of these things move me, neither count I my life dear unto myself, so that I might finish my course with joy, and the ministry, which I have received of the Lord Jesus, to testify the Gospel of the grace

of God. *Ac. xx. 25.* Be followers together of me. *Ph. iii. 17.*
Watch thou in all things, endure afflictions, make full proof of
thy ministry. *2 Ti. iv. 5.* I know thy works, and thy labour,
and how thou hast borne, and for my name's sake hast laboured, and hast not fainted. *Re. ii. 2, 3.* I am jealous over
you with godly jealousy. *2 Co. xi. 2.* Endeavouring to keep
the unity of the Spirit in the bond of peace. There is one
body, and one Spirit, even as ye are called in one hope of
your calling; one Lord, one faith, one baptism, one God and
Father of all. *Ep. iv. 3 to 6.* Therefore leaving the principles of the doctrine of Christ, let go on unto perfection. *He.
vi. 1.* For this cause I bow my knees unto the Father of our
Lord Jesus Christ, that he would grant you, according to the
riches of his glory, to be strengthened with might by his
Spirit in the inner man; that Christ may dwell in your hearts
by faith; that ye, being rooted and grounded in love, may be
able to comprehend with all saints what is the breadth, and
length, and depth, and height; and to know the love of
Christ, which passeth knowledge, that ye might be filled with
all the fulness of God. *Ep. iii. 14. 16 to 19.* Till we all come
in the unity of the faith, and of the knowledge of the Son of
God, unto a perfect man, unto the measure of the stature of
the fulness of Christ : that we henceforth be no more children, tossed to and fro, and carried about with every wind of
doctrine; but may grow up into him in all things, which is
the head even Christ. *Ep. iv. 13, 14, 15.* Whom we preach,
warning every man, and teaching every man in all wisdom;
that we may present every man perfect in Christ Jesus.
Col. i. 28.

9. Foras-
much then as
your Office is
both of so great
excellency, and
of so great dif-
ficulty, ye see
with how great
care and study
ye ought to ap-
ply yourselves,
as well that ye
may shew your-
selves dutiful
and thankful

9. I speak to you Gentiles, inasmuch as I am the apostle of
the Gentiles, I magnify mine Office. *Ro. xi. 13.* We are
ambassadors for Christ. *2 Co. v. 20.* We are labourers together with God : ye are God's husbandry, ye are God's
building. According to the grace of God which is given
unto me, as a wise master-builder, I have laid the foundation,
and another buildeth thereon. But let every man take heed
how he buildeth thereupon. For other foundation can no man
lay than that is laid, which is Jesus Christ. Now if any man
build upon this foundation gold, silver, precious stones, wood,

unto that Lord, who hath placed you in so high a Dignity ; as also to beware, that neither you your-selves offend, nor be occasion that others offend.

hay, stubble, every man's work shall be made manifest : for the day shall declare it, because it shall be revealed by fire ; and the fire shall try every man's work of what sort it is. If any man's work abide which he hath built thereupon, he shall receive a reward. If any man's work shall be burned, he shall suffer loss : but he himself shall be saved ; yet so as by fire. 1 Co. iii. 9 to 15. Therefore seeing we have this ministry, we faint not. But we have this treasure in earthen vessels, that the excellency of the power may be of God, and not of us. We are troubled on every side, yet not distressed ; we are perplexed, but not in despair ; persecuted, but not forsaken ; cast down, but not destroyed ; always bearing about in the body the dying of the Lord Jesus, that the life also of Jesus might be made manifest in our body. For we which live are alway delivered unto death for Jesus' sake, that the life also of Jesus might be made manifest in our mortal flesh. 2 Co. iv. 1. 7 to 11. Thanks be unto God which always causeth us to triumph in Christ, and maketh manifest the savour of his knowledge by us in every place. For we are unto God a sweet savour of Christ, in them that are saved, and in them that perish : to the one we are the savour of death unto death ; and to the other the savour of life unto life. And who is sufficient for these things ? 2 Co. ii. 14, 15, 16. Say to Archippus, Take heed to the ministry which thou hast received in the Lord, that thou fulfil it. Col. iv. 17. Study to shew thyself approved unto God, a workman that needeth not to be ashamed. 2 Ti. ii. 15. I thank Christ Jesus our Lord, who hath enabled me, for that he counted me faithful, putting me into the ministry. 1 Ti. i. 12. By the grace of God I am what I am : and his grace which was bestowed upon me was not in vain ; but I laboured more abundantly than they all ; yet not I, but the grace of God which was with me. 1 Co. xv. 10. I therefore so run, not as uncertainly ; so fight I, not as one that beateth the air : but I keep under my body, and bring it into subjection : lest that by any means, when I have preached to others, I myself should be a castaway. 1 Co. ix. 26, 27. As we were allowed of God to be put in trust with the gospel, even so we speak ; not as pleasing men, but God, which trieth our hearts. 1 *Th.* 2. 4. Am I not an apostle? am I not free? have I not seen Jesus Christ our Lord? are not ye my work in the Lord? Have we not power to eat and to drink? 1 *Co. ix.* 1. 4. Take heed lest by any means this liberty of yours become a stumblingblock to them that are weak. And through thy knowledge shall the weak brother perish, for whom Christ died. Wherefore, if meat make my brother to offend, I will eat no flesh while the world standeth, lest I make my brother to offend. 1 *Co. viii.* 9. 11. 13. It is good neither to eat flesh, nor to drink wine, nor any thing whereby thy brother stumbleth, or is made weak. *Ro. xiv.* 21. Abstain from all appearance of evil. 1 *Th. v.* 22. *See also,* 2 *Co. xi.* 22 to 31.

10. Howbeit, ye cannot have a mind and will thereto of yourselves; for that will and ability is given of God alone: therefore ye ought, and have need, to pray earnestly for his Holy Spirit.

10. Not that we are sufficient of ourselves to think any thing as of ourselves; but our sufficiency is of God; who also hath made us able ministers of the new testament. 2 *Co. iii.* 5, 6. For it is God which worketh in you both to will and to do of his good pleasure. *Ph. ii.* 13. Without me ye can do nothing. *John xv.* 5. That, according as it is written, He that glorieth, let him glory in the Lord. 1 *Co. i.* 31. For God, who commanded the light to shine out of darkness, hath shined in our hearts, to give the light of the knowledge of the glory of God in the face of Jesus Christ. 2 *Co. iv.* 6. So neither is he that planteth any thing, neither he that watereth; but God that giveth the increase. 1 *Co. iii.* 7. Likewise the Spirit also helpeth our infirmities: and He that searcheth the hearts knoweth what is the mind of the Spirit. *Ro. viii.* 26, 27. Finally, brethren, pray for us, that the word of the Lord may have free course, and be glorified. 2 *Th. iii.* 1. Pray without ceasing. 1 *Th. v.* 17. Verily, verily, I say unto you, Whatsoever ye shall ask the Father in my name, he will give it you. Hitherto have ye asked nothing in my name: ask, and ye shall receive, that your joy may be full. *John xvi.* 23, 24. If ye then, being evil, know how to give good gifts unto your children: how much more shall your heavenly Father give the Holy Spirit to them that ask him. *Lu. xi.* 13. *See also,* 1 *Pe. i.* 12.

11. And seeing that you

11. Can the blind lead the blind? shall they not both fall into the ditch? *Lu. vi.* 39. Ye are the salt of the earth: but

cannot by any other means compass the doing of so weighty a work, pertaining to the salvation of man, but with doctrine and exhortation taken out of the holy Scriptures, and with a life agreeable to the same; consider how studious ye ought to be in reading and learning the Scriptures, and in framing the manners both of yourselves, and of them that specially pertain unto you, according to the rule of the same Scriptures: and for this selfsame cause, how ye ought to forsake and set aside (as much as you may) all worldly cares and studies.

if the salt have lost his savour, wherewith shall it be salted? *Mat. v.* 13. Till I come, give attendance to reading, to exhortation, to doctrine. Continue in them: for in doing this thou shalt both save thyself, and them that hear thee. 1 *Ti. iv.* 13. 16. Continue thou in the things which thou hast learned and hast been assured of, knowing of whom thou hast learned them; and that from a child thou hast known the Holy Scriptures, which are able to make thee wise unto salvation through faith which is in Christ Jesus. All Scripture is given by inspiration of God, and is profitable for doctrine, for reproof, for correction, for instruction in righteousness: that the man of God may be perfect, throughly furnished unto all good works. 2 *Ti. iii.* 14 *to* 17. To the law and to the testimony: if they speak not according to this word, it is because there is no light in them. *Is. viii.* 20. Wherefore I put thee in remembrance that thou stir up the gift of God, which is in thee by the putting on of my hands. Hold fast the form of sound words, which thou hast heard of me, in faith and love, which is in Christ Jesus. That good thing which was committed unto thee keep by the Holy Ghost which dwelleth in us. 2 *Ti. i.* 6. 13, 14. Every scribe which is instructed unto the kingdom of heaven is like unto a man that is an householder, which bringeth forth out of his treasure things new and old. *Mat. xiii.* 52. Holding fast the faithful word, as he hath been taught, that he may be able by sound doctrine both to exhort and to convince the gainsayers. *Tit. i.* 9. Take heed unto thyself. 1 *Ti. iv.* 16. Keep thyself pure. 1 *Ti. v.* 22. Flee also youthful lusts: but follow righteousness, faith, charity, peace. The servant of the Lord must not strive; but be gentle unto all men, apt to teach, patient, in meekness instructing those that oppose themselves. 2 *Ti. ii.* 22. 24, 25. In all things shewing thyself a pattern of good works. *Tit. ii.* 7. Why beholdest thou the mote that is in thy brother's eye, but perceivest not the beam that is in thine own eye? Either how canst thou say to thy brother, Brother, let me pull out the mote that is in thine eye, when thou thyself beholdest not the beam that is in thine own eye? Thou hypocrite, cast out first the beam out of thine own eye, and then shalt thou see clearly to pull out the mote that is in thy brother's eye. *Lu. vi.*

41, 42. Our exhortation was not of deceit, nor of uncleanness, nor in guile. 1 *Th. ii.* 3. A Bishop must be blameless, the husband of one wife, vigilant, sober, of good behaviour, given to hospitality, apt to teach; not given to wine, no striker, not greedy of filthy lucre; but patient, not a brawler, not covetous; one that ruleth well his own house, having his children in subjection, with all gravity. For if a man know not how to rule his own house, how shall he take care of the Church of God? 1 *Ti. iii.* 2 *to* 5. Thy word is a lamp unto my feet, and a light unto my path. *Ps. cxix.* 105. These words, which I command thee this day, shall be in thine heart: and thou shalt teach them diligently unto thy children, and shalt talk of them when thou sittest in thine house, and when thou walkest by the way, and when thou liest down, and when thou risest up. *De. vi.* 6, 7. Meditate upon these things; give thyself wholly to them. 1 *Ti. iv.* 15. Demas hath forsaken me, having loved this present world. 2 *Ti. iv.* 10. That which fell among thorns are they, which, when they have heard, go forth, and are choked with cares and riches and pleasures of this life, and bring no fruit to perfection. *Lu. viii.* 14. They that will be rich fall into temptation and a snare, and into many foolish and hurtful lusts, which drown men in destruction and perdition. For the love of money is the root of all evil. But thou, O man of God, flee these things; and follow after righteousness, godliness, faith, love, patience, meekness: Fight the good fight of faith. I give thee charge in the sight of God, who quickeneth all things, and before Christ Jesus, who before Pontius Pilate witnessed a good confession; that thou keep this commandment without spot, unrebukeable, until the appearing of our Lord Jesus Christ. 1 *Ti. vi.* 9 *to* 14. Then Peter began to say unto him, Lo, we have left all, and have followed thee. *Mar. x.* 28. Jesus said unto Simon, Fear not; from henceforth thou shalt catch men. And when they had brought their ships to land, they forsook all, and followed him. After these things he went forth, and saw a Publican, named Levi, sitting at the receipt of custom: and he said unto him, Follow me. And he left all, rose up, and followed him. *Lu. v.* 10, 11. 27, 28. What things were gain to me, those I counted loss for Christ. Yea doubtless, and I count all things but loss for the excellency of the knowledge of Christ Jesus my Lord: for whom I have suffered the loss of all things, and do count them but dung, that I may win Christ. *Ph. iii.* 7, 8. No man can serve two masters: ye cannot serve God and mammon. *Mat. vi.* 24. Thou therefore endure hardness, as a good soldier of Jesus Christ. No man that warreth entangleth himself with the affairs of this life; that he may please him who hath chosen him to be a soldier. Therefore I endure all things for the elect's sakes, that they may also obtain the salvation which is in Christ Jesus with eternal glory. *2 Ti. ii.* 3, 4. 10.

12. We have good hope, that you have well weighed and pondered these things with yourselves long before this time; and that you have clearly determined, by God's grace, to give yourselves wholly to this Office, whereunto it hath pleased God to call you; so that, as much as lieth in you, you will apply yourselves wholly to this one thing, and draw all your cares and studies this way;

12. Which of you, intending to build a tower, sitteth not down first, and counteth the cost, whether he hath sufficient to finish it? Or what king, going to make war against another king, sitteth not down first, and consulteth whether he be able with ten thousand to meet him that cometh against him with twenty thousand? So likewise, whosoever he be of you that forsaketh not all that he hath he cannot be my disciple. *Lu. xiv.* 28, 31. 33. He found Elisha the son of Shaphat, and cast his mantle upon him. And he left the oxen, and ran after Elijah, and ministered unto him. 1 *Ki. xix.* 19, 20, 21. Then Paul answered, What mean ye to weep and to break mine heart? for I am ready not to be bound only, but also to die at Jerusalem for the name of the Lord Jesus. *Ac. xxi.* 13. I will very gladly spend and be spent for you; though the more abundantly I love you, the less I be loved. *2 Co.* 15. Jesus answered and said, Verily I say unto you, There is no man that hath left house, or brethren, or sisters, or father, or mother, or wife, or children, or lands, for my sake, and the gospel's, but he shall receive an hundred fold now in this time, houses, and brethren, and sisters, and mothers, and children, and lands, with persecutions; and in the world to come eternal life. *Mar. x.* 29, 30. Wist ye not that I must be about my Father's business? *Lu. ii.* 49. Jesus saith unto them, My meat is to do the will of him that sent me, and to finish his work. *John iv.* 34. For I came down from heaven, not to do mine own will, but the will of him that sent me. *John vi.* 38. Wherefore, holy brethren, partakers of the heavenly calling, consider the Apostle and High Priest of our

profession, Christ Jesus; who was faithful to him that appointed him. *He. iii.* 1, 2. Meditate upon these things; give thyself wholly to them; that thy profiting may appear to all. 1 *Ti. iv.* 15.

13. and that you will continually pray to God the Father, by the mediation of our only Saviour Jesus Christ, for the heavenly assistance of the Holy Ghost; that by daily reading and weighing of the Scriptures, ye may wax riper and stronger in your Ministry; and that ye may so endeavour yourselves, from time to time, to sanctify the lives of you and yours, and to fashion them after the Rule and Doctrine of Christ, that ye may be wholesome and godly examples, and patterns for the people to follow. And now that this present Congregation of Christ here assembled, may also understand your minds and wills in these things, and that this your promise may the more move you to do your duties, ye shall answer plainly to these things, which we, in the Name of

13. Pray without ceasing. 1 *Th. v.* 17. Praying always with all prayer and supplication in the Spirit, and watching thereunto with all perseverance. *Ep. vi.* 18. Seek the Lord and his strength, seek his face continually. 1 *Ch. xvi.* 11. Ye have not chosen me, but I have chosen you, and ordained you, that ye should go and bring forth fruit, and that your fruit should remain: that whatsoever ye shall ask of the Father in my name, he may give it you. When the Comforter is come, whom I will send unto you from the Father, even the Spirit of truth, which proceedeth from the Father, he shall testify of me. If ye abide in me and my words abide in you, ye shall ask what ye will, and it shall be done unto you. *John xv.* 16. 26. 7. Verily, verily, I say unto you, Whatsoever ye shall ask the Father in my name, he will give it you. Hitherto have ye asked nothing in my name: ask, and ye shall receive, that your joy may be full. *John xvi.* 23, 24. What is written in the law? how readest thou? *Lu. x.* 26. Search the Scriptures; for in them ye think ye have eternal life: and they are they which testify of me. *John v.* 39. These were more noble than those in Thessalonica, in that they received the word with all readiness of mind, and searched the Scriptures daily, whether these things were so. *Ac. xvii.* 11. A certain Jew named Apollos, an eloquent man, and mighty in the Scriptures, mightily convinced the Jews, and that publicly, shewing by the Scriptures that Jesus was Christ. *Ac. xviii.* 24. 28. Saul increased the more in strength, and confounded the Jews which dwelt at Damascus, proving that this is very Christ. *Ac. ix.* 22. Then he said unto them, O fools, and slow of heart to believe all that the prophets have spoken: Ought not Christ to have suffered these things, and to enter into his glory? And beginning at Moses and all the Prophets, he expounded unto them in all the Scriptures the things concerning himself. *Lu. xxiv.* 25, 26, 27. Which things also we speak, not in the words which man's wisdom teacheth, but which the Holy Ghost teacheth; comparing spiritual things

God and of his
Church, shall
demand of you
touching the
same.

with spiritual. 1 *Co. ii.* 13. For the word of God is quick, and powerful, and sharper than any twoedged sword, piercing even to the dividing asunder of soul and spirit, and of the joints and marrow, and is a discerner of the thoughts and intents of the heart. *He. iv.* 12. Blessed art thou, O Lord; teach me thy statutes. I will meditate in thy precepts, and have respect unto thy ways. Thy word have I hid in mine heart, that I might not sin against thee. My hands also will I lift up unto thy commandments, which I have loved; and I will meditate in thy statutes. O how love I thy law! it is my meditation all the day. Thy word is a lamp unto my feet, and a light unto my path. *Ps. cxix.* 12. 15. 11. 48. 97. 105. Teach me to do thy will; for thou art my God: thy Spirit is good; lead me into the land of uprightness. *Ps. cxliii.* 10. Every one that useth milk is unskilful in the word of righteousness: for he is a babe. But strong meat belongeth to them that are of full age, even those who by reason of use have their senses exercised to discern both good and evil. *He. v.* 13, 14. In nothing am I behind the very chiefest Apostles. 2 *Co. xii.* 11. Brethren, I count not myself to have apprehended: but this one thing I do, forgetting those things which are behind, and reaching forth unto those things which are before, I press toward the mark for the prize of the high calling of God in Christ Jesus. *Ph. iii.* 13, 14. Be ye followers of me, even as I also am of Christ. 1 *Co. xi.* 1. Brethren, be followers together of me, and mark them which walk so as ye have us for an ensample. *Ph. iii.* 17. Follow after righteousness, godliness, faith, love, patience, meekness. 1 *Ti. vi.* 11. As ye have therefore received Christ Jesus the Lord, so walk ye in him: rooted and built up in him, and stablished in the faith, as ye have been taught, abounding therein with thanksgiving. Beware lest any man spoil you through philosophy and vain deceit, after the tradition of men, after the rudiments of the world, and not after Christ. *Col. ii.* 6, 7, 8. Wherefore gird up the loins of your mind, be sober, and hope to the end for the grace that is to be brought unto you at the revelation of Jesus Christ; as obedient children, not fashioning yourselves according to the former lusts in your ignorance: but as he which hath called you is holy, so be ye holy in all manner of conversation. 1 *Pe. i.* 13, 14, 15. Feed the flock of God which is among you ; being ensamples to the flock. 1 *Ps. v.* 2, 3. Let no man despise thy youth ; but be thou an example of the believers, in word, in conversation, in charity, in spirit, in faith, in purity. 1 *Ti. iv.* 12.

Let these also first be proved. 1 *Ti. iii.* 10. *See also, Mat. iv.* 1 *to* 11.—1 *Pe. i.* 13, 14, 15.—*Ps. i.* 1, 2.

CCLXII. The solemn Questions to the Candidates for the Priesthood.

The Bishop.—1. Do you think in your heart, that you be truly called, according to the Will of our Lord Jesus Christ, and the Order of this Church of *England,* to the Order and Ministry of Priesthood ?
Ans. I think it.

1. *See Sections* 3, 4, *in CCLV.*

The Bishop. 2. Are you persuaded that the holy Scriptures contain sufficiently all Doctrine required of necessity for eternal salvation through faith in Jesus Christ ? And are you determined, out of the said Scriptures to instruct the people committed to your charge, and to teach nothing, as required of necessity to eternal salvation, but that which you shall be persuaded may be concluded and proved by the Scripture?

Ans. I am so persuaded, and have so determined, by God's grace.

2. From a child thou hast known the holy Scriptures which are able to make thee wise unto salvation through faith which is in Christ Jesus. All Scripture is given by inspiration of God, and is profitable for doctrine, for reproof, for correction, for instruction in righteousness : that the man of God may be perfect, throughly furnished unto all good works. 2 *Tim. iii.* 15, 16, 17. Search the Scriptures ; for in them ye think ye have eternal life : and they are they which testify of me. *John v.* 39. Whatsoever things were written aforetime were written for our learning, that we through patience and comfort of the Scriptures might have hope. *Ro. xv.* 4. These are written, that ye might believe that Jesus is the Christ, the Son of God ; and that believing ye might have life through his name. *John xx.* 31. Ye shall not add unto the word which I command you, neither shall ye diminish ought from it, that ye may keep the commandments of the Lord your God which I command you. *De. iv.* 2. Add thou not unto his words, lest he reprove thee, and thou be found a liar. *Pr. xxx.* 6. I testify unto every man that heareth the words of the prophecy of this book, If any man shall add unto these things, God shall add unto him the plagues that are written in this book : and if any man shall take away from the words of the book of this prophecy, God shall take away his part out of the book of life, and out of the holy city, and from

the things which are written in this book. *Re. xxii.* 18, 19. What thing soever I command you, observe to do it: thou shalt not add thereto, nor diminish from it. *De. xii.* 32. And I, brethren, when I came to you, came not with excellency of speech or of wisdom, declaring unto you the testimony of God. For I determined not to know any thing among you, save Jesus Christ, and him crucified. 1 *Co. ii.* 1, 2. *See also, Mat. v.* 21, 22. 27, 28. 33, 34. 43, 44.

The Bishop.—3. Will you then give your faithful diligence, always so to minister the Doctrine and Sacraments, and the Discipline of Christ, as the Lord hath commanded, and as this Church and Realm hath received the same, according to the commandments of God; so that you may teach the people committed to your Cure and Charge, with all diligence to keep and observe the same?—*Ans.* I will do so, by the help of the Lord.

3. And Jehoshaphat charged them, [the Levites and the priests,] saying, Thus shall ye do in the fear of the Lord, faithfully, and with a perfect heart. 2 *Ch. xix.* 9. Say to Archippus, Take heed to the ministry which thou hast received in the Lord, that thou fulfil it. *Col. iv.* 17. In all things shewing thyself a pattern of good works; in doctrine shewing uncorruptness. *Tit. ii.* 7. Let every soul be subject unto the higher powers. *Ro. xiii.* 1. I besought thee to abide still at Ephesus, that thou mightest charge some that they teach no other doctrine. 1 *Ti. i.* 3. We have sent with them our brother, whom we have oftentimes proved diligent in many things, but now much more diligent. 2 *Co. viii.* 22. Having then gifts differing according to the grace that is given to us, whether prophecy, let us prophesy according to the proportion of faith; or ministry, let us wait on our ministering; or he that teacheth, on teaching; or he that exhorteth, on exhortation; he that giveth, let him do it with simplicity; he that ruleth, with diligence; he that sheweth mercy, with cheerfulness. *Ro. xii.* 6, 7, 8. Feed the flock of God which is among you. 1 *Pe. v.* 2. Teaching them to observe all things whatsoever I have commanded you: and, lo, I am with you alway, even unto the end of the world. *Mat. xxviii.* 20. See also, *Lu. viii.* 15.

The Bishop. 4. Beware of false prophets, which come to you in sheep's
4. Will you be clothing, but inwardly they are ravening wolves. By their
ready, with all
faithful dili- fruits ye shall know them. *Mat. vii.* 15. 20. He that entereth

gence to ba-
nish and drive
away all erro-
neous and
strange doc-
trines contrary
to God's Word;
and to use both
public and pri-
vate moni-
tions and ex-
hortations, as
well to the sick
as to the whole,
within your
Cures, as need
shall require,
and occasion
shall be given?

Ans. I will,
the Lord being
my helper.

not by the door into the sheepfold, but climbeth up some other way, the same is a thief and a robber. *John x.* 1. I know this, that after my departing shall grievous wolves enter in among you, not sparing the flock. Also of your ownselves shall men arise, speaking perverse things, to draw away disciples after them. *Ac. xx.* 29, 30. And their word will eat as doth a canker. But foolish and unlearned questions avoid, knowing that they do gender strifes. In meekness instructing those that oppose themselves; if God peradventure will give them repentance to the acknowledging of the truth; and that they may recover themselves out of the snare of the devil, who are taken captive by him at his will. 2 *Ti. ii.* 17. 23. 25, 26. There are many unruly and vain talkers and deceivers, whose mouths must be stopped, who subvert whole houses, teaching things which they ought not, for filthy lucre's sake. They profess that they know God; but in works they deny him: wherefore rebuke them sharply, that they may be sound in the faith. But speak thou the things that become sound doctrine. *Tit. i.* 10, 11. 16. 13. *ii.* 1. A man that is an heretick after the first and second admonition reject; knowing that he that is such is subverted, and sinneth, being condemned of himself. *Tit. iii.* 10, 11. For there must be also heresies among you, that they which are approved may be made manifest among you. 1 *Co. xi.* 19. The Spirit speaketh expressly, that in the latter times some shall depart from the faith, giving heed to seducing spirits, and doctrines of devils; speaking lies in hypocrisy; forbidding to marry, and commanding to abstain from meats, which God hath created to be received with thanksgiving. But refuse profane and old wives' fables, and exercise thyself rather unto godliness. 1 *Ti. iv.* 1, 2, 3. 7. If any man teach otherwise, and consent not to wholesome words, even the words of our Lord Jesus Christ, and to the doctrine which is according to godliness; he is proud, knowing nothing, but doating about questions and strifes of words; from such withdraw thyself. O Timothy, keep that which is committed to thy trust, avoiding profane and vain babblings, and oppositions of science falsely so called: which some professing have erred concerning the faith. 1 *Ti. vi.* 3, 4, 5. 20, 21. Evil men and seducers shall wax worse and worse, deceiving, and being deceived : of this sort are they which creep into houses, and lead captive silly women laden with sins, led away with divers lusts, ever learning, and never able to come to the knowledge of the truth. *2 Ti. iii.* 13. 6, 7. They that are such serve not our Lord Jesus Christ, but their own belly ; and by good words and fair speeches deceive the hearts of the simple. *Ro. xvi.* 18. And of some have compassion, making a difference : and others save with fear, pulling them out of the fire; hating even the garment spotted by the flesh. *Jude* **22, 23.** He that heareth you heareth me ; and he that despiseth you despiseth me ; and he that despiseth me despiseth him that sent me. *Lu. x.* 16. Is any sick among you ? let him call for the elders of the Church ; and let them pray over him. *Ja. v.* 14. Now we exhort you, brethren, warn them that are unruly, comfort the feeble minded, support the weak, be patient toward all men. 1 *Th. v.* 14.

The Bishop.
5. Will you be diligent in Prayers, and in reading of the holy Scriptures, and in such studies as help to the knowledge of the same, laying aside the study of the world and the flesh ?

Ans. I will endeavour myself so to do, the Lord being my helper.

5. Praying always with all prayer and supplication in the Spirit. *Ep. vi.* 18. We will give ourselves continually to prayer and to the ministry of the word. *Ac. vi.* 4. God is my witness, whom I serve with my spirit in the Gospel of his Son, that without ceasing I make mention of you always in my prayers. *Ro. i.* 9. Epaphras, who is one of you, a servant of Christ, labouring fervently for you in prayers, that ye may stand perfect and complete in all the will of God. *Col. iv.* 12. Though I preach the Gospel, I have nothing to glory of : for necessity is laid upon me ; yea, woe is unto me if I preach not the Gospel ! 1 *Co. ix.* 16. Till I come, give attendance to reading, to exhortation, to doctrine. Neglect not the gift that is in thee, which was given thee by prophecy, with the laying on of the hands of the presbytery. Meditate upon these things ; give thyself wholly to them ; that thy profiting may appear to all. Take heed unto thyself, and unto the doctrine ; continue in them : for in doing this thou shalt both save thyself, and them that hear thee. 1 *Ti. iv.* 13 *to* 16. And I, brethren, when I came to you, came not with excellency of speech or of wisdom, declaring unto you the testimony of God. For I determined not to know any thing among you, save Jesus Christ and him crucified.

1 *Co. ii.* 1, 2. What things were gain to me, those I counted loss for Christ. Yea, doubtless, and I count all things but loss for the excellency of the knowledge of Christ Jesus my Lord: for whom I have suffered the loss of all things, and do count them but dung, that I may win Christ. *Ph. iii.* 7, 8.

The Bishop.—6. Will you be diligent to frame and fashion your ownselves, and your families, according to the Doctrine of Christ; and to make both yourselves and them, as much as in you lieth, wholesome examples and patterns to the flock of Christ?
Ans. I will apply myself thereto, the Lord being my helper.

6. *See Section 2, in CCLVI.*

The Bishop:
7. Will you maintain and set forwards, as much as lieth in you, quietness, peace, and love, among all christian people, and especially among them that are, or shall be, committed to your charge?

Ans. I will so do, the Lord being my helper.

7. Follow peace with them that call on the Lord out of a pure heart. 2 *Ti. ii.* 22. Follow peace with all men. *He. xii.* 14. Do good; seek peace, and pursue it. *Ps. xxxiv.* 14. How beautiful are the feet of them that preach the Gospel of peace. *Ro. x.* 15. Blessed are the peacemakers; for they shall be called the children of God. *Mat. v.* 9. Stand, having your feet shod with the preparation of the gospel of peace. *Ep. vi.* 14, 15. Glory to God in the highest, and on earth peace, good will toward men. *Lu. ii.* 14. The ornament of a meek and quiet spirit, which is in the sight of God of great price. 1 *Pe. iii.* 4. And the Lord make you to increase and abound in love one toward another, and toward all men, even as we do toward you: to the end he may stablish your hearts unblameable in holiness before God, even our Father, at the coming of our Lord Jesus Christ with all his saints. 1 *Th. iii.* 12.

The Bishop.—8. Will you reverently obey your Ordinary, and other chief Ministers, unto whom is committed the charge and government over you; following with a glad mind and will their godly admonitions, and submitting yourselves to their godly judgments?
Ans. I will so do, the Lord being my helper.

8. *See Section 3. in CCLVI.*

The Bishop.
9. Almighty God, who hath given you this will to do all these things; Grant also unto you strength

9. It is God which worketh in you both to will and to do of his good pleasure. *Ph. ii.* 13. Not that we are sufficient of ourselves to think any thing as of ourselves; but our sufficiency is of God. 2 *Co. iii.* 5. Whosoever hath, to him shall be given, and he shall have more abundance. *Mat. xiii.* 12.

and power to perform the same; that he may accomplish his work, which he hath begun in you, through Jesus Christ our Lord. *Amen.*

Being confident of this very thing, that he which hath begun a good work in you will perform it. And this I pray, that your love may abound yet more and more in knowledge and in all judgment; that ye may approve things that are excellent; that ye may be sincere and without offence till the day of Christ; being filled with the fruits of righteousness, which are by Jesus Christ, unto the glory and praise of God. *Ph. i.* 6. 9, 10, 11. Lo, I am with you alway, even unto the end of the world. *Mat. xxviii.* 20. Brethren, pray for us. 1 *Th. v.* 25.

CCLXIII. An Hymn, called, Veni Creator. No. 1.

1. Come, Holy Ghost, our souls inspire, And lighten with celestial fire.

1. And there appeared unto them cloven tongues like as of fire, and it sat upon each of them. And they were all filled with the Holy Ghost. *Ac. ii.* 3, 4. God, who hath also given unto us his Holy Spirit. 1 *Th. iv.* 8. God, who commanded the light to shine out of darkness, hath shined in our hearts, to give the light of the knowledge of the glory of God in the face of Jesus Christ. 2 *Co. iv.* 6. *See also, Ps. xix.* 8.

2. Thou the anointing Spirit art, Who dost thy sev'n-fold gifts impart.

2. Their anointing shall surely be an everlasting priesthood. *Ex. xl.* 15. These things saith he that hath the seven Spirits of God. *Re. iii.* 1. Grace be unto you, and peace, from Him which is, and which was, and which is to come; and from the seven Spirits which are before his throne. *Re. i.* 4. And I beheld, and, lo, a Lamb as it had been slain, having seven horns and seven eyes, which are the seven Spirits of God. *Re. v.* 6. And the Spirit of the Lord shall rest upon him, the Spirit of wisdom and understanding, the Spirit of counsel and might, the Spirit of knowledge and of the fear of the Lord; and shall make him of quick understanding in the fear of the Lord. *Is. xi.* 2, 3.

3. Thy blessed Unction from above, Is comfort, life, and fire of love.

3. Ye have an unction from the Holy One, and ye know all things. The anointing which ye have received of him abideth in you, and ye need not that any man teach you: but as the same anointing teacheth you of all things, and is truth, and is no lie, and even as it hath taught you, ye shall abide in him. 1 *John ii.* 20. 27. The Comforter, which is the Holy Ghost, whom the Father will send in my name, He shall teach

you all things, and bring all things to your remembrance, whatsoever I have said unto you. *John xiv.* 26. Ye, beloved, building up yourselves on your most holy faith, praying in the Holy Ghost, keep yourselves in the love of God, looking for the mercy of our Lord Jesus Christ unto eternal life. *Jude* 20, 21. Quench not the Spirit. 1 *Th. v,* 19.

4. Enable with perpetual light

The dulness of our blinded sight.

4. Consider and hear me, O Lord my God: lighten mine eyes. *Ps. xiii.* 3. Thou wilt light my candle: the Lord my God will enlighten my darkness, *Ps. xviii.* 28. When for the time ye ought to be teachers, ye have need that one teach you again which be the first principles of the oracles of God. *He. v,* 12. Then he said unto them, O fools, and slow of heart to believe all that the prophets have spoken; Ought not Christ to have suffered these things, and to enter into his glory? And beginning at Moses and all the prophets, he expounded unto them in all the Scriptures the things concerning himself. *Lu. xxiv.* 25, 26, 27. Open thou mine eyes, that I may behold wondrous things out of thy law. *Ps. cxix.* 18. Anoint thine eyes with eyesalve, that thou mayest see. *Re. iii.* 18.

5. Anoint and cheer our soiled face

With the abundance of thy grace:

5. Then will I sprinkle clean water upon you, and ye shall be clean: from all your filthiness, will I cleanse you. And I will put my Spirit within you; I will also save you from all your uncleannesses. *Eze. xxxvi.* 25. 27. 29. Lord, lift thou up the light of thy countenance upon us. *Ps. iv.* 6. The Lord is a Sun and Shield: the Lord will give grace and glory. *Ps. lxxxiv.* 11. The grace of our Lord was exceeding abundant with faith and love which is in Christ Jesus. 1 *Ti. i.* 14. The Holy Ghost, which is shed on us abundantly. *Tit. iii.* 5, 6. See also, *Ep. i.* 13.

6. Keep far our foes, give peace at home:

Where thou art guide, no ill can come.

6. Preserve me, O God: for in thee do I put my trust. *Ps. xvi.* 1. Let God arise, let his enemies be scattered: let them also that hate him flee before him. As smoke is driven away, so drive them away: as wax melteth before the fire, so let the wicked perish in the presence of God. *Ps. lxviii.* 1, 2. Pray for the peace of Jerusalem. Peace be within thy walls. *Ps. cxxii.* 1, 7. Now the Lord of peace himself give you peace always by all means. 2 *Th. iii.* 16. The fruit of the Spirit is love, joy, peace. *Ga. v.* 22. The Lord is my light and my salvation; whom shall I fear? the Lord is the

strength of my life; of whom shall I be afraid? *Ps. xxvii.* 1. Because thou hast made the Lord which is my refuge, even the Most High, thy habitation; there shall no evil befall thee, neither shall any plague come nigh thy dwelling. *Ps. xci.* 9, 10. Thou shalt guide me with thy counsel, and afterward receive me to glory. *Ps. lxxiii.* 24. The Lord shall deliver me from every evil work, and will preserve me unto his heavenly kingdom. *2 Ti. iv.* 18.

7. Teach us to know the Father, Son, And Thee, of both, to be but One;

7. This is life eternal, that they might know thee the only true God, and Jesus Christ, whom thou hast sent. *John xvii.* 3. The Comforter, which is the Holy Ghost, whom the Father will send in my name, He shall teach you. *John xiv.* 26. The Comforter, whom I will send unto you from the Father, even the Spirit of truth, which proceedeth from the Father, He shall testify of me. *John xv.* 26. Holy Father, keep through thine own name those whom thou hast given me, that they may be one as we are. *John xvii.* 11.

8. That through the ages all along, This, this may be our endless song; Praise to thy eternal merit, Father, Son, and Holy Spirit.

8. Worthy is the Lamb that was slain to receive power, and riches, and wisdom, and strength, and honour, and glory, and blessing. Blessing, and honour, and glory, and power, be unto him that sitteth upon the throne, and unto the Lamb for ever and ever. Holy, Holy, Holy, Lord God Almighty. *Re. v.* 12, 13. *iv.* 8.

CCLXIV. *An Hymn called* Veni Creator. *No.* 2.

1. Come, Holy Ghost, eternal God,
   Proceeding from above,
   Both from the Father and the Son,
   The God of peace and love.

2. Visit our minds, into our hearts
   Thy heavenly grace inspire;
   That truth and godliness we may
   Pursue with full desire.

3. Thou art the very Comforter
   In grief and all distress:
   The heavenly gift of God Most High:
   No tongue can it express.

4. The fountain and the living spring
   Of joy celestial;
   The fire so bright, the love so sweet,
   The Unction spiritual.

5. Thou in thy gifts art manifold,
   By them Christ's Church doth stand:
   In faithful hearts thou writ'st thy law
   The finger of God's hand.

6. According to thy promise, Lord,
   Thou givest speech with grace;
   That through thy help, God's praises may
   Resound in every place.

7. O Holy Ghost, into our minds
   Send down thy heavenly light;
   Kindle our hearts with fervent zeal,
   To serve God day and night.

8. Our weakness strengthen and confirm,
   (For, Lord, thou know'st us frail)
   That neither devil, world, nor flesh,
   Against us may prevail.

9. Put back our enemies far from us,
    And help us to obtain
Peace in our hearts with God and man,
    (The best, the truest gain ;)

10. And grant that thou being, O Lord,
    Our leader and our guide,
We may escape the snares of sin,
    And never from thee slide.

11. Such measures of thy powerful grace
    Grant, Lord, to us, we pray ;
That Thou may'st be our Comforter
    At the last dreadful day.

12. Of strife and of dissention,
    Dissolve, O Lord, the bands,
And knit the knots of peace and love
    Throughout all Christian lands.

13. Grant us the grace, that we may know
    The Father of all might,
That we of his beloved Son
    May gain the blissful sight ;

14. And that we may with perfect faith
    Ever acknowledge Thee,
The Spirit of Father, and of Son,
    One God in Persons Three.

15. To God the Father laud and praise,
    And to his blessed Son,
And to the Holy Spirit of grace,
    Co-equal three in one.

16. And pray we, that our only Lord
    Would please his Spirit to send
On all that shall profess his Name,
    From hence to the world's end. Amen.

CCLXV. *Praise to God for his goodness in appointing Ministers of his Word ; and Prayer that his Name may be glorified and his Kingdom enlarged.*

Let us pray.

1. Almighty God and heavenly Father, who, of thine infinite love and goodness towards us, hast given to us thy only and most dearly beloved Son Jesus Christ, to be our Redeemer, and the Author of everlasting life ;

1. I appeared unto Abraham, unto Isaac, and unto Jacob, by the name of God Almighty. *Ex. vi.* 3. Our Father which art in heaven. *Mat. vi.* 9. God so loved the world, that he gave his only begotten Son, that whosoever believeth in him should not perish, but have everlasting life. *John iii.* 16. In whom we have redemption through his blood. *Ep. i.* 7. God commendeth his love toward us, in that, while we were yet sinners, Christ died for us. *Ro. v.* 8. In this was manifested the love of God toward us, because that God sent his only begotten Son into the world, that we might live through him. 1 *John iv.* 9. This is my beloved Son, in whom I am well pleased. *Mat. iii.* 17. Being made perfect, he became the Author of eternal salvation unto all them that obey him. *He. v.* 2. Having obtained eternal redemption for us. *He. ix.* 12.

2. Who, after he had made perfect our redemption by his death, and was ascended into heaven, sent abroad in to the world his Apostles, Prophets, Evangelists, Doctors,

2. When Jesus had received the vinegar, he said, It is finished : and he bowed his head, and gave up the ghost. *John xix.* 30. For by one offering he hath perfected for ever them that are sanctified. *He. x.* 14. For thou wast slain, and hast redeemed us to God by thy blood out of every kindred, and tongue, and people, and nation. *Re. v.* 9. Ye shall receive power, after that the Holy Ghost is come upon you : and ye shall be witnesses unto me both in Jerusalem,

and Pastors, by whose labour and ministry he gathered together a great flock in all the parts of the world, to set forth the eternal praise of thy holy name:

and in all Judea, and in Samaria, and unto the uttermost part of the earth *Ac. i.* 8. Wherefore he saith, When he ascended up on high, he led captivity captive, and gave gifts unto men. And he gave some, apostles; and some, prophets; and some, evangelists: and some, pastors and teachers; for the perfecting of the saints, for the work of the ministry, for the edifying of the body of Christ: till we all come in the unity of the faith, and of the knowledge of the Son of God, unto a perfect man, unto the measure of the stature of the fulness of Christ. *Ep. iv.* 8. 11, 12, 13. Whosoever shall call upon the name of the Lord shall be saved. How shall they call on him in whom they have not believed? and how shall they believe in him of whom they have not heard? and how shall they hear without a preacher? and how shall they preach, except they be sent? as it is written, How beautiful are the feet of them that preach the Gospel of peace, and bring glad tidings of good things! But I say, Have they not heard? Yea, verily, their sound went into all the earth, and their words unto the ends of the world. *Ro. x.* 13, 14, 15. 18. If any man speak, let him speak as the oracles of God; if any man minister, let him do it as of the ability which God giveth: that God in all things may be glorified through Jesus Christ, to whom be praise and dominion for ever and ever. Amen. 1 *Pe. iv.* 11. All thy works shall praise thee, O Lord; and thy saints shall bless thee. They shall speak of the glory of thy kingdom, and talk of thy power; to make known to the sons of men his mighty acts, and the glorious majesty of his kingdom. *Ps. cxlv.* 10, 11, 12. Save us, O God of our salvation, and gather us together, and deliver us from the heathen, that we may give thanks to thy holy Name, and glory in thy praise. 1 *Ch. xvi.* 35.

3. For these so great benefits of thy eternal goodness, and for that thou hast vouchsafed to call these thy servants here present to the same Office and Ministry ap-

3. The mercy of the Lord is from everlasting to everlasting. *Ps. ciii.* 17. The goodness of God endureth continually. *Ps. lii.* 1. I will give you pastors according to mine heart, which shall feed you with knowledge and understanding. *Je. iii.* 15. Go ye therefore, and teach all nations: and, lo, I am with you alway, even unto the end of the world. *Mat. xxviii.* 19, 20. Wherefore of these men which companied with us, must one be ordained to be a witness with us. And

pointed for the salvation of mankind, we render unto thee most hearty thanks, we praise and worship thee;

they prayed, and said, Thou, Lord, which knowest the hearts of all men, shew whether of these two thou hast chosen. *Ac. i.* 21, 22. 24. It pleased God, who separated me from my mother's womb, and called me by his grace, to reveal his Son in me, that I might preach him among the heathen. *Ga. i.* 15, 16. The things that thou hast heard of me among many witnesses, the same commit thou to faithful men, who shall be able to teach others also. 2 *Ti. ii.* 2. We are ambassadors for Christ, as though God did beseech you by us: we pray you in Christ's stead, be ye reconciled to God. 2 *Co. v.* 20. We then, as workers together with him, beseech you also that ye receive not the grace of God in vain. 2 *Co. vi.* 1. Who will have all men to be saved. 1 *Ti. ii.* 4. Blessed be the God and Father of our Lord Jesus Christ, which according to his abundant mercy hath begotten us again unto a lively hope. 1 *Pe. i.* 3. Blessed be the Lord, who daily loadeth us with benefits, even the God of our salvation. *Ps. lxviii.* 19. Unto thee, O God, do we give thanks, unto thee do we give thanks: for that thy name is near thy wondrous works declare. *Ps. lxxv.* 1. O come, let us worship and bow down: let us kneel before the Lord our Maker. *Ps. xcv.* 6. I will praise thee, O Lord, with my whole heart; I will shew forth all thy marvellous works. *Ps. ix.* 1.

4. and we humbly beseech thee, by the same thy blessed Son, to grant unto all, which either here, or elsewhere, call upon thy holy Name, that we may continue to shew ourselves thankful unto thee for these and all other thy benefits; and that we may daily increase and go forwards in the knowledge and faith of thee and

4. If ye abide in me, and my words abide in you, ye shall ask what ye will, and it shall be done unto you. *John* xv. 7. And this is the confidence that we have in him, that, if we ask any thing according to his will, he heareth us: and if we know that he hear us, whatsoever we ask, we know that we have the petitions that we desired of him. 1 *John v.* 14, 15. Paul, unto the Church of God which is at Corinth, with all that in every place call upon the name of Jesus Christ our Lord, both their's and our's. I thank my God always on your behalf, for the grace of God which is given you by Jesus Christ. 1 *Co.* 1. 2, 4. Giving thanks always for all things unto God and the Father in the name of our Lord Jesus Christ. *Ep. v.* 20. Wherefore I also, after I heard of your faith in the Lord Jesus, and love unto all the saints, cease not to give thanks for you, making mention of you in my prayers. *Ep. i.* 15, 16. We give thanks to God always for you all, making mention of

thy Son, by the
Holy Spirit.

you in our prayers. 1 *Th. i.* 2. I will bless the Lord at all times: his praise shall continually be in my mouth. O magnify the Lord with me, and let us exalt his name together. *Ps. xxxiv.* 1. 3. Bless the Lord, O my soul: and all that is within me, bless his holy name. Bless the Lord, O my soul, and forget not all his benefits. *Ps. ciii.* 1, 2. Grow in grace, and in the knowledge of our Lord and Saviour Jesus Christ. 2 *Pe. iii.* 18. This is life eternal, that they might know thee the only true God, and Jesus Christ, whom thou hast sent. *John xvii.* 3. Then shall we know, if we follow on to know the Lord. *Ho. vi.* 3. The Gospel of Christ is the power of God unto salvation to every one that believeth. For therein is the righteousness of God revealed from faith to faith: as it is written, The just shall live by faith. *Ro. i.* 16, 17. Strengthened with might by his Spirit in the inner man. *Ep. iii.* 16. Brethren, I count not myself to have apprehended: but this one thing I do, forgetting those things which are behind, and reaching forth unto those things which are before, I press toward the mark for the prize of the high calling of God in Christ Jesus. Yea doubtless, and I count all things but loss for the excellency of the knowledge of Christ Jesus my Lord: for whom I have suffered the loss of all things, and do count them but dung, that I may win Christ, and be found in him. *Ph. iii.* 13, 14. 8, 9. Till we all come in the unity of the faith and of the knowledge of the Son of God unto a perfect man, unto the measure of the stature of the fulness of Christ. *Ep. iv.* 13.

5. So that as well by these thy Ministers, as by them, over whom they shall be appointed thy Ministers, thy holy Name may be for ever glorified, and thy blessed kingdom enlarged, through the same thy Son Jesus Christ our Lord; who liveth and reign-

5. O sing unto the Lord a new song: let the congregation of saints praise him. *Ps. cxlix.* 1. Bless the Lord, O house of Aaron: bless the Lord, O house of Levi: ye that fear the Lord, bless the Lord. Blessed be the Lord out of Zion, which dwelleth at Jerusalem. Praise ye the Lord. *Ps. cxxxv.* 19, 20, 21. Bless ye God in the congregations, even the Lord, from the fountain of Israel. *Ps. lxviii.* 26. Let all those that seek thee rejoice and be glad in thee: let such as love thy salvation say continually, The Lord be magnified. *Ps. xl.* 16. All nations whom thou hast made shall come and worship before thee, O Lord; and shall glorify thy name. I will praise thee, O Lord my God, with all my heart: and I will

<table>
<tr><td>eth with thee, in the unity of the same Holy Spirit, world without end. *Amen.*</td><td>glorify thy name for evermore. *Ps. lxxxvi.* 9. 12. Enlarge the place of thy tent, and let them stretch forth the curtains of thine habitations: spare not, lengthen thy cords, and strengthen thy stakes. *Is. liv.* 2. Thou hast increased the nation, O</td></tr>
</table>

Lord; thou art glorified. *Is. xxvi.* 15. Whether our brethren are enquired of, they are the messengers of the churches, and the glory of Christ. 2 *Co. viii.* 23. God hath highly exalted him and given him a name which is above every name: that at the name of Jesus every knee should bow, of things in heaven, and things in earth, and things under the earth; and that every tongue should confess that Jesus Christ is Lord, to the glory of God the Father. *Ph. ii.* 9, 10, 11. Thanks be unto God, which always causeth us to triumph in Christ, and maketh manifest the savour of his knowledge by us in every place. 2 *Co. ii.* 14. Wherefore also we pray that the name of our Lord Jesus Christ may be glorified in you, and ye in him, according to the grace of our God and the Lord Jesus Christ. 2 *Th. i.* 11, 12. There were great voices in heaven, saying, The kingdoms of this world are become the kingdoms of our Lord, and of his Christ; and he shall reign for ever and ever. *Re. xi.* 15. Thy kingdom come. *Mat. vi.* 10. O our God, hear the prayer of thy servant, and his supplications, and cause thy face to shine upon thy sanctuary, for the Lord's sake. *Da. ix.* 17. He ever liveth to make intercession for them. *He. vii.* 25. And every creature which is in heaven, and on the earth, and under the earth, and such as are in the sea, and all that are in them, heard I saying, Blessing, and honour, and glory, and power, be unto him that sitteth upon the throne, and unto the Lamb for ever and ever. And the four beasts said, Amen. And the four and twenty elders fell down and worshipped him that liveth for ever and ever. *Re. v.* 13, 14.

CCLXVI. The solemn Words to the Candidates for the Office of Priest, used with imposition of hands. See CCLVII.

<table>
<tr><td>1. Receive the Holy Ghost for the Office and Work of a Priest in the Church of God,</td><td>1. Then said Jesus to them again, Peace be unto you: as my Father hath sent me, even so send I you. And when he had said this, he breathed on them, and saith unto them, Receive ye the Holy Ghost: whosoever sins ye remit, they are</td></tr>
</table>

now committed unto thee by the Imposition of our hands. Whose sins thou dost forgive, they are forgiven; and whose sins thou dost retain, they are retained. And be thou a faithful Dispenser of the Word of God, and of his holy Sacraments; In the name of the Father, and of the Son, and of the Holy Ghost. Amen.

remitted unto them; and whosoever sins ye retain, they are retained. *John xx.* 21, 22, 23. Wherefore I put thee in remembrance that thou stir up the gift of God, which is in thee by the putting on of my hands. That good thing which was committed unto thee keep by the Holy Ghost which dwelleth in us. Hold fast the form of sound words, which thou hast heard of me, in faith and love which is in Christ Jesus. *2 Ti. i.* 6. 14. 13. Study to shew thyself approved unto God; a workman that needeth not to be ashamed, rightly dividing the word of truth. *2 Ti. ii.* 15. Let a man so account of us, as of the ministers of Christ, and stewards of the mysteries of God. Moreover it is required in stewards, that a man be found faithful. *1 Co. iv.* 1, 2. I charge thee therefore before God, and the Lord Jesus Christ, who shall judge the quick and the dead at his appearing and his kingdom; preach the word; be instant in season, out of season; reprove, rebuke, exhort with all longsuffering and doctrine. *2 Ti. iv.* 1, 2. Speak thou the things which become sound doctrine. *Tit. ii.* 1. Go ye therefore, and teach all nations, baptizing them in the name of the Father, and of the Son, and of the Holy Ghost: teaching them to observe all things whatsoever I have commanded you: and, lo, I am with you alway, even unto the end of the world. Amen. *Mat. xxviii.* 19, 20. I have received of the Lord that which also I delivered unto you, That the Lord Jesus the same night in which he was betrayed took bread: and when he had given thanks, he brake it, and said, Take, eat: this is my body, which is broken for you: this do in remembrance of me. After the same manner also he took the cup, when he had supped, saying, This cup is the new testament in my blood: this do ye, as oft as ye drink it, in remembrance of me. *1 Co. xi.* 23, 24, 25. Watch thou in all things, endure afflictions, do the work of an evangelist, make full proof of thy ministry. *2 Ti. iv.* 5. Cursed be he that doeth the work of the Lord deceitfully. *Je. xlviii.* 10. Who then is that faithful and wise steward, whom his Lord shall make ruler over his houshold, to give them their portion of meat in due season? Blessed is that servant, whom his lord when he cometh shall find so doing. *Lu. xii.* 42, 43. Be thou faithful unto death, and I will give thee a crown of life. *Re. ii.* 10.

2. Take thou authority to preach the Word of God, and to minister the holy Sacraments in the Congregation, where thou shalt be lawfully appointed thereunto.	2. No man taketh this honour unto himself, but he that is called of God, as was Aaron. *He. v.* 4. We will not boast of things without our measure, but according to the measure of the rule which God hath distributed to us, a measure to reach even unto you. For we stretch not ourselves beyond our measure, as though we reached not unto you: for we are come as far as to you also in preaching the Gospel of Christ: not boasting of things without our measure, that is, of other men's labours; but having hope, when your faith is increased, that we shall be enlarged by you according to our rule abundantly, to preach the Gospel in the regions beyond you, and not to boast in another man's line of things made ready to our hand. *2 Co. x.* 13 *to* 16.

CCLXVII. A Prayer that the Newly-ordered Priests may have great Success in their Ministry.

1. Most merciful Father, we beseech thee to send upon these thy servants thy heavenly blessing; that they may be clothed with righteousness, and that thy Word, spoken by their mouths, may have such success, that it may never be spoken in vain.	1. The blessing of the Lord be upon you: we bless you in the name of the Lord. *Ps. cxxix.* 8. Bless thine inheritance. *Ps. xxviii.* 9. Who shall ascend into the hill of the Lord? or who shall stand in his holy place? He that hath clean hands, and a pure heart; who hath not lifted up his soul unto vanity, nor sworn deceitfully. He shall receive the blessing from the Lord. *Ps. xxiv.* 3, 4, 5. Let thy priests be clothed with righteousness. *Ps. cxxxii.* 9. And Samuel grew, and the Lord was with him, and did let none of his words fall to the ground. *1 Sa. iii.* 19. It is not ye that speak, but the Spirit of your Father which speaketh in you. *Mat. x.* 20. As the rain cometh down, and the snow from heaven, and returneth not thither, but watereth the earth, and maketh it bring forth and bud, that it may give seed to the sower, and bread to the eater: so shall my word be that goeth forth out of my mouth: it shall not return unto me void, but it shall accomplish that which I please, and it shall prosper in the thing whereto I sent it. *Is. lv.* 10, 11. For this cause thank we God without ceasing, because, when ye received the word of God which ye heard of us, ye received it not as the word of men, but as it is in truth, the word of God, which effectually worketh also in you that believe. *1 Th. ii.* 13. Brethren, pray for us, that the

word of the Lord may have free course, and be glorified. *2 Th. iii.* 1.

2. Grant also, that we may have grace to hear and receive what they shall deliver out of thy most holy Word, or agreeable to the same, as the means of our salvation; that in all our words and deeds we may seek thy glory, and the increase of thy kingdom, through Jesus Christ our Lord. *Amen.*

2. The hearing ear, and the seeing eye, the Lord hath made even both of them. *Pr. xx.* 12. Be ye not unwise, but understanding what the will of the Lord is. *Ep. v.* 17. Who will have all men to be saved, and to come to the knowledge of the truth. 1 *Ti. ii.* 4. Being born again, not of corruptible seed, but of incorruptible, by the word of God, which liveth and abideth for ever. 1 *Pe. i.* 23. The seed is the word of God. That on the good ground are they, which in an honest and good heart, having heard the word, keep it, and bring forth fruit with patience. *Lu. viii.* 11. 15. The word of the Lord endureth for ever. And this is the word which by the Gospel is preached unto you. Wherefore laying aside all malice, and all guile, and hypocrisies, and envies, and all evil speakings, as newborn babes, desire the sincere milk of the word, that ye may grow thereby. 1 *Pe. i.* 25. *ii.* 1, 2. If any man speak, let him speak as the oracles of God; that God in all things may be glorified through Jesus Christ. 1 *Pe. iv.* 11. Let your speech be alway with grace, seasoned with salt. *Col. iv.* 6. Whatsoever ye do, do all to the glory of God. 1 *Co. x.* 31. Let your light so shine before men, that they may see your good works, and glorify your Father which is in heaven. *Mat. v.* 16. Having your conversation honest among the Gentiles; that, whereas they speak against you as evil doers, they may by your good works which they shall behold, glorify God in the day of visitation. 1 *Pe. ii.* 12.

THE FORM OF ORDAINING OR CONSECRATING OF AN ARCHBISHOP, OR BISHOP.

CCLXVIII. A Prayer that the Bishops of God's Church may have grace to be diligent.

1. Almighty God, who by thy Son Jesus Christ, didst give to thy holy Apostles many excellent

1. Then said Jesus to them again, Peace be unto you: as my Father hath sent me, even so send I you. And when he had said this, he breathed on them, and saith unto them, Receive ye the Holy Ghost. *John xx.* 21, 22. Behold, I send the promise of my Father upon you: but tarry ye in the city

gifts, and didst
charge them to
feed thy flock;

2. Give
grace we be-
seech thee to
all Bishops,
the Pastors of
thy Church,
that they may
diligently
preach thy
word, and duly
administer the

of Jerusalem, until ye be endued with power from on high. *Lu. xxiv.* 49. Behold, I give unto you power to tread on serpents and scorpions, and over all the power of the enemy. *Lu. x.* 19. He gave them power against unclean spirits, to cast them out, and to heal all manner of sickness and all manner of disease. Heal the sick, cleanse the lepers, raise the dead, cast out devils. *Mat. x.* 1. 8. They were all filled with the Holy Ghost, and began to speak with other tongues, as the Spirit gave them utterance. *Ac. ii.* 4. But the manifestation of the Spirit is given to every man to profit withal. For to one is given by the Spirit the word of wisdom; to another the word of knowledge by the same Spirit; to another faith by the same Spirit; to another the gifts of healing by the same Spirit; to another the working of miracles; to another prophecy; to another discerning of spirits; to another divers kinds of tongues; to another the interpretation of tongues. 1 *Co. xii.* 7 *to* 10. When they had dined, Jesus saith to Simon Peter, Simon, son of Jonas, lovest thou me more than these? He saith unto him, Yea, Lord; thou knowest that I love thee. He saith unto him, Feed my lambs. He saith to him again the second time, Simon, son of Jonas, lovest thou me? He saith unto him, Yea, Lord; thou knowest that I love thee. He saith unto him, Feed my sheep. *John xxi.* 15, 16. A Bishop must be apt to teach. 1 *Ti. iii.* 2. A Bishop must be blameless, as the steward of God. *Ti. i.* 7. Take heed unto yourselves and to all the flock over the which the Holy Ghost hath made you overseers, to feed the Church of God, which he hath purchased with his own blood. *Ac. xx.* 28. The elders which are among you I exhort, who am also an elder, and a witness of the sufferings of Christ, and also a partaker of the glory that shall be revealed: Feed the flock of God which is among you, taking the oversight thereof. 1 *Pe. v.* 1, 2, 3.

2. And grant unto thy servants, that with all boldness they may speak thy word. *Ac. iv.* 29. Praying always with all prayer and supplication in the Spirit, and watching thereunto with all perseverance and supplication for all saints; and for me, that utterance may be given unto me, that I may open my mouth boldly, to make known the mystery of the Gospel, that therein I may speak boldly, as I ought to speak.

godlyDiscipline
thereof ; and
grant to the
people, that
they may obe-
diently follow
the same ; that
all may receive
the crown of
everlasting
glory, through
Jesus Christ
our Lord.
Amen.

Ep. vi. 18, 19, 20. I have not shunned to declare unto you all the counsel of God. *Ac. xx.* 27. Let all things be done decently and in order. For God is not the Author of confusion, but of peace, as in all churches of the saints. 1 *Co. xiv.* 40. 33. If any man seem to be contentious, we have no such custom, neither the churches of God. 1 *Co. xi.* 16. I charge thee before God, and the Lord Jesus Christ, who shall judge the quick and the dead at his appearing and his kingdom ; Preach the word ; be instant in season, out of season ; reprove, rebuke, exhort with all longsuffering and doctrine. But watch thou in all things, endure afflictions, do the work of an evangelist, make full proof of thy ministry: I have finished my course, I have kept the faith : henceforth there is laid up for me a crown of righteousness, which the Lord, the righteous Judge, shall give me at that day : and not to me only, but unto all them also that love his appearing. 2 *Ti. iv.* 1, 2, 3. 5. 7, 8. Remember them which have the rule over you, who have spoken unto you the word of God : whose faith follow. Obey them that have the rule over you, and submit yourselves : for they watch for your souls, as they that must give account, that they may do it with joy, and not with grief : for that is unprofitable for you. *He. xiii.* 7. 17. Be ye followers of me, even as I also am of Christ. Ye became followers of us, and of the Lord, having received the Word in much affliction, with joy of the Holy Ghost. 1 *Co. xi.* 1. 1 *Th. i.* 6. The Lord make you to increase and abound in love one toward another, and toward all men, even as we do toward you : to the end he may stablish your hearts unblameable in holiness before God, even our Father, at the coming of our Lord Jesus Christ with all his saints. 1 *Th. iii.* 12, 13. Wherefore also we pray always for you, that our God would count you worthy of his calling, and fulfil all the good pleasure of his goodness, and the work of faith with power: that the name of our Lord Jesus Christ may be glorified in you, and ye in him, according to the grace of our God and the Lord Jesus Christ. 2 *Th. i.* 11, 12. Be thou faithful unto death, and I will give thee a crown of life. *Re. ii.* 10.

The Epistle.—1 Tim. iii. 1 *to* 6.—*This is a true saying, If a man desire the Office of a Bishop, he desireth a good work. A Bishop then must be blameless, the husband of one wife, vigilant, sober, of good behaviour, given to hospitality, apt to teach ; not given to wine, no striker, not greedy of filthy lucre, but patient ; not a brawler, not covetous ; one that ruleth well his own house, having his children in subjection with all gravity ; (For if a man know not how to rule his own house, how shall he take care of the Church of God ?) Not a novice, lest being lifted up with pride, he fall into the condemnation of the devil. Moreover, he must have a good report of them which are without : lest he fall into reproach, and the snare of the devil.*

Or this.—For the Epistle.—Acts 20. 17 to 35.—*From Miletus Paul sent to Ephesus, and called the elders of the church. And when they were come to him, he said unto them, Ye know from the first day that I came into Asia, after what manner I have been with you at all seasons, serving the Lord with all humility of mind, and with many tears and temptations, which befel me by the lying in wait of the Jews : And how I kept back nothing that was profitable unto you, but have shewed you, and have taught you publicly, and from house to house, testifying both to the Jews and also to the Greeks, repentance toward God, and faith toward our Lord Jesus Christ. And now behold, I go bound in the spirit unto Jerusalem, not knowing the things that shall befal me there ; save that the Holy Ghost witnesseth in every city, saying, That bonds and afflictions abide me. But none of these things move me, neither count I my life dear unto myself, so that I might finish my course with Joy, and the ministry which I have received of the Lord Jesus, to testify the Gospel of the grace of God. And now behold, I know that ye all, among whom I have gone preaching the kingdom of God, shall see my face no more. Wherefore I take you to record this day, that I am pure from the blood of all men. For I have not shunned to declare unto you all the counsel of God. Take heed therefore unto yourselves, and to all the flock, over the which the Holy Ghost hath made you overseers, to feed the Church of God, which he hath purchased with his own blood. For I know this, that after my departing shall grievous wolves enter in among you, not sparing the flock. Also of your ownselves shall men arise, speaking perverse things, to draw away disciples after them. Therefore watch, and remember, that by the space of three years, I ceased not to warn every one night and day with tears. And now, brethren, I commend you to God, and to the word of his grace, which is able to build you up, and to give you an inheritance among all them which are sanctified. I have coveted no man's silver, or gold, or apparel : yea, ye yourselves know, that these hands have ministered unto my necessities, and to them that were with me. I have shewed you all things, how that so labouring ye ought to support the weak ; and to remember the words of the Lord Jesus, how he said, It is more blessed to give than to receive.*

The Gospel. John xxi. 15 to 17.—*Jesus saith to Simon Peter, Simon, son of Jonas, lovest thou me more than these ? He saith unto him, Yea, Lord ; thou knowest that I love thee. He saith unto him, Feed my lambs. He saith to him again the second time, Simon, son of Jonas, lovest thou me ? He saith unto him, Yea, Lord ; thou knowest that I love thee. He saith unto him, Feed my sheep. He saith unto him the third time, Simon, son of Jonas, lovest thou me ? Peter was grieved because he saith unto him the third time, Lovest thou me ? And he saith unto him, Lord, thou knowest all things ; thou knowest that I love thee. Jesus saith unto him, Feed my sheep.*

Or else this. John xx. 19 to 23.—*The same day at evening, being the first day of the week, when the doors were shut, where the disciples were assembled for fear of the Jews, came Jesus and stood in the midst, and saith unto them, Peace be unto you. And when he had so said, he shewed unto them his hands and his side. Then were the disciples glad, when they saw the Lord. Then saith Jesus to them again, Peace be unto you : as my Father hath sent me, even so send I you. And when he had said this, he breathed on them, and saith unto them, Receive ye the Holy Ghost. Whosesoever sins ye remit, they are remitted unto them : and whosoever sins ye retain, they are retained.*

Or this. Mat. xxviii. 18, 19, 20.—*Jesus came and spake unto them, saying, All power is given unto me in heaven and in earth. Go ye therefore and teach all nations, baptizing them In the Name of the Father, and of the Son, and of the Holy Ghost ; teaching them to observe all things whatsoever I have commanded you : and lo, I am with you always even unto the end of the world.*

CCLXIX. *The Presentation of the Bishop-elect for consecration.*

Most Reverend Father in God, we present unto you this godly and well-learned man, to be Ordained and Consecrated Bishop.

CCLXX. The Oath of due obedience to the Archbishop.

In the name of God, Amen. I. N. chosen Bishop of the Church and See of *N.* do profess and promise all due reverence and obedience to the Archbishop, and to the metropolitical Church of *N.* and to their Successors : So help me God, through Jesus Christ.

Obey them that have the rule over you and submit yourselves. *He. xiii.* 17.

CCLXXI. An Invitation to the Congregation to unite in prayer for the Bishop-elect.

Brethren, it is written in the Gospel of Saint Luke, That our Saviour Christ continued the whole night in Prayer, before he did choose and send forth his twelve Apostles. It is written also in the Acts of the Apostles, That the Disciples who were at Antioch, did fast and pray, before they laid hands on Paul and Barnabas, and sent them forth. Let us therefore, following the example of our Saviour Christ and his Apostles, first fall to prayer before we admit, and send forth this person presented unto us, to the work whereunto we trust the Holy Ghost hath called him.

And it came to pass in those days, that he went out into a mountain to pray, and continued all night in prayer to God. And when it was day, he called unto him his disciples : and of them he chose twelve, whom he also named apostles. *Lu. vi.* 12, 13. Now there were in the church that was at Antioch certain prophets and teachers. As they ministered to the Lord, and fasted, the Holy Ghost said, Separate me Barnabas and Saul for the work whereunto I have called them. And when they had fasted and prayed, and laid their hands on them, they sent them away. So they, being sent forth by the Holy Ghost, departed. *Ac. xiii.* 1 *to* 4. Wherefore, holy brethren, partakers of the heavenly calling, consider the Apostle and High Priest of our profession, Christ Jesus. *He. iii.* 1. Be ye followers of me, even as I also am of Christ. *1 Co. xi.* 1.

CLXXII. A Petition that the Bishop-elect, may have grace duly to execute the Episcopal Office.

That it may please thee to bless this our Brother elected, and to send thy grace upon him, that he may duly execute the Office

Ye have not chosen me, but I have chosen you, and ordained you, that ye should go and bring forth fruit. *John xv.* 16. He gave some, apostles ; and some, prophets ; and some, evangelists ; and some, pastors and teachers ; for the perfecting of the saints, for the work of the ministry, for the edifying of the body of Christ. *Ep. iv.* 11, 12. The Church which is his

whereunto he is called to the edifying of thy Church, and to the honour, praise, and glory of thy Name.

body. *Ep. i.* 22, 23. As every man hath received the gift, even so minister the same one to another, as good stewards of the manifold grace of God. If any man speak, let him speak as the oracles of God; if any man minister, let him do it as of the ability which God giveth: that God in all things may be glorified through Jesus Christ, to whom be praise and dominion for ever and ever. Amen. 1 *Pe. iv.* 10, 11.

CCLXXIII. *nearly the same as CCLIII.*

Almighty God, giver of all good things, who, by thy Holy Spirit hast appointed divers Orders of Ministers in thy Church; Mercifully behold this thy servant now called to the Work and Ministry of a Bishop; and replenish him so with the truth of thy doctrine, and adorn him with innocency of life, that both by word and deed he may faithfully serve thee in this Office, to the glory of thy Name, and the edifying and well governing of thy Church, through the merits of our Saviour Jesus Christ, who liveth and reigneth with thee and the Holy Ghost, world without end. *Amen.*

CCLXXIV. *An Address, and solemn Questions to the Bishop-elect.*

The Archbishop.—1. Brother, forasmuch as the Holy Scripture and the ancient Canons command, that we should not be hasty in laying on Hands, and admitting any Person to Government in the Church of Christ, which he hath purchased with no less price than the effusion of his own blood; before I admit you to this Administration, I will examine you in certain Articles, to the end that the Congregation present may have a trial, and bear witness, how you be minded to behave yourself in the Church of God.

1. Lay hands suddenly on no man, neither be partaker of other men's sins: keep thyself pure. 1 *Ti. v.* 22. Take heed therefore unto yourselves, and to all the flock, over the which the Holy Ghost hath made you overseers, to feed the Church of God, which he hath purchased with his own blood. *Ac. xx.* 28. A Bishop must be blameless. Moreover he must have a good report among them which are without; lest he fall into reproach and the snare of the devil. 1 *Ti. iii.* 2. 7.

2. Are you persuaded that you be truly called to this Ministration, according to the will of our Lord Jesus Christ, and the Order of this Realm? *Ans.* I am so persuaded.

2. See Sections, 1, 2. *in CCLV.*

The Archbishop.—3. Are you persuaded, that the holy Scriptures contain sufficiently all doctrine required of necessity to eternal salvation, through faith in Jesus Christ? And are you determined out of the same holy Scriptures to instruct the people committed to your charge, and to teach or maintain nothing, as required of necessity to eternal salvation, but that which you shall be persuaded may be concluded and proved by the same? *Ans.* I am so persuaded, and determined by God's grace.

3. The Holy Scriptures which are able to make thee wise unto salvation through faith which is in Christ Jesus. 2 *Ti.*

M 2

iii. 15. A Bishop must be blameless, as the steward of God.
Holding fast the faithful word as he hath been taught, that he
may be able by sound doctrine both to exhort and to convince
the gainsayers. *Tit. i.* 7. 9. Speak thou the things which
become sound doctrine. *Tit. ii.* 1.

See also, Sections 3, 4. *in* CCLV.

The Archbishop.—4. Will you then faithfully exercise yourself in the same holy
Scriptures, and call upon God by prayer, for the true understanding of the same : so as
ye may be able by them to teach and exhort with wholesome Doctrine, and to withstand
and convince the gain-sayers?
Ans. I will so do, by the help of God.

4. Search the scriptures. *John v.* 39. Open thou mine
eyes, that I may see the wondrous things of thy law. *Ps. cxix.*
18. Son of Man, I have made thee a watchman unto the
house of Israel: therefore hear the word at my mouth, and
give them warning from me. *Eze. iii.* 17. Refuse profane and
old wives' fables, and exercise thyself rather unto godliness.
1 *Ti. iv.* 7. In doctrine shewing uncorruptness, gravity, sincerity, sound speech, that cannot be condemned; that he that
is of the contrary part may be ashamed. *Tit. ii.* 7, 8. Reprove, rebuke, exhort with all longsuffering and doctrine.
2 *Ti. iv.* 2.

The Archbishop.—5. Are you ready, with all faithful diligence to banish and drive
away all erroneous and strange doctrine, contrary to God's Word, and both privately and
openly to call upon and encourage others to the same?
Ans. I am ready, the Lord being my helper.

5. *See Section* 5. *in* CCLXII.

The Archbi-
shop.—6. Will
you deny all
ungodliness
and worldly
lusts, and live
soberly, righ-
teously, and
godly in this
present world;
that you may
shew your-
self in all
things an ex-
ample of good
works unto
others, that

6. The grace of God that bringeth salvation hath appeared
to all men, teaching us that, denying ungodliness and worldly
lusts, we should live soberly, righteously, and godly, in this
present world. *Tit. ii.* 11, 12. If a man desire the office of a
Bishop, he desireth a good work. A Bishop then must be blameless, the husband of one wife, vigilant, sober, of good behaviour,
given to hospitality, apt to teach; not given to wine, no striker,
not greedy of filthy lucre; but patient, not a brawler, not covetous; one that ruleth well his own house, having his children
in subjection with all gravity; (for if a man know not how to
rule his own house, how shall he take care of the Church of

the adversary may be ashamed, having nothing to say against you?

God?) not a novice, lest being lifted up with pride he fall into the condemnation of the devil. Moreover he must have a good report of them which are without, lest he fall into reproach and the snare of the devil. 1 *Ti. iii.* 1 *to* 7. Be thou an example

Ans. I will so do, the Lord being my helper.

of the believers, in word, in conversation, in charity, in spirit, in faith, in purity. 1 *Ti. iv.* 12. In all things shewing thyself a pattern of good works: in doctrine shewing uncorruptness, gravity, sincerity, sound speech, that cannot be condemned; that he that is of the contrary part may be ashamed, having no evil thing to say of you. *Tit. ii.* 7,8. Give none occasion to the adversary to speak reproachfully. 1 *Ti. v.* 14. Having a good conscience; that they may be ashamed that falsely accuse your good conversation in Christ. 1 *Pe. iii.* 16. *See also,* *Tit. i.* 6. 8.

The Archbishop.—7. Will you maintain and set forward, as much as shall lie in you, quietness, love, and peace, among all men; and such as be unquiet, disobedient, and criminous, within your Diocese, correct and punish, according to such authority as you have by God's Word, and as to you shall be committed by the Ordinance of this Realm?

7. Follow righteousness, faith, charity, peace, with them that call on the Lord out of a pure heart. But foolish and unlearned questions avoid, knowing that they do gender strifes. And the servant of the Lord must not strive; but be gentle unto all men, apt to teach, patient, in meekness instructing those that oppose themselves. Shun profane and vain babblings: for they will increase unto more ungodliness. 2 *Ti. ii.* 22 *to* 25. 16. Be instant in season, out of season; reprove, rebuke, exhort with all longsuffering and doctrine. 2 *Ti. iv.* 2. Them that sin rebuke before all, that others may fear. 1 *Ti. v.* 20. Knowing this, that the law is not made for a righteous man, but for the lawless and disobedient, for the ungodly and for sinners, for unholy and profane, for murderers of fathers and murderers of mothers, for man-

Ans. 1 will so do, by the help of the Lord.

slayers, for whoremongers, for them that defile themselves with mankind, for men-stealers, for liars, for perjured persons, and if there be any other thing that is contrary to sound doctrine; according to the glorious Gospel of the blessed God. 1 *Ti. i.* 9, 10, 11. Rebuke them sharply, that they may be sound in the faith. *Tit. i.* 13. I write these things being absent, lest being present I should use sharpness, according to the power which the Lord hath given me to edification, and not to destruction. 2 *Co. xiii.* 10. Against an elder receive not an accusation, but before two or three witnesses. 1 *Ti. v.* 19. The Spirit of the Lord spake by me, and his word was

in my tongue. The God of Israel said, the Rock of Israel
spake to me, he that ruleth over men must be just, ruling in
the fear of God. And he shall be as the light of the morning
when the sun riseth, even a morning without clouds; as the
tender grass springing out of the earth by clear shining after
rain. 2 *Sa. xxiii.* 2, 3, 4. *See also, Section 7. in* CCLXII.

The Archbi-
shop.—8. Will
you be faithful
in ordaining,
sending, or
laying hands
upon others ?
Ans. I will
so be, by the
help of God.

8. For this cause left I thee in Crete, that thou shouldest
set in order the things that are wanting, and ordain elders in
every city, as I had appointed thee. *Tit. i.* 5. The things
that thou hast heard of me among many witnesses, the same
commit thou to faithful men, who shall be able to teach others
also. 2 *Ti. ii.* 2. Lay hands suddenly on no man, neither be
partaker of other men's sins: keep thyself pure. 1 *Ti. v.* 22.
And when they [Paul and Barnabas] had ordained them
elders in every church, and had prayed with fasting, they
commended them to the Lord, on whom they believed. *Ac.*
xiv. 23.

The Archbi-
shop.—9. Will
you shew your-
self gentle, and
be merciful for
Christ's sake,
to poor and
needy people,
and to all
strangers des-
titute of help ?
Ans. I will
so shew myself,
by God's help.

9. The servant of the Lord must be gentle unto all men.
2 *Ti. ii.* 24. Yourselves, brethren, know our entrance in unto
you, that we were gentle among you, even as a nurse cherisheth her children. 1 *Th. ii.* 1, 7. Hold fast the form of
sound words, which thou hast heard of me, in faith and love
which is in Christ Jesus. 2 *Ti. i.* 13. Follow charity. 2 *Ti. ii.*
22. Be ye therefore merciful, as your Father also is merciful. *Lu. vi.* 36. Blessed are the merciful : for they shall obtain mercy. *Mat. v.* 7. Whosoever shall give to drink unto
one of these little ones a cup of cold water only in the name of
a disciple, verily I say unto you, he shall in no wise lose his
reward. *Mat. x.* 42. Whosoever shall give you a cup of
water to drink in my name, because ye belong to Christ,
verily I say unto you, he shall not lose his reward. *Mar. ix.*
41. Be not forgetful to entertain strangers. *He. xiii.* 2.
Whoso hath this world's good, and seeth his brother have
need, and shutteth up his bowels of compassion from him,
how dwelleth the love of God in him? 1 *John iii.* 17. He
shall deliver the needy when he crieth, the poor also, and him
that hath no helper. He shall spare the poor and needy, and
shall save the souls of the needy. *Ps. lxxii.* 12, 13. The
Lord your God is a God of gods, and Lord of lords, a great

God, and a mighty, which regardeth not persons, nor taketh reward: he doth execute the judgment of the fatherless and widow, and loveth the stranger, in giving him food and raiment. Love ye therefore the stranger. *De. x.* 17, 18, 19.

The Archbishop.—10. Almighty God, our heavenly Father, who hath given you a good will to do all these things; Grant also unto you strength and power to perform the same; that he accomplishing in you the good work which he hath begun, you may be found perfect and irreprehensible at the latter day, through Jesus Christ our Lord. *Amen.*

10. *See Section 9. in* CCLXII.

CCLXXV. *A Prayer that the Bishop-elect may have grace to make known the glad tidings of salvation; and duly to administer the discipline of the Church.*

The Archbishop.—Lord, hear our prayers.—*Ans.* And let our cry come unto thee.
Let us pray.—1, 2. Almighty God, and most merciful Father, who of thine infinite goodness, hast given thine only and dearly beloved Son Jesus Christ to be our Redeemer, and the Author of everlasting life; who, after that he had made perfect our Redemption by his death, and was ascended into heaven; poured down his gifts abundantly upon men, making some, Apostles, some, Prophets, some, Evangelists, some, Pastors and Doctors, to the edifying and making perfect his Church;

1, 2. *See Sections* 1, 2. *in* CCLXV.

3. Grant, we beseech thee, to this thy servant such grace, that he may be evermore ready to spread abroad thy Gospel, the glad tidings of reconciliation with thee; and use the authority given him, not to destruction, but to salvation; not to hurt, but to help;

3. Every good gift and every perfect gift cometh down from the Father of lights. *Ja. i.* 17. He giveth more grace. *Ja. iv.* 6. A bishop must be apt to teach. 1 *Ti. iii.* 2. As much as in me is, I am ready to preach the Gospel to you that are at Rome also. For I long to see you, that I may impart unto you some spiritual gift, to the end ye may be established; now I would not have you ignorant, brethren, that oftentimes I purposed to come unto you, (but was let hitherto,) that I might have some fruit among you also, even as among other Gentiles. *Ro. i.* 15. 11. 13. We are come as far as unto you also in preaching the Gospel of Christ. 2 *Cor. x.* 14. How beautiful are the feet of them that preach the Gospel of peace, and bring glad tidings of good things! *Ro. x.* 15. All things are of God, who hath reconciled us to himself by Jesus Christ, and given to us the ministry of reconciliation; to wit, that God was in Christ, reconciling the world unto himself, not imputing their trespasses unto them; and hath committed unto us the word of reconciliation. Now then we are ambassadors for Christ, as though God did beseech you by us: we

pray you in Christ's stead, be ye reconciled to God. 2 *Co. v.* 18, 19, 20. Our authority which the Lord hath given us for edification, and not for your destruction. 2 *Co. x.* 8. Not that we have dominion over your faith, but are helpers of your joy. 2 *Co. i.* 24. In meekness instructing those that oppose themselves; if God peradventure will give them repentance to the acknowledging of the truth; and that they may recover themselves out of the snare of the devil, who are taken captive by him at his will. 2 *Ti. ii.* 25, 26.

4. so that as a wise and faithful servant, giving to thy Family their portion in due season, he may at last be received into everlasting joy, through Jesus Christ our Lord; who, with thee and the Holy Ghost, liveth and reigneth one God, world without end. Amen.

4. Who then is a faithful and wise servant, whom his lord will make ruler over his houshold, to give them their portion of meat in due season? Blessed is that servant, whom his lord when he cometh shall find so doing. Of a truth I say unto you, that he will make him ruler over all that he hath. *Mat. xxiv.* 45. *Lu. xii.* 42, 43, 44. And his lord said unto him, Well done, thou good and faithful servant: thou hast been faithful over a few things, I will make thee ruler over many things: enter thou into the joy of thy lord. *Mat. xxv.* 21. I thank Christ Jesus our Lord, who hath enabled me, for that he counted me faithful, putting me into the ministry. 1 *Ti. i.* 12. Henceforth there is laid up for me a crown of righteousness, which the Lord, the righteous judge, shall give me at that day: and not to me only, but unto all them also that love his appearing. 2 *Ti. iv.* 8.

CCLXXVI. *The solemn Words to the Bishop-elect, with Imposition of hands.*

‡ Receive the Holy Ghost, for the Office and Work of a Bishop in the Church of God, now committed unto thee by the Imposition of our Hands; In the Name of the Father, and of the Son, and of the Holy Ghost. Amen. And remember that thou stir up the grace of God which is given thee by this Imposition of our Hands: for God hath not given us the Spirit of fear, but of power, and love, and soberness.

Then said Jesus to them again, Peace be unto you: as my Father hath sent me, even so send I you. And when he had said this, he breathed on them, and saith unto them, Receive ye the Holy Ghost. *John. xx.* 21, 22. Lo, I am with you alway, even unto the end of the world. *Mat. xxviii.* 20. When Paul laid his hands upon them, the Holy Ghost came on them. *Ac. xix.* 6. And from Miletus he sent to Ephesus, and called the elders of the Church. And when they were come to him, he said unto them, Take heed unto yourselves, and to all the flock, over the which the Holy Ghost hath made you overseers, to feed the Church of God. *Ac. xx.* 17, 18. 28. As every man hath received the gift, even so minister the same one to another, as good stewards of the manifold grace of God: 1 *Pe. iv.* 10. I put thee in remembrance that thou stir up the gift of God, which is in thee by the putting on of my hands. For God hath not given us the spirit of fear; but of power, and of love, and of a sound mind. 2 *Ti. i.* 6, 7.

CCLXXVII. Caution, and Exhortation to the Newly-consecrated Bishop.

1. Give heed unto Reading, Exhortation, and Doctrine. Think upon the things contained in this Book. Be diligent in them, that the increase coming thereby may be made manifest unto all men. Take heed unto thyself, and to Doctrine, and be diligent in doing them : for by so doing thou shalt both save thyself, and them that hear thee.

1. Give attendance to reading, to exhortation, to doctrine. Neglect not the gift that is in thee. Meditate on these things; give thyself wholly to them ; that thy profiting may appear to all. Take heed unto thyself, and unto the doctrine ; continue in them : for in doing this thou shalt save both thyself, and them that hear thee. 1 *Ti. iv.* 13 *to* 16.

2. Be to the flock of Christ a shepherd, not a wolf; feed them, devour them not. Hold up the weak, heal the sick, bind up the broken, bring again the outcasts, seek the lost. Be so merciful, that ye be not too remiss ; so minister discipline, that you forget not mercy : that when the chief Shepherd shall appear, ye may receive the never-fading crown of glory,

2. He that entereth in by the door is the shepherd of the sheep. The wolf catcheth and scattereth the sheep. *John x.* 2. 12. Feed the church of God. I know this, that after my departing shall grievous wolves enter in among you, not sparing the flock. *Ac. xx.* 28, 29. The elders which are among you I exhort, who am also an elder, Feed the flock of God which is among you, taking the oversight thereof, not by constraint, but willingly; not for filthy lucre, but of a ready mind ; neither as being lords over God's heritage, but being ensamples to the flock. 1 *Pe. v.* 1, 2, 3. Thus saith the Lord God unto the shepherds; Woe be to the shepherds of Israel that do feed themselves! Ye eat the fat, and ye clothe you with the wool, ye kill them that are fed ; but ye feed not the flock. The diseased have ye not strengthened, neither have ye healed that which was sick, neither have ye bound up that which was broken, neither have ye brought again that which was driven away, neither have ye sought that which

through Jesus
Christ our
Lord. Amen.

was lost; but with force and with cruelty have ruled them. Thus saith the Lord God, Behold, I, even I, will both search my sheep, and seek them out. I will seek that which was lost, and bring again that which was driven away, and will bind up that which was broken, and will strengthen that which was sick. *Eze. xxxiv.* 2, 3, 4. 11. 15.   The Spirit of the Lord is upon me, because he hath anointed me to preach the Gospel to the poor; he hath sent me to heal the broken hearted, to preach deliverance to the captives, and recovering of sight to the blind, to set at liberty them that are bruised. *Lu. iv.* 18. The Son of Man is come to seek and to save that which was lost. *Lu. xix.* 10.   Comfort the feebleminded, support the weak. 1 *Th. v.* 14.   Heal the sick. *Mat. x.* 8.   The Lord gathereth together the outcasts of Israel. *Ps. cxlvii.* 2.   Be ye therefore merciful, as your Father also is merciful. *Lu. vi.* 36. Now I Paul myself beseech you by the meekness and gentleness of Christ, that I may not be bold when I am present with that confidence, wherewith I think to be bold against some, which think of us as if we walked according to the flesh. Though I should boast somewhat more of our authority, which the Lord hath given us for edification, and not for your destruction, I should not be ashamed: that I may not seem to terrify you by letters. 2 *Co. x.* 1, 2. 8, 9.   I verily, as absent in body, but present in spirit, have judged already, as though I were present, concerning him that hath so done this deed,   In the name of our Lord Jesus Christ, when ye are gathered together, and my spirit, with the power of our Lord Jesus Christ, to deliver such an one unto satan for the destruction of the flesh, that the spirit may be saved in the day of the Lord Jesus. 1 *Co. v.* 3, 4, 5.   I wrote unto you, lest, when I came, I should have sorrow from them of whom I ought to rejoice; but if any have caused grief, he hath not grieved me, but in part.   Sufficient to such a man is this punishment.   To whom ye forgive any thing, I forgive also. 2 *Co. ii.* 3. 5, 6. 10.   When the Chief Shepherd shall appear, ye shall receive a crown of glory that fadeth not away. 1 *Pe. v.* 4.

CCLXXVIII. A Prayer for God's blessing upon the Newly-consecrated Bishop in the discharge of his high office.

Most merciful Father, we beseech thee to send down upon this thy servant thy heavenly blessing; and so endue him with thy Holy Spirit, that he, preaching thy Word, may not only be earnest to reprove, beseech, and rebuke, with all patience and doctrine; but also may be to such as believe a wholesome example, in word, in conversation, in love, in faith, in chastity, and in purity; that, faithfully fulfilling his course, at the latter day he may receive the crown of righteousness laid up by the Lord the righteous Judge, who liveth and reigneth one God with the Father, and the Holy Ghost, world without end. *Amen.*

God be merciful unto us, and bless us: and shew us the light of his countenance, and be merciful unto us. *Ps. lxvii.* 1. God, the Father of our Lord Jesus Christ, the Father of mercies. *2 Co. i.* 3. Grace, mercy, and peace, from God the Father and Christ Jesus our Lord. *2 Ti. i.* 2. Grace be with thee. Amen. *1 Ti. vi.* 21. Preach the word; be instant in season, out of season; reprove, rebuke, exhort with all longsuffering and doctrine. *2 Ti. iv.* 2. Be thou an example of the believers, in word, in conversation, in charity, in spirit, in faith, in purity. *1 Ti. iv.* 12. Flee also youthful lusts: but follow righteousness, faith, charity, peace, with them that call on the Lord out of a pure heart. *2 Ti. ii.* 22. Watch thou in all things, endure afflictions, do the work of an evangelist, make full proof of [*marginal reading,* fulfil] thy ministry. For I am now ready to be offered, and the time of my departure is at hand. I have fought a good fight, I have finished my course, I have kept the faith: henceforth there is laid up for me a crown of righteousness, which the Lord, the righteous Judge, shall give me at that day: and not to me only, but unto all them also that love his appearing. *2 Ti. iv.* 5 to 8. Be thou faithful unto death, and I will give thee a crown of life. *Rs. ii.* 10. I give thee charge in the sight of God, who quickeneth all things, and before Christ Jesus, who before Pontius Pilate witnessed a good confession; that thou keep this commandment without spot, unrebukable, until the appearing of our Lord Jesus Christ: which in his times he shall shew, who is the blessed and only Potentate, the King of kings, and Lord of lords: who only hath immortality, dwelling in the light which no man can approach unto; whom no man hath seen, nor can see: to whom be honour and power everlasting. Amen. *1 Ti. vi.* 13 *to* 16.

Prevent us, O Lord, &c. *as* *CLI.*

The peace of God, &c. *as* *CXVII.*

A FORM OF

PRAYER WITH THANKSGIVING,

To be yearly used upon the Fifth Day of November.

The Sentences.—*The Lord is full of compassion, and mercy: long-suffering, and of great goodness. He will not always be chiding : neither keepeth he his anger for ever. He hath not dealt with us after our sins : nor rewarded us according to our wickedness. Psalm ciii. 8, 9, 10.*

The Hymn.—*O give thanks unto the Lord, for he is gracious : and his mercy endureth for ever. Let them give thanks, whom the Lord hath redeemed : and delivered from the hand of the enemy. Psalm cvii. 1, 2.—Many a time have they fought against me from my youth up : may Israel now say. Yea, many a time have they vexed me from my youth up : but they have not prevailed against me. Psalm cxxix. 1, 2.—They have privily laid their net to destroy me without a cause : yea, even without a cause have they made a pit for my soul. Psalm xxxv. 7.—They have laid a net for my feet, and pressed down my soul : they have digged a pit before me, and are fallen into the midst of it themselves. Psalm lvii. 7.— Great is our Lord, and great is his power : yea, and his wisdom is infinite. The Lord setteth up the meek : and bringeth the ungodly down to the ground. Psalm cxlvii. 5, 6.—Let thy hand be upon the man of thy right hand : and upon the son of man whom thou madest so strong for thy own self. And so will not we go back from thee : O let us live, and we shall call upon thy name. Psalm lxxx. 17, 18.*

Glory be to the Father, &c.
As it was in the, &c.

*Proper Psalms, LIV. CXXIV, CXXV.
The Proper Lessons, 2 Sam. XXII.—Acts XXIII.*

CCLXXIX. *The Suffrages or Responses.*

1, 2.
O Lord, save the king; who putteth his trust in thee.

1, 2. Save now, I beseech thee, O Lord : O Lord, I beseech thee, send now prosperity. *Ps. cxviii.* 25. And Samuel said to all the people, See ye him whom the Lord hath chosen, that there is none like him among all the people? 1 *Sa. x.* 24. O thou my God, save thy servant that trusteth in thee. *Ps. lxxxvi.* 2·

3, 4. Send him help from thy holy place; and evermore mightily defend him.

3, 4. The Lord hear thee in the day of trouble ; the name of the God of Jacob defend thee. Send thee help from the sanctuary, and strengthen thee out of Zion. *Ps. xx.* 1, 2. The Almighty shall be thy defence. *Job xxii.* 25.

5, 6. Let his enemies have no advantage against him ; let not the wicked approach to hurt him.

5, 6. Deliver me, O Lord, from the evil man: preserve me from the violent man. *Ps. cxl.* 1. The enemy shall not be able to do him violence: the son of wickedness shall not hurt him. I will smite down his foes before his face: and plague them that hate him. *Ps. lxxxix.* 23, 24. When the wicked, even mine enemies and my foes, came upon me to eat up my flesh, they stumbled and fell. *Ps. xxvii.* 2.

CCLXXX. *A Thanksgiving.*

I. Almighty God, who hast in all ages shewed thy Power and Mercy in the miraculous and gracious deliverances of thy Church, and in the protection of righteous and religious Kings and States professing thy holy and eternal truth, from the wicked conspiracies, and malicious practices of all the enemies thereof:

1. We have heard with our ears, O God, our fathers have told us, what work thou didst in their days, in the times of old. Thou art my King, O God: command deliverances for Jacob. Thou hast saved us from our enemies, and hast put them to shame that hated us. *Ps. xliv.* 1. 4. 7. Thou art the Lord the God, who shewedst signs and wonders upon Pharaoh, and on all his servants, and on all the people of his land: for thou knewest that they dealt proudly against them. So didst thou get thee a name, as it is this day. And thou didst divide the sea before them, so that they went through the midst of the sea on the dry land; and their persecutors thou threwest into the deeps, as a stone into the mighty waters. *Ne. ix.* 7. 10, 11. There arose up a new king over Egypt, and he said unto his people, Behold, the people of the children of Israel are more and mightier than we: Come on, let us deal wisely with them; lest they multiply. Therefore they did set over them taskmasters to afflict them. And the Lord hardened the heart of Pharaoh king of Egypt, and he pursued after the children of Israel. And Moses said unto the people, Fear ye not, stand still, and see the salvation of the Lord. The Lord shall fight for you, and ye shall hold your peace. And the Lord looked unto the host of the Egyptians, and troubled the host of the Egyptians; and took off their chariot wheels. And the waters returned, and covered the chariots, and the horsemen, and all the host of Pharaoh. *Ex. i.* 8 *to* 11.—*xiv.* 8. 13, 14. 24, 25. 28. When the Lord raised them up judges, then the Lord delivered them out of the hand of their enemies all the days of the judge. *Jud. ii.* 18. It is God that avengeth me, and subdueth the people unto me. He delivereth me from mine enemies: yea, thou liftest me up above those that rise up against me: thou hast delivered me from the violent man. Therefore will I give thanks unto thee, O Lord, among the heathen, and sing praises unto thy name. Great deliverance giveth he to his king; and sheweth mercy to his anointed, to David, and to his seed for evermore. *Ps. xviii.* 47 *to* 50. David said, O Lord, I pray thee, turn the counsel of Ahithophel into foolishness. 2 *Sa. xv.* 31. And Absalom and all the men of Israel said, The counsel of Hushai the Archite is better

than the counsel of Ahithophel. For the Lord had appointed
to defeat the good counsel of Ahithophel, to the intent that the
Lord might bring evil upon Absalom. 2 *Sa. xvii.* 14. He
taketh the wise in their own craftiness : and the counsel of the
froward is carried headlong. *Job v.* 13. O Lord our God, save
thou us out of his [Sennacherib's] hand, that all the kingdoms
of the earth may know that thou art the Lord God, even thou
only. Thus saith the Lord concerning the king of Assyria,
He shall not come into this city, nor shoot an arrow there, nor
come before it with shield, nor cast a bank against it. By the
way that he came, by the same shall he return, and shall not
come into this city, saith the Lord. For I will defend this
city, to save it, for mine own sake, and for my servant David's
sake. And it came to pass that night, that the angel of the
Lord went out, and smote in the camp of the Assyrians an
hundred fourscore and five thousand. 2 *Ki. xix.* 19, 32 *to* 35.
See also, *The Book of* ESTHER.—2 *Sa.* XV. XVI. XVII. XVIII.

2. We yield
thee our un-
feigned thanks
and praise, for
the wonderful
and mighty
Deliverance
of our gracious
Sovereign
King *James*
the First, the
Queen, the
Prince, and all
the Royal
Branches, with
the Nobility,
Clergy, and
Commons of
England, then
assembled in
Parliament,
by Popish
treachery
appointed as
sheep to the
slaughter, in
a most barba-
rous and savage
manner, be-
yond the ex-
amples of for-
mer ages.

2. Now therefore, our God, we thank thee, and praise thy
glorious name. 1 *Ch. xxix.* 13. Praise ye the Lord. I will
praise the Lord with my whole heart, in the assembly of the
upright, and in the congregation. *Ps. cxi.* 1. Thou art the
God that doest wonders : thou hast declared thy strength
among the people. Thou hast with thine arm redeemed thy
people, the sons of Jacob and Joseph. *Ps. lxxvii.* 14, 15. Thou
art my hiding place ; thou shalt preserve me from trouble ;
thou shalt compass me about with songs of deliverance. *Ps.
xxxii.* 7. Great deliverance giveth he to his king ; and sheweth mercy to his anointed, to David, and to his seed for evermore. *Ps. xviii.* 50. When it was day, certain of the Jews
banded together, and bound themselves under a curse, saying
that they would neither eat nor drink till they had killed Paul.
And they were more than forty which had made this conspiracy. And they came to the chief priests and elders, and
said, We have bound ourselves under a great curse, that we
will eat nothing until we have slain Paul. Now therefore ye
with the council signify to the chief captain that he bring him
down unto you to-morrow, as though ye would enquire something more perfectly concerning him : and we, or ever he
come near, are ready to kill him. *Ac. xxiii.* 12 *to* 15. We

are counted as sheep for the slaughter. *Ps. xliv.* 22. *See also,* *Je. xli.* 1 *to* 7.—*Jud. ix.* 2 *to* 5.

3. From this unnatural Conspiracy, not our merit, but thy mercy; not our foresight, but thy providence delivered us: and therefore not unto us, O Lord, not unto us, but unto thy Name be ascribed all honour and glory, in all Churches of the saints, from generation to generation; through Jesus Christ our Lord. Amen.

3. The conspiracy was strong. 2 *Sa. xv.* 12. If it had not been the Lord who was on our side, when men rose up against us: then they had swallowed us up quick. *Ps. cxxiv.* 2, 3. Thou hast with thine arm redeemed thy people. *Ps. lxxvii.* 15. For mine own sake, even for mine own sake, will I do it : for how should my name be polluted? and I will not give my glory unto another. *Is. xlviii.* 11. Not for your sakes do I this, saith the Lord God, be it known unto you, O house of Israel. *Eze. xxxvi.* 32. I wrought for my name's sake, that it should not be polluted before the heathen. *Eze. xx.* 14. Not unto us, O Lord, not unto us, but unto thy name give glory, for thy mercy, and for thy truth's sake. *Ps. cxv.* 1. Thou art worthy, O Lord, to receive glory and honour and power. *Re. iv.* 11. In all churches of the saints. 1 *Co. xiv.* 33. One generation shall praise thy works to another, and shall declare thy mighty acts. *Ps. cxlv.* 4. So we that are thy people, and sheep of thy pasture, shall give thee thanks for ever : and will alway be shewing forth thy praise from generation to generation. *Ps. lxxix.* 14.

CCLXXXI. A Prayer that a sense of God's goodness may lead us to use diligence and zeal in our duties.

1. Accept also, most gracious God, of our unfeigned thanks for filling our hearts again with joy and gladness, after the time that thou hadst afflicted us, and putting a new song into our mouths, by bringing his Majesty, King William, upon this day, for the Deliverance of our Church and Nation from Popish Ty-

1. Unto thee, O God, do we give thanks, unto thee do we give thanks : for that thy name is near thy wondrous works declare. *Ps. lxxv.* 1. We will be glad and rejoice in his salvation. *Is. xxv.* 9. The Jews had joy and gladness, a feast and a good day. *Est. viii.* 17. Make us glad according to the days wherein thou hast afflicted us, and the years wherein we have seen evil. *Ps. xc.* 15. He hath put a new song in my mouth, even praise unto our God. *Ps. xl.* 3. All these men of war came with a perfect heart to Hebron, to make David king over all Israel. And there they were with David three days, eating and drinking : for their brethren had prepared for them. Moreover they that were nigh them, even unto Issachar and Zebulun and Naphtali, brought bread on asses, and on camels, and on mules, and on oxen, and meat, meal, cakes of figs, and bunches of raisins, and wine, and oil,

ranny and arbitrary power.

and oxen, and sheep abundantly. 1 *Ch. xii.* 38, 39, 40. Praise the Lord, O Jerusalem; praise thy God, O Zion. For he hath strengthened the bars of thy gates; he hath blessed thy children within thee. *Ps. cxlvii.* 12, 13. I delivered you out of the hand of the Egyptians, and out of the hand of all that oppressed you. *Jud. vi.* 9. Great deliverance giveth he to his king; and sheweth mercy to his anointed, to David, and to his seed for evermore. *Ps. xviii.* 50.

2. We adore the wisdom and justice of thy Providence, which so timely interposed in our extreme danger, and disappointed all the designs of our enemies.

2. Great and marvellous are thy works, Lord God Almighty: just and true are thy ways, thou King of saints. *Re. xv.* 3. There is no wisdom, nor understanding, nor counsel against the Lord. *Pr. xxi.* 30. Justice and judgment are the habitation of thy throne: mercy and truth shall go before thy face. *Ps. lxxxix.* 14. Our soul is escaped as a bird out of the snare of the fowlers: the snare is broken, and we are escaped. *Ps. cxxiv.* 7. He disappointeth the devices of the crafty, so that their hands cannot perform their enterprise. He taketh the wise in their own craftiness: and the counsel of the froward is carried headlong. *Job v.* 12, 13. Truly there is but a step between me and death. And David made haste to get away for fear of Saul; for Saul and his men compassed David and his men round about to take them. But there came a messenger unto Saul, saying, Haste thee, and come; for the Philistines have invaded the land. Wherefore Saul returned from pursuing after David. 1 *Sa. xx.* 3.—*xxiii.* 26, 27, 28. The enemy said, I will pursue, I will overtake, I will divide the spoil; my lust shall be satisfied upon them; I will draw my sword, my hand shall destroy them. Thou didst blow with thy wind, the sea covered them: they sank as lead in the mighty waters. *Ex. xv.* 9, 10.

3. We beseech thee, give us such a lively and lasting sense of what thou didst then, and hast since that time done for us, that we may not grow secure and careless in our obedience, by pre-

3. Bless the Lord, O my soul: and all that is within me, bless his holy name. Bless the Lord, O my soul, and forget not all his benefits. *Ps. ciii.* 1, 2. I will open my mouth in a parable: I will utter dark sayings of old. We will not hide them from their children, shewing to the generation to come the praises of the Lord, and his strength, and his wonderful works that he hath done. That they might set their hope in God, and not forget the works of God, but keep his commandments. *Ps. lxxviii.* 2. 4. 7. When thou hast eaten and art

...ing upon thy great and undeserved goodness ;

full, then thou shalt bless the Lord thy God for the good land which he hath given thee. Beware that thou forget not the Lord thy God, in not keeping his commandments, and his judgments, and his statutes which I command thee this day. Lest when thou hast eaten and art full, and hast built goodly houses, and dwelt therein; and when thy herds and thy flocks multiply, and thy silver and thy gold is multiplied, and all that thou hast is multiplied; then thine heart be lifted up, and thou forget the Lord thy God. *De. viii.* 10 to 14. And they returned to Joshua, and said unto him, Let not all the people go up; but let about two or three thousand men go up and smite Ai; and make not all the people to labour thither; for they are but few. So there went up thither of the people about three thousand men: and they fled before the men of Ai. And the men of Ai smote of them about thirty and six men: for they chased them from before the gate even unto Shebarim, and smote them in the going down: wherefore the hearts of the people melted. *Jos. vii.* 3, 4, 5. Let thy hand be upon the man of thy right hand, upon the son of man whom thou madest strong for thyself. So will not we go back from thee: quicken us, and we will call upon thy name. *Ps. lxxx.* 17, 18.

4. but that it may lead us to repentance, and move us to be the more diligent and zealous in all the duties of our Religion, which thou hast in a marvellous manner preserved to us.

4. Despisest thou the riches of his goodness and forbearance and longsuffering; not knowing that the goodness of God leadeth thee to repentance? *Ro. ii.* 4. I thought on my ways, and turned my feet unto thy testimonies. I made haste, and delayed not to keep thy commandments. Make me to go in the path of thy commandments; for therein do I delight. *Ps. cxix.* 59, 60. 35. Only fear the Lord, and serve him in truth with all your heart: for consider how great things he hath done for you. 1 *Sa. xii.* 24. Now the end of the commandment is charity out of a pure heart, and of a good conscience, and of faith unfeigned. 1 *Ti. i.* 5. Thine enemies said, Let us take to ourselves the houses of God in possession. *Ps. lxxxiii.* 2. 12. If it had not been the Lord who was on our side, when men rose up against us: then they had swallowed us up quick, when their wrath was kindled against us: then the waters had overwhelmed us, the stream had gone over our soul. Our soul is escaped as a bird out of the

snare of the fowlers. Our help is in the name of the Lord, who made heaven and earth. *Ps. cxxiv.* 2, 3, 4. 7, 8. *See also,* 2 *Co. vii.* 11.

5. Let truth and justice, brotherly kindness and charity, devotion and piety, concord and unity, with all other virtues, so flourish among us, that they may be the stability of our times, and make this Church a praise in the earth. All which we humbly beg for the sake of our blessed Lord and Saviour. *Amen.*

5. Buy the truth, and sell it not. *Pr. xxiii.* 23. Let not mercy and truth forsake thee : bind them about thy neck ; write them upon the table of thine heart. *Pr. iii.* 3. He hath shewed thee, O man, what is good ; and what doth the Lord require of thee, but to do justly, and to love mercy, and to walk humbly with thy God ? *Mi. vi.* 8. Beside this, giving all diligence, add to your faith virtue ; and to virtue knowledge ; and to knowledge temperance ; and to temperance patience ; and to patience godliness ; and to godliness brotherly kindness ; and to brotherly kindness charity. 2 *Pe. i.* 5 *to* 7. Thou shalt love the Lord thy God with all thine heart, and with all thy soul, and with all thy might. *De. vi.* 5. Be of the same mind one toward another. *Ro. xii.* 16. Endeavouring to keep the unity of the Spirit in the bond of peace. *Ep. iv.* 3. Finally, brethren, whatsoever things are true, whatsoever things are honest, whatsoever things are just, whatsoever things are pure, whatsoever things are lovely, whatsoever things are of good report ; if there be any virtue, and if there be any praise, think on these things. *Ph. iv.* 8. The Lord commanded us to do all these statutes, to fear the Lord our God, for our good always, that he might preserve us alive, as it is at this day. *De. vi.* 24. The righteous shall flourish like the palm tree. Those that be planted in the house of the Lord shall flourish in the courts of our God. They shall still bring forth fruit in old age ; they shall be fat and flourishing ; to shew that the Lord is upright : he is my rock, and there is no unrighteousness in him. *Ps. xcii.* 12 *to* 15. At that time will I bring you again, even in the time that I gather you : for I will make you a name and a praise among all people of the earth. *Zep. iii.* 20. Wisdom and knowledge shall be the stability of thy times, and strength of salvation : the fear of the Lord is his treasure. *Is. xxxiii.* 6. Give him no rest, till he establish, and till he make Jerusalem a praise in the earth. *Is. lxii.* 7. Whatsoever ye do in word or deed, do all in the name of the Lord Jesus. *Col. iii.* 17. He is before all things, and by him all things consist. And he

is the Head of the body, the Church. *Col. i.* 17, 18. In whom all the building fitly framed together groweth unto an holy temple in the Lord : in whom ye also are builded together for an habitation of God through the Spirit. *Ep. ii.* 21, 22.

CCLXXXII. *A prayer for grace that we may adorn our Christian Profession.*

1. Almighty God and heavenly Father, who of thy gracious Providence, and tender mercy towards us, didst prevent the malice and imaginations of our enemies, by discovering and confounding their horrible and wicked Enterprize, plotted and intended this day to have been executed against the King, and the whole State of *England,* for the subversion of the Government and Religion established among us ; and didst likewise upon this day wonderfully conduct thy Servant King *William,* and bring him safely into *England,* to preserve us from the attempts of our enemies to bereave us of our Religion and Laws :

1. The Lord hath prepared his throne in the heavens ; and his kingdom ruleth over all. *Ps. ciii.* 19. The Lord is in his holy temple, the Lord's throne is in heaven : his eyes behold, his eyelids try, the children of men. *Ps. xi.* 4. Are not two sparrows sold for a farthing ? and one of them shall not fall on the ground without your Father. But the very hairs of your head are all numbered. Fear ye not therefore, ye are of more value than many sparrows. *Mat. x.* 29, 30, 31. The Lord is very pitiful, and of tender mercy. *Ja. v.* 11. As for you, ye thought evil against me ; but God meant it unto good, to bring to pass, as it is this day, to save much people alive. *Ge. l.* 20. The heathen are sunk down in the pit that they made : in the net which they hid is their own foot taken. The Lord is known by the judgment which he executeth : the wicked is snared in the work of his own hands. *Ps. ix.* 15, 16. He made a pit, and digged it, and is fallen into the ditch which he made. His mischief shall return upon his own head, and his violent dealing shall come down upon his own pate. *Ps. vii.* 15, 16. Shall the throne of iniquity have fellowship with thee, which frameth mischief by a law ? They gather themselves together against the soul of the righteous, and condemn the innocent blood. But the Lord is my defence, and my God is the rock of my refuge. And he shall bring upon them their own iniquity, and shall cut them off in their own wickedness ; yea, the Lord our God shall cut them off. *Ps. xciv.* 20 *to* 23. Then we departed from the river of Ahava on the twelfth day of the first month, to go unto Jerusalem : and the hand of our God was upon us, and he delivered us from the hand of the enemy, and of such as lay in wait by the way. *Ezr. viii.* 31. See also, *Ne.* vi.—*Ex.* iii, iv, v, vi, vii, viii, ix.—*Ps.* lix. 1 *to* 16.—cxviii.

2. We most humbly praise and magnify

2. Now therefore, our God, we thank thee, and praise thy glorious name. 1 *Ch. xxix.* 13. Stand up and bless the Lord

thy most glo-
rious Name, for
thy unspeak.
able goodness
towards us,
expressed in
both these acts
of thy mercy.

your God for ever and ever: and blessed be thy glorious name, which is exalted above all blessing and praise. *Ne. ix.* 5. Our help is in the name of the Lord, who made heaven and earth. *Ps, cxxiv.* 8. Many, O Lord my God, are thy wonderful works which thou hast done, and thy thoughts which are to us-ward: they cannot be reckoned up in order unto thee: if I would declare and speak of them, they should be more than I am able to express. *Ps. xl.* 5. 7. And Mordecai sent letters unto all the Jews, to stablish this among them, that they should keep the fourteenth day of the month Adar, and the fifteenth day of the same, yearly, as the days wherein the Jews rested from their enemies, and the month which was turned unto them from sorrow to joy, and from mourning into a good day: that they should make them days of feasting and joy, and of sending portions one to another, and gifts to the poor. And the Jews undertook to do as Mordecai had written unto them; because Haman, the enemy of all the Jews, had devised against the Jews to destroy them: but when Esther came before the king, he commanded that his wicked device, which he devised against the Jews, should return upon his own head. *Est. ix.* 20 to 25.

3. We confess it has been of thy mercy alone, that we are not consumed: for our sins have cried to heaven against us; and our iniquities justly called for vengeance upon us.

3. It is of the Lord's mercies that we are not consumed, because his compassions fail not. *La. iii.* 22. I am the Lord, I change not; therefore ye sons of Jacob are not consumed. *Mal. iii.* 6. O my God, I am ashamed and blush to lift up my face to thee, my God: for our iniquities are increased over our head, and our trespass is grown up unto the heavens. *Ezr. ix.* 6. See also, *Ps. lxxviii.* 38, 39.—*Ne. ix.* 31.

4. But thou hast not dealt with us after our sins, nor rewarded us after our iniquities; nor given us over, as we deserved, to be a prey to our enemies; but hast in mercy delivered us from their malice, and preserved us from death and destruction. Let the consideration of this thy repeated goodness, O Lord, work in us true repentance, that iniquity may not be our ruin.

4. He hath not dealt with us after our sins; nor rewarded us according to our iniquities. *Ps. ciii.* 10. Thou our God hast punished us less than our iniquities deserve, and hast given us such deliverance as this. *Ezr. ix.* 13. Know therefore that

God exacteth of thee less than thine iniquity deserveth. *Job xxi. 6.* Blessed be the Lord, who hath not given us as a prey to their teeth. *Ps. cxxiv. 6.* Thou hast considered my trouble; thou hast known my soul in adversities; and hast not shut me up into the hand of the enemy: thou hast set my foot in a large room. *Ps. xxxi. 7, 8.* I called upon the Lord in distress: the Lord answered me, and set me in a large place. *Ps. cxviii. 5.* Thou hast delivered my soul from death, mine eyes from tears, and my feet from falling. I will walk before the Lord in the land of the living. *Ps. cxvi. 8, 9.* Despisest thou the riches of his goodness, and forbearance, and longsuffering; not knowing that the goodness of God leadeth thee to repentance? *Ro. ii. 4.* Repent and turn yourselves from all your transgressions; so iniquity shall not be your ruin. *Eze. xviii. 30.*

5. And the apostles said unto the Lord, Increase our faith. *Lu. xvii. 5.* We are bound to thank God always for you, brethren, as it is meet, because that your faith groweth exceedingly, and the charity of every one of you all toward each other aboundeth. *2 Th. i. 3.* The Lord make you to increase and abound in love one toward another, and toward all men. *1 Th. iii. 12.* Keep yourselves in the love of God. *Jude 21.* This is the love of God, that we keep his commandments. *1 John v. 3.* Being fruitful in every good work. *Col. i. 10.* We give thanks to God and the Father of our Lord Jesus Christ, praying always for you, since we heard of your faith in Christ Jesus, and of the love which ye have to all the saints, for the hope which is laid up for you in heaven, whereof ye heard before in the word of the truth of the Gospel; which is come unto you, as it is in all the world; and bringeth forth fruit, as it doth also in you, since the day ye heard of it, and knew the grace of God in truth. *Col. i. 3 to 6.* Behold, I set before you a blessing;—a blessing, if ye obey the commandments of the Lord your God. *De. xi. 26, 27.* Thou shalt keep therefore his statutes, and his commandments, which I command thee this day, that it may go well with thee, and with thy children after thee, and that thou mayest prolong thy days upon the earth, which the Lord thy God giveth thee, for ever. *De. iv. 40.* O continue thy lovingkindness unto them that know thee; and thy righteous-

Marginal note: 5. And increase in us more and more a lively faith and love, fruitful in all holy obedience; that thou mayest still continue thy favour, with the light of thy Gospel, to us and our posterity for evermore; and that for thy dear Son's sake, Jesus Christ our only Mediator and Advocate. Amen.

ness to the upright in heart. *Ps. xxxvii. 10.* The promise is
unto you, and to your children, and to all that are afar off,
even as many as the Lord our God shall call. *Ac. ii. 39.* No
man cometh unto the Father, but by me. If ye shall ask
any thing in my name, I will do it. *John xiv. 6, 14.* There is
one Mediator between God and men, the man Christ Jesus.
1 Ti. ii. 5. If any man sin, we have an Advocate with the
Father, Jesus Christ the righteous. *1 John ii. 1.*

CCLXXXIII. *A Prayer for God's continued Protection.*

1. O Lord, who didst this day discover the snares of death that were laid for us, and didst wonderfully deliver us from the same; Be thou still our mighty Protector, and scatter our enemies that delight in blood: Infatuate and defeat their counsels, abate their pride, assuage their malice, and confound their devices.

1. And the man of God sent unto the king of Israel, saying,
Beware that thou pass not such a place; for thither the Syrians are come down. And the king of Israel sent to the
place which the man of God told and warned him of, and
saved himself there, not once nor twice. *2 Ki. vi. 9, 10.* Thou
hast delivered my soul from death. *Ps. cxvi. 8.* Hear my
voice, O God, in my prayer: preserve my life from fear of
the enemy. Hide me from the secret counsel of the wicked;
from the insurrection of the workers of iniquity: who whet
their tongue like a sword, and bend their bows, that they may
shoot in secret at the perfect: suddenly do they shoot at him,
and fear not. They encourage themselves in an evil matter:
they commune of laying snares privily; they say, Who shall
see them? The inward thought of every one of them, and
the heart, is deep. But God shall shoot at them with an
arrow; suddenly shall they be wounded. And all men shall
fear, and shall declare the work of God; for they shall wisely
consider of his doing. *Ps. lxiv. 1 to 7. 9.* Preserve me, O
God: for in thee do I put my trust. *Ps. xvi. 1.* Rebuke the
company of spearmen, the multitude of the bulls, with the
calves of the people, till every one submit himself with pieces
of silver: scatter thou the people that delight in war. *Ps.
lxviii. 30.* And David said, O Lord, I pray thee, turn the
counsel of Ahithophel into foolishness. *2 Sa. xv. 31.* And the
afflicted people thou wilt save: but thine eyes are upon the
haughty, that thou mayest bring them down. *2 Sa. xxii. 28.*
He shall bring down their pride together with the spoils of
their hands. *Is. xxv. 11.* Break thou the power of the un-

godly and malicious. *Ps. x.* 17. Let them all be confounded
and turned back that hate Zion; *Ps. cxxix.* 5. The Lord
bringeth the counsel of the heathen to nought: he maketh
the devices of the people of none effect. *Ps. xxxiii.* 10. He
disappointeth the devices of the crafty, so that their hands
cannot perform their enterprize. *Job v.* 12.

2. Strengthen the hands of our gracious Sovereign, King *William,* and all that are put in authority under him, with judgment and justice to cut off all such workers of iniquity, as turn Religion into Rebellion, and Faith into Faction;

2. The Lord hear thee in the day of trouble; the name of
the God of Jacob defend thee. Send thee help from the
sanctuary, and strengthen thee out of Zion. *Ps. xx.* 1, 2.
Give the king thy judgments, O God, and thy righteousness
unto the king's son. He shall judge the poor of the people,
he shall save the children of the needy, and shall break in
pieces the oppressor. *Ps. lxxii.* 1. 4. Charge Joshua, and encourage him, and strengthen him. *De. iii.* 28. Thus saith
the Lord, Keep ye judgment, and do justice. *Is. lvi.* 1.
Blessed be the Lord thy God, which delighted in thee to set
thee on his throne, to be king for the Lord thy God: because
thy God loved Israel, to establish them for ever, therefore
made he thee king over them, to do judgment and justice.
2 Ch. ix. 8. He is the minister of God to thee for good. But
if thou do that which is evil, be afraid; for he beareth not
the sword in vain: for he is the minister of God, a revenger
to execute wrath upon him that doeth evil. *Ro. xiii.* 4. Evil
doers shall be cut off. *Ps. xxxvii.* 9. He shall bring upon them
their own iniquity, and shall cut them off in their own wickedness; yea, the Lord our God shall cut them off. *Ps. xciv.* 23.
For, lo, thine enemies, O Lord, for, lo, thine enemies shall
perish; all the workers of iniquity shall be scattered. *Ps.
xcii.* 9. I will early destroy all the wicked of the land; that
I may cut off all wicked doers from the city of the Lord. *Ps.
ci.* 8. I wrote unto the church: but Diotrephes, who loveth
to have the pre-eminence among them, receiveth us not.
Wherefore, if I come, I will remember his deeds which he
doeth, prating against us with malicious words: and not content therewith, neither doth he himself receive the brethren,
and forbiddeth them that would, and casteth them out of the
church. *3 John* 9, 10. There be some that trouble you, and
would pervert the Gospel of Christ. But though we, or an
angel from heaven, preach any other Gospel unto you than

that which we have preached unto you, let him be accursed. *Gal. i.* 7, 8. And it came to pass after forty years, that Absalom said unto the king, I pray thee, let me go and pay my vow, which I have vowed unto the Lord, in Hebron. For thy servant vowed a vow while I abode at Geshur in Syria, saying, If the Lord shall bring me again indeed to Jerusalem, then I will serve the Lord. But Absalom sent spies throughout all the tribes of Israel, saying, As soon as ye hear the sound of the trumpet then ye shall say, Absalom reigneth in Hebron. 2 *Sa. xv.* 7, 8. 10. Now Korah, the son of Izhar, the son of Kohath, the son of Levi, and Dathan and Abiram, the sons of Eliab, and On, the son of Peleth, sons of Reuben, took men: and they rose up before Moses, with certain of the children of Israel, two hundred and fifty princes of the assembly, famous in the congregation, men of renown; and they gathered themselves together against Moses and against Aaron, and said unto them, Ye take too much upon you, seeing all the congregation are holy, every one of them, and the Lord is among them: wherefore then lift ye up yourselves above the congregation of the Lord? And when Moses heard it, he fell upon his face: and he spake unto Korah and unto all his company, saying, Even to-morrow the Lord will shew who are his, and who is holy; and will cause him to come near unto him: even him whom he hath chosen will he cause to come near unto him. This do; Take you censers, Korah, and all his company; and put fire therein, and put incense in them before the Lord to-morrow: and it shall be that the man whom the Lord doth choose, he shall be holy: ye take too much upon you, ye sons of Levi. And Moses said unto Korah, Hear, I pray you, ye sons of Levi: seemeth it but a small thing unto you, that the God of Israel hath separated you from the congregation of Israel, to bring you near to himself to do the service of the tabernacle of the Lord, and to stand before the congregation to minister unto them? And he hath brought thee near to him, and all thy brethren the sons of Levi with thee: and seek ye the priesthood also? For which cause both thou and all thy company are gathered together against the Lord: and what is Aaron, that ye murmur against him? And Moses sent to call Dathan and Abiram, the sons of Eliab: which said, We will not come up: Is it a small thing that thou hast brought us up out of a land that floweth with milk and honey, to kill us in the wilderness, except thou make thyself altogether a prince over us? Moreover thou hast not brought us into a land that floweth with milk and honey, or given us inheritance of fields and vineyards: wilt thou put out the eyes of these men? we will not come up. And Moses was very wroth, and said unto the Lord, Respect not thou their offering: I have not taken one ass from them, neither have I hurt one of them. And Moses said unto Korah, Be thou and all thy company before the Lord, thou, and they, and Aaron, to-morrow: and take every man his censer, and put incense in them, and bring ye before the Lord every man his censer, two hundred and fifty censers; thou also, and Aaron, each of you his censer. And they took every man his censer, and put fire in them, and laid incense thereon, and stood in the door of the tabernacle of the congregation with Moses and Aaron. And Korah gathered all the congregation against them unto the door of the tabernacle of the congregation: and the glory of the Lord appeared unto all the congregation. And the Lord spake unto Moses and unto Aaron, saying, Separate yourselves from among this congregation, that I may consume them in a moment. And they fell upon their faces, and said, O God, the God of the spirits of all flesh, shall one man sin, and wilt thou be wroth with all the congregation? And the Lord spake unto Moses, saying, Speak unto the congregation, saying, Get you up from about the tabernacle of Korah, Dathan, and Abiram. And Moses rose up and went unto Dathan and Abiram; and the elders of Israel followed him. And he spake unto the congregation, saying, Depart, I pray you, from the tents of these wicked men, and touch nothing of their's, lest ye be consumed in all their sins. So they gat up from the tabernacle of Korah, Dathan, and Abiram, on every side: and Dathan and Abiram came out, and stood in the door of their tents, and their wives, and their sons, and their little children. And Moses said, Hereby ye shall know that the Lord hath sent me to do all these works; for I have not done them of mine own mind. If these men die the common death of all men, or if they be visited after the visitation of all men; then the Lord hath not sent me. But if the Lord make a new thing, and the earth open her mouth, and swallow them up, with all that appertain unto them, and they go down quick into the pit; then ye shall understand that these men have provoked the Lord. And it came to pass, as he had made an end of speaking all these words, that the ground clave asunder that was under them. And the earth opened her mouth, and swallowed them up, and their houses, and all the men that appertained unto Korah, and all their goods. They, and all that appertained to them, went down alive into the pit, and the earth closed upon them: and they perished from among the congregation. And all Israel that were round about them fled at the cry of them : for they said, Lest the earth swallow us up also. And there came out a fire from the Lord, and consumed the two hundred and fifty men that offered incense. *Nu. xvi.* 1 to 35.

3. *that they may never prevail against us, or triumph in the ruin of thy Church among us.*

3. Arise, O Lord ; let not man prevail. *Ps. ix.* 19. They have said, Let us take to ourselves the houses of God in possession. O my God, fill their faces with shame ; that they may seek thy name, O Lord. *Ps. lxxxiii.* 4. 12, 13. 16. Let them not say in their hearts, Ah, so would we have it: let them not say, We have swallowed him up. *Ps. xxxv.* 25.

4. *but that our gracious Sovereign, and his Realms, being preserved in thy true Religion, and by thy merciful goodness protected in the same, we may all duly serve thee, and give thee thanks in thy holy congregation ; through Jesus Christ our Lord. Amen.*

4. Let thy hand be upon the man of thy right hand, upon the son of man whom thou madest strong for thyself. So will not we go back from thee : quicken us, and we will call upon thy name. *Ps. lxxx.* 17, 18. Know thou the God of thy father, and serve him with a perfect heart and with a willing mind. *1 Ch. xxviii.* 9. O continue thy lovingkindness unto them that know thee ; and thy righteousness to the upright in heart. *Ps. xxxvi.* 10. So we thy people and sheep of thy pasture will give thee thanks for ever: we will shew forth thy praise to all generations. *Ps. lxxix.* 13. We will rejoice in thy salvation, and in the name of our God we will set up our banners. *Ps. xx.* 5. The king shall joy in thy strength, O Lord ; and in thy salvation how greatly shall he rejoice ! *Ps. xxi.* 1. I will give thee thanks in the great congregation : I will praise thee among much people. *Ps. xxxv.* 18. So they brought the ark of God, and set it in the midst of the tent that David had pitched for it : and they offered burnt sacri-

fices and peace offerings before God. And when David had made an end of offering the burnt offerings and the peace offerings, he blessed the people in the name of the Lord. And he appointed certain of the Levites to minister before the ark of the Lord, and to record, and to thank and praise the Lord God of Israel. 1 *Ch. xvi.* 1, 2. 4. And the Lord was with Jehoshaphat, because he walked in the first ways of his father David, and sought not unto Baalim ; but sought to the Lord God of his father, and walked in his commandments, and not after the doings of Israel. Therefore the Lord stablished the kingdom in his hand ; and all Judah brought to Jehoshaphat presents ; and he had riches and honour in abundance. And his heart was lifted up in the ways of the Lord. 2 *Ch. xvii.* 3 to 6.—*See also particularly,* 2 *Ch.* XXIX. XXX.

CCLXXXIV. *A Prayer for the King, and the Royal Family.*

1. Eternal God, and our most mighty Protector, we thy unworthy servants do humbly present ourselves before thy Majesty, acknowledging thy power, wisdom, and goodness, in preserving the King, and the Three Estates of the Realm of *England* assembled in Parliament, from the Destruction this day intended against them.

1. The eternal God is thy refuge, and underneath are the everlasting arms. *De. xxxiii.* 27. The Lord is my rock, and my fortress, and my deliverer; the God of my rock ; in him will I trust: he is my shield, and the horn of my salvation, my high tower, and my refuge, my Saviour ; thou savest me from violence. I will call on the Lord, who is worthy to be praised: so shall I be saved from mine enemies. 2 *Sa. xxii.* 2, 3, 4. Thou hast been a shelter for me, and a strong tower from the enemy. *Ps. lxi.* 3. O Lord God of hosts, who is a strong Lord like unto thee ? *Ps. lxxxix.* 8. Behold now, I have taken upon me to speak unto the Lord, which am but dust and ashes. *Ge. xviii.* 27. I am not worthy of the least of all the mercies, and of all the truth, which thou hast shewed unto thy servant. *Ge. xxxii.* 10. Thine, O Lord, is the greatness, and the power, and the glory, and the victory, and the majesty. Now therefore, our God, we thank thee, and praise thy glorious name. 1 *Ch. xxix.* 11, 13. O how great is thy goodness, which thou hast laid up for them that fear thee! *Ps. xxxi.* 19. The king trusteth in the Lord, and through the mercy of the Most High, he shall not be moved. For thou preventest him with the blessings of goodness: thou settest a crown of pure gold on his head, *Ps. xxi.* 7. 3. The

Lord saved Israel that day out of the hand of the Egyptians. *Ex. xiv.* 30. Thine hand shall find out all thine enemies : thy right hand shall find out those that hate thee. For they intended evil against thee : and imagined a mischievous device, which they are not able to perform. *Ps. xxi.* 8. 11. Our adversaries said, They shall not know, neither see, till we come in the midst among them, and slay them, and cause the work to cease. *Ne. iv.* 11.

2. Make us, we beseech thee, truly thankful for this, and for all other thy great mercies towards us; particularly for making this day again memorable, by a fresh instance of thy loving-kindness towards us. We bless thee for giving his late Majesty King *William*, a safe arrival here, and for making all opposition fall before him, till he became our King and Governor.

2. Give thanks unto the Lord, call upon his name, make known his deeds among the people. Sing unto him, sing psalms unto him, talk ye of all his wondrous works. Glory ye in his holy name : let the heart of them rejoice that seek the Lord. 1 *Ch. xvi.* 8, 9, 10. O that men would praise the Lord for his goodness; and declare the wonders that he doeth for the children of men! *Ps. cvii.* 8. I will praise the Lord with my whole heart. *Ps. cxi.* 1. In the time of their trouble, when they cried unto thee, thou heardest them from heaven; and according to thy manifold mercies thou gavest them saviours, who saved them out of the hand of their enemies. Many times didst thou deliver them according to thy mercies. *Ne. ix.* 27, 28. He hath made his wonderful works to be remembered : the Lord is gracious and full of compassion. *Ps. cxi.* 4. Great deliverance giveth he to his king; and sheweth mercy to his anointed. *Ps. xviii.* 50. *See also, Est. ix.* 20, 21, 22.—1 *Ch. xi.* 1, 2, 3.

3. We beseech thee to protect and defend our Sovereign King *William*, and all the Royal Family, from all Treasons and Conspiracies;

3. God save the king. 1 *Sa. x.* 24. Then said Abishai to David, God hath delivered thine enemy into thine hand this day : now therefore let me smite him, I pray thee, with the spear even to the earth at once, and I will not smite him the second time. And David said to Abishai, Destroy him not : for who can stretch forth his hand against the Lord's anointed, and be guiltless? 1 *Sa. xxvi.* 8, 9. And Joab said unto the man that told him, And, behold, thou sawest him, and why didst thou not smite him there to the ground? and I would

have given thee, ten shekels of silver, and a girdle. And the men said unto Joab, Though I should receive a thousand shekels of silver, yet would I not put forth mine hand against the king's son. *2 Sa. xviii.* 11, 12. Thou hast girded me with strength unto the battle : thou hast subdued under me those that rose up against me. Thou hast also given me the necks of mine enemies; that I might destroy them that hate me. Thou hast delivered me from the strivings of the people. *Ps. xviii.* 39, 40. 43. Shew thy marvellous lovingkindness, O thou that savest by thy right hand them which put their trust in thee from those that rise up against them. *Ps. xvii.* 7. The king trusteth in the Lord, and through the mercy of the Most High he shall not be moved. Thine hand shall find out all thine enemies : thy right hand shall find out those that hate thee. *Ps. xxi.* 7, 8. *See also,* 2 *Ki. xi.* 2.—*Ps. xci.* 3, 4.— *Je. xxxix.* 18.

4. *Preserve him in thy Faith, Fear, and Love; Prosper his Reign with long happiness here on earth ; and crown him with everlasting glory hereafter : through Jesus Christ our only Saviour and Redeemer. Amen.*

4. Give the king thy judgments, O God, and thy righteousness unto the king's son. *Ps. lxxii.* 1. He that ruleth over men must be just, ruling in the fear of God. *2 Sa. xxiii.* 3. Teach me thy way, O Lord ; I will walk in thy truth : unite my heart to fear thy name. *Ps. lxxxvi.* 11. Hold up my goings in thy paths, that my footsteps slip not. *Ps. xvii.* 5. And thou, Solomon my son, know thou the God of thy father, and serve him with a perfect heart and with a willing mind. 1 *Ch. xxviii.* 9. O Lord God of Abraham, Isaac, and of Israel, give unto Solomon my son a perfect heart, to keep thy commandments, thy testimonies, and thy statutes. 1 *Ch. xxix.* 18, 19. As the Lord hath been with my lord the king, even so be he with Solomon, and make his throne greater than the throne of my lord king David. 1 *Ki. i.* 37. Remember all thy offerings, and accept thy burnt sacrifice. Grant thee according to thine own heart, and fulfil all thy counsel. *Ps. xx.* 3, 4. Jehoshaphat sought to the Lord God of his father, and walked in his commandments. And his heart was lifted up in the ways of the Lord. *2 Ch. xvii.* 1. 4. 6. Hezekiah the son of Ahaz king of Judah began to reign. And he did that which was right in the sight of the Lord, according to all that David his father did. He trusted in the Lord God of Israel ; so that after him was none like him among all the kings of Judah,

nor any that were before him. For he clave to the Lord, and departed not from following him, but kept his commandments, which the Lord commanded Moses. *2 Ki. xviii.* 1. 3. 5, 6. Although my house be not so with God; yet he hath made with me an everlasting covenant, ordered in all things, and sure: for this is all my salvation, and all my desire. *2 Sa. xxiii.* 5. Henceforth there is laid up for me a crown of righteousness, which the Lord, the righteous Judge, shall give me at that day: and not to me only, but unto all them also that love his appearing. *2 Ti. iv.* 8. Unto him that loved us, and washed us from our sins in his own blood, and hath made us kings and priests unto God and his Father; to him be glory and dominion for ever and ever. Amen. *Re. i.* 5, 6.

The Epistle. Rom. 13. 1 to 8.—*Let every soul be subject unto the higher powers. For there is no power but of God; the powers that be, are ordained of God. Whosoever therefore resisteth the power, resisteth the Ordinance of God, and they that resist shall receive to themselves damnation. For rulers are not a terror to good works, but to the evil. Wilt thou then not be afraid of the power? do that which is good, and thou shalt have praise of the same : for he is the minister of God to thee for good. But if thou do that which is evil, be afraid ; for he beareth not the sword in vain : for he is the minister of God, a revenger to execute wrath upon him that doeth evil. Wherefore ye must needs be subject, not only for wrath but also for Conscience sake. For, for this cause pay you tribute also : for they are God's ministers, attending continually upon this very thing. Render therefore to all their dues ; tribute to whom tribute is due, custom to whom custom, fear to whom fear, honour to whom honour.*

The Gospel. St. Luke 9. 51 to 57.—*And it came to pass, when the time was come that he should be received up, he steadfastly set his face to go to Jerusalem, and sent messengers before his face : and they went and entered into a village of the Samaritans, to make ready for him. And they did not receive him, because his face was as though he would go to Jerusalem. And when his disciples James and John saw this, they said, Lord, wilt thou that we command fire to come down from heaven, and consume them, even as Elias did? But he turned and rebuked them, and said, Ye know not what manner of spirit ye are of. For the Son of Man is not come to destroy men's lives, but to save them. And they went to another village.*

CCLXXXV. *A Prayer for a spirit of Thankfulness and of Obedience.*

1. O God, whose name is excellent in all the earth, and thy glory above the heavens ; who on this day didst miraculously preserve our Church and State from the secret contrivance and hel-

1. O Lord our Lord, how excellent is thy Name in all the earth! who hast set thy glory above the heavens. *Ps. viii.* 1. The Lord is high above all nations, and his glory above the heavens. Who is like unto the Lord our God, who dwelleth on high? *Ps. cxiii.* 4, 5. But it came to pass, that when Sanballat, and Tobiah, and the Arabians, and the Ammonites, and the Ashdodites, heard that the walls of Jerusalem were made up, and that the breaches began to be stopped, then they were very wroth, and conspired all of them together to

lish malice of Popish Conspirators ; and on this day also didst begin to give us a mighty deliverance from the open tyranny and oppression of the same cruel and bloodthirsty enemies;

come and to fight against Jerusalem, and to hinder it. Nevertheless we made our prayer unto our God, and set a watch against them day and night, because of them. And our adversaries said, They shall not know, nor see, till we come in the midst among them, and slay them, and cause the work to cease. *Ne. iv.* 7, 8, 9. 11. The wall was finished in the twenty fifth day of the month Elul, in fifty and two days. And it came to pass, that when all our enemies heard thereof, and all the heathen that were about us saw these things, they were much cast down in their own eyes; for they perceived that this work was wrought of our God. *Ne. vi.* 15, 16. Certain of the Jews banded together, and bound themselves under a curse, saying that they would neither eat nor drink till they had killed Paul. And they were more than forty which had made this conspiracy. And he [the chief captain] wrote a letter after this manner: Claudius Lysias unto the most excellent governor Felix sendeth greeting. This man was taken of the Jews, and should have been killed of them : then came I with an army, and rescued him. *Ao. xxiii.* 12, 13. 25, 26, 27. I have also heard the groaning of the children of Israel, whom the Egyptians keep in bondage ; and I have remembered my covenant. Wherefore say unto the children of Israel, I am the Lord, and I will bring you out from under the burdens of the Egyptians, and I will rid you out of their bondage, and I will redeem you with a stretched out arm, and with great judgments : and I will take you to me for a people, and I will be to you a God : and ye shall know that I am the Lord your God, which bringeth you out from under the burdens of the Egyptians. *Ex. vi.* 5, 6, 7.

2. We bless and adore thy glorious Majesty, as for the former; so for this thy late marvellous loving-kindness to our Church and Nation, in the preservation of our Religion and Liberties.

2. Now therefore, our God, we thank thee, and praise thy glorious Name. *1 Ch. xxix.* 13. We will bless the Lord from this time forth and for evermore. Praise the Lord. *Ps. cxv.* 18. Bless the Lord, O my soul : and all that is within me, bless his holy name. Bless the Lord, O my soul : and forget not all his benefits. *Ps. ciii.* 1, 2. Blessed be the Lord God, the God of Israel, who only doeth wondrous things. And blessed be his glorious name for ever : and let the whole earth be filled with his glory : Amen, and Amen. *Ps. lxxii.* 18, 19. Blessed be the Lord : for he hath shewed me his

marvellous kindness in a strong city. *Ps. xxxi.* 21. We have thought of thy lovingkindness, O God, in the midst of thy temple. God is known in her palaces for a refuge. For, lo, the kings were assembled, they passed by together. They saw it, and so they marvelled; they were troubled, and hasted away. *Ps. xlviii.* 9. 3, 4, 5. The Lord loveth the gates of Zion more than all the dwellings of Jacob. Glorious things are spoken of thee, O city of God. *Ps. lxxxvii.* 2, 3. He is the tower of salvation for his king : and sheweth mercy to his anointed, unto David, and to his seed for evermore. 2 *Sa. xxii.* 51. He had peace on all sides round about him. And Judah and Israel dwelt safely, every man under his vine and under his figtree. 1 *Ki. vi.* 24, 25. Blessed be the Lord, who hath not given us as a prey to their teeth. Our soul is escaped as a bird out of the snare of the fowlers: the snare is broken, and we are escaped. Our help is in the name of the Lord, who made heaven and earth. *Ps. cxxiv.* 6, 7, 8. And Mordecai wrote these things, and sent letters unto all the Jews that were in all the provinces of the king Ahasuerus, both nigh and far, to stablish this among them, that they should keep the fourteenth day of the month Adar, and the fifteenth day of the same, yearly, as the days wherein the Jews rested from their enemies, and the month which was turned unto them from sorrow to joy, and from mourning into a good day: that they should make them days of feasting and joy, and of sending portions one to another, and gifts to the poor. The Jews ordained, and took upon them, and upon their seed, and upon all such as joined themselves unto them, so as it should not fail, that they would keep these two days according to their writing, and according to their appointed time every year; and that these days should be remembered and kept throughout every generation, every family, every province, and every city; and that these days of Purim should not fail from among the Jews, nor the memorial of them perish from their seed. *Est. ix.* 20, 21, 22. 27, 28.

3. And we humbly pray, that the devout sense of this thy repeated mercy may renew and increase in us a spirit of love

3. O Lord, I beseech thee, let now thine ear be attentive to the prayer of thy servants, who desire to fear thy name. *Ne. i.* 11. Many a time have they afflicted me from my youth: yet they have not prevailed against me. *Ps. cxxix.* 2. He saved them from the hand of him that hated them, and redeemed them from the hand of the enemy. Many times did

and thankful-
ness to thee
its only Author;
a spirit of
peaceable sub-
mission and
obedience to
our gracious
Sovereign Lord,
King *William*;
and a spirit of
fervent zeal
for our holy
Religion, which
thou hast so
wonderfully
rescued, and
established, a
blessing to us
and our pos-
terity. And
this we beg
for Jesus Christ
His sake.
Amen.

he deliver them. *Ps. cvi.* 10. 43. I love the Lord, because he hath heard my voice and my supplications. *Ps. cxvi.* 1. I will love thee, O Lord, my strength. *Ps. xviii.* 1. I will extol thee, O Lord; for thou hast lifted me up, and hast not made my foes to rejoice over me. *Ps. xxx.* A. My mouth shall shew forth thy righteousness and thy salvation all the day: for I know not the numbers thereof. *Ps. lxxi.* 15. And all men shall fear, and shall declare the work of God; for they shall wisely consider of his doing. *Ps. lxiv.* 9. And Israel saw that great work which the Lord did upon the Egyptians: and the people feared the Lord, and believed the Lord, and his servant Moses. *Ex. xiv.* 31. Submit yourselves to every ordinance of man for the Lord's sake: whether it be to the king, as supreme; or unto governors, as unto them that are sent by him for the punishment of evil doers, and for the praise of them that do well. For so is the will of God. 1 *Pe. ii.* 13, 14, 15. Then Solomon sat on the throne as king instead of David his father, and prospered; and all Israel obeyed him. And all the princes, and the mighty men, and all the sons likewise of king David, submitted themselves unto Solomon the king. 1 *Ch. xxix.* 23, 24. The zeal of thine house hath eaten me up. *Ps. lxix.* 9. Phinehas, the son of Eleazar, the son of Aaron the priest, hath turned my wrath away from the children of Israel, while he was zealous for my sake among them, that I consumed not the children of Israel in my jealousy. Wherefore, Behold, I give unto him my covenant of peace: and he shall have it, and his seed after him, even the covenant of an everlasting priesthood; because he was zealous for his God, and made an atonement for the children of Israel. *Nu. xxv.* 11, 12, 13. Pray for the peace of Jerusalem: they shall prosper that love thee. Peace be within thy walls, and prosperity within thy palaces. For my brethren and companions' sakes, I will now say, Peace be within thee. Because of the house of the Lord our God I will seek thy good. *Ps. cxxii.* 6 to 9. Let thy work appear unto thy servants, and thy glory unto their children. And let the beauty of the Lord our God be upon us: and establish thou the work of our hands upon us; yea, the work of our hands establish thou it. *Ps. xc.* 16, 17. In his temple doth every one speak of his glory. *Ps. xxix.* 9. *See also, the Books of* EZRA *and* NEHEMIAH.

A FORM OF

PRAYER WITH FASTING,

To be used yearly on the Thirtieth day of January.

The Sentences.—*To the Lord our God belong mercies and forgivenesses, though we have rebelled against him : neither have we obeyed the voice of the Lord our God, to walk in his laws which he set before us.* Dan. ix. 9, 10. *Correct us, O Lord, but with judgment ; not in thine anger : lest thou bring us to nothing.* Jer. x. 24. *Enter not into judgment with thy servants, O Lord : for in thy sight shall no man living be justified.* Psal. cxliii. 2.

The Hymn.—*Righteous art thou, O Lord : and just art thy judgments!* Psal. cxix. 137. *Thou art just, O Lord, in all that is brought upon us : for thou hast done right, but we have done wickedly.* Neh. ix. 33. *Nevertheless, our feet were almost gone : our treadings had well nigh slipped. For why? we were grieved at the wicked : we did also see the ungodly in such prosperity.* Psal. lxxiii. 2, 3. *The people stood up, and the rulers took counsel together : against the Lord, and against his Anointed.* Psal. ii. 2. *They cast their heads together with one consent : and were confederate against him.* Psal. lxxxiii. 5. *He heard the blasphemy of the multitude, and fear was on every side : while they conspired together against him, to take away his life.* Psal. xxxi. 15. *They spake against him with false tongues, and compassed him about with words of hatred : and fought against him without a cause.* Psal. cix. 2. *Yea, his own familiar friends, whom he trusted : they that eat of his bread, laid great wait for him.* Psal. xli. 9. *They rewarded him evil for good : to the great discomfort of his soul.* Psal. xxxv. 12. *They took their counsel together, saying, God hath forsaken him : persecute him, and take him, for there is none to deliver him.* Psal. lxxi. 9. *The breath of our nostrils, the Anointed of the Lord was taken in their pits : of whom we said, Under his shadow we shall be safe. The adversary and the enemy entered into the gates of Jerusalem : saying, When shall he die and his name perish? Let the Sentence of guiltiness proceed against him : and now that he lieth, let him rise up no more.* Psal. xli. 5. 8. La. iv. 20. 12. *False witnesses also did rise up against him : they laid to his charge things that he knew not.* Psal. xxxv. 11. *For the sins of the people, and the iniquities of the priests : they shed the blood of the just in the midst of Jerusalem.* Lam. iv. 13. *O my soul, come not thou into their secret ; unto their Assembly, mine honour, be not thou united : for in their anger they slew a man.* Gen. xlix. 6. *Even the man of thy right hand : the son of man, whom thou hadst made so strong for thine own self.* Psal. lxxx. 17. *In the sight of the unwise he seemed to die : and his departure was taken for misery.* Wisd. iii. 2. *They fools counted his life madness, and his end to be without honour : but he is in peace.* Wisd. v. 4. & iii. 3. *For though he was punished in the sight of men : yet was his hope full of immortality.* Wisd. iii. 4. *How is he numbered with the children of God : and his lot is among the saints!* Wisd. v. 5. *But, O Lord God, to whom vengeance belongeth, thou God, to whom vengeance belongeth : be favourable and gracious unto Sion.* Psal. xciv. 1. & li. 18. *Be merciful, O Lord, unto thy people, whom thou hast redeemed : and lay not innocent blood to our charge.* Deut. xxi. 8. *O shut not up our souls with sinners : nor our lives with the blood-thirsty.* Psal. xxvi. 9. *Deliver us from blood-guiltiness, O God, thou that art the God of our salvation : and our tongue shall sing of thy righteousness.* Psal. li. 14. *For thou art the God that hast no pleasure in wickedness ; neither shall any evil dwell with thee. Thou wilt destroy them that speak leasing : the Lord abhors both the blood-thirsty and deceitful man.* Psal. v. 4. 6. *O how suddenly do they consume : perish, and come to a fearful end! Yea, even like as a dream, when one awaketh : so didst thou make their image to vanish out of the city.* Psal. lxxiii. 18, 19. *Great and marvellous are thy works, O Lord God Almighty : just and true are thy ways, O King of saints!* Re. xv. 3. *Righteous art thou, O Lord : and just are thy judgments!* Psal. cxix. 137.

Glory be to the Father, &c.
As it was in the beginning, &c.

Proper Psalms, IX, X, XI.
The Proper Lessons, 2 Sam. I.—Mat. XXVII.

2 q

CCLXXXVI.—*A deprecation of God's righteous Judgments.*

1. O most mighty God, terrible in thy judgments, and wonderful in thy doings toward the children of men ;

1. The Lord your God is God of gods, and Lord of lords, a great God, a mighty, and a terrible, which regardeth not persons, nor taketh reward. *De. x.* 17.   Say unto God, How terrible art thou in thy works! through the greatness of thy power shall thine enemies submit themselves unto thee.   Come and see the works of God: he is terrible in his doing toward the children of men. *Ps. lxvi.* 3. 5.   By terrible things in righteousness wilt thou answer us, O God of our salvation ; who art the confidence of all the ends of the earth, and of them that are afar off upon the sea. *Ps. lxv.* 5.   Oh the depth of the riches both of the wisdom and knowledge of God! how unsearchable are his judgments, and his ways past finding out ! *Ro. xi.* 33.

2. Who in thy heavy displeasure didst suffer the life of our gracious Sovereign King *Charles* the First, to be (as this day) taken away by the hands of cruel and bloody men :

2. O God, thou hast cast us off, thou hast scattered us, thou hast been displeased ; O turn thyself to us again. *Ps. lx.* 1. Put me not to rebuke, O Lord, in thine anger: neither chasten me in thy heavy displeasure. *Ps. xxxviii.* 1.   The breath of our nostrils, the Anointed of the Lord, was taken in their pits. *La. iv.* 20.   When they saw him afar off, they conspired against him to slay him.   *Ge. xxxvii.* 18.   Their feet run to evil, and they make haste to shed innocent blood : their thoughts are thoughts of iniquity ; wasting and destruction are in their paths.   The way of peace they know not; and there is no judgment in their goings: they have made them crooked paths: whosoever goeth therein shall not know peace. *Is. lix.* 7, 8. The Lord will abhor the bloody and deceitful man. *Ps. v.* 6. Deliver me, O my God, out of the hand of the wicked, out of the hand of the unrighteous and cruel man. *Ps. lxxi.* 4. *See also, Ps. lxi.* 2, 3, 4. 6, 7.

3. We thy sinful creatures here assembled before thee, do, in the behalf of all the people of this land, humbly confess, that they were the crying sins of

3. Then all the children of Israel, and all the people, went up, and came unto the house of God, and wept, and sat there before the Lord, and fasted that day until even. *Jud. xx.* 26. O Lord, we have sinned, and have committed iniquity, and have done wickedly, and have rebelled, even by departing from thy precepts and from thy judgments ; neither have we obeyed the voice of the Lord our God, to walk in his laws, which he set before us.   Yea, all Israel have transgressed thy law, even

this Nation, which brought down this heavy judgment upon us.

by departing, that they might not obey thy voice; therefore the curse is poured upon us; for the Lord our God is righteous in all his works which he doeth. *Da. ix.* 4, 5. 10, 11. 14. Righteous art thou, O Lord, and upright are thy judgments. *Ps. cxix.* 137. Thou art just in all that is brought upon us; for thou hast done right, but we have done wickedly: neither have our kings, our princes, our priests, nor our fathers, kept thy law, nor hearkened unto thy commandments and thy testimonies, wherewith thou didst testify against them. For they have not served thee in their kingdom; neither turned they from their wicked works. *Ne. ix.* 33, 34, 35. Since the days of our fathers have we been in a great trespass unto this day; and for our iniquities have we, our kings, and our priests, been delivered into the hand of the kings of the lands, to the sword, to captivity, and to a spoil, and to confusion of face, as it is this day. *Ezr. ix.* 7.

4. But, O gracious God, when thou makest inquisition for blood, lay not the guilt of this innocent blood, (the shedding whereof nothing but the blood of thy Son can expiate,) lay it not to the charge of the people of this land, nor let it ever be required of us, or our posterity.

4. Thus saith the Lord God; The city sheddeth blood in the midst of it. Thou art become guilty in thy blood that thou hast shed. *Eze. xxii.* 3, 4. Surely your blood of your lives will I require; at the hand of every beast will I require it, and at the hand of man; at the hand of every man's brother will I require the life of man. *Ge. ix.* 5. And David said to Abishai, Destroy him not: for who can stretch forth his hand against the Lord's anointed, and be guiltless? 1 *Sa. xxvi.* 9. When he maketh inquisition for blood, he remembereth them: he forgetteth not the cry of the humble. *Ps. ix.* 12. O Lord, according to all thy righteousness, I beseech thee, let thine anger and thy fury be turned away from thy city Jerusalem, thy holy mountain: because of our sins, and the iniquities of our fathers, Jerusalem and thy people are become a reproach to all that are about us. *Da. ix.* 16. The blood of Jesus Christ his Son cleanseth us from all sin. 1 *John i.* 7. The blood of sprinkling, that speaketh better things than that of Abel. *He. xii.* 24. They cried unto the Lord, and said, We beseech thee, O Lord, we beseech thee, let us not perish for this man's life, and lay not upon us innocent blood: for thou, O Lord, hast done as it pleased thee. *Jon. i.* 14. The soul that sinneth, it shall die. The son shall not bear the

iniquity of the fathers, neither shall the father bear the iniquity of the son: the righteousness of the righteous shall be upon him, and the wickedness of the wicked shall be upon him. *Eze. xviii.* 20. Deliver me from bloodguiltiness, O God, thou God of my salvation. *Ps. li.* 14. Lay not innocent blood unto thy people of Israel's charge. *De. xxi.* 8.

5. *Be merciful, O Lord, be merciful unto thy people, whom thou hast redeemed; and be not angry with us for ever: But pardon us for thy mercy's sake, through the merits of thy Son Jesus Christ our Lord. Amen.*

5. Be merciful unto me, O God, be merciful unto me. *Ps. lvii.* 1. Remember thy congregation, which thou hast purchased of old; the rod of thine inheritance, which thou hast redeemed. *Ps. lxxiv.* 2. Wilt thou be angry with us for ever? Wilt thou draw out thine anger to all generations? Wilt thou not revive us again: that thy people may rejoice in thee? Shew us thy mercy, O Lord, and grant us thy salvation. *Ps. lxxxv.* 5, 6, 7. O Lord God of hosts, how long wilt thou be angry with thy people that prayeth? *Ps. lxxx.* 4. Turn us, O God of our salvation, and cause thine anger toward us to cease. *Ps. lxxxv.* 4. For thy name's sake, O Lord, pardon mine iniquity; for it is great. *Ps. xxv.* 11. Help us, O God of our salvation, for the glory of thy name. *Ps. lxxix.* 9. Oh save me for thy mercies' sake. *Ps. vi.* 4. For my name's sake will I defer mine anger, and for my praise will I refrain for thee, that I cut thee not off. *Is. xlviii.* 2. If any man sin, we have an Advocate with the Father, Jesus Christ the righteous: and he is the Propitiation for our sins. 1 *John ii.* 1, 2. Unto him that loved us, and washed us from our sins in his own blood, to him be glory and dominion for ever and ever. Amen. *Re.* i. 5, 6.

CCLXXXVII.—*A Prayer for Grace to follow good examples.*

1. *Blessed Lord, in whose sight the death of thy saints is precious; We magnify thy Name for thine abundant grace bestowed upon our martyred Sovereign; by which he was enabled so cheerfully to*

1. Precious in the sight of the Lord is the death of his saints. *Ps. cxvi.* 15. He shall redeem their soul from deceit and violence; and precious shall their blood be in his sight. *Ps. lxxii.* 14. And Mary said, My soul doth magnify the Lord. *Lu. i.* 46. The grace of our Lord was exceeding abundant with faith and love which is in Christ Jesus. 1 *Ti. i.* 14. Then Paul answered, What mean ye to weep and to break mine heart? for I am ready not to be bound only, but also to die at Jerusalem for the name of the Lord Jesus. *Ac. xxi.* 13. Unto you it is given in the behalf of Christ, not only to believe on

follow the steps of his blessed Master and Saviour, in a constant meek suffering of all barbarous indignities, and at last resisting unto blood; and even then, according to the same pattern, praying for his murderers.

him, but also to suffer for his sake. *Ph. i.* 29. That I may know him, and the power of his resurrection, and the fellowship of his sufferings, being made conformable unto his death. *Ph. iii.* 10. For even hereunto were ye called: because Christ also suffered for us, leaving us an example, that ye should follow his steps. 1 *Pe. i.* 21. Put on, as the elect of God, meekness, longsuffering. *Col. iii.* 12. And they lifted up their voices, and said, Away with such a fellow from the earth: for it is not fit that he should live. *Ac. xxii.* 22. Ye have not yet resisted unto blood, striving against sin. *He. xii.* 4. Then said Jesus, Father, forgive them; for they know not what they do. *Lu. xxiii.* 34. And they stoned Stephen, calling upon God, and saying, Lord Jesus, receive my spirit. And he kneeled down, and cried with a loud voice, Lord, lay not this sin to their charge. *Ac. vii.* 59, 60. See also, 2 *Ch. xxiv.* 20, 21.—*And, in the Holy Gospels, the account of the Sufferings of our Lord Jesus Christ, and of the barbarous Indignities offered to him.*

2. Let his memory, O Lord, be ever blessed among us; that we may follow the example of his courage and constancy, his meekness and patience, and great charity.

2. The memory of the just is blessed: but the name of the wicked shall rot. *Pr. x.* 7. The righteous shall be in everlasting remembrance. *Ps. cxii.* 6. Be ye followers of me, even as I also am of Christ. 1 *Co. xi.* 1. Be not slothful, but followers of them who through faith and patience inherit the promises. For God is not unrighteous to forget your work and labour of love, which ye have shewed toward his name. *He. vi.* 12. 10. And I said, should such a man as I flee? and who is there, that, being as I am, would go into the temple to save his life? I will not go in. *Ne. vi.* 11. In the Lord put I my trust: how say ye to my soul, Flee as a bird to your mountain? *Ps. xi.* 1. Be thou faithful unto death, and I will give thee a crown of life. *Re. ii.* 10. And the king said unto Zadok, Carry back the ark into the city: if I shall find favour in the eyes of the Lord, he will bring me again, and shew me both it, and his habitation, but if he thus say, I have no delight in thee: behold, here am I, let him do to me as seemeth good unto him. 2 *Sa. xv.* 25, 26. I will bear the indignation of the Lord, because I have sinned against him, until he plead my cause, and execute judgment for me: he will bring me forth to the light, and I shall behold his righteousness. *Mi. vii.* 9.

And I will very gladly spend and be spent for you ; though the more abundantly I love you, the less I be loved. 2 *Co. xii.* 15.

3. And grant, that this our land may be freed from the vengeance of his righteous blood, and thy mercy glorified in the forgiveness of our sins ; and all for Jesus Christ his sake, our only Mediator and Advocate. Amen.

3. And they shall answer and say, our hands have not shed this blood, neither have our eyes seen it. Be merciful, O Lord, unto thy people Israel, whom thou hast redeemed, and lay not innocent blood unto thy people of Israel's charge. And the blood shall be forgiven them. *De. xxi.* 7, 8. If any man hate his neighbour, and rise up against him, and smite him mortally that he die ; the elders of his city shall deliver him into the hand of the avenger of blood, that he may die. Thine eye shall not pity him, but thou shalt put away the guilt of innocent blood from Israel, that it may go well with thee. *De. xix.* 11, 12, 13. Pardon, I beseech thee, the iniquity of this people according unto the greatness of thy mercy. *Nu. xiv,* 19. Who is a God like unto thee, that pardoneth iniquity, and passeth by the transgression of the remnant of his heritage ? He retaineth not his anger for ever, because he delighteth in mercy. *Mi. vii.* 18. I, even I, am he that blotteth out thy transgressions for mine own sake, and will not remember thy sins. *Is. xliii.* 25. Christ is the Mediator of the new testament. *He. ix.* 15. He ever liveth to make intercession. *He. vii.* 25. In whom we have redemption through his blood, the forgiveness of sins, according to the riches of his grace. To the praise of the glory of his grace, wherein he hath made us accepted in the Beloved. *Ep. i.* 7. 6. Who is over all, God blessed for ever. Amen. *Ro. ix.* 15.

O Lord, we beseech thee, &c. *as CCXXXVII.*

O most mighty God and merciful, &c. *as CCXXXVIII.*

Turn thou us, O good Lord, &c, *as CCXXXIX.*

The Epistle. 1 *Pe.* ii. 13 to 23.—*Submit yourselves to every ordinance of man for the Lord's sake ; whether it be to the King, as supreme ; or unto governors, as unto them that are sent by him, for the punishment of evil doers, and for the praise of them that do well. For so is the will of God, that with well-doing, ye may put to silence the ignorance of foolish men : as free, and not using your liberty for a cloke of maliciousness, but as the servants of God. Honour all men. Love the brotherhood. Fear God. Honour the King. Servants, be subject to your masters with all fear, not only to the good and gentle, but also to the froward. For this is thankworthy, if a man for conscience toward God endure grief, suffering wrongfully. For what glory is it, if when ye be buffeted for your faults ye shall take it patiently ? but if when ye do well, and suffer for it, ye take it patiently ; this is acceptable with God. For even hereunto were ye called ; because Christ also suffered for us, leaving us an example, that ye should follow his steps ; who did no sin, neither was guile found in his mouth.*

The Gospel. Mat. xxi. 33 to 42.— *There was a certain housholder which planted a vineyard, and hedged it round about, and digged a wine-press in it, and built a tower, and let it out to husbandmen, and went into a far country. And when the time of the fruit drew near, he sent his servants to the husbandmen, that they might receive the fruits of it. And the husbandmen took his servants, and beat one, and killed another, and stoned another. Again, he sent other servants, more than the first: and they did unto them likewise. But last of all he sent unto them his son, saying, They will reverence my son. But when the husbandmen saw the son, they said among themselves, This is the heir, come, let us kill him, and let us seize on his inheritance. And they caught him, and cast him out of the vineyard, and slew him. When the lord therefore of the vineyard cometh, what will he do unto those husbandmen? They say unto him, He will miserably destroy those wicked men, and will let out his vineyard unto other husbandmen, which shall render him the fruits in their seasons.*

CCLXXXVIII.—*A Prayer that the King may reign long and happily.*

1. O Lord, our heavenly Father, who didst not punish us as our sins have deserved, but hast in the midst of judgment remembered mercy; We acknowledge it thine especial favour, that, though for our many and great provocations, thou didst suffer thine anointed blessed King *Charles* the First (as on this day) to fall into the hands of violent and blood-thirsty men, and barbarously to be murdered by them,

1. Thou our God hast punished us less than our iniquities deserve. *Ezr. ix.* 13. Know therefore that God exacteth of thee less than thine iniquity deserveth. *Job xi.* 6. He hath not dealt with us after our sins; nor rewarded us according to our iniquities. *Ps. ciii.* 10. But he, being full of compassion, forgave their iniquity, and destroyed them not: yea, many a time turned he his anger away, and did not stir up all his wrath. *Ps. lxxviii.* 38. O Lord, revive thy work in the midst of the years, in the midst of the years make known; in wrath remember mercy. *Hab. iii.* 2. They got not the land in possession by their own sword, neither did their own arm save them: but thy right hand, and thine arm, and the light of thy countenance, because thou hadst a favour unto them. *Ps. xliv.* 3. Wherefore the king hearkened not unto the people; for the cause was from the Lord, that he might perform his saying, which the Lord spake by Ahijah the Shilonite unto Jeroboam the son of Nebat. 1 *Ki. xii.* 15. And David said unto his men, The Lord forbid that I should do this thing unto my master, the Lord's anointed, to stretch forth mine hand against him, seeing he is the anointed of the Lord. 1 *Sa. xxiv.* 6. *See also, The Character and History of king Josiah, and his removal " from the evil to come."* 2 *Ki.* xxii. xxiii.—2 *Ch.* xxxiv, xxxv. *and the Character of the Jewish nation as set forth in the Book of the Prophet Jeremiah, his cotemporary and surviver.*

2. yet thou didst not leave us for ever, as sheep without a

2. The Lord our God be with us, as he was with our fathers: let him not leave us, nor forsake us. 1 *Ki. viii.* 57. And he said, I saw all Israel scattered upon the hills, as sheep that

shepherd; but by thy gracious providence didst miraculously preserve the undoubted Heir of his Crowns, our then gracious Sovereign King *Charles* the Second, from his bloody enemies, hiding him under the shadow of thy wings, until their tyranny was overpast;

have not a shepherd. 1 *Ki. xxii.* 17. Will the Lord cast off for ever? and will he be favourable no more? *Ps. lxxvii.* 7. The Lord will not cast off his people, neither will he forsake his inheritance. *Ps. xciv.* 14. But Jehosheba, the daughter of king Joram, sister of Ahaziah, took Joash the son of Ahaziah, and stole him from among the king's sons which were slain; and they hid him, even him and his nurse, in the bed-chamber from Athaliah, so that he was not slain. And he was with her hid in the house of the Lord six years. 2 *Ki. xi.* 2, 3. Keep me as the apple of the eye, hide me under the shadow of thy wings, from the wicked that oppress me, from my deadly enemies, who compass me about. *Ps. xvii.* 8, 9. Deliver me from the workers of iniquity, and save me from bloody men. For, lo, they lie in wait for my soul: the mighty are gathered against me; not for my transgression, nor for my sin, O Lord. *Ps. lix.* 2, 3. Be merciful unto me, O God, be merciful unto me: for my soul trusteth in thee: and under the shadow of thy wings shall be my refuge, until this tyranny be overpast. *Ps. lvii.* 1.

3. And didst bring him back in thy good appointed time, to sit upon the throne of his Father; and together with the Royal Family didst restore to us our ancient Government in Church and State.

3. And the seventh year Jehoiada sent and fetched the rulers over hundreds, with the captains and the guard, and brought them to him into the house of the Lord, and made a covenant with them, and took an oath of them in the house of the Lord, and shewed them the king's son. And he brought forth the king's son, and put the crown upon him, and gave him the testimony; and they made him king, and anointed him; and they clapped their hands, and said, God save the king. And Jehoiada made a covenant between the Lord and the king and the people, that they should be the Lord's people; between the king also and the people. And all the people of the land went into the house of Baal, and brake it down; his altars and his images brake they in pieces thoroughly, and slew Mattan the priest of Baal before the altars. And the priest appointed officers over the house of the Lord. And he took the rulers over hundreds, and the captains, and the guard, and all the people of the land; and they brought down the king from the house of the Lord, and came by the way of the gate of the guard to the king's house. And he sat on the throne of the kings. And all the people of the land

rejoiced, and the city was in quiet. 2 *Ki. xi.* 4. 12. 17 *to* 20. *See also,* 2 *Sa. xix.* 9 *to* 12.—1 *Ki. i.* 47.—1 *Ch. xxix.* 22 *to* 25.

4. For these thy great and unspeakable mercies we render to thee our most humble and unfeigned thanks ; beseeching thee, still to continue thy gracious protection over the whole Royal-Family,

4. Now therefore, our God, we thank thee, and praise thy glorious name. 1 *Ch. xxix.* 13. Blessed be the Lord, who hath not given us a prey to their teeth. *Ps. cxxiv.* 6. Blessed be the Lord : for he hath shewed me his marvellous kindness in a strong city. *Ps. xxxi.* 21. Praise ye the Lord. O give thanks unto the Lord ; for he is good : for his mercy endureth for ever. Who can utter the mighty acts of the Lord ? who can shew forth all his praise? *Ps. cvi.* 1, 2. O give thanks unto the Lord ; for he is good ; for his mercy endureth for ever. And say ye, Save us, O God of our salvation, and deliver us, that we may give thanks to thy holy name, and glory in thy praise. Blessed be the Lord God of Israel, for ever and ever. 1 *Ch. xvi.* 34, 35, 36. Blessed be the Lord God of Israel, which hath given one to sit on my throne this day. 1 *Ki. i.* 48. Thus saith the Lord of hosts, I will set up thy seed after thee, and I will establish his kingdom. And now, O Lord God, thou art that God, and thy words be true, and thou hast promised this goodness unto thy servant : therefore now let it please thee to bless the house of thy servant, that it may continue for ever before thee : for thou, O Lord God, hast spoken it : and with thy blessing let the house of thy servant be blessed for ever. 2 *Sa. vii.* 8. 12. 28, 29. Hide me from the secret counsel of the wicked ; from the insurrection of the workers of iniquity. *Ps. lxiv.* 2. Keep me as the apple of the eye, hide me under the shadow of thy wings. *Ps. xvii.* 8. *See also,* 2 *Sa. xviii.* 28.

5. and to grant to our gracious Sovereign King *William,* a long and a happy Reign over us : So we that are thy people will give thee thanks for ever, and will alway be shewing forth thy praise from generation to

5. Hear my cry, O God ; attend unto my prayer. From the end of the earth will I cry unto thee, when my heart is overwhelmed : lead me to the rock that is higher than I. For thou hast been a shelter for me, and a strong tower from the enemy. I will abide in thy tabernacle for ever : I will trust in the covert of thy wings. For thou, O God, hast heard my vows : thou hast given me the heritage of those that fear thy name. Thou wilt prolong the king's life : and his years as many generations. He shall abide before God for ever : O prepare mercy and truth, which may preserve him. So will I sing praise unto thy name for ever, that I may daily perform

2 R

generation ; through Jesus Christ our Lord and Saviour. *Amen.*

my vows. *Ps.* LXI. The king shall joy in thy strength, O Lord; and in thy salvation how greatly shall he rejoice ! For thou preventest him with the blessings of goodness : thou settest a crown of pure gold on his head. He asked life of thee, and thou gavest it him, even length of days for ever and ever. *Ps. xxi.* 1. 3, 4. King Solomon shall be blessed, and the throne of David shall be established before the Lord for ever. And the kingdom was established in the hand of Solomon. 1 *Ki.* ii. 45, 46. Thou hast confirmed to thyself thy people Israel to be a people unto thee for ever : and thou, Lord, art become their God. And now, O Lord God, the word that thou hast spoken concerning thy servant, and concerning his house, establish it for ever, and do as thou hast said. And let thy name be magnified for ever, saying, The Lord of hosts is the God over Israel : and let the house of thy servant David be established before thee. 2 *Sa. vii.* 24, 25, 26. One generation shall praise thy works to another, and shall declare thy mighty acts. I will speak of the glorious honour of thy majesty, and of thy wondrous works. And men shall speak of the might of thy terrible acts : and I will declare thy greatness. They shall abundantly utter the memory of thy great goodness, and shall sing of thy righteousness. *Ps. cxlv.* 4 *to* 7. So we thy people and sheep of thy pasture will give thee thanks for ever : we will shew forth thy praise to all generations. *Ps. lxxix.* 13.

And grant, O Lord, we beseech thee, &c. *as* LXXXIII.

THE ORDER FOR EVENING PRAYER.

The Hymn.—Righteous art thou, &c.
The Proper Psalms, LXXIX, XCIV, LXXXV.
The Proper Lessons.—Je. XII. or Da. IX. 1 *to* 22. *and He. XI.* 32 *to* 40.—*and XII.* 1 *to* 7.

CCLXXXIX. *A Prayer that the guilt of innocent blood may be averted from the Land.*

1. O Almighty Lord God, who by thy wisdom not only guidest and orderest all things most suitably to thine own justice ; but also performest thy

1. Lord God Almighty. *Re. iv.* 8. Behold, God is mighty ; he is mighty in strength and wisdom. *Job xxxvi.* 5. He is wise in heart. *Job ix.* 4. For ever, O Lord, thy word is settled in heaven. Thy faithfulness is unto all generations : thou hast established the earth, and it abideth. They continue this day according to thine ordinances ; for all things serve thee. *Ps. cxix.* 89, 90, 91. Justice and judgment are the habitation of thy throne. *Ps. lxxxix.* 14. Righteous art thou, O

pleasure in such a manner, that we cannot but acknowledge thee to be righteous in all thy ways, and holy in all thy works :

Lord, and upright are thy judgments. *Ps. cxix.* 137. Shall not the Judge of all the earth do right? *Ge. xviii.* 25. Whatsoever the Lord pleased, that did he in heaven, and in earth, in the seas, and all deep places. *Ps. cxxxv.* 6. The just Lord is in the midst thereof; he will not do iniquity: every morning doth he bring his judgment to light, he faileth not. *Zep. iii.* 5. The Lord's voice crieth unto the city, and the man of wisdom shall see thy name. *Mi. vi.* 9. The Lord is righteous in all his ways, and holy in all his works. *Ps. cxlv.* 17.

2. We thy sinful people do here fall down before thee, confessing that thy judgments were right, in permitting cruel men, sons of Belial, (as on this day) to imbrue their hands in the blood of thine Anointed ; we having drawn down the same upon ourselves, by the great and long provocations of our sins against thee.

2. We have sinned with our fathers, we have committed iniquity, we have done wickedly. *Ps. cvi.* 6. I know, O Lord, that thy judgments are right, and that thou in faithfulness hast afflicted me. *Ps. cxix.* 75. Thou art just in all that is brought upon us ; for thou hast done right, but we have done wickedly. *Ne. ix.* 33. He is the Rock, his work is perfect: for all his ways are judgment: a God of truth and without iniquity, just and right is he. *De. xxxii.* 4. The crown is fallen from our head: woe unto us, that we have sinned! for this our heart is faint ; for these things our eyes are dim. *La. v.* 16, 17. Because they have shed innocent blood in their land. *Joel iii.* 19. O Lord, righteousness belongeth unto thee, but unto us confusion of faces, as at this day ; to the men of Judah, and to the inhabitants of Jerusalem, and unto all Israel, that are near, and that are far off, through all the countries whither thou hast driven them, because of their trespass that they have trespassed against thee. O Lord, to us belongeth confusion of face, to our kings, to our princes, and to our fathers, because we have sinned against thee. *Da. ix.* 7, 8.

3. For which we do therefore here humble ourselves before thee ; beseeching thee to deliver this Nation from bloodguiltiness, (that of this day especially,) and to turn from us and our poste-

3. Humble yourselves therefore under the mighty hand of God, that he may exalt you in due time. 1 *Pe. v.* 6. Humble yourselves in the sight of the Lord, and he shall lift you up. *Ja. iv.* 10. Deliver me from bloodguiltiness, O God, thou God of my salvation. *Ps. li.* 14. When David heard it, he said, I and my kingdom are guiltless before the Lord for ever from the blood of Abner, the son of Ner : let it rest on the head of Joab, and on all his father's house. 2 *Sa. iii.* 28, 29. I the Lord thy God am a jealous God, visiting the iniquity of the fathers upon the children unto the third and fourth gene-

rity, all those judgments, which we by our sins have worthily deserved: Grant this, for the all-sufficient merits of thy Son our Saviour Jesus Christ. Amen.

ration of them that hate me. *Ex. xx.* 5. I pray before thee now and confess the sins of the children of Israel, which we have sinned against thee : both I and my father's house have sinned. We have dealt very corruptly against thee, and have not kept the commandments, nor the statutes, nor the judgments, which thou commandedst. *Ne. i.* 6, 7. Turn away my reproach which I fear : for thy judgments are good. *Ps. cxix.* 39. We acknowledge, O Lord, our wickedness, and the iniquity of our fathers : for we have sinned against thee. Do not abhor us, for thy name's sake, do not disgrace the throne of thy glory : remember, break not thy covenant with us. *Je. xiv.* 20, 21. Help us, O God of our salvation, for the glory of thy name : and deliver us, and purge away our sins, for thy name's sake. *Ps. lxxix.* 9. Hear thou their prayer and their supplication in heaven thy dwelling place, and forgive thy people that have sinned against thee. 1 *Ki. viii.* 49, 50. Thus saith the Lord; Like as I have brought all this great evil upon this people, so will I bring upon them all the good that I have promised them. *Je. xxxii.* 42. The blood of Jesus Christ his Son cleanseth us from all sin. 1 *John i.* 7. Unto him that loved us, and washed us from our sins in his own blood, and hath made us kings and priests unto God and his Father; to him be glory and dominion for ever and ever. Amen. *Re. i.* 5, 6.

CCXC. *A Commemoration of God's goodness to King Charles the First.*

I. Blessed God, just and powerful, who didst permit thy dear Servant, our dread Sovereign King Charles the First, to be (as upon this day) given up to the violent outrages of wicked men, to be despitefully used, and at the last murdered by them :

1. There is no God else beside me; a just God and a Saviour; there is none beside me. *Is. xlv.* 21. God hath spoken once, yea; twice have I heard this, that power belongeth unto God. *Ps. lxii.* 11. Shall there be evil in a city, and the Lord hath not done it ? *Am. iii.* 6. Behold, O Lord, and consider to whom thou hast done this. *La. ii.* 20. O God, the proud are risen against me, and the assemblies of violent men have sought after my soul; and have not set thee before them. *Ps. lxxxvi.* 14. The breath of our nostrils, the anointed of the Lord, was taken in their pits. *La. vi.* 20. Fear was on every side : while they took counsel together against me, they devised to take away my life. *Ps. xxxi.* 13.

2. Though we cannot reflect upon so foul an act, but with horror and astonishment; yet do we most gratefully commemorate the glories of thy grace, which then shined forth in thine Anointed; whom thou wast pleased, even at the hour of death, to endue with an eminent measure of exemplary patience, meekness, and charity, before the face of his cruel enemies.

2. Horror hath taken hold upon me because of the wicked that forsake thy law. My flesh trembleth for fear of thee; and I am afraid of thy judgments. I beheld the transgressors, and was grieved. *Ps. cxix.* 53. 120. 158. Thou hast shewed thy people hard things: thou hast made us to drink the wine of astonishment. *Ps. lx.* 3. God is our refuge and strength, a very present help in trouble. *Ps. xlvi.* 1. I will be glad and rejoice in thy mercy; for thou hast considered my trouble; thou hast known my soul in adversities. *Ps. xxxi.* 7. He said unto me, My grace is sufficient for thee: for my strength is made perfect in weakness. *2 Co. xii.* 9. The Lord preserveth the simple: I was brought low, and he helped me. *Ps. cxvi.* 6. Strengthened with all might according to his glorious power, unto all patience. *Col. i.* 11. The fruit of the Spirit is meekness. *Ga. v.* 22, 23. And they stoned Stephen, calling upon God, and saying, Lord Jesus, receive my spirit. And he kneeled down, and cried with a loud voice, Lord, lay not this sin to their charge. And when he had said this, he fell asleep. *Ac. vii.* 59, 60. Blessed are ye, when men shall revile you, and persecute you, and shall say all manner of evil against you falsely, for my sake. I say unto you, Love your enemies, bless them that curse you, do good to them that hate you, and pray for them which despitefully use you, and persecute you. *Mat. v.* 11. 44. Though I walk through the valley of the shadow of death, I will fear no evil: for thou art with me; thy rod and thy staff they comfort me. Thou preparest a table before me in the presence of mine enemies. *Ps. xxiii.* 4, 5.

3. And albeit thou didst suffer them to proceed to such an height of violence, as to kill him, and to take possession of his Throne; yet didst thou in great mercy preserve his Son, whose right it was, and at length by a wonderful providence bring him

3. Thus saith the Lord, Hast thou killed, and also taken possession? *1 Ki. xxi.* 19. He that sitteth in the heaven shall laugh: the Lord shall have them in derision. *Ps. ii.* 4. The Lord bringeth the counsel of the heathen to nought: he maketh the devices of the people of none effect. *Ps. xxxiii.* 10. When Athaliah the mother of Ahaziah saw that her son was dead, she arose and destroyed all the seed royal of the house of Judah. But Jehoshabeath, the daughter of the king, took Joash the son of Ahaziah, and stole him from among the king's sons that were slain, and put him and his nurse in a bed-chamber. And he was with them hid in the house of God six years. *2 Ch. xxii.* 10, 11, 12. And I will bring the blind by a way that

back, and set him thereon, to restore thy true Religion, and to settle peace amongst us : For these thy great mercies we glorify thy Name, through Jesus Christ our blessed Saviour. *Amen.*

they know not; I will lead them in paths that they have not known : I will make darkness light before them, and crooked things straight. These things will I do unto them, and not forsake them. *Is. xlii.* 16. Then they brought out the king's son, and put upon him the crown, and gave him the testimony, and made him king. And Jehoiada and his sons anointed him, and said, God save the king. And Jehoiada made a covenant between him, and between all the people, and between the king, that they should be the Lord's people. Then all the people went to the house of Baal and brake it down, and brake his altars and his images in pieces, and slew Mattan the priest of Baal before the altars. Also Jehoiada appointed the officers of the house of the Lord by the hand of the priests the Levites, whom David had distributed in the house of the Lord to offer the burnt offerings of the Lord, as it is written in the law of Moses, with rejoicing and with singing, as it was ordained by David. And they came through the high gate into the king's house, and set the king upon the throne of the kingdom. And all the people of the land rejoiced : and the city was quiet. *2 Ch. xxiii.* 11. 16, 17, 18. 20, 21. And Judah and Israel dwelt safely, every man under his vine, and under his figtree, from Dan even to Beersheba, all the days of Solomon. *1 Ki. iv.* 25. Peace be within thy walls, and prosperity within thy palaces. For my brethren and companion's sakes, I will now say, Peace be within thee. *Ps. cxxii.* 7, 8. Give unto the Lord the glory due unto his name. *Ps. xxix.* 2. His mercies are great. *2 Sa. xxiv.* 14. I will glorify thy name for evermore. *Ps. lxxxvi.* 12. Giving thanks always for all things unto God and the Father in the name of our Lord Jesus Christ. *Ep. v.* 20.

CCXCI. *A Prayer for Grace to persevere in a life of holiness.*

1. Almighty and everlasting God, whose righteousness is like the strong mountains, and thy judgments like the great deep ; and who, by that barba-

1. The Lord reigneth : clouds and darkness are round about him : righteousness and judgment are the habitation of his throne. *Ps. xcvii.* 1, 2. Thy righteousness standeth like the strong mountains : thy judgments are like the great deep. *Ps. xxxvi.* 6. Ahithophel said unto Absalom, Let me now choose out twelve thousand men, and I will arise and pursue after David this night : and I will come upon him while he

rous murder(as is weary and weak-handed; and I will smite the king only.
on this day)
committed 2 *Sa. xvii.* 1, 2. They said one to another, Behold this
upon the dreamer cometh. Come now, therefore, and let us slay him,
sacred Person
of thine and cast him into some pit, and we will say, Some evil beast
Anointed, hast hath devoured him. *Ge. xxxvii.* 19, 20. And the archers
taught us, that
neither the shot at king Josiah; and the king said to his servants, Have
greatest of
Kings, nor the me away; for I am sore wounded. 2 *Ch. xxxv.* 23. Then
best of men, said these men, We shall not find any occasion against this
are more secure
from violence Daniel, except we find it against him concerning the law of
than from
natural death: his God. They assembled, and found Daniel praying and
making supplication before his God. Then they came near,
and spake before the king concerning the king's decree. Then
the king commanded, and they brought Daniel, and cast him
into the den of lions. *Da. vi.* 5. 11, 12. 16. Others had
trial of cruel mockings and scourgings, yea, moreover of
bonds and imprisonment: they were stoned, they were sawn
asunder, were tempted, were slain with the sword: they wandered about in sheepskins and goatskins; being destitute, afflicted, tormented; (of whom the world was not worthy;)
they wandered in deserts, and in mountains, and in dens and
caves of the earth. *He. xi.* 36, 37, 38.

2. Teach us 2. So teach us to number our days, that we may apply
also hereby so our hearts unto wisdom. *Ps. xc.* 12. Whatsoever thy
to number our
days, that we hand findeth to do, do it with thy might. *Ec. ix.* 10. O that
may apply our men were wise, that they understood this, that they would
hearts unto
wisdom. And consider their latter end! *De. xxxii.* 29. Mind not high
grant, that
neither the things. *Ro. xii.* 16. In my prosperity I said, I shall never
splendour of be moved. Lord, by thy favour thou hast made my mountain
any thing that
is great, nor to stand strong: thou didst hide thy face, and I was troubled.
the conceit of *Ps. xxx.* 6, 7. The king spake, and said, Is not this great
any thing that
is good in us, Babylon, that I have built for the house of the kingdom by the
may withdraw might of my power, and for the honour of my majesty? While
our eyes from
looking upon the word was in the king's mouth, there fell a voice from hea-
ourselves as
sinful dust and ven, saying, O king Nebuchadnezzar, to thee it is spoken;
ashes; The kingdom is departed from thee. And they shall drive
thee from men, and thy dwelling shall be with the beasts of
the field. *Da. iv.* 30, 31, 32. The Pharisee stood and prayed
thus with himself, God, I thank thee, that I am not as other
men are, or even as this publican.—The ruler said, All

these have I kept from my youth up. Now when Jesus heard these things, he said unto him, Yet lackest thou one thing. *Lu. xviii.* 11. 21, 22. Let him that thinketh he standeth take heed lest he fall. 1 *Co. x.* 12. Be not wise in thine own eyes : fear the Lord, and depart from evil. *Pr. iii.* 7. I know that in me, that is, in my flesh, dwelleth no good thing. *Ro. vii.* 18. Dust thou art, and unto dust shalt thou return. *Ge. iii.* 19. And Abraham answered and said, Behold now, I have taken upon me to speak unto the Lord, which am but dust and ashes. *Ge. xviii.* 27.

3. but that, according to the example of this thy blessed Martyr, we may press forward to the prize of the high calling that is before us, in faith and patience, humility and meekness, mortification and self-denial, charity and constant perseverance unto the end : And all this for thy Son our Lord Jesus Christ his sake, to whom with thee and the Holy Ghost be all honour and glory, world without end. *Amen.*

3. Be not slothful, but followers of them who through faith and patience inherit the promises. *He. vi.* 12. I press toward the mark for the prize of the high calling of God in Christ Jesus. *Ph. iii.* 14. The Holy Ghost witnesseth in every city, saying that bonds and afflictions abide me. But none of these things move me, neither count I my life dear unto myself, so that I might finish my course with joy. *Ac. xx.* 23, 24. Put on therefore, as the elect of God, holy and beloved, bowels of mercies, kindness, humbleness of mind, meekness, longsuffering; forbearing one another, and forgiving one another, if any man have a quarrel against any : even as Christ forgave you, so also do ye. *Col. iii.* 12, 13. Then said Jesus unto his disciples, If any man will come after me, let him deny himself, and take up his cross, and follow me. *Mat. xvi.* 24. They that are Christ's have crucified the flesh with the affections and lusts. *Ga. v.* 24. Mortify therefore your members which are upon the earth. *Col. iii.* 5. Beside this, giving all diligence, add to your faith virtue ; and to virtue knowledge ; and to knowledge temperance ; and to temperance patience ; and to patience godliness; and to godliness brotherly kindness ; and to brotherly kindness charity. 2 *Pe. i.* 5, 6, 7. Be not weary in well doing. 2 *Th. iii.* 13. Watching thereunto with all perseverance. *Ep. vi.* 18. He that shall endure unto the end, the same shall be saved. *Mat. xxiv.* 13. For we are made partakers of Christ, if we hold the beginning of our confidence stedfast unto the end. *He. iii.* 14. I thank Christ Jesus our Lord, who hath enabled me. The grace of our Lord was exceeding abundant with faith and love which is in Christ Jesus. Now to the king eternal, immortal, invisible, the only wise God, be honour and glory for ever and ever. Amen. 1 *Ti. i.* 12. 14. 17.

A FORM OF

PRAYER WITH THANKSGIVING,

To be used yearly on the Twenty-ninth day of May.

The Sentences.—*To the Lord our God belong mercies and forgivenesses, though we have rebelled against him : neither have we obeyed the voice of the Lord our God, to walk in his laws which he set before us.* Dan. ix. 9, 10. *It is of the Lord's mercies that we were not consumed : because his compassions fail not.* Lam. iii. 22.

The Hymn.—*My song shall be alway of the loving-kindness of the Lord : with my mouth will I ever be shewing forth his truth from one generation to another.* Psal. lxxxix. 1. *The merciful and gracious Lord hath so done his marvellous works ; that they ought to be had in remembrance.* Psal. cxi. 4. *Who can express the noble acts of the Lord : or shew forth all his praise ?* Psal. cvi. 2. *The works of the Lord are great : sought out of all them that have pleasure therein.* Psal. cxi. 2. *The Lord setteth up the meek : and bringeth the ungodly down to the ground.* Psal. cxlvii. 6. *The Lord executeth righteousness and judgment : for all them that are oppressed with wrong. For he will not alway be chiding : neither keepeth he his anger for ever. He hath not dealt with us after our sins : nor rewarded us according to our wickedness. For look how high the heaven is in comparison of the earth : so great is his mercy toward them that fear him. Yea, like as a father pitieth his own children : even so is the Lord merciful unto them that fear him.* Psal. ciii. 6. 9, 10, 11. 13. *Thou, O God, hast proved us : thou also hast tried us, even as silver is tried. Thou sufferedst men to ride over our heads, we went through fire and water : but thou hast brought us out into a wealthy place.* Psal. lxvi. 9. 11. *O how great troubles and adversities hast thou shewed us ! and yet didst thou turn and refresh us : yea, and broughtest us from the deep of the earth again.* Psal. lxxi. 18. *Thou didst remember us in our low estate, and redeem us from our enemies : for thy mercy endureth for ever.* Psal. cxxxvi. 23, 24. *Lord, thou art become gracious unto thy land : thou hast turned away the captivity of Jacob.* Psal. lxxxv. 1. *God hath shewed us his goodness plenteously : and God hath let us see our desire upon our enemies.* Psal. lix. 10. *They are brought down and fallen : but we are risen and stand upright.* Psal. xx. 8. *There are they fallen, all that work wickedness : they are cast down, and shall not be able to stand.* Psal. xxxvi. 12. *The Lord hath been mindful of us, and he shall bless us : even he shall bless the house of Israel, he shall bless the house of Aaron. He shall bless them that fear the Lord : both small and great.* Psal. cxv. 12, 13. *O that men would therefore praise the Lord for his goodness : and declare the wonders that he doeth for the children of men ! That they would offer unto him the sacrifice of thanksgiving : and tell out his works with gladness !* Psal. cvii. 21, 22. *And not hide them from the children of the generations to come : but shew the honour of the Lord, his mighty and wonderful works that he hath done ! That our posterity may also know them, and the children that are yet unborn : and not be as their forefathers a faithless and stubborn generation.* Psal. lxxviii. 4. 6. 9. *Give thanks, O Israel, unto God the Lord in the congregations ; from the ground of the heart. Praised be the Lord daily ; even the God who helpeth us, and poureth his benefits upon us.* Psal. lxviii. 26. 19. *O let the wickedness of the wicked come to an end : but establish thou the righteous.* Psal. vii. 9. *Let all those that seek thee be joyful and glad in thee ; and let all such as love thy salvation say alway, The Lord be praised.* Psal. xl. 19.

Glory be to the Father, &c.

As it was in the beginning, &c.

Proper Psalms, CXXIV. CXXVI. CXXXIX. CXVIII.
The Proper Lessons, 2 Sam. XIX. 9. *or Numb. XVI. Epistle of St. Jude.*

2 s

CCXCII. *The Suffrages or Responses.*

1, 2. O Lord, shew thy mercy upon us ; and grant us thy salvation.

1, 2. Shew us thy mercy, O Lord, and grant us thy salvation. *Ps. lxxxv.* 7.

3, 4. O Lord, save the King, who putteth his trust in thee.

3, 4. And Samuel said to all the people, See ye him whom the Lord hath chosen, that there is none like him among all the people ? And all the people shouted, and said, God save the king. 1 *Sa. x.* 24. For the king trusteth in the Lord, and through the mercy of the Most High he shall not be moved. *Ps. xxi.* 7. Preserve my soul: for I am holy : O thou my God, save thy servant that trusteth in thee. *Ps. lxxxvi.* 2.

5, 6. Send him help from thy holy place ; and evermore mightily defend him.

5, 6. The Lord hear thee in the day of trouble ; the name of the God of Jacob defend thee. Send thee help from the sanctuary, and strengthen thee out of Zion. *Ps. xx.* 1, 2.

7, 8. Let his enemies have no advantage against him ; let not the wicked approach to hurt him.

7, 8. The enemy shall not be able to do him violence: the son of wickedness shall not hurt him. I will smite down his foes before his face : and plague them that hate him. *Ps. lxxxix.* 23, 24.

9, 10. Endue thy Ministers with righteousness ; and make thy chosen people joyful.

9, 10. Let thy priests be clothed with righteousness ; and let thy saints shout for joy. I will also clothe her priests with salvation : and her saints shall shout aloud for joy. *Ps. cxxxii.* 9. 16.

11, 12. Give peace in our time, O Lord ; because there is none other that fighteth for us, but only thou, O God.

11, 12. Lord, thou wilt ordain peace for us : for thou also hast wrought all our works in us. *Is. xxvi.* 12. Behold, a son shall be born to thee, who shall be a man of rest ; and I will give him rest from all his enemies round about: for his name shall be Solomon, and I will give peace and quietness unto Israel in his days. 1 *Ch. xxii.* 9. Give us help from trouble : for vain is the help of man. *Ps. lx.* 2. The Lord shall fight for you, and ye shall hold your peace. *Ex. xiv.* 14. With him is an arm of flesh; but with us is the Lord our God to fight our battles. *2 Ch. xxxii.* 8.

13, 14. Be unto us, O Lord, a strong tower, from the face of our enemies.

13, 14. Thou hast been a shelter for me, and a strong tower from the enemy. *Ps. lxi.* 3.

15, 16. O Lord, hear our prayer; and let our cry come unto thee.

15, 16. Hear my cry, O God; attend unto my prayer. *Ps. lxi.* 1.

CCXCIII. *A Thanksgiving for deliverance from the Rebellion.*

1. O Almighty God, who art a strong tower of defence unto thy servants against the face of their enemies; We yield thee praise and thanksgiving for the wonderful deliverance of these Kingdoms from THE GREAT REBELLION, and all the Miseries and Oppressions consequent thereupon, under which they had so long groaned.

1. And David spake unto the Lord the words of this song in the day that the Lord had delivered him out of the hand of all his enemies, and out of the hand of Saul: and he said, The Lord is my rock, and my fortress, and my deliverer; the God of my rock; in him will I trust: he is my shield, and the horn of my salvation, my high tower, and my refuge. Thou hast girded me with strength to battle: them that rose up against me hast thou subdued under me. The Lord liveth; and blessed be my rock; and exalted be the God of the rock of my salvation. Therefore I will give thanks unto thee, O Lord, among the heathen, and I will sing praises unto thy name. *2 Sa. xxii.* 1, 2, 3. 40. 47. 50. It is God that avengeth me, and subdueth the people unto me. Thou hast delivered me from the strivings of the people. He delivereth me from mine enemies: yea, thou liftest me up above those that rise up against me: thou hast delivered me from the violent man. Great deliverance giveth he to his king; and sheweth mercy to his anointed, to David, and to his seed for evermore. *Ps. xviii.* 47. 43. 48. 50. For thou, O God, hast proved us: thou hast tried us, as silver is tried. Thou broughtest us into the net; thou laidest affliction upon our loins. Thou hast caused men to ride over our heads; we went through fire and through water: but thou broughtest us out into a wealthy place. *Ps. lxvi.* 10, 11, 12. And in those times there was no

peace to him that went out, nor to him that came in, but great vexations were upon all the inhabitants of the countries. And nation was destroyed of nation, and city of city : for God did vex them with all adversity. 2 *Ch. xv.* 5, 6. God heard their groaning, and God remembered his covenant. *Ex. ii.* 24. They that are delivered from the noise of archers in the places of drawing water, there shall they rehearse the righteous acts of the Lord, even the righteous acts toward the inhabitants of his villages in Israel. *Jud. v.* 11,

2. We acknowledge it thy goodness, that we were not utterly delivered over as a prey unto them; beseeching thee still to continue such thy mercies towards us, that all the world may know that thou art our Saviour and mighty Deliverer; through Jesus Christ our Lord. *Amen.*

2. Blessed be the Lord, who hath not given us as a prey to their teeth. *Ps. cxxiv.* 6. The Lord was my stay. He brought me forth also into a large place: he delivered me, because he delighted in me. He sent from above, he took me; he drew me out of many waters; he delivered me from my strong enemy, and from them that hated me: for they were too strong for me. 2 *Sa. xxii.* 19, 20. 17, 18. Not unto us, O Lord, not unto us, but unto thy name give glory, for thy mercy, and for thy truth's sake. *Ps. cxv.* 1. Continue thy lovingkindness unto them that know thee; and thy righteousness to the upright in heart. *Ps. xxxvi.* 10. Help me, O Lord my God: O save me according to thy mercy: that they may know that this is thy hand; that thou, Lord, hast done it. *Ps. cix.* 26, 27. That men may know that thou, whose name alone is JEHOVAH, art the Most High over all the earth. *Ps. lxxxiii.* 18. That all the earth may know that there is a God in Israel. 1 *Sa. xvii.* 46. O sing unto the Lord a new song; for he hath done marvellous things: his right hand, and his holy arm, hath gotten him the victory. The Lord hath made known his salvation: his righteousness hath he openly shewed in the sight of the heathen. He hath remembered his mercy and his truth toward the house of Israel: all the ends of the earth have seen the salvation of our God. *Ps. xcviii.* 1, 2, 3. Thou art my help and my deliverer. *Ps. lxx.* 5. O the hope of Israel, the Saviour thereof in time of trouble! *Je. xiv.* 8. I will make my holy name known in the midst of my people Israel; and the heathen shall know that I am the Lord, the Holy One in Israel. *Eze. xxxix.* 7.

CCXCIV. *A Promise of obedience to God and the King.*

1. O Lord God of our salvation, who hast been exceedingly gracious unto this land, and by thy miraculous providence didst deliver us out of our miserable confusions; by restoring to us, and to his own just and undoubted Rights, our then most gracious Sovereign Lord, King *Charles* the Second, notwithstanding all the power and malice of his enemies;

1. O God of our salvation, who art the confidence of all the ends of the earth, and of them that are afar off upon the sea. *Ps. lxv.* 5. Lord, thou art become gracious unto thy land, thou hast turned away the captivity of Jacob. Thou hast taken away all thy displeasure: and turned thyself from thy wrathful indignation. *Ps. lxxxv.* 1. 3. Now for a long season Israel hath been without the true God, and without a teaching priest, and without law. And in those times there was no peace to him that went out, nor to him that came in. *2 Ch. xv.* 3. 5. And Jehoiada sent and fetched the rulers over hundreds, with the captains and the guard, and shewed them the king's son. And he brought forth the king's son, and put the crown upon him, and gave him the testimony; and they made him king, and anointed him; and they clapped their hands, and said, God save the king. *2 Ki. xi.* 4. 12. It is God that avengeth me, and that bringeth down the people under me, and that bringeth me forth from mine enemies: thou also hast lifted me up on high above them that rose up against me. *2 Sa. xxii.* 48, 49. They are brought down and fallen: but we are risen, and stand upright. *Ps. xx.* 8.

2. and, by placing him on the Throne of these Kingdoms, didst restore also unto us the public and free profession of thy true Religion and Worship, together with our former Peace and Prosperity, to the great comfort and joy of our hearts:

2. Thou hast caused men to ride over our heads; we went through fire and through water: but thou broughtest us out into a wealthy place. *Ps. lxvi.* 12. The Most High ruleth in the kingdom of men, and giveth it to whomsoever he will. *Da. iv.* 25. And Jehoiada made a covenant between the Lord and the king and the people, that they should be the Lord's people; between the king also and the people. And he took the rulers over hundreds; and the captains, and the guard, and all the people of the land; and they brought down the king from the house of the Lord; and he sat on the throne of the kings. And all the people of the land rejoiced, and the city was in quiet. *2 Ki. xi.* 17. 19, 20. And they entered into a covenant to seek the Lord God of their fathers, with all their heart and with all their soul; that whosoever would not seek the Lord God of Israel should be put to death, whether small or great, whether man or woman. And all Judah rejoiced at the oath: and the Lord gave them rest round about. *2 Ch. xv.* 12, 13. 15.

3. We are here now before thee, with all due thankfulness, to acknowledge thine unspeakable goodness herein, as upon this day shewed unto us, and to offer unto thee our sacrifice of praise for the same;

3. Now therefore are we all here present before God. *Ac. x.* 33. Now therefore, our God, we thank thee, and praise thy glorious name. 1 *Ch. xxxix.* 13. And Ezra blessed the Lord, the great God. And all the people answered, Amen, Amen, with lifting up their hands: and they bowed their heads, and worshipped the Lord with their faces to the ground. *Ne. viii.* 6. David blessed the Lord before all the congregation: and David said, Blessed be thou, Lord God of Israel our Father, for ever and ever. And David said to all the congregation, Now bless the Lord your God. And all the congregation blessed the Lord God of their fathers, and bowed down their heads, and worshipped the Lord. 1 *Ch. xxix.* 10. 20. Oh that men would praise the Lord for his goodness, and for his wonderful works to the children of men! And let them sacrifice the sacrifices of thanksgiving, and declare his works with rejoicing. *Ps. cvii.* 21, 22. I will offer unto thee the sacrifice of thanksgiving, and will call upon the name of the Lord. *Ps. cxvi.* 17. At that time Solomon held a feast, and all Israel with him, a great congregation, before the Lord our God. On the eighth day the people went unto their tents joyful and glad of heart for all the goodness that the Lord had done for David his servant, and for Israel his people. 1 *Ki. viii.* 65, 66.

4. humbly beseeching thee to accept this our unfeigned, though unworthy oblation of ourselves; vowing all holy obedience in thought, word, and work, unto thy Divine Majesty; and promising all loyal and dutiful Allegiance to thine Anointed Servant now set over us, and to his Heirs after him;

4. I beseech you, brethren, by the mercies of God, that ye present your bodies a living sacrifice, holy, acceptable unto God, which is your reasonable service. *Ro. xii.* 1. Bringing into captivity every thought to the obedience of Christ. 2 *Co. x.* 5. Accept, I beseech thee, the free-will offerings of my mouth, O Lord. *Ps. cxix.* 108. All the people answered with one voice, and said, All the words which the Lord hath said, will we do. And he took the book of the covenant, and read in the audience of the people: and they said, All that the Lord hath said will we do, and be obedient. *Ex. xxiv.* 3. 7. In mine holy mountain, in the mountain of the height of Israel, saith the Lord God, there shall all the house of Israel serve me: there will I accept them. I will accept you with your sweet savour, when I bring you out from the people, and gather you out of the countries wherein ye have been scattered. *Eze. xx.* 40, 41. Jehoiada made

a covenant between him, and between all the people, and between the king, that they should be the Lord's people. 2. *Ch. xxiii.* 16. And the king went up into the house of the Lord, and all the people, great and small : and the king stood in his place, and made a covenant before the Lord, to walk after the Lord, and to keep his commandments, and his testimonies, and his statutes, with all his heart, and with all his soul, to perform the words of the covenant. And he caused all that were present in Jerusalem and Benjamin to stand to it. And the Inhabitants of Jerusalem did according to the covenant of God, the God of their fathers. 2 *Ch. xxxiv.* 30, 31, 32. So all the elders of Israel came to the king to Hebron ; and king David made a league with them in Hebron before the Lord : and they anointed David king over Israel. 2 *Sa. v.* 3. *See also,* 1 *Ki. i.* 32 *to* 39.

5. Whom we beseech thee to bless with all increase of grace, honour and happiness, in this world, and to crown him with immortality and glory in the world to come, for Jesus Christ his sake our only Lord and Saviour. *Amen.*

5. I exhort therefore, that, first of all, supplications, prayers, intercessions, and giving of thanks, be made for all men ; for kings, and for all that are in authority ; that we may lead a quiet and peaceable life in all godliness and honesty. 1 *Ti. ii.* 1, 2. Let it please thee to bless the house of thy servant, that it may be before thee for ever : for thou blessest, O Lord, and it shall be blessed for ever. 1 *Ch. xvii.* 27. Give the king thy judgments, O God, and thy righteousness unto the king's son. *Ps. lxxii.* 1. The Lord that made heaven and earth bless thee out of Zion. *Ps. cxxxiv.* 3. Be thou faithful unto death, and I will give thee a crown of life. *Re. ii.* 10. The salvation which is in Christ Jesus with eternal glory. 2 *Ti. ii.* 10. The world to come. *He. ii.* 5. *See also, Ps. xxi.* 3 *to* 6.

CCXCV. *A Thanksgiving and Ascription of Praise to God.*

1. Almighty God, who hast in all ages shewed forth thy power and mercy in the miraculous and gracious deliverances of thy Church, and in the protection of

1. Lord, thou hast been our dwelling place in all generations. *Ps. xc.* 1. He ruleth by his power for ever. *Ps. lxvi.* 7. His mercy is everlasting. *Ps. c.* 5. He will ever be mindful of his covenant. *Ps. cxi.* 5. This is he, that was in the church in the wilderness. *Ac. vii.* 38. And the waters returned, and covered the chariots, and the horsemen, and all the host of Pharaoh that came into the sea after them ; there remained not so much as one of them. Thus the Lord saved

righteous and religious Kings and States, professing thy holy and eternal truth, from the malicious Conspiracies and wicked Practices of all their enemies:

Israel that day out of the hand of the Egyptians; and Israel saw the Egyptians dead upon the sea shore. *Ex. xiv.* 28. 30. The Lord our God, he it is that brought us up and our fathers out of the land of Egypt, from the house of bondage, and which did those great signs in our sight, and preserved us in all the way wherein we went, and among all the people through whom we passed. *Jos. xxiv.* 17. Many a time have they afflicted me from my youth, may Israel now say: many a time have they afflicted me from my youth: yet they have not prevailed against me. *Ps. cxxix.* 1, 2. The Lord preserved David whithersoever he went. 2 *Sa. viii.* 6. Thus saith the Lord concerning the king of Assyria, He shall not come into this city, nor shoot an arrow there, nor come before it with shield, nor cast a bank against it. For I will defend this city, to save it, for mine own sake, and for my servant David's sake. *2 Ki. xix.* 32. 34. Then I proclaimed a fast there, at the river of Ahava, that we might afflict ourselves before our God, to seek of him a right way for us, and for our little ones, and for all our substance. For I was ashamed to require of the king a band of soldiers and horsemen to help us against the enemy in the way: because we had spoken unto the king, saying, The hand of our God is upon all them for good that seek him; but his power and his wrath is against all them that forsake him. So we fasted and besought our God for this: and he was intreated of us. Then we departed from the river of Ahava on the twelfth day of the first month, to go unto Jerusalem; and the hand of our God was upon us, and he delivered us from the hand of the enemy, and of such as lay in wait by the way. *Ezr. viii.* 21, 22, 23. 31. Blessed is the nation whose God is the Lord; and the people whom he hath chosen for his own inheritance. *Ps. xxxiii.* 12. Blessed be the Lord God of Israel; for he hath visited and redeemed his people, and hath raised up an horn of salvation for us in the house of his servant David. That we should be saved from our enemies, and from the hand of all that hate us. *Lu. i.* 68, 69. 71.

2. We yield unto thee our unfeigned thanks and

2. O give thanks unto the Lord; call upon his name: make known his deeds among the people. Sing unto him, sing psalms unto him; talk ye of all his wondrous works. Glory ye

praise, as for his holy name: let the heart of them rejoice that seek the
thy many other Lord. *Ps. cv.* 1, 2, 3. And Israel saw that great work which
great and pub- the Lord did upon the Egyptians: and the people feared the
lic mercies, so
especially for Lord, and believed the Lord, and his servant Moses. *Ex. xiv.*
that signal and 31. The merciful and gracious Lord hath so done his marvel-
wonderful De-
liverance, by lous works: that they ought to be had in remembrance. *Ps. cxi.*
thy wise and 4. O give thanks unto the Lord; for he is good. O give
good Provi-
dence as upon thanks unto the God of gods; to him who alone doeth great
this Day com- wonders; for his mercy endureth for ever. *Ps. cxxxvi.* 1, 2. 4.
pleted, and
vouchsafed to And David perceived that the Lord had established him king
our then most over Israel, and that he had exalted his kingdom for his peo-
gracious Sove-
reign King ple Israel's sake. 2. *Sa. v.* 12. And David spake unto the
Charles the Lord the words of this song in the day that the Lord had de-
Second, and all
the Royal Fa- livered him out of the hand of all his enemies, and out of the
mily, and in hand of Saul. I will call on the Lord, who is worthy to be
them, to this
whole Church praised. He delivered me from my strong enemy, and from
and State, and them that hated me, for they were too strong for me. Thou
all orders and
degrees of men hast also given me the necks of mine enemies. Thou also hast
in both, from delivered me from the strivings of my people. Thou hast de-
the unnatural
Rebellion, livered me from the violent man. 2 *Sa. xxii.* 1. 4. 18. 41. 44.
Usurpation, 49. Great deliverance giveth he to his king; and sheweth
and Tyranny
of ungodly and mercy to David and to his seed for evermore. *Ps. xviii.* 50.
cruel men, and 3. They got not the land in possession by their own sword,
from the sad
confusions and neither did their own arm save them: but thy right hand, and
ruin thereupon thine arm, and the light of thy countenance, because thou hadst
ensuing.
a favour unto them. Thou hast saved us from our enemies,
3. From all and hast put them to shame that hated us. In God we boast
these, O gra-
cious and mer- all the day long, and praise thy name for ever. *Ps. xliv.* 3.
ciful Lord God, 7, 8. It is of the Lord's mercies that we are not consumed,
not our merit,
but thy mercy; because his compassions fail not. *La. iii.* 22. Asa cried un-
not our fore- to the Lord his God, and said, Lord, it is nothing with thee
sight, but thy
Providence; to help, whether with many, or with them that have no power:
not our own help us, O Lord our God; for we rest on thee, and in thy
arm, but thy
right hand, and name we go against this multitude. 2 *Ch. xiv.* 11. See *also,*
thine arm, did *Est. viii.* 7, 8. 10, 11. 16.—*ix.* 21, 22.
rescue and
deliver us.

4. And there- 4. Not unto us, O Lord, not unto us, but unto thy name
fore, not unto give glory, for thy mercy, and for thy truth's sake. *Ps. cxv.* 1.
us, O Lord, not
unto us, but Thine is the kingdom, and the power, and the glory, for ever.
unto thy Name Amen. *Mat. vi.* 13. Blessing, and honour, and glory, and
be ascribed all

2 T

Honour, and Glory, and Praise, with most humble and hearty thanks, in all Churches of the Saints: Even so blessed be the Lord our God, who alone doeth wondrous things, and blessed be the Name of his Majesty for ever; through Jesus Christ our Lord and only Saviour. *Amen.*	power, be unto him that sitteth upon the throne, and unto the Lamb for ever and ever. *Re. v.* 13. Unto thee, O God, do we give thanks, unto thee do we give thanks; for that thy name is near thy wondrous works declare. For promotion cometh neither from the east, nor from the west, nor from the south. But God is the Judge, he putteth down one, and setteth up another. *Ps. lxxv.* 1. 6, 7. Now unto him that is able to do exceeding abundantly above all that we ask or think, according to the power that worketh in us, unto him be glory in the Church by Christ Jesus throughout all ages, world without end. Amen. *Ep. iii.* 20, 21. In his temple doth every one speak of his glory. *Ps. xxix.* 9. Blessed be the Lord God, even the God of Israel; which only doeth wondrous things; and blessed be the name of his Majesty for ever: and all the earth shall be filled with his Majesty. Amen, Amen. *Ps. lxxii.* 18, 19.

The Epistle. 1 Pe. ii. 11.—*Dearly beloved, I beseech you as strangers and pilgrims, abstain from fleshly lusts, which war against the soul; having your conversation honest among the Gentiles: that, whereas they speak against you as evil doers, they may, by your good works which they shall behold, glorify God in the day of visitation. Submit yourselves to every ordinance of man for the Lord's sake; whether it be to the King, as supreme; or unto governors, as unto them that are sent by him for the punishment of evil doers, and for the praise of them that do well. For so is the will of God, that with well-doing ye may put to silence the ignorance of foolish men: as free, and not using your liberty for a cloke of maliciousness, but as the servants of God. Honour all men. Love the brotherhood. Fear God. Honour the King.*

The Gospel. Mat. xxii. 16.—*And they sent out unto him their disciples, with the Herodians, saying, Master, we know that thou art true, and teachest the way of God in truth, neither carest thou for any man: for thou regardest not the person of men. Tell us therefore, What thinkest thou? Is it lawful to give tribute unto Cæsar, or not? But Jesus perceived their wickedness, and said, Why tempt ye me, ye hypocrites? Shew me the tribute-money. And they brought unto him a penny. And he saith unto them, whose is this image and superscription? They say unto him, Cæsar's. Then saith he unto them, Render therefore unto Cæsar, the things which are Cæsar's; and unto God, the things that are God's. When they had heard these words, they marvelled, and left him, and went their way.*

CCXCVI. *A Thanksgiving for deliverance from enemies, and Prayer for future protection.*

1. Almighty God and heavenly Father, who, of thine infinite and unspeakable goodness towards us, didst in a most extraordinary and wonderful	1. Our God hath not forsaken us in our bondage, but hath extended mercy unto us, to give us a reviving, to set up the house of our God, and to repair the desolations thereof, and to give us a wall in Judah and in Jerusalem. *Ezr. ix.* 9. For thy great mercies' sake thou didst not utterly consume them, for thou art a gracious and merciful God. *Ne. ix.* 31. The Lord bringeth the counsel of the heathen to nought: he

manner disappoint and overthrow the wicked designs of those traiterous, heady, and highminded men, who, under the pretence of Religion, and thy most holy Name, had contrived, and well-nigh effected the utter destruction of this Church and Kingdom:

maketh the devices of the people of none effect. The counsel of the Lord standeth for ever, the thoughts of his heart to all generations. *Ps. xxxiii.* 10, 11. He disappointeth the devices of the crafty, so that their hands cannot perform their enterprise. He taketh the wise in their own craftiness: and the counsel of the froward is carried headlong. *Job v.* 12, 13. The heathen are sunk down in the pit that they made: in the net which they hid is their own foot taken. The Lord is known by the judgment which he executeth: the wicked is snared in the work of his own hands. *Ps. ix.* 15, 16. And they [Korah, Dathan, and Abiram] gathered themselves together against Moses and against Aaron, and said unto them, Ye take too much upon you, seeing all the congregation are holy. And Moses said, Hereby ye shall know that the Lord hath sent me to do all these works; for I have not done them of mine own mind. If these men die the common death of all men, or if they be visited after the visitation of all men; then the Lord hath not sent me. But if the Lord make a new thing, and the earth open her mouth, and swallow them up, with all that appertain unto them, and they go down quick into the pit; then ye shall understand that these men have provoked the Lord.—And the earth opened her mouth, and swallowed them up, and their houses, and all the men that appertained unto Korah, and all their goods. And there came out a fire from the Lord, and consumed the two hundred and fifty men that offered incense. And Aaron stood between the dead and the living; and the plague was stayed. Now they that died in the plague were fourteen thousand and seven hundred, beside them that died about the matter of Korah. *Nu. xvi.* 3. 28, 29, 30. 32. 35. 48, 49.

2. As we do this day most heartily and devoutly adore and magnify thy glorious Name for this thine infinite goodness already vouchsafed to us; so do we most humbly beseech thee to

2. The Jews ordained, and took upon them, and upon their seed, and upon all such as joined themselves unto them, so as it should not fail, that they would keep these two days according to their writing, and according to their appointed time every year; and that these days should be remembered and kept throughout every generation, every family, every province, and every city; and that these days of Purim should not fail from among the Jews, nor the memorial of them perish from their seed. *Est. ix.* 27, 28. Oh that men would

continue thy grace and favour towards us, that no such dismal calamity may ever again fall upon us.

praise the Lord for his goodness, and for his wonderful works to the children of men! *Ps. cvii.* 21. Now therefore, our God, we thank thee, and praise thy glorious name. 1 *Ch. xxix.* 13. O continue thy lovingkindness unto them that know thee; and thy righteousness to the upright in heart. Let not the foot of pride come against me, and let not the hand of the wicked remove me. *Ps. xxxvi.* 10, 11. Deliver me not over unto the will of mine enemies. *Ps. xxvii.* 12.

3. Infatuate and defeat all the secret counsels of deceitful and wicked men against us. Abate their pride, assuage their malice, and confound their devices.

3. And David said, O Lord, I pray thee, turn the counsel of Ahithophel into foolishness. 2 *Sa. xv.* 31. Keep me, O Lord, from the hands of the wicked; preserve me from the violent man; who have purposed to overthrow my goings. The proud have hid a snare for me, and cords; they have spread a net by the way-side; they have set gins for me. Grant not, O Lord, the desires of the wicked; further not his wicked device; lest they exalt themselves. *Ps. cxl.* 4, 5. 8. Hide me from the secret counsel of the wicked; from the insurrection of the workers of iniquity. *Ps. lxiv.* 2. The wicked in his pride doth persecute the poor: let them be taken in the devices that they have imagined. *Ps. x.* 2. And the afflicted people thou wilt save: but thine eyes are upon the haughty, that thou mayest bring them down. 2 *Sa. xxii.* 28. And he shall bring down their pride together with the spoils of their hands. *Is. xxv.* 11. Let them be confounded and put to shame that seek after my soul: let them be turned back and brought to confusion that devise my hurt. *Ps. xxxv.* 4. The Lord bringeth the counsel of the heathen to nought: and maketh the devices of the people to be of none effect. *Ps. xxxiii.* 10. See also, *Is. xliv.* 24, 25.

4. Strengthen the hands of our gracious Sovereign King William, and all that are put in authority under him, with judgment and justice to cut off all such workers of iniquity, as turn Religion into Rebellion, and Faith into Fac-

4. I exhort that, first of all, supplications, prayers, intercessions, and giving of thanks, be made for all men; for kings, and for all that are in authority. 1 *Ti. ii.* 1, 2. The Lord send thee help from the sanctuary, and strengthen thee out of Zion. *Ps. xx.* 1, 2. Give the king thy judgments, O God, and thy righteousness unto the king's son. He shall judge the poor of the people, he shall save the children of the needy, and shall break in pieces the oppressor. *Ps. lxxii.* 1. 4. He is the minister of God to thee for good. But if thou do that which is evil, be afraid; for he beareth not the sword in

tion; that they may never again prevail against us, nor triumph in the ruin of the Monarchy and thy Church among us.

vain: for he is the minister of God, a revenger to execute wrath upon him that doeth evil. *Ro. xiii.* 4. He shall bring upon them their own iniquity, and shall cut them off in their own wickedness; yea, the Lord our God shall cut them off. *Ps. xciv.* 23. For, lo, thine enemies, O Lord, for, lo, thine enemies shall perish; all the workers of iniquity shall be scattered. But my horn shalt thou exalt like the horn of an unicorn: I shall be anointed with fresh oil. *Ps. xcii.* 9, 10. O Lord, thou art our God; let not man prevail against thee. 2 *Ch. xiv.* 11. And it came to pass after forty years, that Absalom said unto the king, I pray thee, let me go and pay my vow, which I have vowed unto the Lord, in Hebron. For thy servant vowed a vow while I abode at Geshur in Syria, saying, If the Lord shall bring me again indeed to Jerusalem, then I will serve the Lord. But Absalom sent spies throughout all the tribes of Israel, saying, As soon as ye hear the sound of the trumpet, then ye shall say, Absalom reigneth in Hebron. 2 *Sa. xv.* 7, 8. 10. Arise, O Lord; save me, O my God: for thou hast smitten all mine enemies upon the cheek bone; thou hast broken the teeth of the ungodly. Salvation belongeth unto the Lord: thy blessing is upon thy people. *Ps. iii.* [" *a psalm of David when he fled from Absalom*"] 7, 8. And Nathan said, My lord, O king, hast thou said, Adonijah shall reign after me, and he shall sit upon my throne? For he is gone down this day, and hath slain oxen and fat cattle and sheep in abundance, and hath called all the king's sons, and the captains of the host, and Abiathar the priest; and, behold, they eat and drink before him, and say, God save king Adonijah. But me, even me thy servant, and Zadok the priest, and Benaiah the son of Jehoiada, and thy servant Solomon, hath he not called. Is this thing done by my lord the king? Then king David answered and said, Call me Bathsheba. And she came into the king's presence and stood before the king. And the king sware, and said, As the Lord liveth, that hath redeemed my soul out of all distress, even as I sware unto thee by the Lord God of Israel, saying, Assuredly Solomon thy son shall reign after me, and he shall sit upon my throne in my stead; even so will I certainly do this day. Then Bathsheba bowed with her face to the earth, and did reverence to the king. And king David said, Call me Zadok the priest, and Nathan the prophet, and Benaiah the son of Jehoiada. And they came before the king. The king also said unto them, Take with you the servants of your lord, and cause Solomon my son to ride upon mine own mule, and bring him down to Gihon: and let Zadok the priest and Nathan the prophet anoint him there king over Israel: and blow ye with the trumpet, and say, God save king Solomon. And Zadok the priest took an horn of oil out of the tabernacle, and anointed Solomon. And they blew the trumpet; and all the people said, God save king Solomon. So king Solomon sent, and they brought Adonijah down from the altar. And Solomon said unto him, Go to thine house. 1 *Ki. i.* 24 *to* 34. 39. 53. *See also,* 1 *Ki. ii.* 26 *to* 46.

5. Protect and defend our Sovereign Lord the King, with the whole Royal Family, from all Treasons and Conspiracies. Be unto him an helmet of salvation, and a strong tower of defence against the face of all his enemies; clothe them with shame and confusion, but upon Himself and hisPosterity let the Crown for ever flourish.

5. The Lord hear thee in the day of trouble, the name of the God of Jacob defend thee. *Ps. xx.* 1. The king shall joy in thy strength, O Lord; and in thy salvation how greatly shall he rejoice! For the king trusteth in the Lord, and through the mercy of the Most High he shall not be moved. *Ps. xxi.* 1. 7. No weapon that is formed against thee shall prosper; and every tongue that shall rise against thee in judgment thou shalt condemn. This is the heritage of the servants of the Lord. *Is. liv.* 17. O God the Lord, the strength of my salvation, thou hast covered my head in the day of battle. *Ps. cxl.* 7. Thou hast been a shelter for me, and a strong tower from the enemy. *Ps. lxi.* 3. The name of the Lord is a strong tower; the righteous runneth into it, and is safe. *Pr. xviii.* 10. Let them be ashamed and confounded that seek after my soul; let them be turned backward, and put to confusion, that desire my hurt. *Ps. lxx.* 2. His enemies will I clothe with shame: but upon himself shall his crown flourish. *Ps. cxxxii.* 18. And it shall come to pass, when thy days be expired that thou must go to be with thy fathers, that I will raise up thy seed after thee, which shall be of thy sons; and I will establish his kingdom. I will be his Father, and he shall be my son. Now therefore let it please thee to bless the house of thy servant, that it may be before thee for ever. 1 *Ch. xvii.* 11. 13. 27.

6. So we thy people, and the sheep of thy pasture, will give thee thanks for ever, and will always be shewing forth thy praise from generation to generation; through Jesus Christ our only Saviour and Redeemer, to whom with thee O Father, and the Holy Ghost, be glory in the Church throughout all ages, world without end. Amen.

6. So we, that are thy people, and sheep of thy pasture, shall give thee thanks for ever : and will alway be shewing forth thy praise from generation to generation. *Ps. lxxix.* 14. the eighth day he sent the people away : and they blessed the king, and went unto their tents joyful and glad of heart for all the goodness that the Lord had done for David his servant, and for Israel his people. 1 *Ki. viii.* 66. O Lord my God, I will give thanks unto thee for ever. *Ps. xxx.* 12. I will mention the lovingkindnesses of the Lord, and the praises of the Lord, according to all that the Lord hath bestowed on us, and the great goodness toward the house of Israel, which he hath bestowed on them according to his mercies, and according to the multitude of his lovingkindnesses. He was their Saviour. In all their affliction he was afflicted, and the angel of his presence saved them: in his love and in his pity he redeemed them. *Is. lxiii.* 7, 8, 9. Now unto him that is able to do exceeding abundantly above all that we can ask or think, according to the power that worketh in us, unto him be glory in the Church by Christ Jesus throughout all ages, world without end. Amen. *Ep. iii.* 20, 21.

A FORM OF

PRAYER WITH THANKSGIVING,

To be used on the Anniversary of the King's Accession.

The Sentences.—*I exhort that first of all, Supplications, Prayers, Intercessions, and giving of Thanks, be made for all men; for Kings, and for all that are in authority; that we may lead a quiet and peaceable life, in all godliness and honesty: for this is good and acceptable unto God our Saviour.* 1 Ti. ii. 1, 2, 3. *If we say that we have no sin, we deceive ourselves, and the truth is not in us; but, if we confess our sins, he is faithful and just to forgive us our sins, and to cleanse us from all unrighteousness.* 1 John i. 8, 9.

The Hymn.—*O Lord our Governor: how excellent is thy name in all the world!* Ps. viii. 1. *Lord, what is man, that thou hast such respect unto him: or the son of man, that thou so regardest him?* Ps. cxliv. 3. *The merciful and gracious Lord hath so done his marvellous works: that they ought to be had in remembrance.* Ps. cxi. 4. *Oh that men would therefore praise the Lord for his goodness: and declare the wonders that he doeth for the children of men!* Ps. cvii. 21. *Behold, O God our Defender: and look upon the face of thine Anointed.* Ps. lxxxiv. 9. *O hold thou up his goings in thy paths: that his footsteps slip not.* Ps. xvii. 5. *Grant the King a long life: and make him glad with the joy of thy countenance. Let him dwell before thee for ever: O prepare thy loving mercy and faithfulness, that they may preserve him.* Ps. lxi. 6, 7. and xxi. 6. *In his time let the righteous flourish: and let peace be in all our borders.* Ps. lxxii. 7. and cxlvii. 14. *As for his enemies, clothe them with shame: but upon himself let his crown flourish.* Ps. cxxxii. 19. *Blessed be the Lord God, even the God of Israel; which only doeth wondrous things. And blessed be the Name of his Majesty for ever; and all the earth shall be filled with his Majesty. Amen, Amen.* Ps. lxxii. 18, 19.

Proper Psalms, XX. XXI. CI.
The Proper Lessons, Josh. I. 1 to 9.—Rom. XIII.

The Suffrages, as CCXCII.

CCXCVII.—A Thanksgiving for his Majesty's Accession to the Throne.

1. Almighty God, who rulest over all the kingdoms of the world, and disposest of them according to thy good pleasure; We yield thee unfeigned thanks, for that thou wast pleased, as on this day, to place thy Servant our Sovereign Lord, King William

1. And Hezekiah prayed before the Lord, and said, O Lord God of Israel, which dwellest between the cherubims, thou art the God, even thou alone, of all the kingdoms of the earth; thou hast made heaven and earth. *2 Ki. xix.* 15. And [Jehoshaphat] said, O Lord God of our fathers, art not thou God in heaven? and rulest not thou over all the kingdoms of the heathen? and in thine hand is there not power and might, so that none is able to withstand thee? *2 Ch. xx.* 6. God putteth down one, and setteth up another. *Ps. lxxv.* 7. The Most High ruleth in the kingdom of men, and giveth it to whomsoever he will. *Da. iv.* 25. O praise the Lord; for it is a good thing to sing praises unto our God: yea, a joyful and pleasant thing it is to be thankful. *Ps. cxlvii.* 1. Let us

2 u

upon the Throne of this Realm.

come before his presence with thanksgiving, and make a joyful noise unto him with psalms. *Ps. xcv.* 2. Enter into his gates with thanksgiving, and into his courts with praise : be thankful unto him, and bless his name. *Ps. c.* 4. Then they brought out the king's son, and put upon him the crown, and gave him the testimony, and made him king. And Jehoiada and his sons anointed him, and said, God save the king. And, behold, the king stood at his pillar, and the princes and the trumpets by the king : and all the people of the land rejoiced, and sounded with trumpets, also the singers with instruments of music, and such as taught to sing praise. 2 *Ch. xxiii.* 11. 13. And it came to pass, when Hiram heard the words of Solomon, that he rejoiced greatly, and said, Blessed be the Lord this day, which hath given unto David a wise son over this great people. 1 *Ki. v.* 7.

2. Let thy wisdom be his guide, and let thine arm strengthen him ; let justice, truth, and holiness, let peace and love, and all those virtues that adorn the Christian Profession, flourish in his days ;

2. Now, my son, the Lord be with thee ; and prosper thou. Only the Lord give thee wisdom and understanding, and give thee charge concerning Israel, that thou mayest keep the law of the Lord thy God. 1 *Ch. xxii.* 11, 12. And Solomon said unto God, Thou hast made me king over a people like the dust of the earth in multitude. Give me now wisdom and knowledge, that I may go out and come in before this people. 2 *Ch. i.* 8, 9, 10. Thou shalt guide me with thy counsel. *Ps. lxxiii.* 24. I have found David my servant ; with my holy oil have I anointed him : with whom my hand shall be established : mine arm also shall strengthen him. *Ps. lxxxix.* 20, 21. Pray for the peace of Jerusalem : they shall prosper that love thee. Peace be within thy walls, and prosperity within thy palaces. *Ps. cxxii.* 6, 7. That they may adorn the doctrine of God our Saviour in all things. *Tit. ii.* 10. Give the king thy judgments, O God, and thy righteousness unto the king's son. He shall judge thy people with righteousness, and thy poor with judgment. He shall judge the poor of the people, he shall save the children of the needy, and shall break in pieces the oppressor. In his days shall the righteous flourish ; and abundance of peace so long as the moon endureth. *Ps. lxxii.* 1, 2. 4. 7.

3. direct all his counsels

3. Thou, Solomon my son, know thou the God of thy father, and serve him with a perfect heart and with a willing

and endeavours to thy glory and the welfare of his people;

mind. 1 *Ch. xxviii.* 9. In all thy ways acknowledge him, and he shall direct thy paths. *Pr. iii.* 6. Whatsoever ye do, do all to the glory of God. 1 *Co. x.* 31. Solomon sent to Hiram, saying, Now the Lord my God hath given me rest on every side, so that there is neither adversary nor evil occurrent. And, behold, I purpose to build an house unto the name of the Lord my God. 1 *Ki. v.* 2. 4, 5. And thus did Hezekiah throughout all Judah, and wrought that which was good and right and truth before the Lord his God. And in every work that he began in the service of the house of God, and in the law, and in the commandments, to seek his God, he did it with all his heart, and prospered. 2 *Ch. xxxi.* 20, 21. And now, O Lord my God, thou hast made thy servant king instead of David my father: and I am but a little child: I know not how to go out or come in. Give therefore thy servant an understanding heart to judge thy people, that I may discern between good and bad. 1 *Ki. iii.* 7. 9. It is he that giveth salvation unto kings: who delivereth David his servant from the hurtful sword. Rid me, and deliver me from the hand of strange children. That our sons may be as plants grown up in their youth; that our daughters may be as corner stones, polished after the similitude of a palace: that our garners may be full, affording all manner of store: that our sheep may bring forth thousands and ten thousands in our streets: that our oxen may be strong to labour; that there be no breaking in, nor going out; that there be no complaining in our streets. *Ps. cxliv.* 10 to 14.

4. and give us grace to obey him cheerfully and willingly for conscience sake; that neither our sinful passions, nor our private interests, may disappoint his cares for the public good;

4. My son, fear thou the Lord and the king: and meddle not with them that are given to change. *Pr. xxiv.* 21. He is the minister of God to thee for good. Wherefore ye must needs be subject, not only for wrath, but also for conscience sake. *Ro. xiii.* 4, 5. Thus saith the Lord, Behold, I will bring evil upon this place, and upon the inhabitants thereof, even all the words of the book which the king of Judah hath read: because they have forsaken me, and have burned incense unto other gods, that they might provoke me to anger with all the works of their hands. 2 *Ki. xxii.* 16, 17. I [Nehemiah] made treasurers over the treasuries, and their office was to distribute unto their brethren. In those days saw I in

Judah some treading wine presses on the sabbath, and bringing in sheaves, and lading asses; as also wine, grapes, and
figs, and all manner of burdens, which they brought into Jerusalem on the sabbath day : and I testified against them in
the day wherein they sold victuals. There dwelt men of
Tyre also therein, which brought fish, and all manner of
ware, and sold on the sabbath unto the children of Judah, and
in Jerusalem. And I commanded the Levites that they should
cleanse themselves, and that they should come and keep the
gates, to sanctify the sabbath day. In those days also saw I
Jews that had married wives of Ashdod, of Ammon, and of
Moab : and I contended with them, and cursed them, and
smote certain of them, and plucked off their hair, and made
them swear by God, saying, Ye shall not give your daughters unto their sons, nor take their daughters unto your sons,
or for yourselves. Did not Solomon king of Israel sin by
these things ? *Ne. xiii.* 13. 15, 16. 22, 23. 25, 26.

5. let him always possess the hearts of his people, that they may never be wanting in honour to his Person, and dutiful sub-mission to his Authority; let his Reign be long and pros-perous, and crown him with immorta-lity in the life to come; through Jesus Christ our Lord. *Amen.*

5. If thou wilt be a servant unto this people this day, and
wilt serve them, and answer them, and speak good words to
them, then they will be thy servants for ever. 1 *Ki. xii.* 7.
And all the people took notice of it, and it pleased them : as
whatsoever the king did pleased all the people. 2 *Sa. iii.* 36.
But the people answered, Thou shalt not go forth: for if we
flee away, they will not care for us; neither if half of us
die, will they care for us : but now thou art worth ten thousand of us. And he bowed the heart of all the men of Judah,
even as the heart of one man; so that they sent this word
unto the king, Return thou, and all thy servants. 2 *Sa. xviii.*
3.—*xix.* 14. Honour the king. 1 *Pe. ii.* 17. Then Bathsheba bowed with her face to the earth, and did reverence to
the king, and said, Let my Lord king David live for ever.
1 *Ki. i.* 31. Submit yourselves to every ordinance of man
for the Lord's sake: whether it be to the king, as supreme;
or unto governors, as unto them that are sent by him for the
punishment of evil doers, and for the praise of them that do
well. 1 *Pe. ii.* 13, 14. It is God that subdueth the people
unto me. *Ps. xviii.* 47. His glory is great in thy salvation:
honour and majesty hast thou laid upon him. *Ps. xxi.* 5. Thou
wilt prolong the king's life: and his years as many genera-

tions. He shall abide before God for ever: O prepare mercy and truth, which may preserve him. *Ps. lxi.* 6, 7. O Lord, I beseech thee, send now prosperity. *Ps. cxviii.* 25. Henceforth there is laid up for me a crown of righteousness, which the Lord, the righteous Judge, shall give me at that day: and not to me only, but unto all them also that love his appearing. *2 Ti. iv.* 8. Be thou faithful unto death, and I will give thee a crown of life. *Re. ii.* 10.

CCXCVIII.—*A Prayer for the King and the Royal Family.*

1. O Lord our God, who upholdest and governest all things in heaven and earth; receive our humble prayers, with our hearty thanksgivings, for our Sovereign Lord William, as on this day, set over us by thy grace and providence to be our King; and so together with him bless our gracious Queen Adelaide, and all the Royal Family;

1. The kingdom is the Lord's: and he is the governor among the nations. *Ps. xxii.* 28. Upholding all things by the word of his power. *He. i.* 3. O Lord God of hosts, hear my prayer: give ear, O God of Jacob. *Ps. lxxxiv.* 8. Hear my prayer, O God; give ear to the words of my mouth. I will freely sacrifice unto thee: I will praise thy name, O Lord; for it is good. *Ps. liv.* 2. 6. Accept, I beseech thee, the freewill offerings of my mouth, O Lord. *Ps. cxix.* 108. I will praise thee, O Lord my God, with all my heart. *Ps. lxxxvi.* 12. I will offer to thee the sacrifice of thanksgiving. *Ps. cxvi.* 17. And it came to pass, when Hiram heard the words of Solomon, that he rejoiced greatly, and said, Blessed be the Lord this day, which hath given unto David a wise son over this great people. *1 Ki. v.* 7. The Most High ruleth in the kingdom of men, and giveth it to whomsoever he will. *Da. iv.* 17. I have found David my servant; with my holy oil have I anointed him: with whom my hand shall be established: mine arm also shall strengthen him. *Ps. lxxxix.* 20, 21. And the king said, As the Lord liveth, that hath redeemed my soul out of all distress, even as I sware unto thee by the Lord God of Israel, saying, Assuredly Solomon thy son shall reign after me, and he shall sit upon my throne in my stead: even so will I certainly do this day. And Zadok the priest took an horn of oil and anointed Solomon. And they blew the trumpet; and all the people said, God save king Solomon. And all the people came up after him; and the people piped with pipes, and rejoiced with great joy, so that the earth rent with the sound of them. Then sat Solomon upon the throne of David his father; and his kingdom

was established greatly. The king said moreover, King Solomon shall be blessed, and the throne of David shall be established before the Lord for ever. And the kingdom was established in the hand of Solomon. 1 *Ki. i.* 29, 30. 39, 40. *ii.* 12. 44, 45, 46. He sheweth mercy to his anointed, unto David, and to his seed for evermore. 2 *Sa. xxii.* 51. That they may offer sacrifices of sweet savours unto the God of heaven, and pray for the life of the king, and of his sons. *Ezr. vi.* 10.

2. that they all, ever trusting in thy goodness, protected by thy power, and crowned with thy gracious and endless favour, may continue before thee in health, peace, joy, and honour, and may live long and happy lives upon earth, and after death obtain everlasting life and glory in the kingdom of heaven, by the Merits and Mediation of Christ Jesus our Saviour, who with the Father and the Holy Spirit, liveth and reigneth ever one God, world without end. *Amen.*

2. The king shall joy in thy strength, O Lord; and in thy salvation how greatly shall he rejoice! Thou preventest him with the blessings of goodness: thou settest a crown of pure gold on his head. He asked life of thee, and thou gavest it him, even length of days for ever and ever. His glory is great in thy salvation: honour and majesty hast thou laid upon him. Thou hast made him exceeding glad with thy countenance. For the king trusteth in the Lord, and through the mercy of the Most High he shall not be moved. *Ps. xxi.* 1. 3 *to* 7. God is my strength and power. 2 *Sa. xxii.* 33. Remember me, O Lord, with the favour that thou bearest unto thy people. *Ps. cvi.* 4. In his favour is life. *Ps. xxx.* 5. O Lord, I beseech thee, send now prosperity. *Ps. cxviii.* 25. I am continually with thee: thou hast holden me by my right hand. *Ps. lxxiii.* 23. Surely he shall deliver thee from the snare of the fowler, and from the noisome pestilence. He shall cover thee with his feathers, and under his wings shalt thou trust: his truth shall be thy shield and buckler. *Ps. xci.* 3, 4. The steps of a good man are ordered by the Lord: and he delighteth in his way. For the Lord loveth judgment, and forsaketh not his saints; they are preserved for ever. Wait on the Lord, and keep his way, and he shall exalt thee to inherit the land. Mark the perfect man, and behold the upright: for the end of that man is peace. *Ps. xxxvii.* 23. 28. 34. 37. I have also given thee that which thou hast not asked, both riches, and honour. And if thou wilt walk in my ways, to keep my statutes and my commandments, as thy father David did walk, then I will lengthen thy days. 1 *Ki. iii.* 13, 14. Be thou faithful unto death, and I will give thee a crown of life. *Re. ii.* 10. For thou shalt give the king everlasting felicity. *Ps.*

xxi. 6. To them who by patient continuance in well doing seek for glory and honour and immortality, eternal life. *Ro. ii.* 7. For so an entrance shall be ministered unto you abundantly into the everlasting kingdom of our Lord and Saviour Jesus Christ. 2 *Pe. i.* 11. When Christ, who is our life, shall appear, then shall ye also appear with him in glory. *Col. iii.* 4. For as in Adam all die, even so in Christ shall all be made alive. 1 *Co. xv.* 22. Now unto the king eternal, immortal, invisible, the only wise God, be honour and glory for ever and ever. Amen. 1 *Ti. i.* 17.

CCXCIX. A Prayer for God's protection of the King against all his Enemies.

1. Most gracious God, who hast set thy Servant *William* our King upon the Throne of his Ancestors, we most humbly beseech thee to protect him on the same from all the dangers to which he may be exposed;	1. The Lord hath sought him a man after his own heart, and the Lord hath commanded him to be captain over his people. 1 *Sa. xiii.* 14. And David perceived that the Lord had established him king over Israel, and that he had exalted his kingdom for his people Israel's sake. 2 *Sa. v.* 12. I have found David my servant: with my holy oil have I anointed him: with whom my hand shall be established: mine arm also shall strengthen him. The enemy shall not exact upon him; nor the son of wickedness afflict him. And I will beat down his foes before his face, and plague them that hate him. *Ps. lxxxix.* 20 *to* 23. The king trusteth in the Lord, and through the mercy of the Most High he shall not be moved. *Ps. xxi.* 7.
2. Hide him from the gathering together of the froward, and from the insurrection of wicked doers; Do thou weaken the hands, blast the designs, and defeat the enterprizes of all his enemies, that no secret conspiracies, nor open	2. Hide me from the gathering together of the froward: and from the insurrection of wicked doers. *Ps. lxiv.* 2. Thou shalt hide them in the secret of thy presence from the pride of man: thou shalt keep them secretly in a pavilion from the strife of tongues. *Ps. xxxi.* 20. He weakeneth the hands of the men of war. *Je. xxxviii.* 4. Let mine adversaries be clothed with shame, and let them cover themselves with their own confusion, as with a mantle. *Ps. cix.* 29. Break their teeth, O God, in their mouth, break out the great teeth of the young lions, O Lord. Let them melt away as waters which run continually: when he bendeth his bow to shoot his arrows, let them be as cut in pieces. *Ps. lviii.* 6, 7. He poureth

violences, may contempt upon princes, and weakeneth the strength of the
disquiet his mighty.   He discovereth deep things out of darkness, and
Reign ; bringeth out to light the shadow of death. *Job xii.* 21, 22.
His enemies will I clothe with shame : but upon himself shall
his crown flourish. *Ps. cxxxii.* 18.   Peace be within thy
walls, and plenteousness within thy palaces. *Ps. cxxii.* 7.

3 but that, 3. Keep me as the apple of the eye, hide me under the
being safely shadow of thy wings. *Ps. xvii.* 8.   He that dwelleth in the
kept under the
shadow of thy secret place of the Most High shall abide under the shadow
wing, and sup- of the Almighty.   Surely he shall deliver thee/from the snare
ported by thy
power, he may of the fowler, and from the noisome pestilence.   He shall
triumph over
all opposition ; cover thee with his feathers, and under his wings shalt thou
that so the trust: his truth shall be thy shield and buckler. *Ps. xci.* 1. 3, 4·
world may ac-
knowledge thee With whom my hand shall be established : mine arm shall
to be his defen- strengthen him. *Ps. lxxxix.* 21.   The Lord taketh my part
der and mighty
deliverer in all with them that help me ; therefore shall I see my desire upon
difficulties and
adversities ; them that hate me. *Ps. cxviii.* 7.   Through God we shall do
through Jesus valiantly, for he it is that shall tread down our enemies.
Christ our
Lord. *Amen.* *Ps. lx.* 12.   And all men shall fear, and shall declare the work
of God ; for they shall wisely consider of his doing. *Ps. lxiv.*
9.   Save us, O Lord our God, and gather us from among the
heathen, to give thanks unto thy holy name, and to triumph
in thy praise. *Ps. cvi.* 47.   Fear thou not ; for I am with
thee : he not dismayed ; for I am thy God : I will strengthen
thee ; yea, I will help thee ; yea, I will uphold thee with the
right hand of my righteousness.   Behold, all they that were
incensed against thee shall be ashamed and confounded : they
shall be as nothing ; and they that strive with thee shall perish.   Thou shalt seek them, and shalt not find them, even
them that contended with thee : they that war against thee
shall be as nothing, and as a thing of nought.   For I the
Lord thy God will hold thy right hand, saying unto thee,
Fear not ; I will help thee. *Is. xli.* 10 *to* 13.   And all flesh
shall know that I the Lord am thy Saviour and thy Redeemer,
the mighty One of Jacob. *Is. xlix.* 26.

CCC. *A Prayer for the King as supreme Governor of the Church.*

1. Blessed 1. Thus saith the Lord God, Behold, I will lift up mine
Lord, who hast hand to the Gentiles, and set up my standard to the people :

hast called Christian Princes to the defence of thy Faith, and hast made it their duty to promote the spiritual welfare, together with the temporal interest of their people ;

and they shall bring thy sons in their arms, and thy daughters shall be carried upon their shoulders. And kings shall be thy nursing fathers, and their queens thy nursing mothers. Thus saith the Lord, the Redeemer of Israel, and his Holy One, to him whom man despiseth, to him whom the nation abhorreth, to a servant of rulers, Kings shall see and arise, princes also shall worship, because of the Lord that is faithful. *Is. xlix.* 22, 23. 7. Blessed be the Lord God of our fathers, which hath put such a thing as this in the king's heart to beautify the house of the Lord which is in Jerusalem. *Ezr. vii.* 27. Blessed be the Lord thy God, which delighteth in thee to set thee on his throne, to be king for the Lord thy God : because thy God loved Israel, to establish them for ever, therefore made he thee king over them. *2 Ch. ix.* 8.

2. We acknowledge with humble and thankful hearts thy great goodness to us, in setting thy Servant our most gracious King over this Church and Nation ; Give him, we beseech thee, all those heavenly graces that are requisite for so high a trust ;

2. Blessed be the Lord this day, which hath given unto David a wise son over this great people. *1 Ki. v.* 7. The Lord said to thee, Thou shalt feed my people Israel. *2 Sa. v.* 2. O give thanks unto the Lord, for he is good : for his mercy endureth for ever. *Ps. cvii.* 1. And all the congregation blessed the Lord God of their fathers, and bowed down their heads, and worshipped the Lord, and the king. And they sacrificed sacrifices unto the Lord, and offered burnt offerings unto the Lord ; and did eat and drink before the Lord on that day with great gladness. And they made Solomon the son of David king the second time, and anointed him unto the Lord to be the chief governor. And David said, Give unto Solomon my son a perfect heart, to keep thy commandments, thy testimonies, and thy statutes. *1 Ch. xxix.* 20, 21, 22. 10. 19. Give therefore thy servant an understanding heart to judge thy people, that I may discern between good and bad. *1 Ki. iii.* 9.

3. Let the work of thee his God prosper in his hands ; Let his eyes behold the success of his designs for the service of thy true Religion established amongst

3. Now, my son, the Lord be with thee ; and prosper thou, and build the house of the Lord thy God, as he hath said of thee. Only the Lord give thee wisdom and understanding, and give thee charge concerning Israel, that thou mayest keep the law of the Lord thy God. Then shalt thou prosper. *1 Ch. xxii.* 11, 12, 13. Remember me, O Lord, with the favour that thou bearest unto thy people : O visit me with thy salvation ; that I may see the good of thy chosen, that I may rejoice

us; And make
him a blessed
instrument of
protecting and
advancing thy
Truth, wher-
ever it is perse-
cuted and op-
pressed;

in the gladness of thy nation, that I may glory with thine inheritance. *Ps. cvi.* 4, 5. The Lord shall bless thee out of Zion: and thou shalt see the good of Jerusalem, and peace upon Israel. *Ps. cxxviii.* 5, 6. Then spake Solomon, The Lord said that he would dwell in the thick darkness. I have surely built thee an house to dwell in, a settled place for thee to abide in for ever. And the Lord hath performed his word that he spake, and I am risen up in the room of David my father, and sit in the throne of Israel. And I have set there a place for the ark, wherein is the covenant of the Lord, which he made with our fathers. 1 *Ki. viii.* 12, 13. 20, 21. O God, the heathen are come into thine inheritance; thy holy temple have they defiled; they have laid Jerusalem on heaps. *Ps. lxxix.* 1. Let thy hand be upon the man of thy right hand, upon the son of man whom thou madest strong for thyself. *Ps. lxxx.* 17. Give the king thy judgments, O God, and thy righteousness unto the king's son. For he shall deliver the needy when he crieth; the poor also, and him that hath no helper. *Ps. lxxii.* 1. 12. Our God hath not forsaken us in our bondage, but hath extended mercy unto us in the sight of the kings of Persia, to give us a reviving, to set up the house of our God, and to repair the desolations thereof, and to give us a wall in Judah and in Jerusalem. *Ezr. ix.* 9. They shall bring thy sons in their arms, and thy daughters shall be carried upon their shoulders. And kings shall be thy nursing fathers, and their queens thy nursing mothers. *Is. xlix.* 22, 23. *See also, Est.* VIII. IX. X.

4. Let Hy-
poerisy and
Profaneness,
Superstition
and Idolatry,
fly before his
face; Let not
Heresies and
false Doctrines
disturb the
peace of the
Church, nor
Schisms and
causeless Di-
visions weaken
it; But grant
us to be of one
heart and one

4. A king that sitteth in the throne of judgment scattereth away all evil with his eyes. A wise king scattereth the wicked, and bringeth the wheel over them. *Pr. xx.* 8. 26. O when wilt thou come unto me? I will walk within my house with a perfect heart. I will set no wicked thing before mine eyes: I hate the work of them that turn aside; it shall not cleave to me. A froward heart shall depart from me: I will not know a wicked person. Whoso privily slandereth his neighbour, him will I cut off: him that hath an high look and a proud heart will not I suffer. He that worketh deceit shall not dwell within my house: he that telleth lies shall not tarry in my sight. I will early destroy all the wicked of the land:

mind in serving thee our God, and obeying him according to thy will:

that I may cut off all wicked doers from the city of the Lord. *Ps. ci.* 2 to 5. 7, 8. That the hypocrite reign not, lest the people be ensnared. *Job xxxiv.* 30. They shall not profane the holy things of the children of Israel. *Le. xxii.* 15. When Asa heard the prophecy of Oded the prophet, he took courage, and put away the abominable idols out of all the land of Judah and Benjamin, and out of the cities which he had taken from Mount Ephraim, and renewed the altar of the Lord. *2 Ch. xv.* 8. He [Josiah] put down the idolatrous priests. *2 Ki. xxiii.* 5. The Lord send thee help from the sanctuary, and strengthen thee out of Zion. *Ps. xx.* 1, 2. A man that is an heretic after the first and second admonition reject. *Tit. iii.* 10. There be some that trouble you, and would pervert the gospel of Christ. *Ga. i.* 7. I would they were even cut off which trouble you. *Ga. v.* 12. Now the Spirit speaketh expressly, that in the latter times some shall depart from the faith, giving heed to seducing spirits, and doctrines of devils ; speaking lies in hypocrisy. 1 *Ti. iv.* 1, 2. Be not carried about with divers and strange doctrines. For it is a good thing that the heart be established with grace. *He. xiii.* 9. Now I beseech you, brethren, mark them which cause divisions and offences contrary to the doctrine which ye have learned ; and avoid them. *Ro. xvi.* 17. That there should be no schism in the body. 1 *Co. xii.* 25. Finally, brethren, farewell. Be perfect, be of good comfort, be of one mind, live in peace ; and the God of love and peace shall be with you. *2 Co. xiii.* 11 Whereto we have already attained, let us walk by the same rule, let us mind the same thing. *Ph. iii.* 16. The multitude of them that believed were of one heart and of one soul. *Ac. iv.* 32. Submit yourselves to every ordinance of man for the Lord's sake : whether it be to the king, as supreme; or unto governors; for so is the will of God. Honour all men. Love the brotherhood. Fear God. Honour the king. 1 *Pe. ii.* 13, 14, 15. 17.

5. And that these blessings may be continued to afterages, let there never be one wanting in his house to

5. O continue thy lovingkindness unto them that know thee. *Ps. xxxvi.* 10. Now let it please thee to bless the house of thy servant, that it may continue for ever before thee: for thou, O Lord God, hast spoken it: and with thy blessing let the house of thy servant be blessed for ever. *2 Sa. vii.* 29.

succeed him in the government of this United Kingdom, that our posterity may see his children's children, and peace upon Israel. So we that are thy people, and sheep of thy pasture, shall give thee thanks for ever, and will always be shewing forth thy praise from generation to generation. Amen.

If his children forsake my law, and walk not in my judgments: if they break my statutes, and keep not my commandments; then will I visit their transgression with the rod, and their iniquity with stripes. Nevertheless my lovingkindness will I not utterly take from him, nor suffer my faithfulness to fail. My covenant will I not break. Once have I sworn by my holiness that I will not lie unto David. *Ps. lxxxix.* 30 *to* 35. And the Lord hath performed his word that he spake, and I am risen up in the room of David my father, and sit on the throne of Israel, as the Lord promised. 1 *Ki. viii.* 20. Thou shalt see thy children's children, and peace upon Israel. *Ps. cxxviii.* 6. Pray for the peace of Jerusalem: they shall prosper that love thee. Peace be within thy walls, and prosperity within thy palaces. For my brethren and companions' sakes, I will now say, Peace be within thee. Because of the house of the Lord our God I will seek thy good. *Ps. cxxii.* 6 *to* 9. So we, that are thy people, and sheep of thy pasture, shall give thee thanks for ever: and will alway be shewing forth thy praise from generation to generation. *Ps. lxxix.* 14.

The Epistle.—1 Pet. ii. 11 to 17, as in the Office for *The Restoration.*
The Gospel.—Mat. xii. 16 to 22, as in the same Office.

CCCI. *A Prayer for Unity.*

1. O God the Father of our Lord Jesus Christ, our only Saviour, the Prince of Peace;

1. Blessed be the God and Father of our Lord Jesus Christ, who hath blessed us with all spiritual blessings in heavenly places in Christ. *Ep. i.* 3. I, even I, am the Lord ; and beside me there is no Saviour. *Is. xliii.* 11. Unto us a Child is born, unto us a Son is given: and the government shall be upon his shoulder : and his name shall be called Wonderful, Counsellor, the Mighty God, the Everlasting Father, the Prince of Peace. *Is. ix.* 6.

2. Give us grace seriously to lay to heart the great dangers we are in by our unhappy divisions.

2. If a kingdom be divided against itself, that kingdom cannot stand. And if a house be divided against itself, that house cannot stand. *Mar. iii.* 24, 25. For the divisions of Reuben there were great searchings of heart. *Jud. v.* 16. Whereas there is among you envying, and strife, and divisions, are ye not carnal, and walk as men? 1 *Co. iii.* 3. Where

envying and strife is, there is confusion and every evil work. *Ja. iii.* 16. Grudge not one against another, brethren, lest ye be condemned: behold, the Judge standeth before the door. *Ja. v.* 9. Now I beseech you, brethren, mark them which cause divisions and offences contrary to the doctrine which ye have learned; and avoid them. *Ro. xvi.* 17.

3. Take away all hatred and prejudice, and whatsoever else may hinder us from godly Union and Concord:

3. I beseech thee, O Lord, take away the iniquity of thy servant. *2 Sa. xxiv.* 10. Let all bitterness, and wrath, and anger, and clamour, and evil speaking, be put away from you, with all malice. *Ep. iv.* 31. Doing nothing by partiality. *1 Ti. v.* 21. Hatred stirreth up strifes: but love covereth all sins. *Pr. x.* 12. Put on therefore, as the elect of God, holy and beloved, bowels of mercies, kindness, humbleness of mind, meekness, longsuffering; forbearing one another, and forgiving one another, if any man have a quarrel against any: even as Christ forgave you, so also do ye. And above all these things put on charity, which is the bond of perfectness. And let the peace of God rule in your hearts, to the which also ye are called in one body. *Col. iii.* 12 *to* 15. Now I beseech you, brethren, by the name of our Lord Jesus Christ, that ye all speak the same thing, and that there be no divisions among you; but that ye be perfectly joined together in the same mind and in the same judgment. *1 Co. i.* 10. Let nothing be done through strife or vainglory; but in lowliness of mind let each esteem other better than themselves. *Ph. ii.* 3. The wisdom that is from above is first pure, then peaceable, gentle, and easy to be entreated, full of mercy and good fruits, without partiality, and without hypocrisy. And the fruit of righteousness is sown in peace of them that make peace. *Ja. iii.* 17, 18. Let us not therefore judge one another any more: but judge this rather, that no man put a stumblingblock or an occasion to fall in his brother's way. Let not your good be evil spoken of: for the kingdom of God is not meat and drink; but righteousness, and peace, and joy in the Holy Ghost. Let us therefore follow after the things which make for peace, and things wherewith one may edify another. *Ro. xiv.* 13. 16, 17. 19.

4. that, as there is but one

4. As the body is one, and hath many members, and all the members of that one body, being many, are one body: so also

Body, and one Spirit, and one Hope of our Calling, one Lord, one Faith, one Baptism, one God and Father of us all, so we may henceforth be all of one heart, and of one soul, united in one holy bond of Truth and Peace, of Faith and Charity, and may with one mind and one mouth glorify thee ; through Jesus Christ our Lord, Amen.

is Christ. For by one Spirit are we all baptized into one body, whether we be Jews or Gentiles, whether we be bond or free ; and have been all made to drink into one Spirit. 1 *Co. xii.* 12, 13. I therefore, the prisoner of the Lord, beseech you that ye walk worthy of the vocation wherewith ye are called, with all lowliness and meekness, with longsuffering, forbearing one another in love ; endeavouring to keep the unity of the Spirit in the bond of peace. There is one body, and one Spirit, even as ye are called in one hope of your calling ; one Lord, one faith, one baptism, one God and Father of all, who is above all, and through all, and in you all. *Ep. iv.* 1 *to* 6. Peace I leave with you, my peace I give unto you. *John xiv.* 27. These things I command you, that ye love one another. *John xv.* 17. He that loveth his brother abideth in the light, but he that hateth his brother is in darkness. 1 *John ii.* 10, 11. Now I am no more in the world, but these are in the world, and I come to thee. Holy Father, keep through thine own name those whom thou hast given me, that they may be one, as we are. Neither pray I for these alone, but for them also which shall believe on me through their word ; that they all may be one ; as thou, Father, art in me, and I in thee, that they also may be one in us. *John xvii.* 11. 20, 21. If there be therefore any consolation in Christ, if any comfort of love, if any fellowship of the Spirit, if any bowels and mercies, fulfil ye my joy, that ye be likeminded, having the same love, being of one accord, of one mind. *Ph. ii.* 1, 2. Only let your conversation be as it becometh the Gospel of Christ : that whether I come and see you, or else be absent, I may hear of your affairs, that ye stand fast in one spirit, with one mind striving together for the faith of the Gospel. *Ph. i.* 27. And be at peace among yourselves. 1 *Th. v.* 13. And I will give them one heart, and one way, that they may fear me for ever, for the good of them, and of their children after them. *Je. xxxii.* 39. In Judah the hand of God was to give them one heart to do the commandment of the king and of the princes, by the word of the Lord. 2 *Ch. xxx.* 12. And the multitude of them that believed were of one heart and of one soul. *Ac. iv.* 32. Behold, how good and how pleasant it is for brethren to dwell together in unity ! It is

like the precious ointment upon the head, that ran down upon
the beard, even Aaron's beard : that went down to the skirts
of his garments ; as the dew of Hermon, and as the dew that
descended upon the mountains of Zion : for there the Lord
commanded the blessing, even life for evermore. *Ps.* cxxxiii.
Be renewed in the spirit of your mind. *Ep. iv.* 23.   Peace be
to the brethren, and love with faith, from God the Father and
the Lord Jesus Christ. *Ep. vi.* 23. Finally, brethren, farewell.
Be perfect, be of good comfort, be of one mind, live in peace ;
and the God of love and peace shall be with you. 2 *Co. xiii.*
11.   Now the God of patience and consolation grant you to
be likeminded one toward another according to Christ Jesus :
that ye may with one mind and one mouth glorify God, even
the Father of our Lord Jesus Christ. *Ro. xv.* 5, 6.

Grant, O Lord, we beseech thee, *as LXXXIII.*

Grant, we beseech thee, Almighty God, *as CL.*

Almighty God, the fountain of all, *as CLII.*

The peace of God which passeth all understanding, keep your hearts and minds in the
knowledge and love of God, and of his Son Jesus Christ our Lord : And the blessing of
God Almighty, the Father, the Son, and the Holy Ghost, be amongst you, and remain
with you always. *Amen.*

ARTICLES OF RELIGION.

CCCII. Article I. Of Faith in the Holy Trinity.

1. There is but one living and true God, 1. There is none other God but one. 1 *Co. viii.* 4. Thus saith the Lord the King of Israel, and his Redeemer the Lord of hosts; I am the First, and I am the Last; and beside me there is no God; I know not any. *Is. xliv.* 6. 8. I am He, and there is no God with me. *De. xxxii.* 39. The scribe said unto him, Well, Master, thou hast said the truth: for there is one God; and there is none other but he. *Mar. xii.* 32. Thou believest that there is one God; thou doest well: the devils also believe. *Ja. ii.* 19. Thou shalt have no other gods before me. *Ex. xx.* 3. He is the living God, and stedfast for ever. *Da. vi.* 26. The Lord is the true God, he is the living God, and an everlasting King: the gods that have not made the heavens and the earth, even they shall perish. *Je. x.* 10, 11. Ye turned to God from idols to serve the living and true God. 1 *Th. i.* 9. Ye are the temple of the living God. 2 *Co. vi.* 16. We know that the Son of God is come, and hath given us an understanding, that we may know him that is true, and we are in him that is true, even in his Son Jesus Christ. This is the true God, and eternal life. 1 *John v.* 20. Look unto me, and be ye saved, all ye ends of the earth: for I am God, and there is none else. *Is. xlv.* 22.

2. everlasting, 2. Before the mountains were brought forth, or ever thou hadst formed the earth and the world, even from everlasting to everlasting, thou art God. *Ps. xc.* 2. Art thou not from everlasting, O Lord my God? *Hab. i.* 12. Thy throne is established of old: thou art from everlasting. *Ps. xciii.* 2. Now unto the King eternal, immortal, invisible, the only wise God, be honour and glory for ever and ever. 1 *Ti. i.* 17. *See also, Ro. xvi.* 25, 26.

3. without body, parts, or passions; 3. God is a Spirit: and they that worship him must worship him in spirit and in truth. *John iv.* 24. Behold my hands and my feet, that it is I myself: handle me and

Y2

see; for a spirit hath not flesh and bones, as ye see me have. *Lu. xxiv.* 39. To whom will ye liken God? or what likeness will ye compare unto him? *Is. xl.* 18. When they knew God, they glorified him not as God; and changed the glory of the uncorruptible God into an image made like to corruptible man, and to birds, and fourfooted beasts, and creeping things. *Ro. i.* 21. 23. We ought not to think that the Godhead is like unto gold, or silver, or stone, graven by art and man's device. *Ac. xvii.* 29. Do not I fill heaven and earth? saith the Lord. *Je. xxiii.* 24. Hast thou not known? hast thou not heard, that the everlasting God, the Lord, the Creator of the ends of the earth, fainteth not, neither is weary? *Is. xl.* 28. Of old hast thou laid the foundation of the earth : and the heavens are the work of thy hands. They shall perish, but thou shalt endure : thou art the same, and thy years shall have no end. *Ps. cii.* 25, 26, 27. God cannot be tempted with evil. *Ja. i.* 13. If thou sinnest, what doest thou against him? or if thy transgressions be multiplied, what doest thou unto him? If thou be righteous, what givest thou him? or what receiveth he of thine hand? Thy wickedness may hurt a man as thou art; and thy righteousness may profit the son of man. *Job xxxv.* 6, 7, 8. Can a man be profitable unto God, as he that is wise may be profitable unto himself? Is it any pleasure to the Almighty, that thou art righteous? or is it gain to him, that thou makest thy ways perfect? Will he reprove thee for fear of thee? will he enter with thee into judgment? *Job xxii.* 2, 3, 4.

4. of infinite power, wisdom, and goodness; 4. The Lord appeared to Abram, and said unto him, I am the Almighty God. *Ge. xvii.* 1. With God all things are possible. *Mat. xix.* 26. Whatsoever the Lord pleased, that did he in heaven, and in earth, in the seas, and all deep places. *Ps. cxxxv.* 6. Great is our Lord, and of great power: his understanding is infinite. *Ps. cxlvii.* 5. He is mighty in strength and wisdom. *Job xxxvi.* 5. Blessed be the name of God for ever and ever: for wisdom and might are his: He giveth wisdom unto the wise. *Da. ii.* 20, 21. O the depth of the riches both of the wisdom and knowledge of God! how unsearchable are his judgments, and his ways past finding out! *Ro. xi.* 33. The earth is full of the good-

ness of the Lord. *Ps. xxxiii.* 5. The goodness of God endureth continually. *Ps. lii.* 1. The Lord is good to all: and his tender mercies are over all his works. *Ps. cxlv.* 9. Truly God is good to Israel, even to such as are of a clean heart. *Ps. lxxiii.* 1. My people shall be satisfied with my goodness, saith the Lord. *Je. xxxi.* 14. You are kept by the power of God through faith unto salvation. 1 *Pe. i.* 5. See also, *Ps. xxxiv.* 8.—*Ex. xxxiv.* 6.—*Ja. i.* 17.

5. the Maker, and Preserver of all things, both visible and invisible.

5. In the beginning God created the heaven and the earth. *Ge. i.* 1. By him were all things created, that are in heaven, and that are in earth, visible and invisible, whether they be thrones, or dominions, or principalities, or powers: all things were created by him, and for him: and he is before all things, and by him all things consist. *Col. i.* 16, 17. Upholding all things by the word of his power. *He. i.* 3. Thou, even thou, art Lord alone; thou hast made heaven, the heaven of heavens, with all their host, the earth, and all things that are therein, the seas, and all that is therein, and thou preservest them all. *Ne. ix.* 6. By the word of the Lord were the heavens made: and all the host of them by the breath of his mouth. *Ps. xxxiii.* 6. He hath made the earth by his power, he hath established the world by his wisdom, and hath stretched out the heavens by his discretion. The Portion of Jacob is not like them: [*graven images:*] for he is the Former of all things. *Je. x.* 12. 16. Thus saith God the Lord, he that created the heavens, and stretched them out; he that spread forth the earth, and that which cometh out of it; he that giveth breath unto the people upon it, and spirit to them that walk therein: I the Lord have called thee in righteousness. *Is. xlii.* 5, 6. See also, *John i.* 1, 2, 3.—*He. i.* 2.

6. And in unity of this Godhead there be three Persons, of one substance, power, and eternity; the Father, the Son, and the Holy Ghost.

6. Hear, O Israel: The Lord our God is one Lord. *De. vi.* 4. There is one God; and there is none other but he. *Mar. xii.* 32. I and my Father are One. *John x.* 30. In him dwelleth all the fulness of the Godhead bodily. *Col. ii.* 9. The Comforter, whom I will send unto you from the Father, even the Spirit of truth, which proceedeth from the Father, he shall testify of me. *John xv.* 26. There are three that bear record in heaven, the Father, the Word, and the Holy Ghost: and these Three are One. 1 *John v.* 7. The Lord appeared unto

Abram, and said unto him, I am the Almighty God. *Ge. xvii.* 1.

I am Alpha and Omega, the Beginning and the Ending, saith the Lord, [*Jesus Christ, see Re. xxii.* 13. 16.] which is, and which was, and which is to come, the Almighty. *Re. i.* 8. The inspiration of the Almighty [*the Holy Ghost, see* 1 Co. ii. 10.—xii. 8.—2 Pe. i. 21.] giveth them understanding. *Job xxxii.* 8.

According to the gift of the grace of God given unto me by the effectual working of his Power. *Ep. iii.* 7. Most gladly therefore will I rather glory in mine infirmities, that the Power of Christ may rest upon me. 2 *Co. xii.* 9. Through mighty signs and wonders, by the Power of the Spirit of God. *Ro. xv.* 19.

The mystery, which was kept secret since the world began, but now is made manifest according to the commandment of the Everlasting God. *Ro. xvi.* 25, 26. I [Jesus Christ] am Alpha and Omega, the Beginning and the End, the First and the Last. *Re. xxii.* 13. Who through the Eternal Spirit offered himself without spot to God. *He. ix.* 14.

Go ye therefore, and teach all nations, baptizing them in the name of the Father, and of the Son, and of the Holy Ghost. *Mat. xxviii.* 19. The grace of the Lord Jesus Christ, and the love of God, and the communion of the Holy Ghost, be with you all. 2 *Co. xiii.* 14. Elect according to the foreknowledge of God the Father, through sanctification of the Spirit, unto obedience and sprinkling of the blood of Jesus Christ. 1 *Pe. i.* 2. Because ye are sons, God hath sent forth the Spirit of his Son into your hearts. *Ga. iv.* 6. Praying in the Holy Ghost, keep yourselves in the love of God, looking for the mercy of our Lord Jesus Christ unto eternal life. *Jude* 20, 21.

CCCIII. Article II. Of the Word or Son of God, which was made very man.

1. The Son, which is the Word of the Father, begotten from everlasting of the Father, 1. Lo a voice from heaven, saying, This is my beloved Son, in whom I am well pleased. *Mat. iii.* 17. And devils also came out of many, crying out, and saying, Thou art Christ the Son of God. *Lu. iv.* 41. In the beginning was the Word, and the Word was with God, and the Word was God.

The same was in the beginning with God. And the Word was made flesh, and dwelt among us, (and we beheld his glory, the glory as of the only begotten of the Father,) full of grace and truth. No man hath seen God at any time; the only begotten Son, which is in the bosom of the Father, he hath declared him. *John i.* 1, 2. 14. 18. His name is called, The Word of God. *Re. xix.* 13. God hath in these last days spoken unto us by his Son: the brightness of his glory, and the express image of his person. Unto which of the angels said he at any time, Thou art my Son, this day have I begotten thee? And again, I will be to him a Father, and he shall be to me a Son? And again, when he bringeth in the First-begotten into the world, he saith, And let all the angels of God worship him. *He. i.* 1, 2, 3. 5, 6. Thou Beth-lehem Ephrahta, though thou be little among the thousands of Judah, yet out of thee shall he come forth unto me that is to be ruler in Israel; whose goings forth have been from of old, from everlasting. *Mi. v.* 2.

2. the very and eternal God, and of one substance with the Father,

2. Jesus said unto them, Verily, verily, I say unto you, Before Abraham was, I am. *John viii.* 58. I am Alpha and Omega, the Beginning and the End, the First and the Last. *Re. xxii.* 13. God was manifest in the flesh. 1 *Ti. iii.* 16. We know that the Son of God is come, and hath given us an understanding, that we may know him that is true, and we are in him that is true, even in his Son Jesus Christ. This is the true God, and eternal life. 1 *John v.* 20. Unto the Son he saith, Thy throne, O God, is for ever and ever. *He. i.* 8. Of whom as concerning the flesh Christ came, who is over all, God blessed for ever. *Ro. ix.* 5. Thus saith the Lord the King of Israel, and his Redeemer the Lord of hosts; I am the First, and I am the Last; and beside me there is no God. *Is. xliv.* 6. I and my Father are one. *John x.* 30. Jesus said, He that believeth on me, believeth not on me, but on him that sent me. And he that seeth me seeth him that sent me. *John xii.* 44, 45.

3. took man's nature in the womb of the blessed Virgin, of her substance:

3. I will put enmity between thee and the woman, and between thy seed and her seed; it shall bruise thy head, and thou shalt bruise his heel. *Ge. iii.* 15. When the fulness of the time was come, God sent forth his Son, made of a woman,

made under the law. *Ga. iv.* 4. The Lord himself shall give you a sign, Behold, a virgin shall conceive, and bear a Son, and shall call his name Immanuel. *Is. vii.* 14. The angel Gabriel was sent from God unto a city of Galilee, named Nazareth, to a virgin espoused to a man whose name was Joseph, of the house of David; and the virgin's name was Mary. And the angel came in unto her, and said, Hail, thou that art highly favoured, the Lord is with thee: blessed art thou among women. And the angel said unto her, Fear not, Mary: for thou hast found favour with God. And, behold, thou shalt conceive in thy womb, and bring forth a Son, and shalt call his name JESUS. He shall be great, and shall be called the Son of the Highest. And Mary said, Behold, from henceforth all generations shall call me blessed. *Lu. i.* 26, 27, 28. 30, 31, 32. 46. 48.

4. so that two whole and perfect Natures, that is to say, the Godhead and Manhood, were joined together in one Person, never to be divided,

4. They shall call his name Emmanuel, which being interpreted is, God with us. *Mat. i.* 23. In him dwelleth all the fulness of the Godhead bodily. *Col. ii.* 9. Christ Jesus, who being in the form of God, thought it not robbery to be equal with God: but made himself of no reputation, and took upon him the form of a servant, and was made in the likeness of men: and being found in fashion as a man, he humbled himself, and became obedient unto death, even the death of the cross. *Ph. ii. 5 to* 8. Take heed therefore unto yourselves, and to all the flock, over the which the Holy Ghost hath made you overseers, to feed the Church of God, which he hath purchased with his own blood. *Ac. xx.* 28. The Word was made flesh, and dwelt among us, (and we beheld his glory, the glory as of the only begotten of the Father,) full of grace and truth. *John i.* 14. The fathers, of whom as concerning the flesh Christ came, who is over all, God blessed for ever. Amen. *Ro. ix.* 5. Which [angels] also said, Ye men of Galilee, why stand ye gazing up into heaven? this same Jesus, which is taken up from you into heaven, shall so come in like manner as ye have seen him go into heaven. *Ac. i.* 11. I am the First and the Last: I am he that liveth, and was dead; and, behold, I am alive for evermore. *Re. i.* 17, 18. Jesus Christ the same yesterday, and to day, and for ever. *He. xiii.* 8. The kingdoms of this world are become the kingdoms of our Lord, and of his Christ; and he shall reign for ever and ever. *Re. xi.* 15.

And every creature which is in heaven, and on the earth, and under the earth, and such as are in the sea, and all that are in them, heard I saying, Blessing, and honour, and glory, and power, be unto him that sitteth upon the throne, and unto the Lamb for ever and ever. *Re. v.* 13. The Son abideth ever. *John viii.* 35. Seeing we have a great High Priest, that is passed into the heavens, Jesus the Son of God, let us hold fast our profession. *He. iv.* 14. This man, because he continueth ever, hath an unchangeable priesthood. Wherefore he is able also to save them to the uttermost that come unto God by him, seeing he ever liveth to make intercession for them. *He. vii.* 24, 25.

5. whereof is one Christ, very God, and very Man;

5. To us there is but one Lord Jesus Christ, by whom are all things, and we by him. 1 *Co. viii.* 6. And Simon Peter answered and said, Thou art the Christ, the Son of the living God. *Mat. xvi.* 16. Unto you is born this day in the city of David, a Saviour, which is Christ the Lord. *Lu. ii.* 11. And his name shall be called Wonderful, Counsellor, The Mighty God, The everlasting Father, The Prince of Peace. *Is. ix.* 6. Wherefore let all the house of Israel know assuredly, that God hath made that same Jesus, whom ye have crucified, both Lord and Christ. *Ac. ii.* 36. Looking for the blessed hope, and the glorious appearing of the great God and our Saviour Jesus Christ. *Tit. ii.* 13. And they stoned Stephen, calling upon God, and saying, Lord Jesus, receive my spirit. *Ac. vii.* 50. Thomas answered and said unto him, My Lord and my God. *John xx.* 28. Without controversy great is the mystery of godliness: God was manifest in the flesh. 1 *Ti. iii.* 16. Every spirit that confesseth not that Jesus Christ is come in the flesh is not of God. 1 *John iv.* 3. Hereby perceive we the love of God, because he laid down his life for us. 1 *John iii.* 16. There is one Mediator between God and men, the man Christ Jesus. 1 *Ti. ii.* 5.

6. who truly suffered, was crucified, dead and buried,

6. Christ also hath once suffered for sins, the just for the unjust, that he might bring us to God, being put to death in the flesh, but quickened by the Spirit. 1 *Pe. iii.* 18. He is despised and rejected of men; a man of sorrows, and acquainted with grief: and we hid as it were our faces from him; he was despised, and we esteemed him not. He poured out his soul

unto death : and he was numbered with the transgressors ; and he bare the sin of many. *Is. liii.* 3. 12. Forasmuch then as Christ hath suffered for us in the flesh, arm yourselves likewise with the same mind. 1 *Pe. iv.* 1. And when they were come to the place, which is called Calvary, there they crucified him. And when Jesus had cried with a loud voice, he said, Father, into thy hands I commend my spirit : and having said thus, he gave up the ghost. *Lu. xxiii.* 33. 46. When they came to Jesus, and saw that he was dead already, they brake not his legs. *John xix.* 33. Our Lord Jesus Christ died for us. 1 *Th. v.* 9, 10. I lay down my life, that I might take it again. No man taketh it from me, but I lay it down of myself. I have power to lay it down, and I have power to take it again. *John x.* 17, 18. When the even was come, there came a rich man of Arimathea, named Joseph, who also himself was Jesus' disciple : he went to Pilate, and begged the body of Jesus. Then Pilate commanded the body to be delivered. And when Joseph had taken the body, he wrapped it in a clean linen cloth, and laid it in his own new tomb. *Mat. xxvii.* 57 *to* 60. He made his grave with the wicked, and with the rich in his death. *Is. liii.* 9.

7. to reconcile his Father to us,   7. We were reconciled to God by the death of his Son. *Ro. v.* 10. You, that were sometime alienated and enemies in your mind by wicked works, yet now hath he reconciled in the body of his flesh through death. *Col. i.* 21, 22. That he might reconcile both unto God in one body by the cross, having slain the enmity thereby : and came and preached peace to you which were afar off, and to them that were nigh. For through him we both have access by one Spirit unto the Father. *Ep. ii.* 16, 17, 18. Wherefore in all things it behoved him to be made like unto his brethren, that he might be a merciful and faithful High Priest in things pertaining to God, to make reconciliation for the sins of the people. *He. ii.* 17. And hath given to us the ministry of reconciliation, to wit, that God was in Christ, reconciling the world unto himself, not imputing their trespasses unto them. He made him to be sin for us, who knew no sin ; that we might be made the righteousness of God in him. 2 *Co. v.* 18, 19. 21. *See also, Mat. xx.* 28.— 1 *Ti. ii.* 5, 6.

8. and to be a sacrifice, not only for original guilt, but also for actual sins of men.

8. Christ our passover is sacrificed for us. 1 *Co. v.* 7. Christ hath loved us, and hath given himself for us an offering and a sacrifice to God for a sweet smelling savour. *Ep. v.* 2. Now once in the end of the world hath he appeared to put away sin by the sacrifice of himself. *He. ix.* 26. Behold the Lamb of God, which taketh away the sin of the world. *John i.* 29. As by the offence of one judgment came upon all men to condemnation; even so by the righteousness of one the free gift came upon all men unto justification of life. *Ro. v.* 18. For as in Adam all die, even so in Christ shall all be made alive. 1 *Co. xv.* 22. If any man sin, we have an Advocate with the Father, Jesus Christ the righteous: and he is the Propitiation for our sins: and not for ours only, but also for the sins of the whole world. 1 *John ii.* 1, 2. The blood of Jesus Christ his Son cleanseth us from all sin. 1 *John i.* 7. Christ hath redeemed us from the curse of the law, being made a curse for us. *Ga. iii.* 13. Blotting out the handwriting of ordinances that was against us, which was contrary to us, and took it out of the way, nailing it to his cross. *Col. ii.* 14. Christ was once offered to bear the sins of many. *He. ix.* 28. Surely he hath borne our griefs, and carried our sorrows: yet we did esteem him stricken, smitten of God, and afflicted. But he was wounded for our transgressions, he was bruised for our iniquities: the chastisement of our peace was upon him; and with his stripes we are healed. All we like sheep have gone astray; we have turned every one to his own way; and the Lord hath laid on him the iniquity of us all. *Is. liii.* 4, 5, 6.

CCCIV. Article III. Of the going down of Christ into Hell.

As Christ died for us, and was buried, so also is it to be believed that he went down into Hell.

I delivered unto you first of all that which I also received, how that Christ died for our sins according to the Scriptures; and that he was buried. 1 *Co. xv.* 3, 4. David speaketh concerning him, I foresaw the Lord always before my face, for he is on my right hand, that I should not be moved: therefore did my heart rejoice, and my tongue was glad; moreover also my flesh shall rest in hope: because thou wilt not leave my soul in hell, neither wilt thou suffer thine Holy One to see corruption. David being a prophet, and knowing that God had sworn with an oath to him, that of the fruit of his loins, according to the flesh, he would raise up Christ to sit on his throne ; he seeing this before spake of the resurrection of Christ, that his soul was not left in hell, neither his flesh did see corruption. *Ac. ii.* 25, 26, 27. 29, 30, 31. Now that he ascended, what is it but that he also descended first into the lower parts of the earth? He that descended is the same also that ascended up far above all heavens, that he might fill all things. *Ep. iv.* 9, 10. Jesus said unto him, Verily I say unto thee, To day shalt thou be with me in paradise. *Lu. xxiii.* 43.

CCCV. Article IV. Of the Resurrection of Christ.

1. Christ did truly rise again from death,

1. Christ rose again the third day according to the Scriptures. *1 Co. xv.* 3, 4. He is not here: for he is risen, as he said. Come, see the place where the Lord lay. *Mat. xxviii.* 6. Now when Jesus was risen early the first day of the week, he appeared first to Mary Magdalene. *Mar. xvi.* 9. Remember how he spake unto you when he was yet in Galilee, saying, The Son of man must be delivered into the hands of sinful men, and be crucified, and the third day rise again. *Lu. xxiv.* 6, 7. This is now the third time that Jesus shewed himself to his disciples, after that he was risen from the dead. *John xxi.* 14. Him God raised up the third day, and shewed him openly ; not to all the people, but unto witnesses chosen before of God, even to us, who did eat and drink with him after he rose from the dead. *Ac. x.* 40, 41. To whom also he shewed himself alive after his passion by many infallible proofs, being seen of them forty days, and speaking of the things pertaining to the kingdom of God. *Ac. i.* 3. To this end Christ both died, and rose, and revived, that he might be Lord both of the dead and living. *Ro. xiv.* 9. Blessed be the God and Father of our Lord Jesus Christ, which according to his abundant mercy hath begotten us again unto a lively hope by the resurrection of Jesus Christ from the dead. *1 Pe. i.* 3. Who was delivered for our offences, and was raised again for our justification. *Ro. iv.* 25. Then saith he to Thomas, Reach hither thy finger, and behold my hands:

and reach hither thy hand, and thrust it into my side: and be not faithless, but believing. *John xx.* 27.

2. and took again his body, with flesh, bones, and all things appertaining to the perfection of man's nature, wherewith he ascended into Heaven, and there sitteth until he return to judge all men at the last day.

2. Jesus himself stood in the midst of them, and saith unto them, Peace be unto you. But they were terrified and affrighted, and supposed that they had seen a spirit. And he said unto them, Why are ye troubled? and why do thoughts arise in your hearts? Behold my hands and my feet, that it is I myself: handle me, and see; for a spirit hath not flesh and bones, as ye see me have. And when he had thus spoken, he shewed them his hands and his feet. And they gave him a piece of a broiled fish, and of an honeycomb. And he took it, and did eat before them. And said unto them, Thus it is written, and thus it behoved Christ to suffer, and to rise from the dead the third day. And it came to pass, while he blessed them, he was parted from them, and carried up into heaven. *Lu. xxiv.* 36 *to* 40. 42, 43. 46.*51. And while they looked stedfastly toward heaven as he went up, behold, two men stood by them in white apparel; which also said, Ye men of Galilee, why stand ye gazing up into heaven? this same Jesus, which is taken up from you into heaven, shall so come in like manner as ye have seen him go into heaven. *Ac. i.* 10, 11. So then after the Lord had spoken unto them, he was received up into heaven, and sat on the right hand of God. *Mar. xvi.* 19. God hath highly exalted him, and given him a name which is above every name. *Ph. ii.* 9. The Lord said unto my Lord, Sit thou at my right hand, until I make thine enemies thy footstool. *Ps. cx.* 1. Who being the brightness of his glory, and the express image of his person, and upholding all things by the word of his power, when he had by himself purged our sins, sat down on the right hand of the Majesty on high. *He. i.* 3. We have such an High Priest, who is set on the right hand of the throne of the Majesty in the heavens; a Minister of the sanctuary, and of the true tabernacle. *He. viii.* 1, 2. If ye then be risen with Christ, seek those things which are above, where Christ sitteth on the right hand of God. *Col. iii.* 1. Whom the heaven must receive until the times of restitution of all things. *Ac. iii.* 21. For the Lord himself shall descend from heaven with a shout, with the voice of the archangel, and with the trump of God: and the dead in Christ

shall rise first. 1 *Th. iv.* 16. The Father hath committed all judgment unto the Son: and hath given him authority to execute judgment also. *John v.* 22. 27. He hath appointed a day, in the which he will judge the world in righteousness by that Man whom he hath ordained. *Ac. xvii.* 31. The Lord Jesus who shall judge the quick and the dead at his appearing and his kingdom. 2 *Ti. iv.* 1. He commanded us to preach unto the people, and to testify that it is he which was ordained of God to be the Judge of quick and dead. *Ac. x.* 42. We must all appear before the judgment seat of Christ; that every one may receive the things done in his body, according to that he hath done, whether it be good or bad. 2 *Co. v.* 10. The day of the Lord will come as a thief in the night; in the which the heavens shall pass away with a great noise, and the elements shall melt with fervent heat, the earth also and the works that are therein shall be burned up. Seeing then that all these things shall be dissolved, what manner of persons ought ye to be in all holy conversation and godliness, looking for and hasting unto the coming of the day of God. 2 *Pe. iii.* 10, 11, 12. *See also,* 1 *Pe. iv.* 3. 5.—*Ro. ii.* 12. 16.

CCCVI. *Article V. Of the Holy Ghost.*

The Holy Ghost, proceeding from the Father and the Son, is of one substance, majesty, and glory, with the Father and the Son, very and eternal God.

The Comforter, which is the Holy Ghost, whom the Father will send in my name, he shall teach you all things. *John xiv.* 26. But when the Comforter is come, whom I will send unto you from the Father, even the Spirit of truth, which proceedeth from the Father, he shall testify of me. *John xv.* 26. It is expedient for you that I go away: for if I go not away, the Comforter will not come unto you; but if I depart, I will send him unto you. *John xvi.* 7. Therefore being by the right hand of God exalted, and having received of the Father the promise of the Holy Ghost, he hath shed forth this, which ye now see and hear. *Ac. ii.* 33. Ye are not in the flesh, but in the Spirit, if so be that the Spirit of God dwell in you. Now if any man have not the Spirit of Christ, he is none of his. *Ro. viii.* 9. Searching what, or what manner of time the Spirit of Christ which was in them [the prophets] did signify, when it testified beforehand the sufferings

of Christ, and the glory that should follow. 1 *Pe. i.* 11. God
hath revealed them unto us by his Spirit: for the Spirit searcheth all things, yea, the deep things of God. For what man
knoweth the things of a man, save the spirit of man which is in
him? even so the things of God knoweth no man, but the Spirit
of God. 1 *Co. ii.* 10, 11. Know ye not that ye are the temple of
God, and that the Spirit of God dwelleth in you? If any
man defile the temple of God, him shall God destroy. Know
ye not that your body is the temple of the Holy Ghost which
is in you, which ye have of God? 1 *Co. iii.* 16, 17. *vi.* 19.
Now the Lord is that Spirit: and where the Spirit of the
Lord is, there is liberty. But we all, with open face beholding as in a glass the glory of the Lord, are changed into the
same image from glory to glory, even as by the Spirit of the
Lord. 2 *Co. iii.* 17, 18. If ye be reproached for the name of
Christ, happy are ye; for the Spirit of glory and of God
resteth upon you. 1 *Pe. iv.* 14. Peter said, Ananias, Why
hath Satan filled thine heart to lie to the Holy Ghost? Thou
hast not lied unto men, but unto God. How is it that ye have
agreed together to tempt the Spirit of the Lord? *Ac. v.* 3,
4. 9. Prophecy came not in old time by the will of man:
but holy men of God spake as they were moved by the Holy
Ghost. 2 *Pe. i.* 21. All Scripture is given by inspiration of
God. 2 *Ti. iii.* 16. It is written in the prophets, And they
shall be all taught of God. *John vi.* 45. The Holy Ghost,
whom the Father will send in my name, he shall teach you
all things. *John xiv.* 26. How much more shall the blood of
Christ, who through the eternal Spirit offered himself without spot to God, purge your conscience from dead works to
serve the living God? *He. ix.* 14. Go ye therefore, and
teach all nations, baptizing them in the name of the Father,
and of the Son, and of the Holy Ghost. *Mat. xxviii.* 19.

*CCCVII. Article VI. Of the Sufficiency of the Holy Scriptures
for Salvation.*

**1. Holy
Scripture con-
taineth all
things neces-
sary to salva-
tion :**
1. From a child thou hast known the holy Scriptures, which
are able to make thee wise unto salvation through faith which
is in Christ Jesus. All Scripture is given by inspiration of
God, and is profitable for doctrine, for reproof, for correction,

for instruction in righteousness: that the man of God may be perfect, throughly furnished unto all good works. *2 Ti. iii.* 15, 16, 17. The law of the Lord is perfect, converting the soul: the testimony of the Lord is sure, making wise the simple. The statutes of the Lord are right, rejoicing the heart : the commandment of the Lord is pure, enlightening the eyes. The fear of the Lord is clean, enduring for ever: the judgments of the Lord are true and righteous altogether. *Ps. xix.* 7, 8, 9. These [signs] are written, that ye might believe that Jesus is the Christ, the Son of God; and that believing ye might have life through his name. *John xx.* 31.

2. so that whatsoever is not read therein, nor may be proved thereby, is not to be required of any man, that it should be believed as an article of the Faith, or be thought requisite or necessary to salvation. In the name of the holy Scripture we do understand those Canonical Books of the Old and New Testament, of whose authority was never any doubt in the Church.

Of the Names and Number of the Canonical Books.

Genesis,	The I Book of Chronicles,
Exodus,	The II Book of Chronicles,
Leviticus,	The I Book of Esdras,
Numbers,	The II Book of Esdras,
Deuteronomy,	The Book of Esther,
Joshua,	The Book of Job,
Judges,	The Psalms,
Ruth,	The Proverbs,
The I Book of Samuel,	Ecclesiastes or Preacher,
The II Book of Samuel,	Cantica, or Songs of Solomon,
The I Book of Kings,	IV. Prophets the greater,
The II Book of Kings,	XII. Prophets the less.

And the other Books (as *Hierome* saith) the Church doth read for example of life and instruction of manners ; but yet doth it not apply them to establish any doctrine ; such as these following,

The III Book of Esdras,	Baruch the Prophet,
The IV. Book of Esdras,	The Song of the three Children,
The Book of Tobias,	The Story of Susanna,
The Book of Judith,	Of Bel and the Dragon,
The rest of the Book of Esther,	The Prayer of Manasses,
The Book of Wisdom,	The I Book of Maccabees,
Jesus the son of Sirach,	The II Book of Maccabees.

All the Books of the New Testament, as they are commonly received, we do receive and account them Canonical.

2. Preach the word ; be instant in season, out of season; reprove, rebuke, exhort with all longsuffering and doctrine. For the time will come when they will not endure sound doctrine ; but after their own lusts shall they heap to themselves teachers, having itching ears ; and they shall turn away their ears from the truth, and shall be turned unto fables. *2 Ti. iv.* 2, 3, 4. There be some that trouble you, and would pervert the Gospel of Christ. But though we, or an angel from

heaven, preach any other Gospel unto you than that which we have preached unto you, let him be accursed. As we said before, so say I now again, If any man preach any other Gospel unto you than that ye have received, let him be accursed. *Ga. i.* 7, 8, 9. In vain they do worship me, teaching for doctrines the commandments of men. Thus have ye made the commandment of God of none effect by your tradition. *Mat. xv.* 9. 6. To the law and to the testimony: if they speak not according to this word, it is because there is no light in them. *Is. viii.* 20. Every word of God is pure. Add thou not unto his words, lest he reprove thee, and thou be found a liar. *Pr. xxx.* 5, 6. What thing soever I command you, observe to do it: thou shalt not add thereto, nor diminish from it. *De. xii.* 32. Ye shall not add unto the word which I command you, neither shall ye diminish ought from it, that ye may keep the commandments of the Lord your God, which I command you. *De. iv.* 2. Prophecy came not in old time by the will of man: but holy men of God spake as they were moved by the Holy Ghost. *2 Pe. i.* 21. I testify unto every man that heareth the words of the prophecy of this book, If any man shall add unto these things, God shall add unto him the plagues that are written in this book: And if any man shall take away from the words of the book of this prophecy, God shall take away his part out of the book of life, and out of the holy city, and from the things which are written in this book. *Re. xxii.* 18, 19.

CCCVIII. *Article VII. Of the Old Testament.*

1. The Old Testament is not contrary to the New,

1. God, who at sundry times and in divers manners spake in time past unto the fathers by the prophets, hath in these last days spoken unto us by his Son. *He. i.* 1, 2. Think not that I am come to destroy the Law, or the Prophets: I am not come to destroy, but to fulfil. For verily I say unto you, Till heaven and earth pass, one jot or one tittle shall in no wise pass from the law, till all are fulfilled. *Mat. v.* 17, 18. And he said unto them, These are the words which I spake unto you, while I was yet with you, that all things must be fulfilled, which were written in the Law of Moses, and in the Prophets, and in the Psalms, concerning me. *Lu. xxiv.* 44. Wherefore the law was our schoolmaster to bring us unto Christ. *Ga. iii.* 24.

He mightily convinced the Jews, and that publickly, shewing by the Scriptures that Jesus was Christ. *Ac. xviii.* 28.

2. Search the Scriptures; for in them ye think ye have eternal life : and they are they which testify of me. Had ye believed Moses, ye would have believed me : for he wrote of me. *John v.* 39. 46. Now the righteousness of God without the law is manifest, being witnessed by the Law and the Prophets. *Ro. iii.* 21. The mystery which was kept secret since the world began, but now is made manifest, and, by the Scriptures of the prophets, according to the commandment of the everlasting God, made known to all nations for the obedience of faith. *Ro. xvi.* 25, 26. Many came into his lodging; to whom he expounded and testified the kingdom of God, persuading them concerning Jesus, both out of the law of Moses, and out of the prophets, from morning until evening. *Ac. xxviii.* 23. It is written in the prophets, And they shall be all taught of God. Every man therefore that hath heard, and hath learned of the Father, cometh unto me. *John vi.* 45. To him give all the prophets witness, that through his name whosoever believeth in him shall receive remission of sins. *Ac. x.* 43. I will put enmity between thee and the woman, and between thy seed and her seed ; it shall bruise thy head, and thou shalt bruise his heel. *Ge. iii.* 15. In thy seed shall all the nations of the earth be blessed. *Ge. xxii.* 18. The Scripture, foreseeing that God would justify the heathen through faith, preached before the Gospel unto Abraham, saying, In thee shall all nations be blessed. So then they which be of faith are blessed with faithful Abraham. That the blessing of Abraham might come on the Gentiles through Jesus Christ. If ye be Christ's then are ye Abraham's seed, and heirs according to the promise. *Ga. iii.* 8, 9. 14. 29. For unto us was the Gospel preached, as well as unto them. *He. iv.* 2. And many of them, that sleep in the dust of the earth shall awake, some to everlasting life, and some to shame and everlasting contempt. And they that be wise shall shine as the brightness of the firmament; and they that turn many to righteousness as the stars for ever and ever. *Da. xii.* 2, 3. Ho, every one that thirsteth, come ye to the waters, and he that hath no money ; come ye, buy,

(margin note) 2. for both in the Old and New Testament everlasting life is offered to mankind by Christ.

and eat; yea, come, buy wine and milk without money and without price. *Is. lv.* 1. And he said unto them, Go ye into all the world, and preach the Gospel to every creature. He that believeth and is baptized shall be saved; but he that believeth not shall be damned. *Mar. xvi.* 15, 16. *See also, Re. xxii.* 17.—*Ac. iii.* 20.—1 *Pe. i.* 10.

3. who is the only Mediator between God and Man, being both God and Man. Wherefore they are not to be heard, which feign that the old Fathers did look only for transitory promises.

3. There is one God, and one Mediator between God and men, the man Christ Jesus. 1 *Ti. ii.* 5. The man that is my fellow, saith the Lord of hosts. *Ze. xiii.* 7. He is the Mediator of the new testament. *He. ix.* 15. If any man sin, we have an Advocate with the Father, Jesus Christ the righteous. 1 *John ii.* 1. He ever liveth to make intercession for them. *He. vii.* 25. Verily I say unto you, That many prophets and righteous men have desired to see those things which ye see, and have not seen them; and to hear those things which ye hear, and have not heard them. *Mat. xiii.* 17. Your father Abraham rejoiced to see my day: and he saw it, and was glad. *John viii.* 56. By faith Noah became heir of the righteousness which is by faith. Abraham looked for a city which hath foundations, whose builder and maker is God. By faith Moses refused to be called the son of Pharaoh's daughter; choosing rather to suffer affliction with the people of God, than to enjoy the pleasures of sin for a season; esteeming the reproach of Christ greater riches than the treasures in Egypt: for he had respect unto the recompense of the reward. Women received their dead raised to life again: and others were tortured, not accepting deliverance; that they might obtain a better resurrection. These all died in faith, not having received the promises, but having seen them afar off, and embraced them, and confessed that they were strangers and pilgrims on the earth. For they that say such things declare plainly that they seek a country. They desire a better country, that is, an heavenly: wherefore God is not ashamed to be called their God; for he hath prepared for them a city. *He. xi.* 7. 10. 24, 25, 26. 35. 13, 14. 16. *See also,* 1 *Co. x.* 1 *to* 4.

4. Although the Law given from God by Moses, as touching Cere- monies and

4. Behold, the days come, saith the Lord, that I will make a new covenant with the house of Israel, and with the house of Judah: not according to the covenant that I made with their fathers in the day that I took them by the hand to bring

A A

Rites, do not bind Christian men, nor the Civil Precepts thereof ought of necessity to be received in any commonwealth: yet notwithstanding, no Christian man whatsoever is free from the obedience of the Commandments which are called Moral.

them out of the land of Egypt; which my covenant they brake. *Je. xxxi.* 31, 32. The law was our schoolmaster to bring us unto Christ: but after that faith is come, we are no longer under a schoolmaster. *Ga. iii.* 24, 25. Having abolished in his flesh the enmity, even the law of commandments contained in ordinances; for to make in himself of twain one new man, so making peace. *Ep. ii.* 15. The priesthood being changed, there is made of necessity a change also of the law. For there is verily a disannulling of the commandment going before for the weakness and unprofitableness thereof. For the law made nothing perfect, but the bringing in of a better hope did; by the which we draw nigh unto God. The law maketh men high priests which have infirmity; but the word of the oath, which was since the law, maketh the Son, who is consecrated for evermore. *He. vii.* 12. 18, 19. 28. The sceptre shall not depart from Judah, nor a lawgiver from between his feet, until Shiloh come; and unto him shall the gathering of the people be. *Ge. xlix.* 10. Then said Paul, I stand at Cæsar's judgment seat, where I ought to be judged. *Ac. xxv.* 10. Submit yourselves to every ordinance of man for the Lord's sake. 1 *Pe. ii.* 13. Render therefore to all their dues: tribute to whom tribute is due; custom to whom custom; fear to whom fear; honour to whom honour. *Ro. xiii.* 7. Stand fast therefore in the liberty wherewith Christ hath made us free; and be not entangled again with the yoke of bondage. *Ga. v.* 1. Do we then make void the law through faith? God forbid: yea, we establish the law. *Ro. iii.* 31. The law is holy, and the commandment holy, and just, and good. *Ro. vii.* 12. Think not that I am come to destroy the Law, or the Prophets: I am not come to destroy, but to fulfil. For verily I say unto you, Till heaven and earth pass, one jot or one tittle shall in no wise pass from the law, till all be fulfilled. Whosoever therefore shall break one of these least commandments, and shall teach men so, he shall be called the least in the kingdom of heaven: but whosoever shall do and teach them, the same shall be called great in the kingdom of heaven. For I say unto you, That except your righteousness shall exceed the righteousness of the scribes and

Pharisees, ye shall in no case enter into the kingdom of heaven. *Mat. v.* 17 *to* 20. If ye fulfil the royal law according to the Scripture, Thou shalt love thy neighbour as thyself, ye do well. Whosoever shall keep the whole law, and yet offend in one point, he is guilty of all. For he that said, Do not commit adultery, said also, Do not kill. Now if thou commit no adultery, yet if thou kill, thou art become a transgressor of the law. *Ja. ii.* 8. 10, 11. Sin is the transgression of the law. 1 *John iii.* 4. Fear God, and keep his commandments: for this is the whole duty of man. *Ec. xii.* 13. *See particularly, Ac.* xv.

CCCIX. *Article VIII. Of the Three Creeds.*

The three Creeds, Nicene Creed, Athanasius's Creed, and that which is commonly called the Apostles' Creed, ought thoroughly to be received and believed: for they may be proved by most certain warrants of holy Scripture.

Hold fast the form of sound words, which thou hast heard of me, in faith and love which is in Christ Jesus. 2 *Ti. i.* 13. Holding the mystery of the faith in a pure conscience. 1 *Ti. iii.* 9. Beloved, when I gave all diligence to write unto you of the common salvation, it was needful for me to write unto you, and exhort you that ye should earnestly contend for the faith which was once delivered unto the saints. Beloved, remember ye the words which were spoken before of the apostles of our Lord Jesus Christ. Ye, beloved, building up yourselves on your most holy faith, praying in the Holy Ghost, keep yourselves in the love of God, looking for the mercy of our Lord Jesus Christ unto eternal life. *Jude* 3. 17. 20, 21. See the Creeds, Nos. *VI.—XVI.—CXXV.*

CCCX. *Article IX. Of Original or Birth-sin.*

1. Original Sin standeth not in the following of Adam, (as the Pelagians do vainly talk;) but it is the fault and corruption of the nature of every man, that naturally is engendered of the offspring of *Adam* :

1. Adam begat a son in his own likeness. *Ge. v.* 3. That which is born of the flesh is flesh. *John iii.* 6. Death reigned from Adam to Moses, even over them that had not sinned after the similitude of Adam's transgression. By one man's offence death reigned by one. By the offence of one judgment came upon all men to condemnation. By one man's disobedience many were made sinners. *Ro. v.* 14. 17, 18, 19. How then can man be justified with God? or how can he be clean that is born of a woman? *Job xxv.* 4. Who can bring a clean thing out of an unclean? not one. *Job xiv.* 4. Behold, I was shapen in iniquity; and in sin did my mother conceive me. *Ps. li.* 5. The wicked are estranged from the womb: they

go astray as soon as they be born, speaking lies. *Ps. lviii.* 3. I know that in me, (that is, in my flesh,) dwelleth no good thing. *Ro. vii.* 18. The natural man receiveth not the things of the Spirit of God: for they are foolishness unto him: neither can he know them, because they are spiritually discerned. 1 *Co. ii.* 14. Except a man be born again, he cannot see the kingdom of God. *John iii.* 3.

2. whereby man is very far gone from original righteousness, and is of his own nature inclined to evil,

2. In my flesh dwelleth no good thing: for to will is present with me; but how to perform that which is good I find not. *Ro. vii.* 18. God saw that the wickedness of man was great in the earth, and that every imagination of the thoughts of his heart was only evil continually. *Ge. vi.* 5. And the Lord said in his heart, I will not again curse the ground any more for man's sake; for the imagination of man's heart is evil from his youth. *Ge. viii.* 21. There is no man that sinneth not. 1 *Ki. viii.* 46. The whole world lieth in wickedness. 1 *John v.* 19. The heart is deceitful above all things, and desperately wicked: who can know it? *Je. xvii.* 9. Lo, this only have I found, that God hath made man upright; but they have sought out many inventions. *Ec. vii.* 29. They are sottish children, and they have none understanding: they are wise to do evil, but to do good they have no knowledge. *Je. iv.* 22. Having the understanding darkened, being alienated from the life of God through the ignorance that is in them, because of the blindness of their heart. *Ep. iv.* 18. Out of the heart proceed evil thoughts, murders, adulteries, fornications, thefts, false witness, blasphemies. *Mat. xv.* 19. The fool hath said in his heart, There is no God. They are corrupt, they have done abominable works, there is none that doeth good. The Lord looked down from heaven upon the children of men, to see if there were any that did understand, and seek God. They are all gone aside, they are all together become filthy: there is none that doeth good, no, not one. *Ps. xiv.* 1, 2, 3. Every man is tempted, when he is drawn away of his own lust, and enticed. Then when lust hath conceived, it bringeth forth sin: and sin, when it is finished, bringeth forth death. *Ja. i.* 14, 15. Put off the old man, which is corrupt according to the deceitful lusts. *Ep. iv.* 22.

3. so that the flesh lust.

3. The flesh lusteth against the Spirit, and the Spirit against the flesh: and these are contrary the one to the other: so that

eth always contrary to the Spirit ; and therefore in every person born into this world, it deserveth God's wrath and damnation.

ye cannot do the things that ye would. *Ga. v.* 17. I delight in the law of God after the inward man : but I see another law in my members, warring against the law of my mind, and bringing me into captivity to the law of sin which is in my members. *Ro. vii.* 22, 23. Among whom also we all had our conversation in times past in the lusts of our flesh, fulfilling the desires of the flesh and of the mind ; and were by nature the children of wrath, even as others. *Ep. ii.* 3. If ye live after the flesh, ye shall die. To be carnally minded is death. *Ro. viii.* 13. 6. The wages of sin is death. *Ro. vi.* 23. By the offence of one judgment came upon all men to condemnation. *Ro. v.* 18. Now we know that what things soever the law saith, it saith to them who are under the law : that every mouth may be stopped, and all the world may become guilty before God. *Ro. iii.* 19. Abstain from fleshly lusts, which war against the soul. 1 *Pe. ii.* 11. Be not deceived ; God is not mocked : for whatsoever a man soweth, that shall he also reap. For he that soweth to his flesh shall of the flesh reap corruption. *Ga. vi.* 7, 8.

4. And this infection of nature doth remain, yea, in them that are regenerated; whereby the lust of the flesh, called in the Greek *phronema sarkos,* which some do expound the wisdom, some sensuality, some the affection, some the desire, of the flesh, is not subject to the law of God.

4. We know that the law is spiritual : but I am carnal, sold under sin. I know that in me, (that is, in my flesh,) dwelleth no good thing : for to will is present with me ; but how to perform that which is good I find not. For the good that I would, I do not : but the evil which I would not, that I do. I find then a law, that, when I would do good, evil is present with me. For I delight in the law of God after the inward man : but I see another law in my members, warring against the law of my mind, and bringing me into captivity to the law of sin which is in my members. *Ro. vii.* 14. 18, 19. 21, 22, 23. The flesh lusteth against the Spirit, and the Spirit against the flesh. *Ga. v.* 17. If we say that we have no sin, we deceive ourselves, and the truth is not in us. If we say that we have not sinned, we make him a liar, and his word is not in us. 1 *John i.* 8. 10. There is not a just man upon earth, that doeth good, and sinneth not. *Ec. vii.* 20. Who can say, I have made my heart clean, I am pure from my sin ? *Pr. xx.* 9. We are all as an unclean thing, and all our righteousnesses are as filthy rags. *Is. lxiv.* 6. In many things we offend all. *Ja. iii.* 2. Διότι τὸ Φρόνημα τῆς σαρκὸς, ἔχθρα εἰς Θεὸν.

Τῶ γάρ νόμω τοῦ Θεοῦ οὐχ ὑποτάσσεται· οὐδὲ γάρ δύναται. Because the carnal mind is enmity against God : for it is not subject to the law of God, neither indeed can be. *Ro. viii.* 7.

5. And although there is no condemnation for them that believe and are baptized, yet the Apostle doth confess, that concupiscence and lust hath of itself the nature of sin.

5. There is therefore now no condemnation to them which are in Christ Jesus, who walk not after the flesh, but after the Spirit. *Ro. viii.* 1.   He that believeth and is baptized shall be saved. *Mar. xvi.* 16.   God sent not his Son into the world to condemn the world.   He that believeth on him is not condemned. *John iii.* 17, 18.   Verily, verily, I say unto you, He that heareth my word, and believeth on him that sent me, hath everlasting life, and shall not come into condemnation ; but is passed from death unto life. *John v.* 24.   Is the law sin? God forbid.   Nay, I had not known sin, but by the law : for I had not known lust, except the law had said, Thou shalt not covet.   But sin, taking occasion by the commandment, wrought in me all manner of concupiscence. *Ro. vii.* 7, 8. Whosoever looketh on a woman to lust after her, hath committed adultery with her already in his heart. *Mat. v.* 28.   When lust hath conceived, it bringeth forth sin: and sin, when it is finished, bringeth forth death. *Ja. i.* 15.   There is a sin not unto death. 1 *John v.* 17.

CCCXI. Article X. Of Free-Will.

1. The condition of man after the fall of *Adam* is such, that he cannot turn and prepare himself, by his own natural strength and good works, to faith and calling upon God :

1. They that are in the flesh cannot please God. *Ro. viii.* 8. The natural man receiveth not the things of the Spirit of God : for they are foolishness unto him : neither can he know them, because they are spiritually discerned. 1 *Co. ii.* 14. No man can come to me, except the Father which hath sent me draw him. *John vi.* 44.   No man can say that Jesus is the Lord, but by the Holy Ghost. 1 *Co. xii.* 3.   Turn thou me, and I shall be turned ; for thou art the Lord my God.   Surely after that 1 was turned, I repented. *Je. xxxi.* 18, 19.   The preparations of the heart in man, and the answer of the tongue, is from the Lord. *Pr. xvi.* 1.   We know not what we should pray for as we ought. *Ro. viii.* 26. *See also, Col. ii.* 13.

2. Wherefore we have no power to do good works pleasant and

2. Abide in me, and I in you.   As the branch cannot bear fruit of itself, except it abide in the vine ; no more can ye, except ye abide in me.   I am the vine, ye are the branches : He that abideth in me, and I in him, the same bringeth forth

acceptable to God, without the grace of God by Christ preventing us that we may have a good will, and working with us, when we have that good will.

much fruit: for without me ye can do nothing. *John xv.* 4, 5. Not that we are sufficient of ourselves to think any thing as of ourselves; but our sufficiency is of God. *2 Co. iii.* 5. Can the Ethiopian change his skin, or the leopard his spots? then may ye also do good, that are accustomed to do evil. *Je. xiii.* 23. They that are in the flesh cannot please God. *Ro. viii.* 8. A new heart will I give you, and a new spirit will I put within you: and I will take away the stony heart out of your flesh, and I will give you an heart of flesh. And I will put my Spirit within you, and cause you to walk in my statutes, and ye shall keep my judgments, and do them. *Eze. xxxvi.* 26, 27. We were by nature children of wrath, even as others. But God, who is rich in mercy, for his great love wherewith he loved us, even when we were dead in sins, hath quickened us together with Christ; for by grace are ye saved through faith; and that not of yourselves: it is the gift of God: not of works. And you hath he quickened, who were dead in trespasses and sins. For we are his workmanship, created in Christ Jesus unto good works, which God hath before ordained that we should walk in them. *Ep. ii.* 3, 4, 5. 8, 9. 1. 10. O Lord, I know that the way of man is not in himself: it is not in man that walketh to direct his steps. *Je. x.* 23. A certain woman named Lydia, a seller of purple, of the city of Thyatira, which worshipped God, heard us: whose heart the Lord opened, that she attended unto the things which were spoken of Paul. *Ac. xvi.* 14. God, who commanded the light to shine out of darkness, hath shined in our hearts, to give the light of the knowledge of the glory of God in the face of Jesus Christ. *2 Co. iv.* 6. By the grace of God I am what I am: and his grace which was bestowed upon me was not in vain; but I laboured more abundantly than they all: yet not I, but the grace of God which was with me. *1 Co. xv.* 10. I can do all things through Christ which strengtheneth me. *Ph. iv.* 13. He said, My grace is sufficient for thee: for my strength is made perfect in weakness. Most gladly therefore will I rather glory in my infirmities, that the power of Christ may rest upon me. *2 Co. xii.* 9. Lord, thou hast wrought all our works in us. *Is. xxvi.* 12. It is God which worketh in you both to will and to do of his good pleasure. *Ph. ii.* 13. Now the God of peace, that brought again from the dead our Lord Jesus, that great Shepherd of the sheep, through the blood of the everlasting covenant, make you perfect in every good work to do his will, working in you that which is well-pleasing in his sight, through Jesus Christ. *He. xiii.* 20, 21. For of him, and through him, and to him, are all things : to whom be glory for ever. Amen. *Ro. xi.* 36.

CCCXII. *Article XI. Of the Justification of Man.*

We are accounted righteous before God, only for the merit of our Lord and Saviour Jesus Christ by Faith, and not for our own works or deservings : Wherefore, that we are justified by Faith only, is a most wholesome Doctrine, and very full of comfort, as more largely is expressed in the Homily of Justification.

Enter not into judgment with thy servant : for in thy sight shall no man living be justified. *Ps. cxliii.* 2. By the deeds of the law there shall no flesh be justified in his sight. But now the righteousness of God without the law is manifested, even the righteousness of God which is by faith of Jesus Christ unto all and upon all them that believe : for there is no difference : for all have sinned, and come short of the glory of God; being justified freely by his grace, through the redemption that is in Christ Jesus : whom God hath set forth to be a Propitiation through faith in his blood, to declare his righteousness for the remission of sins that are past, through the forbearance of God. *Ro. iii.* 20 *to* 25. By grace are ye saved through faith; and that not of yourselves : it is the gift of God : not of works, lest any man should boast. *Ep. ii.* 8, 9. He hath made him to be sin for us, who knew no sin ; that we might be made the righteousness of God in him. 2 *Co. ii.* 21. With the heart man believeth unto righteousness. *Ro. x.* 10. Behold, the days come, saith the Lord, that I will raise unto David a righteous Branch ; and a King shall reign and prosper. And this is his name whereby he shall be called, THE LORD OUR RIGHTEOUSNESS. *Je. xxiii.* 5, 6. Be it known unto you, men and brethren, that through this man is preached unto you the forgiveness of sins : and by him all that believe are justified from all things, from which ye could not be justified by the law of Moses. *Ac. xiii.* 38, 39. That no man is justified by the law in the sight of God, it is evident : for, The just shall live by faith. And the law is not of faith : but, The man that doeth them shall live in them. For as many as are of the works of the law are under the curse : for it is written,

Cursed is every one that continueth not in all things which are written in the book of the law to do them. *Ga. iii.* 11, 12. 10. Knowing that a man is not justified by the works of the law, but by the faith of Jesus Christ, even we have believed in Jesus Christ, that we might be justified by the faith of Christ, and not by the works of the law : for by the works of the law shall no flesh be justified. *Gal. ii.* 16. They being ignorant of God's righteousness, and going about to establish their own righteousness, have not submitted themselves unto the righteousness of God. For Christ is the end of the law for righteousness to every one that believeth. *Ro. x.* 3, 4. What saith the Scripture? Abraham believed God, and it was counted unto him for righteousness. Now to him that worketh is the reward not reckoned of grace, but of debt. But to him that worketh not, but believeth on him that justifieth the ungodly, his faith is counted for righteousness. *Ro. iv.* 3, 4, 5. Abraham believed God, and it was accounted to him for righteousness. Know ye therefore that they which are of faith, the same are the children of Abraham. And the Scripture, foreseeing that God would justify the heathen through faith, preached before the Gospel unto Abraham, saying, In thee shall all nations be blessed. So then they which be of faith are blessed with faithful Abraham. *Ga. iii.* 6 *to* 9. Not by works of righteousness which we have done, but according to his mercy he saved us; that being justified by his grace, we should be made heirs according to the hope of eternal life. *Tit. iii.* 5. 7. Where is boasting then? it is excluded. By what law? of works? Nay: but by the law of faith. Therefore we conclude that a man is justified by faith without the deeds of the law. *Ro. iii.* 27, 28. Of him are ye in Christ Jesus, who of God is made unto us wisdom, and righteousness, and sanctification, and redemption: that, according as it is written, He that glorieth, let him glory in the Lord. 1 *Co. i.* 30, 31. Surely, shall one say, In the Lord have I righteousness and strength: even to him shall men come. In the Lord shall all the seed of Israel be justified, and shall glory. *Is. xlv.* 24, 25. Being justified by faith, we have peace with God through our Lord Jesus Christ : by whom also we have access by faith into this grace wherein we stand, and rejoice in hope of the glory of God. *Ro. v.* 1, 2. Doubtless, I count all things but loss for the excellency of the knowledge of Christ Jesus my Lord: for whom I have suffered the loss of all things, and do count them but dung, that I may win Christ, and be found in him, not having mine own righteousness, which is of the law, but that which is through the faith of Christ, the righteousness which is of God by faith. *Ph. iii.* 8, 9. We are more than conquerors through him that loved us. *Ro. viii.* 37. Let thy merciful kindness be for my comfort. *Ps. cxix.* 76. Comfort ye, comfort ye my people, saith your God. Speak ye comfortably to Jerusalem, and cry unto her, that her iniquity is pardoned: for she hath received of the Lord's hand double for all her sins. *Is. xl.* 1, 2. Now our Lord Jesus Christ himself, and God, even our Father, which hath loved us, and hath given us everlasting consolation and good hope through grace, comfort your hearts, and stablish you in every good word and work. 2 *Th. ii.* 16, 17.

CCCXIII. *Article XII. Of Good Works.*

Albeit that Good Works, which are the fruits of Faith, and follow after Justification, cannot put away our sins, and endure the severity of God's Judgment; yet are they pleasing and acceptable to God in Christ, and do spring out necessarily of a true and lively Faith; insomuch that by them a lively Faith may be as evidently known as a tree discerned by the fruit.

We are his workmanship, created in Christ Jesus unto good works, which God hath before ordained that we should walk in them. *Ep. ii.* 10. Faith, if it hath not works, is dead, being alone. Yea, a man may say, Thou hast faith, and I have works: shew me thy faith without thy works, and I will shew thee my faith by my works. By works was faith made perfect. For as the body without the spirit is dead, so faith without works is dead also. *Ja. ii.* 17, 18. 22. 26. The Gospel which is come unto you, as it is in all the world; and bringeth forth fruit, as it doth also in you, since the day ye heard of it, and knew the grace of God in truth. *Col. i.* 5, 6. Filled with the fruits of righteousness which are by Jesus Christ, unto the glory and praise of God. *Ph. i.* 11. Being made free from sin, ye became the servants of righteousness. Ye have your fruit unto holiness. *Ro. vi.* 18. 22. He that abideth in me, and I in him, the same bringeth forth much fruit. Herein is my Father glorified, that ye bear much fruit; so shall ye be my disciples. I have chosen you, and ordained you, that ye should go and bring forth fruit, and that your fruit should remain. *John xv.* 5. 8. 16. In Jesus Christ neither circumcision availeth any thing, nor uncircumcision; but faith which worketh by love. *Ga. v.* 6. When ye shall have done all those things which are commanded you, say, We are unprofitable servants: we have done that which was our duty to do. *Lu. xvii.* 10. If we walk in the light, as he is in the light, we have fellowship one with another, and the blood of Jesus Christ his Son cleanseth us from all sin. 1 *John i.* 7. Enter not into judgment with thy servant: for in thy sight shall no man living be justified. *Ps. cxliii.* 2. How should man be just with God? If he will contend with him, he cannot answer him one of a thousand. *Job ix.* 2, 3. If thou, Lord, shouldest mark iniquities, O Lord, who shall stand? *Ps. cxxx.* 3. Do we then make void the law through faith? God forbid: yea, we establish the law. *Ro. iii.* 31. What shall we say then? Shall we continue in sin, that grace may abound? God forbid. How shall we, that are dead to sin, live any longer therein? What then? shall we sin, because we are not under the law, but under grace? God forbid. But now being made free from sin, and become servants to God, ye have your fruit unto holiness, and the end everlasting life. *Ro. vi.* 1, 2. 15. 22. The grace of God that bringeth salvation hath appeared to all men, teaching us that, denying ungodliness and worldly lusts, we should live soberly, righteously, and godly, in this present world; looking for that blessed hope, and the glorious appearing of the great God and our Saviour Jesus Christ; who gave himself for us, that he might redeem us from all iniquity, and purify unto himself a peculiar people, zealous of good works. *Tit. ii.* 11 *to* 14. I beseech you therefore, brethren, by the mercies of God, that ye present your bodies a living sacrifice, holy, acceptable unto God, which is your reasonable service. Be ye transformed by the renewing of your mind, that ye may prove what is that good, and acceptable, and perfect will of God. *Ro. xii.* 1, 2. This is a faithful saying, and these things I will that thou affirm constantly, that they which have believed in God might be careful to maintain good works. *Tit. iii.* 8. To do good and to communicate forget not: for with such sacrifices God is well pleased. Now the God of peace, that brought again from the dead our Lord Jesus, that Great Shepherd of the sheep, through the blood of the everlasting covenant,

make you perfect in every good work to do his will, working
in you that which is well pleasing in his sight, through
Jesus Christ. *He. xiii.* 16. 20, 21.   Without faith it is
impossible to please him. *He. xi.* 6.   A man may say, Thou
hast faith, and I have works: shew me thy faith without thy
works, and I will shew thee my faith by my works. *Ja. ii.* 18.
Beloved, now are we the sons of God, and it doth not yet
appear what we shall be: but we know that, when he shall
appear, we shall be like him; for we shall see him as he is.
And every man that hath this hope in him purifieth himself,
even as he is pure.   In this the children of God are manifest,
and the children of the devil: whosoever doeth not righteousness is not of God.   He that doeth righteousness is righteous,
even as he is righteous. 1 *John iii.* 2, 3. 10. 7.   Hereby we
do know that we know him, if we keep his commandments.
He that saith, I know him, and keepeth not his commandments,
is a liar, and the truth is not in him.   He that saith he is in the
light, and hateth his brother, is in darkness even until now.
He that loveth his brother abideth in the light, and there is
none occasion of stumbling in him. 1 *John ii.* 3, 4. 9, 10.   Ye
shall know them by their fruits.   Do men gather grapes of
thorns or figs of thistles? even so every good tree bringeth forth
good fruit; but a corrupt tree bringeth forth evil fruit.   By
their fruits ye shall know them. *Mat. vii.* 16, 17. 20.   Either
make the tree good, and his fruit good; or else make the
tree corrupt, and his fruit corrupt: for the tree is known by
his fruit. *Mat. xii.* 33.   Let your light so shine before men,
that they may see your good works, and glorify your Father
which is in heaven. *Mat. v.* 16.   Giving all diligence, add to
your faith virtue; and to virtue knowledge; and to knowledge
temperance; and to temperance patience; and to patience
godliness; and to godliness brotherly kindness; and to brotherly kindness charity.   For if these things be in you, and
abound, they make you that ye shall neither be barren nor
unfruitful in the knowledge of our Lord Jesus Christ. 2 *Pe. i.*
5 *to* 8.   Blessed is the man that walketh not in the counsel of
the ungodly, but his delight is in the law of the Lord; he
shall be like a tree planted by the rivers of water, that
bringeth forth his fruit in his season; his leaf also shall not
wither; and whatsoever he doeth shall prosper. *Ps. i.* 1 *to* 4.

CCCXIV. *Article XIII. Of Works before Justification.*

Works done before the grace of Christ, and the Inspiration of his Spirit, are not pleasant to God, forasmuch as they spring not of faith in Jesus Christ, neither do they make men meet to receive grace, or (as the school-authors say) deserve grace of congruity : yea rather, for that they are not done as God hath willed and commanded them to be done, we doubt not but they have the nature of sin.

What then? are we better than they? No, in no wise: for we have before proved both Jews and Gentiles, that they are all under sin : as it is written, There is none righteous, no, not one. Now we know that what things soever the law saith, it saith to them who are under the law : that every mouth may be stopped, and all the world may become guilty before God. Therefore by the deeds of the law there shall no flesh be justified in his sight : for by the law is the knowledge of sin. *Ro. iii.* 9, 10. 19, 20. We are all as an unclean thing, and all our righteousnesses are as filthy rags. *Is. lxiv.* 6. Every good tree bringeth forth good fruit; but a corrupt tree bringeth forth evil fruit. A good tree cannot bring forth evil fruit, neither can a corrupt tree bring forth good fruit. *Mat. vii.* 17, 18. The carnal mind is enmity against God : for it is not subject to the law of God, neither indeed can be. So then they that are in the flesh cannot please God. But ye are not in the flesh, but in the Spirit, if so be that the Spirit of God dwell in you. Now if any man have not the Spirit of Christ, he is none of his. *Ro. viii.* 7, 8, 9. The sacrifice of the wicked is an abomination to the Lord. *Pr. vi.* 8. As the branch cannot bear fruit of itself, except it abide in the vine; no more can ye, except ye abide in me. I am the vine, ye are the branches: he that abideth in me, and I in him, the same bringeth forth much fruit: for without me ye can do nothing. *John xv.* 4, 5. Without faith it is impossible to please God. *He. xi.* 6. He that believeth and is baptized shall be saved; but he that believeth not shall be damned. *Mar. xvi.* 16. He that believeth on the Son hath everlasting life : and he that believeth not the Son shall not see life; but the wrath of God abideth on him. *John iii.* 36. If Abraham were justified by works, he hath whereof to glory; but not before God. For what saith the Scripture? Abraham believed God, and it was counted unto him for righteousness. Now to him that worketh is the reward not reckoned of grace, but of debt. But to him that worketh not, but believeth on him that justifieth the ungodly, his faith is counted for righteousness. Even as David also describeth the blessedness of the man, unto whom

God imputeth righteousness without works. *Ro. iv.* 2 *to* 6. Not by works of righteousness which we have done, but according to his mercy he saved us. *Tit. iii.* 5. It is not of him that willeth, nor of him that runneth, but of God that sheweth mercy. *Ro. ix.* 16. Who hath first given to him, and it shall be recompensed unto him again? *Ro. xi.* 35. Who maketh thee to differ from another? and what hast thou that thou didst not receive? 1 *Co. iv.* 7. God, even when we were dead in sins, hath quickened us together with Christ; by grace are ye saved through faith; and that not of yourselves: it is the gift of God: not of works, lest any man should boast. For we are his workmanship, created in Christ Jesus unto good works, which God hath before ordained that we should walk in them. Wherefore remember, that ye being in time past Gentiles in the flesh, who are called Uncircumcision by that which is called the Circumcision in the flesh made by hands; that at that time ye were without Christ, being aliens from the commonwealth of Israel, and strangers from the covenants of promise, having no hope, and without God in the world: but now in Christ Jesus ye who sometimes were far off are made nigh by the blood of Christ. *Ep. ii.* 4, 5. 8 *to* 13. Whatsoever ye do in word or deed, do all in the name of the Lord Jesus, giving thanks to God and the Father by him. *Col. iii.* 17. I know that in me, (that is, in my flesh,) dwelleth no good thing: for to will is present with me; but how to perform that which is good I find not. *Ro. vii.* 18. Whatsoever is not of faith is sin. *Ro. xiv.* 23.

CCCXV. *Article XIV. Of Works of Supererogation.*

1. Voluntary Works besides, over and above, God's Commandments, which they call Works of Supererogation, cannot be taught without arrogancy and impiety.

1. Thou shalt love the Lord thy God with all thy heart, and with all thy soul, and with all thy strength, and with all thy mind; and thy neighbour as thyself. *Lu. x.* 27. Be ye therefore perfect, even as your Father which is in heaven is perfect. *Mat. v.* 48. What thing soever I command you, observe to do it: thou shalt not add thereto, nor diminish from it. *De. xii.* 32. As many as are of the works of the law are under the curse: for it is written, Cursed is every one that continueth not in all things which are written in the book of the law to do them. *Ga. iii.* 10. Who maketh thee to differ from another? and what hast thou that thou didst not receive?

now if thou didst receive it, why dost thou glory, as if thou hadst not received it? 1 *Co. iv.* 7. In vain do they worship me, teaching for doctrines the commandments of men. *Mat. xv.* 9. There is none righteous, no, not one. *Ro. iii.* 10. Beware lest any man spoil you through philosophy and vain deceit, after the tradition of men, after the rudiments of the world, and not after Christ. Let no man judge you in meat, or in drink, or in respect of an holyday, or of the new moon, or of the sabbath days. Let no man beguile you of your reward in a voluntary humility and worshipping of angels, intruding into those things which he hath not seen, vainly puffed up by his fleshly mind, and not holding the Head. If ye be dead with Christ from the rudiments of the world, why, as though living in the world, are ye subject to ordinances, (touch not; taste not; handle not;) after the commandments and doctrines of men? which things have indeed a shew of wisdom in will worship, and humility, and neglecting of the body; not in any honour to the satisfying of the flesh. *Col. ii.* 8. 16. 18 *to* 23.

2. For by them men do declare, that they do not only render unto God as much as they are bound to do, but that they do more for his sake, than of bounden duty is required: whereas Christ saith plainly, When ye have done all that are commanded to you, say, We are unprofitable servants.

2. Enter not into judgment with thy servant: for in thy sight shall no man living be justified. *Ps. cxliii.* 2. Can a man be profitable unto God, as he that is wise may be profitable unto himself? Is it any pleasure to the Almighty, that thou art righteous? or is it gain to him, that thou makest thy ways perfect? *Job xxii.* 2, 3. If thou be righteous, what givest thou him? or what receiveth he of thine hand? *Job xxxv.* 7. All things come of thee, and of thine own have we given thee. 1 *Ch. xxix.* 14. Two men went up into the temple to pray; the one a Pharisee, and the other a Publican. The Pharisee stood and prayed thus with himself, God, I thank thee, that I am not as other men are, extortioners, unjust, adulterers, or even as this Publican. I fast twice in the week, I give tithes of all that I possess. And the Publican, standing afar off, would not lift up so much as his eyes unto heaven, but smote upon his breast, saying, God be merciful to me a sinner. I tell you, this man went down to his house justified rather than the other: for every one that exalteth himself shall be abased; and he that humbleth himself shall be exalted. *Lu. xviii.* 10 *to* 14. Which of you, having a servant plowing or

feeding cattle, will say unto him by and by, when he is come from the field, Go and sit down to meat? and will not rather say unto him, Make ready wherewith I may sup, and gird thyself, and serve me, till I have eaten and drunken; and afterward thou shalt eat and drink? Doth he thank that servant because he did the things that were commanded him? I trow not. So likewise ye, when ye shall have done all those things which are commanded you, say, We are unprofitable servants: we have done that which was our duty to do. *Lu. xvii.* 7 *to* 10.

CCCXVI. *Article XV. Of Christ alone without Sin.*

1. Christ in the truth of our nature, was made like unto us in all things, (sin only except,) from which he was clearly void, both in his flesh, and in his spirit.

1. God sent forth his Son, made of a woman, made under the law. *Ga. iv.* 4. Jesus Christ our Lord, which was made of the seed of David according to the flesh. *Ro. i.* 3. The Word was made flesh, and dwelt among us. *John i.* 14. Forasmuch then as the children are partakers of flesh and blood, he also himself likewise took part of the same: for verily he took not on him the nature of angels; but he took on him the seed of Abraham. *He. ii.* 14. 16. He hath made him to be sin for us, who knew no sin. 2 *Co. v.* 21. We have not an High Priest which cannot be touched with the feeling of our infirmities; but was in all points tempted like as we are, yet without sin. *He. iv.* 15. Such an High Priest became us, who is holy, harmless, undefiled, separate from sinners. *He. vii.* 26. Who did no sin, neither was guile found in his mouth. 1 *Pe. ii.* 22. The prince of this world cometh, and hath nothing in me. *John xiv.* 30. Which of you convinceth me of sin? *John viii.* 46.

2. He came to be the Lamb without spot, who, by sacrifice of himself once made, should take away the sins of the world, and sin, (as St. John saith,) was not in him.

2. The next day John seeth Jesus coming unto him and saith, Behold the Lamb of God, which taketh away the sin of the world. *John i.* 29. The Lamb slain from the foundation of the world. *Re. xiii.* 8. Now once in the end of the world hath he appeared to put away sin by the sacrifice of himself. *He. ix.* 26. Ye know that ye were not redeemed with corruptible things, as silver and gold, from your vain conversation received by tradition from your fathers; but with the precious blood of Christ, as of a lamb without blemish and without spot. 1 *Pe. i.* 18, 19. How much more shall the

blood of Christ, who through the eternal Spirit offered himself without spot to God, purge your conscience from dead works to serve the living God ? *He. ix.* 14. Christ our Passover is sacrificed for us. 1 *Co. v.* 7. Christ was once offered to bear the sins of many. *He. ix.* 28. Who his ownself bare our sins in his own body on the tree. 1 *Pe. ii.* 24. In whom we have redemption through his blood, the forgiveness of sins, according to the riches of his grace. *Ep. i.* 7. The blood of Jesus Christ his Son cleanseth us from all sin. 1 *John i.* 7. Jesus Christ the righteous is the Propitiation for our sins : and not for ours only, but also for the sins of the whole world. 1 *John ii.* 1, 2. And ye know that he was manifested to take away our sins ; and in him is no sin. 1 *John iii.* 5.

3. But all we the rest, although baptized, and born again in Christ, yet offend in many things ; and if we say we have no sin, we deceive ourselves, and the truth is not in us.

3. The Scripture hath concluded all under sin. *Ga. iii.* 22. There is none righteous, no, not one. *Ro. iii.* 10. There is not a just man upon earth, that doeth good, and sinneth not. *Ec. vii.* 20. That which I do I allow not: for what I would, that do I not: but what I hate, that do I. I find then a law, that, when I would do good, evil is present with me. *Ro. vii.* 15. 21. For the flesh lusteth against the Spirit, and the Spirit against the flesh : and these are contrary the one to the other : so that ye cannot do the things that ye would. *Ga. v.* 17. Cleanse thou me from secret faults. *Ps. xix.* 12. In many things we offend all. *Ja. iii.* 2. If we say that we have no sin, we deceive ourselves, and the truth is not in us. If we say that we have not sinned, we make him a liar, and his word is not in us. 1 *John i.* 8. 10.

CCCXVII. Article XVI. Of Sin after Baptism.

Not every deadly sin willingly committed after Baptism is sin against the Holy Ghost, and unpardonable. Wherefore the grant of repentance is not to be denied to such as fall into sin after Baptism.

The soul that sinneth, it shall die. *Eze. xviii.* 4. The wages of sin is death. *Ro. vi.* 23. I say unto you, All manner of sin and blasphemy shall be forgiven unto men: but the blasphemy against the Holy Ghost shall not be forgiven unto men. And whosoever speaketh a word against the Son of man, it shall be forgiven him : but whosoever speaketh against the Holy Ghost, it shall not be forgiven him, neither in this world, neither in the world to come. *Mat. xii.* 31, 32. If any man see his brother sin a sin which is not unto death, he shall ask, and he shall give him life for them that sin not unto death. There

c c

After we have received the Holy Ghost, we may depart from grace given, and fall into sin, and by the grace of God we may arise again, and amend our lives. And therefore they are to be condemned, which say, they can no more sin as long as they live here, or deny the place of forgiveness to such as truly repent.

is a sin unto death : I do not say that he shall pray for it. All unrighteousness is sin : and there is a sin not unto death. 1 *John v.* 16, 17. And the Lord said, Simon, Simon, behold, satan hath desired to have you, that he may sift you as wheat : but I have prayed for thee, that thy faith fail not : and when thou art converted, strengthen thy brethren. And he said unto him, Lord, I am ready to go with thee, both into prison, and to death. And he said, I tell thee, Peter, the cock shall not crow this day, before that thou shalt thrice deny that thou knowest me. *Lu. xxii.* 31 *to* 34. Peter said unto him, Though I should die with thee, yet will I not deny thee. Likewise also said all the disciples.—Then began Peter to curse and to swear, saying, I know not the man. And immediately the cock crew. And the Lord turned, and looked upon Peter. And Peter remembered the word of Jesus which said unto him, Before the cock crow, thou shalt deny me thrice. And he went out, and wept bitterly. *Mat. xxvi.* 35. 74, 75. *Lu. xxii.* 61. Repent therefore of this thy wickedness, and pray God, if perhaps the thought of thine heart may be forgiven thee. *Ac. viii.* 22. Take heed, brethren, lest there be in any of you an evil heart of unbelief, in departing from the living God. But exhort one another daily, while it is called To day ; lest any of you be hardened through the deceitfulness of sin. *He. iii.* 12, 13. Lead us not into temptation, but deliver us from evil. *Mat. vi.* 13. And Nathan said to David, Thou art the man. And David said unto Nathan, I have sinned against the Lord. And Nathan said unto David, The Lord also hath put away thy sin. 2 *Sa. xii.* 7. 13. Wash me throughly from mine iniquity, and cleanse me from my sin. For I acknowledge my transgressions : and my sin is ever before me. *Ps. li.* 2, 3. I thought on my ways, and turned my feet unto thy testimonies. I made haste, and delayed not to keep thy commandments. *Ps. cxix.* 59, 60. Who can say, I have made my heart clean, I am pure from my sin ? *Pr. xx.* 9. There is not a just man upon earth, that doeth good, and sinneth not. *Ec. vii.* 20. If we say that we have no sin, we deceive ourselves, and the truth is not in us. 1 *John i.* 8. To the Lord our God belong mercies and forgivenesses, though we have rebelled against him ; neither have we obeyed the voice of the Lord our God, to walk in his laws, which he set before us. *Da. ix.* 9, 10. Thou, Lord, art good, and ready to forgive. *Ps. lxxxvi.* 5. Brethren, if a man be overtaken in a fault, ye which are spiritual, restore such an one in the spirit of meekness; considering thyself, lest thou also be tempted. *Ga. vi.* 1. Sufficient to such a man is this punishment, which was inflicted of many. So that contrariwise ye ought rather to forgive him, and comfort him, lest perhaps such an one should be swallowed up with overmuch sorrow. Wherefore I beseech you that ye would confirm your love toward him. 2 *Co. ii.* 6, 7, 8.

CCCXVIII. *Article XVII. Of Predestination and Election.*

1. Predestination to Life is the everlasting purpose of God, whereby (before the foundations of the world were laid) he hath constantly decreed by his counsel secret to us, to deliver from curse and damnation those whom he hath chosen in Christ out of mankind, and to bring them by Christ to everlasting salvation, as vessels made to honour.

1. Blessed be the God and Father of our Lord Jesus Christ, who hath blessed us with all spiritual blessings in heavenly places in Christ: according as he hath chosen us in him before the foundation of the world, that we should be holy and without blame before him in love : having predestinated us unto the adoption of children by Jesus Christ to himself, according to the good pleasure of his will; in whom also we have obtained an inheritance, being predestinated according to the purpose of him who worketh all things after the counsel of his own will. *Ep. i.* 3, 4, 5. 11. Elect according to the foreknowledge of God the Father, through sanctification of the Spirit, unto obedience and sprinkling of the blood of Jesus Christ. 1 *Pe. i.* 2. According to the eternal purpose which he purposed in Christ Jesus our Lord. *Ep. iii.* 11. The Lamb slain from the foundation of the world. *Re. xiii.* 8. Who hath saved us, and called us with an holy calling, not according to our works, but according to his own purpose and grace, which was given us in Christ Jesus before the world began. 2 *Ti. i.* 9. Then shall the King say unto them on his right hand, Come, ye blessed of my Father, inherit the kingdom prepared for you from the foundation of the world. *Mat. xxv.* 34. And they that dwell on the earth shall wonder, whose names were not written in the book of life from the foundation of the world. *Re. xvii.* 8. Who hath known the mind of the Lord? or who hath been his counsellor? *Ro. xi.*

34. Why dost thou strive against him? for he giveth not account of any of his matters. *Job xxxiii.* 13. The counsel of the Lord standeth for ever, and the thoughts of his heart to all generations. *Ps. xxxiii.* 11. The secret things belong unto the Lord our God: but those which are revealed belong unto us and to our children for ever. *De. xxix.* 29. Oh the depth of the riches both of the wisdom and knowledge of God! how unsearchable are his judgments, and his ways past finding out! *Ro. xi.* 33. Hath not the potter power over the clay, of the same lump to make one vessel unto honour, and another unto dishonour? And that he might make known the riches of his glory on the vessels of mercy, which he had afore prepared unto glory, even us, whom he hath called. *Ro. ix.* 21. 24, 25. The Father, who hath delivered us from the power of darkness, and hath translated us into the kingdom of his dear Son: in whom we have redemption through his blood, even the forgiveness of sins. *Col. i.* 12, 13, 14. As many as are of the works of the law are under the curse: for it is written, Cursed is every one that continueth not in all things which are written in the book of the law to do them. Christ hath redeemed us from the curse of the law, being made a curse for us. *Ga. iii.* 10. 13. But we are bound to give thanks alway to God for you, brethren beloved of the Lord, because God hath from the beginning chosen you to salvation through sanctification of the Spirit and belief of the truth: whereunto he called you by our Gospel, to the obtaining of the glory of our Lord Jesus Christ. *2 Th. ii.* 13, 14. Ye are not of the world, but I have chosen you out of the world. *John xv.* 19. As in Adam all die, even so in Christ shall all be made alive. *1 Co. xv.* 22. Of him are ye in Christ Jesus, who of God is made unto us wisdom, and righteousness, and sanctification, and redemption. *1 Co. i.* 30. By whom also we have access by faith into this grace wherein we stand, and rejoice in hope of the glory of God. *Ro. v.* 2. Whom he did foreknow, he also did predestinate to be conformed to the image of his Son. Moreover whom he did predestinate, them he also called: and whom he called, them he also justified: and whom he justified, them he also glorified. *Ro. viii.* 29, 30. In a great house there are not only vessels of gold and of silver, but also of

wood and of earth; and some to honour, and some to dishonour. If a man therefore purge himself from these, he shall be a vessel unto honour, sanctified, and meet for the master's use. *2 Ti. ii.* 20, 21.

2. Wherefore, they which be endued with so excellent a benefit of God be called according to God's purpose by his Spirit working in due season: they through Grace obey the calling:

2. But ye are a chosen generation, a royal priesthood, an holy nation, a peculiar people; that ye should shew forth the praises of him who hath called you out of darkness into his marvellous light: which in time past were not a people, but are now the people of God: which had not obtained mercy, but now have obtained mercy. *1 Pe. ii.* 9, 10. No man can come to me, except the Father which hath sent me draw him. Every man that hath heard, and hath learned of the Father, cometh unto me. *John vi.* 44, 45. God, who hath saved us, and called us with an holy calling, not according to our works, but according to his own purpose and grace, which was given us in Christ Jesus before the world began. *2 Ti. i.* 8, 9. In whom also we have obtained an inheritance, being predestinated according to the purpose of him who worketh all things after the counsel of his own will. *Ep. i.* 11. God is faithful, by whom ye were called unto the fellowship of his Son Jesus Christ our Lord. *1 Co. i.* 9. This is the word of the Lord, Not by might, nor by power, but by my Spirit, saith the Lord of hosts. *Zec. iv.* 6. Having made known unto us the mystery of his will, according to his good pleasure which he hath purposed in himself: that in the dispensation of the fulness of times he might gather together in one all things in Christ, both which are in heaven, and which are on earth; even in him. *Ep. i.* 9, 10. As the rain cometh down, and the snow from heaven, and returneth not thither, but watereth the earth, and maketh it bring forth and bud; so shall my word be that goeth forth out of my mouth: it shall not return unto me void, but it shall accomplish that which I please, and it shall prosper in the thing whereto I sent it. *Is. lv.* 10, 11. It is the Spirit that quickeneth. *John vi.* 63. Thy people shall be willing in the day of thy power. *Ps. cx.* 3. God be thanked, that ye were the servants of sin, but ye have obeyed from the heart that form of doctrine which was delivered you. *Ro. vi.* 17. They that are with him are called, and chosen, and faithful. *Re. xvii.* 14. It is God which worketh in you both to will and to do of his good pleasure. *Ph. ii.* 13.

3. They be justified freely: they be made sons of God by adoption :

3. Whom he called, them he also justified. *Ro. viii.* 30. Being justified freely by his grace through the redemption that is in Christ Jesus. *Ro. iii.* 24. Not by works of righteousness which we have done, but according to his mercy he saved us, by the washing of regeneration, and renewing of the Holy Ghost; that being justified by his grace, we should be made heirs according to the hope of eternal life. *Tit. iii.* 5. 7. In the Lord shall all the seed of Israel be justified, and shall glory. *Is. xlv.* 25. Therefore being justified by faith, we have peace with God through our Lord Jesus Christ: by whom also we have access by faith into this grace wherein we stand. *Ro. v.* 1, 2. As many as received him, to them gave he power to become the sons of God, even to them that believe on his name: which were born, not of blood, nor of the will of the flesh, nor of the will of man, but of God. *John i.* 12, 13. Having predestinated us unto the adoption of children by Jesus Christ to himself, according to the good pleasure of his will, to the praise of the glory of his grace. *Ep. i.* 5, 6. God sent forth his Son, to redeem them that were under the law, that we might receive the adoption of sons. And because ye are sons, God hath sent forth the Spirit of his Son into your hearts, crying, Abba, Father. Wherefore thou art no more a servant but a son, and if a son, then an heir of God through Christ. *Ga. iv.* 4 *to* 7. As many as are led by the Spirit of God, they are the sons of God. Ye have not received the spirit of bondage again to fear; but ye have received the Spirit of adoption whereby we cry, Abba, Father. *Ro. viii.* 14, 15. Behold, what manner of love the Father hath bestowed upon us, that we should be called the sons of God. Beloved, now are we the sons of God, and it doth not yet appear what we shall be: but we know that, when he shall appear, we shall be like him. 1 *John iii.* 1, 2.

4. they be made like the image of his only-begotten Son Jesus Christ :

4. Whom he did foreknow, he also did predestinate to be conformed to the image of his Son, that he might be the first-born among many brethren. *Ro. viii.* 29. If any man be in Christ, he is a new creature: old things are passed away; behold, all things are become new. *Co. v.* 17. As we have borne the image of the earthy, we shall also bear the image of the heavenly. 1 *Co. xv.* 49. For if we have been planted

together in the likeness of his death, we shall be also in the likeness of his resurrection : knowing this, that our old man is crucified with him, that the body of sin might be destroyed, that henceforth we should not serve sin. For he that is dead is freed from sin. Likewise reckon ye also yourselves to be dead indeed unto sin, but alive unto God through Jesus Christ our Lord. *Ro. vi.* 5, 6, 7. 11. As many of you as have been baptized into Christ have put on Christ. *Ga. iii.* 27. And have put on the new man, which is renewed in knowledge after the image of him that created him. *Col. iii.* 10. I have manifested thy name unto the men which thou gavest me out of the world. Holy Father, keep through thine own name those whom thou hast given me, that they may be one, as we are. They are not of the world, even as I am not of the world. The glory which thou gavest me I have given them ; that they may be one, even as we are one: I in them, and thou in me, that they may be made perfect in one. *John xvii.* 6. 11. 16. 22, 23. As for me, I will behold thy face in righteousness: I shall be satisfied, when I awake, with thy likeness. *Ps. xvii.* 15.

5. they walk religiously in good works, and at length, by God's mercy, they attain to everlasting felicity.

5. For we are his workmanship, created in Christ Jesus unto good works, which God hath before ordained that we should walk in them. *Ep. ii.* 10. The grace of God that bringeth salvation hath appeared to all men, teaching us that, denying ungodliness and worldly lusts, we should live soberly, righteously, and godly, in this present world. *Tit. ii.* 11, 12. Ye have not chosen me, but I have chosen you, and ordained you, that ye should go and bring forth fruit, and that your fruit should remain. Abide in me, and I in you. As the branch cannot bear fruit of itself, except it abide in the vine ; no more can ye, except ye abide in me. Herein is my Father glorified, that ye bear much fruit. *John xv.* 16. 4. 8. We do not cease to pray for you, that ye might walk worthy of the Lord unto all pleasing, being fruitful in every good work. *Col. i.* 9, 10. He that goeth forth and weepeth, bearing precious seed, shall doubtless come again with rejoicing, bringing his sheaves with him. *Ps. cxxvi.* 6. Keep yourselves in the love of God, looking for the mercy of our Lord Jesus Christ unto eternal life. *Jude* 21. In whom also we have obtained

an inheritance, being predestinated according to the purpose of him who worketh all things after the counsel of his own will. *Ep. i.* 11. Looking for that blessed hope, and the glorious appearing of the great God and our Saviour Jesus Christ. *Tit. ii.* 13. And this is the Father's will which hath sent me, that of all which he hath given me I should lose nothing, but should raise it up again at the last day. And this is the will of him that sent me, that every one which seeth the Son, and believeth on him, may have everlasting life: and I will raise him up at the last day. Verily, verily, I say unto you, He that believeth on me hath everlasting life. *John vi.* 39, 40. 47. He which hath begun a good work in you will perform it until the day of Jesus Christ. *Ph. i.* 6. Whom he justified, them he also glorified. *Ro. viii.* 30. Thou wilt shew me the path of life: in thy presence is fulness of joy, at thy right hand there are pleasures for evermore. *Ps. xvi.* 11. Thou shalt guide me with thy counsel, and afterward receive me to glory. *Ps. lxxiii.* 24. Blessed be the God and Father of our Lord Jesus Christ, which according to his abundant mercy hath begotten us again unto a lively hope by the resurrection of Jesus Christ from the dead, to an inheritance incorruptible, and undefiled, and that fadeth not away, reserved in heaven for you, who are kept by the power of God through faith unto salvation ready to be revealed in the last time. 1 *Pe. i.* 3, 4, 5. Now unto him that is able to keep you from falling, and to present you faultless before the presence of his glory with exceeding joy, to the only wise God our Saviour, be glory and majesty, dominion and power, both now and ever. Amen. *Jude* 24, 25.

6. As the godly consideration of Predestination, and our Election in Christ, is full of sweet, pleasant, and unspeakable comfort to godly persons, and such as feel in themselves the working of the Spirit of

6. My sheep hear my voice, and I know them, and they follow me: and I give unto them eternal life; and they shall never perish, neither shall any man pluck them out of my hand. My Father, which gave them me, is greater than all; and no man is able to pluck them out of my Father's hand. *John x.* 27, 28, 29. Behold, God is my salvation; I will trust, and not be afraid: for the Lord JEHOVAH is my strength and my song; he also is become my salvation. Therefore with joy shall ye draw water out of the wells of salvation. Sing unto the Lord; for he hath done excellent

Christ, mortifying the works of the flesh, and their earthly members, and drawing up their mind to high and heavenly things,

things : for great is the Holy One of Israel. *Is. xii.* 2, 3. 5, 6. I know that my Redeemer liveth, and though after my skin worms destroy this body, yet in my flesh shall I see God : whom I shall see for myself, and mine eyes shall behold, and not another. *Job xix.* 25, 26, 27. And not only so, but we also joy in God through our Lord Jesus Christ, by whom we have now received the atonement. We rejoice in hope of the glory of God. *Ro. v.* 11. 2. Whom having not seen, ye love : in whom, though now ye see him not, yet believing, ye rejoice with joy unspeakable and full of glory : receiving the end of your faith, even the salvation of your souls. 1 *Pe. i.* 8, 9. I am in a strait betwixt two, having a desire to depart, and to be with Christ ; which is far better. *Ph. i.* 23. Looking for that blessed hope, and the glorious appearing of the great God and our Saviour Jesus Christ. *Tit. ii.* 13. For we know that if our earthly house of this tabernacle were dissolved, we have a building of God, an house not made with hands, eternal in the heavens. Therefore we are always confident, I say, and willing rather to be absent from the body, and to be present with the Lord. 2 *Co. v.* 1. 6. 8. I am crucified with Christ : nevertheless I live ; yet not I, but Christ liveth in me : and the life which I now live in the flesh I live by the faith of the Son of God, who loved me, and gave himself for me. *Ga. ii.* 20. Every man that hath this hope in him purifieth himself, even as he is pure. 1 *John iii.* 3. According to the power that worketh in us. *Ep. iii.* 20. They that are Christ's have crucified the flesh with the affections and lusts. *Ga. v.* 24. It is a faithful saying : For if we be dead with him, we shall also live with him ; if we suffer, we shall also reign with him. 2 *Ti. ii.* 11, 12. And hope maketh not ashamed ; because the love of God is shed abroad in our hearts by the Holy Ghost which is given unto us. *Ro. v.* 5. I keep under my body, and bring it into subjection : lest that by any means, when I have preached to others, I myself should be a castaway. 1 *Co. ix.* 27. We look not at the things which are seen, but at the things which are not seen : for the things which are seen are temporal, but the things which are not seen are eternal. 2 *Co. iv.* 18. We walk by faith, not by sight. 2 *Co. v.* 7. Our conversation is in heaven ; from whence also we

look for the Saviour, the Lord Jesus Christ. *Ph. iii.* 20. Truly
our fellowship is with the Father, and with his Son Jesus
Christ. 1 *John i.* 3. Now our Lord Jesus Christ himself, and
God, even our Father, which hath loved us, and given us everlasting consolation and good hope through grace, comfort your
hearts, and stablish you in every good word and work. 2 *Th.*
ii. 16, 17.

7. as well
because it doth
greatly estab-
lish and
confirm their
faith of eternal
salvation to be
enjoyed
through
Christ, as be-
cause it doth
fervently
kindle their
love towards
God :

7. Who shall lay any thing to the charge of God's elect?
It is God that justifieth. Who is he that condemneth? It is
Christ that died, yea rather, that is risen again, who is even
at the right hand of God, who also maketh intercession for
us. Who shall separate us from the love of Christ? shall
tribulation, or distress, or persecution, or famine, or nakedness,
or peril, or sword? Nay, in all these things we are more than
conquerors through him that loved us. For I am persuaded,
that neither death, nor life, nor angels, nor principalities, nor
powers, nor things present, nor things to come, nor height,
nor depth, nor any other creature, shall be able to separate us
from the love of God, which is in Christ Jesus our Lord. *Ro.*
viii. 33, 34, 35. 37, 38, 39. Ye have not chosen me, but I have
chosen you. *John xv.* 16. We love him, because he first
loved us. *John iv.* 19. Whom have I in heaven but thee?
and there is none upon earth that I desire beside thee. *Ps.*
lxxiii. 25.

8. So, for
curious and
carnal persons,
lacking the
Spirit of
Christ, to have
continually
before their
eyes the sen-
tence of God's
Predestina-
tion, is a most
dangerous
downfal,
whereby the
Devil doth
thrust them
either into
desperation,
or into wretch-
lessness of
most unclean
living, no less

8. Beware lest any man spoil you through philosophy or
vain deceit, after the tradition of men, after the rudiments of
the world, and not after Christ: intruding into those things
which he hath not seen, vainly puffed up by his fleshly mind,
and not holding the Head, from which all the body by joints
and bands having nourishment ministered, and knit together,
increaseth with the increase of God. *Col. ii.* 8. 18, 19. These
be they who separate themselves, sensual, having not the
Spirit. *Jude* 19. The carnal mind is enmity against God:
for it is not subject to the law of God, neither indeed can be.
Ro. viii. 7. The natural man receiveth not the things of the
Spirit of God: for they are foolishness unto him: neither can
he know them, because they are spiritually discerned. 1 *Co.*
ii. 14. Account that the longsuffering of our Lord is salvation; even as our beloved brother Paul also according to the

perilous than desperation.

wisdom given unto him hath written unto you; as also in all his epistles, speaking in them of these things; in which are some things hard to be understood, which they that are unlearned and unstable wrest, as they do also the other Scriptures, unto their own destruction. Ye therefore, beloved, seeing ye know these things before, beware lest ye also, being led away with the error of the wicked, fall from your own stedfastness. *2 Pet. iii.* 15, 16, 17. And they said, There is no hope : but we will walk after our own devices, and we will every one do the imaginations of his evil heart. *Je. xviii.* 12. And he said, Behold, this evil is of the Lord; what should I wait for the Lord any longer? *2 Ki. vi.* 33. O thou son of man, speak unto the house of Israel; Thus ye speak, saying, If our transgressions and our sins be upon us, and we pine away in them, how should we then live ? Say unto them, As I live, saith the Lord God, I have no pleasure in the death of the wicked : but that the wicked turn from his way and live. *Eze. xxxiii.* 10, 11. Despisest thou the riches of his goodness and forbearance and longsuffering ; not knowing that the goodness of God leadeth thee to repentance? *Ro. ii.* 4. The Lord is not willing that any should perish, but that all should come to repentance. *2 Pe. iii.* 9. If after they have escaped the pollutions of the world through the knowledge of the Lord and Saviour Jesus Christ, they are again entangled therein, and overcome, the latter end is worse with them than the beginning. For it had been better for them not to have known the way of righteousness, than, after they have known it, to turn from the holy commandment delivered unto them. But it is happened unto them according to the true proverb, The dog is turned to his own vomit again; and the sow that was washed to her wallowing in the mire. *2 Pe. ii.* 20, 21, 22. See also, *He. vi.* 7, 8. —*xii.* 15.

9. Furthermore, we must receive God's promises in such wise, as they be generally set forth to us in holy Scripture :

9. The secret things belong unto the Lord our God : but those things which are revealed belong unto us and to our children for ever, that we may do all the words of this law. *De. xxix.* 29. Let the wicked forsake his way, and the unrighteous man his thoughts : and let him return unto the Lord, and he will have mercy upon him ; and to our God, for he will abundantly pardon. *Is. lv.* 7. Go ye into all the world, and preach the

Gospel to every creature. He that believeth and is baptized shall be saved. *Mar. xvi.* 15, 16. He that receiveth whomsoever I send receiveth me; and he that receiveth me receiveth him that sent me. *John xiii.* 20. Come unto me, all ye that labour and are heavy laden, and I will give you rest. *Mat. xi.* 28. Him that cometh to me I will in no wise cast out. *John vi.* 37. Whosoever will, let him take the water of life freely. *Re. xxii.* 17. For God so loved the world, that he gave his only begotten Son, that whosoever believeth in him should not perish, but have everlasting life. *John iii.* 16. God our Saviour, who will have all men to be saved, and come unto the knowledge of the truth. For there is one God, and one Mediator between God and men, the man Christ Jesus; who gave himself a ransom for all, to be testified in due time. 1 *Ti. ii.* 3 *to* 6.

10. and, in our doings, that Will of God is to be followed, which we have expressly declared unto us in the Word of God.

10. Then said they unto him, What shall we do, that we might work the works of God? Jesus answered and said unto them, This is the work of God, that ye believe on him whom he hath sent. And this is the will of him that sent me, that every one which seeth the Son, and believeth on him, may have everlasting life. *John vi.* 28, 29. 40. Behold, a certain lawyer stood up and tempted him, saying, Master, what shall I do to inherit eternal life? He said unto him, What is written in the law? how readest thou? And he answering said, Thou shalt love the Lord thy God with all thy heart, and with all thy soul, and with all thy strength, and with all thy mind; and thy neighbour as thyself. And he said unto him, Thou hast answered right: this do, and thou shalt live. *Lu. x.* 25 *to* 28. He hath shewed thee, O man, what is good; and what doth the Lord require of thee, but to do justly, and to love mercy, and to walk humbly with thy God? *Mi. vi.* 8. Whatsoever things were written aforetime were written for our learning. *Ro. xv.* 4. The Holy Scriptures, which are able to make thee wise unto salvation, through faith which is in Christ Jesus. All Scripture is given by inspiration of God, and is profitable for doctrine, for reproof, for correction, for instruction in righteousness: that the man of God may be perfect, throughly furnished unto all good works. 2 *Ti. iii.* 15, 16, 17. I am the light of the world: he that followeth me shall not walk in

darkness, but shall have the light of life. If ye continue in my word, then are ye my disciples indeed; and ye shall know the truth. *John viii.* 12. 31, 32. If any man will do his will, he shall know of the doctrine, whether it be of God. *John vii.* 17. Let us therefore, as many as be perfect, be thus minded: and if in any thing ye be otherwise minded, God shall reveal even this unto you. Nevertheless, whereto we have already attained, let us walk by the same rule, let us mind the same thing. *Ph. iii.* 15, 16. Let us hear the conclusion of the whole matter: Fear God, and keep his commandments. For God shall bring every work into judgment, with every secret thing, whether it be good, or whether it be evil. *Ec. xii.* 13, 14. Blessed are they that do his commandments, that they may have right to the tree of life, and may enter in through the gates into the city. *Re. xxii.* 14.

CCCXIX. *Article XVIII. Of obtaining eternal Salvation only by the Name of Christ.*

There be some that trouble you, and would pervert the Gospel of Christ. But though we, or an angel from heaven, preach any other Gospel unto you than that which we have preached unto you, let him be accursed. *Ga. i.* 7, 8. If any man love not the Lord Jesus Christ, let him be Anathema Maran-atha. 1 *Co. xvi.* 22. We have proved both Jews and Gentiles, that they are all under sin. They are all gone out of the way, they are together become unprofitable; there is none that doeth good, no, not one. All have sinned, and come short of the glory of God. *Ro. iii.* 9. 12. 23. By the works of the law shall no flesh be justified. *Ga. ii.* 16. He that believeth and is baptized shall be saved. *Mar. xvi.* 16. Jesus saith unto him, I am the Way, and the Truth, and the Life: no man cometh unto the Father, but by me. *John xiv.* 6. Other foundation can no man lay than that is laid, which is Jesus Christ. 1 *Co. iii.* 11. To him give all the prophets witness, that through his name whosoever believeth in him shall receive remission of sins. *Ac. x.* 43. Neither is there salvation in any other: for there is none other name under heaven given among men, whereby we must be saved. *Ac. iv.* 12. This is the record, that God hath given to us eternal life, and this

Marginal note: They also are to be had accursed that presume to say, That every man shall be saved by the Law or Sect which ho professeth, so that he be diligent to frame his life according to that Law, and the light of Nature. For holy Scripture doth set out unto us only the Name of Jesus Christ, whereby men must be saved.

life is in his Son. He that hath the Son hath life; and he that
hath not the Son of God hath not life. These things have I
written unto you that believe on the name of the Son of God;
that ye may know that ye have eternal life, and that ye may
believe on the name of the Son of God. 1 *John v.* 11, 12,
13.   He that believeth on the Son hath everlasting life: and
he that believeth not the Son shall not see life: but the wrath
of God abideth on him. *John iii.* 36.   Many deceivers are
entered into the world, who confess not that Jesus Christ is
come in the flesh.   This is a deceiver and an antichrist.
Whosoever transgresseth, and abideth not in the doctrine
of Christ, hath not God. He that abideth in the doctrine of
Christ, he hath both the Father and the Son. If there come
any unto you, and bring not this doctrine, receive him not
into your house, neither bid him God speed: for he that bid-
deth him God speed is partaker of his evil deeds. 2 *John*
7. 9, 10, 11.

CCCXX. *Article XIX.   Of the Church.*

The visible Church of Christ is a congregation of faithful men, in the which the pure Word of God is preached, and the Sacraments be duly ministered according to Christ's ordinance in all those things that of necessity are requisite to the same. As the Church of *Jerusalem, Alexandria,* and *Antioch,* have erred; so also the Church of *Rome* hath erred, not only in their living and manner of Ceremonies, but also in matters of Faith.

Unto the Church of God which is at Corinth, to them that
are sanctified in Christ Jesus, called to be saints, with all that
in every place call upon the name of Jesus Christ our Lord,
both their's and our's. 1 *Co. i.* 2.   To the saints and faithful
brethren in Christ which are at Colosse. *Col. i.* 2.   That thou
mayest know how thou oughtest to behave thyself in the
house of God, which is the Church of the living God, the
pillar and ground of the truth. 1 *Ti. iii.* 15.   If any man
speak, let him speak as the oracles of God. 1 *Pe. iv.* 11.
Moses of old time hath in every city them that preach him,
being read in the synagogues every sabbath day. *Ac. xv.* 21.
When they believed Philip preaching the things concerning
the kingdom of God, and the name of Jesus Christ, they were
baptized, both men and women. *Ac. viii.* 12.   Jesus came
and spake unto them, saying, All power is given unto me in
heaven and in earth.   Go ye therefore, and teach all nations,
baptizing them in the name of the Father, and of the Son,
and of the Holy Ghost: teaching them to observe all things
whatsoever I have commanded you : and, lo, I am with you
alway, even unto the end of the world. Amen. *Mat. xxviii.*
18, 19, 20: I have received of the·Lord that which also I

delivered unto you, That the Lord Jesus the same night in which he was betrayed took bread : and when he had given thanks, he brake it, and said, Take, eat : this is my body which is broken for you: this do in remembrance of me. After the same manner also he took the cup, when he had supped, saying, This cup is the New Testament in my blood: this do ye, as oft as ye drink it, in remembrance of me. For as often as ye eat this bread, and drink this cup, ye do shew the Lord's death till he come. 1 *Co. xi.* 23 *to* 26. And they continued stedfastly in the Apostles' doctrine and fellowship, and in breaking of bread, and in prayers. And the Lord added to the Church daily such as should be saved. *Ac. ii.* 42. 47. And he ordained twelve, that they should be with him, and that he might send them forth to preach. *Mar. iii.* 14. After these things the Lord appointed other seventy also, and sent them two and two before his face into every city and place, whither he himself would come. *Lu. x.* 1. Of these men which have companied with us all the time that the Lord Jesus went in and out among us, beginning from the baptism of John, unto that same day that he was taken up from us, must one be ordained to be a witness with us of his resurrection. *Ac. i.* 21, 22. No man taketh this honour unto himself, but he that is called of God, as was Aaron. *He. v.* 4. And they withstood Uzziah the king, and said unto him, It appertaineth not unto thee, Uzziah, to burn incense unto the Lord, but to the priests the sons of Aaron, that are consecrated to burn incense : go out of the sanctuary; for thou hast trespassed : neither shall it be for thine honour from the Lord God. 2 *Ch. xxvi.* 18. Now the Spirit speaketh expressly, that in the latter times some shall depart from the faith, giving heed to seducing spirits, and doctrines of devils ; speaking lies in hypocrisy ; having their conscience seared with a hot iron ; forbidding to marry, and commanding to abstain from meats. 1 *Ti. iv.* 1, 2, 3. Be not soon shaken in mind, or be troubled. Let no man deceive you by any means. For the mystery of iniquity doth already work: even him, whose coming is after the working of satan with all power and signs and lying wonders, and with all deceivableness of unrighteousness in them that perish; because they received not the love of the truth, that they might be saved. 2 *Th. ii.* 2, 3. 7. 9, 10. Many false prophets shall rise and shall deceive many. And because iniquity shall abound, the love of many shall wax cold. *Mat. xxiv.* 11, 12. I charge thee therefore before God, and the Lord Jesus Christ, who shall judge the quick and the dead at his appearing and his kingdom, preach the word : be instant in season, out of season ; reprove, rebuke, exhort with all longsuffering and doctrine. For the time will come when they will not endure sound doctrine ; but after their own lusts shall they heap to themselves teachers, having itching ears ; and they shall turn away their ears from the truth, and shall be turned unto fables. But watch thou in all things, do the work of an evangelist, make full proof of thy ministry. 2 *Ti. iv.* 1 to 5.

CCCXXI. *Article XX. Of the Authority of the Church.*

1. The Church hath power to decree Rites or Ceremonies, and Authority in Controversies of Faith :

1. Let all things be done unto edifying. Let all things be done decently and in order. 1 *Co. xiv.* 26. 40. For this cause left I thee in Crete, that thou shouldest set in order the things that are wanting. *Tit. i.* 5. The Jews ordained, and took upon them, and upon their seed, and upon all such as joined themselves unto them, so as it should not fail, that they would keep these two days according to their writing, and according to their appointed time every year ; and that these days should be remembered and kept throughout every generation, every family, every province, and every city ; and that these days of Purim should not fail from among the Jews, nor the memorial of them perish from their seed. *Est. ix.* 27, 28. And it was at Jerusalem the feast of the dedication,* and it was winter. And Jesus walked in the temple in Solomon's porch. *John x.* 22, 23. There rose up certain of the sect of the Pharisees which believed, saying, That it was needful to circumcise them, and to command them to keep the law of Moses. And the apostles and elders came together for to consider of this matter. Then pleased it the apostles and elders, with the whole Church, to send chosen men of their own company to Antioch with Paul and Barnabas ; namely,

* *This feast, according to the best authorities, was instituted by the Jews about 1300 years after the giving of the law, and 165 B. C., to commemorate the purifying of the Temple from the idolatrous pollutions introduced into it by Antiochus Epiphanes.*

Judas surnamed Barsabas, and Silas, chief men among the brethren: and they wrote letters by them after this manner; The apostles and elders and brethren send greeting unto the brethren which are of the Gentiles in Antioch and Syria and Cilicia. Forasmuch as we have heard, that certain which went out from us have troubled you with words, saying, Ye must be circumcised, and keep the law : to whom we gave no such commandment : it seemed good unto us, being assembled with one accord, to send chosen men unto you with our beloved Barnabas and Paul. We have sent therefore Judas and Silas, who shall also tell you the same things by mouth. For it seemed good to the Holy Ghost, and to us, to lay upon you no greater burden than these necessary things; That ye abstain from meats offered to idols, and from blood, and from things strangled, and from fornication : from which if ye keep yourselves, ye shall do well. *Ac. xv.* 5, 6. 22 *to* 25. 27, 28, 29. As they went through the cities, they delivered them the decrees for to keep, that were ordained of the apostles and elders which were at Jerusalem. And so were the churches established in the faith, and increased in number daily. *Ac. xvi.* 4, 5. As I besought thee to abide still at Ephesus, when I went into Macedonia, that thou mightest charge some that they teach no other doctrine. 1 *Ti. i.* 3. There are many unruly and vain talkers and deceivers, specially they of the circumcision : whose mouths must be stopped. *Tit. i.* 10, 11. A man that is an heretic after the first and second admonition reject. *Tit. iii.* 10. Now I beseech you, brethren, mark them which cause divisions and offences contrary to the doctrine which ye have learned ; and avoid them. For they that are such serve not our Lord Jesus Christ, but their own belly. *Ro. xvi.* 17, 18. Teaching them to observe all things whatsoever I have commanded you: and, lo, I am with you alway, even unto the end of the world. *Mat. xxviii.* 20. Obey them that have the rule over you, and submit yourselves: for they watch for your souls, as they that must give account. *He. xiii.* 17.

2. And yet it is not lawful for the Church to ordain any
2. To the law and to the testimony : if they speak not according to this word, it is because there is no light in them. *Is. viii.* 20. What thing soever I command you, observe to do it : thou

E E

thing that is contrary to God's Word written, neither may it so expound one place of Scripture, that it be repugnant to another. Wherefore, although the Church be a witness and a keeper of holy Writ, yet, as it ought not to decree any thing against the same, so besides the same ought it not to enforce any thing to be believed for necessity of Salvation.

shalt not add thereto, nor diminish from it. *De. xii.* 32. He said unto them, Why do ye transgress the commandment of God by your tradition? for God commanded, saying, Honour thy father and mother: but ye say, Whosoever shall say to his father or his mother, It is a gift, by whatsoever thou mightest be profited by me; and honour not his father or his mother, he shall be free. Thus have ye made the commandment of God of none effect by your tradition. But in vain do they worship me, teaching for doctrines the commandments of men. *Mat. xv.* 3 *to* 6. 9. If any man speak, let him speak as the oracles of God; if any man minister, let him do it as of the ability which God giveth: that God in all things may be glorified through Christ Jesus. 1 *Pe. iv.* 11. Having then gifts differing according to the grace that is given to us, whether prophecy, let us prophesy according to the proportion of faith; or ministry, let us wait on our ministering; or he that teacheth, on teaching; or he that exhorteth, on exhortation. *Ro. xii.* 6, 7, 8. Which things also we speak, comparing spiritual things with spiritual. 1 *Co. ii.* 13. Hold fast the form of sound words, which thou hast heard of me, in faith and love which is in Christ Jesus. 2 *Ti. i.* 13. Prove all things; hold fast that which is good. 1 *Th. v.* 21. Let God be true, but every man a liar. What advantage then hath the Jew? Much every way: chiefly, because that unto them were committed the oracles of God. *Ro. iii.* 4. 1, 2. These things write I unto thee, hoping to come unto thee shortly: but if I tarry long, that thou mayest know how thou oughtest to behave thyself in the house of God, which is the Church of the living God, the pillar and ground of the truth. 1 *Ti. iii.* 14, 15. Peter and John answered and said unto them, Whether it be right in the sight of God to hearken unto you more than unto God, judge ye. For we cannot but speak the things which we have seen and heard. *Ac. iv.* 19, 20. I speak after the manner of men; Though it be but a man's covenant, yet if it be confirmed, no man disannulleth, or addeth thereto. *Ga. iii.* 15. But though we, or an angel from heaven, preach any other Gospel unto you than that which we have preached unto you, let him be accursed. As we said before, so say I now again, If any man preach any other Gospel unto you than that ye have received, let him be accursed. *Ga. i.* 8, 9.

CCCXXII. Article XXI. Of the Authority of General Councils.

1. General Councils may not be gathered together without the commandment and will of Princes.

> 1. Let every soul be subject unto the higher powers. For there is no power but of God: the powers that be are ordained of God. *Ro. xiii.* 1.

2. And when they be gathered together, (forasmuch as they be an assembly of men, whereof all be not governed with the Spirit and Word of God,) they may err, and sometimes have erred, even in things pertaining unto God. Wherefore things ordained by them as necessary to salvation have neither strength nor authority, unless it may be declared that they be taken out of Holy Scripture.

> 2. Now therefore hearken, O Israel, unto the statutes and unto the judgments, which I teach you. Ye shall not add unto the word which I command you, neither shall ye diminish ought from it. *De. iv.* 1, 2. Walk ye not in the statutes of your fathers, neither observe their judgments: I am the Lord your God; walk in my statutes, and keep my judgments, and do them. *Eze. xx.* 18, 19. To the law and to the testimony: if they speak not according to this word, it is because there is no light in them. *Is. viii.* 20.

CCCXXIII. Article XXII. Of Purgatory.

1. The Romish Doctrine concerning Purgatory, Pardons, Worshipping and Adoration, as well of Images as of Reliques, and also Invocation of Saints, is a fond thing, vainly invented, and grounded upon no warranty of Scripture,

> 1. The blood of Jesus Christ his Son cleanseth us from all sin. 1 *John i.* 7. I heard a voice from heaven saying unto me, Write, Blessed are the dead which die in the Lord from henceforth: Yea, saith the Spirit, that they may rest from their labours; and their works do follow them. *Re. xiv.* 13. And Jesus said unto him, Verily I say unto thee, To day shalt thou be with me in paradise. *Lu. xxiii.* 43. Whatsoever thy hand findeth to do, do it with thy might; for there is no work, nor device, nor knowledge, nor wisdom, in the grave, whither thou goest. *Ec. ix.* 10. None of them can by any means redeem his brother, nor give to God a ransom for him. *Ps. xlix.* 7. I, even I, am he that blotteth out thy transgressions for mine own sake, and will not remember thy sins. *Is. xliii.* 25. Behold the Lamb of God, which taketh away the sin of the world. *John i.* 29. Ye are washed, ye are sanctified, ye are justified in the name of the Lord Jesus, and by the Spirit

of our God. 1 *Co. vi.* 11.   By one offering he hath perfected
for ever them that are sanctified. *He. x.* 14.   And he said to
me, These are they which came out of great tribulation, and
have washed their robes, and made them white in the blood
of the Lamb.   Therefore are they before the throne of God,
and serve him day and night in his temple. *Re. vii.* 14, 15.
To the Lord our God belong mercies and forgivenesses, though
we have rebelled against him. *Da. ix.* 9.   If we confess our
sins, he is faithful and just to forgive us our sins, and to cleanse
us from all unrighteousness. 1 *John i.* 9.   Why doth this man
thus speak blasphemies? who can forgive sins but God only?
Mar. ii. 7.   Thou shalt have no other gods before me.   Thou
shalt not make unto thee any graven image, or any likeness of
any thing that is in heaven above, or that is in the earth
beneath, or that is in the water under the earth: thou shalt
not bow down thyself to them, nor serve them: for I the Lord
thy God am a jealous God. *Ex. xx.* 3, 4, 5.   Cursed be the
man that maketh any graven or molten image, an abomination unto the Lord, the work of the hands of the craftsman,
and putteth it in a secret place.   And all the people shall
answer and say, Amen. *De. xxvii.* 15.   I am the Lord: that
is my name: and my glory will I not give to another, neither
my praise to graven images. *Is. xlii.* 8.   He removed the
high places, and brake the images, and cut down the groves,
and brake in pieces the brazen serpent that Moses had made:
for unto those days the children of Israel did burn incense to
it: and he called it Nehushtan. 2 *Ki. xviii.* 4.   And as Peter
was coming in, Cornelius met him, and fell down at his feet,
and worshipped him: but Peter took him up, saying, Stand
up; I myself also am a man. *Ac. x.* 25, 26.   Then the priest
of Jupiter, which was before their city, brought oxen and
garlands unto the gates, and would have done sacrifice with
the people.   Which when the Apostles, Barnabas and Paul,
heard of, they rent their clothes, and ran in among the people,
crying out, and saying, Sirs, why do ye these things?   We
also are men of like passions with you, and preach unto you
that ye should turn from these vanities unto the living God,
which made heaven, and earth, and the sea, and all things
that are therein. *Ac. xiv.* 13, 14, 15.   And I fell at his feet to

worship him. And he said unto me, See thou do it not: I am thy fellowservant. *Re. xix.* 10. Then saith Jesus unto him, Get thee hence, Satan: for it is written, Thou shalt worship the Lord thy God, and him only shalt thou serve. *Mat. iv.* 10. He feedeth on ashes: a deceived heart hath turned him aside, that he cannot deliver his soul, nor say, Is there not a lie in my right hand? *Is. xliv.* 20.

2. but rather repugnant to the Word of God.

2. I am in a strait betwixt two, having a desire to depart, and to be with Christ; which is far better. *Ph. i.* 23. We are confident, I say, and willing rather to be absent from the body, and to be present with the Lord. 2 *Co. v.* 8. There is therefore now no condemnation to them which are in Christ Jesus. *Ro. viii.* 1. Let no man beguile you of your reward in a voluntary humility and worshipping of angels, intruding into those things which he hath not seen, vainly puffed up by his fleshly mind. *Col. ii.* 11. Thou, when thou prayest, enter into thy closet, and when thou hast shut thy door, pray to thy Father which is in secret. *Mat. vi.* 6. There is one God, and one Mediator between God and men, the man Christ Jesus. 1 *Ti. ii.* 5. He is able also to save them to the uttermost that come unto God by him, seeing he ever liveth to make intercession for them. *He. vii.* 25. O thou that hearest prayer, unto thee shall all flesh come. *Ps. lxv.* 2. Little children, keep yourselves from idols. 1 *John v.* 21.

CCCXXIV. Article XXIII. Of Ministering in the Congregation.

It is not lawful for any man to take upon him the Office of public preaching, or ministering the Sacraments in the Congregation, before he be lawfully called, and sent to execute the same. And those we ought to judge lawfully called and sent, which be chosen and called to this

I have not sent these prophets, yet they ran: I have not spoken to them, yet they prophesied. *Je. xxiii.* 21. And no man taketh this honour unto himself, but he that is called of God, as was Aaron. So also Christ glorified not himself to be made an High Priest; but he that said unto him, Thou art my Son, To day have I begotten thee. *He. v.* 4, 5.—*See Lev. viii.* They gathered themselves together against Moses and against Aaron, and said unto them, Ye take too much upon you, seeing all the congregation are holy, every one of them, and the Lord is among them. And there came out a fire from the Lord, and consumed the two hundred and fifty men that offered incense. The censers of these sinners against their own souls, let them make them broad plates for a covering of

work, by men who have public author-ity given unto them in the Congregation, to call and send Ministers into the Lord's vineyard.

the altar: for they offered them before the Lord, therefore they are hallowed: and they shall be a sign unto the children of Israel. *Nu. xvi.* 3. 35. 38. But when Uzziah was strong, his heart was lifted up to his destruction: for he transgressed against the Lord his God, and went into the temple of the Lord to burn incense upon the altar of incense. And Azariah the priest went in after him, and with him fourscore priests of the Lord, that were valiant men: and they withstood Uzziah the king, and said unto him, It appertaineth not unto thee, Uzziah, to burn incense unto the Lord, but to the priests the sons of Aaron, that are consecrated to burn incense: go out of the sanctuary; for thou hast trespassed; neither shall it be for thine honour from the Lord God. Then Uzziah was wroth, and had a censer in his hand to burn incense: and while he was wroth with the priests, the leprosy even rose up in his forehead before the priests in the house of the Lord, from beside the incense altar. And Azariah the chief priest, and all the priests, looked upon him, and, behold, he was leprous in his forehead, and they thrust him out from thence; yea, himself hasted also to go out, because the Lord had smitten him. *2 Ch. xxvi.* 16 *to* 23. And he ordained twelve, that they should be with him, and that he might send them forth to preach. *Mar. iii.* 14. After these things the Lord appointed other seventy also, and sent them two and two before his face into every city and place, whither he himself would come. *Lu. x.* 1. Then said Jesus to them again, Peace be unto you: as my Father hath sent me, even so send I you. *John xx.* 21. Go ye therefore, and teach all nations: teaching them to observe all things whatsoever I have commanded you: and, lo, I am with you alway, even unto the end of the world. Amen. *Mat. xxviii.* 19, 20. Wherefore of these men which have companied with us all the time that the Lord Jesus went in and out among us, beginning from the baptism of John, unto that same day that he was taken up from us, must one be ordained to be a witness with us of his resurrection. *Ac. i.* 21, 22. As they ministered to the Lord, and fasted, the Holy Ghost said, Separate me Barnabas and Saul for the work whereunto I have called them. And when they had fasted and prayed, and laid their hands on them, they sent them away. *Ac. xiii.* 2, 3. Paul, an Apostle, not of men, neither by man, but by Jesus Christ, and God the Father, who raised him from the dead. *Ga. i.* 1. God hath given to us the ministry of reconciliation; now then we are ambassadors for Christ, as though God did beseech you by us: we pray you in Christ's stead, be ye reconciled to God. *2 Co. v.* 18. 20. And when they had preached the Gospel to that city, and had taught many, they returned again to Lystra, confirming the souls of the disciples, and exhorting them to continue in the faith. And when they had ordained them elders in every church, and had prayed with fasting, they commended them to the Lord, on whom they believed. *Ac. xiv.* 21, 22, 23. For this cause left I thee in Crete, that thou shouldest set in order the things that are wanting, and ordain elders in every city, as I had appointed thee. *Tit. i.* 5. Neglect not the gift that is in thee, which was given thee by prophecy, with the laying on of the hands of the presbytery. *1 Ti. iv.* 14. I put thee in remembrance that thou stir up the gift of God, which is in thee by the putting on of my hands. *2 Ti. i.* 6. The things that thou hast heard of me among many witnesses, the same commit thou to faithful men, who shall be able to teach others also. *2 Ti. ii.* 2. Take heed therefore unto yourselves, and to all the flock, over the which the Holy Ghost hath made you overseers, to feed the Church of God, which he hath purchased with his own blood. *Ac. xx.* 28. The harvest truly is plenteous, but the labourers are few; Pray ye therefore the Lord of the harvest, that he will send forth labourers into his harvest. *Mat. ix.* 37, 38.

CCCXXV. Article XXIV. Of Speaking in the Congregation, in such a tongue as the people understandeth.

It is a thing plainly repugnant to the Word of God, and the Custom of the Primitive Church, to have Public Prayer in the Church, or to minister the Sacraments, in I would that ye all spake with tongues, but rather that ye prophesied : for greater is he that prophesieth than he that speaketh with tongues, except he interpret, that the Church may receive edifying. Likewise ye, except ye utter by the tongue words easy to be understood, how shall it be known what is spoken? for ye shall speak into the air. If I know not the meaning of the voice I shall be unto him that speaketh a barbarian, and he that speaketh shall be a barbarian unto me. If

a tongue not
understanded
of the people.

I pray in an unknown tongue, my spirit prayeth, but my understanding is unfruitful. What is it then? I will pray with the
spirit, and I will pray with the understanding also. Else when
thou shalt bless with the spirit how shall he that occupieth the
room of the unlearned say Amen at thy giving of thanks, seeing he understandeth not what thou sayest? In the church I
had rather speak five words with my understanding, that by
my voice I might teach others also, than ten thousand words
in an unknown tongue. If therefore the whole church be come
together into one place, and all speak with tongues, and there
come in those that are unlearned, or unbelievers, will they not
say that ye are mad? but if all prophesy, and there come in
one that believeth not, or one unlearned, he is convinced of all,
he is judged of all: and thus are the secrets of his heart made
manifest; and so falling down on his face he will worship God.
Let all things be done unto edifying. If any man speak in an
unknown tongue, let it be by two, or at the most by three, and
that by course; and let one interpret. But if there be no in-
terpreter, let him keep silence in the church. 1 *Co. xiv.* 5.
9. 11. 14, 15, 16. 19. 23 *to* 28. God is a Spirit: and they
that worship him must worship him in Spirit and in truth.
John iv. 24.

CCCXXVI. *Article XXV. Of the Sacraments.*

1. Sacra-
ments ordained
of Christ be no
only badges or
tokens of Chris-
tian men's
profession:
but rather
they be certain
sure witnesses,
and effectual
signs of grace,
and God's good
will towards
us, by the
which he doth
work invisibly
in us, and doth
not only
quicken but
also strengthen
and confirm
our Faith in
him.

1. Then Peter said unto them, Repent, and be baptized every
one of you in the name of Jesus Christ for the remission of sins,
and ye shall receive the gift of the Holy Ghost. Then they
that gladly received his word were baptized: and the same
day there were added unto them about three thousand souls.
And they continued stedfastly in the Apostles' doctrine and
fellowship, and in breaking of bread, and in prayers. *Ac. ii.*
38. 41, 42. As many of you as have been baptized into Christ
have put on Christ. *Ga. iii.* 27. Know ye not, that so many
of us as were baptized into Jesus Christ were baptized into his
death? Therefore we are buried with him by baptism into
death: that like as Christ was raised up from the dead by the
glory of the Father, even so we also should walk in newness
of life. For if we have been planted together in the likeness
of his death, we shall be also in the likeness of his resurrection.

Ro. vi. 3, 4, 5. Buried with him in baptism, wherein also ye are risen with him through the faith of the operation of God. *Col. ii.* 12. The longsuffering of God waited in the days of Noah, while the ark was a preparing, wherein few, that is, eight souls were saved by water. The like figure whereunto even baptism doth also now save us (not the putting away of the filth of the flesh, but the answer of a good conscience toward God,) by the resurrection of Jesus Christ. 1 *Pe. iii.* 20, 21. The cup of blessing which we bless, is it not the communion of the blood of Christ? The bread which we break, is it not the communion of the body of Christ? 1 *Co. x.* 16.

2, 3, 4, There are two Sacraments ordained of Christ our Lord in the Gospel, that is to say, Baptism, and the Supper of the Lord.—Those five commonly called Sacraments, that is to say, Confirmation, Penance, Orders, Matrimony, and extreme Unction, are not to be counted for Sacraments of the Gospel, being such as have grown partly of the corrupt following of the Apostles, partly are states of life allowed in the Scriptures; but yet have not like nature of Sacraments with Baptism, and the Lord's Supper, for that they have not any visible sign or ceremony ordained of God.—The Sacraments were not ordained of Christ to be gazed upon, or to be carried about, but that we should duly use them. And in such only as worthily receive the same they have a wholesome effect or operation: but they that receive them unworthily purchase to themselves damnation, as St. *Paul* saith.

2, 3, 4. Go ye therefore, and teach all nations, baptizing them in the name of the Father, and of the Son, and of the Holy Ghost. *Mat. xxviii.* 19. He that believeth and is baptized shall be saved; but he that believeth not shall be damned. *Mar. xvi.* 16. I received of the Lord that which also I delivered unto you, That the Lord Jesus the same night in which he was betrayed took bread: and when he had given thanks, he brake it, and said, Take, eat: This is my body, which is broken for you: this do in remembrance of me. After the same manner also he took the cup, when he had supped, saying, This cup is the new testament in my blood: this do ye, as oft as ye drink it, in remembrance of me. For as often as ye eat this bread, and drink this cup, ye do shew the Lord's death till he come. Wherefore whosoever shall eat this bread, and drink this cup of the Lord, unworthily, shall be guilty of the body and blood of the Lord. But let a man examine himself, and so let him eat of that bread, and drink of that cup. For he that eateth and drinketh unworthily, eateth and drinketh damnation to himself, not discerning the Lord's body. For this cause many are weak and sickly among you, and many sleep. For if we would judge ourselves, we should not be judged. But when we are judged, we are chastened of the Lord, that we should not be condemned with the world. 1 *Co. xi.* 23 *to* 32.

CCCXXVII. *Article XXVI. Of the Unworthiness of the Ministers, which hinders not the Effect of the Sacrament.*

1. Although in the visible Church the evil be ever mingled with the good, and sometimes the evil have chief authority in the Ministration of the Word and Sacraments,

1. Another parable put he forth unto them, saying, The kingdom of heaven is likened unto a man which sowed good seed in his field : but while men slept, his enemy came and sowed tares among the wheat, and went his way. But when the blade was sprung up, and brought forth fruit, then appeared the tares also. Again, the kingdom of heaven is like unto a net, that was cast into the sea, and gathered of every kind. They gathered the good into vessels, but cast the bad away. *Mat. xiii.* 24, 25, 26. 47, 48. In the last days perilous times shall come. For men shall be lovers of their own selves, covetous, boasters, proud, blasphemers, disobedient to parents, unthankful, unholy, without natural affection, trucebreakers, false accusers, incontinent, fierce, despisers of those that are good, traitors, heady, high-minded, lovers of pleasures more than lovers of God; having a form of godliness, but denying the power thereof. Of this sort are they which creep into houses, and lead captive silly women laden with sins, led away with divers lusts, ever learning, and never able to come to the knowledge of the truth. 2 *Ti. iii.* 1 *to* 7. Jesus answered them, Have not I chosen you twelve, and one of you is a devil? *John vi.* 70. Many will say to me in that day, Lord, Lord, have we not prophesied in thy name? and in thy name have cast out devils? and in thy name done many wonderful works? And then will I profess unto them, I never knew you: depart from me, ye that work iniquity. *Mat. vii.* 22, 23. *See particularly the state of the Seven Churches of Asia as given in Re.* ii. iii. *See also,* 2 *Co. xi.* 13, 14, 15.

2. yet forasmuch as they do not the same in their own name, but in Christ's, and do minister by his commission

2. We are ambassadors for Christ, as though God did beseech you by us: we pray you in Christ's stead, be ye reconciled to God. 2 *Co. v.* 20. Let a man so account of us, as of the ministers of Christ, and stewards of the mysteries of God. 1 *Co. iv.* 1. Who then is Paul, and who is Apollos, but minis-

and authority, ters by whom ye believed, even as the Lord gave to every
we may use
their Ministry, man? 1 *Co. iii.* 5. The Scribes and the Pharisees sit in
both in hearing Moses' seat: all therefore whatsoever they bid you observe,
the Word of
God, and in re- that observe and do. *Mat. xxiii.* 2, 3. For we preach not our-
ceiving of the selves, but Christ Jesus the Lord. *2 Co. iv.* 5.
Sacraments.

3. Neither is the effect of Christ's ordinance taken away by their wickedness, nor the
grace of God's gifts diminished from such as by faith and rightly do receive the Sacraments ministered unto them: which be effectual, because of Christ's institution and
promise, although they be ministered by evil men. Nevertheless, it appertaineth to the
discipline of the Church, that enquiry be made of evil Ministers, and that they be accused
by those that have knowledge of their offences; and finally being found guilty, by just
judgment be deposed.

3. But we have this treasure in earthen vessels, that the excellency of the power may be of God, and not of us. *2 Co. iv.*
7. We are labourers together with God: ye are God's husbandry, ye are God's building. I have planted, Apollos
watered; but God gave the increase. So then neither is he that
planteth any thing, neither he that watereth; but God that
giveth the increase. 1 *Co. iii.* 9. 6, 7. Some indeed preach
Christ even of envy and strife; and some also of good will.
What then? notwithstanding, every way, whether in pretence,
or in truth, Christ is preached; and I therein do rejoice, yea,
and will rejoice. *Ph. i.* 15. 18. *See also the account of the
Institution of the Sacrament of Baptism, Mat. xxviii.* 19, 20 :
and that of the Lord's Supper, 1 *Co. xi.* 23 *to* 26. Against an
elder receive not an accusation, but before two or three witnesses. 1 *Ti. v.* 19. Diotrephes, who loveth to have the pre-
eminence among them, receiveth us not. Wherefore, if I come,
I will remember his deeds which he doeth, prating against us
with malicious words: and not content therewith, neither doth
he himself receive the brethren, and forbiddeth them that
would, and casteth them out of the church. 3 *John* 9, 10. He
that troubleth you shall bear his judgment, whosoever he be.
I would they were even cut off which trouble you. *Ga. v.* 10. 12.

CCCXXVIII. Article XXVII. Of Baptism.

1. Baptism   1. Then they that gladly received his word were baptized:
is not only a
sign of profes- and the same day there were added unto them about three
sion, and mark thousand souls. *Ac. ii.* 41. Then answered Peter, Can any
of difference,
whereby Chris- man forbid water, that these should not be baptized, which

tian men are discerned from others that be not christened; but it is also a sign of Regeneration, or new Birth, whereby, as by an instrument, they that receive Baptism rightly are grafted into the Church;

have received the Holy Ghost as well as we? And he commanded them to be baptized in the name of the Lord. *Ac. x.* 46, 47, 48. If any man be in Christ, he is a new creature. *2 Co. v.* 17. Jesus answered and said unto him, Verily, verily, I say unto thee, Except a man be born again, he cannot see the kingdom of God. Except a man be born of water and of the Spirit, he cannot enter into the kingdom of God. *John iii.* 3. 5. Not by works of righteousness which we have done, but according to his mercy he saved us, by the washing of regeneration, and renewing of the Holy Ghost. *Tit. iii.* 5. Buried with him in baptism, wherein also ye are risen with him through the faith of the operation of God, who hath raised him from the dead. *Col. ii.* 12. Know ye not, that so many of us as were baptized into Jesus Christ were baptized into his death? Therefore we are buried with him by baptism into death: that like as Christ was raised up from the dead by the glory of the Father, even so we also should walk in newness of life. For if we have been planted together in the likeness of his death, we shall be also in the likeness of his resurrection. *Ro. vi.* 3, 4, 5. By one Spirit are we all baptized into one body. *1 Co. xii.* 13. The Church which is his body, the fulness of him that filleth all in all. *Ep. i.* 22, 23.

2. the promises of forgiveness of sin, and of our adoption to be the sons of God by the Holy Ghost, are visibly signed and sealed; Faith is confirmed, and Grace increased by virtue of prayer unto God.

2. Then Peter said unto them, Repent, and be baptized every one of you in the name of Jesus Christ for the remission of sins, and ye shall receive the gift of the Holy Ghost. For the promise is unto you, and to your children, and to all that are afar off, even as many as the Lord our God shall call. *Ac. ii.* 38, 39. And now why tarriest thou? arise, and be baptized, and wash away thy sins, calling on the name of the Lord. *Ac. xxii.* 16. Ye are all the children of God by faith in Christ Jesus. For as many of you as have been baptized into Christ have put on Christ. *Ga. iii.* 26, 27. And because ye are sons, God hath sent forth the Spirit of his Son into your hearts, crying, Abba, Father. *Ga. iv.* 6. Who hath also sealed us, and given us the earnest of the Spirit in our hearts. *2 Co. i.* 22. Ye were sealed with that Holy Spirit of promise, which is the earnest of our inheritance. *Ep. i.* 13, 14. Let us draw near with a true heart in full assurance of faith, having our hearts sprinkled from an evil conscience, and our bodies washed with

pure water. *He. x.* 22. And they continued stedfastly in the Apostles' doctrine and fellowship, and in breaking of bread, and in prayers. *Ac. ii.* 42. If ye then, being evil, know how to give good gifts unto your children: how much more shall your heavenly Father give the Holy Spirit to them that ask him. *Lu. xi.* 13. *See also, Col. i.* 9, 10.

3. The Baptism of young Children is in any wise to be retained in the Church, as most agreeable with the institution of Christ.

3. And God said unto Abraham, Thou shalt keep my covenant therefore, thou, and thy seed after thee in their generations. This is my covenant, which ye shall keep, between me and you and thy seed after thee; Every man child among you shall be circumcised. And he that is eight days old shall be circumcised among you, every man child in your generations. *Ge. xvii.* 9, 10. 12. And they brought young children to him, that he should touch them: and his disciples rebuked those that brought them. But when Jesus saw it, he was much displeased, and said unto them, Suffer the little children to come unto me, and forbid them not: for of such is the kingdom of God. And he took them up in his arms, put his hands upon them, and blessed them. *Mar. x.* 13, 14. 16. They brought unto him also infants, that he would touch them. Jesus called them unto him, and said, Suffer little children to come unto me, and forbid them not: for of such is the kingdom of God. *Lu. xviii.* 15, 16. And Jesus came and spake unto them, saying, All power is given unto me in heaven and in earth. Go ye therefore, and teach all nations, baptizing them in the name of the Father, and of the Son, and of the Holy Ghost. *Mat. xviii.* 18, 19. The promise is unto you, and to your children. *Ac. ii.* 39. She was baptized and her houshold. And he was baptized, he and all his, straightway. *Ac. xvi.* 15. 33. I baptized the houshold of Stephanas. *1 Co. i.* 16. The unbelieving husband is sanctified by the wife, and the unbelieving wife is sanctified by the husband: else were your children unclean; but now are they holy. *1 Co. vii.* 14.

CCCXXIX. *Article XXVIII. Of the Lord's Supper.*

1. The Supper of the Lord is not only a sign of the love that Christians

1. Herein is love, not that we loved God, but that he loved us, and sent his Son to be the Propitiation for our sins. Beloved, if God so loved us, we ought also to love one another. *1 John iv.* 10, 11. And this is his commandment, That we should believe

ought to have
among them-
selves one to
another; but
rather is a
Sacrament of
our Redemp-
tion by Christ's
death: inso-
much that to
such as rightly,
worthily, and
with faith,
receive the
same, the Bread
which we
break is a par-
taking of the
Body of Christ;
and likewise
the Cup of
Blessing is a
partaking of
the Blood of
Christ.

on the name of his Son Jesus Christ, and love one another, as he gave us commandment. 1 *John iii.* 23. By this shall all men know that ye are my disciples, if ye have love one to another. *John xiii.* 35. We being many, are one body in Christ, and every one members one of another. *Ro. xii.* 5. We being many are one bread, and one body: for we are all partakers of that one bread. 1 *Co. x.* 17. And as they were eating, Jesus took bread, and blessed it, and brake it, and gave it to the disciples, and said, Take, eat; this is my body. And he took the cup, and gave thanks, and gave it to them, saying, Drink ye all of it; for this is my blood of the new testament, which is shed for many for the remission of sins. *Mat. xxvi.* 26, 27, 28. And he took bread, and gave thanks, and brake it, and gave unto them, saying, This is my body which is given for you: this do in remembrance of me. Likewise also the cup after supper, saying, This cup is the new testament in my blood, which is shed for you. *Lu. xxii.* 19, 20. In whom we have redemption through his blood, the forgiveness of sins, according to the riches of his grace. *Ep. i.* 7. The cup of blessing which we bless, is it not the communion of the blood of Christ? the bread which we break, is it not the communion of the body of Christ? 1 *Co. x.* 16. Let a man examine himself, and so let him eat of that bread, and drink of that cup. 1 *Co. xi.* 28. Verily, verily, I say unto you, He that believeth on me hath everlasting life. I am that bread of life. This is the bread which cometh down from heaven, that a man may eat thereof, and not die. *John vi.* 47, 48. 50. We are made partakers of Christ, if we hold the beginning of our confidence stedfast unto the end. *He. iii.* 14.

2. 3. Transubstantiation (or the change of the substance of Bread and Wine,) in the Supper of the Lord, cannot be proved by holy Writ, but is repugnant to the plain words of Scripture, overthroweth the nature of a Sacrament, and hath given occasion to many superstitions.—The Body of Christ is given, taken, and eaten, in the Supper, only after an heavenly and spiritual manner. And the mean whereby the Body of Christ is received and eaten in the Supper is Faith.—The Sacrament of the Lord's Supper was not by Christ's ordinance reserved, carried about, lifted up, or worshipped.

2. As often as ye eat this bread, and drink this cup, ye do shew the Lord's death till he come. 1 *Co. xi.* 26. Whom the heaven must receive until the times of restitution of all things. *Ac. iii.* 21. This is my blood of the new testament,

which is shed for many for the remission of sins. But I say unto you, I will not drink henceforth of this fruit of the vine, until that day when I drink it new with you in my Father's kingdom. *Mat. xxvi.* 28, 29. Jesus said unto them, Verily, verily, I say unto you, Except ye eat the flesh of the Son of man, and drink his blood, ye have no life in you. *John vi.* 53. God is a Spirit; and they that worship him must worship him in Spirit and in truth. *John iv.* 24. I am the bread of life : he that cometh to me shall never hunger ; and he that believeth on me shall never thirst. I am the living bread which came down from heaven: if any man eat of this bread, he shall live for ever : and the bread that I will give is my flesh, which I will give for the life of the world. Whoso eateth my flesh, and drinketh my blood, hath eternal life; and I will raise him up at the last day. Many therefore of his disciples, when they had heard this, said, This is an hard saying; who can hear it? When Jesus knew in himself that his disciples murmured at it, he said unto them, Doth this offend you? It is the Spirit that quickeneth; the flesh profiteth nothing : the words that I speak unto you, they are Spirit, and they are life. *John vi.* 35. 51. 54. 60, 61. 63. I am crucified with Christ: nevertheless I live ; yet not I, but Christ liveth in me : and the life which I now live in the flesh I live by the faith of the Son of God, who loved me, and gave himself for me. *Ga. ii.* 20. I bow my knees unto the Father of our Lord Jesus Christ, that he would grant, that Christ may dwell in your hearts by faith, ye being rooted and grounded in love. *Ep. iii.* 14. 16, 17. Jesus said, Take, eat; Drink ye all of it. *Mat. xxvi.* 26, 27. Whosoever shall eat this bread, and drink this cup of the Lord, unworthily, shall be guilty of the body and blood of the Lord. 1 *Co. xi.* 27. *See above in Sec.* 1.

CCCXXX. *Article XXIX. Of the Wicked which do not eat the Body of Christ in the Use of the Lord's Supper.*

The wicked, and such as be void of a lively faith, although they do carnally and visi- nally and visi- If we say that we have fellowship with him, and walk in darkness, we lie, and do not the truth: but if we walk in the light, as he is in the light, we have fellowship one with another, and the blood of Jesus Christ his Son cleanseth us from all sin.

bly press with their teeth (as St. *Augustine* saith) the Sacrament of the Body and Blood of Christ, yet in no wise are they partakers of Christ; but rather, to their condemnation, do eat and drink the Sign or Sacrament of so great a thing.

1 *John i.* 6, 7. Then shall ye begin to say, We have eaten and drunk in thy presence, and thou hast taught in our streets. But he shall say, I tell you, I know you not whence ye are; depart from me, all ye workers of iniquity. *Lu. xiii.* 26, 27. Without faith it is impossible to please him. *He. xi.* 6. The natural man receiveth not the things of the Spirit of God : for they are foolishness unto him : neither can he know them, because they are spiritually discerned. 1 *Co. ii.* 14. Ye cannot drink the cup of the Lord, and the cup of devils : ye cannot be partakers of the Lord's table, and of the table of devils. 1 *Co. x.* 21. What concord hath Christ with Belial? 2 *Co. vi.* 15. He that eateth and drinketh unworthily, eateth and drinketh damnation to himself, not discerning the Lord's body. 1 *Co. xi.* 29. Purge out therefore the old leaven, that ye may be a new lump. Let us keep the feast, not with old leaven, neither with the leaven of malice and wickedness ; but with the unleavened bread of sincerity and truth. 1 *Co. v.* 7, 8. Examine yourselves, whether ye be in the faith; prove your own selves. Know ye not your own selves, how that Jesus Christ is in you, except ye be reprobates? 2 *Co. xiii.* 5. For if we would judge ourselves, we should not be judged. 1 *Co. xi.* 31.

CCCXXXI. *Article XXX. Of both Kinds.*

The Cup of the Lord is not to be denied to the Lay-people: for both the parts of the Lord's Sacrament, by Christ's ordinance and commandment, ought to be ministered to all Christian men alike.

And he took the cup, and gave thanks, and gave it to them, saying, Drink ye all of it. *Mat. xxvi.* 27. And he took the cup, and when he had given thanks, he gave it to them : and they all drank of it. *Mar. xiv.* 23. And he took bread, and gave thanks, and brake it, and gave unto them, saying, This is my body which is given for you: this do in remembrance of me. Likewise also the cup after supper, saying, This cup is the new testament in my blood, which is shed for you. *Lu. xxii.* 19, 20. The cup of blessing which we bless, is it not the communion of the blood of Christ? 1 *Co. x.* 16. As often as ye eat this bread, and drink this cup, ye do shew the Lord's death till he come. 1 *Co. xi.* 26.—*See also the connecting verses from 23 to 32, in sections 2, 3, 4. in No.* cccxxvi.

CCCXXXII. *Article XXXI. Of the one Oblation of Christ finished upon the Cross.*

The Offering of Christ once made is that perfect redemption, propitiation, and satisfaction, for all the sins of the whole world, both original and actual; and there is none other satisfaction for sin, but that alone. Wherefore the sacrifices of Masses, in the which it was commonly said, that the Priest did offer Christ for the quick and the dead, to have remission of pain or guilt, were blasphemous fables, and dangerous deceits.

Behold the Lamb of God, which taketh away the sin of the world. *John i.* 29. If any man sin, we have an Advocate with the Father, Jesus Christ the righteous: and he is the Propitiation for our sins: and not for ours only, but also for the sins of the whole world. 1 *John ii.* 1, 2. 7. The blood of Jesus Christ his Son cleanseth us from all sin. 1 *John i.* 7. By the which will we are sanctified through the offering of the body of Jesus Christ once for all. This man, after he had offered one sacrifice for sins, for ever sat down on the right hand of God. By one offering he hath perfected for ever them that are sanctified. Now where remission of these is, there is no more offering for sin. If we sin wilfully after that we have received the knowledge of the truth, there remaineth no more sacrifice for sins. *He. x.* 10. 12. 14. 18. 26. How much more shall the blood of Christ, who through the eternal Spirit offered himself without spot to God, purge your conscience from dead works to serve the living God?—Nor yet that he should offer himself often, as the high priest entereth into the holy place every year with blood of others; for then must he often have suffered since the foundation of the world: but now once in the end of the world hath he appeared to put away sin by the sacrifice of himself. Christ was once offered to bear the sins of many. *He. ix.* 14. 25, 26. 28. Christ hath loved us, and hath given himself for us an offering and a sacrifice to God for a sweet smelling savour. Christ loved the Church, and gave himself for it; that he might sanctify and cleanse it with the washing of water by the word, that he might present it to himself a glorious Church, not having spot, or wrinkle, or any such thing: but that it should be holy and without blemish. *Ep. v.* 2. 25, 26, 27. God was in Christ, reconciling the world unto himself, not imputing their trespasses unto them. 2 *Co. v.* 19. In whom we have redemption through his blood, even the forgiveness of sins. *Col. i.* 14. Without shedding of blood is no remission. *He. ix.* 22. Ye as lively stones, are built up a spiritual house, an holy priesthood, to offer up spiritual sacrifices, acceptable to God by Jesus Christ. 1 *Pe. ii.* 5.

G G

CCCXXXIII. *Article XXXII. Of the Marriage of Priests.*

Bishops, Priests, and Deacons, are not commanded by God's Law, either to vow the estate of single life, or to abstain from marriage: therefore it is lawful for them, as for all other Christian men, to marry at their own discretion, as they shall judge the same to serve better to godliness.

Now the Spirit speaketh expressly, that in the latter times some shall depart from the faith, giving heed to seducing spirits, and doctrines of devils; forbidding to marry. 1 *Ti. iv.* 1. 3. Have we not power to lead about a sister, a wife, as well as other apostles, and as the brethren of the Lord, and Cephas? 1 *Co. ix.* 5. A Bishop then must be blameless, the husband of one wife, vigilant, sober, one that ruleth well his own house, having his children in subjection with all gravity. Likewise must the Deacons be grave, not doubletongued. Even so must their wives be grave, not slanderers, sober, faithful in all things. Let the Deacons be the husbands of one wife, ruling their children and their own houses well. 1 *Ti. iii.* 2. 4. 8. 11, 12. The Lord said unto Moses, Speak unto the priests the sons of Aaron, and say unto them, They shall not take a wife that is profane; neither shall they take a woman put away from her husband: for he is holy unto his God. *Le. xxi.* 1. 7. Marriage is honourable in all, and the bed undefiled. *He. xiii.* 4.

CCCXXXIV. *Article XXXIII. Of excommunicate Persons, how they are to be avoided.*

That person which by open denunciation of the Church is rightly cut off from the unity of the Church, and excommunicated, ought to be taken of the whole multitude of the faithful, as an Heathen and Publican, until he be openly reconciled by penance, and received into the Church by a Judge that hath authority thereunto.

I verily, as absent in body, but present in spirit, have judged already, as though I were present, concerning him that hath so done this deed, In the name of our Lord Jesus Christ, when ye are gathered together, and my spirit, with the power of our Lord Jesus Christ, to deliver such an one unto Satan for the destruction of the flesh, that the spirit may be saved in the day of the Lord Jesus. Now I have written unto you not to keep company, if any man that is called a brother be a fornicator, or covetous, or an idolater, or a railer, or a drunkard, or an extortioner; with such an one no not to eat. Therefore put away from among yourselves that wicked person. 1 *Co. v.* 3, 4, 5. 11. 13. If thy brother shall trespass against thee, go and tell him his fault between thee and him alone: if he shall hear thee, thou hast gained thy brother. But if he will not hear thee, then take with thee one or two more, that in the mouth of two or three witnesses every word may be established. And if he shall neglect to hear them, tell it unto the Church:

but if he neglect to hear the Church, let him be unto thee as an heathen man and a Publican. Verily I say unto you, Whatsoever ye shall bind on earth shall be bound in heaven: and whatsoever ye shall loose on earth shall be loosed in heaven. *Mat. xviii.* 15 *to* 18. Now we command you, brethren, in the name of our Lord Jesus Christ, that ye withdraw yourselves from every brother that walketh disorderly, and not after the tradition which ye received of us. If any man obey not our word by this epistle, note that man, and have no company with him, that he may be ashamed. 2 *Th. iii.* 6. 14. If I make you sorry, who is he then that maketh me glad, but the same which is made sorry by me? Sufficient to such a man is this punishment, which was inflicted of many. So that contrariwise, ye ought rather to forgive him, and comfort him, lest perhaps such an one should be swallowed up with overmuch sorrow. Wherefore I beseech you that ye would confirm your love toward him. For to this end also did I write that I might know the proof of you, whether ye be obedient in all things. To whom ye forgive any thing, I forgive also: for if I forgave any thing, to whom I forgave it, for your sakes forgave I it in the person of Christ. 2 *Co. ii.* 2. 6 *to* 10. What have I to do to judge them that are without? do not ye judge them that are within? 1 *Co. v.* 12.

CCCXXXV. Article XXXIV. Of the Traditions of the Church.

1, 2. It is not necessary that Traditions and Ceremonies be in all places one, and utterly like; for at all times they have been divers, and may be changed according to the diversities of countries, times, and men's manners, so that nothing be ordained against God's Word. Whosoever through his private judgment, willingly and purposely, doth openly break the traditions and ceremonies of the Church, which be not repugnant to the Word of God, and be ordained and approved by common authority, ought to be rebuked openly, (that others may fear to do the like,) as he that offendeth against the common order of the Church, and hurteth the authority of the Magistrate, and woundeth the consciences of the weak brethren.

1, 2. Let all things be done decently and in order. 1 *Co. xiv.* 40. Let every soul be subject unto the higher powers. For there is no power but of God: the powers that be are ordained of God. Wherefore ye must needs be subject, not only for wrath, but also for conscience sake. *Ro. xiii.* 1. 5. Judge this, that no man put a stumblingblock or an occasion to fall in his brother's way. For the kingdom of God is not meat and drink; but righteousness, and peace, and joy in the Holy Ghost. Let us therefore follow after the things which make for peace, and things wherewith one may edify another. *Ro. xiv.* 13. 17. 19. Though I be absent in the flesh, yet I am with you in the spirit, joying and beholding your order, and the stedfastness of your faith in Christ. *Col. ii.* 5. Diotrephes, who loveth to have the preeminence among them, receiveth us not. Wherefore, if I come, I will remember his deeds which he doeth, prating against us with malicious words : and not content therewith, neither doth he himself receive the brethren, and forbiddeth them that would, and casteth them out of the church. *3 John* 9, 10. Now we command you, brethren, in the name of our Lord Jesus Christ, that ye withdraw yourselves from every brother that walketh disorderly, and not after the tradition which ye received of us. *2 Th. iii.* 6. If any man seem to be contentious, we have no such custom, neither the churches of God. *1 Co. xi.* 16. Now we exhort you, brethren, warn them that are unruly. *1 Th. v.* 14. Them that sin rebuke before all, that others also may fear. *1 Ti. v.* 20. I beseech you, brethren, mark them which cause divisions and offences contrary to the doctrine which ye have learned; and avoid them. For they that are such serve not our Lord Jesus Christ. *Ro. xvi.* 17, 18. When ye sin so against the brethren, and wound their weak conscience, ye sin against Christ. *1 Co. viii.* 12.

3. Every particular or national Church hath authority to ordain, change, and abolish ceremonies or rites of the Church ordained only by man's authority, so that all things be done to edifying.

3. Submit yourselves to every ordinance of man for the Lord's sake. *1 Pe. ii.* 13. Obey them that have the rule over you, and submit yourselves : for they watch for your souls, as they that must give account, that they may do it with joy, and not with grief : for that is unprofitable for you. *He. xiii.* 17. Let all things be done unto edifying. *1 Co. xiv.* 26.

CCCXXXVI. *Article XXXV. Of the Homilies.*

The second Book of Homilies, the several titles whereof we have joined under this Article, doth contain a godly and wholesome Doctrine, and necessary for these times, as doth the former Book of Homilies, which were set forth in the time of *Edward* the Sixth ; and therefore we judge them to be read in Churches by the Ministers, diligently and distinctly, that they may be understanded of the people.

Of the Names of the Homilies.

1. *Of the right use of the Church.*
2. *Against Peril of Idolatry.*
3. *Of repairing and keeping clean of Churches.*
4. *Of good Works : first of Fasting.*
5. *Against Gluttony and Drunkenness.*
6. *Against Excess of Apparel.*
7. *Of Prayer.*
8. *Of the Place and Time of Prayer.*
9. *That common Prayers, and Sacraments ought to be ministered in a known tongue.*
10. *Of the reverent estimation of God's Word.*
11. *Of Almsdoing.*
12. *Of the Nativity of Christ.*
13. *Of the Passion of Christ.*
14. *Of the Resurrection of Christ.*
15. *Of the worthy receiving of the Sacrament of the Body and Blood of Christ.*
16. *Of the Gifts of the Holy Ghost.*
17. *For the Rogation-days.*
18. *Of the State of Matrimony.*
19. *Of Repentance.*
20. *Against Idleness.*
21. *Against Rebellion.*

CCCXXXVII.*Article XXXVI. Of Consecration of Bishops and Ministers.*

The Book of Consecration of Archbishops and Bishops, and Ordering of Priests and Deacons, lately set forth in the time of *Edward* the Sixth, and confirmed at the same time by authority of Parliament, doth contain all things necessary to such Consecration and Ordering : neither hath it any thing, that of itself is superstitious and ungodly. And therefore whosoever are consecrated or ordered according to the Rites of that Book, since the second year of the forenamed King *Edward* unto this time, or hereafter shall be consecrated or ordered according to the same Rites ; we decree all such to be rightly, orderly, and lawfully consecrated and ordered.

And the Lord spake unto Moses, saying, Take Aaron and his sons with him, and gather thou all the congregation together unto the door of the tabernacle of the congregation. This is the thing which the Lord commanded to be done. And Moses took the anointing oil, and he poured of the anointing oil upon Aaron's head, and anointed him, to sanctify him. And Moses took of the anointing oil, and of the blood which was upon the altar, and sprinkled it upon Aaron, and upon his sons, and sanctified Aaron, and his sons. *Le. viii.* 1, 2, 3. 5. 10. 12. 30. Thou shalt bring the Levites before the tabernacle of the congregation : and thou shalt gather the whole assembly of the children of Israel together : and thou shalt bring the Levites before the Lord : and the children of Israel shall put their hands upon the Levites : and Aaron shall offer the Levites before the Lord for an offering of the children of Israel, that they may execute the service of the Lord. *Nu. viii.* 9, 10, 11. Then said Jesus, As my Father hath sent me, even so send I you. And when he had said this, he breathed on them, and saith unto them, Receive ye the Holy Ghost : Whose soever sins ye remit, they are remitted unto them ; and whose soever sins ye retain, they are retained. *John xx.* 21, 22, 23. Paul, to all the saints in Christ Jesus which are at Philippi, with the Bishops and Deacons. *Ph. i.* 1. For this cause left I thee in Crete, that thou should-est set in order the things that are wanting, and ordain elders in every city, as I had appointed thee. *Ti. i.* 5. If a man de-sire the office of a Bishop, he desireth a good work. A Bishop must be blameless. Likewise must the Deacons be grave, holding the mystery of the faith in a pure conscience. Let these also first be proved; then let them use the office of a Deacon, being found blameless. 1 *Ti. iii.* 1, 2. 8, 9, 10. Whom they set before the Apostles: and when they had prayed, they laid their hands on them. *Ac. vi.* 6. Take heed unto your-selves, and to all the flock, over the which the Holy Ghost hath made you overseers, to feed the church of God, which he hath purchased with his own blood. *Ac. xx.* 28. Wherefore I put thee in remembrance that thou stir up the gift of God which is in thee, by the putting on of my hands. 2 *Ti. i.* 6. Neglect not the gift that is in thee, which was given thee by prophecy, with the laying on of the hands of the pres-bytery. 1 *Ti. iv.* 14. *See the Offices for Ordering Deacons and Priests; and that for the Consecration of Bishops: pages* 215 —274.

CCCXXXVIII. Article XXXVII. Of the Civil Magistrates.

1, 2. The King's Majesty hath the chief power in this Realm of *England,* and other his Dominions, unto whom the chief Government of all Estates of this Realm, whether they be Ecclesiastical or Civil, in all causes doth appertain, and is not, nor ought to be, subject to any foreign Jurisdiction.—Where we attribute to the King's Majesty the chief govern-ment, by which Titles we understand the minds of some slanderous folks to be offended; we give not to our Princes the ministering either of God's Word, or of the Sacraments, the which thing the injunctions also lately set forth by *Elizabeth* our Queen do most plainly testify; but that only prerogative, which we see to have been given always to all godly Princes in holy Scriptures by God himself; that is, that they should rule all states and degrees committed to their charge by God, whether they be Ecclesiastical or Temporal, and restrain with the civil sword the stubborn and evil-doers.

1, 2. Let every soul be subject unto the higher powers. *Ro. xiii.* 1. Submit yourselves to every ordinance of man for the Lord's sake: whether it be to the king, as supreme; or unto governors, as unto them that are sent by him for the punish-ment of evil doers, and for the praise of them that do well. 1 *Pe. ii.* 13, 14. And he set judges in the land throughout all the fenced cities of Judah, city by city. Moreover in Jerusa-lem did Jehoshaphat set of the Levites, and of the chief of the

fathers of Israel, for the judgment of the Lord, and for controversies. 2 *Ch. xix.* 5. 8.   And Asa appointed certain of the
Levites to minister before the ark of the Lord, and to record,
and to thank and praise the Lord God of Israel. 1 *Ch. xvi.* 4.

3. The Bishop of *Rome* hath no jurisdiction in this Realm of *England*. The Laws of the Realm may punish Christian men with death, for heinous and grievous offences. It is lawful for Christian men, at the commandment of the Magistrate, to wear weapons, and serve in the wars.

3.   When Uzziah was strong, his heart was lifted up
to his destruction: for he transgressed against the Lord his
God, and went into the temple of the Lord to burn incense
upon the altar of incense.   And Azariah the priest went
in after him, and with him fourscore priests of the Lord,
that were valiant men : and they withstood Uzziah the king,
and said unto him, It appertaineth not unto thee, Uzziah, to
burn incense unto the Lord, but to the priests the sons of
Aaron, that are consecrated to burn incense.   And while he
was wroth with the priests, the leprosy even rose up in his
forehead before the priests in the house of the Lord, from
beside the incense altar. 2 *Ch. xxvi.* 16 *to* 19.   And kings shall
be thy nursing fathers, and their queens thy nursing mothers.
Is. xlix. 23.   Then king Jehoash called for Jehoiada the priest,
and the other priests, and said unto them, Why repair ye not
the breaches of the house? now therefore receive no more
money of your acquaintance, but deliver it for the breaches of
the house. 2 *Ki. xii.* 7.   And Hezekiah appointed the courses
of the priests and the Levites after their courses, every man
according to his service, the priests and Levites for burnt offerings and for peace offerings, to minister, and to give thanks,
and to praise in the gates of the tents of the Lord. 2 *Ch. xxxi.* 2.
And the king commanded all the people, saying, Keep the
passover unto the Lord your God, as it is written in the book
of this covenant. 2 *Ki. xxiii.* 21.   So Solomon thrust out
Abiathar from being priest unto the Lord ; and Zadok the
priest did the king put in the room of Abiathar. 1 *Ki.
ii.* 27. 35.   Let none of you suffer as a busybody in other
men's matters. 1 *Pe. iv.* 15. The powers that be are ordained
of God.   The ruler is the minister of God to thee for good.
He beareth not the sword in vain: for he is the minister of
God, a revenger to execute wrath upon him that doeth evil.
Ro. xiii. 1. 4.   A wise king scattereth the wicked, and
bringeth the wheel over them. *Pr. xx.* 26.   There was a certain man in Cæsarea called Cornelius, a centurion of the band
called the Italian band, a devout man, and one that feared God

with all his house, which gave much alms to the people, and prayed to God alway. *Ac. x.* 1, 2. And the soldiers likewise demanded of him, saying, And what shall we do? And he said unto them, Do violence to no man, neither accuse any falsely; and be content with your wages. *Lu. iii.* 14.—See also, 2 *Ch. xvii.* 7, 8, 9.—*viii.* 14.—xxxiv.—*Jon. iii.* 5 to 9.

CCCXXXIX. *Article XXXVIII. Of Christian men's Goods, which are not common.*

The Riches and Goods of Christians are not common, as touching the right, title, and possession of the same, as certain Anabaptists do falsely boast. Notwithstanding, every man ought, of such things as he possesseth, liberally to give alms to the poor, according to his ability.

And the multitude of them that believed were of one heart and of one soul: neither said any of them that ought of the things which he possessed was his own; but they had all things common. Neither was there any among them that lacked: for as many as were possessors of lands or houses sold them, and brought the prices of the things that were sold, and laid them down at the Apostles' feet: and distribution was made unto every man according as he had need. *Ac. iv.* 32. 34, 35. Peter said, Ananias, why hath Satan filled thine heart to lie to the Holy Ghost, and to keep back part of the price of the land? Whiles it remained, was it not thine own? and after it was sold, was it not in thine own power? *Ac. v.* 3, 4. We hear that there are some which walk disorderly, working not at all, but are busybodies. Now them that are such we command and exhort by our Lord Jesus Christ, that with quietness they work, and eat their own bread. 2 *Th. iii.* 11, 12. Give alms of such things as ye have. *Lu. xi.* 41. Charge them that are rich in this world, that they be not highminded, nor trust in uncertain riches, but in the living God, who giveth us richly all things to enjoy; that they do good, that they be ready to distribute, willing to communicate. 1 *Ti. vi.* 17, 18. Whoso hath this world's good, and seeth his brother have need, and shutteth up his bowels of compassion from him, how dwelleth the love of God in him? 1 *John iii.* 17. To do good and to communicate forget not: for with such sacrifices God is well pleased. *He. xiii.* 16. Distributing to the necessity of saints; given to hospitality. *Ro. xii.* 13. As we have therefore opportunity, let us do good unto all men, especially unto them who are of the houshold of faith. *Ga. vi.* 10. God is not unrighteous to forget your work and labour of love, which ye have shewed toward his name, in that ye have ministered to the saints, and do minister. *He. vi.* 10. Upon the first day of the week let every one of you lay by him in store, as God hath prospered him, that there be no gatherings when I come. *Co. xvi.* 2. The liberal deviseth liberal things; and by liberal things shall he stand. *Is. xxxii.* 8. As touching the ministering to the saints, it is superfluous for me to write to you. But this I say, He which soweth sparingly shall reap also sparingly; and he which soweth bountifully shall reap also bountifully. Every man according as he purposeth in his heart, so let him give; not grudgingly, or of necessity: for God loveth a cheerful giver: as a matter of bounty, and not as of covetousness. *2 Co. ix.* 1. 6, 7. 5. The poor shall never cease out of the land: therefore I command thee, saying, Thou shalt open thine hand wide unto thy brother, to thy poor, and to thy needy, in thy land. *De. xv.* 11. Remember the words of the Lord Jesus, how he said, It is more blessed to give than to receive. *Ac. xx.* 35. Godliness with contentment is great gain. *1 Ti. vi.* 7.

CCCXL. Article XXXIX. Of a Christian man's Oath.

As we confess that vain and rash Swearing is forbidden Christian men by our Lord Jesus Christ, and *James* his Apostle, so we judge, that Christian Religion doth not prohibit, but that a man may swear when the Magistrate requireth, in a cause of faith and charity, so it be done according to the Prophet's teaching, in justice, judgement, and truth.

Ye have heard that it hath been said by them of old time, Thou shalt not forswear thyself, but shalt perform unto the Lord thine oaths: but I say unto you, Swear not at all; neither by heaven; for it is God's throne: nor by the earth; for it is his footstool: neither by Jerusalem; for it is the city of the great King. Neither shalt thou swear by thy head, because thou canst not make one hair white or black. But let your communication be, Yea, yea; Nay, nay; for whatsoever is more than these cometh of evil. *Mat. v.* 33 to 37. But above all things, my brethren, swear not, neither by heaven, neither by the earth, neither by any other oath: but let your yea, be yea; and your nay, nay; lest ye fall into condemnation. *Ja. v.* 12. Thou shalt not take the name of the Lord thy God in vain; for the Lord will not hold him guiltless that taketh his name in vain. *Ex. xx.* 7. I will come near to you to judgment; and I will be a swift witness against false swearers. *Mal. iii.* 5. Ye shall not swear by my name falsely, neither shalt thou profane the name of thy God: I am the Lord. *Le. xix.* 12. Thou shalt fear the Lord thy God, and serve him, and shalt

H H

swear by his name. *De. vi.* 13. Swear now therefore unto me by the Lord, that thou wilt not cut off my seed after me, and that thou wilt not destroy my name out of my father's house. And David sware unto Saul. 1 *Sa. xxiv.* 21, 22. And they entered into a covenant to seek the Lord God of their fathers with all their heart and with all their soul. And they sware unto the Lord with a loud voice; And all Judah rejoiced at the oath: for they had sworn with all their heart, and sought him with their whole desire; and he was found of them. 2 *Ch. xv.* 12. 14, 15. Men verily swear by the greater; and an oath for confirmation is to them an end of all strife. Wherein God, willing more abundantly to shew unto the heirs of promise the immutability of his counsel, confirmed it by an oath. *He. vi.* 16, 17. Jesus held his peace. And the high priest answered and said unto him, I adjure thee by the living God, that thou tell us whether thou be the Christ, the Son of God. Jesus saith unto him, Thou hast said. *Mat. xxvi.* 63, 64. Moreover I call God for a record upon my soul, that to spare you I came not as yet unto Corinth. 2 *Co. i.* 23. God is my witness, that without ceasing I make mention of you always in my prayers. *Ro. i.* 9. Thou shalt swear, The Lord liveth, in truth, in judgment, and in righteousness: and the nations shall bless themselves in him, and in him shall they glory. *Je. iv.* 2.

THE END.

T. INKERSLEY, PRINTER,
BRADFORD.

Lightning Source UK Ltd.
Milton Keynes UK
UKHW020043280720
367273UK00011B/610